Microsoft Office Projects for Windows

William J. Belisle
Gary R. Brent
James A. Folts
Marianne B. Fox
Pauline A. Johnson
Tony Lima
Lawrence C. Metzelaar
Carl A. Scharpf

The Benjamin/Cummings Publishing Company, Inc.
Redwood City, California • Menlo Park, California
Reading, Massachusetts • New York • Don Mills, Ontario
Wokingham, U.K. • Amsterdam • Bonn • Sydney
Singapore • Tokyo • Madrid • San Juan

Senior Editor: *Maureen A. Allaire*

Project Editor: *Nancy E. Davis*

Developmental Editors: *Rebecca Johnson, Shelly Langman, Evelyn Spire*

Executive Editor; B & E, CIS, MIS: *Michael Payne*

Production Manager: *Adam Ray*

Production Coordinator: *Jeni Englander*

Marketing Manager: *Melissa Baumwald*

Custom Publishing Operations Specialist: *Michael Smith*

Senior Manufacturing Coordinator: *Janet Weaver*

Copy Editor: *Barbara Conway*

Proofreader: *Holly McLean Aldis*

Indexer: *Mark Kmetzko*

Cover Design: *Annabelle Ison*

Preface

*M*icrosoft Office Projects for Windows is the newest addition to Benjamin/Cummings' best-selling list of microcomputer application texts. The text teaches students basic and advanced skills in each of the four applications of the Microsoft Office suite—Word 6, Excel 5, Access 2, and PowerPoint 4. After each section, the student learns the basics of how to link documents created in the different applications using the object linking and embedding (OLE) functionality that has made this package the one of choice both in education and industry.

Microsoft Office Projects for Windows teaches the user to use the Office suite to its fullest potential. The projects build student confidence and problem-solving skills through the proven project approach of the SELECT series modules. Each of the projects has been written by an experienced author and instructor and follows a consistent, pedagogically sound format to facilitate the learning process.

This text is intended for the introductory computer course. The projects were designed to be accessible for a first-time user, but they also offer more advanced topics for those students with a little more experience.

ORGANIZATION OF THE TEXT: THE PROJECT APPROACH

Each section begins with an overview that introduces the basic concepts of the application and provides hands-on instructions that allow students to begin using the software almost immediately. Students learn how to start the application, explore the online Help feature included in each application, exit the application, and more.

Students then learn problem-solving techniques as they work through four to five projects. These projects help students master the key concepts and problem-solving techniques they will need as they use the applications in their personal lives, school work, and careers. The projects provide a mix of academic, business, and real-life scenarios that students can relate to.

One of the strengths of the Microsoft Office suite is the ability to integrate the four individual software applications. *Microsoft Office Projects for Windows* provides several projects to help students understand the integration capabilities found in Microsoft Office. An "Introduction to Microsoft Office" is designed to familiarize students with the different software applications available in the Microsoft Office suite; teach how the applications can be integrated using the Microsoft Office Manager; teach how to open and use the Microsoft Office Manager; teach how to customize the Manager Toolbar and Menu; and show how to get help from the online help system.

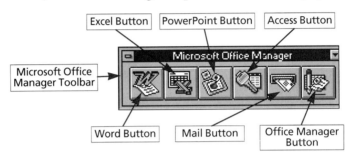

Students also work through three integrated projects in *Microsoft Office Projects for Windows.* These three projects, "Embedding an Excel Worksheet in a Word Document," "Linking an Access Database File to a Word Document," and "Embedding and Linking Word, Excel, Access, and PowerPoint," build on the skills learned in the individual application projects and teach how to use and integrate the powerful components of the Microsoft Office suite. Finally, a supplementary project called "Electronic Mail and the Internet" helps students gain a greater understanding of this valuable and growing area of computing. They learn what e-mail is and how it is used, how to send e-mail, how to access an FTP site and a World Wide Web site, and more.

The comprehensive Operations Reference found in the backmatter provides a visual reference to the menu commands in the applications and includes a grid that indicates whether an operation can be found in a particular application. Button and keystroke combinations for these operations are also included. The comprehensive Glossary includes definitions for all the key terms found in the text, and the Indexes provide an extra navigational tool for students who find they need a refresher in certain topics. *Microsoft Office Projects for Windows* is destined to become a valuable reference text after students complete the projects.

PROJECT FEATURES

The following elements are found in each section of *Microsoft Office Projects for Windows*.

■ Each project begins with **Learning Objectives** that describe the skills and commands you will master.

■ Projects revolve around **Case Studies,** real-world scenarios that allow you to learn an application in a broader context. Case studies give you a sense of when, how, and where an application can serve as an effective tool.

■ **Designing the Solution** introduces you to important problem-solving techniques. You will see how to analyze the case study and design a solution before you sit down at the computer. Thinking through the problem before working with the application allows you to identify the larger issues that must be resolved in order to successfully complete the project.

■ Each topic begins with a brief explanation of concepts you will learn and the operations you will perform.

■ The computer icon provides a cue that you should begin working at the computer. **Numbered steps** guide you step-by-step through each project, providing detailed instructions on how to perform operations. Instructions are provided for both mouse and keyboard where appropriate.

🖥 *To open a blank window for a new document:*

1 Select New on the File menu or press (ALT) + (F7) and then type **n**
The New dialog box appears, as shown in Figure 1.1. This dialog box allows you to select from a variety of *templates* and *wizards*. **Templates** are preformatted skeleton documents ranging from memos to newsletters. **Wizards** ask a series of questions about a document format and then use that information to build a document for you to use. Right now, you need the default general-purpose template named Normal.

Figure 1.1

2 If Normal does not appear in the Template box, type **Normal**

3 Select OK.

■ Visual cues such as *screen shots* reinforce key concepts and help you check your work. Screen shots provide examples of what you will see on your own computer screen.

■ *Exit points* identify good places in each project to take a break.

■ *Margin figures* introduce tools from the computer interface. These tools are often convenient alternatives to the menu commands presented in the numbered steps.

■ *Tips, Reminders, Cautions,* and *Quick Fixes* appear throughout each project to highlight important, helpful, or pertinent information about each application. This extra level of support clearly identifies useful reference material and helps you work independently.

Tip   You can open a new document with a click of the mouse. Use the New document button on the standard toolbar to open a Normal document with a single click.

■ *Key Terms* are boldfaced and italicized and appear throughout each project.

■ Each project ends with *The Next Step,* a *Summary* of concepts covered in the projects, and a list of *Key Terms and Operations.* The Next Step discusses the concepts from the project and proposes other uses and applications for the skills you have learned.

■ At the end of each project, you'll find *Study Questions* (multiple choice, short answer, and discussion) which may be used as a self-test or as a homework assignment.

■ *Review Exercises* present hands-on tasks with abbreviated instructions to help you build on skills acquired in the project.

■ *Assignments* draw on skills introduced in the projects. They encourage you to synthesize and integrate what you have learned using problems that require analysis and critical thinking to complete.

SUPPLEMENTS

The text has a corresponding Instructor's Manual with a Test Bank and Transparency Masters. For each project in the student text, the Instructor's Manual includes Expanded Student Objectives, Answers to Study Questions, and Additional Assessment Techniques. The Test Bank contains two separate tests with answers, and consists of multiple choice, true/false, and fill-in questions referenced to pages in the student's text. Transparency Masters illustrate over one hundred key concepts and screen captures from the text.

The Instructor's Data Disk contains student data files, answers to selected Review Exercises, answers to selected Assignments, and the test files from the Instructor's Manual in ASCII format.

ACKNOWLEDGEMENTS

The Benjamin/Cummings Publishing Company would like to thank our reviewers for their valuable contributions:

Joseph Aieta
Babson College

Bob Barber
Lane Community College

Jacquelyn Crowe
Spokane Community College

Ralph Duffy
North Seattle Community College

Dan Flynn
Shoreline Community College

Jonathan Frank
Suffolk University

Patrick Gilbert
University of Hawaii

Maureen Greenbaum
Union County College

Sunil Hazari
East Carolina University

William Hightower
Elon College

Seth Hock
Columbus State Community College

Cynthia Kachik
Santa Fe Community College

Ron Leake
Johnson County Community College

Randy Marak
Hill College

Gail Miles
Lenoir-Rhyne College

Carolyn Monroe
Baylor University

John Passafiume
Clemson University

Louis Pryor
Garland County Community College

Tonia Queen
Brevard Community College

Michael Reilly
University of Denver

Dick Ricketts
Lane Community College

Cynthia Thompson
Carl Sandburg College

JoAnn Weatherwax
Saddleback College

David Whitney
San Francisco State University

James Wood
Tri-County Technical College

Allen Zilbert
Long Island University

Contents

PART 2: MICROSOFT WORD 6

OVERVIEW   WRD-1

PROJECT 1: CREATING A DOCUMENT   WRD-10

PROJECT 2: EDITING A DOCUMENT   WRD-28

PROJECT 3: CHARACTER FORMATTING   WRD-51

PROJECT 4: PARAGRAPH FORMATTING   WRD-68

PROJECT 5: SECTION FORMATTING   WRD-90

PART 3: MICROSOFT EXCEL 5

OVERVIEW   EX-1

PROJECT 1: BUILDING A SMALL WORKSHEET EX-23

PROJECT 5: VISUALIZING INFORMATION WITH CHARTS   EX-131

PART 4:
INTEGRATED PROJECT 1

INTEGRATED PROJECT 1: EMBEDDING AN EXCEL WORKSHEET IN A WORD DOCUMENT   INT1-1

PART 5:
MICROSOFT ACCESS 2

OVERVIEW   ACC-1

PROJECT 2: POLISHING A PRESENTATION   PP-44

PROJECT 3: WORKING WITH TEXT OBJECTS   PP-66

PROJECT 4: COMBINING TEXT AND ART   PP-95

PROJECT 5: PRESENTING A SLIDE SHOW   PP-119

PART 8:
INTEGRATED PROJECT 3

PROJECT 3: EMBEDDING AND LINKING WORD, EXCEL, ACCESS, AND POWERPOINT   INT3-1

PART 9: ADDITIONAL PROJECT

ADDITIONAL PROJECT: ELECTRONIC MAIL AND THE INTERNET   ADD-1

COMPREHENSIVE OPERATIONS REFERENCE

COMPREHENSIVE GLOSSARY

INDEXES

Introduction to Microsoft Office

Objectives

After completing this introduction, you should be able to:

▶ Open more than one Office software application concurrently

▶ Open the Microsoft Office Manager

▶ Customize the Office Manager toolbar and menu

▶ Exit Microsoft Office

▶ Get online Help

Microsoft Office is a *software suite*, which is several software products in one package. Microsoft Word, Excel, Access and PowerPoint are all individual *software applications*, or programs, in their own right, which means they can be purchased and used separately. But Microsoft has gone one step further by creating the Microsoft Office Manager utility, which unites these separate applications into one powerful unit.

The Office Manager *integrates* the worksheet, word processing, database, and presentation packages, allowing you to share information from one application to another. Integrating means that the separate packages can act like one software program. You can create a worksheet in Excel, and while Excel is still open, you can open Word and copy data from Excel into Word. You can then open PowerPoint and copy the Excel or Word data into your presentation. There are virtually no limitations. All four packages can be open at the same time, with data being shared and used across all four applications simultaneously. The only limitation may be in the type of computer hardware you are using. Because Office requires at least 6 MB of RAM and 58 MB of hard disk space for a typical installation, your ability to use Office to its fullest capacity will depend on the amount of computing resources you have available to you.

There are two versions of the Microsoft Office product: the standard Microsoft Office, and Microsoft Office Professional. The only difference between these two packages, besides cost (the Professional is more expensive), is that the Professional comes with the Access database, and the standard version does not. Both packages include one ***workstation license*** to use Microsoft Mail 3.2, which is Microsoft's electronic mail system for PC networks. If you are connected to a PC network that uses Microsoft Mail, the license allows you to set up your workstation on the network mail server. The Microsoft Mail network version, which is what you need to use the mail license, is a separate network product and must be purchased separately.

OPENING MICROSOFT OFFICE APPLICATIONS

When you start Windows, you start the Microsoft Office Manager at the same time. When you see the Program Manager on the screen, you may also see the Microsoft Office startup announcement. This is an optional announcement and may not be displayed on your computer or network. Once Office is started, however, you will see the Office toolbar, which will look similar to Figure I.1.

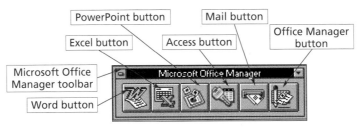

Figure I.1

When you are ready to open one of the Office applications, you simply select the appropriate button on the toolbar. You can use the toolbar to move from one application to another quickly and easily.

To open Office applications simultaneously:

1 Select the Word button on the Office toolbar.

2 Type your name at the beginning of the new document.

3 While Word is open, select the Excel button on the Office toolbar.

4 While Excel is open, select the Word button on the Office toolbar.

Notice that Office returned you back to the Word document that was open when you started Excel rather than starting a new document.

5 Select the Excel button.

6 Choose Exit from the File menu to close Excel.

7 Choose Exit from the File menu to close Word. Do not save the document.

USING THE OFFICE MANAGER

The Office Manager does more than integrate Office's products. With the Office Manager you can move directly to the File Manager, customize the toolbar with other Microsoft applications, such as Microsoft FoxPro, Microsoft Publisher, Paintbrush—any software applications you use frequently. You can also change the look of Office Manager by displaying the title bar or only the toolbar. You can even change the size of the toolbar icons.

Customizing the Office Manager

When you select the Office Manager, you see the menu shown in Figure I.2. The Office Manager menu has three sections separated by a horizontal line: 1) Office products, 2) Windows products, and 3) Setup and customize options. You can open each application by selecting the button on the toolbar or by choosing the application on the menu. You can remove and add to the different menu and toolbar options by customizing the toolbar.

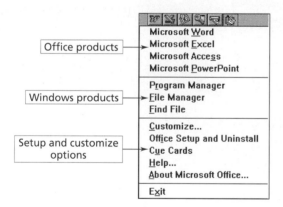

Figure I.2

You should customize the toolbar by adding your most frequently used programs or programs you will use to share data. Add items that you don't use quite as often to the menu.

To customize the toolbar:

1 Select the Office Manager button.

2 Choose Customize from the Office Manager menu.
The Customize dialog box appears as shown in Figure I.3.

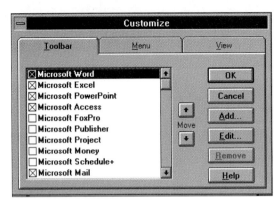

Figure I.3

3 Select the applications from the Toolbar list box that you want displayed as buttons on the Office Manager toolbar.
A checkmark appears in the box to the left of each application name you selected.

4 Use the scroll bar to the right of the list box to view all applications, and select the toolbar applications as shown in Figures I.3 and I.4 and click OK to continue.

5 If an application is selected but you do not want it on the toolbar, select it again to remove the checkmark from the box.

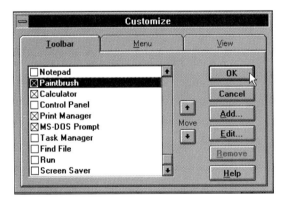

Figure I.4

The toolbar now looks like Figure I.5.

Figure I.5

Ordering the Toolbar and Menu

The Office Manager menu and toolbar may display the selected items in a different order than those shown in the figures in this module. You can determine the order, from left to right, of the toolbar buttons and the order, from top to bottom, of the menu items. You customize these two features in the same way. You will customize the toolbar now, and you can customize the menu items at your leisure.

When you open the Customize dialog box, you will see the two Move buttons shown in Figure I.6. Using these buttons, you will move items on the toolbar or menu. The up-arrow Move button will move the item up the menu or left on the toolbar; the down-arrow Move button moves the item down the menu or right on the toolbar.

Figure I.6

 To order the toolbar buttons:

1 Choose Customize from the Office Manager menu.

2 Select the toolbar tab.

Tip To modify the menu items you can select the Menu tab.

3 Select the MS-DOS Prompt item by clicking on the name, not on the marked box.

4 Use the Move buttons to move this item to the top of the list, and then click OK.
The toolbar now looks like Figure I.7.

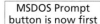

Figure I.7

5 Customize the toolbar again so it displays only the buttons shown in Figure I.8.

Figure I.8

Modifying the Office Buttons

The last customizing option lets you change the way the Office Manager displays the entire Office toolbar. You can add the Office Manager title bar, choose to display the title screen when Office starts, and control whether the toolbar is always displayed or is hidden. You can also change the size of the buttons from small to large.

 To modify Office buttons:

1 Open the Office Manager and choose Customize.

2 Select the View tab.

The screen now looks similar to Figure I.9. Because computer systems are configured differently, your settings may not be exactly the same as those shown here.

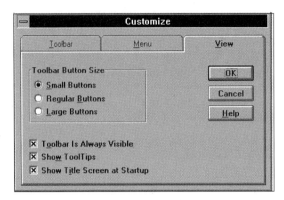

Figure I.9

3 Select one of the view options that is different from your standard setup. If Small Buttons is selected in the Toolbar Button Size box, select Large Buttons, or vice versa.

4 Select OK.

EXITING OFFICE MANAGER

Usually, when you are through with a Microsoft software program, you choose Exit from the File menu. As you work with the individual programs, such as Word and Excel, you will usually exit them before you open another package or exit Windows. The Office Manager is a bit different.

The Office Manager usually remains open, displaying the Office buttons in the upper-right corner of the screen. Those buttons remain on the screen as long as the Office Manager is open, even if you work in another software program that is not part of the Microsoft Office product.

You can, however, exit the Office Manager by choosing Exit from the Office Manager menu. The Office Manager closes down, and the Office Manager buttons are no longer displayed on the screen. To start the Office Manager again, you select Microsoft Office from the Startup window or from the appropriate window on your computer system.

ADDITIONAL MICROSOFT OFFICE PROGRAMS

Microsoft Office includes some additional programs, or tools, that you can use in every Office application. These include WordArt, the Equation Editor, the ClipArt Gallery, Graph, the PowerPoint Viewer, and Microsoft Organization Chart. You'll learn more about these tools as you work through the projects in this book.

GETTING ONLINE HELP

Anytime you work with a new software package, it is important to know how to get assistance and how to get your questions answered. The Office Manager has an online Help utility, very similar to the Windows help system. You'll find the Help utility in the Office Manager menu.

THE NEXT STEP

What applications do you use frequently? What Windows accessories do you like to have available to you quickly? Think carefully about how you work, and then use the Office Manager to customize your desktop. The more efficient your workspace, the more energy you have to create your files. As the old saying goes, "work smarter, not harder." Make the Office Manager work for you.

SUMMARY AND EXERCISES

Summary

- Microsoft Office is an integrated software package.
- Office includes the applications Word, Excel, Mail, PowerPoint, and the professional edition includes Access.
- Microsoft Mail is a workstation license that lets you set up your workstation on a PC network.
- Multiple Office applications can be open concurrently.
- Information can be shared between all of the Office applications.
- The Office Manager controls the Office toolbar and menu items.
- The toolbar and menu items can be customized to display any and all of the Office products, as well as other Microsoft programs and accessories.
- The toolbar and menu items can also be ordered to display the programs in any order.
- The toolbar itself can be modified to display the Office title bar.
- Microsoft Office normally remains open while you work in Windows, but it can be exited and started again.

Key Terms and Operations

Key Terms	Operations
integrate	Customize the toolbar
software applications	Modify the buttons display
software suite	Open the Office Manager
workstation license	Open Word and Excel simultaneously
	Order the toolbar

Study Questions

Multiple Choice

1. Microsoft Office is
   a. available only to businesses for office use.
   b. a word processing package.
   c. an accounting program.
   d. a software suite.

2. A software suite
   a. is a group of networked software programs.
   b. has products that can be used together to share information.
   c. is a program that can be used in multiple languages at the same time, such as French and German.
   d. must be bought from the same store.

3. The only real limitation(s) to using a software suite
   a. is when the software suite is loaded on a stand-alone PC and not on a network.
   b. is the availability of the software on the network and the number of users.
   c. are found in the hardware capacities of the computer being used.
   d. are the security levels granted to nonnetwork users.

4. A Microsoft Mail workstation license is
   a. a piece of paper granting you network access.
   b. a program that lets you set up your PC on a PC network running Microsoft Mail
   c. the authority granted to the user by Microsoft to send electronic mail directly to the company.
   d. never issued to an end user, only to a network manager.

5. The Microsoft Office Manager toolbar
   a. can be modified to display all or some of the Office products.
   b. is always an icon in the Program Manager window.
   c. cannot display Windows accessories or programs.
   d. closes when one of the Office products is started.

Short Answer

1. What products make up the standard Microsoft Office suite?

2. What products make up the Microsoft Office Professional?

3. How do you customize the toolbar and menu?

4. What software programs can be added to the toolbar?

5. What menu items can be added to the menu?

For Discussion

1. What are some advantages to using a software suite?

2. Discuss some reasons why you would share information between different applications.

3. What are you looking forward to the most about learning how to use the Microsoft Office products?

PART I

Windows 3.1

Windows 3.1

Objectives

After completing this overview, you should be able to:

▶ Recognize graphical operating environments

▶ Identify the system requirements for Windows' two operating modes

▶ Differentiate between Windows applications and non-Windows applications

▶ Use a mouse

▶ Start and exit Windows

▶ Get help in Windows

USING A GRAPHICAL OPERATING ENVIRONMENT

An *operating environment* simplifies the interface between the user and the computer's operating system. In a graphical operating environment, a *desktop* (the screen background) serves as a graphics-based work area. Applications and documents are found inside *windows* (rectangular areas on the desktop). Figure 0.1 shows a sample graphical operating environment. Users communicate with the computer by selecting menu options and small graphical images instead of typing hard-to-remember text commands such as those found in DOS. A graphical operating environment is an integrated environment with a consistent user interface. Applications designed for graphical environments have the same basic command structure and a similar design. This basic consistency among programs greatly simplifies the learning of new applications and reduces the anxiety that many computer users experience when delving into new products.

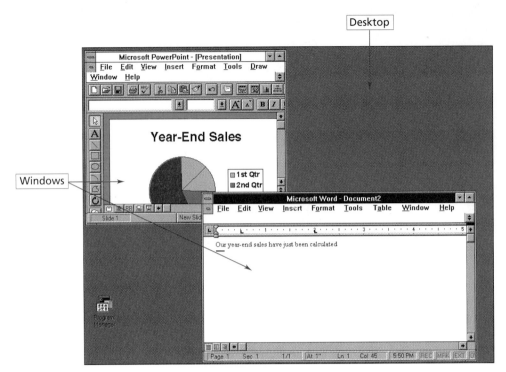

Figure 0.1

The high degree of integration among applications also allows the seamless exchange of data from one document to another. Data can be either copied or cut from one document and placed into a temporary holding area called the *Clipboard*. This data can then be pasted into a document in the same or another application. Figure 0.2 shows an example of how you can use the Clipboard. You can create a chart in Microsoft Excel (a spreadsheet program) and then copy the chart into a report in Microsoft Word (a word processing program). The resulting synthesized document has a much greater impact than the parts have standing on their own.

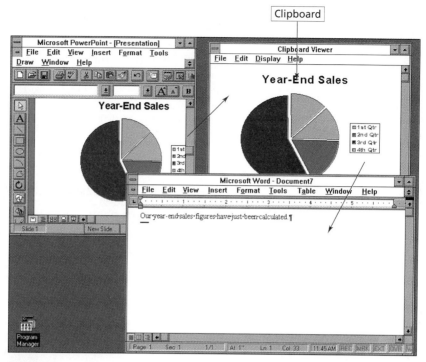

Figure 0.2

A graphical environment also provides the computer with the capability of displaying a document on the screen just as it will appear on a printout. That is, the text fonts and graphic shapes that you see on the screen are virtually the same as the ones that you will get on your printout. This feature, called **WYSIWYG** (an acronym for What You See Is What You Get), has led to the development of sophisticated word processors and desktop publishing programs that produce high-quality, professional-looking documents.

Graphics-based computer systems have been around since the late 1970s, when the Xerox Palo Alto Research Center (PARC) developed the Xerox Star. Although easy to use, its exorbitant price limited its widespread use as a commercial product. It was not until 1984, when Apple released the highly popular Macintosh, that graphics-based computer systems began to find their way into the hands of average users.

Microsoft released Windows in late 1985 as a graphical operating environment for DOS-based computers. For the next five years it underwent many changes as it slowly grew in popularity. In 1990 Microsoft released Windows 3.0, and shortly thereafter an enhanced version called Windows 3.1. Soaring sales figures and widespread industry acceptance have made Windows the DOS-based graphical computer interface of the 1990s.

USING WINDOWS 3.1

Windows 3.1 is a full-featured graphical operating environment that greatly extends the capabilities of DOS. Windows is not an operating system per se but an operating environment that runs "on top of" DOS. You first load DOS and then Windows. Application programs, such as Microsoft Excel and Microsoft Word, are then loaded under Windows.

With Windows you no longer have to deal directly with DOS. The DOS command line is replaced with a ***graphical user interface (GUI)*** that is much easier to learn than DOS's text-based interface. In a graphical user interface, operations are executed by selecting ***icons,*** graphical representations of Windows elements, and by choosing options from lists of commands called ***menus***. These basic elements of the Windows GUI are shown in Figure 0.3. For example, to initialize a diskette in DOS, you would type FORMAT A:. In Windows you would choose the Format Disk command from a menu. You are then prompted for the desired disk drive. The main difference is that you don't have to type the word FORMAT; in fact, you don't even have to know the name of the command, since in Windows it is listed on the menu for you. This is such a useful feature that the latest versions of DOS, beginning with version 4.0, have adopted a graphical user interface that is very similar to the one in Windows.

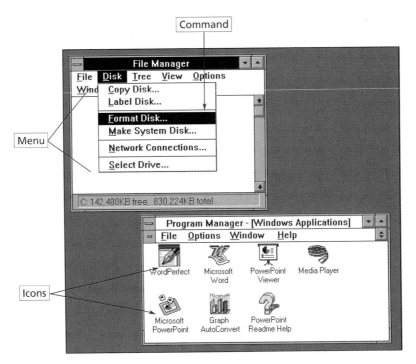

Figure 0.3

In addition to providing easy access to DOS commands, Windows provides a simple method for starting application programs. In DOS you start an application by entering the appropriate command at the DOS prompt. If you don't know the correct file name you're out of luck until you find it. In Windows, programs are represented graphically as icons. The previous figure displays many icons each telling you something about the program it represents.

In this module, you will learn how to use the mouse to choose icons, open windows, and start application programs. You will examine Windows' sophisticated memory management capabilities that transform DOS from a singletasking operating system, which runs one program at a time, into a *multitasking* operating system, which runs two or more programs simultaneously, with each program contained in a separate window. For example, if you need to look up financial figures in Microsoft Excel while you are typing a report in Microsoft Word, you can run Excel in a window in the upper left corner of the screen and run Word in a window in the lower right.

System Requirements

Depending on what type of processor you have and how much memory is available, Windows automatically loads itself in one of two modes: standard mode or 386 enhanced mode.

Standard mode is Windows' basic operating mode. Non-Windows applications run in full-screen windows that cannot be sized into smaller windows. Standard mode requires

- MS-DOS 3.1 or higher
- A computer with an Intel 80286 processor or better
- An EGA monitor (VGA or better is preferred)
- 1 MB of RAM (2 MB are highly recommended)
- A hard disk with 6 MB of free space (9 MB are preferred)

386 enhanced mode provides access to the advanced memory management features of the Intel 80386 processor. You have virtual memory capabilities, in which free space on the hard disk is used as an extension of RAM. In addition, non-Windows applications can run in sizable windows. 386 enhanced mode requires

- MS-DOS 3.1 or higher
- A computer with an Intel 80386 processor or better
- An EGA monitor (VGA or better is preferred)
- 2 MB of RAM (4 MB are highly recommended)
- A hard disk with 8 MB of free space (10 MB are preferred)

In addition to the required hardware, the following are recommended:

- A pointing device, such as a mouse or trackball
- A high-resolution printer, if you want to print with Windows

SELECTING WINDOWS APPLICATIONS

To take full advantage of all of the features in Windows 3.1, you must buy special versions of software programs, known as *Windows applications*. When you buy an application software package, the product's box will indicate whether it has been written specifically for Windows. For example, WordPerfect, a popular word processor, comes in three versions: WordPerfect for DOS, WordPerfect for Windows and WordPerfect for Macintosh. Both versions work under Windows, but only WordPerfect for Windows can use all of Windows' graphical features. Some programs have only a Windows version. Excel and PageMaker (a desktop publishing program) will not run unless you have first loaded Windows.

This does not mean that only Windows applications can run under Windows. Almost all programs run under Windows, but *non-Windows applications*, programs not designed specifically for Windows, cannot take advantage of many of Windows' features. For example, dBASE IV runs under Windows, but because it is a non-Windows application, it does not have a consistent graphical user interface, as do Microsoft Excel or WordPerfect for Windows.

A Note to the Student

Windows can be customized in many different configurations. The screen examples shown in this module reflect Windows' standard configuration, in which only the Program Manager appears when Windows is started. If you perform all of the procedures correctly, and if your copy of Windows is configured in the standard manner, your screen should look the same as the screen examples shown in the module.

You can execute Windows commands in two ways: by using a mouse or a keyboard. To accommodate both methods, the instructions in the projects will describe how to execute commands as follows:

Choose Exit Windows from the File menu.

Select the BOXES.BMP file from the pull-down list.

Specific instructions for using the keyboard are not included in the projects unless the keyboard method is the only available option. The following section explains how to use a mouse to execute Windows commands.

USING A MOUSE

Windows 3.1 is designed to be used with a pointing device such as a mouse or trackball. A *mouse* is a hand-held input device that is rolled on a small flat surface, usually a table or mouse pad. The movement of the mouse causes a corresponding movement of a pointer on the screen. A *trackball* performs the same function as a mouse but works somewhat differently. You use your fingers to roll a ball that is exposed on the top of the device, which causes the pointer to move on the screen.

A mouse designed for use with an IBM PC or a compatible has two or three buttons. Most systems assume you will hold the mouse in your right hand and press the left button. If you wish to hold the mouse in your left hand and press the right button, you need to change the way the mouse has been set up.

Familiarity with some common terms will help you use a mouse. The *pointer* is a symbol (usually an arrow) that moves around the screen as you move the mouse. To *click* means to position the pointer on an object, and then quickly press and release the left mouse button. A *double-click* involves the same motion as a click, but it is done twice in rapid succession. Usually this causes a small hour glass icon to appear on the screen for a few seconds. The hour glass indicates that you need to wait while Windows loads something. When you *drag* an object, you place the pointer on the object, hold down the left mouse button while moving the mouse and then release the left mouse button when the object is placed where you want it. Dragging is used for moving or sizing an object or choosing commands.

The *menu bar* lists available menus. An application usually has File, Edit, and Help menus, in addition to the application's unique menus. To use a mouse to choose a command, you click the name of the menu on the menu bar. A **_pull-down menu_**, a menu that you have "pulled down" onto the screen, appears. While holding down the left mouse button, you select the desired command and then release the button to execute the command. Alternatively, you can execute a command by clicking the command in the pull-down menu.

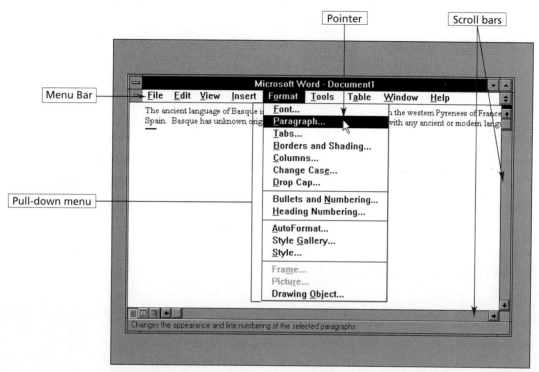

Figure 0.4

Some windows have bars called **_scroll bars_** along the right and/or bottom borders. Figure 0.4 displays scroll bars for scrolling through a document. Figure 0.5 displays a scroll bar that lets you browse through a list of available fonts (character designs). You can move through the document or the list of choices one line at a time by clicking either arrow at the end of the scroll bar. For example, if you click the downward-pointing arrow, you move down one line in the document or list. You can move to a specific location by dragging the **_scroll box_**, the box within the scroll bar. For example, if you drag the scroll box to the middle of the bar, you move to the middle of the document or list.

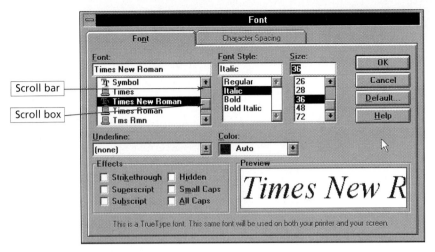

Figure 0.5

You also can scroll with the keyboard one line at a time by pressing ⊕ or ⊕ or one screen at a time by pressing (PGUP) or (PGDN).

STARTING WINDOWS

The following steps describe the standard method for starting Windows. How you start Windows depends on how your computer is set up. For example, your computer may be running a menu system or DOS shell that facilitates the starting of Windows, or your computer may be set up to start Windows automatically.

To start Windows:

1 Type **win** and press (ENTER) at the DOS prompt.

The first screen to appear displays the Windows 3.1 logo, which is soon followed by a window called the Program Manager. Your screen may look different from Figure 0.6, depending on how your system is set up. You will learn more about this window later.

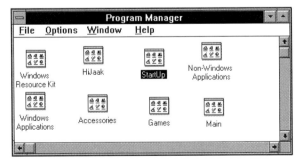

Figure 0.6

GETTING ONLINE HELP

The Help menu within the Program Manager provides assistance for the Program Manager and for most Windows concepts, commands, and terms. You access Help by choosing the Help command from the menu system. If you are in the process of executing a command, you can press (F1) for help to get an explanation of how the command operates.

To access Help and then access Contents:

1 Make sure you are in Windows.

2 Choose Help from the menu bar.

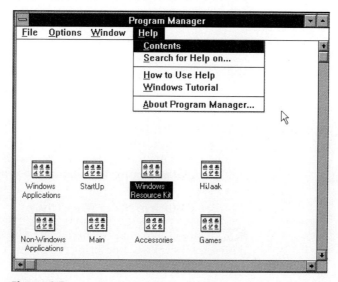

Figure 0.7

3 Choose Contents from the Help menu, as shown in Figure 0.7 The Contents screen appears as shown in Figure 0.8.

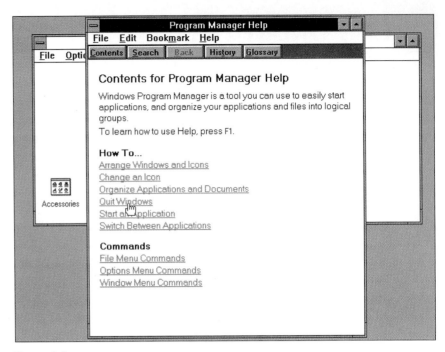

Figure 0.8

The Contents screen displays the topics for the Program Manager Help. Notice that the pointer has changed to a hand.

 ### To get help quitting Windows:

1 Select Quit Windows under the How To heading.
The screen displays a description of how to exit Windows, as shown in Figure 0.9.

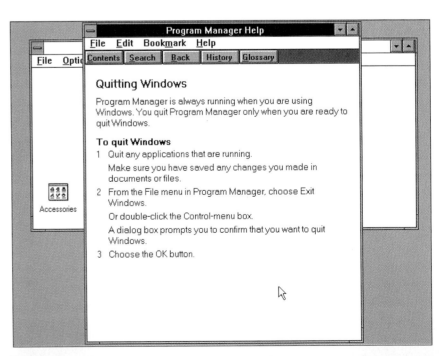

Figure 0.9

Notice in Figure 0.9 the five buttons at the top of the Help screen. The Contents button displays the topics for the Program Manager Help, Search enables you to type keywords to look up Help information, Back takes you back to a previous Help screen, History lists the names of the Help screens that you have displayed, and Glossary provides a list of definitions for important words.

To go back to the previous Help screen:

1 Select the Back button.
The screen displays the Contents for the Program Manager Help screen. Notice that the Back button is dimmed to indicate that you cannot go back to any other Help screens; that is, this is the screen from which you started.

The Search button enables you to type in a keyword and then have Windows search for any information related to it. For example, if you type STARTING, Windows gives you information on starting applications.

To search for Help on starting an application:

1 Select the Search button.
The screen now looks like Figure 0.10.

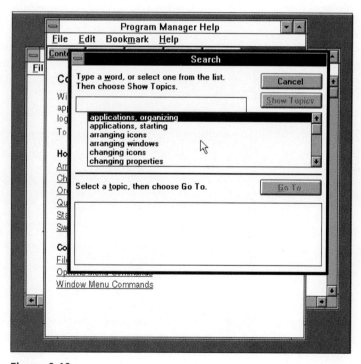

Figure 0.10

2 Type **starting** and press (ENTER)
The search screen displays five topics found under *starting applications*, as shown in Figure 0.11.

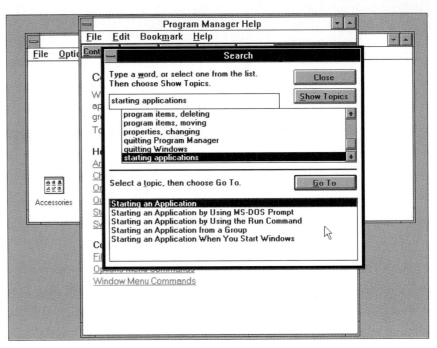

Figure 0.11

3 Double-click *Starting an Application from a Group*.
The screen displays the Starting an Application from a Group screen, as shown in Figure 0.12. The highlighted words are included in the Windows Glossary.

Figure 0.12

 To look up a word in the Glossary:

1 Select the word *group*.
The screen displays the definition of *group*, as shown in Figure 0.13.

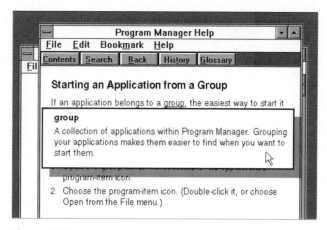

Figure 0.13

2 Select the Back button to return to the previous window.

Tip An alternative method for looking up the definition of a word is to click the Glossary button for a complete list of all items in the Windows Glossary.

To exit Help:

1 Choose Exit from the File menu.

If you access Help from within a software application, you will receive help on that particular application. The Help feature will work in the same way, but the command options and the Help screens will pertain to the application. In many applications Help will be context-sensitive. For example, if you are in the process of saving a document in Microsoft Word and you press (F1), you will get help on saving a document in Word and avoid searching through the Help screens to find the right screen.

Windows offers three methods to exit the program. Two methods use the Control menu and will be explored in Project 1. In the steps that follow, you will use the File menu.

To exit Windows:

1 Choose File from the menu bar.
The screen now looks like Figure 0.14.

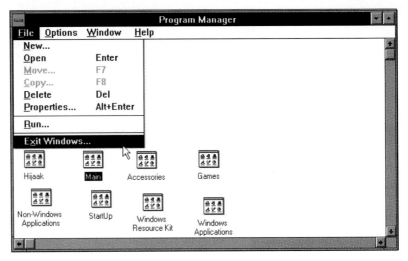

Figure 0.14

2 Choose Exit Windows from the File menu.
You should see a dialog box.

3 Click OK to close the dialog box.

This concludes the Overview. You can review the material presented in the Overview by working through the Study Questions or go on to the next project.

SUMMARY AND EXERCISES

Summary

- Graphical operating environments offer a consistent, easy-to-use graphical user interface.
- Windows is not an operating system by itself but an operating environment that greatly extends the capabilities of DOS.
- Windows supports a multitasking environment, which allows several applications to run simultaneously in separate windows.
- Almost all programs designed for DOS should run under Windows; however, to take full advantage of the powerful Windows features, you should get special Windows applications.
- Windows 3.1 has two operating modes: standard and 386 enhanced. Windows automatically loads itself into one of these two modes depending on what kind of computer is being used and how much memory is available.
- The pointer is a symbol that moves around the screen as you move your mouse. To click means to position the pointer on an object and then quickly press and release the left mouse button. A double-click has the same motion as a click but it is done twice in rapid succession. To drag an object means to hold down the left mouse button while moving the mouse.

- Scroll bars enable you to scroll through documents or lists of choices.
- The Help menu within the Program Manager provides assistance for the Program Manager and for most Windows concepts, commands, and terms.

Key Terms and Operations

Key Terms
click
Clipboard
desktop
double-click
drag
graphical user interface (GUI)
icon
menu
menu bar
mouse
multitasking
non-Windows application
operating environment
pointer

pull-down menu
scroll bar
scroll box
standard mode
386 enhanced mode
trackball
window
Windows application
WYSIWYG

Operations
Access online Help
Exit Windows
Start Windows

Study Questions

True/False

1. Microsoft Windows was the first graphical operating environment released on the market. **T   F**

2. A trackball has a ball on the top which is rolled in order to move the pointer. **T   F**

3. Windows by itself is considered to be a complete operating system. **T   F**

4. It is possible to format a disk from within Windows. **T   F**

5. Windows will be an important graphical computer interface in the 1990s. **T   F**

Short Answer

1. _____ is the Windows operating mode that gives you the most power.

2. _____ are applications that have been designed specifically for use in the Windows environment.

3. A graphical representation of a Windows element is called a(n) _____.

4. The _____ is the symbol on the screen that can be moved around by moving the mouse.

5. When you _____ something, you hold down the left mouse button while moving the mouse.

For Discussion

1. Why do you no longer need the DOS prompt after loading Windows?

2. What is multitasking, and how can it be useful to you?

3. What does the Clipboard allow you to do?

Objectives

After completing this project, you should be able to:

▶ Access the Program Manager and the Control menu

▶ Use a dialog box

▶ Move and size a window

▶ Maximize, minimize, and restore a window

▶ Move and neatly arrange icons

▶ Scroll through a window

USING THE PROGRAM MANAGER

The *Program Manager* performs a pivotal role in the operation of Windows. It automatically opens every time you start Windows and remains in the background during your entire Windows session. When you are ready to quit Windows, you do so by closing the Program Manager.

In addition to opening and closing Windows, the Program Manager performs two important functions. First, it gives you a quick and easy way to start applications. Second, it enables you to group programs and documents logically.

 To display the Program Manager:

1 If you have not done so already, start Windows.
Figure 1.1 shows a typical Program Manager window. The names and the arrangement of the program group icons on your screen may be different.

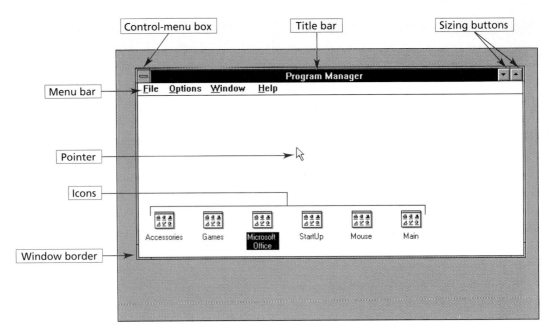

Figure 1.1

The Program Manager window has several features that all other windows have:

- A **Control-menu box** appears in the upper-left corner of each window. When you click the Control-menu box, a pull-down menu appears that lists commands for controlling that window.
- The **sizing buttons** are used to change the dimensions of the window quickly.
- The **title bar** displays the name of the application or document.
- The **window border** defines the outside edge of the window.

Within Windows, you perform many operations by choosing menu options. The Program Manager's menus provide basic commands for managing windows and applications. For example, you can open, copy, and delete applications. You also can get help on the Program Manager and on other parts of Windows.

When you select menus from the menu bar, the resulting pull-down menus follow three conventions that are common among most Windows menus: checkmarks, dimmed commands, and ellipses.

A **checkmark** next to a command name indicates that a command is active. Only optional commands that can be **toggled** (turned on and off) are displayed with checkmarks. For example, under the Options menu shown in Figure 1.2, the Auto Arrange command can be toggled on and off depending on your preference. If the Auto Arrange command is on, a checkmark appears next to the command and icons will be automatically arranged when a window is resized.

 ### To toggle the Auto Arrange command on and off:

1 Choose Options from the menu bar.

The pull-down menu shown in Figure 1.2 appears. You may see a checkmark next to the Auto Arrange option.

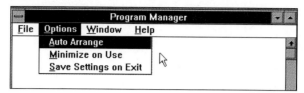

Figure 1.2

2 Choose Auto Arrange.
The pull-down menu disappears.

3 Choose Options again.
If you *did not* previously see a checkmark, you will see one now, as shown in Figure 1.3. If you *did* previously see a checkmark, you will not see one now.

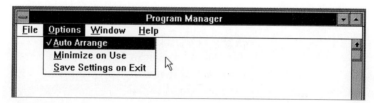

Figure 1.3

4 Choose Auto Arrange again if necessary to display a checkmark next to the option name. Otherwise, cancel the current command by clicking anywhere on the desktop.

A ***dimmed command*** on a menu is not available at the current time. Some commands are available only during certain situations; when they are dimmed, they cannot be executed. When you click on the File command, several dimmed commands are displayed.

To view dimmed commands in the File menu:

1 Choose File.
Move and Copy are dimmed and currently inaccessible, as shown in Figure 1.4.

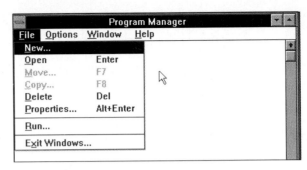

Figure 1.4

2 Click anywhere on the desktop to cancel the command.

An *ellipsis*, the three dots (...) that follow certain commands, denotes that a dialog box will appear when you choose the command. A *dialog box* is a rectangular box that either prompts the user to provide more information or provides information of its own, such as a warning or error message. For example, Windows displays its operating mode in a dialog box.

 To display Windows' current operating mode:

1 Choose Help.
The menu shown in Figure 1.5 appears. Notice that the command About Program Manager has an ellipsis.

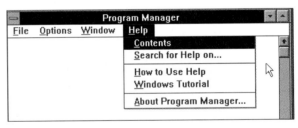

Figure 1.5

2 Choose About Program Manager.
The dialog box shown in Figure 1.6 appears. In addition to the operating mode, you can see information on the version, memory, and system resources.

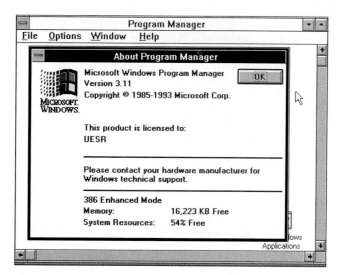

Figure 1.6

3 Select OK to exit the dialog box.

USING THE CONTROL MENU

Application windows, document windows, and some dialog boxes have **Control menus.** When you select the Control-menu box in the upper-left corner of a window, the Control menu appears. If you are using a keyboard, the Control menu enables you to control window operations, such as moving, sizing, and closing windows. Mouse users can perform these window operations by clicking, double-clicking, or dragging windows. Mouse users should be familiar with the Control menu, however, because it is common to all windows and it provides a sure way to close any window.

You can use the Control menu to close any window, including the Program Manager. When you close a window, the window disappears from the screen, but when you close the Program Manager, you also exit Windows. Before exiting Windows, however, you will see a dialog box that allows you to proceed with or cancel the exit process. In the steps that follow, you will explore the Program Manager Control menu as a means of exiting Windows and see how to cancel the command using the dialog box.

 ### *To close the active window:*

1 Select the Control-menu box.
Mouse users must be sure to click the Control-menu box only once.

The Control menu appears as shown in Figure 1.7.

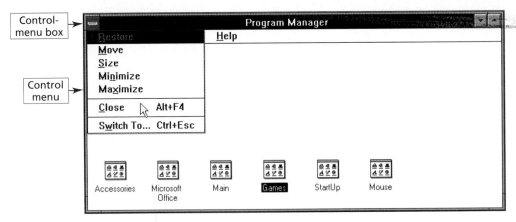

Figure 1.7

2 Choose Close.
A dialog box appears, confirming that you want to exit Windows.

3 Select Cancel to remain in Windows.
If you had wanted to exit Windows you would have selected OK. Most dialog boxes contain a Cancel button that enables you to cancel a command.

MOVING A WINDOW

Occasionally one window will hide another. A window can be moved by dragging its title bar or by using the Control menu. In the steps that follow, you will use the dragging method.

 To move the Program Manager window:

1 Place the pointer anywhere on the Program Manager title bar.

2 Click the title bar and hold down the left mouse button.

3 Drag the pointer a little to the right.

4 Release the mouse button.

5 Move the Program Manager window back to its original position.

SIZING A WINDOW

Sizing a window requires a steady hand. In the sets of steps that follow, you will move the pointer to the edge of the window until the pointer's shape changes and then drag the edges. Figure 1.8 describes different pointer shapes.

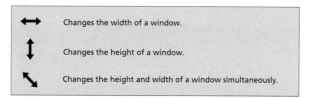

↔	Changes the width of a window.
↕	Changes the height of a window.
↖	Changes the height and width of a window simultaneously.

Figure 1.8

Caution Do not click the mouse in these operations until the pointer changes into the appropriate shape.

To increase the height of a window:

1 Place the pointer on the upper border of the window until the pointer becomes double-pointed.

2 Drag the pointer up a short distance and then release the mouse button.

You can also change the height of a window by dragging the lower border up or down.

To increase the width of a window:

1 Place the pointer on the right side of the window border until the pointer becomes double-pointed.

2 Drag the pointer a short distance to the right and then let go of the mouse button.

You can also change a window's width by dragging its left border left or right.

To simultaneously change the height and width of a window:

1 Place the pointer in the lower right corner of the window until the pointer becomes diagonal and double-pointed.

2 Drag the pointer a short distance upward and to the left.

If necessary, you can exit Windows now and continue this project later.

MAXIMIZING, MINIMIZING, AND RESTORING A WINDOW

You often will want to concentrate all of your attention on one particular window, especially if that window contains an application like a word processing program or an electronic spreadsheet. Enlarging the window to its maximum size makes it easier to work on. To ***maximize*** a window, or to fill the entire screen with the window, you will use the Maximize button shown in Figure 1.9.

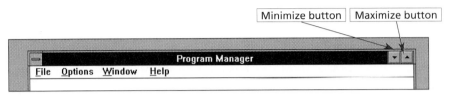

Figure 1.9

 ## To maximize a window:

1 If necessary, start Windows.

2 Select the Maximize button.
The Program Manager window fills the entire screen. Notice that the Restore button has replaced the Maximize button, as shown in Figure 1.10.

To *restore* a window means to bring it back to its previous size.

Figure 1.10

 ## To restore a window after it has been maximized:

1 Select the Restore button.
Sometimes you will be temporarily finished with the current window and will need to move on to something else. In such cases you don't necessarily want to close the window, you just want to put it away temporarily. To *minimize* a window reduces it to an icon, which Windows places at the bottom of the screen. Later you can easily restore the application to its former size by double-clicking the icon.

An icon is usually easy to identify by its distinct shape. The application's name always appears below the icon.

 ## To minimize and then restore the Program Manager:

1 Select the Minimize button.
Compare your minimized Program Manager with Figure 1.11.

Figure 1.11

2 Double-click the Program Manager icon.

Tip If you are using the keyboard and have multiple application icons on the screen, you will need to press (ALT)+(ESC) to select the Program Manager icon, before you can restore the Program Manager.

WORKING WITH ICONS

Windows has three basic types of icons: application icons, group icons, and program-item icons, as shown in Figure 1.12.

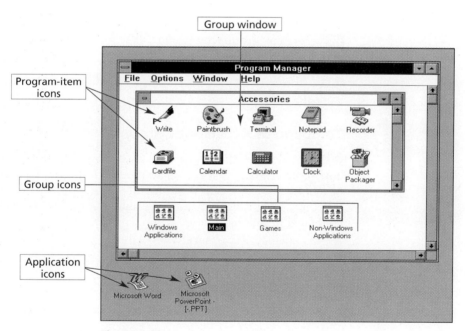

Figure 1.12

- *Application icons* represent programs that have been minimized. In Figure 1.12, Word and PowerPoint are represented as application icons. These programs are running and can be easily restored to a window.
- *Group icons* in the Program Manager represent groups of programs. Group icons open into *group windows* filled with programs. In general, group icons look the same except for their labels. Figure 1.12 has four

group icons—Windows Applications, Main, Games, and Non-Windows Applications—and one group window—Accessories. Accessories is represented as a group icon when it is not open.

■ ***Program-item icons*** are used to start applications. When you open a program-item icon, a window opens with the program inside. The Accessories group in Figure 1.12 contains program-item icons for programs such as Paintbrush, Notepad, and Cardfile. If you were to open the Windows Applications group icon, you would see the Word and Excel program-item icons in the group window. Word and Excel's program-item icons look the same as their application icons.

Using the mouse, you can move the icons to arrange them as you like and open applications you need to work with.

To move an application icon:

1 Minimize the Program Manager by selecting the Minimize button. The Program Manager is now running as an application icon.

2 Drag the Program Manager application icon to a new location.

3 Restore the Program Manager by double-clicking its icon.

To move a group icon:

1 Drag any group icon inside the Program Manager.

2 Practice dragging other group icons.

3 Choose Arrange Icons from the Window menu to arrange the group icons neatly.

To open the Accessories group:

1 Double-click the Accessories group icon.
The screen should look similar to the one in Figure 1.13, although the size of the Accessories group window and the order of the programs may be different. You probably will not be able to see all of the programs that are contained in the Accessories group window.

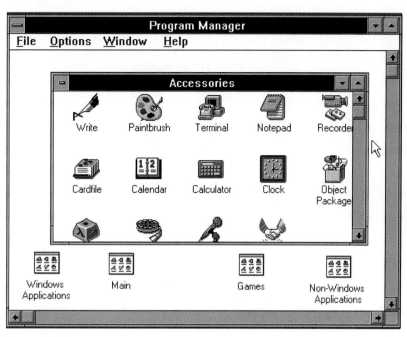

Figure 1.13

USING SCROLL BARS

Scroll bars enable you to see text and graphics that do not fit inside a window. Scroll bars appear on the right side and bottom borders of a window only when the contents of a window are larger than the window itself. For example, in Figure 1.13 the Accessories group window has several program-item icons that do not fit within the boundaries of its window. You can use scroll bars to view all of the icons.

> **Reminder** To move to a specific location in a window, you can drag the scroll box within the scroll bar.

 ### To scroll through and then close
the Accessories group window:

1 If you do not see any scroll bars, reduce the size of the Accessories group window so that you can no longer see one or more program-item icons.

2 Use the scroll bar arrows to see more programs.

3 Double-click the Control-menu box to close the Accessories group window.

EXITING WINDOWS

So far you have used two methods for closing Windows: choosing Exit Windows from the Program Manager File menu and choosing Close from the Program Manager Control menu. A shortcut method of exiting Windows is to double-click the Program Manager Control-menu box.

To exit Windows:

1 Use one of the methods that you have learned to exit Windows.

This concludes Project 1. You can continue with the Study Questions and Review Exercises, or go on to the next project.

SUMMARY AND EXERCISES

Summary

- The Program Manager automatically opens when you start Windows and stays in the background during your entire Windows session. It provides a quick way to start applications and group applications together.
- Menus can contain checkmarks, dimmed commands, and ellipses.
- Dialog boxes ask for information, present information, display warnings, and describe errors.
- The Control menu, which is present in all windows, can be used to close any window. It can also move, size, minimize, maximize, and restore a window for users who don't have a mouse.
- If you wish to concentrate on a particular window, you can maximize it to fill the screen.
- If you are temporarily not using a window, you can reduce it to an icon.
- Icons can be dragged and placed anywhere on the screen.
- Clicking the scroll bars enables you to move horizontally or vertically through a window.

Key Terms and Operations

Key Terms
application icon
checkmark
Control menu
Control-menu box
dialog box
dimmed command
ellipsis
group icon
group window
maximize
minimize
Program Manager
program-item icon
restore
sizing buttons

title bar
toggle
window border

Operations
Display Windows' current operating
    mode
Maximize a window
Minimize a window
Move a window
Move an icon
Open a group window
Restore a window
Size a window
Toggle a command
Use scroll bars
Use the Control menu

Study Questions

True/False

1. The Program Manager is opened automatically when you start Windows. **T   F**

2. Group icons look alike except for their names. **T   F**

3. Application icons look alike except for their names. **T   F**

4. The Control-menu box is located in the upper left corner of every window. **T   F**

5. Scroll bars are always present in all windows. **T   F**

Short Answer

1. A(n) _____ is a small box that prompts the user to provide more information in order to complete a command.

2. In order to fill the entire screen with a particular window, you must _____ that window.

3. When you _____ a window, you reduce it to an icon.

4. _____ appear on the edge of a window when the information in that window is too big to fit within its boundaries.

5. An ellipsis (...) following a command indicates the presence of a(n) _____.

For Discussion

1. List and describe three types of icons.

2. How do you increase the width of a window?

3. Describe how to move a window.

4. Describe three ways to exit Windows.

5. What are dimmed commands?

Review Exercises

1. Check to see how much main memory is available.

2. Size and move the Program Manager window so that it takes up only the upper half of the screen.

3. Open the Main group window.

4. Size and move the Main group window so that it is easily visible on the screen.

5. Close the Main group window.

6. Reduce the Program Manager to an icon.

7. Move the Program Manager icon to the upper right corner of the screen.

8. Restore the Program Manager.

9. Exit Windows.

PROJECT 2: MANAGING PROGRAMS

Objectives

After completing this project, you should be able to:

▶ Use the Program Manager to start a program

▶ Start multiple programs

▶ Switch among programs

▶ Manage multiple programs with the Task List

▶ Concentrate on one program

▶ Set dialog box options

▶ Exit multiple programs

STARTING A PROGRAM

One of the Program Manager's main roles is to start programs. When you start a program, the Program Manager opens a window and places the program into it. Programs and their associated documents are contained in application and document windows.

An *application window* contains a running *application*, a program designed for a particular type of work. For example, the Program Manager runs in an application window as does a word processing program such as Microsoft Word. Figure 2.1 displays a Microsoft Word application window.

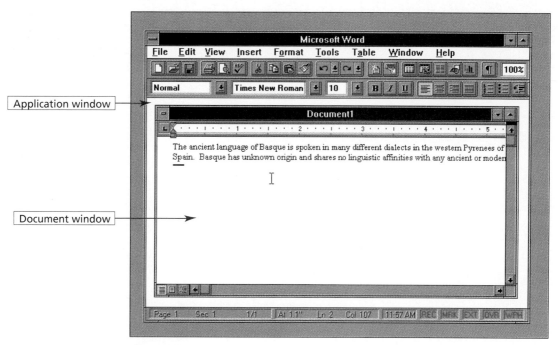

Application window

Document window

Figure 2.1

A *document window* is found inside an application window and contains a *document*, such as a letter, memo, or report. If you are working on multiple documents simultaneously, you will have multiple document windows open within one application window, as shown in Figure 2.2.

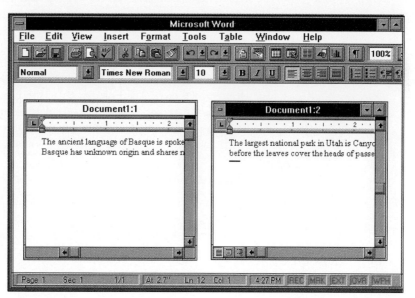

Figure 2.2

A few special applications do not contain document windows. The Program Manager uses group windows, which are similar to document windows because they reside within an application window. For example, the Accessories group window resides within the Program Manager application window.

To open the Accessories group window:

1 If you have not done so already, start Windows.

2 Choose Options from the menu bar. Make sure Minimize On Use is *not* checked. If it is not checked, click anywhere in the desktop. If it is checked, choose Minimize On Use to toggle it off.
When Minimize On Use is checked, the Program Manager will minimize itself every time that you open an application. In this project you don't want that to happen.

3 Open Accessories by double-clicking the Accessories group icon.

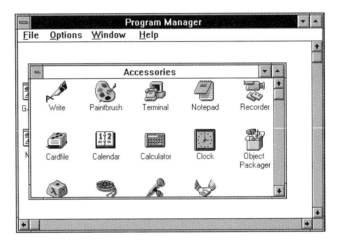

Figure 2.3

The Accessories group window includes utility programs provided as part of the Windows software package. Some of the program icons are shown in Figure 2.3. For example, the **Clock** displays the current time, the **Calculator** allows you to do calculations as you would on any typical calculator, and the **Calendar** serves as an electronic appointment book with an alarm to remind you of important appointments.

To open and close the Calendar program:

1 Double-click the Calendar program-item icon. If necessary, scroll through Accessories to find the Calendar.
The screen looks similar to Figure 2.4. Your Calendar may be positioned differently.

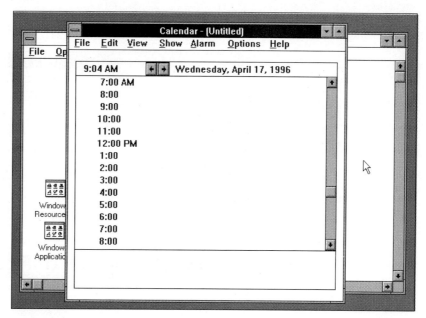

Figure 2.4

2 Choose Exit from the File menu.

STARTING MULTIPLE PROGRAMS (MULTITASKING)

Multitasking—the capability to run multiple programs simultaneously—is one of the main strengths of Windows 3.1. This capability is called multitasking because programs are often referred to as *tasks*. In this exercise you will reopen the Calendar and then open the Cardfile. The *Cardfile*, another utility program, is an electronic set of index cards that you can use to keep track of names, addresses, telephone numbers, and so on. To switch from one program to another, you will click any part of the desired window.

To run programs simultaneously:

1 Double-click the Calendar program-item icon.

2 Click any part of the Program Manager window.
If the Program Manager is difficult to see in the background, you may have to downsize the Calendar window or move it to one side.

3 Double-click the Cardfile program-item icon.

4 Switch back and forth among the open windows by clicking any part of the desired window. You may have to resize or move windows.
Figure 2.5 shows how the screen can look with four windows open simultaneously.

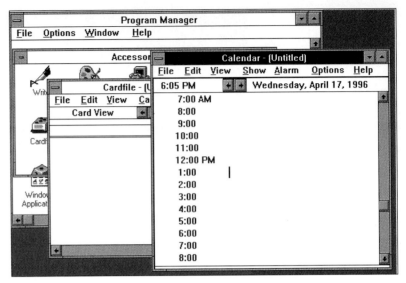

Figure 2.5

Your screen may look somewhat different, but, essentially, you will have three open application windows: the Program Manager, the Calendar, and the Cardfile. Notice that the Accessories group window is also open within the Program Manager. Because the Accessories window is contained in the Program Manager, its size and placement on the screen depend on the Program Manager's size and placement on the screen.

MANAGING PROGRAMS WITH THE TASK LIST

The **Task List** is a window that enables you to switch from one program to another, to arrange programs neatly, and to close programs.

Tip Using the Task List is one of the few operations in which mouse users may want to use the keyboard. Mouse users can pull up the Task List by double-clicking the desktop, but since the desktop is often covered with open windows, it may be easier to press (CTRL) + (ESC) to pull up the Task List.

 To open the Task List:

1 Double-click anywhere on the desktop area.
The Task List dialog box is displayed as shown in Figure 2.6.

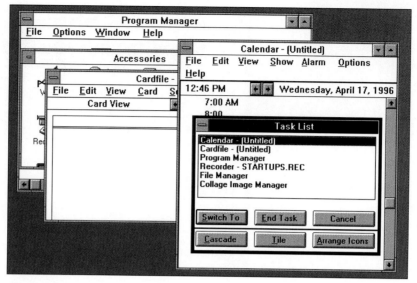

Figure 2.6

Switching Programs

You can switch from one program to another by clicking any part of the target window, but if one window is completely covering another, you can always switch programs with the Task List.

To switch programs with the Task List:

1 Double-click the Program Manager from the Task List.

2 Press (CTRL) + (ESC) to pull up the Task List.

3 Double-click the Cardfile from the Task List.

4 Press (CTRL) + (ESC) to pull up the Task List.

5 Double-click the Calendar from the Task List.

Cascading and Tiling Windows

Often it is difficult to work with several open windows that have been arbitrarily positioned on the screen. Windows 3.1 offers two methods for arranging open windows: cascading and tiling. *Cascading* causes all windows to overlap so that their title bars are visible. *Tiling* reduces all open windows to a size in which they can be accommodated side-by-side on the screen, like tiles. This "bird's-eye view" might be best suited for copying and pasting between windows.

To cascade multiple windows with the Task List:

1 Press (CTRL) + (ESC) to pull up the Task List.

2 Select Cascade.

The screen now looks like Figure 2.7.

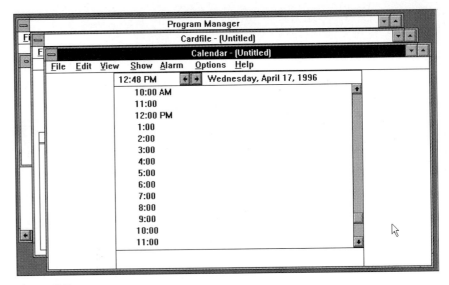

Figure 2.7

 ### To tile windows with the Task List:

1 Press (CTRL) + (ESC) to pull up the Task List.

2 Select Tile.

The screen now looks like Figure 2.8.

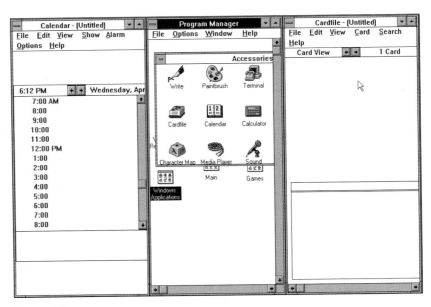

Figure 2.8

EXITING PROGRAMS

You are now done with the Calendar and the Cardfile. You can close most programs in Windows by choosing the Exit command from the File menu. Before you can exit the Cardfile, however, you will need to restore it.

To exit the Calendar and the Cardfile:

1 Choose Exit from the File menu.
A dialog box appears, asking you if you wish to save your appointments.

2 Select No.

3 Double-click the Cardfile to restore it.

4 Choose Exit from the File menu.

5 Restore the Program Manager.

EXIT   If necessary, you can exit Windows now and continue this project later.

CONCENTRATING ON ONE PROGRAM

If you have several open windows, they can end up appearing rather small and difficult to work with. You will find that you normally use only one or two applications at a time, so it's a good idea to reduce unused programs to icons so that they are out of the way. Your main applications can then be sized to workable dimensions. Since a minimized application is still running in memory, you can resume working at the spot where you left off when you restore it.

In the steps that follow, you will enter appointments in the Calendar and print them out. To concentrate on the Calendar, you will minimize unused programs and then adjust the Calendar to a workable size.

To concentrate on the Calendar:

1 If necessary, start Windows and open the Cardfile and Calendar programs.

2 Minimize the Program Manager.

3 Minimize the Cardfile.

4 Resize the Calendar so that you can work with it comfortably.
The screen now looks similar to Figure 2.9.

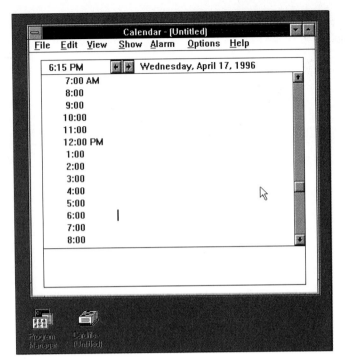

Figure 2.9

 To enter appointments for the following day:

1 Choose Next from the Show menu.

2 Enter a list of things that you will be doing tomorrow.
The screen now looks similar to Figure 2.10, but your appointments will be different.

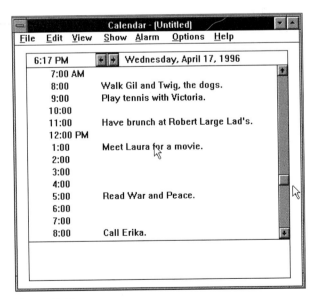

Figure 2.10

SETTING DIALOG BOX OPTIONS

Dialog boxes display information and prompt you to enter text. You can also adjust the settings of Windows options by using option buttons, command buttons, and check boxes. You move the cursor from one option to another by selecting the option.

Option buttons appear in small groups of related options from which you can select only one item. For example, you use option buttons in the Print Setup dialog box to set up the printer.

To set printer options:

1 Choose Print Setup from the File menu.

The Print Setup dialog box appears as shown in Figure 2.11. In the box labeled Orientation, you can choose one of two option buttons: Portrait or Landscape. A portrait orientation means that your document will be printed vertically on the paper. A landscape orientation prints horizontally.

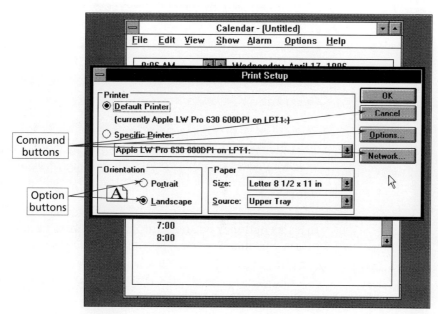

Figure 2.11

2 Select Landscape.

Command buttons are rectangular buttons labeled with an action. The Print Setup dialog box contains the two most common command buttons, OK and Cancel, and the Options and Network command buttons. When you select OK the dialog box closes, and any new settings are saved. Selecting Cancel closes the dialog box without saving new settings. Notice that Options and Network are each followed by an ellipsis (...), which indicates that another dialog box will appear if you choose this option.

To view more options for setting up the printer:

1 Select Options.
A dialog box similar to Figure 2.12 is displayed, if you are using a laser printer.

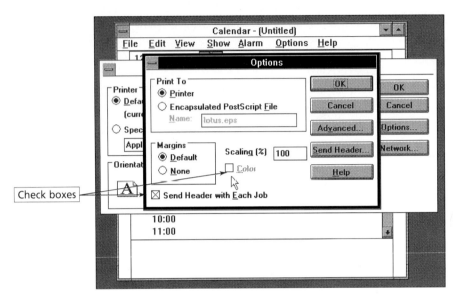

Figure 2.12

In Figure 2.12, Send Header with Each Job has a ***check box*** to the left, which indicates that this option can be toggled on and off. When the box is checked, the option is on; when the boxed is not checked, the option is off.

If your screen does not display Send Header with Each Job, it means that this option is not relevant to your printer's setup, and you should proceed to step 2 of the following numbered steps.

To toggle a check box option and cancel any new settings:

1 Select Send Header with Each Job.
You should see an *X* in the check box.

2 Select Cancel to close the dialog box without saving any of the new settings.

Now you can print your appointment calendar and then close all the windows you have open.

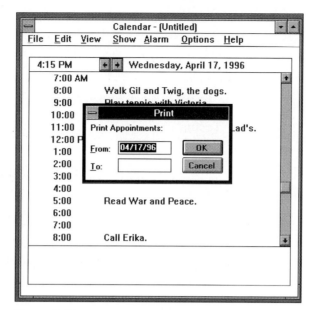

Figure 2.13

 ## To print your appointments:

1 Choose Print from the File menu.
The Print dialog box appears as shown in Figure 2.13.

2 Select OK in the Print dialog box.

3 Exit the Calendar and Cardfile programs, using the method you learned earlier in the project.

This concludes Project 2. You can either exit Windows or go on to work the Study Questions and Review Exercises.

SUMMARY AND EXERCISES

Summary

- You use the Program Manager to start and manage programs.
- Programs and their associated documents are contained in two types of windows: application and document. An application window contains an application. A document window contains documents and is found within an application window.
- You start a program by double-clicking its program-item icon.
- You can close most programs by choosing Exit from the File menu.
- Windows provides multitasking capabilities.
- The Task List arranges open programs, switches among open programs, and closes programs.
- Multiple open windows can be arranged with the Cascade or Tile options.

- To concentrate on one program, you can minimize unused running applications.
- Dialog box settings can be adjusted with option buttons, command buttons, and check boxes.

Key Terms and Operations

Key Terms

application
application window
Calculator
Calendar
Cardfile
cascading
check box
Clock
command button
document

document window
option button
task
Task List
tiling

Operations

Manage programs with the Task List
Set dialog box options
Start and exit a program
Start multiple programs

Study Questions

True/False

1. To restore a minimized program with a mouse, you double-click its icon. **T   F**

2. A document is a file created by application software. **T   F**

3. The Task List is not used to switch between programs. **T   F**

4. A program is also known as a task. **T   F**

5. Exiting a program means reducing it to an icon. **T   F**

Short Answer

1. You can adjust the settings of Windows options by using option buttons, command buttons, and _____.

2. The ability to run several programs at one time is called _____.

3. When Minimize On Use is checked, the _____ minimizes itself every time that you open an application.

4. The Calendar and the _____ are two accessories provided with Windows.

5. To open a program with a mouse, you _____ its icon.

For Discussion

1. Describe the two basic types of windows associated with applications.

2. What type of window contains the Program Manager?

3. What is the difference between cascading windows and tiling windows?

4. How do you bring up the Task List?

5. What is meant by restoring a program?

Review Exercises

1. Go into the Accessories group and open the Clock.

2. From the Accessories group, open the Calculator.

3. Switch back and forth among the open windows by using the Task List.

4. Tile all of your open windows.

5. Cascade all of your open windows.

6. Size the clock so that it is in a small window in the upper right corner of the screen.

7. Reduce the Program Manager to an application icon.

8. Make sure the Calculator is selected, and then press (F1) to get help on using the Calculator.

9. Select Enter Calculations from the Help screen.

10. Choose Print Topic from the File menu. The printout explains how to enter calculations.

11. Choose Exit from the File menu to exit Help.

12. Exit from all programs, including the Program Manager.

Objectives

After completing this project, you should be able to:

▶ Use the File Manager to view disks, directories, and files

▶ Use the File Manager to copy a file

▶ Temporarily exit to DOS to run a command

▶ Create a document with Windows Write

▶ Copy data with the Clipboard

▶ View the contents of the Clipboard

ORGANIZING A DISK WITH DIRECTORIES

Imagine how inefficiently a hospital would be run if patients were randomly placed in rooms despite the reason for admittance or level of care required. Think about the staff time and other resources that would be consumed if expectant mothers in labor and patients requiring intensive care were placed in widely scattered rooms on several floors.

Consider another example. Have you ever looked through a catalog to order merchandise? Think about how long it would take you to find all the garden supplies if individual products were organized by size instead of by category.

One reason hospitals group similar patients and catalogs group similar items is to shorten processing time. In a computer environment, improvements in processing a large number of program files and user-developed data files can also be made if similar files are grouped together. DOS groups files stored on disk using a *directory*. You could think of a directory as the disk's table of contents.

DOS automatically creates the first directory each time a new disk is prepared to accept data. Once DOS has created this *root directory*, you can create additional directories within the root directory and *subdirectories* within directories. For example, you can create separate directories for your word processing, spreadsheet, and database files. Then you can create separate subdirectories to organize your different word processing files.

Figure 3.1 illustrates a typical directory structure, including directories for three software programs: DB (database), SS (spreadsheet), and WP (word processing).

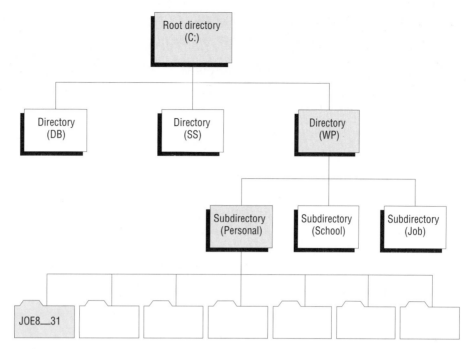

Figure 3.1

When you refer to a file in a DOS command, you must specify a *path,* which describes the route a program must follow to access data stored on disk. The path to the JOE8__31 word-processed document in the previous figure would be stated as

C:\WP\PERSONAL\JOE8_31

Drive   Directory   Subdirectory   File

Note that the drive, directory, and file within a path are separated by a backslash (\). You will learn how to create and maintain directories in Project 3.

OPENING THE FILE MANAGER

The *File Manager* is a powerful Windows program that enables you to manage your files and directories. It possesses counterparts to most DOS operations and adds a few commands of its own. For example, the File Manager allows you to copy, move, delete, rename, and search for files; make, display, and remove directories; and even format system and data disks.

When you open the File Manager, you see a *directory window* that is split in two, as shown in Figure 3.2. The left half of the window displays the directory structure of the current drive, and the right half displays the contents of the current directory.

To open the File Manager:

1 If you have not done so already, start Windows.

2 Double-click the Main group icon from the Program Manager.

3 Double-click the File Manager program-item icon.
The screen now looks like Figure 3.2.

Don't worry if your directory structure looks somewhat different than the figure. Directory structures are set up according to the preference of the user.

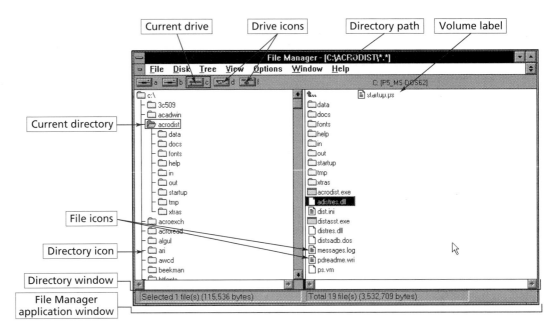

Figure 3.2

The directory window contains two descriptive labels: the directory path and the volume label. The ***directory path*** displays the current drive letter and directory. The ***volume label***, which is typically assigned during formatting, is a name used to refer to a drive or diskette.

Three icons enable you to manage drives, directories, and files. **Drive icons** represent floppy and hard disk drives, optical drives, or other storage devices. **Directory icons** look like small folders and represent directories on the current disk. The open folder icon is the current directory; its contents are listed in the right half of the directory window. Next to each file name is a **file icon**. Documents and programs have different file icons.

VIEWING DISKS, DIRECTORIES, AND FILES

When you first enter the File Manager, you will see a display of directories of the current drive. Most likely, the current drive will be a hard disk with many directories, such as the one in the previous figure. You can display the contents of any drive by selecting the drive icon.

Note the following instructions assume that you are working with a 3½-inch disk.

To change disk drives:

1 Look at the disk drive icons across the top of the directory window. Note which drive is currently selected.

2 Make sure a diskette is in drive A: (for some computers, drive B:), and then select the drive icon for drive A: by clicking it.
You should see the contents of drive A: in the directory window.

3 Go back to the hard disk drive by selecting the appropriate disk drive icon.

To open the Windows directory:

1 Look for a directory named Windows.

2 If Windows is *not* selected, double-click the Windows directory.
The screen now looks similar to Figure 3.3.

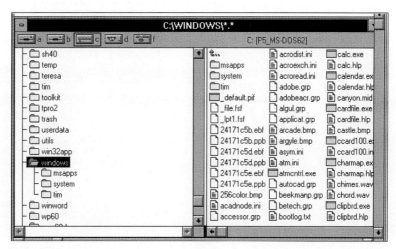

Figure 3.3

In the right half of the directory window, Windows displays file names in alphabetical order. You can change the view to display file details such as sizes, dates, and times along with file names, as shown in Figure 3.4. This view is important if you need to see things such as a file's last modification date.

To view files with their details:

1 Choose All File Details from the View menu.

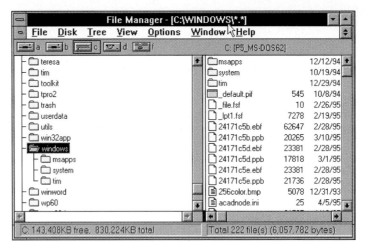

Figure 3.4

2 Size the directory window so that you can see all of the file details. Your directory window now looks similar to Figure 3.5. The file size is in bytes, the date is the last modification date, and the time is the last modification time.

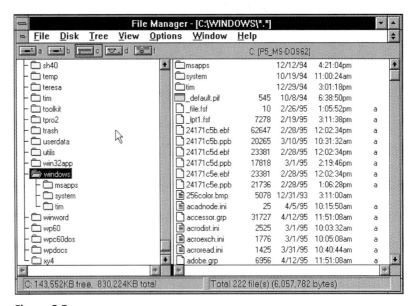

Figure 3.5

If file sizes, dates, and times are not essential, you can change the view back to file names only. More files can be displayed on the screen when only their names are listed.

To view files by name:

1 Chose Name from the View menu.
Typically, files are displayed in alphabetical order. Another common way of listing files is by their type, that is, by their extension.

To sort files by their type:

1 Choose Sort by Type from the View menu.
Notice that all files are grouped by their extensions.

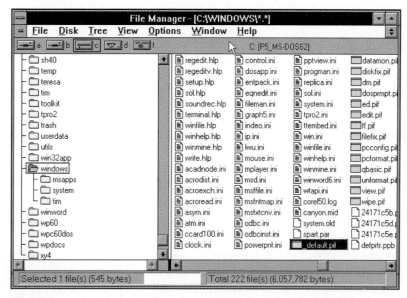

Figure 3.6

COPYING A FILE WITH THE FILE MANAGER

At times you will need to transfer a file from one disk to another. For example, if you are working in an office and saving all of your work on a hard disk, you can back up your files or take your work home with you by copying the files to a floppy disk. The File Manager can be used to copy files. BOXES.BMP is a graphics file that you are going to copy to drive A:. Be sure a floppy disk is in drive A:.

To copy a file:

1 Select the file BOXES.BMP or any other file with the .BMP extension if BOXES.BMP does not appear on your screen.

2 Choose Copy from the File menu.

3 Type **A:** in the dialog box and then click OK.
A copy of BOXES.BMP is now on drive A:

4 Choose Exit from the File menu to exit the File Manager.

The File Manager is a powerful program. You have just used it to perform two of the most common DOS operations: listing files and copying files. Later, spend some time exploring more of the File Manager's useful features.

EXIT If necessary, you can exit Windows now and continue this project later.

USING DOS COMMANDS

Within the File Manager, with just a click of the mouse, you can do many things that would otherwise require a text-based DOS command. There will be times, however, when you will need to go to the DOS prompt and type a command. CHKDSK is a DOS command that has no real equivalent within Windows. In addition to providing a disk's status, CHKDSK checks your disk for errors. You can access the DOS prompt through the Main group window.

 To run the CHKDSK command from the DOS prompt:

1 If necessary, start Windows.

2 Double-click the MS-DOS Prompt icon in the Main program group.

3 At the DOS prompt type **CHKDSK A:** and then press ⟨ENTER⟩
The screen now looks similar to Figure 3.7.

```
          Press ALT+TAB to switch to Windows or another application.
          Press ALT+ENTER to switch this MS-DOS Prompt between a
          window and full screen.




Microsoft(R)  MS-DOS(R) Version 5.00
                    (C)Copyright Microsoft Corp 1981-1991.

D:\WINDOWS>chkdsk a:

Volume 104011AB500 created 07-17-1990 12:02p


    362496 bytes total disk space
    349184 bytes in 85 user files
     13312 bytes available on disk


      1024 bytes in each allocation unit
       354 total allocation units on disk
        13 available allocation units on disk


    655360 total bytes memory
     43448 bytes free

D:\WINDOWS>
```

Figure 3.7

If you see any error messages when you run CHKDSK, you must *completely* exit Windows by choosing Exit Windows from the Program Manager's File menu. Then type CHKDSK A: /F at the DOS prompt. If you do not completely exit Windows before executing this command, you could lose some data.

To exit DOS and return to Windows:

1 Type EXIT and press (ENTER)

2 Double-click the Control-menu box for the Main group window. You are now back at the Program Manager window.

CREATING A DOCUMENT WITH WRITE

The Accessories group in the Program Manager contains several utility programs for performing simple tasks. For example, if you're working in a program and realize you forgot to write your grocery list, you can pull up the electronic *Notepad* and list your items. The Accessories group also contains a small word processing program called *Write* and a painting program called *Paintbrush.* Some programs here you have seen, such as the Calendar and the Cardfile. Accessories such as Write and Paintbrush enable you to create and save documents. Accessories such as the Clock aren't used to create documents. The Clock simply displays the current time.

The Write program works well for creating memos and other short documents. Many people use it daily when they don't need the power of a full-featured word processor.

To open Write:

1 Double-click the Accessories group icon.

2 Double-click the Write program-item icon.

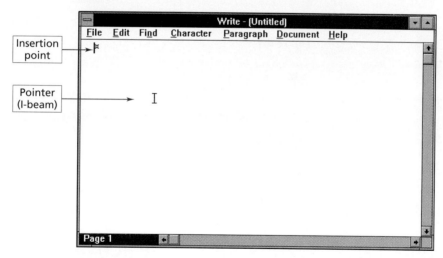

Figure 3.8

As soon as you enter Write, you can begin typing. As you type, the text appears on the screen at a vertical blinking line called the **insertion point**, as shown in Figure 3.8. The insertion point can be moved by positioning the pointer at the desired location and then clicking the mouse. Notice that the pointer changes from an arrow to an I-beam when it is in Write's work area.

In the following steps, you will create, save, and print a Write document. Be sure you have a floppy disk in drive A:

To enter text:

1 Type **The Bob Westbrook Story,** using *your* name instead of Bob's.

2 Press (ENTER) twice.

3 Type a short description of yourself, a one paragraph autobiography.

To save a document:

1 Choose Save from the File menu.

2 Type the file name **A:AUTOBIO**

The screen now looks similar to Figure 3.9. Write automatically adds the extension .WRI to the file name when it saves the document.

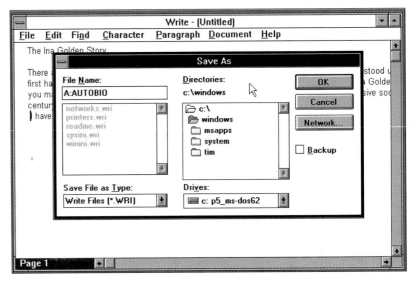

Figure 3.9

3 Select OK.

To print a document and exit Write:

1 Choose Print from the File menu.
The Print dialog box appears.

2 Select OK.

3 Choose Exit from the File menu.

COPYING DATA WITH THE CLIPBOARD

Recall that the Clipboard is used to transfer data between documents. Data that has been copied from a document is temporarily placed into the Clipboard, and from there it can then be pasted into almost any other Windows document. In the steps that follow you will create a new Write document and use the clipboard to paste it onto the document you created earlier.

To open Write and enter text:

1 Select the Write program-item icon from the Accessories group window.

2 Type a short descriptive paragraph of your favorite sport.

 To copy information:

1 With the mouse, position the insertion point at the beginning of the paragraph.

2 Drag the mouse so that the entire paragraph is selected.

3 Choose Copy from the Edit menu.
This places the highlighted data into the Clipboard.

 To open another Write document:

1 Use the Task List to return to the Program Manager.

2 Select the Write program-item icon from the Accessories group window.

3 Choose Open from the File menu.

4 Type **A:AUTOBIO.WRI** and then press (ENTER)
Note that Write automatically added the extension .WRI when it saved the file.

5 Move the insertion point to the end of the document.

6 Choose Paste from the Edit menu.
The text from the Clipboard now appears.

 To exit both documents:

1 Choose Exit from the File menu.

2 Select Yes when asked to save your file.

3 Use the Task List to return to the other Write document, which is listed as Write-[Untitled].

4 Choose Exit from the File menu.

5 Select No when asked to save your file.

6 Double-click the Accessories group Control-menu box to close the Accessories window.
You are now back at the Program Manager window.

VIEWING THE CONTENTS OF THE CLIPBOARD

After you have placed data in the Clipboard, the contents of the Clipboard remain the same until you replace them with more data. Because it can be difficult to remember what was last placed there, Windows allows you to view the Clipboard's contents.

To view the contents of the Clipboard:

1 Double-click the Main group icon.

2 Double-click the Clipboard program-item icon.

You can see the text that you copied earlier. If you were to paste something into any document right now, this is the data that would be pasted.

3 Choose Exit from the File menu to exit the Clipboard.

4 Double-click the Main group window Control-menu box to close the current window.

You are now at the Program Manager window.

This concludes Project 3. You can either exit Windows or go on to work the Study Questions and Review Exercises.

SUMMARY AND EXERCISES

Summary

- The File Manager is a powerful Windows program for managing files and directories. It employs a graphical interface to perform many of the same operations that you would otherwise execute from the DOS prompt.
- You can select the MS-DOS Prompt icon to display the DOS prompt for commands such as CHKDSK that have no equivalent in Windows.
- Write is a word processing program designed for creating small documents.
- The Clipboard can be used to copy data between documents, even documents created by different applications.

Key Terms and Operations

Key Terms
directory
directory icon
directory path
directory window
drive icon
file icon
File Manager
insertion point
Notepad
Paintbrush
path
root directory
subdirectories

volume label
Write

Operations
Change disk drives
Copy a file
Create a document with Write
Open the File Manager
Run the CHKDSK command
Use the Clipboard to copy and paste data
View the contents of the Clipboard
View the contents of a directory

Study Questions

True/False

1. The DOS prompt program-item icon is contained in the Accessories group. **T** **F**

2. The Clipboard program-item icon is contained in the Main group.   **T**   **F**

3. The File Manager has an equivalent command for many DOS commands.   **T**   **F**

4. You can copy files with the File Manager.   **T**   **F**

5. Windows has an electronic notepad.   **T**   **F**

Short Answer

1. The insertion point is positioned on the screen by a pointer that looks like a(n) _____.

2. If you go to DOS by clicking the DOS program-item icon, you can return by typing _____.

3. Windows' word processing program is called _____.

4. Windows' drawing program is called _____.

5. The _____ is a Windows feature that enables you to manage files and directories.

For Discussion

1. Why would you want to run a DOS command from within Windows?

2. Describe the relationship between the directory window and the File Manager application window.

3. In the File Manager, what is meant by file details?

4. What is the purpose of the Clipboard?

5. Describe two utility programs contained in the Accessories group.

Review Exercises

1. Use the File Manager to go into the DOS subdirectory on the hard disk.

2. Copy TREE.COM to drive A: (or drive B: if you are using drive B:).

3. Change drives from the hard disk to drive A:.

4. Delete TREE.COM from drive A: by selecting the file name and then choosing Delete from the File menu.

5. Delete BOXES.BMP from drive A:.

6. Exit the File Manager.

7. From the Main program group go to the DOS prompt by selecting the correct program-item icon.

8. Type **A:** and then press (ENTER)

9. At the DOS prompt type **DIR** > **PRN** and then press (ENTER)
   This command prints a list of the file names on your default disk. You should not see TREE.COM or BOXES.COM, since they have both been deleted.

10. Type **EXIT** to return to Windows.

PART II

Microsoft Word 6

Overview

People have been processing words for centuries using chisels, quills, pens, and pencils. In the mid-1800s, the first typewriters added mechanical precision and speeded matters up somewhat, but were still clumsy and relatively inefficient. Revision and editing required cutting and pasting, and ultimately retyping. It was not uncommon for a letter or manuscript to be retyped several times before it was complete. If the manuscript was for publication, it would then need to be completely retyped by a typographer to put it into publishable form.

The first real word processor was the IBM Magnetic Tape/Selectric typewriter, introduced in 1964. It recorded the typist's keystrokes on a magnetic tape and allowed the tape to be revised and then played back on an electric typewriter directly from the tape. It was awkward and slow by today's standards, but it reduced the amount of retyping needed to produce finished documents. Today, *word processing* involves the use of a computer to write, edit, format, store, and print documents.

USING A WORD PROCESSOR

Not only have modern word processors eliminated cutting, pasting, and retyping, but they also have combined writing, revising, editing, and often the publication process itself into one integrated system. With your word processor, you can pull together elements from many sources, such as charts, graphs, photographs, or drawings, as well as words. You can format your documents as only commercial typesetters could a decade ago—using different typefaces and sizes, using columns and borders, or including graphics with your words. Word processing will make your written communication easier, and probably more effective and more attractive.

Most people who use personal computers use them for word processing. Many use them for nothing else. Word processors vastly simplify the creation and development of documents. Text that is typed on the computer keyboard is stored on a magnetic disk. The text can be called back up on the computer screen and revised and saved repeatedly. At any time in the preparation process, the text can be printed out.

Modern word processors offer a variety of tools to assist in the document preparation process. Today's full-fledged word processors do much more than manipulate words. They are an integral part of the desktop publishing process, allowing you to combine words, pictures, charts, equations—even sound—in your documents. They allow extensive formatting choices and can print on anything from a simple dot-matrix printer to a complex typesetting machine.

USING WORD FOR WINDOWS

Word processing programs vary widely in their capabilities and ease of use. Microsoft Word 6.0 for Windows is an industrial-strength word processor, as capable of producing the Great American Novel or a complex technical document as it is preparing a one-page memo or the envelope to put that memo in. Word 6.0 for Windows probably contains more features and capabilities than you'll ever need. Despite its power, however, you should find it relatively easy to learn and use for basic writing needs. As your needs as a writer grow, those advanced features will be there for you to use, but they won't be in the way in the meantime.

Word 6.0 for Windows can make your writing easier and more polished. Correcting and editing your writing with a word processor allows your ideas to flow onto paper more easily. Then you can use a variety of features to revise and develop your document. You can easily insert, delete, and correct words. You can move, copy, and delete blocks of text. You can use the Word for Windows electronic dictionary to check the spelling of every word in your document. You can use the electronic thesaurus to find alternative word choices while you're writing or revising. You can use a grammar checker that looks for common style and usage problems. Word 6.0 for Windows will even correct keyboarding errors as you type. For example, if you accidentally type *adn*, it will automatically substitute *and*.

Sophisticated formatting capabilities allow you to create professional-quality documents that look like they came from the printer rather than out of a printer. Word for Windows is a ***WYSIWYG*** word processor, which means what you see is what you get. Because what you see on-screen is what you will get from your printer, you can see how formatting changes will affect your final document. With a click of the mouse, you can create numbered lists, bulleted lists, or indentations. With another click you can create a table and then format it to present data you either type in or import from spreadsheets or databases. Click again for the Word for Windows integrated charting program or illustration program. For a term paper or lab report, you can add headers and footers, footnotes, or a table of contents. You can add columns and pictures to the format for your organization's newsletter. Word for Windows also contains a number of templates and automatic formatting features to help you give your documents a polished, professional look.

Word for Windows is a powerful writing, editing, and publishing tool. You'll find your investment in learning how to use it rewarded in added ease and flexibility in writing, in the creative options it lends to your written communication, and in the polish it allows you to give your written presentation.

STARTING WORD FOR WINDOWS

In this module you will create, edit, save, and print several documents. Work all numbered steps in order so your document content and screen displays will coincide with those described. You can interrupt your work at the end of any series of numbered steps and exit Word for Windows. If you wish to retrieve the document later and continue where you stopped, be sure to save your document (*file*) before exiting. You can print your document at any point.

To start Word for Windows:

1 Start Windows running on your computer.

2 Double-click the Word for Windows icon.

You may need to open an Applications group window first, depending on the way the system and desktop are organized. Check with your instructor or lab assistant if you need help with this step.

> **Tip:** When you see a button or icon next to a numbered step, you can select the button or icon on the screen in place of the menu command in the numbered step.

The Word for Windows screen will appear on the monitor, along with a Tip of the Day box in the middle of the screen, as shown in Figure 0.1. If the Tip of the Day box does not appear on the screen, this feature has probably been turned off on your system, and you can skip step 3.

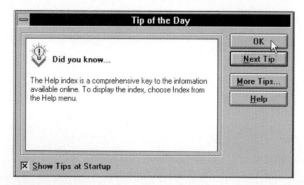

Figure 0.1

3 Select OK.

The monitor should now look like Figure 0.2.

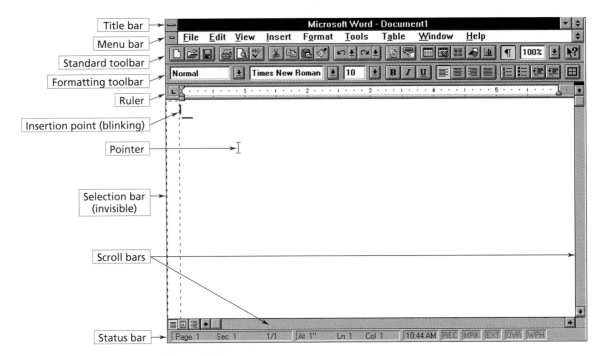

Figure 0.2

THE WORD FOR WINDOWS SCREEN

The Word for Windows screen is organized into several areas that allow you not only to view your document, but also to manipulate it in a variety of ways.

Title bar: contains the title of the application (Microsoft Word) and of the document file you're working on (probably Document1 if you haven't named the file yet).

Menu bar: gives you access to word processing commands.

Standard toolbar: contains buttons that allow you to perform many word processing tasks with one click of the mouse.

Formatting toolbar: contains information, menus, and buttons related to formatting your document.

Ruler: displays and allows you to control margins, indents, tab settings, and so on.

Scroll bars: used to move around in your document. The horizontal scroll bar also includes buttons to display your document in different ways.

Status bar: gives basic information about your document or about word processing modes.

Selection bar: use to select part of your document with a mouse.

You can customize the Word for Windows screen to suit your preferences and working habits. The standard toolbar, formatting toolbar, and ruler can all be individually turned on or off. You can also add other specialized toolbars. You can even display your document full-screen, with no menus, rulers, or toolbars showing.

To turn the standard toolbar off and on:

1 Choose Toolbars from the View menu.
The dialog box shown in Figure 0.3 should appear on the screen.

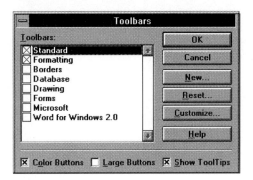

Figure 0.3

2 Click Standard to clear the check box.

3 Select OK.
Note that the standard toolbar disappears. You can turn it back on by reversing the procedure.

4 Choose Toolbars from the View menu.

5 Click Standard to put an "X" in the check box.

6 Select OK.

If you want to see your text alone, with no menus or toolbars showing, you can switch to full-screen view.

 ### To change to full-screen view:

1 Choose Full Screen from the View menu.
When you want the menus and toolbars back, you can drop out of full-screen view easily.

 2 Click the center of the Full Screen button, located near the bottom of the screen to exit full screen view.

GETTING ONLINE HELP

Word for Windows offers two styles of Help on-screen, while you're working at the computer. You can open a contents screen that will direct you to information about using Word for Windows, will give on-screen examples and demonstrations, or will supply reference information. You can also get help with the specific feature you want to use by accessing *context-sensitive Help*. This Help approach takes you directly to the information about a feature you have selected or are using without requiring you to search through a list of topics.

 ### To open Word Help Contents:

1 Choose Contents from the Help menu.

The screen should look like Figure 0.4:

Help buttons →

Press F1 for
Help instructions

Click these icons
for more information
about Word →

Figure 0.4

The menu bar and the five buttons beneath it work just as they do in all Windows Help screens.

2 Press F1 to learn how to use Help.

Many Help topics contain *jumps*, which are references to definitions or further Help information. In this screen, Help Basics is one of many jumps, denoted by an underline and contrasting color. When you use the mouse to position the pointer on a jump, the pointer changes to a pointing hand.

3 Click Help Basics in the Introduction section.

4 Read the instructions on how to use Help.

5 Click "jumps" in the Help text.

6 Read the description of a jump in the pop-up window.

7 Click once to close the window.

8 Choose Exit from the File menu (or double-click the Control menu box at the upper left corner of the Help window) to exit help.

 To get context-sensitive Help on how to save a file:

1 Click File in the menu bar to open the drop-down File menu.

2 Use ↓ and ↑ to select the Save option.

3 Press F1 to get Help on saving a file.

4 Choose Exit from the File menu.

You can also use the mouse to get context-sensitive Help. To do the following steps, you must be using a mouse.

To use the Help pointer to get context-sensitive Help on the Save File button:

1 Use the mouse to position the pointer on the Help button on the standard toolbar, but don't click yet.
Note that after a few moments a *ToolTip* appears below the pointer, indicating the function of the button.

2 Click the Help button to change the pointer to a Help pointer that combines a question mark with the usual pointer.

3 Use the mouse to position the Help pointer on the Save button on the toolbar.

4 Click to open the Help window.

5 Choose Exit from the File menu to exit Help.

EXITING WORD FOR WINDOWS

Word for Windows has a safety feature to prevent the loss of text. If you attempt to quit the program without first saving your file, Word for Windows will automatically ask if you want to save changes to your file. To see how this safety feature works, you must first type something on the screen.

To exit Word for Windows:

1 Type some text on the screen. It can be anything: your name, the name of your dog or cat, the name of your favorite rock star. It can be only a few characters—just so you've changed the document a little bit.

2 Choose Exit from the File menu (or double-click the Control menu box at the upper left corner of the Word window).
Because you made changes to your document before quitting, you'll get the warning shown in Figure 0.5:

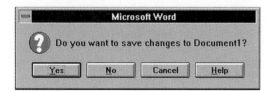

Figure 0.5

If you select Yes, the Save As dialog box will appear so you can save your file (you'll see how to do that in the next project). If you select No, Word will quit without saving changes to the file. If you select Cancel, Word will return you to the document without quitting. If you select Help, you'll get information about these options.

3 Select No.
This should return you to the Windows desktop.

This concludes the Overview. You can either exit Word, or go on to work the Study Questions.

SUMMARY AND EXERCISES

Summary

- Word processing is using a computer to write, edit, format, store, and print documents.
- Word for Windows is a powerful word processing program with extensive features for creating, saving, retrieving, editing, and printing documents.
- You can modify the Word for Windows screen to suit your working habits.
- Whenever you get stuck with menus, commands, or concepts, you can use the Word for Windows on-screen Help facility instead of having to page through a manual.

Key Terms and Operations

Key Terms	
context-sensitive Help	scroll bar
file	selection bar
formatting toolbar	standard toolbar
jump	status bar
menu bar	title bar
ruler	word processing
	WYSIWYG

Study Questions

Multiple Choice

1. If you try to quit Word for Windows without first saving changes to your document:
    a. The changes will be lost.
    b. Word for Windows will save the changes automatically.
    c. You will be asked if you want to save changes before quitting.
    d. You will destroy your document file.

2. To change the pointer to its Help shape (a question mark) to access context-sensitive Help:
    a. Press (CTRL) + **H**
    b. Click the Help button.
    c. Double-click the Help menu.
    d. Press and hold down the (ALT) and (SHFT) keys.

3. What is the major reason a word processor like Word for Windows saves time and effort?
    a. You don't have to retype the entire document each time you make changes or additions.
    b. You can type faster on a computer.
    c. You can format text using different typefaces and sizes.
    d. You can integrate pictures and text.

4. You can turn toolbars on and off by:
   a. pressing (CTRL) + T
   b. using the Tools menu.
   c. double-clicking the toolbar.
   d. using the View menu.

5. You normally start Word for Windows:
   a. at the DOS prompt.
   b. from the Windows Program Manager.
   c. from within the document you are editing.
   d. from the Windows File Manager.

Short Answer

1. The _____ at the bottom of the screen gives basic information about your document or about word processing modes.

2. _____ is an acronym indicating that the screen shows your document exactly as the document will be printed.

3. Word's _____-sensitive Help provides information about the feature you have selected or are about to use.

4. A _____ contains a row of buttons that allow you to perform common word processing tasks with a click of the mouse.

5. To retrieve a document to edit it later, you must first save it as a _____.

For Discussion

1. How do you start Word for Windows on your system?

2. Describe three ways to access the Help system in Word for Windows.

3. What writing and editing functions are included in a modern word processor such as Word for Windows?

Objectives

After completing this project, you should be able to:

▶ Open a new document

▶ Enter text

▶ Display nonprinting characters

▶ Move around in a document

▶ Save a document

▶ Make backup copies of your document

In this project you will create a new document, type text, move around in the document, make simple corrections, and save the document. You'll begin preparing a résumé that could be sent to prospective employers. When you finish this project, you'll know the rudiments of word processing with Word for Windows.

CASE STUDY: CREATING A RÉSUMÉ

Assume that you are a recent graduate in photojournalism looking for an advanced internship or a first job on a daily newspaper. Your portfolio is ready to show, but you need a résumé to send to editors or leave with them following an interview.

Because a résumé represents your professional qualifications, it must look professional: polished but not flashy, substantial but not stodgy.

Designing the Solution

Like almost any résumé, yours should include details about your educational background, honors or awards, relevant work experience, and an employment history. Within each of these categories, you should list items so the most recent appears first. Your résumé should list a concise career objective, one that is ambitious but not unrealistic. You should list special skills or interests that might be relevant to an employer. You should not list references by name, but offer instead to make such references available. And because equipment is important for a photojournalist, your résumé should list what camera gear you own and are prepared to use on the job. Your résumé should be brief and to the point. A rule of thumb is that the résumé of a recent college graduate should never be longer than a single page.

Most writing projects are not strictly linear—that is, you rarely begin writing with the first word and write straight through to the last, ending with a final product. Instead, most of us get a few ideas down on paper, add more words, move things around, delete some words and add others, revise and reshape, change words, smooth transitions, and so on. A word processor can be a powerful tool in this evolutionary process because you can make changes without throwing any of your work away.

Your résumé is a fairly straightforward document, but even it will evolve over the next four projects. You'll begin by typing the beginnings of the text. You'll add more text. You'll revise and rearrange text, as is typical in the preparation of any résumé. Then you'll polish the final product by choosing the type style and formatting the paragraph arrangement. In the end you'll have a professional-looking résumé, one that would represent you well with any prospective employer.

OPENING A NEW DOCUMENT

Word for Windows normally opens with a blank window and is ready to create a new document. If someone was using the computer before you, however, the window may already contain text. In that case, you'll need to open a blank window for your new document. (If Word for Windows isn't running already, start it by double-clicking the Word for Windows icon in the Windows Program Manager.)

 To open a blank window for a new document:

1 Choose New from the File menu.

The New dialog box will appear, as shown in Figure 1.1. This dialog box allows you to select from a variety of templates and wizards. **Templates** are preformatted skeleton documents ranging from memos to newsletters. A template is like a blank, formatted document that you can fill in with your own text. **Wizards** ask a series of questions about a document format and then use your answers to build a document for you to use. Right now, you need the default general-purpose template, named Normal.

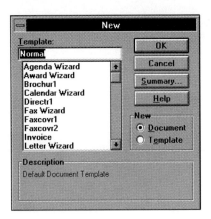

Figure 1.1

2 If Normal doesn't appear in the Template box, type **Normal**

3 Select OK.

 Tip If you're using a mouse, you can click the New Document button on the Standard toolbar to open a Normal document.

The document area of the screen will be blank except for the blinking insertion point (|), the end mark(___), and possibly a paragraph mark (¶). The *insertion point* marks the position where text will be inserted or deleted when you type on the keyboard. The *end-of-document mark* (end mark) shows where the document ends; you cannot insert characters after the end mark. A *paragraph mark* indicates the end of a paragraph and forces the beginning of a new line. The paragraph mark may not show on the screen. If not, you'll see shortly how to make the paragraph mark visible.

ENTERING TEXT

In this project, you will create and edit a résumé, the beginnings of which are shown in Figure 1.2.

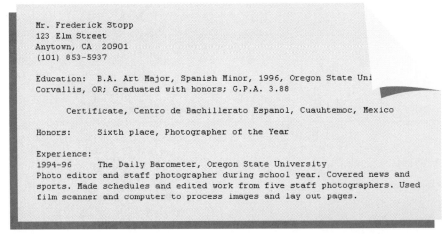

```
Mr. Frederick Stopp
123 Elm Street
Anytown, CA  20901
(101) 853-5937

Education:  B.A. Art Major, Spanish Minor, 1996, Oregon State Uni
Corvallis, OR; Graduated with honors; G.P.A. 3.88

         Certificate, Centro de Bachillerato Espanol, Cuauhtemoc, Mexico

Honors:     Sixth place, Photographer of the Year

Experience:
1994-96     The Daily Barometer, Oregon State University
Photo editor and staff photographer during school year. Covered news and
sports. Made schedules and edited work from five staff photographers. Used
film scanner and computer to process images and lay out pages.
```

Figure 1.2

Don't worry if you make errors as you type. These errors will just give you more to practice with when you learn how to make corrections later.

To enter the name and address:

1 Type **Mr. Frederick Stopp** and press (ENTER)
Notice as you type that the insertion point moves just ahead of the last character you typed. Note also that pressing (ENTER) forces the beginning of a new line.

2 Type **123 Elm Street** and press (ENTER)

3 Type **Anytown, CA 20901** and press (ENTER)

4 Type **(101) 853-5937** and press (ENTER)

The résumé is started. Before continuing with it, you will learn how to display nonprinting characters and how to move the insertion point around in the document.

DISPLAYING ALL CHARACTERS

Most of the characters you've just typed are printable: they will appear on the sheet of paper that eventually comes out of your printer. But some, such as the spaces between words, will not be printed. *Nonprinting characters* include not only spaces, but also paragraph marks (inserted with (ENTER)) and tab characters. Often it's helpful to be able to see some or all of these characters on the screen. Word for Windows allows you to turn nonprinting characters on or off to suit yourself.

You can change the display of nonprinting characters by using the Tools menu.

To display nonprinting characters using the Tools menu:

1 Choose Options from the Tools menu.

The Options dialog box, shown in Figure 1.3, appears. You can customize Word for Windows in many ways by changing the settings in this dialog box. Right now, we're interested only in the options on the View tab.

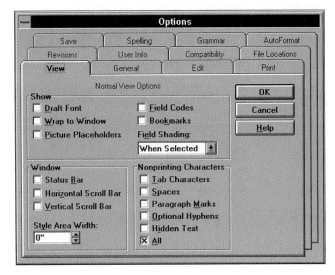

Figure 1.3

2 Select the View tab if it is not already visible, as shown in Figure 1.3.

3 Select All within the Nonprinting Characters box, so an "X" appears inside the check box to its left.

4 Clear all other check boxes (except All) under Nonprinting Characters.

5 Select OK.

You can also use a mouse to quickly flip back and forth between displaying and hiding nonprinting characters.

To use the mouse to turn nonprinting characters on and off:

1 Make sure the standard toolbar appears at the top of the screen. If the toolbar does not appear, choose Toolbars from the View menu and use the Toolbar dialog box to turn the toolbar on.

 2 Click the Show/Hide ¶ button near the right side of the standard toolbar.

Note that each time you click the Show/Hide ¶ button, the paragraph marks (¶) at the end of each line toggle on or off. Notice also that spaces between words, represented by a small raised dot (·), toggle on or off. If you had tabs in your document, they would be represented by an arrow (→).

Figure 1.4 shows the screen with all nonprinting characters displayed.

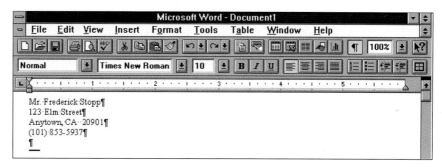

Figure 1.4

MOVING AROUND IN A DOCUMENT

The blinking insertion point indicates a specific location in a document: a position where some action might take place, such as changing a character or inserting and deleting text. Note that the insertion point and the mouse pointer are similar but different. The insertion point blinks and is a plain vertical line; the pointer does not blink and is shaped like an I-beam.

You can reposition the insertion point using either the mouse or the keyboard. To use the mouse, move the pointer to the new location and click once.

To position the insertion point with the mouse:

1 Position the pointer between the two *e*'s in *Street*.

2 Click the left mouse button.

3 Note that the blinking insertion point is now positioned between the two *e*'s.

The insertion point can only be positioned within the text of your document. The insertion point will not move into the white space at the right of the text. If you try to position it there, the insertion point will move to the end of the nearest line.

You can also use the keyboard to move the insertion point. Table 1.1 describes the actions associated with various keystrokes.

Table 1.1

Keys	Action
↑, ↓, ←, →	Moves the insertion point up or down one line, or left or right one character
(HOME)	Moves the insertion point to the beginning of the line
(END)	Moves the insertion point to the end of the line
(PGUP)	Moves the insertion point up one screen
(PGDN)	Moves the insertion point down one screen
(CTRL)+→ (or ←)	Moves the insertion point to the beginning of the next (or previous) word
(CTRL)+↓ (or ↑)	Moves the insertion point to the beginning of the next (or previous) paragraph
(CTRL)+(PGUP) (or (PGDN))	Moves the insertion point to the top (or bottom) of the screen
(CTRL)+(HOME) (or (END))	Moves the insertion point to beginning (or end) of the document

In the numbered steps that follow, be sure that (NUM LOCK) is turned *off* if you are using the numeric keypad. Note as you move the insertion point how the center portion of the status bar at the bottom of the screen indicates changes in the position of the insertion point.

To move the cursor one line or one character at a time:

1 Press ↑ until the insertion point reaches the top of the screen.

2 Press ↓ until the insertion point reaches the bottom of the current document.

3 Move the cursor up to the city-state line in the address.

4 Press → until the insertion point reaches the end of the line.

5 Press ← until the insertion point reaches the beginning of the line.

6 Practice moving with the arrow keys until you are comfortable with them.

To move the insertion point to the beginning or end of a line:

1 Position the insertion point somewhere within a line of text.

2 Press (HOME) to move the insertion point to the beginning of the line.

3 Press (END) to move the insertion point to the end of the line.

To move the insertion point from word to word:

1 Position the insertion point somewhere within a line of text.

2 Press (CTRL)+→ several times to move from one word to the next word in your document.

3 Press (CTRL)+← several times to move backward from word to word.

MAKING MINOR CORRECTIONS

One of the advantages of a word processor is that you can make corrections at any time during the document preparation process. If the ideas are flowing, you probably won't want to take the time to check the spelling of a word until later. But sometimes you'll notice a typo that you can't put out of your mind until you correct it. You can make minor corrections using the (BACKSPACE) or (DEL) keys. You can also reverse previous typing or editing by using Word's Undo feature. (In Project 2, you'll learn to use even more extensive editing and correcting tools.)

Assume you want to include your middle initial in your résumé.

To make corrections using (BACKSPACE):

1 Position the insertion point immediately in front of the *S* in *Stopp*.

2 Type **W**, then a period, and then press (SPACE)

After looking at it, however, you decide the middle initial is too formal and want to delete it.

3 Press (BACKSPACE) once.

Notice that the insertion point moves one character to the left, erasing the space that was there.

4 Press (BACKSPACE) twice more to remove the period and initial and restore the résumé to its original form.

Now, assume you want to remove *Mr.* from the résumé.

To make corrections using (DEL):

1 Position the insertion point at the beginning of your document, immediately in front of the *M*.

2 Press (DEL) once.

Notice that the character to the right of the insertion point (the *M*) is erased.

3 Press (DEL) three more times to remove *Mr.* from in front of the name.

Now assume you want to see how the résumé looks with the label *Telephone:* in front of the telephone number.

To make corrections using Word's Undo and Redo features:

1 Position the insertion point at the beginning of the fourth line (in front of the opening parenthesis mark for the area code).

2 Type **Telephone:** and press (SPACE)

Once you see it on the screen, however, you can tell that the label isn't really necessary and clutters up the heading, so you decide to delete it. You can use the Undo button, shown in Figure 1.5, to reverse most word processing operations.

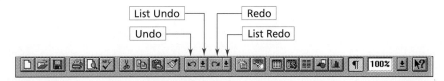

Figure 1.5

3 Select the Undo button on the standard toolbar.

Note that all the characters you typed are removed and the text has been restored to its original form. Assume, however, that you're not sure about the heading and want to see it in place again.

4 Select the Redo button (see Figure 1.5) on the standard toolbar.

Note that this reverses the undo and restores the text. Now you decide finally that the heading really isn't needed.

5 Select the Undo button again to remove the text.

The Undo command will reverse most (but not all) Word for Windows operations. It is not limited to undoing typing or deletion errors. You can usually undo or redo the last several operations you have performed. The number of steps you can undo or redo depends on the complexity of the steps and the configuration of the computer. To see a list of operations that can be undone or redone, click the List Undo button or the List Redo button on the standard toolbar (see Figure 1.5).

COMPOSING PARAGRAPHS

Entering text in Word for Windows is a lot like typing on a typewriter—with one notable exception. You should press (ENTER), the equivalent of the carriage return on a typewriter, only at the end of a paragraph, not at the end of every line within the paragraph. Like most word processors, Word for Windows contains a feature called *word wrap,* which allows it to determine where line endings need to fall. Word wrap allows you to type on your keyboard without having to worry about when to break a line. If you add or delete text from a paragraph, Word for Windows will recast the lines accordingly. If you change the margins in your document so the lines are shorter or longer, Word for Windows will again automatically revise the line endings.

As you type, text fills the line and continues on to the next line automatically. Word for Windows moves the insertion point to the beginning of the next line. Also, the program moves the last word of one line to the next line if the word does not fit. At the end of a paragraph, you will press (ENTER), which inserts a paragraph mark (¶). Only the last line of each paragraph should end with a paragraph mark. To insert a blank line, you will press (ENTER) again.

Check that the beginning lines of the résumé shown in Figure 1.6 are on the screen.

```
Frederick·Stopp¶
123·Elm·Street¶
Anytown,·CA··20901¶
(101)·853-5937¶
¶
```

Figure 1.6

To enter more of the résumé:

1 Position the insertion point on the blank line below the telephone number.

2 Press (ENTER) to leave the blank line and begin a new line.

3 Type **Education:** and press (TAB)
Note that pressing (TAB) produces an arrow (→), which represents a nonprinting tab character in Word. (You'll see how to set tabs in Project 4.)

4 Type the remainder of this portion of the résumé, as shown in Figure 1.7.

If you make a mistake, keep typing. You will be able to correct mistakes later, when you edit the document. Press (TAB) to produce the tab character (→) shown in Figure 1.7. Remember not to press (ENTER) at the end of a line unless it is the end of a paragraph or the end of a short line or unless you want to insert a blank line.

Education: → B.A. Art Major, Spanish Minor, 1996, Oregon State University, Corvallis, Oregon; graduated with honors; G.P.A. 3.88¶
¶
→ Certificate, Centro de Bachillerato Espanol, Cuauhtemoc, Mexico¶
¶
Honors: →Sixth place, Photographer of the Year¶
¶
Experience:¶
1994-96→The Daily Barometer, Oregon State University¶
Photo editor and staff photographer during academic school year. Covered news and sports. Made schedules and edited work from five staff photographers. Used film scanner and computer to process images and lay out pages.¶

Figure 1.7

The content of your letter should be the same as that of the document just shown. However, the distribution of the text on each line may be different. For example, different margin settings might be in effect or a special type font (print style and number of characters per inch) may be set for the printer.

Tip If you learned to type on a typewriter, you may have picked up some habits that won't work well with a word processor. You've already seen that you should press (ENTER) only at the end of a paragraph, not at the end of each line as you would on a typewriter. Here are some other differences:

- The letter *O* and the numeral *0* are different keys—and different characters—on a computer.
- The letter *l* and the numeral *1* are also different.
- You should type only one space following a period.
- Don't use underlining to emphasize text except in manuscripts. Use italic instead. You'll see how to do that in Project 3.
- Use tabs, not spaces, to align text. You already know how to enter tab characters, and you'll see how to set tabs in Project 4.

SAVING A NEW DOCUMENT

Normally, you will want to save your work, with all changes, to disk. The ability to save a document is the real power of word processing or any computer program. Once a file has been saved to disk, you can call your document back to the screen, change the document, and save it again. Word for Windows provides several ways to save your document: choosing the Save or Save As options from the File menu or selecting the Save button on the Standard toolbar.

You must provide a storage location and file name for any document you wish to save. The name may contain one to eight characters. The name cannot include blank spaces or certain other special characters, such as ? or *. Word for Windows will automatically add the file name extension .DOC to your document files. (You can also add your own file name extension, but it makes retrieving documents more awkward.) The instructions in this module assume you are saving your documents to a floppy disk in drive A:. If needed, you can modify the location specification from drive A: to the appropriate disk drive and directory as necessary for the computer system.

To save your document under the file name RESUME:

1 Select Save on the Standard toolbar.
The Save As dialog box should appear, as shown in Figure 1.8.

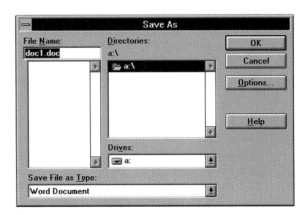

Figure 1.8

2 Type **RESUME** in the File Name box, but do not press (ENTER) yet.

3 Click the Drives box to open a menu of drive choices.

4 Select the a: option.

5 Select OK.

If you get an error message, it's probably because you don't have a formatted disk in the drive you specified.

Notice that as soon as you save your file to disk, a message at the left of the status bar (at the very bottom of the screen) displays the file name and a bar chart shows the progress of the save operation. Notice also that the title bar at the very top of the screen now indicates the new file name, with the file name extension .DOC attached.

To add text to the résumé:

1 Position the insertion point at the bottom of the résumé (after the period in *pages*).

2 Press (ENTER) twice to leave a blank line.

3 Type the additional experience item and objective section shown in Figure 1.9. Remember to press (TAB) where a tab character (→) appears.

> 1996 → The Seattle Times, Seattle, Washington¶
> Summer internship as a staff photographer. Covered general assignment news, sports, and features.¶
> ¶
> Objective: →   General assignment staff photographer for progressive daily newspaper.¶

Figure 1.9

To save changes in an existing document:

1 Select the Save File button on the toolbar.

This time, Word for Windows will not ask you the name of the file. Word assumes you want to save the file under the existing name, thus overwriting the previous version of your document. That way, you'll keep only one copy of the file and your disk won't be cluttered with different versions of the same document. In general this is a good policy, but it's good insurance to keep one extra copy of your document on disk just in case something goes wrong, such as a scratch on the disk or a power interruption that makes the file unusable.

Word for Windows can make automatic backup copies for you, so you always have the most recent and next most recent versions of your document saved to disk. Every time you save your document, the existing file is renamed to give it the file name extension .BAK, and your new file is saved with the file name extension .DOC. If something goes wrong with the .DOC file, you can copy the .BAK file and then work with the copy.

To have Word for Windows make automatic backup copies:

1 Choose Save As from the File menu.

2 Select Options.
The Options dialog box for Save will appear, as shown in Figure 1.10.

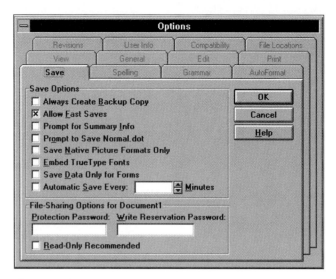

Figure 1.10

3 Select the Always Create Backup Copy box, so that an X appears in the check box to the left.

4 Select OK in the Options Save dialog box.

5 Select OK in the Save As dialog box.

Tip Be sure to save your document regularly. You're probably aware that when you turn off the computer, everything that hasn't been saved to disk is lost. You can lose hours of work in microseconds. Obviously, you should save every time you plan to shut off the computer. You also should save every time you take a break or every time you've typed a few paragraphs—every 10 to 15 minutes at least. You never know when a voltage spike, a power outage, or someone tripping over a power cord will unravel all those electrons that represent your efforts.

EXITING WORD FOR WINDOWS

To quit Word for Windows and return to the Windows desktop:

1 Choose Exit from the File menu (or double-click the Control menu box in the upper left corner).

If you've made changes in your document since you last saved it, you'll get a warning message asking if you want to save changes (Yes) or discard changes (No).

2 If you get the warning message, choose Yes to save changes. Word should return you to the Windows desktop.

THE NEXT STEP

A résumé, of course, is only one of the kinds of documents you can prepare using a word processor. The possibilities are virtually limitless. Anything that involves words can be prepared with a word processor, from simple letters or memos to complex reports or books.

All writing at some point involves selecting that first word. The power of a word processor is that you can easily change that word, add to it, move it, delete it, save it, retrieve it, or print it. The same techniques you used to begin this résumé will also work for a cover letter for the résumé, for a lab report, or for a term paper.

This concludes Project 1. You can either exit Word, or go on to work the Study Questions, Review Exercises, and Assignments.

SUMMARY AND EXERCISES

Summary

- You can set Word to display or hide nonprinting characters such as paragraph marks (¶), spaces (·), and tabs (→).
- You can move the insertion point one or more characters at a time by using different combinations of arrow keys and command keys, or by moving the pointer and clicking.
- Word allows you to undo, and subsequently redo, several previous word processing operations, including typing or deleting text.
- In Word, text automatically "wraps" from the end of one line to the beginning of the next. You need to press (ENTER) (the equivalent of a carriage return on a typewriter) only at the end of a paragraph.
- To insert a blank line, press (ENTER) at the beginning of the line.
- When you save your document, you can choose the drive and directory where you want to store the file. Word uses the same conventions as MS-DOS does for naming files.
- You can set Word to automatically create a backup file for you each time you save a document.
- Remember to save your files frequently. You can save your document quickly by selecting the Save File button on the toolbar.

Key Terms and Operations

Key Terms	Operations
end-of-document mark (end mark)	Save a file
insertion point	Create a new file
nonprinting characters	Redo a command
paragraph mark	Undo a command
templates	
Wizards	
word wrap	

Study Questions

Multiple Choice

1. The end of a paragraph is indicated by which of these symbols?
   - a. ·
   - b. |
   - c. →
   - d. ¶

2. Which of the following is not a nonprinting character?
   - a. #
   - b. ·
   - c. →
   - d. ¶

3. Which of the following key commands moves the insertion point to the beginning of a line?
   - a. (CTRL)+(←)
   - b. (←)+(←)
   - c. (END)
   - d. (HOME)

4. When typing text in Word for Windows, you should press (ENTER) at the end of a:
   - a. line.
   - b. paragraph.
   - c. page.
   - d. document.

5. Word for Windows uses which of the following as a file name extension for document files?
   - a. .TXT
   - b. .DOC
   - c. .WP
   - d. .BAK

6. You can toggle nonprinting characters on and off by selecting
   - a. the selection bar at the left of the text.
   - b. the Hide option from the View menu.
   - c. the Show/Hide ¶ button on the Standard toolbar.
   - d. the Print button on the Standard toolbar.

7. The Save icon on the Standard toolbar looks like:
   - a. a file folder.
   - b. a floppy disk.
   - c. two sheets of paper.
   - d. an envelope.

8. The end of your document is indicated by:
   - a. a ¶ mark.
   - b. a → mark.
   - c. a vertical bar (|).
   - d. a short horizontal bar (___).

9. Which of the following key commands will take you to the end of your document?
   - a. (CTRL)+(↓)
   - b. (END)
   - c. (CTRL)+(PGDN)
   - d. (CTRL)+(END)

10. To delete the character to the right of the insertion point, you would press:
    - a. →
    - b. (BACKSPACE)
    - c. (DEL)
    - d. (TAB)+(BACKSPACE)

Short Answer

1. When you type, characters appear at the spot in the text marked by the _____.

2. You can erase text using either the _____ key or the _____ key.

3. Word can keep your next-most-recent version of a document as a _____ copy.

4. _____ is a word processing feature that automatically breaks a paragraph into individual lines.

5. You can position the insertion point using either the _____ or the _____.

6. Pressing (ENTER) inserts a _____ mark into your document.

7. Pressing (CTRL) + (→) moves the insertion point to the _____ in your document.

8. The → symbol within your document is a nonprinting character that designates a _____.

9. The file name for your document is displayed in the _____.

10. To move immediately to the beginning of your document, press _____.

For Discussion

1. What does the Undo command do? What does the Redo command do?

2. How is a word processor different from a typewriter?

3. What are the rules for naming a file in Word?

4. What is a backup copy of a document? Why is a backup copy useful?

Review Exercises

Creating a Cover Letter

1. Write the cover letter shown in Figure 1.11 to accompany the résumé when it is sent to a newspaper editor. Be sure to use tabs for paragraph indents.

```
Dee Scribe, Editor
The Observer Review
123 4th Street
Centralville, CA    98000

Dear Ms. Scribe:

   I am applying for the opening for a
staff photographer at your newspaper.

   I am a recent graduate of Oregon State
University interested in a career as a
newspaper photographer. I have two year's
experience working on the Daily Barometer,
our student daily.

   Enclosed is a resume and a slide port-
folio of my work. I plan to be in
Centralville in about ten days and will
call to see if I could stop in to talk
with you at that time.

Very truly yours,



Fred Stopp
```

Figure 1.11

2. Add the current date to the top of the cover letter.

3. Delete the name of the editor and substitute a new name. Be sure to change the salutation to match.

4. Add a sentence to the end of the second paragraph saying that you have completed a summer internship at the *Seattle Times.*

5. Change *Very truly yours* to *Sincerely yours.*

6. Change *Fred* to *Frederick.*

7. Save the cover letter under the file name COVERLTR.

Assignments

Modifying the Résumé

Use the Save As option to save the résumé under the name MYRESUME. You should now have two copies of the résumé, one named RESUME and one named MYRESUME. The active file—the one showing in the title bar at the top of the screen—should be MYRESUME.DOC. Use MYRESUME to make the following modifications.

Use (DEL) or (BACKSPACE) to erase *Frederick Stopp* on the top line of the résumé, and substitute your name. Substitute your address and telephone number in the heading. Leave the headings, but change the items under the Education, Honors, Experience, and Objective headings so they pertain to you.

Save the file for later use.

Creating a Telephone List

Enter your personal list of telephone numbers for family, friends, business contacts, emergency services, and so on, using the following format:

```
Last name, first name          →          Telephone number
```

The list can be in any order. You will sort the list in alphabetical order and print it out in a later project. Save the file under the name FONELIST.

PROJECT 2: EDITING A DOCUMENT

Objectives

After completing this project, you should be able to:

▶ Retrieve documents

▶ Insert text

▶ Select text

▶ Delete text

▶ Move text

▶ Copy text

▶ Save documents under different names

▶ Preview and print documents

In this project you will make changes in the résumé you created in Project 1, save the file under a new name, and print the document. The changes will involve inserting, selecting, deleting, copying, and moving text. In the days of the typewriter, you would have been making these changes with a pair of scissors in one hand and a jar of paste in the other. Then you would have had to retype the entire document, probably more than once. With Word, you'll be able to make all changes on-screen, preview the result, and print out the résumé when you're satisfied.

CASE STUDY

You created a résumé in Project 1 that should look like Figure 2.1.

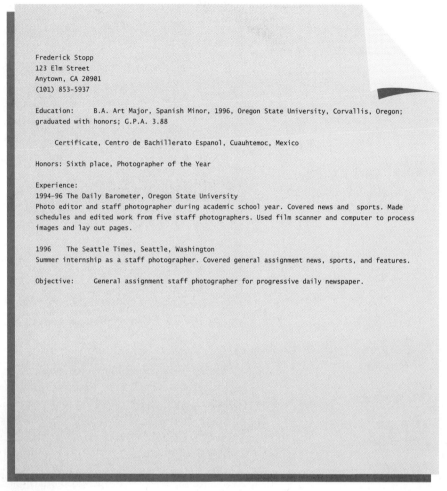

Frederick Stopp
123 Elm Street
Anytown, CA 20901
(101) 853-5937

Education: B.A. Art Major, Spanish Minor, 1996, Oregon State University, Corvallis, Oregon;
graduated with honors; G.P.A. 3.88

      Certificate, Centro de Bachillerato Espanol, Cuauhtemoc, Mexico

Honors: Sixth place, Photographer of the Year

Experience:
1994-96 The Daily Barometer, Oregon State University
Photo editor and staff photographer during academic school year. Covered news and sports. Made
schedules and edited work from five staff photographers. Used film scanner and computer to process
images and lay out pages.

1996   The Seattle Times, Seattle, Washington
Summer internship as a staff photographer. Covered general assignment news, sports, and features.

Objective: General assignment staff photographer for progressive daily newspaper.

Figure 2.1

At this point, your résumé is really a first draft. It needs to be reorganized to look more like a standard résumé and revised to correct inaccuracies.

Designing the Solution

Résumés follow a fairly standard pattern. Figure 2.2 is a typical résumé outline.

```
Name
Address
Telephone

Career objective
Educational history
Honors
Experience
Employment history
Skills or interests
References
```

Figure 2.2

Within each section, items are listed in reverse chronological order—that is, most recent first. In addition, it is critical that a résumé be accurate. All facts, such as dates, titles, and numerical information, must be correct and supportable. At best, mistakes make you look bad and are embarrassing. At worst, they can cost you the position you're seeking.

If you compare the résumé you started in Project 1 with the outline in Figure 2.2, you'll see that certain items in the résumé are out of order. Other items need correction or qualification to make them accurate. In this project, you'll use some of Word's editing tools to rearrange and correct the résumé. Because you saved your file from Project 1, you'll be able to do all this with a minimum of retyping. At the end of this project, you'll preview and print out a copy of the résumé.

RETRIEVING A DOCUMENT

One of the major advantages of a word processing program is its ability to store documents on disk, allowing you to open documents later for revision and printing. That way you don't have to retype an entire document if you want to make changes or corrections. To open a file you've saved before, call up the Open dialog box and indicate the file you want to retrieve.

To retrieve the document RESUME:

1 Choose Open from the File menu or select the Open File button on the Standard toolbar.

The Open dialog box, shown in Figure 2.3, will appear on the screen. If this dialog box looks familiar, it's because this box very similar to the Save As dialog box you used at the end of Project 1.

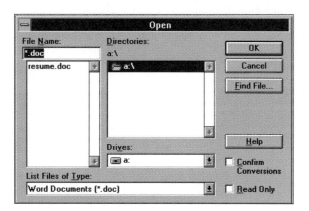

Figure 2.3

2 If needed, change the Directories and Drives boxes to the directory and drive where you saved the RESUME.DOC file in Project 1.

3 Make sure the List Files of Type box contains "Word Documents (*.doc)." If it doesn't, use the drop-down menu to change the setting so .DOC files will be listed.

4 Select resume.doc in the File Name box.

5 Select OK.

The résumé you started in Project 1 should appear on-screen.

Tip If you want to return to exactly where you left off with a file when you were last working with it, press (SHFT)+(F5) before you do anything else. Word will return the insertion point to its last location.

INSERTING TEXT

Word normally operates in *insert mode,* which means characters you type on the keyboard are inserted into whatever text already exists in your document. You can switch to *overtype mode,* in which characters you type replace existing characters. If Word is in overtype mode, OVR appears darkened in the status bar at the bottom of the screen.

To toggle between insert and overtype mode:

1 Double-click OVR in the status bar at the bottom of the screen or press (INS)

Note that OVR appears in the status bar, as shown in Figure 2.4. (If you're using the keyboard and OVR does not appear darkened, (INS) has probably been assigned another function. See the next Tip for instructions on how to reset it.)

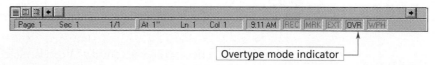

Overtype mode indicator

Figure 2.4

2 Double-click OVR in the status bar again or press (INS) again. Overtype mode will be cleared and OVR will be dimmed in the status bar. Word will be in insert mode again.

Tip The (INS) key can be assigned another function in Word. It can be used to paste in text that has been moved to the clipboard. You'll see how to use the clipboard later in this project, but for now you may need to change what (INS) is used for so you will be able do the steps above. To change the (INS) key assignment, first choose Options from the Tools menu. Second, select the tab labeled *Edit.* Then turn off the *X* in the check box beside the line *Use the INS Key for Paste.* (Note that you can also turn overtype mode on or off using the line just below that one, which is labeled *Overtype Mode.*)

Be sure that Word is in insert mode (OVR should be dimmed in the status bar).

To insert text into your letter:

1 Position the insertion point immediately in front of the first character of *Photographer* in the Honors section of the résumé.

2 Type **Collegiate** and press (SPACE)
Note that Word inserts each character as you type it, moving existing text ahead to make room for the new characters.

To type over text in your letter:

1 Position the insertion point immediately in front of the *2* in the zip code.

2 Switch to overtype mode. OVR will appear darkened in the status bar.

3 Type **90210** which is the corrected zip code.
Note that the characters you type replace those already on the screen.

4 Switch back to insert mode so OVR is again dimmed in the status bar.

Tip Although Word gives you a choice, it's usually best to work in insert mode. Overtyping destroys text, making it easy to accidentally wipe out valuable text or formatting information. Although using insert mode exclusively sometimes results in extra unwanted text, it's not difficult to delete such text, as you'll see shortly.

 If necessary, you can save your file as RESUME.DOC, exit Word now, and continue this project later.

SELECTING TEXT

The general rule when using Word is "select, and then do." Many operations in Word involve selecting a block of text, and then doing something with that block. A text block can be a single character, a word, a sentence, a paragraph, or your entire document. Once you've selected a text block, you can move the block, copy it, delete it, or change the way it looks. As with many other operations, Word gives you several ways to select text. In the numbered steps that follow, you will try different ways to select text, although you won't do anything with the text blocks just yet. You'll see how to select text first with the mouse and then with the keyboard.

To select text by dragging:

1 Position the pointer somewhere inside the word *Sixth* in the Honors section of the résumé.

2 Press the mouse button and hold it down.

3 Without releasing the mouse button, move the pointer to a different part of the screen.

Notice as you drag the pointer that the text you drag over appears highlighted (white letters on a black background) and that your selection is anchored at the point where you initially pressed the mouse button. Notice also that you can select single characters while you stay within the word *Sixth*, but that once the selection expands to include other words, Word automatically "rounds off" to include whole words only (and the space that follows the word).

4 Still holding down the mouse button, position the pointer somewhere within *Year*, at the end of the line.

5 Release the mouse button to select the highlighted text.

6 Check that your selection matches the block shown in Figure 2.5.

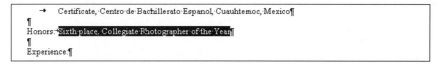

Figure 2.5

If you want to cancel a text selection, you can simply click once or press one of the arrow keys.

To cancel a text selection:

1 Click once or press one of the arrow keys.

You can also select parts of your text using the mouse within the selection bar, the area within the document window just to the left of the text. When the pointer is in the selection bar, it changes from an I-beam shape into an arrow that points upward and to the right.

To select a line of text using the selection bar:

1 Move the pointer into the selection bar just to the left of the Education section of the résumé, as shown in Figure 2.6.

Figure 2.6

Note that the shape of the pointer changes to an arrow.

2 Click to select one line, as shown in Figure 2.7.

Figure 2.7

To select several lines, click and drag the pointer up or down in the selection bar. Table 2.1 describes other ways of selecting text using the mouse.

Table 2.1

Selection	Action
Word	Double-click the word.
Sentence	Hold down (CTRL) and click anywhere within the sentence.
Paragraph	Double-click in the selection bar next to the paragraph, or triple-click anywhere within the paragraph.
Several paragraphs	Drag in the selection bar.
Entire document	Hold down (CTRL) and click in the selection bar, or triple-click in the selection bar.

Sometimes it's faster or more convenient to select text using the keyboard. The simplest way is to use the arrow keys in combination with the (SHFT) key.

To select text using (SHFT) and the arrow keys:

1 Use the arrow keys to position the insertion point immediately in front of *Sixth* in the Honors section of the résumé.

2 Hold down (SHFT) and press (→) several times.
Notice that this works like dragging. As the insertion point moves, the text is highlighted, always anchored where you began the selection. Unlike when you drag the mouse, however, Word does not round off to whole words if the selection includes more than one word.

3 With (SHFT) still pressed, press (↑) several times.

4 Continuing to hold down (SHFT), use the arrow keys to move the insertion point so the selection includes the *r* in *Year* at the end of the line.

5 Release (SHFT) to complete the selection.

6 Cancel the text selection by clicking or by pressing one of the arrow keys.

The (F8) key is the Extend key. When you press (F8) once, it anchors the selection and begins extend mode, signaled by the EXT indicator in the status bar at the bottom of the screen, shown in Figure 2.8. You can extend the selection using the mouse or arrow keys, or you can press (F8) a second time to select a word, a third time to select a sentence, a fourth time to select a paragraph, and a fifth time to select the entire document. To cancel a selection, you must first turn off extend mode. To turn off extend mode, press (ESC) or double-click the EXT indicator in the status bar.

Extend mode indicator

Figure 2.8

You can also extend a selection by using (SHFT) in combination with keys that you might use to move the insertion point to different locations within your document, as summarized in Table 2.2.

Table 2.2

To Extend a Selection	Action
To the end of a word	(CTRL) + (SHFT) + (→)
To the beginning of a word	(CTRL) + (SHFT) + (←)
To the end of a line	(SHFT) + (END)
To the beginning of a line	(SHFT) + (HOME)
To the end of a paragraph	(CTRL) + (SHFT) + (↓)
To the beginning of a paragraph	(CTRL) + (SHFT) + (↑)
To the end of a document	(CTRL) + (SHFT) + (END)
To the beginning of a document	(CTRL) + (SHFT) + (HOME)
To the whole document	(CTRL) + **A**

DELETING TEXT

Once you've selected text, one of the things you can do with that text is delete it. You can delete text permanently, or you can remove it from your document and place it in a temporary storage location called the *clipboard.* Later you can retrieve that text from the clipboard and place it somewhere else in your document or in some other Windows application (such as a spreadsheet or database program).

To delete a word permanently:

1 Select the word *academic*, as shown in Figure 2.9.

Tip Recall that the easiest way to select a single word is to double-click the word.

```
Experience:¶
1994-96•The·Daily·Barometer,·Oregon·State·University¶
Photo·editor·and·staff·photographer·during·academic·school·year.·Covered·news·and·sports.·Made·
schedules·and·edited·work·from·five·staff·photographers.·Used·film·scanner·and·computer·to·process·
images·and·lay·out·pages.·¶
```

Figure 2.9

2 Press either `DEL` or `BACKSPACE`

Note that the word is deleted and that the remaining text closes up to fill in the space where the word used to be. The word wrap feature resets the line endings for the entire paragraph. The word you deleted is gone forever—well, almost. You can still reverse the deletion with Word's Undo feature.

To undo a deletion:

1 Select the Undo button on the Standard toolbar.

2 Note that *academic* is restored.

Remember that you can undo several of the most recent operations in Word in reverse order. So even if you deleted text and went on to perform other word processing operations, you would probably still be able to retrieve that deleted text by repeating the undo operation as many times as needed.

If you have a text block selected and then begin typing on the keyboard, Word ordinarily replaces the selected text with the new text.

To replace schedules *with* assignments:

1 Select *schedules* in the first paragraph of the Experience section, as shown in Figure 2.10.

```
Experience:¶
1994-96•The·Daily·Barometer,·Oregon·State·University¶
Photo·editor·and·staff·photographer·during·academic·school·year.·Covered·news·and·sports.·Made·
schedules·and·edited·work·from·five·staff·photographers.·Used·film·scanner·and·computer·to·process·
images·and·lay·out·pages.·¶
```

Figure 2.10

2 Type **a**

3 Note that as soon as you type the new character, the selected text is deleted and the new text begins to replace it.

4 Finish typing *assignments* to complete the replacement.

Tip Ordinarily it's very convenient to have revised text replace selected text, but like anything that deletes text, this method can be dangerous. If you don't want Word to treat selected text this way, you can set the software to insert new text in front of the selection rather than replacing selected text. To do this, choose Options from the Tools menu. In the dialog box, select the Edit tab, and then set the Typing Replaces Selection box to off (clear the *X* from the box) and select OK.

To delete a text selection from a document and move the text to the clipboard:

1 Select the Seattle Times entry in the Experience section of the résumé, including the blank line just following the entry.

The screen should resemble Figure 2.11.

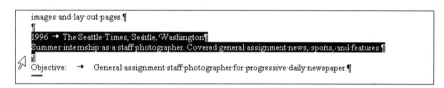

Figure 2.11

2 Choose Cut from the Edit menu (or select the Cut button on the Standard toolbar, or press (CTRL) + **X**).

The text has been removed from your document, but a copy of it is temporarily stored in the clipboard. The text will remain in the clipboard until you copy something else into the clipboard or until you quit Windows. The clipboard is part of Windows and is available to any Windows application, such as a spreadsheet or database. You can use the clipboard to transfer information back and forth between one Word document and another, or between Word and another Windows application.

Tip After you have selected the text to be cut, click the right mouse button, and then select Cut.

MOVING TEXT

By deleting text to the clipboard in the numbered steps just above, you've actually performed the first half of a text-block move operation. You moved text from the document into the clipboard. All that remains is to move that text from the clipboard to some other part of your document. Because a résumé ordinarily lists information in reverse chronological order, you will move the most recent work experience (the one just deleted to the clipboard) ahead of the other entry.

To insert text from the clipboard:

1 Position the insertion point immediately in front of the *1* in *1994–96* as shown in Figure 2.12.

```
Honors: Sixth place, Collegiate Photographer of the Year¶
¶
Experience:¶
|1994-96•The·Daily·Barometer,·Oregon·State·University¶
Photo·editor·and·staff·photographer·during·academic·school·year.·Covered·news·and·sports.·Made·
assignments·and·edited·work·from·five·staff·photographers.·Used·film·scanner·and·computer·to·process·
images·and·lay·out·pages.¶
¶
Objective:    →    General·assignment·staff·photographer·for·progressive·daily·newspaper.¶
```

Figure 2.12

2 Choose Paste from the Edit menu (or select the Paste button on the Standard toolbar, or press ⌐CTRL⌐ + **V**, or click the *right* mouse button and select Paste).

Your screen should resemble Figure 2.13. Note that the two *Experience* entries have now been transposed.

```
Honors: Sixth place, Collegiate Photographer of the Year¶

Experience:¶
1996  →  The·Seattle·Times,·Seattle,·Washington¶
Summer·internship·as·a·staff·photographer.·Covered·general·assignment·news,·sports,·and·features.¶
¶
1994-96•The·Daily·Barometer,·Oregon·State·University¶
Photo·editor·and·staff·photographer·during·academic·school·year.·Covered·news·and·sports.·Made·
assignments·and·edited·work·from·five·staff·photographers.·Used·film·scanner·and·computer·to·process·
images·and·lay·out·pages.¶
¶
Objective:    →    General·assignment·staff·photographer·for·progressive·daily·newspaper.¶
```

Figure 2.13

Tip The clipboard, as you know, still contains the text you just inserted, and you could insert that same text somewhere else if you wanted. If you have to repeat text, you can use this feature of the clipboard to expedite your work.

Word also allows you to move text using the ⌐F2⌐ key. This type of text move doesn't involve the clipboard, so whatever text is already in the clipboard won't be disturbed. To move text with ⌐F2⌐, you would first select the text you want to move, press ⌐F2⌐ to begin the move, position the insertion point where you want the text to appear, and press ⌐ENTER⌐ to complete the move. You will use ⌐F2⌐ to move the Objective section of the résumé so this section appears right after the name, address, and telephone number.

To move the Objective section using ⌐F2⌐*:*

1 Select the Objective section and the blank line just above it.

2 Check to see that the screen resembles Figure 2.14.

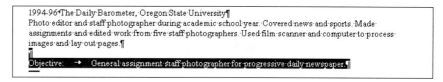

Figure 2.14

3 Press (F2)

Note that the status bar at the bottom of the screen now prompts you for the next step in the move operation, as shown in Figure 2.15.

Figure 2.15

4 Position the insertion point—now a dotted vertical line—at the destination for the move, just in front of the paragraph mark above the Education section, as shown in Figure 2.16.

```
Frederick Stopp¶
123 Elm Street¶
Anytown, CA  90210¶
(101) 853-5937¶
¶
Education:  →  B.A. Art Major, Spanish Minor, 1996, Oregon State University, Corvallis, Oregon;
graduated with honors; G.P.A. 3.88¶
```

Figure 2.16

5 Press (ENTER)

6 The Objective section should now appear just after the name and address block, as shown in Figure 2.17. If you check the end of your document, you'll see that the Objective section doesn't appear there any longer.

```
Frederick Stopp¶
123 Elm Street¶
Anytown, CA  90210¶
(101) 853-5937¶
¶
Objective:  →  General assignment staff photographer for progressive daily newspaper.¶
¶
Education:  →  B.A. Art Major, Spanish Minor, 1996, Oregon State University, Corvallis, Oregon;
graduated with honors; G.P.A. 3.88¶
```

Figure 2.17

Word also allows you to move selected text quickly by dragging it from one spot and dropping it in another using the mouse. This operation is called ***drag and drop.***

To transpose two sentences using drag and drop:

1 Select the third sentence in the last section of the document, as shown in Figure 2.18.

Tip Recall that you can select a sentence by pressing (CTRL) while you click somewhere in the sentence.

> Experience:¶
> 1996 → The·Seattle·Times,·Seattle,·Washington¶
> Summer·internship·as·a·staff·photographer.·Covered·general·assignment·news,·sports,·and·features.¶
> ¶
> 1994-96·The·Daily·Barometer,·Oregon·State·University¶
> Photo·editor·and·staff·photographer·during·academic·school·year.·Covered·news·and·sports.·Made·
> assignments·and·edited·work·from·five·staff·photographers.·Used·film·scanner·and·computer·to·process·
> images·and·lay·out·pages.¶

Figure 2.18

2 Position the pointer somewhere within the selection to change the shape of the pointer to an arrow. Press and hold down the mouse button to "grab" the selected text block, as shown in Figure 2.19.

> Experience:¶
> 1996 → The·Seattle·Times,·Seattle,·Washington¶
> Summer·internship·as·a·staff·photographer.·Covered·general·assignment·news,·sports,·and·features.¶
> ¶
> 1994-96·The·Daily·Barometer,·Oregon·State·University¶
> Photo·editor·and·staff·photographer·during·academic·school·year.·Covered·news·and·sports.·Made·
> assignments·and·edited·work·from·five·staff·photographers.·Used·film·scanner·and·computer·to·process·
> images·and·lay·out·pages.¶

Figure 2.19

Note that the pointer has a small rectangle attached to it, which signifies the block of text you are moving. Note also that you can use the pointer to move the insertion point, which has changed from an I-beam to a dotted vertical bar.

3 Continuing to hold down the mouse button, move the pointer so the dotted insertion point is positioned just in front of *Covered* in the line above, as shown in Figure 2.20.

> Experience:¶
> 1996 → The·Seattle·Times,·Seattle,·Washington¶
> Summer·internship·as·a·staff·photographer.·Covered·general·assignment·news,·sports,·and·features.¶
> ¶
> 1994-96·The·Daily·Barometer,·Oregon·State·University¶
> Photo·editor·and·staff·photographer·during·academic·school·year.·Covered·news·and·sports.·Made·
> assignments·and·edited·work·from·five·staff·photographers.·Used·film·scanner·and·computer·to·process·
> images·and·lay·out·pages.¶

Figure 2.20

4 Release the mouse button.
The two sentences should be transposed, as shown in Figure 2.21.

> Experience:¶
> 1996 → The·Seattle·Times,·Seattle,·Washington¶
> Summer·internship·as·a·staff·photographer.·Covered·general·assignment·news,·sports,·and·features.¶
> ¶
> 1994-96*The·Daily·Barometer,·Oregon·State·University¶
> Photo·editor·and·staff·photographer·during·academic·school·year. **Made·assignments·and·edited·work·from·five·staff·photographers.** Covered·news·and·sports.·Used·film·scanner·and·computer·to·process·images·and·lay·out·pages.¶

Figure 2.21

EXIT If necessary, you can save your file as RESUME.DOC, exit Word now, and continue this project later.

COPYING TEXT

Copying text is very much like moving text. The difference is that the originally selected text is not deleted when a copy of it is inserted elsewhere in your document. As with moving, you can copy by using the clipboard, by using the function keys, or by dragging and dropping. You'll try out all three methods in the following series of numbered steps. But because there is no need to duplicate material in the résumé, you will undo each copy operation after you perform it.

To copy text using the clipboard:

1 Select the name and address block at the top of the résumé, including the blank line below the block.

2 Choose Copy from the Edit menu (or select the Copy button on the Standard toolbar, or press (CTRL)+C, or click the right mouse button and select Copy) to copy the selection to the clipboard.

3 Position the insertion point just in front of the *E* in *Education*.

4 Choose Paste from the Edit menu (or select the Paste button on the Standard toolbar, or press (CTRL)+V).

The top of your document should resemble Figure 2.22, with two name and address blocks separated by the Objective section.

> Frederick·Stopp¶
> 123·Elm·Street¶
> Anytown,·CA··90210¶
> (101)·853-5937¶
> ¶
> Objective: → General·assignment·staff·photographer·for·progressive·daily·newspaper.¶
> ¶
> Frederick·Stopp¶
> 123·Elm·Street¶
> Anytown,·CA··90210¶
> (101)·853-5937¶
> ¶
> Education: → B.A.·Art·Major,·Spanish·Minor,·1996,·Oregon·State·University,·Corvallis,·Oregon;·graduated·with·honors;·G.P.A.·3.88¶

Figure 2.22

5 Undo the copy operation to remove the copied text.

Tip Recall that you can undo the last operation by choosing Undo from the Edit menu or by selecting the Undo button on the Standard toolbar.

 To copy text using (SHFT) + (F2):

1 Select the name and address block, as before.

2 Press (SHFT) + (F2)
A *Copy to where?* prompt appears in the status bar at the bottom of the screen.

3 Position the dotted vertical insertion point just in front of the *E* in *Education*.

4 Press (ENTER) to complete the copy.

5 Undo the copy operation to restore the résumé.

 To copy text by dragging and dropping:

1 Select the name and address block again.

2 Move the pointer inside the selection so the pointer turns into an arrow.

3 Hold down (CTRL) and press the mouse button. Continue to hold down both (CTRL) and the mouse button until you're ready to paste the copied text.
Note that the pointer has a small dotted rectangle attached to it and that a dotted insertion point appears beside the rectangle.

4 Move the dotted insertion point to just in front of the *E* in *Education*.

5 Release both the mouse button and (CTRL) to insert the text.

6 Undo the copy operation to restore the résumé.

Reminder Word allows great flexibility in selecting, moving, and copying text. Sometimes it might seem there are so many different ways to accomplish the same thing that you can't remember any of them. Recall that you can get a list of keyboard or mouse commands at any time through the Help facility. To get options for selecting text, for instance, open the Help Index window and select *selecting text or graphics*. Then select *selecting text and graphics using the keyboard* or *selecting text and graphics using the mouse*. Either choice will give you a complete list of options.

SAVING A DOCUMENT UNDER A DIFFERENT NAME

Saving a file under a new name creates a new file. The new file becomes the active file, which is the file currently being edited. The old file stored under the previous name will remain unchanged unless you deliberately open that file. You can use this feature to save intermediate drafts of a document. For instance, it is usually a good idea to save an extra copy of a document under a different name if you are about to undertake an extensive revision. That gives you a version to fall back on if you get mixed up in the middle of the revision or make a mistake and turn all your hard work into electronic garbage.

 To save an existing document under a new name:

1 Open the Save As dialog box by choosing Save As (*not* Save) from the File menu.

Warning If you choose Save, Word will immediately save the file under its current name and defeat the purpose of separately saving the second draft of the résumé.

2 In the File Name box, type the new name for the document: **RESUME2**

3 If needed, change the drive and directory in the Save As dialog box.

4 Select OK or press (ENTER)

5 Notice that the title bar at the top of the screen now shows the new file name.

PREVIEWING AND PRINTING A DOCUMENT

The end result of a word processing effort is usually a printed document: something you can mail, give to someone else to read, or mark up for further revision. Before you commit your document to paper, however, Word can prepare a preview on-screen. The preview shows just how the printed document will look: where page breaks will fall, where page numbers will appear, how headings and margins will look, and so on.

The Print Preview screen looks like Figure 2.23, with the *Print Preview toolbar* at the top just above the miniature page. You can edit your document in print-preview mode while you check margins, page breaks, heading positions, and so on, to be sure the page will look like you want it to. The Print button calls up the Print dialog box, as you'll see shortly. The *Magnifier button* toggles between edit mode (with the usual I-beam pointer) and zoom mode (with a magnifying-glass pointer). When in *zoom mode*, you can click to switch back and forth between a full-page view and a close-up view. The *One Page button* displays a single page of your document, and the *Multiple Pages button* allows you to view several miniature pages at once. The *Zoom control box* allows you to set the magnification of the preview page. The *View Ruler button* toggles the ruler on and off. The *Shrink to Fit button* may be able to eliminate the last page of your document if that page contains only a few lines of text. The *Full Screen button* toggles to a preview display containing only your document and the Print Preview toolbar. The *Close button* turns off print-preview mode and returns to the display mode you were using before. The Help button can be used to obtain more information about any of these features.

Print Preview toolbar

Vertical ruler

Pointer in zoom mode

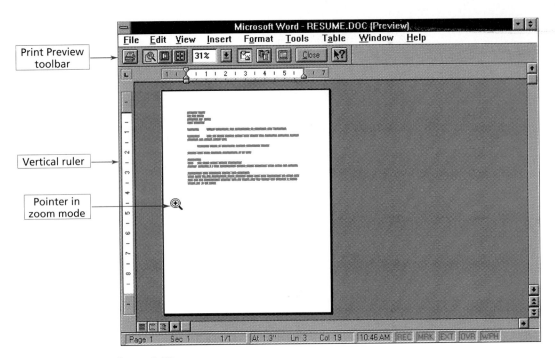

Figure 2.23

To preview and print the document:

1 Select the Print Preview button on the Standard toolbar.

2 Choose Print from the File menu (or press (CTRL) + **P**).
The Print dialog box will appear, as shown in Figure 2.24. The printer for the system will be listed after Printer at the top of the box. The print settings default to printing one copy of your entire document. You can change the number of copies and you can set the range of pages you want if you don't need to print the entire document.

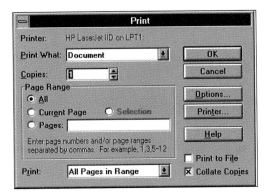

Figure 2.24

3 Select OK in the Print dialog box.

4 Note that a message appears telling you that Word is preparing the document for printing and transmitting information to the printer.

5 Compare your printed copy to the Print Preview display for your document.

If you already know that your document is formatted correctly, you can bypass the preview before printing. You can open the Print dialog box by choosing Print from the File menu, setting the defaults as needed, and then selecting OK.

Tip To really expedite printing, you can simply accept whatever defaults are in effect and print by selecting the Print button on the Standard toolbar.

THE NEXT STEP

You may want to tailor your résumé to fit the type of job or internship you're applying for. Experience that is relevant to one position might actually undercut your chances for another position. One approach would be to create a very complete master résumé that could be revised by deleting sections to customize it to particular situations. What types of information might you add to the outline at the beginning of this project?

You could take a similar approach for a cover letter. By changing the name and address of the person you're writing to, and perhaps making other alterations in the text of the letter, you can quickly produce a personalized letter.

This concludes Project 2. You can either exit Word, or go on to work the Study Questions, Review Exercises, and Assignments.

SUMMARY AND EXERCISES

Summary

- You can retrieve documents you've stored to disk by choosing Open from the File menu or by selecting the Open button on the Standard toolbar.
- You can switch between insert mode and overtype mode by pressing (INS) or by double-clicking OVR in the status bar. It is safest to work in insert mode.
- The general strategy when working in Word is "select, and then do," which means first select a block of text, and then do something with it.
- You can select blocks of text in a variety of ways: dragging with the mouse, using (SHFT) with the arrow keys, clicking in the selection bar, or using (F8).
- You can delete text permanently by using (DEL) or (BACKSPACE). You can delete text to the clipboard by choosing Cut from the Edit menu, by pressing (CTRL)+**X,** or by selecting the Cut button on the Standard toolbar.

- If you type something while a text block is selected, the typed text replaces the selected text.
- You can move text in three ways. You can delete text to the clipboard and then copy it from the clipboard back into your document. You can use (F2). Last, you can drag and drop text selections.
- Copying text is like moving text, except you don't delete the text from its original location. You can copy text to the clipboard, you can use (SHFT)+(F2), or you can drag and drop using the mouse with (CTRL).
- You can save separate drafts of a document by changing the file name when you save the file. To do that, you would choose Save As from the File menu.
- Word will preview your printed document on the screen so you can check page breaks, margins, and so on before you actually print the file.

Key Terms and Operations

Key Terms	**Operation**
drag and drop	Copy
clipboard	Cut
insert mode	Open
overtype mode	Paste
	Print
	Print preview

Study Questions

Multiple Choice

1. When you copy a block of text, it is temporarily stored in the:
   - a. buffer.
   - b. clipboard.
   - c. status bar.
   - d. block file.

2. Which of the following will not select text?
   - a. holding down (SHFT) and pressing one of the arrow keys
   - b. clicking in the selection bar
   - c. holding down (CTRL) and clicking
   - d. clicking at the end of a line

3. Which of the following inserts text from the clipboard?
   - a. (CTRL)+X
   - b. (CTRL)+C
   - c. (CTRL)+I
   - d. (CTRL)+V

4. If Word is in overtype mode:
   - a. OVR appears in the status bar.
   - b. The pointer changes to an X shape.
   - c. The title bar blinks as a warning.
   - d. The insertion point becomes a dotted line.

5. To select a single word:
   a. Press (F8) three times.
   b. Press (CTRL) and click the word.
   c. Press (CTRL) + **W**
   d. Double-click the word.

6. If you delete a text block with (DEL), you can retrieve the text block:
   a. by pressing (CTRL) + **V**
   b. by choosing Paste from the Edit menu.
   c. with the Undo command.
   d. by pressing (F2)

7. To select an entire document:
   a. Hold down (CTRL) and press (F8)
   b. Hold down (CTRL) and click in the selection bar.
   c. Double-click in the selection bar.
   d. Choose Entire from the Select menu.

8. The Copy button on the Standard toolbar looks like:
   a. a pair of scissors.
   b. two sheets of paper.
   c. a sheet of paper and a clipboard.
   d. a printer.

9. If you save a document under a new name:
   a. The old name and associated file are deleted.
   b. The old file gets the new name and the old name is deleted.
   c. The file you are editing retains the old name.
   d. Both the old and the new files will be saved to disk.

10. When it is in the selection bar, the pointer:
    a. has a small rectangle attached to it.
    b. is shaped like an I-beam.
    c. is a vertical blinking line.
    d. becomes an arrow pointing up and to the right.

Short Answer

1. To toggle between insert mode and overtype mode, press _____.

2. The general rule in using Word is, "_____, and then do."

3. To cancel a text selection, click or press one of the _____ keys.

4. The Extend key is the _____ key.

5. The Move key is the _____ key.

6. After you copy text from the clipboard, the clipboard still contains _____.

7. To copy a text selection using the mouse, you must hold down the _____ key while dragging the selection.

8. To select text using the keyboard, you can hold down the _____ key and then press one of the arrow keys.

9. You can delete a block of text using either the _____ or _____ keys.

10. When you exit Windows, the contents of the clipboard are _____.

For Discussion

1. Why is it usually better to use insert mode rather than overtype mode?

2. What is the difference between deleting text using (DEL) or (BACKSPACE) and deleting text using (CTRL)+**X**?

3. Word allows you to move text blocks in several different ways, using both the mouse and the keyboard. What are the advantages and disadvantages of each?

Review Exercises

Correcting a Rough Draft

1. Type a rough draft of the memo shown in Figure 2.25 (without making the corrections yet).

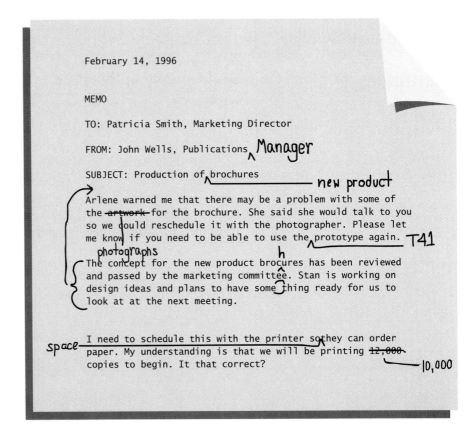

Figure 2.25

2. Make the corrections noted.

3. Save the file under the file name NEWMEMO and print the file.

Creating a Meeting Agenda

1. Type the meeting agenda items shown in Figure 2.26. Use ⬚TAB⬚ to indent the agenda items.

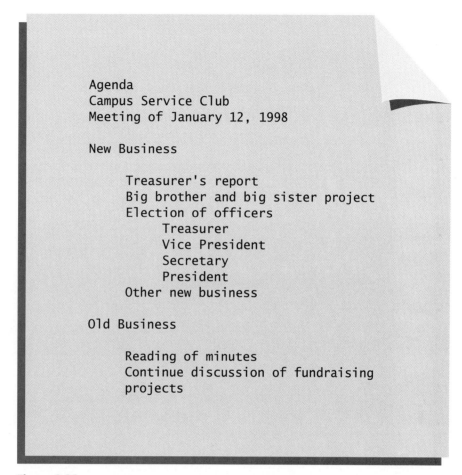

```
Agenda
Campus Service Club
Meeting of January 12, 1998

New Business

        Treasurer's report
        Big brother and big sister project
        Election of officers
                Treasurer
                Vice President
                Secretary
                President
        Other new business

Old Business

        Reading of minutes
        Continue discussion of fundraising
        projects
```

Figure 2.26

2. Substitute today's date for the date in Figure 2.26.

3. Move the Old Business heading and the items under it so this section appears before the New Business section.

4. Move the Election of Officers and positions listed under that heading so this section is the first item under New Business.

5. Reorganize the list of officers so it is more logical.

6. Save the revised agenda under the file name AGENDA.

7. Print a copy of the agenda.

Assignments

Modifying the Résumé

Retrieve your personal version of the résumé you saved under the file name MYRESUME.DOC at the end of Project 1. Reorganize the document so the headings follow the order of the outline at the beginning of this project. Add new headings or information as needed. Put all items within each section in reverse chronological order. Double-check your document for accuracy and completeness. Save your revised document and print a copy of it.

Modifying a Telephone List

Retrieve the telephone list you saved under the file name FONELIST.DOC at the end of Project 1. Reorganize the first five items on your list as follows (you'll reorganize the rest of the list using a faster method in a later project): select what should be the first line by clicking alongside it in the selection bar. Drag and drop that line at the top of the list. Then select what should be the second line and move it under the first. Continue until the first five lines of your list are in alphabetical order. Put a title at the top of the list if you haven't already. Save the list and print a copy of it.

PROJECT 3: CHARACTER FORMATTING

Objectives

After completing this project, you should be able to:

► Apply character styles such as boldface, italic, and underline.

► Change type styles and sizes

► Create subscripts and superscripts

In this project you will begin to polish the appearance of the résumé using character formatting: type styles and sizes, character emphasis, and special characters. You'll begin by formatting the entire résumé so it no longer looks like a draft. You'll add boldface headings in a different type style to set off the headings and help organize the page visually. And you'll add some foreign-language accents to give the résumé a more polished and professional look. All of this is a first step into desktop publishing.

CASE STUDY: POLISHING THE RÉSUMÉ

Printed documents communicate not only by what they say, but also by how they look—by their form and appearance. Even though we're warned not to judge a book by its cover, most of us do exactly that. An attractive book, magazine, or brochure is more likely to be read and will probably have more credibility than one that looks sloppy, hastily put together, or unattractive. The same is true of smaller documents such as résumés, reports, and letters.

Word allows you to control the appearance of whatever document you're preparing in a variety of ways. You can select different typefaces and type sizes. You can make the type boldface or italic. You can use special characters such as foreign-language characters or mathematical symbols. With these capabilities, you can transform a rough draft into a document that looks polished and professional.

The résumé you began in the first project is complete and well organized at this point, but it lacks polish. It looks like the draft that it is. You probably wouldn't hand it to a potential employer any more than you would show up for an interview in ragged jeans. Dressing up the résumé requires the use of Word's extensive character formatting capabilities.

Designing the Solution

A good rule of thumb in designing any document is summed up in the widely used KISS formula: keep it simple, stupid. Smart designers usually try to keep it simple by, for example:

- Using a minimum number of typefaces
- Grouping material that belongs together into blocks
- Making one element (probably an illustration or headline) stand out for emphasis
- Setting tabs and indentations so type blocks line up and the page looks better organized

In this project, you'll format the résumé using typefaces that are professional and polished. You'll provide emphasis and clarity by making the name and headings stand out. You'll use italics and special characters to make the text conform better to common style conventions, thus raising its credibility.

At the end of this project, the résumé should look like Figure 3.1.

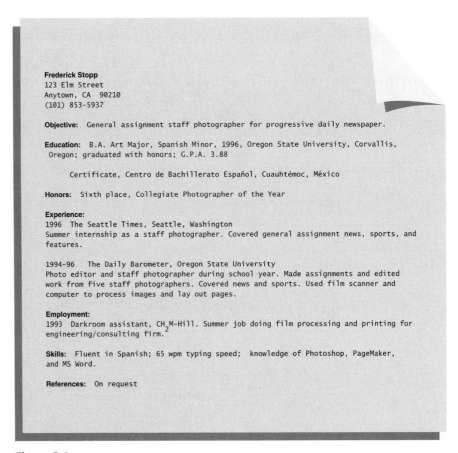

Figure 3.1

CHARACTERS, PARAGRAPHS, AND SECTIONS

Word recognizes three types of building blocks that make up a document: characters, paragraphs, and sections. Each one of these building blocks has specific characteristics and can be formatted in different ways. For instance, characters can be bold or italic, paragraphs can be indented or double spaced, and sections can be page numbered or printed sideways.

As usual in Word, the general rule is "select, and then do." First you select the part of your document you want to format and then you apply the formatting. If you want to underline text, you first select the characters you want to underline, and then you tell Word to underline them. If you want to boldface text, you select the text and then tell Word to boldface it.

Characters can have a variety of formats, as shown in Figure 3.2.

Type style:	Courier	**Bodoni**	Times New Roman
	Brush	Arial	UMBRA
Type size:	Eight point	Fourteen point	Twenty point
	bold *italic*	~~strikethrough~~	SMALL CAPS
	<u>continous underline</u> or <u>word</u> <u>underline</u> or <u>double underline</u>		
	superscript or subscript	condensed or e x p a n d e d character spacing	

Figure 3.2

How you format your documents will affect the legibility and appearance of those documents, and probably influence the documents' credibility and attractiveness to readers. You can use character formats to establish the tone and structure of your document, to provide emphasis, or to produce special effects to gain attention.

APPLYING CHARACTER FORMATS

Once you've selected the text you want to format, you can apply character formats in any of three ways: by using the Font dialog box, the keyboard, or the Formatting toolbar. You'll learn all three in the numbered steps that follow, working with the sample résumé from Projects 1 and 2.

The appearance of a résumé is obviously important. Because it represents you to a potential employer, you want this document to look as professional as possible. Its precise final appearance will depend heavily on the type of printer you're using, but you can do a lot to dress up the résumé regardless. Begin by retrieving your last version of the résumé, saved as RESUME2.DOC in Project 2.

To retrieve the résumé file:

1 Click the Open button in the standard toolbar.

2 Adjust the Drives and Directories boxes if needed.

3 Select RESUME2.DOC from the File Name box.

4 Select OK.

5 Select the Show/Hide ¶ button if needed to make nonprinting characters visible.

Your document should resemble Figure 3.3.

```
Frederick·Stopp¶
123·Elm·Street¶
Anytown,·CA··90210¶
(101)·853-5937¶
¶
Objective:    →    General·assignment·staff·photographer·for·progressive·daily·newspaper.¶
¶
Education:    →    B.A.·Art·Major,·Spanish·Minor,·1996,·Oregon·State·University,·Corvallis,·Oregon;·
graduated·with·honors;·G.P.A.·3.88¶
¶
        →    Certificate,·Centro·de·Bachillerato·Espanol,·Cuauhtemoc,·Mexico¶
¶
Honors:→Sixth·place,·Collegiate·Photographer·of·the·Year¶
¶
Experience:¶
1996 →  The·Seattle·Times,·Seattle,·Washington¶
Summer·internship·as·a·staff·photographer.·Covered·general·assignment·news,·sports,·and·features.¶
¶
1994-96·The·Daily·Barometer,·Oregon·State·University¶
Photo·editor·and·staff·photographer·during·academic·school·year.·Made·assignments·and·edited·work·from·
five·staff·photographers.·Covered·news·and·sports.·Used·film·scanner·and·computer·to·process·images·and·
lay·out·pages.·¶
```

Figure 3.3

In standard style, the names of newspapers, magazines, books, and so on are normally italicized. You'll begin formatting the résumé by italicizing *The Seattle Times.*

To italicize text using the Font dialog box:

1 Select the name of the newspaper, so the text appears as shown in Figure 3.4.

```
Honors:→Sixth·place,·Collegiate·Photographer·of·the·Year¶
¶
Experience:¶
1996 →  The·Seattle·Times,·Seattle,·Washington¶
Summer·internship·as·a·staff·photographer.·Covered·general·assignment·news,·sports,·and·features.¶
¶
```

Figure 3.4

2 Choose Font from the Format menu.

The Font dialog box shown in Figure 3.5 will appear on-screen.

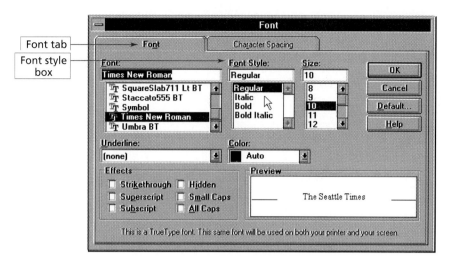

Figure 3.5

3 Select the Font tab, if it is not already on top.

4 Select Italic from the Font Style box.
Note that the Sample box in the lower right corner shows how the text will look with the italic style applied.

5 Select OK.
Note that the name of the newspaper now appears in italics. (Cancel the text selection if necessary to see the formatting clearly.)

To remove the italics using the Font dialog box:

1 Select the name of the newspaper again.

2 Choose Font from the Format menu.

3 Select Regular from the Font Style box.

4 Select OK.
Note that normal characters have replaced the italics.

Tip For quick access to the Font dialog box after you have selected characters to be formatted, click the right mouse button and then select Font.

The Font dialog box is the most powerful character formatting tool you have in Word. You can use it to apply or clear any character formats in any combination. But if you have frequent need for simple character formats, using the dialog box will begin to seem awkward and time-consuming. Word therefore provides two shortcuts: the Formatting toolbar and keyboard formatting commands. The *Formatting toolbar* appears near the top of the screen and allows you to use a mouse to make quick changes in common character and paragraph formats.

To italicize text using the Formatting toolbar:

1 If the Formatting toolbar, shown in Figure 3.6, does not appear near the top of the screen, choose Toolbars from the View menu, select For-matting, and then select OK.

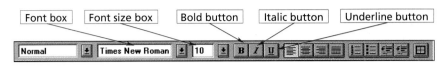

Figure 3.6

2 Select the name of the newspaper again, so *The Seattle Times* is highlighted once more.

3 Select the Italic button in the Formatting toolbar.

4 Select the button again to clear the italic formatting. Note that each click on the button toggles back and forth between italic and nonitalic formatting.

5 Select the Italic button again so the newspaper's name is italicized.

Note that the Formatting toolbar provides two other buttons for quick character formatting: one for boldface and one for underlining.

To italicize text using the keyboard:

1 Select the name of the other newspaper, *The Daily Barometer*.

2 Press (CTRL)+**I** to apply italic.

3 Press (CTRL)+**I** a second time to remove the formatting.

4 Press (CTRL)+**I** a third time to reapply italic.

Word makes available a series of keyboard shortcuts to format characters, as shown in Table 3.1.

Table 3.1

Keyboard Shortcut	Character Style
(CTRL) + (SHFT) + **A**	All caps
(CTRL) + **B**	Bold
(CTRL) + (SHFT) + **D**	Double underline
(CTRL) + (SHFT) + **H**	Hidden text
(CTRL) + **I**	Italic
(CTRL) + (SHFT) + **K**	Small caps
(CTRL) + **U**	Continuous underline
(CTRL) + (SHFT) + **W**	Word underline
(CTRL) + **=**	Subscript
(CTRL) + (SHFT) + **=**	Superscript

EXIT If necessary, you can save your file, exit now, and continue this project later.

CHANGING TYPEFACE AND TYPE SIZE

The terminology that Word uses for type styles and sizes is the same as that used for more than two centuries by commercial printers, book publishers, and newspapers. A particular style of type is known as a *font.* By most classification systems, there are only a few very general categories of type styles; these categories are shown in Figure 3.7.

Serif faces
Sans serif faces
Cursive and script faces
𝕭lackletter faces
𝓝𝓞𝓥𝓔𝓛𝓣𝓨 **faces of** MANY *types*

Figure 3.7

Within these general categories are thousands of type styles or fonts. Which fonts you have available in Word will depend on the printer and what fonts have been installed in Windows on the computer. A typewriter font, such as Courier New, is a *fixed-space* font, which means all letters have equal width and letters line up in columns. A fixed-space font is a good choice for manuscripts or other materials in draft form. Most typefaces are *proportionally spaced,* which means some letters are wider than others. A lowercase *i* is much thinner than an uppercase *W,* for instance, in a proportionally spaced font. *Serif fonts* have small crosslines, called serifs, at the end of the main letter strokes. A serif font such as Times New Roman is a good choice for *body text*—the main reading material in reports, letters, and so on. *Sans serif fonts,* such as Helvetica or Arial, lack those crosslines. Sans serif fonts are slightly difficult to read for large amounts of text, but they are an excellent choice for headings, especially when bold. Cursive, blackletter, and novelty fonts should be avoided except where they are obviously appropriate, such as cursive type for a formal invitation or a particular novelty font for a poster.

Most type fonts are available in different styles, such as bold or italic. You can use styles for emphasis or to provide variation in your document. You might boldface a heading to make it stand out more clearly. Or you might italicize the title of a document to make it distinct from other information on the page.

Tip It's wonderful to have an assortment of type styles and sizes to work with in your documents. Unfortunately, it's tempting to want to use them all. Avoid the temptation, because it leads to a hodgepodge of type styles that looks like it was clipped from old magazines and pasted on paper like a ransom note.

A good rule of thumb is to avoid using more than two different typefaces in any one document. You could use a sans serif face such as Arial or Helvetica (in different styles and sizes) for the headings and a serif face such as Times New Roman (also in various sizes and styles) for body text. The result will be a cleaner, more tightly integrated document, but with enough variety that it doesn't look plain or uninteresting.

Printers measure type size in *points.* A point is 1/72 of an inch, so 72-point type is 1 inch high. Most books are printed using 9- to 11-point type. The headings in this module are in 22-point type. Average newspaper headlines are about 30 to 40 points. Word is capable of producing type sizes from 4 points to 127 points in ½-point increments. Whether that full range of sizes is actually available to you will depend on the font you're using and on the printer.

The numbered steps in the pages that follow assume you have at least a few different type fonts and sizes to work with, although you may not be able to match the exact fonts used in the examples. You will begin by changing the heading lines to a sans serif font. The most common such font is Arial, which is used in the examples below. If Arial isn't available, substitute Helvetica or the closest san serif font you have.

To change typeface and size using the Formatting toolbar:

1 Begin by selecting the top line of the résumé (the name).

2 Click the Down Arrow button to the right of the Font box in the Formatting toolbar, as shown in Figure 3.8.

| Normal | ▼ | Times New Roman | ▼ | 10 | ▼ | **B** *I* U | ≡ ≡ ≡ ≡ | ≣ ≣ ≣ ≣ | ⊞ |

Figure 3.8

3 Select Arial.

4 Select the entire document (triple-click in the selection bar or press (CTRL) + **A**).

5 Open the Font Size box by clicking the Down Arrow button to its right.

6 Select 12.

Changing fonts and point sizes with the Font dialog box works the same way as using the Formatting toolbar. The difference is that although the dialog box isn't as easily accessible, you can change other character attributes at the same time if you need to.

To change font size and character style using the Font dialog box:

1 Select the first line of the document (the name at the top of the résumé).

2 Choose Font from the Format menu to open the Font dialog box.

3 Select the Font tab if it is not on top already.

4 Select Bold in the Font Style box.

5 Select 14 in the Points box.

6 Select OK.

The top of your document should resemble Figure 3.9.

Frederick·Stopp¶
123·Elm·Street¶
Anytown,·CA··90210¶
(101)·853-5937¶

Figure 3.9

Tip When word processors that could use various type fonts in various sizes were first developed, writing instructors noticed an interesting phenomenon. Students using the older word processors, which limited them to one set of characters, seemed to write better than students using the newer, more flexible machines. The problem, apparently, was that students using the newer word processors were being mesmerized by all the formatting options and distracted from the content of their writing. As a result, the quality of their writing suffered.

The solution, of course, is not to get rid of the formatting flexibility—the design and format of a document are part of the way the document communicates. On the other hand, it's not very wise to expect a dazzling design to cover up bad writing. In the end, it's probably best to make writing and design two distinct issues and focus on them separately. Word can help you do this with the Draft font. To use this font, you would choose Options from the Tools menu, select the View tab, and select Draft Font. Your entire document will be displayed in a single type font and size. This option makes it easier to focus on the words themselves. Then, when you are ready to address character formatting issues, go back to the View tab in the Options dialog box and clear the Draft Font selection.

USING SUBSCRIPTS AND SUPERSCRIPTS

Subscripts and superscripts are useful for footnote references, chemical formulas, or mathematical notation. A **_subscript_** appears slightly below the normal baseline for the text (H_2O); a **_superscript_** appears slightly above the baseline ($E = mc^2$). Word will automatically reduce the size of the character so it fits as a superscript or subscript.

To enter a subscript using the Font dialog box:

1 At the bottom of the résumé, type the new text shown in Figure 3.10.

Employment:¶
1993 → Darkroom·assistant,·CH2M-Hill.·Summer·job·doing·film·processing·and·printing·
for·engineering/consulting·firm.¶
¶
Skills:→Fluent·in·Spanish;·65·wpm·typing·speed;·knowledge·of·Photoshop,·PageMaker,·
and·MS·Word.¶
¶
References: → On·request¶

Figure 3.10

2 Style the new text as 12-point Times Roman, as you've already done with the text above it.

3 Select the single character *2* in *CH2M-Hill.*

4 Choose Font from the Format menu to open the Font dialog box.

5 Select the Character Spacing tab if it is not already on top.

6 Select Lowered from the Position drop-down menu, as shown in Figure 3.11.

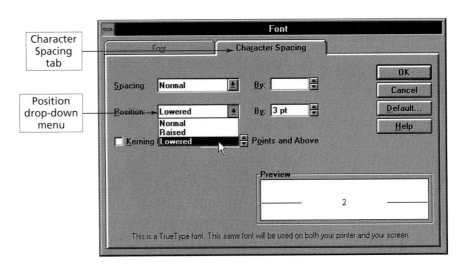

Figure 3.11

7 Select OK.
Your screen should look like Figure 3.12.

Employment:¶
1993 → Darkroom·assistant,·CH2M-Hill.·Summer·job·doing·film·processing·and·printing·
for·engineering/consulting·firm.¶

Figure 3.12

EXIT If necessary, you can save your file, exit now, and continue this project later.

REPEATING AND COPYING CHARACTER FORMATS

To polish the résumé more, it would help to have the headings appear more distinctly, such as in a boldface sans serif font. You could format the headings by selecting each one, then applying the needed format, and then going on to the next heading. Obviously, the more complex the format, the longer this procedure will take. Word provides shortcuts to make this type of operation easier and faster. Repeating character formats is useful if you've just formatted one block of text and want to apply the same format to a series of other blocks. Copying character formats allows you to "borrow" the existing format information from one block of text and apply it to another block.

 To repeat a character format:

1 Select the first heading: *Objective:*

2 Choose Font from the Format menu to open the Font dialog box.

3 Select the Font tab if it is not already on top.

4 Select the same sans serif face that you selected for the name in the top line of the document.

5 Select Bold in the Font Style box.

6 Select OK to complete the format choice.
Check to see that the heading is now displayed in boldface sans serif.

7 Select the next heading: *Education:*

8 Choose Repeat Font Formatting from the Edit menu (or press (CTRL)+**Y**) to repeat the formatting operation.

The Repeat Font Formatting command works well as long as you do all the formatting operations at the same time. If you want to copy existing character formatting in the middle of performing other operations, however, Word allows you to borrow formatting information without copying the content itself. This is a two-step operation that uses the Format Painter button in the Standard toolbar. First you "dip the paintbrush" in the formatting that you want to copy. Then you "brush" across the text you want to format.

 To copy a character format using the Format Painter button:

1 Position the insertion point somewhere within one of the headings you've already formatted (*Objective:* or *Education:*).

2 Select the Format Painter button in the Standard toolbar. Note that the pointer now has a small paintbrush attached to it.

 3 Drag the paintbrush pointer to select the next heading: *Honors:* Note that as soon as you release the mouse button to complete the text selection, the format information, but not the content, is transferred from the already formatted heading to the *Honors:* heading.

4 Use the same procedure to format the other four headings in the résumé.

SPECIAL CHARACTERS

A font of type normally contains many characters that don't appear on the keyboard, such as foreign-language characters, mathematical symbols, and publishing symbols. In addition, special fonts are available that consist entirely of special characters. Word allows you easy access to both through the Insert Symbol command.

 ### *To insert foreign-language accent characters:*

1 Select the *n* in *Espanol* in the Education section of the résumé.

2 Check that the screen matches Figure 3.13.

> **Education:** →B.A.·Art·Major,·Spanish·Minor,·1996,·Oregon·State·University,·Corvallis,·
> Oregon;·graduated·with·honors;·G.P.A.·3.88¶
> ¶
>   →   Certificate,·Centro·de·Bachillerato·Español,·Cuauhtemoc,·Mexico¶
> ¶
> **Honors:**   →   Sixth·place,·Collegiate·Photographer·of·the·Year¶

Figure 3.13

3 Choose Symbol from the Insert menu to open the Symbol dialog box.

4 Select the Symbols tab if it is not already on top.

5 Select Normal Text in the Font box, if it isn't selected already.

6 Select the *ñ* symbol, on the bottom row of the box, as shown in Figure 3.14.

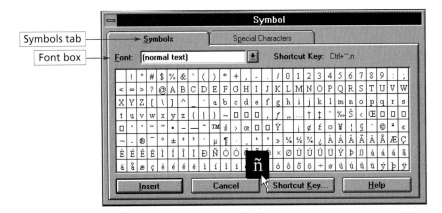

Figure 3.14

Note that the shortcut keystroke for this special character appears at the top of the dialog box.

7 Select Insert to substitute the accented character for the selected character.

8 Select Close to close the Symbol dialog box.

9 Use the same procedure to substitute an *é* for the *e* in both *Cuauhtemoc* and *Mexico*.

Check that the screen now resembles Figure 3.15.

Education: →B.A.·Art·Major,·Spanish·Minor,·1996,·Oregon·State·University,·Corvallis,· Oregon;·graduated·with·honors;·G.P.A.·3.88¶
¶
    →   Certificate,·Centro·de·Bachillerato·Español,·Cuauhtémoc,·México¶
¶
Honors: → Sixth·place,·Collegiate·Photographer·of·the·Year¶

Figure 3.15

To save and print your document:

1 Save your document as RESUME2.DOC.

2 Print a copy of the résumé.

THE NEXT STEP

Explore what other special characters are available on the computer system you are using. In addition to the special characters available in the Normal Text font, many systems have a Symbol font, containing the Greek alphabet and a variety of mathematical symbols, and a Wingdings font, containing different sorts of arrows, highlighted numbers, astrological signs, and so on.

Through these special characters and character formats, the personal computer has brought a new look to all kinds of documents, from business letters, to reports, to newsletters. The widespread availability of different typefaces in different sizes has made it straightforward and inexpensive to do what only commercial printers used to do at relatively high prices. These capabilities are part of the basis of the desktop publishing revolution.

Unfortunately, having the equipment to use typefaces doesn't teach you how to use them. Start collecting examples of documents you think are well designed, particularly documents of a type that are of special interest to you. You can adapt those design ideas to your own work. Watch also for documents you think are poorly designed and note what it would take to transform these documents into an effective format.

SUMMARY AND EXERCISES

Summary

- Word distinguishes three types of building blocks in a document: characters, paragraphs, and sections. Each has its own set of formatting characteristics.
- Characters can be normal, bold, italic, underlined, or a number of other styles. They can be superscripted or subscripted. They can be different fonts or point sizes. They can have expanded or condensed character spacing.
- You can format blocks of characters by first selecting the characters and then applying the format.
- You can apply character formats by using the Font dialog box, the Formatting toolbar, or keyboard commands.
- Type styles are known as fonts. Type sizes are measured in points (1/72 of an inch).
- You can repeat formatting operations by choosing Repeat from the Edit menu (or pressing (CTRL)+**Y**).
- You can copy character formats by using the Format Painter button in the Standard toolbar.
- You can insert special characters using the Insert Symbol command. Most systems have special fonts containing nothing but special characters and symbols.

Key Terms and Operations

Key Terms
body text
fixed-space font
font
Formatting toolbar
points
proportionally spaced font
sans serif font

serif font
subscript
superscript

Operations
Change type font and size
Copy character formats
Insert special characters

Study Questions

Multiple Choice

1. Word recognizes three types of document building blocks. Which of the following is *not* one of them?
   a. characters
   b. words
   c. paragraphs
   d. sections

2. Which of the following key combinations formats selected text as bold?
   a. (SHFT)+**B**
   b. (ALT)+**B**
   c. (CTRL)+**B**
   d. (SHFT)+(CTRL)+**B**

3. A point, the measurement system for type size, is equivalent to:
   - a. 1/8 inch
   - b. 1/35 inch
   - c. 1/72 inch
   - d. 1/100 inch

4. Which of the following type styles is generally best for large amounts of reading matter?
   - a. serif
   - b. sans serif
   - c. cursive
   - d. novelty

5. Which of the following includes a superscript?
   - a. CO_2
   - b. Español
   - c. $A = \pi r^2$
   - d. Française

6. To repeat an operation, press:
   - a. (CTRL)+R
   - b. (CTRL)+Y
   - c. (CTRL)+X
   - d. (CTRL)+O

7. Which of the following is not a character attribute (a character format that can be changed in the Font dialog box)?
   - a. double spacing
   - b. underlining
   - c. font
   - d. color

8. You are most likely to find Greek characters such as π or δ in:
   - a. the Times Roman font.
   - b. the Wingdings font.
   - c. the Helvetica font.
   - d. the Symbol font.

9. Which of the following character formats is not available in the Formatting toolbar?
   - a. bold
   - b. font changes
   - c. superscript
   - d. underline

10. Foreign-language accents and other special symbols are available through which of these menus?
    - a. File
    - b. Edit
    - c. Format
    - d. Insert

Short Answer

1. To format selected text as italic, press _____.

2. To format selected text as bold, press _____.

3. The _____ allows you to set type style, type size, bold, italic, or underline with a few clicks.

4. A particular style of type is called a _____.

5. A line of 18-point type is about _____-inch tall.

6. The name of a serif typeface available on your system is _____.

7. To select a single word prior to italicizing it, place the pointer somewhere within the word and _____.

8. To remove underlining from a word, first select the word and then click _____ in the Formatting toolbar.

9. You can copy format information by using the _____ button in the Formatting toolbar.

10. If you want type that is 1 inch tall for a poster, you should select the text block and set the size to _____ points.

For Discussion

1. How can you copy character formats using the mouse?

2. How can you avoid typographical monotony if you use only two fonts in a document?

3. Take an advertisement from a magazine and classify the fonts used in it according to the following system: serif, sans serif, cursive, text, and novelty.

Review Exercises

Formatting a Memo

1. Retrieve the memo you corrected at the end of Project 2, named NEWMEMO.

2. Format all of the text in a serif face like Times New Roman.

3. Make all of the characters 11 point.

4. Make the *MEMO* heading 14 point in a sans serif face (such as Arial or Helvetica).

5. Boldface the headings *To*, *From*, and *Subject*.

6. Save the file under the same name (NEWMEMO) and print a copy of it.

Formatting a Meeting Agenda

1. Retrieve the agenda you saved under the name AGENDA at the end of Project 2.

2. Format all of the text as 12-point Times New Roman (or a similar serif face).

3. Format the *Agenda* title line as 24-point Arial or Helvetica, in bold.

4. Format the name of the club and the date line as 14-point Arial or Helvetica.

5. Make the old and new business headings bold.

6. Save under the same name (AGENDA) and print a copy of the document.

Assignments

Formatting Your Résumé

Retrieve your personal version of the résumé, saved under the file name MYRESUME. Update the résumé if needed by adding new information or headings. Format your résumé to match the résumé you worked on in Project 2. Save the revised and formatted résumé and print a copy of it.

Formatting the Address List

Typefaces have personalities. Some are conservative, whereas others are flashy. Some are easygoing; others are forceful. Retrieve the telephone list you saved under the file name FONELIST. Just for fun, create a new version of the list under the file name SILLY (you'll need to use the Save As option).

Pick a name on your list and select the line it's on (by clicking once in the selection bar). Format that line with a typeface that matches as closely as possible the personality of the person whose name appears there. Pick a bold, conservative face if that fits, or an elegant, italic face if that fits. Repeat for each of the people on your list. Save the list (under the name SILLY) and print a copy.

Now, retrieve the original version from the file FONELIST. Format it in a way that makes the list easy to read and use. Consider font and size. You may want to boldface names so they stand out better. Format the heading to separate it from the names and addresses. When you're finished, save the list again under the file name FONELIST and print a copy.

PROJECT 4: PARAGRAPH FORMATTING

Objectives

After completing this project, you should be able to:

▶ Set the alignment of lines in a paragraph

▶ Create paragraph indentations

▶ Copy paragraph formats

▶ Create and apply simple styles

▶ Set tab stops

In this project you will continue to polish the appearance of the résumé using paragraph formatting. You will use paragraph indentation to make the different sections stand out more clearly. You will create your own custom indentation style and use it to create consistently formatted paragraphs within the résumé. You will use tabs to organize a new list of photographic equipment.

CASE STUDY: USING PARAGRAPH FORMATS TO STRUCTURE THE RÉSUMÉ

In the last project you began to polish the résumé by using type fonts that look professional, by adding bold and italics for emphasis, and by using special characters for precision and accuracy. The résumé still lacks, however, a visible typographic structure that clearly displays its underlying organization. You can use paragraph indentations and tab stop settings to align blocks of text in a way that makes the organization of the résumé apparent at a glance.

Designing the Solution

To make the section headings stand out, you can indent lines that follow the heading, making each heading prominent at the left edge of the page. To give the page better balance and a more formal appearance, you can center the top lines of the résumé. You'll also be adding a new section,

which is a list of equipment, that will require the use of tab stops to make
the list readable.

When you finish, the résumé should look like Figure 4.1.

Frederick Stopp
123 Elm Street
Anytown, CA 90210
(101) 853-5937

Objective: General assignment staff photographer for progressive daily
newspaper.

Education: B.A. Art Major, Spanish Minor,1996, Oregon State University,
Corvallis, Oregon; graduated with honors; G.P.A. 3.88

Certificate, Centro de Bachillerato Español, Cuauhtémoc, México

Honors: Sixth place, Collegiate Photographer of the Year

Experience:
1996   The Seattle Times, Seattle, Washington
Summer internship as a staff photographer. Covered general
assignment news, sports, and features.

1994-96   *The Daily Barometer*, Oregon State University
Photo editor and staff photographer during academic school year.
Made assignments and edited work from five staff photographers.
Covered news and sports. Used film scanner and computer to
process images and lay out pages.

Employment:
1993   Darkroom assistant, CH_2M-Hill. Summer job doing film processing
and printing for engineering/consulting firm.

Equipment: Nikon F3 body   35 mm Nikkor   105 mm MicroNikkor
Nikon F4 body   50 mm Nikkor   180 mm Nikkor
28 mm Nikkor   85 mm Nikkor   300 mm f/2.8 Nikkor

Skills: Fluent in Spanish; 65 wpm typing speed; knowledge of Photoshop,
PageMaker, and MS Word.

References: On request

Figure 4.1

CHOOSING PARAGRAPH FORMAT OPTIONS

Webster's Dictionary says a paragraph is "a distinct section or subdivision of a written or printed composition that consists of from one to many sentences, forms a rhetorical unit, and is indicated by beginning on a new, usually indented, line."

Word's operating definition is simpler and shorter: a paragraph begins after a paragraph mark (¶) and ends with the next paragraph mark. In Word, strictly speaking, paragraphs have to do with formatting, not grammar, although there is often an obvious parallel.

You can format paragraphs in Word to change the alignment of lines, how lines are indented, tab stops, line spacing, spacing between paragraphs, how the paragraph will be treated at a page break, and borders and shading. It will probably come as no surprise that you format paragraphs by first selecting them and then applying the formatting. A paragraph is considered selected in Word when the insertion point is anywhere within the paragraph or when the current selection includes some part of the paragraph. If you want to format a single paragraph, you can just position the insertion point somewhere inside that paragraph. If you want to format more than one paragraph, you can create a selection block that includes at least some part of each paragraph to be formatted.

As with character styles, you can apply paragraph formatting in any of three ways: by using the Paragraph dialog box, the keyboard, or the Formatting toolbar. You can do almost all common paragraph formatting using your mouse and the Formatting toolbar.

LINE ALIGNMENT

One of the most basic paragraph formats is line alignment. Word can create four kinds of paragraph line alignment: aligned left, centered, aligned right, or justified (see Figure 4.2). For most work, *aligned left* is appropriate and more legible. *Centered alignment* works well for some headings and for small amounts of text that need a formal presentation. *Aligned right* formatting should be avoided except for a very few lines of text, such as a figure caption or short heading. Text with *justified alignment* has an even margin on both left and right sides and usually looks best with multicolumn formats such as newsletters.

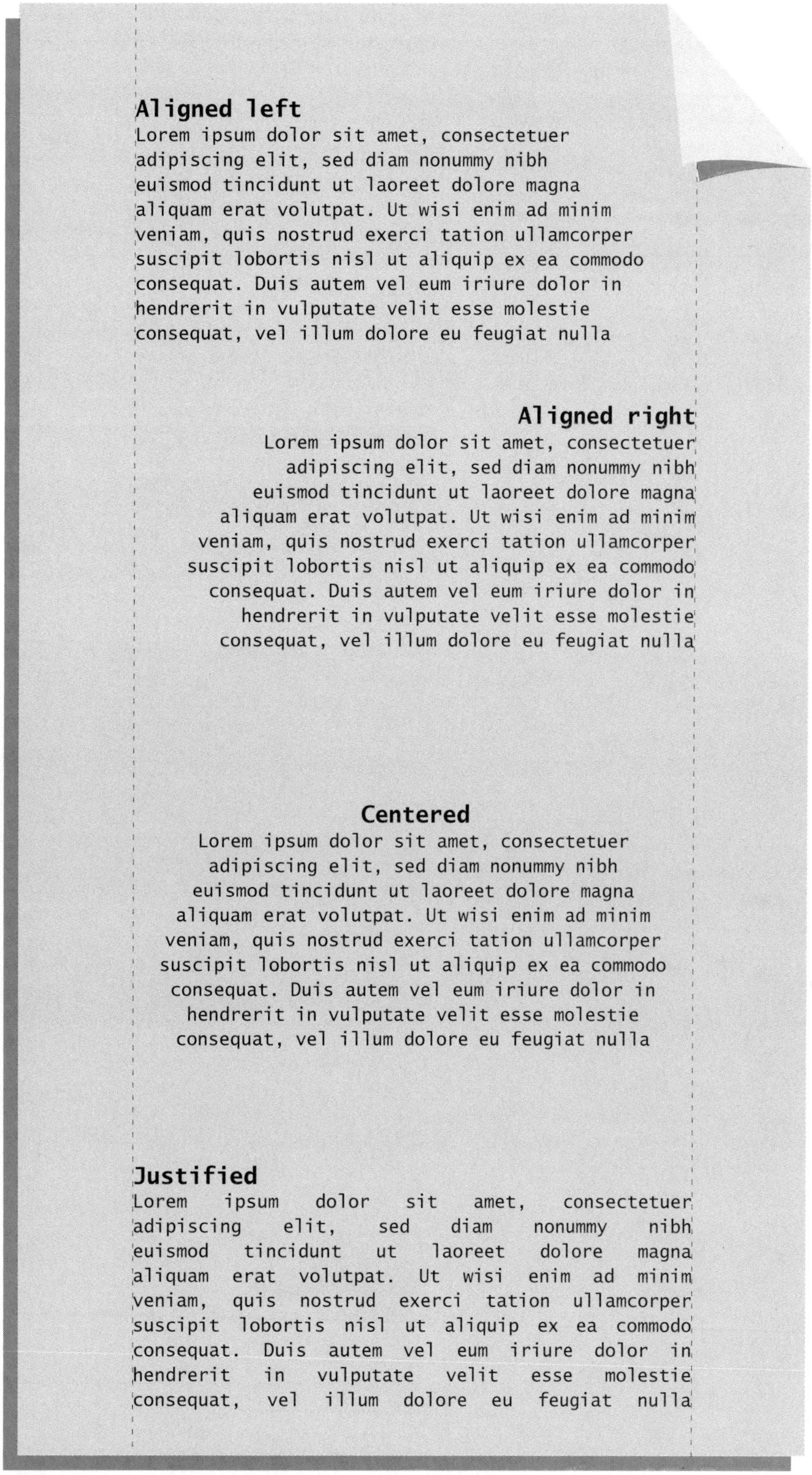

Aligned left

Lorem ipsum dolor sit amet, consectetuer
adipiscing elit, sed diam nonummy nibh
euismod tincidunt ut laoreet dolore magna
aliquam erat volutpat. Ut wisi enim ad minim
veniam, quis nostrud exerci tation ullamcorper
suscipit lobortis nisl ut aliquip ex ea commodo
consequat. Duis autem vel eum iriure dolor in
hendrerit in vulputate velit esse molestie
consequat, vel illum dolore eu feugiat nulla

Aligned right

Lorem ipsum dolor sit amet, consectetuer
adipiscing elit, sed diam nonummy nibh
euismod tincidunt ut laoreet dolore magna
aliquam erat volutpat. Ut wisi enim ad minim
veniam, quis nostrud exerci tation ullamcorper
suscipit lobortis nisl ut aliquip ex ea commodo
consequat. Duis autem vel eum iriure dolor in
hendrerit in vulputate velit esse molestie
consequat, vel illum dolore eu feugiat nulla

Centered

Lorem ipsum dolor sit amet, consectetuer
adipiscing elit, sed diam nonummy nibh
euismod tincidunt ut laoreet dolore magna
aliquam erat volutpat. Ut wisi enim ad minim
veniam, quis nostrud exerci tation ullamcorper
suscipit lobortis nisl ut aliquip ex ea commodo
consequat. Duis autem vel eum iriure dolor in
hendrerit in vulputate velit esse molestie
consequat, vel illum dolore eu feugiat nulla

Justified

Lorem ipsum dolor sit amet, consectetuer
adipiscing elit, sed diam nonummy nibh
euismod tincidunt ut laoreet dolore magna
aliquam erat volutpat. Ut wisi enim ad minim
veniam, quis nostrud exerci tation ullamcorper
suscipit lobortis nisl ut aliquip ex ea commodo
consequat. Duis autem vel eum iriure dolor in
hendrerit in vulputate velit esse molestie
consequat, vel illum dolore eu feugiat nulla

Figure 4.2

The résumé that you've begun is currently all aligned left, the default line alignment in Word. The only adjustment you will need to make here is to center the heading lines—the name, address, and telephone number.

Tip Formatting paragraphs is easier when it's clear where they begin and end. If paragraph marks are not displayed on the screen, select the Show/Hide ¶ button in the Standard toolbar to display them.

To align the heading paragraphs using the Paragraph dialog box:

1 If the résumé is not in the document window, retrieve it now.

2 Check that the screen resembles Figure 4.3.

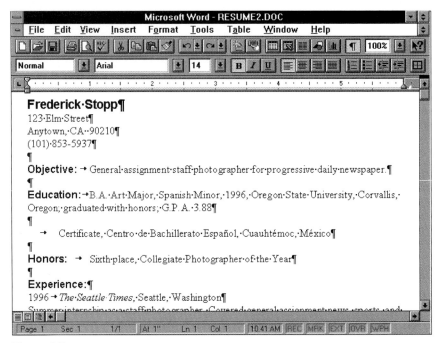

Figure 4.3

3 Select some part of each of the four lines at the top of the résumé. Your selection should look something like the one in Figure 4.4.

Figure 4.4

According to Word's definition, each of these four lines is a separate paragraph because each one ends with a paragraph mark, so you must select some part of each line to format it.

4 Choose Paragraph from the Format menu to open the Paragraph dialog box.

5 Select the Indents and Spacing tab if it is not already on top.

6 Select the Alignment drop-down list box so the four alignment options are revealed, as shown in Figure 4.5.

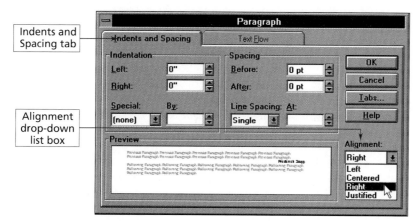

Indents and Spacing tab

Alignment drop-down list box

Figure 4.5

7 Select the Right option.
Note that the bold paragraph on the miniature page in the Preview box changes shape to show how selected paragraphs will look after the formatting is applied.

8 Select OK to complete the formatting choice.

Note the appearance of the heading on the page. If there were many lines, or if the lines were longer, they would be very difficult to read. It's for that reason that right-aligned paragraphs are rarely used. You will be changing these paragraphs in the steps below.

Tip For quick access to the Paragraph dialog box, position the pointer on the paragraph you want to format, click the right mouse button, and then select Paragraph.

The Paragraph dialog box is comprehensive: it gives you access to nearly all of the paragraph formats available in Word. But you'll rarely use all the formats, and the Paragraph dialog box requires several keystrokes or clicks to use. To speed up the process, Word allows you to use the Formatting toolbar and keyboard for the more common paragraph formatting options.

To align the top four lines of the résumé using the Formatting toolbar:

1 Select the heading paragraphs as before (so at least some portion of each of the four lines is selected).

2 Select the Center button in the Formatting toolbar, shown in Figure 4.6.

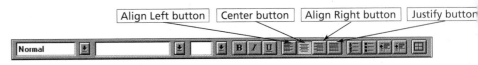

Figure 4.6

3 Select the other three alignment buttons to see how they affect the selected paragraphs.

The justified alignment will look like the left alignment because the paragraphs are all one line long.

4 Click the Align Left button to leave the heading information on the résumé aligned at left.

Word also provides simple keyboard shortcuts for aligning paragraphs. These shortcuts are summarized in Table 4.1.

Table 4.1

Keyboard Shortcut	Paragraph Alignment
(CTRL)+L	Aligned left
(CTRL)+E	Center
(CTRL)+R	Aligned right
(CTRL)+J	Justified

To center the heading paragraphs using the keyboard:

1 Select the heading paragraphs as before, so the screen again resembles Figure 4.4.

2 Press (CTRL)+E to center the paragraphs.

INDENTING PARAGRAPHS

Word allows you to indent a paragraph from the left and right margins and to indent the first line independently on the left. You could, for instance, indent from both left and right margins to indicate a block of quoted material, or you could indent the first line alone to make paragraph breaks more obvious. You also could leave the first line unindented and indent only the subsequent lines in the paragraph, which is called a ***hanging indentation***.

To make the résumé easier to read and make the sections more obvious, you will format most of the paragraphs with hanging indentations. You will establish the hanging indentation with keyboard commands, and then refine the size of the indentations using the ruler.

Table 4.2 shows several keyboard commands you can use to establish paragraph indentations.

Table 4.2

Keyboard Shortcut	Paragraph Indentation
(CTRL) + **M**	Indent to next tab
(CTRL) + (SHFT) + **M**	Decrease indentation by one tab
(CTRL) + **T**	Hanging indentation to next tab
(CTRL) + (SHFT) + **T**	Reduce hanging indentation by one tab

To establish a hanging indentation using the keyboard:

1 Position the insertion point somewhere within the Education section of the résumé.

2 Press (CTRL) + **T**

3 Note that the first line of the section remains unindented, but that the second line is indented, as shown in Figure 4.7.

> **Objective:** → General·assignment·staff·photographer·for·progressive·daily·newspaper.¶
> ¶
> **Education:** →B.A.·Art·Major,·Spanish·Minor,·1996,·Oregon·State·University,·Corvallis,·
> Oregon;·graduated·with·honors;·G.P.A.·3.88¶
> ¶
> → Certificate,·Centro·de·Bachillerato·Español,·Cuauhtémoc,·México¶

Figure 4.7

You can use a mouse to set indentations and tab stops on Word's ruler, which is shown in Figure 4.8. The three triangular ***indent markers*** are used to set indentations. You can "grab" each indent marker with the mouse pointer and slide the marker to the left or right to adjust the indentation. (To grab a marker, position the pointer over it and then click and hold down the mouse button; the marker will move with the pointer.) The top left indent marker sets the amount of indentation for the first line. The bottom left indent marker sets the amount of indentation for the remaining lines in the paragraph; this indentation determines the paragraph's left edge. The indent marker at the right sets the amount of indentation from the right edge. You'll be moving the bottom left indent marker to increase the amount of indentation in the lines following the first line.

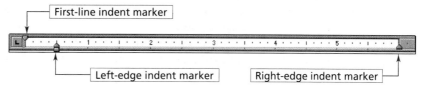

Figure 4.8

Caution When you do the following series of numbered steps, be sure to grab the triangle that represents the left-edge indent marker, not the small box beneath it. If you grab the box, both the first-line and the left-edge indent markers move in tandem. If you grab the triangle, the left-edge indent marker will move independently.

To set indentations with the ruler indent markers:

1 Make sure the ruler is visible on the screen. If not, choose Ruler from the View menu.

2 Make sure the insertion point is positioned somewhere inside the Education section paragraph.

3 Position the pointer on the left-edge indent marker (the bottom left triangle, which should be indented 0.5 inch already).

4 Press and hold down the mouse button to grab the indent marker.

5 Move the indent marker to the right so it is positioned under the 1.5-inch mark on the ruler, as shown in Figure 4.9.

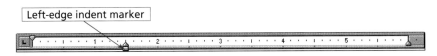

Figure 4.9

If necessary, you can save your file as RESUME2.DOC, exit Word now, and continue this project later.

COPYING PARAGRAPH FORMATS

The formatting information for a paragraph is stored in the paragraph mark (¶) at the end of the paragraph. If you delete the paragraph mark, the formatting information for that paragraph disappears and the paragraph takes on the formatting of the paragraph it is joined with. On the other hand, if the insertion point is inside a paragraph and you press ⒺⓃⓉⒺⓇ to begin a new paragraph, the new paragraph takes on the formatting of the previous one.

Copying Paragraph Formatting to New Paragraphs

Perform the following steps to learn how Word's paragraph formatting information is copied from one paragraph to another.

To create an additional centered paragraph:

1 Position the insertion point at the end of the last centered line at the top of the résumé, as shown in Figure 4.10.

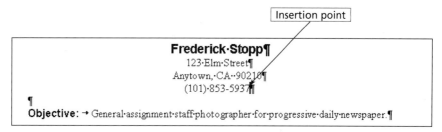

Figure 4.10

2 Press (ENTER) to start a new paragraph.

Note that the new paragraph is centered, just like the one before it, as shown in Figure 4.11.

Figure 4.11

Anything you typed on this new line would be centered, just like the lines above it.

3 Press (BACKSPACE) to delete the new paragraph you just added.

To create an additional left-aligned paragraph:

1 Position the insertion point at the beginning of the first left-aligned paragraph (the blank line just above the Objective section of the résumé), as shown in Figure 4.12.

Figure 4.12

2 Press (ENTER) to start a new paragraph.

3 Note that the new paragraph is left-aligned, as shown in Figure 4.13.

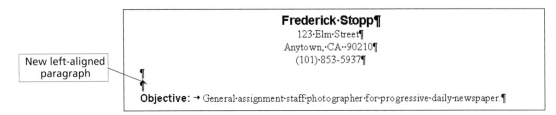

New left-aligned paragraph

Frederick·Stopp¶
123·Elm·Street¶
Anytown,·CA··90210¶
(101)·853-5937¶
¶
¶
Objective: → General·assignment·staff·photographer·for·progressive·daily·newspaper.¶

Figure 4.13

4 Press (BACKSPACE) to remove the new paragraph.

When you create a new paragraph from an old one, the new one receives the same formatting attributes as the old. That's helpful when you're adding text to an existing document. But it doesn't help when you want to copy formatting information from one paragraph to an already existing paragraph.

Copying Paragraph Formatting Using Styles

With the résumé, you need to copy formatting from one paragraph to another existing paragraph. You have formatted the Education section with a hanging indentation, but the other sections are still unindented. It's possible, of course, to format the remaining sections individually—selecting each one in turn, then applying the hanging indent format, and then adjusting it—but that approach would result in a lot of repetitive work and the possibility of errors and inconsistencies. Word provides an easier way: creating your own paragraph styles and then applying them to other paragraphs.

In Word a *style* is a collection of formatting characteristics that is given a name and is accessible from the Style box in the Formatting toolbar. A particular style includes formatting information about the type font and size and formatting information about line alignment, indentations, and all other paragraph characteristics.

You have been using Word's default Normal style all along in preparing your résumé. The style for the current selection appears in the Style box at the far left of the Formatting toolbar, as shown in Figure 4.14.

Style box

| Normal | ⬇ | Times New Roman | ⬇ | 12 | ⬇ | **B** | *I* | U | ≡ ≡ ≡ ≡ | ⊞ |

Figure 4.14

Word has a number of built-in styles such as Normal, but it also allows you to define your own styles. In the following set of numbered steps you will be creating a new style, called HangingIndent, based on the Education section that you have already formatted.

Caution In the following series of numbered steps, be careful about where you put the insertion point. If you put the insertion point in the boldface text, Word will interpret that to mean that you want paragraphs formatted with the new HangingIndent style to be boldfaced. If the insertion point is within normal text, however, Word will not change existing character formatting when the HangingIndent style is applied.

To create a new paragraph style:

1 Position the insertion point within the nonboldface text in the Education section of the résumé.

2 Select the Style box at the left end of the Formatting toolbar.

3 Type **HangingIndent** into the Style box.

4 Press (ENTER) to complete the style definition.

You have defined a new style named HangingIndent that creates a hanging indentation just like the one used in the Education section. Now you can apply the new style to other paragraphs in the résumé.

To apply the HangingIndent style to the Objective section:

1 Select the Objective section and the blank lines above and below it, as shown in Figure 4.15. These are the paragraphs you will be formatting.

Figure 4.15

2 Select the down arrow to the right of the Style box.

The new HangingIndent style will be in the list, as shown in Figure 4.16.

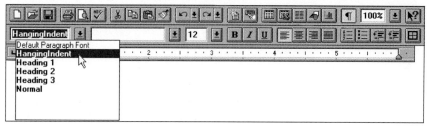

Figure 4.16

3 Select HangingIndent to apply this style.

The text in the Objective section has been reformatted with the new style and should now line up with the text in the Education section, as shown in Figure 4.17.

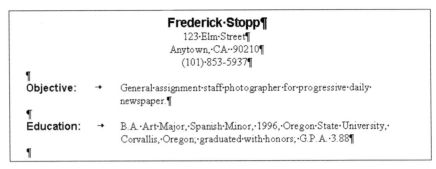

Figure 4.17

 To apply the HangingIndent style to the remainder of the résumé:

1 Select all of the rest of the résumé below the Education section.

2 Select the down arrow to the right of the Style box.

3 Select HangingIndent to apply this style.

The indent formatting will be copied to the other paragraphs and all the indentations in the résumé should line up.

EXIT If necessary, you can save your file as RESUME2.DOC, exit Word now, and continue this project later.

SETTING TAB STOPS

The résumé is now looking quite polished. All that remains is to add one last section, listing the photographer's equipment. This section will require the use of tab stops to make a neat presentation. You will type the information first and set the tab stops afterward. (This approach makes it easier to determine how wide the tab settings must be.)

 To enter the Equipment section of the résumé:

1 Type the information shown in Figure 4.18. The new section should go between the Employment section and the Skills section.
The default tab stop settings will make the items seem jumbled for now.

2 Insert or delete blank lines so that there is one blank line above and one below the new Equipment section.

```
Equipment:   →   Nikon·F3·body  →  35·mm·Nikkor → 105·mm·MicroNikkor¶
         →   Nikon·F4·body   →    50·mm·Nikkor → 180·mm·Nikkor¶
         →   28·mm·Nikkor → 85·mm·Nikkor   →   300·mm·f/2.8·Nikkor¶
```

Figure 4.18

To make this new section consistent with the others in the résumé, you will need to change the formatting of the heading to boldface sans serif.

To style the characters in the Equipment heading:

1 Select one of the already formatted boldface headings.

2 Click the Format Painter button in the Standard toolbar.

3 Use the paintbrush pointer to select *Equipment:*

Check that the Equipment heading is now formatted like the other headings in the résumé.

The default tab stops in Word are normally set at half-inch intervals. They are marked on the ruler with very small hash marks just below the ruler itself, as shown in Figure 4.19. The default settings are often satisfactory, but frequently you'll want to customize the settings to give your material optimum presentation. You can set not only the location of the tab stop, but also its style.

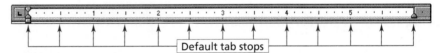

Figure 4.19

Word implements four styles of tab stops: left, center, right, and decimal. The *left tab stop* aligns the text on the left side under the tab stop. The *center tab stop* centers text on the tab stop. The *right tab stop* aligns text on the right side under the tab stop. The *decimal tab stop* aligns text (or, more commonly, numbers) on the decimal point under the tab stop. Figure 4.20 shows examples of each style of tab and the ruler line above, which indicates the tab stop settings.

→	Left tab	→	Center tab	→	Right tab	→	Decimal tab
→	will align	→	will	→	will align	→	195.33
→	along the	→	center	→	along the	→	34.95
→	left edge	→	lines	→	right edge	→	1,234.56

Figure 4.20

Each of the four styles of tab stops is indicated on the ruler by a different symbol and is set using the Tab Alignment button at the left edge of the ruler. You will select the Tab Alignment button until the style of tab stop you want appears. Then you will click on the ruler where you want to set the tab stop. A tab stop of the style you selected will be inserted on the ruler. You can set additional tab stops by clicking at other points on the ruler. If you need to, you can grab the tab stops with the pointer and slide the markers from side to side to adjust the tab settings on the ruler. If you want to delete a tab stop, you can grab the marker with the pointer and drag the marker up or down off the ruler so the tab marker disappears.

Remember that tab stop settings are a paragraph format, so you must select all of the text where you want the tab stops to be in effect before you set the tabs.

To set tab stops for the Equipment section of the résumé:

1 Select at least part of each of the three paragraphs (lines) in the Equipment section.

2 Select the Tab Alignment button on the ruler until the left tab style appears, indicated by the *L*-shaped symbol, as shown in Figure 4.21.

Figure 4.21

3 Click at the 3-inch mark on the ruler to set the tab. Adjust the tab stop if needed by grabbing the marker with the pointer and sliding the marker from side to side.

4 Click again at the 4.5-inch mark on the ruler. Adjust the tab marker if needed.

5 Check that the Equipment section resembles Figure 4.22.

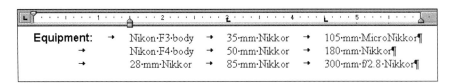

Figure 4.22

Note that the left-edge indent marker acts as a tab marker for the first column. The second and third columns use the tab stops you set using the Formatting toolbar and the ruler.

The résumé is nearly complete, but notice that the two items under the Experience section seem somewhat cluttered. The job description details under each heading need to be indented.

To complete indenting in the Experience section:

1 Position the insertion point just in front of *Summer*, on the third line of the Experience section.

2 Press (TAB) to indent this line.

3 Insert a second tab just in front of *Photo*, just underneath *1994–96* in the Experience section.

The Experience section of your résumé should now look like Figure 4.23.

```
Experience:¶
1996         →      The·Seattle·Times,·Seattle,·Washington¶
             →      Summer·internship·as·a·staff·photographer.·Covered·general·
                    assignment·news,·sports,·and·features.¶
¶
1994-96      →      The·Daily·Barometer,·Oregon·State·University¶
             →      Photo·editor·and·staff·photographer·during·academic·school·year.·
                    Made·assignments·and·edited·work·from·five·staff·photographers.·
                    Covered·news·and·sports.·Used·film·scanner·and·computer·to·
                    process·images·and·lay·out·pages.¶
```

Figure 4.23

Tip If you want a quick look at font and paragraph formats, select the Help button at the right end of the Standard toolbar. The pointer will change into an arrow with a question mark attached to it. Then click anywhere in the text to get a listing of formatting information. When you are done, press (ESC) to cancel Help.

The résumé is finished now except for saving it and printing it.

To save and print the résumé:

1 Save the completed résumé.

2 Print a copy of the résumé.

THE NEXT STEP

You may already have begun adapting the résumé for your own use. As you continue adding and modifying, here are a few résumé guidelines to keep in mind:

- Keep your résumé brief, normally no longer than a page for a recent college graduate.
- List activities (such as work experience) in reverse chronological order; most recent first.
- Double-check all dates, spelling, and grammar.
- You may want to include a section on extracurricular activities, travel, or serious noncareer interests.
- You may want to indicate your willingness to relocate.
- *Don't* list salary expectations, name of husband or wife, or names and addresses of references.

You can also use your word processing skills to prepare a cover letter for your résumé.

SUMMARY AND EXERCISES

Summary

- Word defines a paragraph as any amount of text that ends with a paragraph mark (¶).
- A paragraph in Word can be formatted with different alignments (left, center, right, justified), different indentations, different tab stop settings, different line spacing, and so on.
- You format a paragraph by first selecting it and then applying the formatting.
- A paragraph is selected in Word when it contains the insertion point or when some portion of the paragraph is in the current selection.
- You can apply paragraph formatting using the Paragraph dialog box, the keyboard, or the Formatting toolbar. Nearly all common paragraph formatting can be accomplished using the Formatting toolbar and the ruler.
- The paragraph mark contains the paragraph's formatting information. When you press (ENTER) at the end of a paragraph, that paragraph's formatting information is copied into the new paragraph.
- You can create new paragraph styles using the Style box on the Formatting toolbar and then apply those styles to other paragraphs.
- Word uses four styles of tab stops: left, center, right, and decimal. Each paragraph can have its own settings for tab styles and positions.

Key Terms and Operations

Key Terms
aligned left
aligned right
center tab stop
centered alignment
decimal tab stop
hanging indentation
indent marker
justified alignment
left tab stop

right tab stop
style

Operations
Change paragraph alignment
Copy paragraph formats
Define and use styles
Indent paragraphs
Set tab stops

Study Questions

Multiple Choice

1. To select a paragraph, you must:
   a. Select every character within the paragraph, including the paragraph mark (¶).
   b. Just be sure the paragraph mark (¶) is selected.
   c. Make sure that some part of the paragraph is selected or that the insertion point is somewhere inside the paragraph.
   d. Use the selection bar and mouse.

2. The formatting information for a paragraph is stored in:
   a. the paragraph mark (¶) at the beginning of the paragraph.
   b. the paragraph mark (¶) at the end of the paragraph.
   c. an invisible code at the beginning of the paragraph.
   d. the Formatting toolbar.

3. To create a new style based on an existing formatted paragraph:
   a. Use the Paragraph dialog box.
   b. Press CTRL + S
   c. Use the ruler.
   d. Use the Style box in the Formatting toolbar.

4. Which of the following is *not* one of the tab styles in Word?
   a. left   c. right
   b. center   d. justified

5. Which of the following keyboard commands will create a hanging indentation?
   a. CTRL + H   c. CTRL + T
   b. CTRL + I   d. CTRL + L

6. When you change tab settings or indentations on the ruler, they affect:
   a. the entire document.
   b. the paragraph at the top of the screen.
   c. the selected paragraph(s).
   d. all paragraphs after the insertion point.

7. When you press ENTER at the end of a paragraph, you create a new paragraph that has the same formatting as:
   a. a left-aligned paragraph.
   b. the paragraph below it.
   c. the format shown on the Formatting toolbar.
   d. the paragraph above it.

8. To establish a new tab, you should click:
   a. the selection bar.   c. the Formatting toolbar.
   b. the ruler.   d. the current paragraph.

9. Which of the following *cannot* be set in the Paragraph dialog box?
   a. paragraph alignment
   b. paragraph indentation
   c. extra space above or below the paragraph
   d. type font and size

10. Which of the following cannot be controlled by the indent markers on the ruler?
    a. the first line at left
    b. the right edge of all lines
    c. the left edge of all lines
    d. the right edge of the top line

Short Answer

1. To center a paragraph, select the paragraph and press _____.

2. To adjust paragraph indentations, use the _____ on the ruler.

3. You can set different styles of tab stops on the ruler by clicking first on the _____.

4. To make a paragraph aligned left, press _____.

5. The three triangular indent markers on the ruler give you independent control of the _____, _____, and _____ of a paragraph.

6. If you delete the paragraph mark between two paragraphs, the new combined paragraph will take on the formatting of the _____ paragraph.

7. The tab style that produces proper alignment in a column of figures is called a _____.

8. The paragraph alignment style that produces an even left and right edge is called _____.

9. To delete a tab stop from the ruler using the mouse, you should drag the tab marker _____.

10. You can format paragraphs in Word using the keyboard, the ruler and Formatting toolbar, or the _____.

For Discussion

1. What type of indentations can be established with Word? How is each type used?

2. Describe how to set tabs so a column of figures in an expense report would line up.

3. You produced a three-column list in the sample résumé. Would that be a workable approach to formatting the text in a multicolumn document such as a newsletter? Why or why not?

4. What is a paragraph in Word?

Review Exercises

Formatting Paragraphs in a Memo

1. Retrieve the memo from the file NEWMEMO.

2. Select the date line at the top of the memo and format it with right paragraph alignment.

3. Select the *MEMO* heading and center it.

4. Insert tabs in front of the *To*, *From*, and *Subject* lines.

5. Replace the space following the colon (:) in each of those same three lines with a tab.

6. Select all three lines and insert a right tab at 1 inch and a left tab at 1.25 inches on the ruler.

7. Select the three paragraphs that make up the body of the memo.

8. Use the mouse to adjust the first-line indent marker on the ruler so each line is indented ¼ inch.

The memo should look like Figure 4.24.

February 14, 1996

MEMO

TO: Patricia Smith, Marketing Director

FROM: John Wells, Publications Director

SUBJECT: Production of new product brochures

The concept for the new product brochures has been reviewed and passed by the marketing committee. Stan is working on design ideas and plans to have something ready for us to look at at the next meeting.

Arlene warned me that there may be a problem with some of the photographs for the brochure. She said she would talk to you so we could reschedule it with the photographer. Please let me know if you need to be able to use the T41 prototype again.

I need to schedule this with the printer so they can order paper. My understanding is that we will be printing 10,000 copies to begin. Is that correct?

Figure 4.24

9. Save the memo and print a copy.

Formatting Paragraphs in a Meeting Agenda

1. Retrieve the agenda you saved under the name AGENDA at the end of Project 3.

2. Center the top three lines.

3. Delete the tab characters ($\rightarrow$) in the document.

4. Indent all the items under the Old Business and New Business sections one level (to the first default tab stop).

5. Indent the office titles under *Election of officers* an extra heading level (to the next default tab stop).

6. Save the revised agenda and print a copy of it.

Creating an Invoice

1. Type the information for the invoice shown in Figure 4.25.

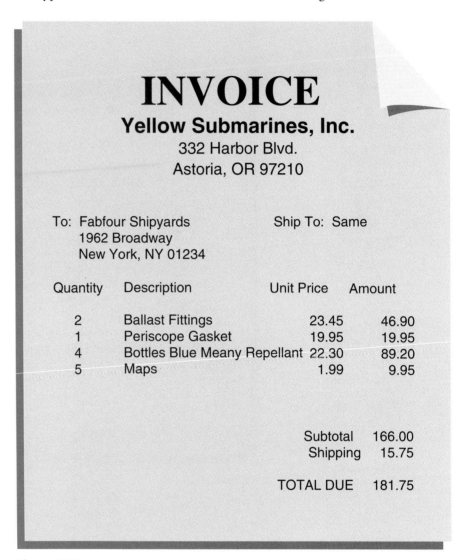

Figure 4.25

2. Format the entire document in a 12-point sans serif face such as Arial or Helvetica.

3. Center the heading lines.

4. Change the *Invoice* heading to 36-point Times New Roman or a similar serif face and boldface the heading.

5. Change the formatting of the name of the company to 18-point bold.

6. Change the formatting of the company address lines to 14-point.

7. Select the company name and address lines in the To and Ship To sections. Insert left tab stops at ⅜ inch, 3 inches, and 3-¾ inches.

8. Select from the *Quantity/Description/Unit Price/Amount* heading to the bottom of the document. Insert a center tab stop at ¼ inch. Insert a left tab stop at 1 inch. Insert decimal tab stops at 4 inches and 5 inches.

9. Save your document as INVOICE.DOC and print a copy of it.

Assignments

Formatting Your Résumé

Retrieve your personal version of the résumé, saved under the file name MYRESUME. Update or revise it if necessary. Change paragraph formats to match the résumé you completed in this project. Save the revised and formatted résumé and print a copy of it.

Formatting the Telephone List with Leader Tabs

Retrieve the version of your telephone list saved under the file name FONELIST. It should be a list of names and telephone numbers separated by tabs. Select all the lines with names and numbers on them and use the ruler to insert a right tab at about 4 inches (adjust the location of the tab as needed to accommodate the names on your list). The names should now align on the left edge and the numbers, on the right edge.

If the gap between the names and numbers is very wide, it makes it difficult to match numbers with names. Commercial printers use a dotted line, called a leader, to tie the parts of the line together and make the line easier to read. Word allows you to insert leader tabs.

Begin by selecting all the lines (paragraphs) you want to format. Choose Tabs from the Format menu. Select item 2 in the Leader box. As soon as you select OK or press (ENTER), the leader will be inserted. Save the list and print a copy of it.

PROJECT 5: SECTION FORMATTING

Objectives

After completing this project, you should be able to:

▶ Change margins

▶ Change paragraph line spacing

▶ Create bulleted lists

▶ Add footnotes

▶ Add headers or footers

In this project you will begin putting together a short research paper. Like many research papers, this will have footnotes, page numbers, and, eventually, a table of data. At the end of this project you'll be able to use basic page formatting and the features of Word that take some of the pain out of preparing reports and papers. You'll have the beginnings of the research paper. In Projects 6 and 7, you'll continue with the paper, working with the tools Word provides for editing and correcting and then adding a table.

CASE STUDY: BEGINNING THE RESEARCH PAPER

Assume you are a student in Sociology 415, a course in sociological research. You've been given an assignment to produce a short analytical paper dealing with a social issue and supported by data from a sample study listed in your textbook. Your paper should include relevant references, including the data you have used to support your findings.

Designing the Solution

The overall organization of almost any research paper follows this general pattern:

■ Placing the study in context: introductory remarks, possibly a review of work and writings in this area, a statement of your hypothesis
■ Description of your study: where your data came from
■ Analysis of your study: results, discussion of results, conclusions or recommendations

We'll assume you've done your research, produced a rough draft following this overall organizational pattern, and made revisions. Now you are ready to format the paper. The standard format for a research paper is essentially the same as for a manuscript submitted for publication. The format is designed to be easy to read—and easy to edit, annotate, and revise.

The standard research paper format has been around since the days of the typewriter and is still based on the characteristics of the typewriter. Research papers are nearly always double spaced, which allows more room to mark corrections and make comments. Even with the many type fonts available with modern personal computers, the standard for a research paper remains a typewriter font such as Courier, which facilitates corrections in spelling and word choice. Margins are set wide enough to accommodate more comments, and binding if necessary. Because research papers usually run several pages, you'll want to number the pages for ease of handling. You'll frequently need to quote other people's writing in your own work and then credit these sources in a footnote reference. Some research paper characteristics, footnotes in particular, were difficult and time-consuming on a typewriter, but are relatively easy to produce using Word.

You'll begin this project by typing the text for the paper, or retrieving it from disk. Then you'll set margins and double space the text. Next, you'll format the heading and title information. You'll create a bulleted list, add footnotes, and add a single-spaced quotation. Last, you'll add a header that prints page numbers automatically at the top of each page.

WORKING WITH SECTIONS AND SECTION BREAKS

A *section* in Word is a portion of a document that can be formatted with specific margin settings, page orientation (vertical or horizontal), page-numbering sequence, or other features affecting page layout. When you begin a new document in Word, the entire document is a single section. If necessary, you can insert section breaks to divide the document into separate sections and vary the section formatting from one section to another. For instance, you could number the first few pages of a report with small roman numerals and then switch to another section to use conventional arabic numerals for the rest of the report. Or you could include a horizontal page in a separate section to accommodate a wide table within a series of conventional vertical pages. For most simple documents, however, the entire document will be a single section. That will be the case with this research paper.

CHANGING THE MARGINS

Formatting sections in Word follows the general rule: select and then do. When formatting sections, you first select the section and then you format it. A section is selected when any part of it is selected. If your whole document is a single section, that makes selecting it very straightforward: you just need to have the insertion point somewhere inside the document to format the whole document.

The nearly complete draft of the research paper is shown in Figure 5.1. Note that some items are missing from the draft. You will add these items later in this and subsequent projects.

If the file SOC415.DOC is available, you will not need to type the text in yourself. If you do need to type the text yourself, the lines in the document window may be longer or shorter, depending on the margin settings on the computer you are using. Don't worry about that; you'll be changing the margins shortly anyway. Note also that there is an intentionally misspelled word—*likelyhood*—that appears several times in the text. It is there to give the spelling checker something to do in the next project. If you are typing and make other mistakes, you can leave the mistakes to be corrected later.

Sociology 415
Professor R. Warner
December 6, 1995

Impact of Educational Level on
Views of Gender Roles
by B.J. Mitchell

I am interested in discovering if there is a relationship between educational level and views on gender roles. I believe I will find that as one's level of education increases, the likelyhood of having non-traditional views toward gender roles increases. Examples of non-traditional views include regarding the following as acceptable lifestyle choices: women working in male-dominated fields, men sharing responsibilityfor work in the home, and women able to hold any job solely on the basis of qualification.
I think there will be a positive connection between higher education and non-traditional views toward gender roles for a variety of reasons. Individuals with greater education are more likely to be aware of the historic and institutional discrimination against women.
[quote will go here]
In addition, persons with higher education are likely to marry others with similar educational background, making the practice of non-traditional gender roles a likely possibility in their relationships. Educated individuals are more likely than uneducated persons to work in areas of employment where women have attained some degree of success in male-dominated environments. Observing these achievements could have the effect of changing a person's views from believing women do not "belong" in the workplace to encouraging their continued success.
The Study
Data for this paper comes from mail surveys sent to probability samples of residents in metropolitan Toronto and Detroit in 1988. The response rate was 69 percent, yielding a total sample size of 1805. The data and percentage distribution of the responses are shown in the table below, along with column and row totals used in the statistical analysis.
[Insert Data Table Here]
Findings
The table shows the results of a probability sample survey. The results support my hypothesis. Specifically, while less than 20 percent of those with a high school education reported having non-traditional views toward gender roles, 42 percent of those with some college and over half of those sampled with college degrees hold non-traditional views. In addition, the data show that almost half of those with high school only and less than 15 percent of those with a college degree hold traditional views. This demonstrates that with increased education, the likelyhood of having non-traditional views also increases.
If there were no correlation between educational level and non-traditional views, the survey responses would be expected to be distributed as shown in the following table.
[Expected response table goes here]
A Chi Square analysis shows the actual data and expected results differ significantly at the 0.01 level. For this reason I must reject the null hypothesis. I conclude that as a person receives more education, the likelyhood that his or her views toward gender roles will become non-traditional increases.

Figure 5.1

To prepare the draft and redefine Normal style:

1 Type the draft as shown, or retrieve the SOC415.DOC file if it is available.

2 Select a few words within the document and format that text as 12-point Courier New (or a similar typewriter-style face).

3 Select Normal in the Style box at the left end of the Formatting toolbar.
The Reapply Style dialog box will appear.

4 Select the top option: *Redefine the style using the selection as an example?*

5 Press (ENTER) to redefine Normal style as 12-point Courier New.
All text in the paper will change to 12-point Courier as soon as you redefine Normal style. Now you need to boldface the two headings.

To boldface the headings:

1 Select the first heading: *The Study.*

2 Select the Bold button on the Formatting toolbar to boldface the heading.

3 Select the second heading: *Findings.*

4 Select the Bold button on the Formatting toolbar to boldface the heading.

5 Save your document as SOC415-2.DOC.

The standard margin settings for a research paper are at least one inch on all sides. You will set the top, bottom, left, and right margins for the paper to one inch exactly.

To set the margins:

1 Choose Page Setup from the File menu.
The Page Setup dialog box, shown in Figure 5.2, appears.

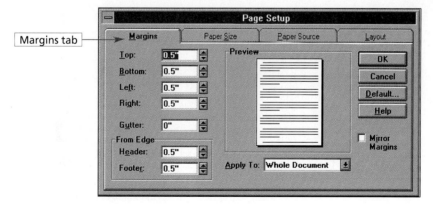

Figure 5.2

The margin settings on your screen may not exactly match those shown in Figure 5.2, but you are about to change them.

2 Select the Margins tab if it is not already on top.

3 Select the measurement within the Top box, as shown in Figure 5.2.

4 Type **1"** in the Top box.

The new measurement you type replaces the old measurement for the top margin. You can also use the arrow keys, (BACKSPACE), and (DEL) to edit the measurement in any of the boxes.

5 Select the measurement within the Bottom box, located just below the Top box.

As soon as you advance to the Bottom box, the Preview display within the dialog box is updated to indicate how the new setting for the top margin will affect general page appearance.

6 Type **1"** in the Bottom box.

7 Change the measurement to 1″ in the Left box.

8 Change the measurement to 1″ in the Right box.

9 Select Whole Document in the Apply To box.

10 Select OK.

To make the document easier to read on screen, you can adjust the magnification of the display using the Zoom Control box at the right edge of the Standard toolbar. For most of the figures in this project the Zoom Control box is set to Page Width so an entire line can be seen on the screen without scrolling from side to side. If you have the Zoom Control set differently, the figures may not exactly match your screen display.

Note that the new margin settings change the length of the lines throughout the document. All the lines, including first lines of paragraphs, are flush to the left margin. Standard research paper format, however, calls for a first-line indent of about five spaces. You can indent first lines by changing the formatting for all text paragraphs in the paper. However, you don't want to indent the heading information or the two headings *The Study* and *Findings*.

The default first-line indent in Word is ½ inch. You can change it if necessary, but ½ inch happens to be the setting that will indent a paragraph of 12-point Courier by five spaces, so you will leave the default as is.

To indent the first line of the text paragraphs:

1 Click the Show/Hide ¶ button on the Standard toolbar if paragraph marks are not visible.

2 Select all paragraphs from the first text paragraph to the paragraph just above the heading *The Study*.

3 Choose Paragraph from the Format menu.

The Paragraph dialog box appears.

4 Select the Indents and Spacing tab if it is not already on top.

5 Select the Special pull-down menu.

6 Select the First Line option, as shown in Figure 5.3.

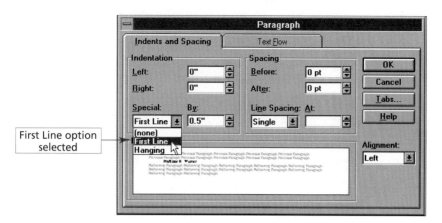

Figure 5.3

7 Select OK to complete the new setting.

The top of the paper should now look like Figure 5.4. You've indented the first paragraphs, but not the paragraphs following the headings below. To do that, you will be using Word's Repeat feature.

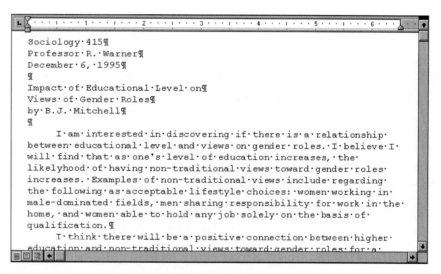

Figure 5.4

To indent the first lines of remaining paragraphs:

1 Position the insertion point somewhere within the paragraph following the heading *The Study*.

2 Choose Repeat Paragraph Formatting from the Edit menu to put the same format in effect.

3 Select some part of all of the remaining paragraphs, following the *Findings* heading.

4 Choose Repeat Paragraph Formatting from the Edit menu.

Now you can double space the lines in the body of the paper. Recall that line spacing is a paragraph format, so you will select the paragraphs to be formatted and then double space them.

To double space the body of the paper:

1 Position the insertion point somewhere within the first paragraph of the body of the paper.

2 Select all text from the insertion point to the end of the document.

3 Click the right mouse button to bring up the short-cut menu.

4 Select Paragraph to bring up the Paragraph dialog box.

5 Select the Indents and Spacing tab if it is not already on top.

6 Set the Line Spacing drop-down list box to Double.

7 Press (ENTER) to double space all selected paragraphs.

Tip You can also use keyboard shortcuts to set paragraph line spacing. To single space, press (CTRL) + 1; to double space, press (CTRL) + 2; and to set spacing at one-and-a-half lines, press (CTRL) + 5.

The paper now should all be doubled spaced except for the heading lines at the beginning of the paper. Next you can turn your attention to formatting the heading. Titles of papers are usually centered, and the course name and date are placed at the right edge of the page.

To make the top three lines flush right:

1 Select the top three lines (the course name, the instructor's name, and the date).

2 Click the Align Right button on the Formatting toolbar to align these lines on the right.

To center the title:

1 Select the three title lines.

2 Click the Center button on the Formatting toolbar to center these lines.

If necessary, you can save your file as SOC415-2.DOC, exit Word now, and continue this project later.

CREATING A BULLETED LIST

To make clearer what you mean by nontraditional views of gender roles, you decide to list on separate lines each of the three example lifestyle choices mentioned in the first paragraph. To make it easier for the reader to compare these examples and understand the pattern of your thought, you will put the three examples in a bulleted list. A **bullet** is a small typographical device, usually a large dot, that indicates separate items in a list, just as numbers do in a numbered list. Unlike numbered lists, however, bulleted lists don't suggest that items are in some particular order.

First you will edit the text so each item in the list appears on a separate line and in a separate paragraph. Then you'll indent the list and add the bullets.

To create an indented list:

1 Place the insertion point just after the colon following *choices*.

2 Press (ENTER) to separate the list from the rest of the paragraph and establish a new paragraph.

3 Remove the first-line indentation using the top left indent marker on the ruler.

The screen may scroll to the left when you move the marker. You can adjust the display using the horizontal scroll bar at the bottom of the screen.

4 Edit the list so it appears as shown in Figure 5.5. Be sure to eliminate all unneeded commas and spaces as well as the word *and* that connects the last item to the rest of the list and the period that ends the list.

```
likelyhood·of·having·non-traditional·views·toward·gender·roles·

increases.·Examples·of·non-traditional·views·include·regarding·

the·following·as·acceptable·lifestyle·choices:¶

women·working·in·male-dominated·fields¶

men·sharing·responsibility·for·work·in·the·home¶

women·able·to·hold·any·job·solely·on·the·basis·of·qualification¶

      I·think·there·will·be·a·positive·connection·between·higher·

education·and·non-traditional·views·toward·gender·roles·for·a·
```

Figure 5.5

5 Select the three new paragraphs that comprise the list.

6 Click the Increase Indent button on the Formatting toolbar to indent these lines.

The list should now look as shown in Figure 5.6, although the way you selected the paragraphs might differ.

```
increases.·Examples·of·non-traditional·views·include·regarding·

the·following·as·acceptable·lifestyle·choices:¶

      women·working·in·male-dominated·fields¶

      men·sharing·responsibility·for·work·in·the·home¶

      women·able·to·hold·any·job·solely·on·the·basis·of·

qualification¶

      I·think·there·will·be·a·positive·connection·between·higher·

education·and·non-traditional·views·toward·gender·roles·for·a·
```

Figure 5.6

Tip If necessary, you can increase the size of the indentation by selecting the Increase Indent button repeatedly or by pressing (CTRL) + M. Each time you increase the indentation, the text moves to the next tab, ordinarily ½ inch. To decrease the size of an indentation, you can select the Decrease Indent button or press (CTRL) + (SHIFT) + M. You can also adjust paragraph indentation using the indent markers on the ruler, as shown in Figure 5.7.

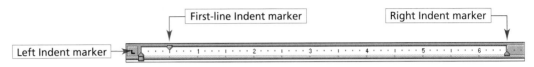

Figure 5.7

To format a series of lines as a bulleted list, you can call up the Bullets and Numbering dialog box, shown in Figure 5.8. You can use this dialog box to create both bulleted lists and numbered lists on a single level (like the one in the research paper) or on multiple levels (like an outline). You can change the character used for a bullet and customize the line spacing. For the list in the research paper, however, the default bullet style will work well. The default bullet style will have a blue border around it.

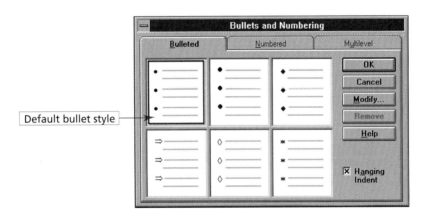

Figure 5.8

To create a bulleted list:

1 Select the three list items, as shown in Figure 5.6.

2 Choose Bullets and Numbering from the Format menu.

3 Select the Bulleted tab if it is not already on top.

4 Select OK to add bullets to the list.

The list should now look as shown in Figure 5.9. Each item in the list stands out clearly and the distinction between traditional and nontraditional views is made apparent.

```
increases. · Examples· of· non-traditional· views· include· regarding·

the· following· as· acceptable· lifestyle· choices:¶

    •  women· working· in· male-dominated· fields¶

    •  men· sharing· responsibility· for· work· in· the· home¶

    •  women· able· to· hold· any· job· solely· on· the· basis· of·

       qualification¶

       I· think· there· will· be· a· positive· connection· between· higher·

education· and· non-traditional· views· toward· gender· roles· for· a·
```

Figure 5.9

 Tip If you want to use the bullet style already selected in the Bullets and Numbering dialog box, you can produce a bulleted list quickly by selecting the list items and then selecting the Bullets button on the Formatting toolbar. The button is a toggle, so selecting it a second time will eliminate the bullets.

ADDING FOOTNOTES AND A QUOTATION

The data for the research paper came from a study published in an academic journal. To credit those who conducted the research, you need to add a footnote citing that study. A *footnote,* as you are probably aware, is a brief block of text at the bottom of a page used for citing authorities or making incidental comments. Footnotes are usually numbered in sequential order.

In the days of the typewriter, footnoting was a painful operation. The typist had to type the body of the text, being careful to stop short of the bottom of the page and leave exactly enough room for the footnote. Then the typist had to switch to single spacing and type whatever footnotes belonged on that page. Word, by contrast, makes the process of footnoting relatively painless. When you insert a footnote reference in the body of a paper, Word automatically numbers and formats the footnote reference as a superscript. Word then opens a footnote window where you can enter the text of the footnote as it should appear at the bottom of the page. If you insert or delete a footnote, Word automatically renumbers all other footnotes. When you print out the paper, Word puts footnotes at the bottom of the appropriate pages, or will place them at the end of the section if you select the *endnotes* option. Unlike footnotes, which always appear at the bottom of the page, endnotes appear at the end of the section.

To add a footnote, you use the Footnote and Endnote dialog box, shown in Figure 5.10. This dialog box allows you to customize footnotes or endnotes to suit nearly any style guide. You can click the Help button if you want more information about available options. For the research paper, however, the default—numbered footnotes—is exactly what you want.

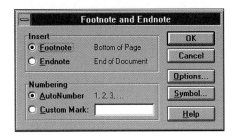

Figure 5.10

 ### To add a footnote reference:

1 In the first paragraph after the heading *The Study*, position the insertion point immediately after the period following *Detroit in 1988*, at the end of the first sentence.

2 Choose Footnote from the Insert menu.

3 Select OK to add the footnote.

The footnote window opens at the bottom of the screen, as shown in Figure 5.11. This is a separate window, with its own vertical scroll bar, and you can switch from one window to the other by clicking inside the window or by pressing (F6). Notice that Word has inserted a superscript footnote reference mark just after *1988* in the text window and at the beginning of the footnote text in the footnote window. Now you will type the reference.

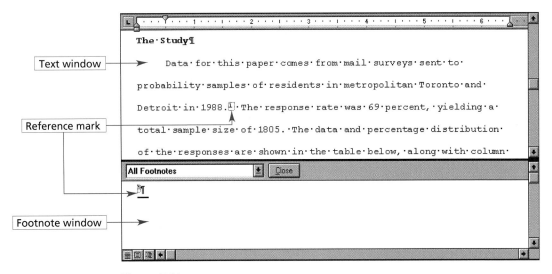

Figure 5.11

 ### To add the footnote text and set the Footnote Text style:

1 Type the footnote text shown in Figure 5.12

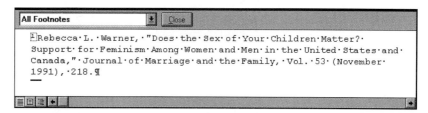

Figure 5.12

2 Select one or two words within the footnote text and change the size to 12 point.

3 Select Footnote Text in the Style box at the left end of the Formatting toolbar.
The Reapply Style dialog box will appear.

4 Select the top option: *Redefine the style using the selection as an example?*

5 Select OK to redefine the Footnote Text style as 12-point Courier New.
All of the footnote text will immediately change to 12-point Courier New. Any future footnotes you enter will also appear in this new Footnote Text style.

Titles of books and journals should be underlined in standard research-paper style. Recall that underlining is a character format in Word, so you will need to select the words you want to underline and then format them as underlined. You can easily select a block of words by dragging the pointer from the first word to the last. The selection will be "rounded off" to include whole words only.

To underline the journal title:

1 Select the title of the journal as shown in Figure 5.13.

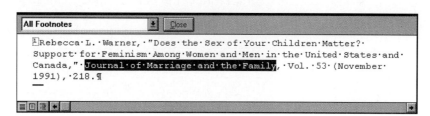

Figure 5.13

2 Click the Underline button on the Formatting toolbar to underline the title.

3 Select the Close button to close the footnote window.

Next you need to add a supporting quotation and footnote it as well. Assume that in the notes for the research paper, there is a quotation that supports the argument that education influences attitudes about gender roles. The quotation will go just after the second paragraph in the body of the paper. The research paper format for longer quotations is to set them off as a separate block of single-spaced text, indented on the left side.

To add the quotation:

1 Select the line [*quote will go here*].

2 Type the quotation shown in Figure 5.14.

```
Education has been argued to have a "liberalizing"
effect upon people by exposing them to divergent world
views and lifestyles.
```

Figure 5.14

The material you type should replace the bracketed note, and it will be double spaced and indented like the other paragraphs in the body of the paper. You will need to single space the block quotation and indent it on the left.

To single space and indent the quotation:

1 Position the insertion point somewhere within the quotation you just added.

2 Press CTRL + 1 to single space the quotation.

3 Remove the first-line indentation using the top left indent marker on the ruler.

4 Select the Increase Indent button on the Formatting toolbar.

5 Position the insertion point immediately following the period at the end of the block quotation and immediately in front of the paragraph mark (¶), if currently displayed.

6 Press ENTER to establish a new single-spaced paragraph, which inserts a blank line after the block quotation.

Now you need to add the footnote that gives the citation for the quotation.

To add a footnote reference for the quotation:

1 Position the insertion point just after the last period in the block quotation.

2 Choose Footnote from the Insert menu.

3 Select OK to add the footnote.

As before, Word inserts a footnote reference in the body of the paper and opens a footnote window for you to type the footnote text. Note that the previous footnote number 1 has already been renumbered and a new number 1 inserted for you where you can type the text for the new footnote.

To add the text for the new footnote:

1 Type the footnote text shown in Figure 5.15 and underline the name of the journal as shown.

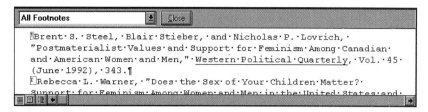

Figure 5.15

2 Position the insertion point somewhere within the second footnote.

Notice that when you move from one footnote to another in the footnote window, Word adjusts the text in the main window so the footnote reference is displayed. This makes it relatively simple to check the correspondence between a footnote reference and the footnote text itself. If the footnote window isn't already open, you can open it by choosing Footnote from the View menu.

Tip To switch quickly between footnote references and text, double-click a footnote reference to open the footnote window and view the associated footnote text. Then double-click the footnote number in the footnote window to close the footnote window and return to the document window.

 EXIT If necessary, you can save your file as SOC415-2.DOC, exit Word now, and continue this project later.

ADDING HEADERS AND FOOTERS

You are nearly done with the basic formatting of the research paper. All that remains is to add a *header,* a repeating section of text at the top of each page. Word also accommodates *footers,* which are like headers but appear at the bottom of the page. Headers and footers often list the title of a book, the name of the chapter, or the page number. The header for this paper will include the name of the author and the page number, a common convention for research papers.

Because the name of the author already appears on the first page, however, and because it is obvious which page that is, you won't put the header on page 1. Thus you will need to make the first page of the paper an exception in the series of headers.

 To make the header for the first page different from other pages:

1 Position the insertion point anywhere within the document, but be sure no text is selected.

2 Choose Page Setup from the File menu.

3 Select the Layout tab, as shown in Figure 5.16.

Layout tab

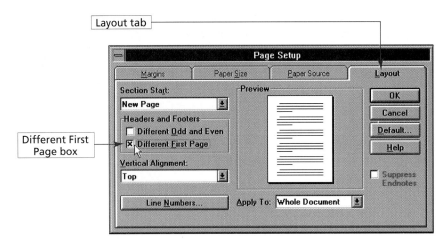

Different First
Page box

Figure 5.16

4 Select Different First Page so an *X* appears in the box.

5 Select OK to complete the formatting choice.

You have just created two types of headers: one for the first page and one for all other pages. You will leave the first page header blank, so no header will appear on page 1, and you will use the other header to print the author name and page number on subsequent pages.

When you insert a header or footer, the display will change to Page Layout view, and a box for the header will appear at the top of the page, as shown in Figure 5.17. If the box is for page 1, it will be labeled *First Page Header*. Otherwise, it will simply be labeled *Header*. If the magnification of the page is too small for you to see what you're doing, you can change it using the Zoom Control box on the Standard toolbar near the right edge. The text of the paper itself appears dimmed because you can't edit the paper when you're working on headers and footers. You can move from page to page by selecting the Previous Page and Next Page buttons at the bottom of the vertical scroll bar or by pressing (PGUP) and (PGDN). You can move between the header and footer on the page by selecting the leftmost button on the Header and Footer toolbar.

Page Number button

Page Zoom control box

Type of header

Previous Page/Next Page buttons

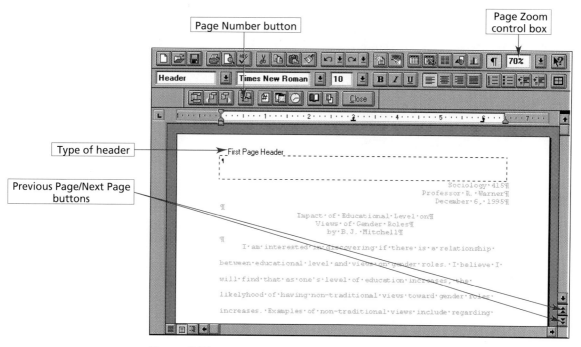

Figure 5.17

To create a header:

1 Choose Header and Footer from the View menu.

2 If you are in the first-page header, move to the next page by selecting the Next Page button on the vertical scroll bar or by pressing (PGDN)

3 Position the insertion point in the Header box.

4 Select Page Width in the Zoom Control box.

5 Type **Mitchell,** then a space, and then a slash character (/), and then another space.

6 Click the Page Number button on the Header and Footer toolbar. You have inserted a special code in the header that Word replaces with the appropriate page number. The code appears as a page number immediately after the header text.

To format the header:

1 Click the Align Right button on the Formatting toolbar to justify the header on the right.

The header should now look like Figure 5.18. Move from page to page to see that the page numbers do change and that the first page has a blank header.

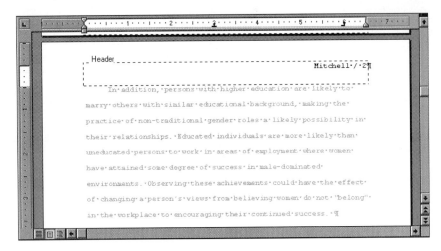

Figure 5.18

2 Select the Close button to close the Header and Footer window.

 ## To save the paper and print a copy of it:

1 Save the revised version of the paper as SOC415-2.DOC. Remember to choose Save As from the File menu to change the file name.

2 Click the Print button on the Standard toolbar or choose Print from the File menu to print a copy of the revised paper.

THE NEXT STEP

When it comes to commonly used document features, Word makes many standard operations nearly automatic. You can produce standard headers, footers, footnotes, endnotes, bulleted lists, or numbered lists with a few clicks or a few keystrokes. For many documents, Word's standard formats work well. For others, you may need to modify the format. You may want to return to the Paragraph dialog box to see how you can control line spacing both within and between paragraphs on the Indents and Spacing tab. You can also switch to the Text Flow tab and format a paragraph so it will not be split at a page break or so a heading will be kept with the text that follows it. You may want to experiment more with the Bullets and Numbering dialog box to try other typographical devices, indentations, or even multilevel lists. You also could experiment with changing the position of headers and footers by changing the From Edge settings on the Margins tab in the Page Setup dialog box. Word can be as flexible as you need it to be, but you'll need to invest some time in learning how to accomplish what you want.

The standard research paper format used here will work for many papers you are asked to write. If you want more detail, a common authority for style and format questions is *The Chicago Manual of Style*, available in nearly any library. An adaptation of *The Chicago Manual of Style* especially for students is *A Manual for Writers of Term Papers, Theses, and Dissertations*, by Kate L. Turabian, also published by The University of Chicago Press. In addition, each academic field tends to have its own particular style and format. Many fields in the humanities use Modern Language Association style, many social sciences use the style of the American Psychological Association, and many life sciences use the style of the Council of Biology Editors. Your field may have its own set of conventions and you should be relatively familiar with what those conventions are.

This concludes Project 5. You can either exit Word, or go on to work the Study Questions, Review Exercises, and Assignments.

SUMMARY AND EXERCISES

Summary

- Page layout—such as margins, page orientation, page numbering, positions of headers and footers—is referred to as section formatting in Word.
- Although most simple documents are a single section, Word allows you to divide a document into many sections and change the page layout choices from section to section.
- You can set page margins in the Page Setup dialog box (choose Page Setup in the File menu).
- You can set paragraph indentation, including the first line indentation, in the Paragraph dialog box from the Format menu, or by moving the indent markers on the ruler.
- You can create a bulleted or numbered list with the Bullets and Numbering dialog box in the Format menu, or by selecting either the Bullets or the Numbering button on the Formatting toolbar.
- To create a footnote, open the Footnote and Endnote dialog box from the Insert menu. Word will open a footnote window where you can type the text of the footnote.
- You can add headers or footers by choosing Header and Footer from the View menu.
- You can have a header and footer for the first page different from those on the other pages in a section if you specify Different First Page on the Layout tab of the Page Setup dialog box.
- Headers and footers can contain a special code that automatically inserts page numbers.

Key Terms and Operations

Key Terms
bullet
endnote
footer
footnote
header
section

Operations
Change margins
Indent paragraphs
Create bulleted lists
Add footnotes
Set up headers and footers

Study Questions

Multiple Choice

1. Which of the following is *not* controlled by section formatting in Word?
   a. page numbering
   b. margins
   c. line spacing
   d. page orientation

2. Which of the following is not a paragraph format in Word?
   a. bulleted lists
   b. line spacing
   c. numbered lists
   d. line width

3. The Center button aligns:
   a. one line of text.
   b. an entire paragraph.
   c. the characters selected.
   d. to the next tab.

4. A typographic device used to set off items in a list is called:
   a. a dingbat.
   b. a logo.
   c. a typo.
   d. a bullet.

5. The Increase Indent button moves text to:
   a. the right ¼ inch.
   b. the next tab.
   c. align with the text above.
   d. the right margin.

6. You can double space text by pressing:
   a. CTRL + S
   b. CTRL + 2
   c. SHIFT + S
   d. CTRL + D

7. The footnote number that goes in the text of the document is called:
   a. the reference mark.
   b. the footnote text.
   c. the subscript.
   d. an asterisk.

8. Document headers or footers often contain:
   a. page numbers.
   b. copyright disclaimers.
   c. charts and graphs.
   d. footnotes.

9. You can indent the first line of a paragraph by using:
   a. the Indent dialog box.
   b. CTRL + I
   c. the Increase Indent button.
   d. the indent markers on the ruler.

10. To select a section:
    a. Triple-click in the selection bar.
    b. Select the entire document.
    c. Position the insertion point inside the section.
    d. Select all text in the section.

Short Answer

1. To change page orientation within a document from vertical to horizontal _____, you must establish a new _____.

2. You can change line spacing in the _____ dialog box.

3. Endnotes appear at the end of a _____.

4. To indent a paragraph from the right, you can use the _____ on the ruler.

5. Footnotes are usually used for _____ or _____.

6. Word's footnote window contains the footnote _____.

7. Most section formatting is done in the _____ dialog box.

8. The buttons for paragraph alignment (center, right, left) are on the _____ toolbar.

9. If you insert or delete a footnote, Word will _____ other footnotes.

10. If you want each chapter in a book to start numbering from page 1, you should make each chapter a separate _____.

For Discussion

1. What is a section in Word? What are sections used for?

2. Explain the general procedure for adding a footnote to a document.

3. How can you suppress a header on the first page of a section or document?

Review Exercises

Changing the Research Paper Format

Reformat the research paper you worked on in this project according to a new set of style guidelines:

1. Change the margin settings to 1 inch for the top and bottom and 1.25 inches for the sides.

2. Reorganize the header and add a footer as follows: for the header, center the date and place the course number at the right edge; for the footer, place the word *Page*, followed by the page number, at the right edge.

3. Turn the bulleted list into a numbered list beginning with number 1.

4 Add a new footnote to the research paper. Place the footnote reference at the end of the first sentence in the last paragraph, which ends "at the 0.01 level." Add the following footnote text:

   `That is, there is only a 1% chance that education and gender role attitudes are not significantly related.`

5. Save the file as NEWSOC.DOC and print it out.

Formatting the Paper in Publication Style

Reformat the research paper in a style suitable for publication as a report or journal article:

1. Set margins to 1.25 inches all around (top, bottom, and sides).

2. Delete the course number, instructor's name, and date.

3. Change the font for the entire document to 12-point Times Roman (or a similar serif face).

4. Change the title to 18-point Times Roman bold.

5. Change all other headings to 14-point Helvetica or Arial (or a similar sans serif face).

6. Single space the entire document.

7. On the Indents and Spacing tab in the Paragraph dialog box, set extra spacing before or after paragraphs as needed to separate headings from the text above them.

8. Format the footnotes in 10-point Times Roman (or equivalent).

9. Save the file as PUB.DOC and print the result.

Assignments

Numbering with Multiple Levels

Use the Multilevel Numbering option in the Bullets and Numbering dialog box to number the agenda created at the end of Projects 2 and 3. (The agenda should be in a file named AGENDA.DOC.)

Formatting Your Own Paper

Take a term paper you've already written and saved to disk and format that paper according to the conventions used for the research paper in this project. Word can read word processing files from many other word processors, so try this even if you didn't use Word to write your paper in the first place. You can almost always transfer text from one word processor to another if you first save the file as an ASCII, or plain text, file. The drawback is that you will lose most of your formatting information this way.

Formatting a Draft as a Finished Publication

Retrieve the file PASTEUR.DOC. This document is the presentation Louis Pasteur gave to the French Academy of Science in 1878 announcing his discoveries in germ theory. The document is formatted as a draft for publication. Your job is to turn it into a finished publication as shown in Figure 5.19.

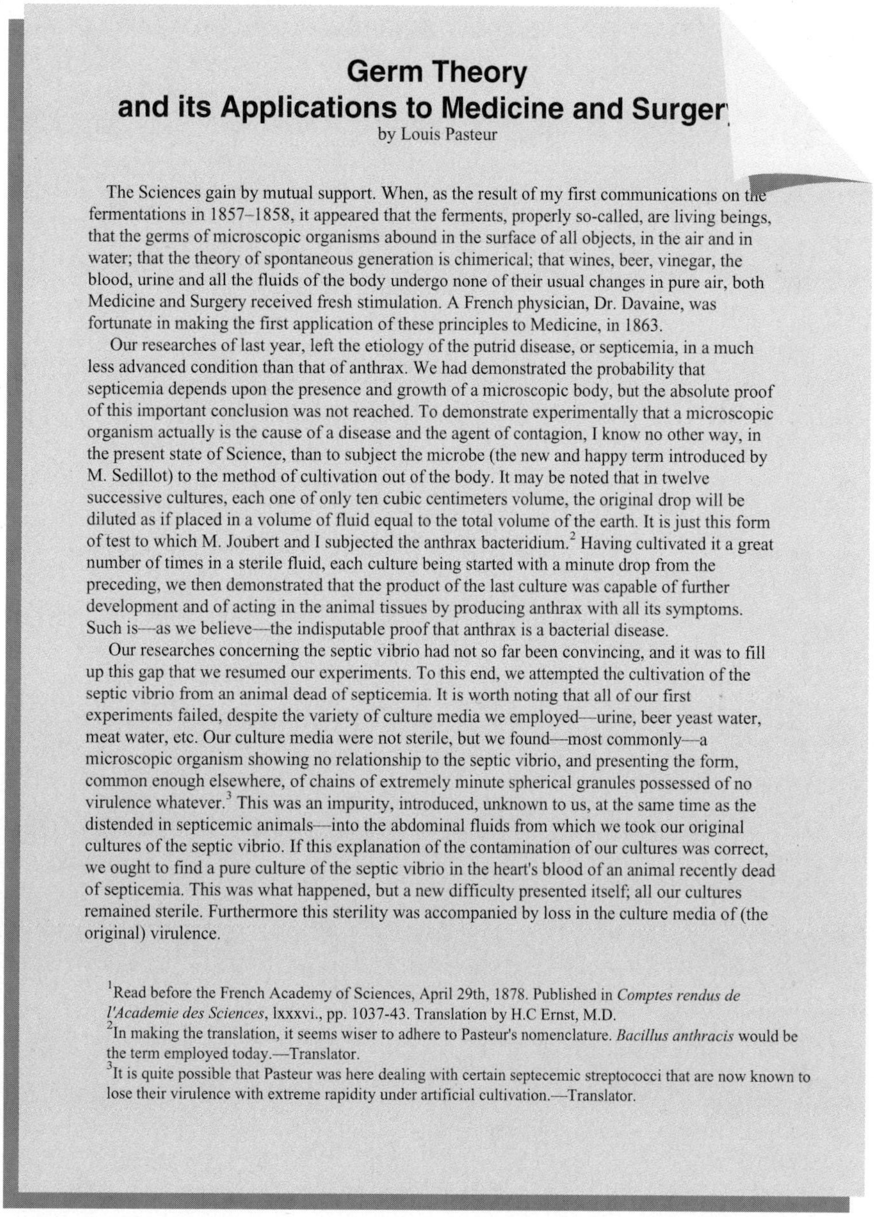

Germ Theory
and its Applications to Medicine and Surgery

by Louis Pasteur

The Sciences gain by mutual support. When, as the result of my first communications on the fermentations in 1857–1858, it appeared that the ferments, properly so-called, are living beings, that the germs of microscopic organisms abound in the surface of all objects, in the air and in water; that the theory of spontaneous generation is chimerical; that wines, beer, vinegar, the blood, urine and all the fluids of the body undergo none of their usual changes in pure air, both Medicine and Surgery received fresh stimulation. A French physician, Dr. Davaine, was fortunate in making the first application of these principles to Medicine, in 1863.

Our researches of last year, left the etiology of the putrid disease, or septicemia, in a much less advanced condition than that of anthrax. We had demonstrated the probability that septicemia depends upon the presence and growth of a microscopic body, but the absolute proof of this important conclusion was not reached. To demonstrate experimentally that a microscopic organism actually is the cause of a disease and the agent of contagion, I know no other way, in the present state of Science, than to subject the microbe (the new and happy term introduced by M. Sedillot) to the method of cultivation out of the body. It may be noted that in twelve successive cultures, each one of only ten cubic centimeters volume, the original drop will be diluted as if placed in a volume of fluid equal to the total volume of the earth. It is just this form of test to which M. Joubert and I subjected the anthrax bacteridium.[2] Having cultivated it a great number of times in a sterile fluid, each culture being started with a minute drop from the preceding, we then demonstrated that the product of the last culture was capable of further development and of acting in the animal tissues by producing anthrax with all its symptoms. Such is—as we believe—the indisputable proof that anthrax is a bacterial disease.

Our researches concerning the septic vibrio had not so far been convincing, and it was to fill up this gap that we resumed our experiments. To this end, we attempted the cultivation of the septic vibrio from an animal dead of septicemia. It is worth noting that all of our first experiments failed, despite the variety of culture media we employed—urine, beer yeast water, meat water, etc. Our culture media were not sterile, but we found—most commonly—a microscopic organism showing no relationship to the septic vibrio, and presenting the form, common enough elsewhere, of chains of extremely minute spherical granules possessed of no virulence whatever.[3] This was an impurity, introduced, unknown to us, at the same time as the distended in septicemic animals—into the abdominal fluids from which we took our original cultures of the septic vibrio. If this explanation of the contamination of our cultures was correct, we ought to find a pure culture of the septic vibrio in the heart's blood of an animal recently dead of septicemia. This was what happened, but a new difficulty presented itself; all our cultures remained sterile. Furthermore this sterility was accompanied by loss in the culture media of (the original) virulence.

[1]Read before the French Academy of Sciences, April 29th, 1878. Published in *Comptes rendus de l'Academie des Sciences*, lxxxvi., pp. 1037-43. Translation by H.C Ernst, M.D.
[2]In making the translation, it seems wiser to adhere to Pasteur's nomenclature. *Bacillus anthracis* would be the term employed today.—Translator.
[3]It is quite possible that Pasteur was here dealing with certain septecemic streptococci that are now known to lose their virulence with extreme rapidity under artificial cultivation.—Translator.

Figure 5.19

Here are the specifications:

- Page margins will be 1 inch top and bottom, 1½ inches at the sides.
- The main text is to be 11-point Times New Roman, single spaced, with a first-line indentation of ¼ inch.
- Underlining in the draft should be changed to italic in the final publication.
- The title of the paper should be 18-point Arial bold.
- Footnote references in the draft are given as ^ 1 for the first footnote, ^ 2 for the second, and so on. Footnote text is given in brackets with a heading such as *Footnote 1 text:* in front of the text. Change the references and text to conventional forms, like those used in the research paper in this project. All footnote text should be formatted as 10-point Times New Roman.

- Add headers and footers as follows: All pages, including the first page, should have a footer containing the page number only. The page number should be on the right side on odd pages and on the left side on even pages. The first page should not have a header. Even pages should have headers that say *Germ Theory* on the left side of the page. Odd pages should have headers that say *by Louis Pasteur* on the right side of the page. All headers and footers should be formatted as 12-point Times New Roman bold italic.
- Save the revised document as NEWGERMS.DOC and print it out.

PART III

Microsoft
Excel 5

Overview

Objectives

After completing this overview, you should be able to:

▶ Start Microsoft Excel

▶ Navigate workbooks and worksheets

▶ Identify common pointer shapes

▶ Change the active cell

▶ Select cells and ranges

▶ Manipulate toolbars

▶ Access Help

▶ Exit Excel

Among the many far-reaching developments of the Renaissance was the widespread application, in fourteenth-century Tuscany, of double-entry bookkeeping. Prior to this, the accounts of bankers and merchants were kept in a haphazard, loosely organized manner. The Tuscan innovation, made possible by the importation of Arabic and Hindu numbers, was to organize accounts into tables with rows and columns, thus making them much easier to maintain.

Now double-entry bookkeeping probably doesn't rank very highly on your list of exciting things, but it contributed to the advent of the commercial and industrial revolution that utterly transformed the Western world.

Until about 1980, most people who created tables of numbers and text worked in much the same way as the Tuscans. Electronic calculators made the job easier, but the use of larger computers was difficult and restricted to major projects.

Accounting tables are called *worksheets* or *spreadsheets,* and if you're creating one the traditional way, you will need some green ledger paper or a lab notebook, a pencil, and a calculator. You'll also need a big eraser, because one of the worst problems with manual worksheets is revision: if one number must change, then it will probably affect dozens of other numbers. The burden of recalculating parts of a traditional worksheet makes it difficult to experiment—to perform "what if" analysis. If you want to make a chart or graph presenting the information pictorially, you will have to get some help from a graphic artist or do your best with colored pens and a ruler.

The invention of personal computers and electronic spreadsheet programs changed this situation dramatically. An electronic spreadsheet presents the table, with its rows and columns, on a computer screen. It is much easier to make modifications, because recalculation happens automatically in response to changes.

The first electronic spreadsheet programs made the basic tasks of building and modifying a worksheet much easier. Contemporary programs, such as Microsoft Excel 5 for Windows, vastly extend these capabilities with such features as data analysis, charting, and typographical formatting. Erasers and green eye-visors are optional.

DESIGNING WORKSHEETS

An electronic spreadsheet program is a tool not only for accountants. Anyone who wants to organize information in tables can benefit from one. Financial analysts, biologists, engineers, attorneys, marketing specialists, physical scientists, managers, political analysts, health professionals, and many others routinely use electronic spreadsheets. Apart from being universally useful, spreadsheet programs are also fun, because building a worksheet is like creating your own little machine—a worksheet is dynamic: it does things and responds to changes.

If you heard about a car that required you to hoist out the engine to change the oil, you would probably think the machine was poorly designed and difficult to maintain. Because, like machines, worksheets should be functional, you must pay close attention to design principles when creating them. You will want to design worksheets that are efficient, easy to use, easy to change, and easy to understand.

The projects in this module use examples that highlight many common design issues. When you finish the module, you will be able to apply your knowledge of Excel commands and worksheet-design techniques to your own area of expertise.

A NOTE TO THE STUDENT

As in other programs, there is often more than one way to perform a particular command or action in Excel. Many commands can be accessed from a regular menu bar, a toolbar button, a shortcut mouse menu, and a keystroke shortcut. Though most mouse actions have keyboard equivalents, in general Excel works best with a mouse. Some powerful features of the program, such as toolbars, are accessible *only* with a mouse. This module presumes that you will be using a mouse with Excel.

If you want to review how to use the mouse, windows, menus, and dialog boxes, refer to the Introduction to Windows.

STARTING EXCEL

The standard name of the group window containing the Excel program icon is Microsoft Office, but on your system the group could have a different name, such as WinApps or Excel 5.

 To start Excel:

1 Open the group window containing the Microsoft Excel icon. Figure 0.1 shows an example of what you will see.

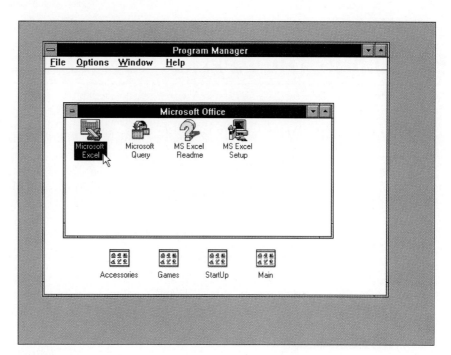

Figure 0.1

2 Double-click the Microsoft Excel icon. The screen should now resemble Figure 0.2.

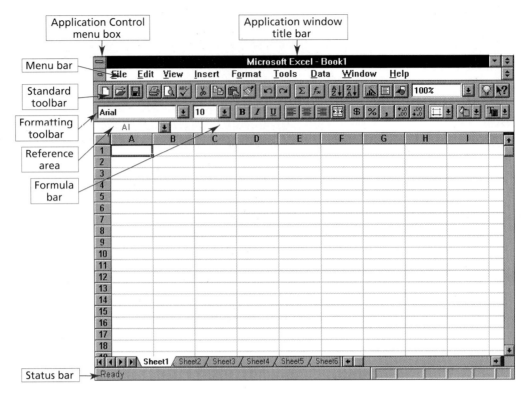

Figure 0.2

EXPLORING THE APPLICATION WINDOW

The two main types of windows in Excel are the ***application window,*** which you can think of as representing the Excel program itself, and ***workbook windows,*** which are composed of ***sheets*** that contain things you create using Excel. The application window, whose title bar when you start Excel reads *Microsoft Excel–Book1,* is a window that frames workbook windows. The workbook window is initially maximized within the application window. Both the application window and the workbook window have Control menu boxes, Minimize buttons, Restore buttons, and Maximize buttons, so it's important not to confuse the two types of windows.

To better understand the difference between these two kinds of windows, you will now reduce the size of the workbook window so its borders are visible, and then you will minimize it to an icon.

To restore and minimize the workbook window:

1 Click the workbook window's Restore button.
The screen should now resemble Figure 0.3. The workbook window is reduced in size so its borders are visible. Notice that the default name for the workbook, *Book1,* appears in its title bar.

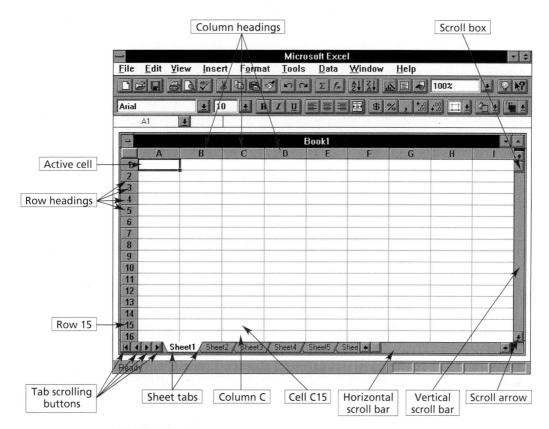

Figure 0.3

2 Click the *workbook* window's Minimize button.
The screen should now resemble Figure 0.4. The workbook window is reduced to an icon in the lower-left corner of the application window.

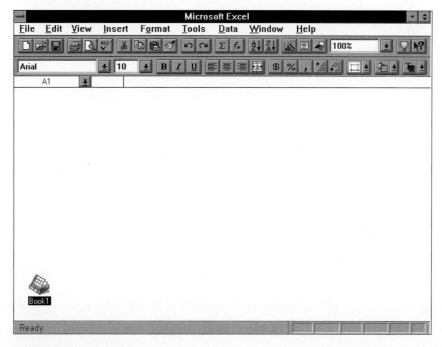

Figure 0.4

3 Double-click the workbook icon.

The screen now resembles Figure 0.3; the workbook window is again visible within the application window. Repeat the minimize-and-restore procedure, if necessary, to clearly distinguish between the application and document windows.

> **Tip**   When you have multiple workbooks open, check the title bar of a window to ascertain which document you are working with.

Excel commands are grouped on the *menu bar* displayed across the top of the application window. You can select the options on a menu bar by clicking them with the mouse or by pressing (ALT) in combination with the underlined letter in the option.

Beneath the menu bar are two rows of buttons: the Standard and Formatting toolbars. A *toolbar* contains buttons and other controls that provide quick access to important commands and functions. Toolbars are accessible only with a mouse.

Below the toolbars is the *formula bar* and the *reference area.* These sections of the application window become active when you type or change information in a worksheet.

At the bottom of the application window is the *status bar,* which includes keyboard-status indicators and displays brief help messages when you use Excel commands.

NAVIGATING THE WORKBOOK

A workbook is composed of one or more sheets, each of which can be a worksheet, chart sheet, or module. A worksheet, designed to hold text and numbers and to perform calculations, is the most common type, and is what you will spend most of your time with when using Excel. A *chart sheet* is used to hold an Excel chart. A *module* or macro sheet is a sheet used to hold Excel macros (programs that you create).

Changing among Sheets

A new, blank workbook contains 16 worksheets. You can add any combination of worksheets, chart sheets, or modules to this. You can also delete any sheets.

The name of each sheet appears on its *sheet tab* near the bottom of the workbook window. Initially, Sheet1 is visible. You can view a sheet by clicking its tab; you can use the *tab scrolling buttons,* as shown in Figure 0.5, to see different tabs.

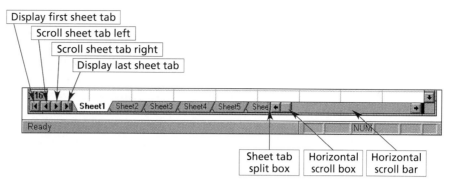

Figure 0.5

 To activate a sheet:

1 Click the tab named Sheet2.
You are now viewing a different worksheet, Sheet2.

2 Click the right sheet-tab scrolling button three times so the tab for Sheet8 is visible.
Note that though the tab for Sheet2 is not currently visible, you are still looking at the Sheet2 worksheet.

3 Click the tab scrolling button to display the last sheet tab.

4 Click the tab for Sheet16.
Sheet16 now appears.

5 Click the tab scrolling button to display the first sheet tab.

6 Click the tab for Sheet1.
The screen should once again resemble Figure 0.3.

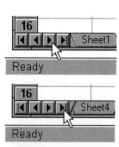

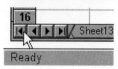

Much of your work in this module will be done with a single worksheet.

Tip

- You can use (CTRL) + (PGDN) to change to the next sheet and (CTRL) + (PGUP) to change to the previous sheet.
- If you hold down (SHFT) and click a sheet-tab scrolling button, you can scroll by several tabs at once.

Navigating within a Worksheet

Each Excel worksheet is composed of **columns** and **rows**. Columns are labeled with the letters of the alphabet, starting with A and continuing through Z, followed by AA, AB, and so forth, to IV for a maximum of 256 columns. Rows are labeled with numbers from 1 to 16,384. The worksheets you will build won't use nearly so large an area; the average worksheet size for this module is about 10 columns by 20 rows.

The basic building block of a worksheet, the intersection of a column and a row, is called a **cell,** and it is identified by its column letter and row number. For example, the **cell reference** C15 refers to the cell at the intersection of column C and row 15.

Scrolling a Worksheet

Think of the workbook window as a frame through which you can see only part of the total worksheet area. To view a different area, you can shift the frame using the scroll bars or arrow keys.

Because Book1 is the only workbook currently in use, you should first maximize its window to make best use of the screen.

Tip Even if you plan primarily to use a mouse, in the steps that follow you should experiment with both the mouse and the keyboard actions.

To scroll the worksheet window:

1 Click the Maximize button in the upper-right corner of the Book1 workbook window.

The screen should appear similar to Figure 0.2.

2 Mouse: Click the down scroll arrow (at the bottom of the vertical scroll bar). Press and hold down the mouse button on a scroll arrow to repeat the scrolling action.

   or Keys: Press and hold down ⬇ until the window begins to move. The window will shift down row by row. You can use the other scroll arrows (and the other arrow keys, ⬅ ➡ ⬆) to move by single columns or rows in other directions. Experiment with the other scroll arrows or arrow keys.

3 Press (CTRL) + (HOME) to return to the upper-left corner of the worksheet, cell A1.

4 Mouse: Click in the middle of the vertical scroll bar. Notice that the scroll box moves to the bottom of the scroll bar. You can click in the vertical scroll bar to shift the window in the opposite direction.

   or Keys: Press (PGDN)

If you pressed (PGDN), the window shifts down by one window's height to show a different portion of the worksheet. Press (PGUP) to shift the window farther up; to shift the window farther down, press (PGDN). Experiment with (PGDN) and (PGUP).

5 Press (CTRL) + (HOME) to return to the upper-left corner of the worksheet, cell A1.

6 Click in the middle of the horizontal scroll bar to move the horizontal scroll box to the right edge of the horizontal scroll bar.

The window shifts right by one window's width to show a different portion of the worksheet. You can also click and drag the scroll boxes.

7 Press (CTRL) + (HOME) to return to the upper-left corner of the worksheet, cell A1.

Positioning the Active Cell

The cell appearing with a heavy border around it indicates the *active cell* rectangle. The active cell (also called the selected cell, current cell, or cell pointer) is where the action will take place if you type data or perform a command. When you first activate a new, empty worksheet, A1 is the active cell.

To position the active cell:

1 Mouse: Move the pointer to cell E2 and click the mouse button.
    or Keys: Use the arrow keys to move the active cell rectangle to E2.
Notice that the cell reference of the active cell is displayed in the reference area.

2 Try scrolling the window (by clicking one of the scroll arrows).

Tip Notice that scrolling with the mouse does *not* change the active cell, whereas using the arrow keys does.

Changing Pointer Shapes

The shape of the pointer changes depending on where the pointer is positioned on-screen. In the steps that follow, you will carefully move the pointer to the locations described and observe the changes in its appearance. Notice that pointer shapes change in response to specific mouse movements and screen locations. Don't worry about memorizing the meanings of all the different pointer shapes at this time.

 ### *To change pointer shapes:*

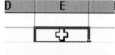

1 Position the pointer in the middle of the active cell or in any other cell.
The pointer appears as a hollow plus sign; this pointer is used to select a new active cell or a group of cells.

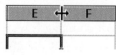

2 Position the pointer on a line separating two column letters.
The pointer appears as a double arrow, which you will use in later projects to change the width of a column.

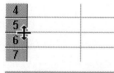

3 Position the pointer on the line separating any two row headings.
This double arrow is similar to the column-width pointer and is used to change the height of a row.

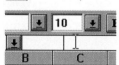

4 Position the pointer in the middle of the formula bar.
The pointer changes to an insertion symbol, called an *I-beam;* you will use this to edit text within the formula bar.

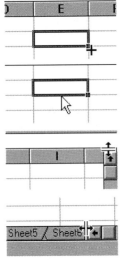

5 Position the pointer so it just touches the lower-right corner of the active cell.

This pointer is called the *fill handle* and is used to copy cell contents.

6 Position the pointer so it just touches any of the edges of the active cell.

The pointer turns into an arrow, which you can use to move the contents of a cell to a new location.

7 Position the pointer on the small black rectangle at the top of the vertical scroll bar.

This area is called the *split bar,* and it is used to split a window into two sections. A horizontal split bar is at the right of the horizontal scroll bar.

8 Position the pointer on the small rectangle just to the left of the left scroll arrow.

You can click and drag this split bar to control the relative width of the scroll bar and sheet-tab scroll areas.

9 Position the pointer on any button within a toolbar, such as the Print button. Do not click.

A small box appears, called a *ToolTip,* which identifies the function of the button that you position the pointer on.

MAKING SELECTIONS

As you use Excel, you will occasionally want to perform an action that affects an entire worksheet, but most of the time you will want to change only a portion of a worksheet. Before using most commands, you first indicate your *selection,* the part of the worksheet you want to change. Most Excel commands operate on a selection. You can select a single cell, a *range* (a rectangular block of cells), or a group of ranges. After you make a selection, you can choose a command to affect that selection.

Selecting a Single Cell

The active cell is the currently selected cell. You can select a single cell by positioning the active-cell rectangle. You can select a cell that is not currently visible by first scrolling the window and then clicking the cell to make a selection. Suppose you want to select cell B5.

 To select cell B5:

1 Mouse: Position the pointer on cell B5 and click.
  or Keys: Use the arrow keys to position the active-cell rectangle on cell B5.

2 Scroll until cell J35 is visible and then select it.

Selecting a Range of Cells

A *range* is a *rectangular* block of cells referred to by its upper-left and lower-right diagonal corner cells. For example, the range whose upper-left corner is cell B2 and whose lower-right corner is cell C5 would be referred to as B2:C5. A range can be as small as a single cell or as large as the entire worksheet.

To select a range, you would first select any corner cell and then use the mouse to extend the selection to cover the entire range. Suppose you want to select the range B2:C5.

To select the range B2:C5:

1 Select cell B2 by clicking in it, and ensure that the pointer forms a hollow plus sign positioned inside the active cell.

2 Hold down the mouse button and drag down to row 5 and across to column C to select the range, then release the mouse button. You could also extend the selection to the right first and then down; the order doesn't matter.

The range B2:C5 is selected, as shown in Figure 0.6.

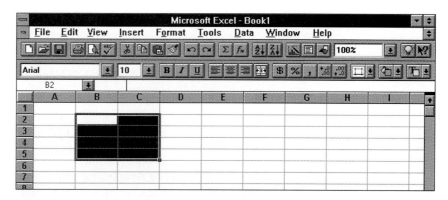

Figure 0.6

> **Tip** If you need to select a large range and don't want to hold down the mouse button for a long time, select a cell that is any corner of the range, use the scroll bars if necessary to shift the window, position the pointer on the cell that is the diagonally opposite corner, hold down (SHFT), and click.

Practice selecting other ranges. Notice that when you make a new selection, the previous selection markings disappear. You will also notice that there's always one cell in the selection that is not darkened, yet is still within the thick bordered area that defines the selection.

Selecting an Entire Column or Row

A complete column or row is just a large range. Selecting an entire column or row is easy: you click the column or row heading. You must be very careful to click directly on the heading letter or number, and not on a dividing line between headings (the dividing line is used to change column widths).

To select an entire column or row:

1 Click the column heading (letter) G.
This selects all of column G (the range G1:G16384).
The screen should resemble Figure 0.7.

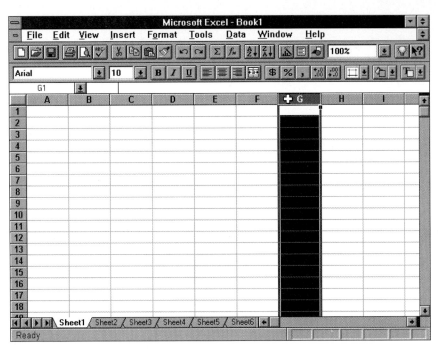

Figure 0.7

2 Click the row heading (number) 7.
This selects all of row 7 (the range A7:IV7). Practice selecting other columns and rows.

Selecting Adjacent Columns or Rows

To select a group of adjacent columns or rows, you first select one column or row and then extend the selection through the other columns or rows.

 To select an adjacent group of columns or rows:

1 Select column C.

2 Hold down the mouse button, drag to column F, and then release the mouse button.
This extends the selection across column headings D, E, and F. The selected range is C1:F16384, which can be abbreviated to C:F.

3 Select row 7. (The previous selection of C:F will be canceled.)

4 Extend the selection down through row 10.
Practice with other column-and-row group selections.

Making Nonadjacent Selections

You will sometimes want to affect an area of the worksheet that is not rectangular and that cannot be selected as a single range. Excel allows you to compose a more complicated selection, called a **nonadjacent selection,** from a group of ranges.

You have noticed that if you move away from a selection and make another cell active, the previous selection is no longer marked. To make a composite selection out of a group of separate ranges, columns, or rows, you will hold down (CTRL) while making your selections with the mouse.

To make nonadjacent selections:

1 Select the range B3:D8. After making this selection, release the mouse button.

2 Position the mouse pointer on cell G10.

3 Hold down (CTRL) and then hold down the mouse button.

4 Drag the mouse to select the range G10:H15, and then release both the mouse button and (CTRL)

The screen should look similar to Figure 0.8. Using this method, practice making other nonadjacent selections.

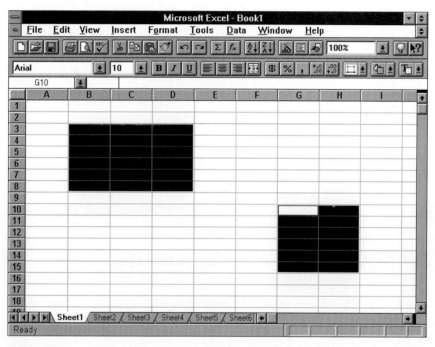

Figure 0.8

Selecting an Entire Sheet

Clicking the button above the heading for row 1 and to the left of the heading for column A selects the entire worksheet.

 ## *To select the entire worksheet:*

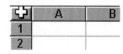

1 Click the Select All button.

The entire worksheet is selected, as shown in Figure 0.9.

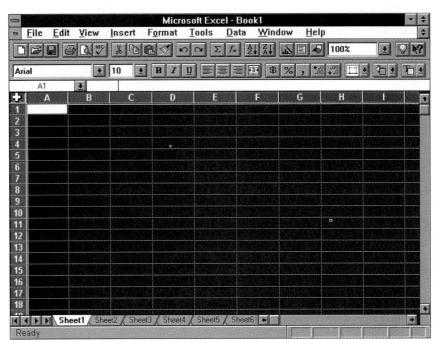

Figure 0.9

2 To cancel the selection, click any individual cell or reposition the active cell using the arrow keys.

WORKING WITH TOOLBARS

Though the Standard and Formatting toolbars appear by default on the screen, 11 other toolbars are available for various kinds of tasks. Any toolbar can be customized to contain tools—buttons and other controls—of your choice. You can also create new toolbars of your own design. More than 200 tools are available for placement in toolbars.

Sometimes a particular toolbar will display automatically, depending on the actions you are performing in Excel. At other times, you may want to hide, display, or rearrange toolbars as you work. You will occasionally want to hide a toolbar just to give yourself more screen space for other information.

Initially, the Standard and Formatting toolbars are *docked* (anchored) to the top section of the application window, but any toolbar can be made into a *floating toolbar*—a small window that can be positioned anywhere on-screen. Any toolbar can be docked to the top or bottom of the window, and most can also be docked to the left or right side of the window.

 To hide a toolbar:

1 Open the **View** menu, and then choose **Toolbars**.
The Toolbars dialog box appears.

2 Select **Formatting** to clear its check box.
The screen should now resemble Figure 0.10.

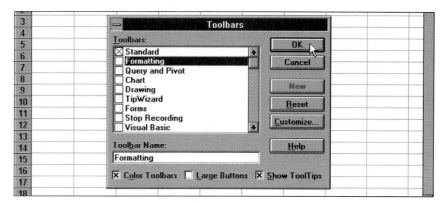

Figure 0.10

3 Select **OK.**

The Formatting toolbar no longer appears, allowing you to see a few more rows of the worksheet.

To display a floating toolbar:

1 Open the **View** menu, and then choose **Toolbars.**
The Toolbars dialog box appears.

2 Scroll down the list of toolbars and select **Auditing.**

3 Select **OK,** as shown in Figure 0.11.

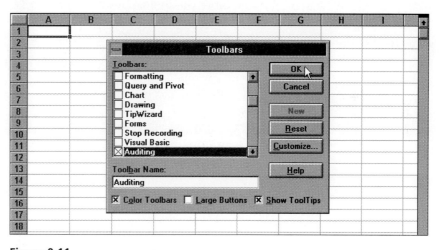

Figure 0.11

The Auditing toolbar appears in a small window of its own, "floating" on the application window. The toolbar can be moved, reproportioned, or docked against an edge.

To dock a floating toolbar:

1 Position the pointer on the Auditing toolbar's title bar.

2 Hold down the mouse button and drag the outline image of the toolbar to the bottom center of the application window, over the status bar, as shown in Figure 0.12.

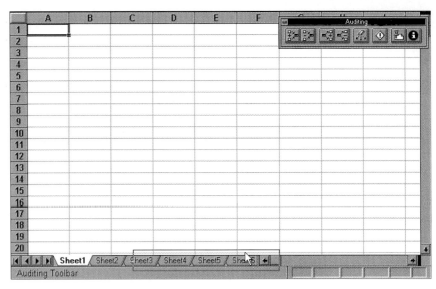

Figure 0.12

3 Release the mouse button.
The Auditing toolbar is now docked to the bottom of the application window.

Every docked toolbar has an outlined background area in which its buttons and controls are placed. If you click and drag this background, you can move the toolbar away from its docked position and make it a floating toolbar. A floating toolbar can be hidden by clicking *once* in its Control menu box.

To undock and hide a docked toolbar:

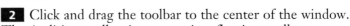

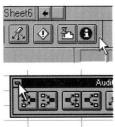

1 Position the pointer within the background of the docked Auditing toolbar.

2 Click and drag the toolbar to the center of the window.
The Auditing toolbar is once again a floating toolbar.

3 Click once in the Auditing toolbar's Control menu box to hide the toolbar.

4 Open the **View** menu, and then choose **Toolbars,** and display the Formatting toolbar.
The screen should once again appear as it did when you first started Excel.

Tip Clicking the *right* mouse button in a toolbar's background displays a shortcut menu to provide quick access to many of the commands discussed in this section.

GETTING ON-SCREEN HELP

The Help system in Microsoft Excel conforms to the standard Help conventions of Windows, which may be familiar to you if you have used other Windows applications. Think of the Help system as a vast reference manual stored on disk, with convenient indexes and cross-references to help you find the information you need. You can type a word naming a topic you're interested in, and Excel will search its alphabetical list of topic areas for that word. The first few characters of the word are often sufficient for Excel to do its search. In the steps that follow, you will use the Help menu to get information on dialog boxes.

To access the Help system:

1 Open the **Help** menu, and then choose **Search for Help on.**

2 Type **dia** in the text box to get help on dialog boxes.

A list of topic areas, including the topic of dialog boxes, appears as shown in Figure 0.13. Dialog boxes is also the selected topic area in the list, because it is the first topic on the list.

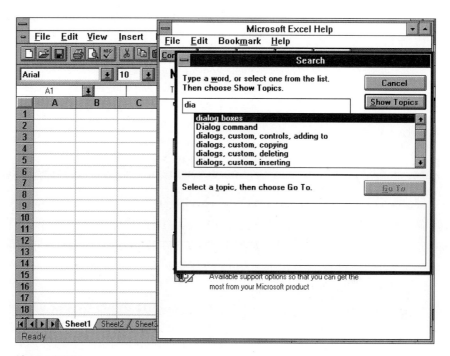

Figure 0.13

3 Select **Show Topics.**

This instructs Excel to show the specific topics concerning dialog boxes for which it can provide help. As shown in Figure 0.14, several topic areas are displayed. The first topic, Choosing dialog box options, is currently selected.

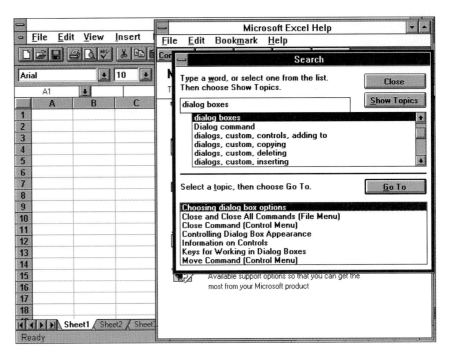

Figure 0.14

4 Select **Go To.**
Help information about choosing dialog box options now appears.

5 Select **Contents.**
A table of contents for Help appears. To read about one of the listed topics, select that topic.

6 In the Help dialog box, open the **File** menu, and then choose **Exit.** (Do not choose Exit from the application window.)

Tip If you want to return to your worksheet but wish to leave the Help window displayed for your reference, then choose Always On Top from the Help menu within the Help window.

Using the Help Tool

The Help tool allows you to get help on a topic by pointing to a particular part of the screen containing that topic or by selecting the topic from a menu. The Help tool is available on the toolbar or by pressing (SHFT) + (F1).

To use the Help tool:

1 Click the **Help** tool.
The pointer should now appear as an arrow with the word *Help.*

2 Open the **Format** menu, and then choose **Auto Format.**
A Help screen about AutoFormat appears. Note that because the Help tool was active, the AutoFormat command was not actually selected.

3 Close the Help window.

> **Tip** Using the mouse, you can also point the Help tool at a part of the screen to get help information. For example, you can activate the Help tool, point to the middle of the formula bar, and click. Help information on the formula bar appears.

Using the TipWizard

The small button depicting a light bulb near the right edge of the Standard toolbar is called the **TipWizard.** This feature monitors your work in Excel and identifies possible shortcuts and alternatives to the actions you perform. When the light bulb turns yellow (or when it displays a question mark on a monochrome screen) it has a tip for you. To see the tip, you would click the TipWizard tool. The text of the tip will appear in the TipWizard box. You can also view previous tips and get additional help on the currently displayed tip. To remove the tip from the screen, you would click the TipWizard tool again.

To use the TipWizard:

1 Click the **TipWizard** tool.
The most recent tip appears in the TipWizard box above the formula bar.

2 Click the Previous Tip button (the upward-pointing arrow near the right of the TipWizard box).
The text of the previous tip appears.

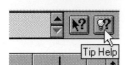

3 Click the **Tip Help** tool (to the right of the TipWizard box).
A Help and How To window opens with additional information on the currently displayed tip.

4 From the Help window's **File** menu, choose **Exit.** Select the **Close** button in the How to window if the window is displayed.

5 Click the **TipWizard** tool.
The TipWizard box disappears.

EXITING EXCEL

You will now exit the Excel program. It is not necessary to save this empty worksheet (although if you happened to have made changes to it, Excel will give you the opportunity to save it before exiting). You can use either of two methods to exit Excel.

To exit Excel:

1 Open the **File** menu, and then choose **Exit.**

2 Because you do not need to save this workbook, select No in the Save Changes dialog box if it appears.

Tip You can also exit Excel by double-clicking the Control menu box in the upper-left corner of the Excel window. Remember that there is also a smaller Control menu box that belongs to the current workbook window. Double-clicking the smaller Control menu box closes only that workbook window, not the Excel program.

Now that you've used the mouse to choose menu commands, the numbered steps will be stated in a more abbreviated form. For example,

1 Open the **File** menu, and then choose **Exit**

will be represented as

2 Choose **File** and then **Exit**.

THE NEXT STEP

Now that you are acquainted with the Excel application and workbook windows, you are ready to enter information into a worksheet and to use commands to affect the information. The next project, Building a Small Worksheet, will illustrate many of the basic aspects of Excel worksheets.

SUMMARY AND EXERCISES

Summary

- Worksheets (spreadsheets) consist of tables of information presented in rows and columns. Beyond its basic ability to perform arithmetic, Excel offers powerful formatting, data analysis, and charting features.
- You can use Excel to build workbooks composed of worksheets, chart sheets, and modules.
- The top portion of the Excel application window contains the menu bar, the Standard toolbar, the Formatting toolbar, and the formula bar.
- An Excel worksheet is composed of columns (labeled A, B, C, . . ., Z, AA, AB, . . ., IV) and rows (labeled 1 through 16384).
- The intersection of a row and a column is called a cell, which is the basic building block of a worksheet. You refer to a cell by its row and column (for example, the cell at the intersection of column C and row 15 is called cell C15).
- The selected cell is where the action takes place in a worksheet. The selected cell appears with a thick outline.
- The pointer can take a variety of shapes, depending on precisely where it is positioned on-screen and on what action it will perform.
- A range is a rectangular block of cells. You can select a range of cells by holding down the mouse button and dragging the pointer through the cells you want to select. You can also select whole columns, rows, and nonadjacent ranges.
- Toolbars contain controls that allow quick access to commands. You can rearrange and customize toolbars.

• A standard Windows Help system is available to explain Excel commands and features. You can search for topics of interest using the Search command from the Help menu.

Key Terms and Operations

Key Terms

active cell
application window
cell
cell reference
chart sheet
column
docked
fill handle
floating toolbar
formula bar
Help tool
I-beam
menu bar
module
nonadjacent selection
range
reference area

row
selection
sheet
sheet tab
split bar
spreadsheet
status bar
tab scrolling buttons
TipWizard
toolbar
ToolTip
workbook window
worksheet

Operations

Exiting Excel
Getting on-screen help

Study Questions

Multiple Choice

1 In Excel, the intersection of a column and a row is called a:
   a. block.
   b. selection.
   c. cell.
   d. range.
   e. formula.

2. How deep (how many rows) is an Excel worksheet?
   a. 100
   b. 500
   c. 1000
   d. 1024
   e. 16,384

3. To position in the upper-left corner of the worksheet (cell A1), press:
   a. CTRL + PGUP
   b. PGUP
   c. HOME
   d. CTRL + HOME
   e. ALT + PGUP

4. A new, blank workbook contains how many worksheets?
   a. 1
   b. 2
   c. 16
   d. 100
   e. 16,384

5. A rectangular block of cells is called a:
   a. data block.
   b. paragraph.
   c. data segment.
   d. code segment.
   e. range.

6. How do you use the mouse to quickly select an entire column in Excel?
   a. click any cell in the column
   b. click the column heading letter
   c. click the top cell and drag to the bottom cell
   d. click the **Column Select** tool on the toolbar
   e. click the top cell of the column and press (F8)

7. What menu command gives you control over the display of toolbars?
   a. choose **View** and then **Toolbars**
   b. ToolTips
   c. choose **Edit** and then **Bars**
   d. choose **Edit** and then **Toolbars**
   e. choose **Tools** and then **View**

Short Answer

1. The intersection of column C and row 5 is referred to as what?

2. The rectangular block of cells whose upper-left corner is B3 and whose lower-right corner is E8 is referred to as what?

3. The location where the "action" takes place in the worksheet is called what?

4. How can nonadjacent selections be made using the mouse in Excel?

For Discussion

1. Who other than accountants might benefit from Excel?

2. How might you use Excel in your own work or area of expertise?

3. What were some of the problems of spreadsheets before spreadsheet computer programs were available? What distinguishes electronic spreadsheets from their manual predecessors?

4. What distinguishes Excel from the first generation of electronic spreadsheets?

Objectives

After completing this project, you should be able to:

▶ Enter text and numeric constants

▶ Change column widths

▶ Build simple formulas

▶ Recalculate a worksheet

▶ Use arithmetic operators

▶ Automatically format a worksheet

▶ Save, close, and open a worksheet

▶ Edit cell entries

▶ Insert and name new worksheets

▶ Open a new workbook

CASE STUDY: CALCULATING NET PAY

In this project you will build a small worksheet that uses each of the three basic kinds of cell entries common to all Excel worksheets: text, numbers, and formulas. First, you will enter text to use for titles, numbers that will serve as the basic data manipulated in the worksheet, and a formula that refers to the numbers and computes a result. You will then learn how to format the worksheet to improve its appearance. Finally, you will save the workbook to disk so the workbook can be used later.

Designing the Solution

This first worksheet will calculate a person's net pay by subtracting taxes withheld from gross pay. A rough version of the worksheet follows:

Gross Pay   853

Taxes Withheld   127

Net Pay   ?

The question mark is a reminder that you will design the Excel worksheet to compute the net pay.

ENTERING CONSTANTS

A cell can contain three basic kinds of data: *text constants, number constants,* and *formulas.* Constants do not change after you type them into a cell. **Number constants** are numbers—mathematical values that can be used in calculations; **text constants** consist of words, comments, titles, and other nonmathematical information.

Formulas compute a result, usually by performing arithmetic on information obtained from other cells. The **value** (result) of a formula can change if any of the cells the formula refers to change. Formulas do the work of a worksheet, and well-designed formulas are the key to building a worksheet that is flexible and powerful.

You will start by entering the text constants of this worksheet. Text constants are usually words that label the different parts of a worksheet to make it easier to understand.

To enter text constants:

1 Start Excel.

2 Select cell A1.

3 Type **Gross Pay**

The screen should appear similar to Figure 1.1. Notice that the text appears in the formula bar as well as in the cell.

| Cancel box | Enter box | Function Wizard |

A1			Gross Pay
A	B	C	D	E	F	G	H	I
1 Gross Pay								
2								
3								
4								
5								

Figure 1.1

Tip To cancel an entry while you are typing it, you can select the Cancel box or press (ESC).

4 Select the Enter box or press (ENTER) or any arrow key to finish entering the text into cell A1.

Tip From now on, when you see a step that tells you to enter something in a cell, it means to type the information and then click the Enter box or press (ENTER).

5 Select cell A2 if necessary, and enter `Taxes Withheld`

6 Enter `Net Pay` in cell A3.

Changing the Width of a Column

The text *Taxes Withheld* in cell A2 appears to spill over into column B. However, the entire text is stored in cell A2. In this section you will learn to manually adjust the width of a column so it accommodates long entries.

You can adjust the width of a column by first positioning the pointer on the right edge of a column heading and then dragging the mouse, or by using the Column command from the Format menu. If, instead of dragging the mouse, you double-click the mouse button, the width will be automatically set to *best fit* (to accommodate the longest entry in that column).

To change the width of column A:

1 Move the pointer to the right edge of the heading for column A (to the boundary line between the headings for columns A and B).
The pointer should change to a double arrow.

2 Hold down the mouse button.
Notice that the current column width is displayed in the reference area.

3 Drag the column width so the column is somewhat wider than the longest text entry (*Taxes Withheld*) as shown in Figure 1.2, and then release the mouse button.

	A	B	C	D	E	F	G	H	I
1	Gross Pay								
2	Taxes Withheld								
3	Net Pay								
4									

Figure 1.2

To set the column width to best fit:

1 Position the pointer on the right edge of the heading for column A (so the pointer becomes a double arrow).

2 Double-click to set the column to best fit.

Tip Sometimes best fit will actually be too narrow, and you will need to manually increase a column's width. A column is too narrow when numeric entries appear as lines of number signs (#).

Entering Numeric Constants

In general, when you type numbers in Excel, you should leave out extra punctuation such as dollar signs and commas. Although Excel will preserve this punctuation in your entry, it is best to assign a consistent appearance to a group of cells by using Excel's extensive formatting commands.

Include a decimal point only if the number has a fractional part. If you type a percent sign after a number, the number will be divided by 100 (and assigned a percent style).

This worksheet contains two numeric constants: gross pay and taxes withheld.

To enter the numeric constants:

1 Select cell B1.

2 Enter the sample gross pay amount, **853** in cell B1.

3 Enter the sample taxes withheld amount, **127** in cell B2.

Notice that Excel aligns a number against the right edge of its cell, and text against the left edge. You will learn later how to adjust the alignment of cell contents.

ENTERING FORMULAS

There are several ways to create a formula in Excel. The simplest and least prone to error is to use **point mode.** In point mode, you use the mouse or arrow keys to point to the various cells that are to be included in the formula, and Excel figures out what the actual cell references are. When you use point mode, you don't have to worry about figuring out cell addresses yourself.

Riddle

Q. How can you tell when people aren't using point mode in Excel?

A. They are trying to figure out cell references by holding a ruler or piece of paper against the computer screen to line up rows and columns.

In the following steps, you will use a formula to calculate net pay. The formula will refer to the gross pay amount and subtract the taxes withheld from that amount. Note that all formulas begin with an equal sign, and you will not press (ENTER) until the entire formula is complete.

To enter the formula to calculate net pay:

1 Select cell B3, the cell to the right of *Net Pay*.

This cell should contain the formula to calculate net pay.

2 Type =

The screen should be similar to Figure 1.3.

B3	↓ X ƒ	=							
	A	B	C	D	E	F	G	H	I
1	Gross Pay	853							
2	Taxes Withheld	127							
3	Net Pay	=							
4									
5									

Figure 1.3

3 Point to the gross pay amount you entered in cell B1 by either clicking on the cell to select it or using the arrow keys to move up to the cell. The screen should resemble Figure 1.4. Notice that Excel is building the formula for you in the formula bar.

B1		ƒ×	=B1						
	A	B	C	D	E	F	G	H	I
1	Gross Pay	✛ 853							
2	Taxes Withheld	127							
3	Net Pay	=B1							
4									
5									

Figure 1.4

4 Type - (a minus sign) as shown in Figure 1.5.
The formula is supposed to subtract taxes withheld from the gross pay amount.

B3		ƒ×	=B1-						
	A	B	C	D	E	F	G	H	I
1	Gross Pay	✛ 853							
2	Taxes Withheld	127							
3	Net Pay	=B1-							
4									
5									

Figure 1.5

5 Point to the taxes withheld amount by either selecting cell B2 or using the arrow keys. See Figure 1.6.

B2		ƒ×	=B1-B2						
	A	B	C	D	E	F	G	H	I
1	Gross Pay	853							
2	Taxes Withheld	✛ 127							
3	Net Pay	=B1-B2							
4									
5									

Figure 1.6

6 To finish the formula, select the Enter box or press (ENTER) (see Figure 1.7).

B2		ƒ×	=B1-B2						
	A	B	C	D	E	F	G	H	I
1	Gross Pay	853							
2	Taxes Withheld	127							
3	Net Pay	=B1-B2							
4									
5									

Figure 1.7

7 Select cell B3, if necessary, to examine the completed formula.

Notice that Excel has built the formula =B1-B2, as shown in the formula bar of Figure 1.8. Cell B3 contains a formula whose result, currently 726, appears in the worksheet.

B3			=B1-B2							
	A	**B**	**C**	**D**	**E**	**F**	**G**	**H**	**I**	
1	Gross Pay	853								
2	Taxes Withheld	127								
3	Net Pay	726								
4										
5										

Figure 1.8

Reminders Here are some reminders about building formulas using the point method:

- All formulas start with an equal sign.
- You will use the mouse or arrow keys to select the cells that the formula refers to.
- You will press (ENTER) (or select the Enter box on the formula bar) only once, when you have completed the entire formula.

Recalculating a Worksheet

The foremost advantage of an electronic spreadsheet is that its formulas can ***recalculate*** and show new results if there are changes in the cells to which the formulas refer. For example, suppose that the taxes withheld changed to 179.

To change and recalculate the worksheet:

1 Select cell B2, where you entered 127 as the taxes withheld.

2 Change the taxes withheld to 179 by typing **179** and pressing (ENTER) or clicking the Enter box.

As shown in Figure 1.9, the new entry replaces the previous one, and the result of the net pay formula adjusts automatically to 674.

B2			179							
	A	**B**	**C**	**D**	**E**	**F**	**G**	**H**	**I**	
1	Gross Pay	853								
2	Taxes Withheld	179								
3	Net Pay	674								
4										
5										

Figure 1.9

Experiment with other changes to gross pay and taxes withheld.

Arithmetic Operators

The formula you just created uses the subtraction operator. Excel has several major operators, which are listed in Table 1.1 in ***priority*** order. The priorities of the various operators in a formula determine the order in which Excel performs the operations. Higher priority operations are performed first. For example, because multiplication and division are operations of higher priority than addition and subtraction, =8-3*2 is calculated with implied parentheses: =8-(3*2), which results in 2, not 10. You can use parentheses to override the standard priorities: =(8-3)*2 is 10.

Table 1.1

Priority	Symbol	Operator	Function	Example Formula	Example Result
1	%	Percent	Divides a number by 100	=5%	0.05
2	^	Exponentiation	Raises a number to a power	=3^2	9
3	*	Multiplication	Multiplies two numbers	=4*2	8
	/	Division	Divides one number by another	=12/3	4
4	+	Addition	Adds two numbers	=3+2	5
	−	Subtraction	Subtracts one number from another	=7-4	3
5	&	Text joining	Connects two text strings	=''Uh''&''Oh''	UhOh
6	=	Equal to	TRUE if a=b, FALSE otherwise	=5=3	FALSE
	<	Less than	TRUE if a<b, FALSE otherwise	=6<7	TRUE
	>	Greater than	TRUE if a>b, FALSE otherwise	=2>3	FALSE
	<=	Less than or equal to	TRUE if a<=b, FALSE otherwise	=17<=17	TRUE
	>=	Greater than or equal to	TRUE if a>=b, FALSE otherwise	=16>=17	FALSE
	<>	Not equal to	TRUE if a<>b, FALSE otherwise	=6<>7	TRUE

Tip When you need to type /, *, −, or +, use the keys on the numeric keypad at the right of the keyboard. This is often quicker than searching the main keyboard for the appropriate symbol.

FORMATTING CELLS

The *format* of a cell indicates how the information in the cell should appear on-screen or in a printout. The many attributes of a cell format include number punctuation (such as dollar signs and commas), alignment, borders, and font.

In the following steps, you will use the *AutoFormat* command to have Excel automatically assign formats to the cells in your worksheet. You will learn more about cell formats in later projects.

To format the worksheet automatically:

1 Select the range A1:B3 by selecting cell A1, holding down the left mouse button, dragging to cell B3, and then releasing the mouse button.

2 Choose **Format** and then **AutoFormat**.
The AutoFormat dialog box appears.

3 Examine samples of the AutoFormat table formats available. To see a sample, click on a table format name in the list box.

4 Select **Accounting 1** from the list, and then select **OK** as shown in Figure 1.10.

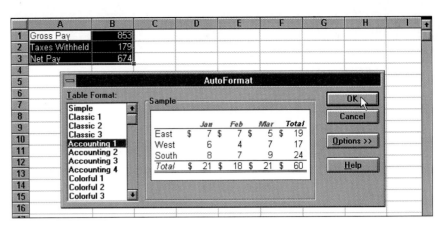

Figure 1.10

The screen should now resemble Figure 1.11.

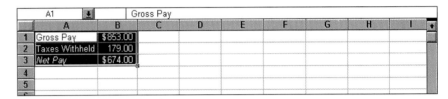

Figure 1.11

5 Click anywhere outside A1:B3 to cancel the selection.

When you use AutoFormat, Excel takes a few seconds to assign customized formats to the worksheet. Notice some of the appearance attributes affected by the AutoFormat command:

- The text *Net Pay* is italic.
- The gross pay and net pay amounts (that is, the first and last rows of numeric values in the worksheet) appear with leading dollar signs.
- All numeric values in the worksheet appear with two digits to the right of the decimal point.
- The two cells comprising the last row of the worksheet have thin top border lines and double bottom border lines.

SAVING, CLOSING, AND UPDATING WORKBOOKS

The worksheet you have built exists only in the computer's *memory* (RAM). If the computer were to be turned off or the power interrupted at this point, you would lose your work.

Tip Save your work often, perhaps every five minutes. A rule of thumb is that it is time to save when (1) it would be troublesome to re-create the work you've done since you last saved, (2) you are about to make a major change or addition to the worksheet, or (3) you are about to use a command whose effects you are not certain of.

Saving a Workbook

You will now save a copy of the workbook to disk.

To save the workbook:

1 Choose **File** and then **Save,** or click the **Save** tool on the Standard toolbar.

Because this is a new file, Excel presents the Save As dialog box, where you can choose the disk drive on which you would like to store the file and type the name you would like to give the file. Excel proposes the name BOOK1.XLS.

2 Use the **Drives** and **Directories** list boxes to choose whatever disk drive and directory you want to save the file to.

3 Double-click in the **File Name** text box.

4 Type **pay1** in the **File Name** text box and then select **OK,** as shown in Figure 1.12.

A Summary Info dialog box appears; you can optionally provide additional descriptive information about the file.

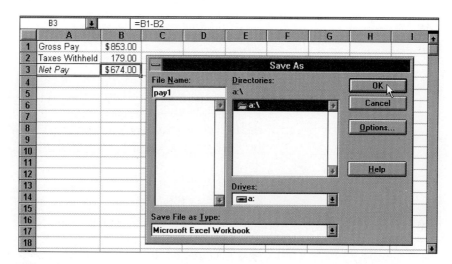

Figure 1.12

5 Type your name in the **Author** section of the Summary Info dialog box and select **OK.**

The Save command does not close the workbook window, so your worksheet remains visible. Notice that the name you just assigned to your file, PAY1.XLS, now appears in the title bar. Excel automatically assigned the file extension .XLS. Because the workbook now has a file name, subsequent uses of the Save command will be quicker; you will not be prompted to type a name.

Tip If you want to save a workbook with a different name than the one that is already assigned to it, use the Save As command from the File menu. With this command, the original file is preserved and a second file, with the new name, is created.

 EXIT If necessary, you can exit Excel now, and continue this project later.

Closing a Workbook

Closing a workbook removes it from the screen.

To close the workbook:

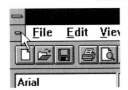

1 Choose **File** and then **Close,** or double-click the *workbook's* Control menu box (which is under the Excel application window's Control menu box).
If you made any changes to the workbook since you last saved it, the Save Changes dialog box will appear, asking whether you want to save the updated version of the worksheet.

2 Click **Yes,** if necessary.

Opening a Workbook

Opening the PAY1 workbook file loads a copy of the workbook from disk into memory, where you can modify the workbook. The original copy of the file remains unchanged on the disk until you save the updated workbook over the original version.

To open a workbook file:

1 Choose **File** and then **Open,** or select the **Open** tool on the Standard toolbar.
The Open dialog box appears.

2 Change the disk drive and the directory, if necessary.

3 Select the file PAY1.XLS from the alphabetical file list.

4 Select **OK.**

Tip If you save your workbooks frequently, you can return to a recently saved version if you "mess up" the workbook currently on-screen. You can use the Close command in the File menu to clear the messed-up workbook from the screen (without saving), and then use the Open command to retrieve the earlier version from disk.

Editing Cell Entries

One way to change the content of a cell is to type a new entry to replace an old one, as you did when you changed the value of the taxes withheld earlier in this project. However, there will be times when you need to change just a piece of a long entry—perhaps you will need to make a small correction to a long title or formula. In such cases, editing the cell entry can save you some typing.

You can edit a cell entry by activating the cell and clicking in the formula bar: this will display an insertion point in the formula bar. You can also double-click directly in the cell: this will allow "in-cell editing" and display the insertion point in the worksheet itself. You can position the insertion point within the text by clicking or by using the arrow keys. Pressing (BKSP) will erase characters to the left of the insertion point; pressing (DEL) will erase characters to the right.

Suppose that the title *Taxes Withheld* needed to be changed to *Tax Withheld*.

To edit a cell entry:

1 Double-click in cell A2, which contains the text *Taxes Withheld*. The insertion point appears in the cell and the Edit indicator appears in the left side of the Status bar.

2 Position the insertion point just after the *s* in *Taxes*.

3 Press (BKSP) twice.
The screen should resemble Figure 1.13.

	A	B	C	D	E	F	G	H	I
	A2		Tax Withheld						
1	Gross Pay	$853.00							
2	Tax Withheld	179.00							
3	Net Pay	$674.00							
4									
5									

Figure 1.13

4 Select the Enter box or press (ENTER) to enter the revised text.

CREATING NEW WORKSHEETS AND WORKBOOKS

When you first start the program, Excel presents you with a workbook containing 16 blank worksheets. A workbook, regardless of how many worksheets it contains, is stored in a single file on disk. If you "use up" the 16 worksheets initially provided, you can insert new, blank worksheets within the workbook. In general, the worksheets within a given workbook should all be concerned with the same topic or related in some way. If you need to create worksheets for some new task unrelated to an existing workbook, then you should open a new workbook.

Inserting a New Worksheet

If at any time during your Excel session you want to insert a new, blank worksheet in the current workbook, you can choose the Worksheet command from the Insert menu. The new worksheet will be inserted immediately preceding the current sheet and will be automatically activated.

To insert a new worksheet:

1 Choose **Insert** and then **Worksheet.**
A new sheet, named Sheet17, is created and activated.

2 Click the **Sheet1** tab to switch back to the pay worksheet.

Naming Sheets

If you use multiple sheets in a workbook, it will be much easier to identify them if you assign names to appear on the sheet tabs. You can double-click on a sheet tab to rename a sheet.

> **Tip** Though a sheet name can be up to 31 characters long, you should try to think of a good abbreviated name, because long names in sheet tabs make it harder to see multiple tabs at once on-screen. A sheet name can contain spaces but cannot be enclosed in square brackets or contain the characters \, /, :, ?, or *. Remember that sheet names are *not* workbook (file) names.

 To rename a sheet:

1 Double-click on the tab for **Sheet1.**
The Rename Sheet dialog box appears.

2 Type **Payroll** and then select **OK,** as shown in Figure 1.14.

Figure 1.14

The sheet tab now shows the name Payroll.

Rearranging Sheets

By clicking and dragging a sheet tab or group of sheet tabs, you can change the order in which the sheets appear. In the steps below, you will drag Sheet17 so it appears after the Payroll sheet.

To change the order of sheet tabs:

1 Click on the tab for **Sheet17** and hold down the mouse button.
A sheet icon appears, along with a small arrowhead indicating the position at which the selected sheet will be inserted, as shown in Figure 1.15.

Figure 1.15

2 Drag the sheet icon so the arrowhead appears between the **Payroll** tab and the **Sheet2** tab, as shown in Figure 1.16.

Figure 1.16

3 Release the mouse button.
The Sheet17 tab now appears after the Payroll sheet tab.
4 Close and save the PAY1 workbook.

Opening a New Workbook

To open a new workbook containing blank worksheets, you can choose the New command from the File menu or select the New Workbook tool on the Standard toolbar.

> **Tip**   Remember, you can have many different workbooks open at once. If you have finished working with one workbook and want to begin a new one, you can reduce the clutter on the screen by closing the first workbook. If you need to switch between (or simultaneously view) the workbooks, you should keep them both open.

To open a new workbook:

1 Click the **New Workbook** tool on the Standard toolbar.
A new workbook window appears.

EXITING EXCEL

You will now exit the Excel program.

To exit Excel:

1 Choose **File** and then **Exit.**

THE NEXT STEP

Now that you have created basic cell entries common to most worksheets, you are ready to create them in a larger worksheet. In the next project, you will build more sophisticated formulas and learn how to copy and move cell contents. You will see how AutoFormat performs in a more complicated context, and you will begin to take more control over the appearance of the worksheet.

This concludes Project 1. You can either exit Excel, or go on to work the Study Questions, Review Exercises, and Assignments.

SUMMARY AND EXERCISES

Summary

- A cell can contain a text constant, a number constant, or a formula.
- Number constants should be entered without extra punctuation.
- A formula's result is called its value.
- You can change the width of a column in a worksheet.
- Formulas do the work in a worksheet. Formulas are built most easily by using point mode.
- When a formula in one cell depends upon the data in another cell, the formula will automatically recalculate if the contents of the other cell change.
- Arithmetic operators are prioritized, and this determines the order in which operations are performed in a formula.
- Workbooks should be saved frequently.
- The appearance of simple worksheets can be quickly improved by using the AutoFormat command.
- A cell entry can be edited rather than retyped.
- The Open command in the File menu is used to open a workbook that was saved to disk; the New command is used to open a new, blank workbook.
- New worksheets can be inserted into a workbook with the Insert command from the Edit menu.
- Worksheets can be rearranged by dragging sheet tabs.

Key Terms and Operations

Key Terms	Operations
AutoFormat	Change column width
best fit	Close a workbook
format	Insert a worksheet
formula	Open a saved workbook
number constant	Rearrange sheets
point mode	Rename a sheet
priority	Save a workbook
recalculate	Start a new workbook
text constant	
value	

Study Questions

Multiple Choice

1. What determines the order in which arithmetic operations are performed in an Excel formula?
   a. The order is strictly left to right.
   b. The order is strictly right to left.
   c. The order is determined by the priority of the operators used.
   d. The order doesn't matter.
   e. The settings you specify in the Operator Precedence menu determine the order.

2. What are the two types of constants?
   a. text and number
   b. formula and value
   c. label and text
   d. relative and absolute
   e. formula and number

3. If you change a cell entry upon which a formula depends (which a formula refers to), what will happen?
   a. The formula will display an error message.
   b. The formula will automatically recalculate to reflect the changed data.
   c. You will need to rebuild the formula before it will display a new result.
   d. You will need to copy the formula upon itself.
   e. Nothing will happen.

4. How many times do you press (ENTER) (or select the Enter box) when building an Excel formula?
   a. once
   b. twice
   c. as many times as there are cell references in the formula
   d. as many times as there are arithmetic operators in the formula
   e. never

5. In Excel, what is the result of the formula $= 3 + 25 + 4$?
   a. 29   d. 17
   b. 72   e. none of the above
   c. 26

6. In Excel, what is the result of the formula $= 3 + (4 - 2) * 3$?
   a. 15   d. 9
   b. 1   e. none of the above
   c. 3

7. The way information appears in a cell (such as its alignment, font, or numeric punctuation) is referred to as the cell's:
   a. style.   d. format.
   b. attributes.   e. AutoFormat.
   c. display mode.

8. When should you save your work in Excel?
   a. when you are about to make a major modification to the worksheet
   b. every 5 or 10 minutes
   c. when it would be time-consuming to re-create the work you've done since you last saved
   d. when you are about to experiment with an unfamiliar Excel command
   e. all of the above

9. What happens when you close a workbook in Excel?
   a. The workbook is automatically saved.
   b. Excel will automatically exit.
   c. If you made changes to the workbook since you last saved, a dialog box will appear and give you the opportunity to save again.
   d. A new, empty workbook will automatically appear.
   e. You will automatically lose all changes made since you last saved the workbook.

10. How do you begin to edit a cell entry?
    a. make the cell active and then choose **Edit** from the menu bar
    b. make the cell active and then select the formula bar or double-click the cell
    c. double-click in the formula bar
    d. all of the above
    e. none of the above

Short Answer

1. What is the result of a formula called?

2. What kind of information is usually represented with text constants?

3. If you enter a text constant that is longer than a cell's width, what does Excel do?

4. When you enter a number constant, should you include punctuation (dollar signs, commas, and so on)? Why?

5. In general what is the best method to use when building formulas that refer to other cells? Why?

6. What determines the order in which arithmetic operations are performed in Excel formulas?

7. What determines the way information in a cell will appear?

8. What command is used to automatically format a range?

9. What command is used to open a new, blank workbook?

10. What steps are required to edit an existing cell entry?

For Discussion

1. What aspects of a cell's appearance does the AutoFormat command affect?

2. What is the single most important feature of electronic spreadsheets? Why?

3. Describe the point method for building formulas.

Review Exercises

Simple Income Statement

Build and format a worksheet based on the information shown in Figure 1.17. Income is calculated by subtracting the cost of goods sold from the sales. Pick out any one of the Accounting table formats when you use the AutoFormat command. Save the workbook as INCOME1.

	A	B	C	D	E	F	G	H	
1	Sales	$57,189.00							
2	Cost of Goods Sold	33,202.00							
3	*Income*	?							
4									
5									

Figure 1.17

Population Report

Build and format a worksheet similar to Figure 1.18. Use an addition formula to compute the total population of the United States, Canada, and Mexico combined. If the column containing the numbers is too narrow, Excel displays a number sign (#) or scientific notation. Once you use AutoFormat or manually widen the columns, the numbers themselves will appear. Pick out any one of the Classic or Colorful table formats. Save the workbook as POPREP1.

	A	B	C	D	E	F	G	H	I	
1	**Country**	*Population*								
2	United States	248710000								
3	Mexico	90007000								
4	Canada	26835500								
5	Total	?								
6										

Figure 1.18

Assignments

Detailed Income Statement

Build a worksheet based on Figure 1.19. Gross income is the sales minus the cost of goods sold. Net income is the gross income minus the expenses. Use AutoFormat and the Accounting 1 table format. Save the file as INCOME2.

	A	B	C	D	E	F	G	H	
1	Sales	$93,126.00							
2	Cost of Goods Sold	32,117.00							
3	*Gross Income*	?							
4	*Expenses*	$16,909.00							
5	**Net Income**	?							
6									

Figure 1.19

Population Density

Build a worksheet based on Figure 1.20. The population density is the number of people per square mile; calculate it by dividing the population of a city by the city's area. Use AutoFormat and experiment with the various non-Accounting table formats. Notice that AutoFormat does not limit the number of digits that display to the right of the decimal point in the non-Accounting formats. Save the file as DENSITY1.

	A	B	C	D	E	F	G	H
1	City	Population	Area (sq. mi.)	Density				
2	Hong Kong	5693000	23	?				
3	Los Angeles	10130000	1110	?				
4								
5								
6								

Figure 1.20

Coffee House Income

Figure 1.21 shows cost and price information for the top-selling coffee at Clem's Coffee Clutch. Enter the data as shown in Figure 1.21. The formula that calculates income will subtract the cost from the selling price and multiply the result by the number sold. You will need to use parentheses in the formula. Adjust column widths as necessary, but do not format the worksheet; it will be used for an exercise in a later project. Save the worksheet as COFFEE1.

	A	B	C	D	E	F	G	H	I
1	Coffee	Cost	Selling Price	No. Sold	Income				
2	House Blend	0.39	0.95	60	?				
3									

Figure 1.21

PROJECT 2: BUILDING A LARGER WORKSHEET

Objectives

After completing this project, you should be able to:

▶ Move a cell

▶ Check the spelling of worksheet data

▶ Use preselected ranges for data entry

▶ Copy the contents of a cell

▶ Use relative cell references in formulas

▶ Use the SUM function and the AutoSum tool

CASE STUDY: SALES OF AUDIO RECORDINGS

From 1975 to 1990, the popularity of the kinds of media used for recorded music shifted dramatically. These changes are illustrated in Figure 2.1. In this project, you will build this Excel worksheet and add formulas to calculate the totals (indicated by question marks in the figure).

	A	B	C	D	E	F	G	H
1	Shipments of Audio Recordings							
2	(in millions of dollars)							
3		1975	1980	1985	1990			
4	Phonograph Records							
5	LP Albums	1485	2290.3	1280.5	86.5			
6	Singles	211.5	269.3	281	94.4			
7	Total Records	?	?	?	?			
8	Tapes							
9	8-tracks	583	526.4	25.3	0			
10	Cassettes	98.8	776.4	2411.5	3472.4			
11	Total Tapes	?	?	?	?			
12	Compact Discs							
13	Regular CDs	0	0	389.5	3451.6			
14	CD Singles	0	0	0	6			
15	Total CDs	?	?	?	?			
16	Grand Total	?	?	?	?			
17								

Figure 2.1

Designing the Solution

The formulas you will create for this worksheet will calculate totals for each year in each media category (records, tapes, and CDs) and grand totals (the totals of records, tapes, and CDs combined). You will then format the worksheet so the information is more readable.

In the steps that follow, as important new concepts and features are introduced, you can refer to Figure 2.1 to orient yourself in the worksheet. Although you might be tempted to jump ahead and type everything in immediately, please follow the steps carefully.

BUILDING THE SKELETON OF A WORKSHEET

When you create a worksheet, it is often easiest to enter the static (unchanging) information first. To establish an overall skeleton or shape for the worksheet, you will enter the row and column titles before you enter the number constants and formulas. In general you should wait until the worksheet is complete and functioning correctly before doing detailed formatting.

To enter the main titles:

1 Start Excel.

2 Select cell A1 on Sheet1 and enter the text **Shipments of Audio Recordings**

3 Enter **(in millions of dollars)** in cell A2.

Moving Cells

In the following steps, you will enter the first row title, *Phonograph Records*, in the wrong cell. You will then use Excel's ***drag-and-drop*** feature to move the title to the correct cell. In Excel, to ***move*** means that you pick up an object from one location (in this case, the original cell) and place it in another location.

To move a cell:

1 Enter **Phonograph Records** in cell A3.
Notice that the sample worksheet in Figure 2.1 shows the first row title, *Phonograph Records*, in row 4, one row *below* the row containing the years. Rather than retyping the information you just entered, you can move it to the correct location, cell A4.

2 Select cell A3, which should contain the text constant *Phonograph Records*.

3 Position the pointer to touch any edge of the active-cell rectangle so the pointer becomes an arrow (Figure 2.2).

2	(in millions of dollars)				
3	Phonograph Records				
4					
5					

Figure 2.2

4 Hold down the mouse button and drag the dimmed image of the cell outline to cell A4, as shown in Figure 2.3. Release the mouse button. The screen should now look like Figure 2.4, with *Phonograph Records* in the new location.

2	(in millions of dollars)							
3	Phonograph Records							
4								
5								

Figure 2.3

2	(in millions of dollars)							
3								
4	Phonograph Records							
5								

Figure 2.4

Entering Row Titles

Notice that the row subtitles in Figure 2.1 are slightly indented to create an outline format. One simple way to accomplish this in Excel is to precede each text entry with two space characters.

To enter the row titles:

1 Select cell A5.

2 Press (SPACE) twice, and then enter **LP Albums**

3 Select cell A6, press (SPACE) twice, and then enter **Singles**

4 Select cell A7, press (SPACE) twice, and then enter **Total Records**

5 Refer back to Figure 2.1 to enter all the remaining row titles. Remember to indent where indicated in the figure.

> **Reminder** If you discover that you have made an incorrect entry in a cell, you can select the cell and double-click in it, or click in the formula bar. As shown in Project 1, you will then be able to type new information or use the editing keys to correct your mistake.

Checking the Spelling in a Worksheet

Once you have entered all the text constants into a worksheet, you can use Excel to check your spelling. The spelling checker will begin its check on the currently selected cell, and then it will proceed toward the lower-right corner of the worksheet. When it finishes checking the lower-right part of the worksheet, you can optionally have it check the upper-left portion. If you plan to check the spelling of the entire worksheet, it is most convenient to start at the top left corner by making A1 the active cell.

The spelling checker will pause on any word in the worksheet that it does not find in the spelling dictionary. The Spelling dialog box will suggest replacements for the possibly misspelled word. If the original word you typed is spelled correctly, you can select Ignore All in the dialog box; the spelling checker then skips over all subsequent occurrences of that spelling. (Choosing Ignore causes only the current occurrence to be skipped.) If the spelling needs to be corrected, you can choose from the list of suggestions or type a new spelling and then select Change. As illustrated in Figure 2.5, the spelling checker paused on an incorrect spelling of the word *Phonograph*. The two suggested words are *Phonograph* and *Photograph*. Because *Phonograph* is selected in the Change To box, you would select Change. The spelling will be corrected, and the spelling checker will continue to any other words that may have been misspelled, giving you a chance to correct them.

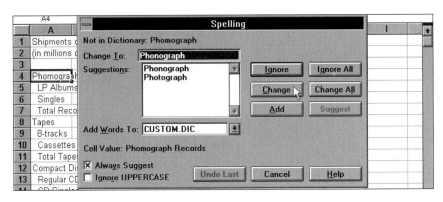

Figure 2.5

To check spelling in the worksheet:

1 Move the active cell to the top left cell (cell A1).
A quick way to do this is by pressing (CTRL) + (HOME)

2 Choose **Tools** and then **Spelling** or select the **Spelling** tool.

3 Correct any misspelled words that occur in your worksheet.

Entering Column Titles

The years *1975, 1980, 1985,* and *1990* need to be entered as column titles. In the steps that follow, you will use several methods for entering data.

To enter the column titles:

1 To make it easier to read the worksheet as you enter data, make column A slightly wider than *Phonograph Records*, the longest of the individual row titles.

2 Select cell B3, type **1975** and press (ENTER)
Depending on how Excel was installed on the system you are using, the active-cell rectangle may move down automatically after you press (ENTER). You can change this option if you wish.

Tip To control whether the active cell (the selection) is moved after you press (ENTER), you can choose Options from the Tools menu, select the Edit tab, and select (or clear) the Move Selection After Enter check box. If the check box is cleared, the effect of pressing (ENTER) is the same as that of clicking the Enter button in the formula bar. If the check box is checked, the active cell will move down after you press (ENTER).

3 Select cell C3, type **1980** and press ⊕

4 Enter the other two years **1985** and **1990** in the appropriate cells.

Tip Pressing an arrow key after you type data will automatically enter the data and position the selection one cell in the direction of the arrow key.

Using Selection to Speed Data Entry

The various sales figures need to be entered in the main section of the worksheet. Although the sales figures could always be entered without the use of a preselected range, in the steps that follow you will learn how to make repetitive entry more convenient by preselecting a data-entry range. At the lower-right corner of a selection, pressing (TAB) or (ENTER) moves to the upper left; at the upper left of a selection, pressing (SHIFT) + (TAB) moves to the lower right. You can use these keys to change which cell is active within a selected range. If (TAB) does not behave in this way, you can choose Options from the Tools menu, select the Transition tab, and clear the Transition Navigation Keys check box. Using (TAB) or (ENTER) will make your entry of multiple columns of numbers somewhat more convenient, because as you complete the last entry in a column, the active cell will "wrap around," or continue, to the next column automatically.

To use selection to speed data entry:

1 Select B5:E6 (as shown in Figure 2.6), the range where you will place sales amounts for LP albums and singles.

	A	B	C	D	E	F	G	H	
1	Shipments of Audio Recordings								
2	(in millions of dollars)								
3		1975	1980	1985	1990				
4	Phonograph Records								
5	LP Albums								
6	Singles								
7	Total Records								

Figure 2.6

2 Practice pressing (ENTER) to move down and (TAB) to move to the right within the selection.

3 Use (TAB) or (ENTER) to make cell B5 the active cell in the selected range, and type **1485** as shown in Figure 2.7.

	A	B	C	D	E	F	G	H	
1	Shipments of Audio Recordings								
2	(in millions of dollars)								
3		1975	1980	1985	1990				
4	Phonograph Records								
5	LP Albums	1485							
6	Singles								
7	Total Records								

Figure 2.7

4 Press (ENTER)

5 Enter the remaining figures for phonograph-record sales in the appropriate cells.

6 Enter the other sales figures for tapes and compact discs. As you enter the data, remember that the cells in Figure 2.1 that have question marks are kept blank for now.

SAVING THE WORKBOOK

In the following steps, you will save the workbook to disk, giving it the name AUDIO1.

 To save the workbook:

1 Choose **File** and then **Save,** or click the **Save** tool.
The Save As dialog box appears.

2 Select the appropriate disk drive and directory.

3 Enter **audio1** for the file name and select **OK.**

4 Enter your name in the Author section of the Summary Info dialog box and select **OK.**

 If necessary, you can quit Excel now and continue this project later.

CONSTRUCTING FORMULAS AND FUNCTIONS

In the steps that follow, you will use point mode to build a formula that calculates total record sales for 1975.

 To enter the formula for total record sales:

1 Select cell B7.
You will build a formula that adds the sales of LP albums and singles.

2 Type = to activate the formula bar.

3 Use the mouse or arrow keys to select cell B5, which contains sales of LP albums for 1975.

4 Type +

5 Use the mouse or arrow keys to select cell B6, which contains sales of singles for 1975.

6 Click the formula bar Enter box, or press (ENTER) to complete the formula.

Compare the screen with Figure 2.8.

B7	⬇	=B5+B6							
	A	**B**	**C**	**D**	**E**	**F**	**G**	**H**	
1	Shipments of Audio Recordings								
2	(in millions of dollars)								
3		1975	1980	1985	1990				
4	Phonograph Records								
5	LP Albums	1485	2290.3	1280.5	86.5				
6	Singles	211.5	269.3	281	94.4				
7	Total Records	1696.5							
8	Tapes								

Figure 2.8

A formula's result is called its value. The value of this formula is 1696.5, which appears in cell B7. If you look in the formula bar, you will see the formula itself: =B5+B6.

Copying Formulas

In Excel, any type of cell entry—text constant, number constant, or formula—can be duplicated in other cells, but duplication of formulas is most useful. Worksheets tend to have repeating patterns. For example, total record sales for 1980, 1985, and 1990 are all calculated in a manner similar to the calculation of total record sales for 1975. Copying allows you to create a formula once and then have its operation duplicated in other cells that require the same computation.

You will now copy the formula to the cells in the range C7:E7, so that you can also calculate total record sales for 1980, 1985, and 1990.

To copy a formula using the fill handle:

1 Select cell B7, which contains the total records formula for 1975.

2 Position the pointer on the lower-right corner of the active-cell rectangle.

As shown in Figure 2.9, the pointer changes to a small plus sign, which is called the *fill handle*.

B7	⬇	=B5+B6							
	A	**B**	**C**	**D**	**E**	**F**	**G**	**H**	
1	Shipments of Audio Recordings								
2	(in millions of dollars)								
3		1975	1980	1985	1990				
4	Phonograph Records								
5	LP Albums	1485	2290.3	1280.5	86.5				
6	Singles	211.5	269.3	281	94.4				
7	Total Records	1696.5							
8	Tapes								

Figure 2.9

3 Press and hold down the mouse button and drag the fill handle across the row through column E for 1990, as shown in Figure 2.10.

	=B5+B6							
	A	B	C	D	E	F	G	H
1	Shipments of Audio Recordings							
2	(in millions of dollars)							
3		1975	1980	1985	1990			
4	Phonograph Records							
5	LP Albums	1485	2290.3	1280.5	86.5			
6	Singles	211.5	269.3	281	94.4			
7	Total Records	1696.5						
8	Tapes							

Figure 2.10

4 Release the mouse button.
Totals should now appear for the years 1980 through 1990, as shown in Figure 2.11.

B7	=B5+B6							
	A	B	C	D	E	F	G	H
1	Shipments of Audio Recordings							
2	(in millions of dollars)							
3		1975	1980	1985	1990			
4	Phonograph Records							
5	LP Albums	1485	2290.3	1280.5	86.5			
6	Singles	211.5	269.3	281	94.4			
7	Total Records	1696.5	2559.6	1561.5	180.9			
8	Tapes							

Figure 2.11

The steps that follow show an alternative method of copying a cell. You will first use the Undo command, which will undo the copy performed in the previous steps. The Undo command reverses the effect of the most recent command performed and returns the worksheet to the state it was in before the command was issued.

To copy a formula using the Copy and Paste commands:

1 Choose **Edit** and then **Undo Auto Fill.**
Because Auto Fill was the most recently issued command, Excel undoes that command.

2 Select cell B7, which contains the formula for calculating total records for 1975.

3 Choose **Edit** and then **Copy,** or select the **Copy** tool.
Notice the message at the bottom of the application window: *Select destination and press ENTER or choose Paste.*

4 Select the destination range, C7:E7.

5 Press (ENTER) to complete the copy operation.

Tip The drag-and-drop move operation you used at the beginning of this project takes data from one location and places it in another. The Copy command *duplicates* the data—the original data remains.

Recognizing Relative Cell References

What was copied when you performed the previous steps? It wasn't the value 1696.5, because different numbers appear in each of the cells showing totals. To see what is actually in a cell, you can activate that cell and then look in the formula bar.

To examine the relative cell references:

1 Select cell B7, which contains the original formula for total record sales for 1975.

2 Examine the formula bar. The formula is $=B5+B6$.

3 Select cell C7, which contains the formula for 1980. The formula in this cell is a copy of the original formula, but the formula bar shows that this formula is $=C5+C6$.

4 Examine the formulas for 1985 and 1990. These formulas read $=D5+D6$ and $=E5+E6$, respectively.

$=B5+B6$ was not literally copied. In a formula, Excel treats cell references as being *relative* to the cell containing the formula. Although the original formula reads $=B5+B6$, Excel interprets the formula to mean "Take what is two cells above (the formula) and add to it what is one cell above." Unless you instruct the program otherwise, Excel will interpret cell references in formulas as being *relative* to the location of the formula; this is called a ***relative cell reference.*** When cell B7's formula is copied to cell C7, Excel shifts all the references one cell to the right, so the formula in cell C7 reads $=C5+C6$.

Relative cell referencing is why the duplicated formulas each read differently from the original. This adjustment of a copied formula to reflect a new location is most often what you will want Excel to do. For example, the formula that calculates total record sales for 1990 *should* read $=E5+E6$ and not $=B5+B6$.

Using Excel Functions

The total sales for tapes and compact discs also need to be calculated. You could use an addition formula identical to that used to calculate total record sales, but instead you will now try another approach: you will build a formula that contains an Excel function.

A ***function*** is an operation whose use simplifies formula building. Functions are similar to the keys on an electronic calculator that perform specialized calculations. For example, a financial calculator will have a button to calculate the periodic payment amount for a loan. Excel has more than 300 functions, including mathematical, financial, engineering, statistical, date, and text functions. Each function has an identifying name, such as SUM, AVERAGE, and PMT.

When you enter a function as part of a formula, you must follow the function name with a pair of parentheses. For most functions, you also must provide additional items of information inside the parentheses. These additional items, called ***arguments*** to the function, give the function the data it needs to complete its task and compute a ***result.*** If you are supplying multiple arguments, you should separate them with commas. Table 2.1 lists several basic Excel functions and provides examples based on Figure 2.12.

	A	B	C	D	E
1	Principal	$16,000			
2	Interest	10% per year			
3	Term	5 years			
4					
5	Vehicle	Mileage	Price		
6	Velocipede	10,000	$12,000		
7	Steam Cart	20,000	$8,000		
8	Sedan Chair	30,000	$16,000		
9					
10					

Figure 2.12

Table 2.1

Function	Syntax	Description	Example Formula	Example Result
SUM	SUM(range)	Totals a range	=SUM(C6:C*)	$36,000
AVERAGE	AVERAGE(range)	Averages a range	=AVERAGE(B6:B8)	20,000
MIN	MIN(range)	Gets smallest value in range	=MIN(C6:C8)	$8,000
MAX	MAX(range)	Gets largest value in range	=MAX(B6:B8)	30,000
COUNT	COUNT(range)	Counts values in range	=COUNT(A5:C8)	6
IF	IF (test, result if true, result if false)	Performs test; result of function depends on whether test is true or false	=IF(B2<0.12,5,10)	5
PMT	PMT (periodic interest rate, number of periods, principal amount)	Calculates periodic payment for a loan	=PMT(B2/ 12,B3*12,B1)	($339.95)

The SUM function, in its basic form, is designed to total the values in a range of cells. The argument you provide to the function indicates the range it is to sum. For example, =SUM(H1:H12) totals all the values in the range H1:H12. The much longer addition formula =H1+H2+H3+H4+H5+H6+H7+H8+H9+H10+H11+H12 arrives at the same result as =SUM(H1:H12), but the SUM function is a more efficient way of creating the formula.

In the steps that follow, you will use point mode to build a SUM function formula that calculates total tape sales for 1975. As with all formulas, you will start by typing an equal sign, followed by SUM and an open parenthesis. Then, using pointing techniques, you will select the range to be summed, and finally you will end the formula with a close parenthesis.

 To enter the SUM function to calculate total tape sales for 1975:

1 Select cell B11.

2 Type =sum(

SUM can be in upper- or lowercase letters. The screen should resemble Figure 2.13.

B11			=sum(					
	A	B	C	D	E	F	G	H
1	Shipments of Audio Recordings							
2	(in millions of dollars)							
3		1975	1980	1985	1990			
4	Phonograph Records							
5	LP Albums	1485	2290.3	1280.5	86.5			
6	Singles	211.5	269.3	281	94.4			
7	Total Records	1696.5	2559.6	1561.5	180.9			
8	Tapes							
9	8-tracks	583	526.4	25.3	0			
10	Cassettes	98.8	776.4	2411.5	3472.4			
11	Total Tapes	=sum(						
12	Compact Discs							
13	Regular CDs	0	0	389.5	3451.6			

Figure 2.13

3 Select cell B10, cassette sales for 1975, and drag up to cell B9, 8-track sales for 1975. Once the range B9:B10 is selected, release the mouse button. The screen should appear similar to Figure 2.14. Notice that a range selection made in point mode appears with a moving border.

B10			=sum(B9:B10					
	A	B	C	D	E	F	G	H
1	Shipments of Audio Recordings							
2	(in millions of dollars)							
3		1975	1980	1985	1990			
4	Phonograph Records							
5	LP Albums	1485	2290.3	1280.5	86.5			
6	Singles	211.5	269.3	281	94.4			
7	Total Records	1696.5	2559.6	1561.5	180.9			
8	Tapes							
9	8-tracks	583	526.4	25.3	0			
10	Cassettes	98.8	776.4	2411.5	3472.4			
11	Total Tapes	=sum(B9:B10						
12	Compact Discs							
13	Regular CDs	0	0	389.5	3451.6			

Figure 2.14

4 Type **)** and press (ENTER) to complete the formula.

5 Select cell B11.

The completed formula reads =SUM(B9:B10), as shown in Figure 2.15.

B11	▼	=SUM(B9:B10)						
	A	B	C	D	E	F	G	H
1	Shipments of Audio Recordings							
2	(in millions of dollars)							
3		1975	1980	1985	1990			
4	Phonograph Records							
5	LP Albums	1485	2290.3	1280.5	86.5			
6	Singles	211.5	269.3	281	94.4			
7	Total Records	1696.5	2559.6	1561.5	180.9			
8	Tapes							
9	8-tracks	583	526.4	25.3	0			
10	Cassettes	98.8	776.4	2411.5	3472.4			
11	Total Tapes	681.8						
12	Compact Discs							
13	Regular CDs	0	0	389.5	3451.6			

Figure 2.15

For totaling such a small range, the SUM function might appear to have little advantage over a regular addition formula. But functions are more flexible. For example, if you insert a new row between 8-track and cassette sales—such as a row for sales of cassette singles—the range reference in the SUM function automatically expands to include the new information. A simple addition formula would not change to include this new row.

The formula =SUM(B9:B10) uses relative cell references; the formula means "sum up the two-cell range immediately above the formula." Because it uses relative addresses, the formula will work correctly if copied. You will now learn about a shortcut method of building SUM formulas before you copy the SUM formula to other cells.

Using the AutoSum Tool

You can always write a SUM formula manually, but *AutoSum* is a convenient feature that writes a SUM formula for you. The AutoSum button is located on the Standard toolbar. It is labeled with a Greek capital sigma (Σ), which is traditionally used in mathematics to indicate summation.

When you choose the AutoSum command, it looks for ranges surrounding the active cell, and makes a guess about what range you want to total. You have the option of accepting AutoSum's proposed range or selecting another range.

To use the AutoSum tool:

1 Select cell C11, which is to contain total tape sales for 1980.

2 Click the AutoSum tool.
AutoSum writes a formula for you. As shown in Figure 2.16, the formula =SUM(C9:C10) appears in the formula bar. After examining the contents of cells neighboring C11, AutoSum guesses that the range you want to sum is C9:C10, which is correct. At this point, if you wanted to select a different range to be summed, you could.

C9		=SUM(C9:C10)					
	A	**B**	**C**	**D**	**E**	**F**	**G**	**H**
1	Shipments of Audio Recordings							
2	(in millions of dollars)							
3		1975	1980	1985	1990			
4	Phonograph Records							
5	LP Albums	1485	2290.3	1280.5	86.5			
6	Singles	211.5	269.3	281	94.4			
7	Total Records	1696.5	2559.6	1561.5	180.9			
8	Tapes							
9	8-tracks	583	526.4	25.3	0			
10	Cassettes	98.8	776.4	2411.5	3472.4			
11	Total Tapes	681.8	=SUM(C9:C10)					
12	Compact Discs							
13	Regular CDs	0	0	389.5	3451.6			

Figure 2.16

3 Accept this formula by clicking the formula bar Enter box or by pressing (ENTER)

4 Copy the formula for 1980 total tape sales to the other cells designated for total tapes (for the years 1985 and 1990).

5 Select B15:E15, the range of cells that are to contain total CD sales.

6 Select the AutoSum tool.
A SUM formula is entered automatically in each cell of the selected range. The screen should now resemble Figure 2.17.

B15		=SUM(B13:B14)					
	A	**B**	**C**	**D**	**E**	**F**	**G**	**H**
1	Shipments of Audio Recordings							
2	(in millions of dollars)							
3		1975	1980	1985	1990			
4	Phonograph Records							
5	LP Albums	1485	2290.3	1280.5	86.5			
6	Singles	211.5	269.3	281	94.4			
7	Total Records	1696.5	2559.6	1561.5	180.9			
8	Tapes							
9	8-tracks	583	526.4	25.3	0			
10	Cassettes	98.8	776.4	2411.5	3472.4			
11	Total Tapes	681.8	1302.8	2436.8	3472.4			
12	Compact Discs							
13	Regular CDs	0	0	389.5	3451.6			
14	CD Singles	0	0	0	6			
15	Total CDs	0	0	389.5	3457.6			
16	Grand Total							

Figure 2.17

Calculating Grand Totals

You can compute the grand total for a year by adding total records, total tapes, and total CDs. This cannot be calculated using a SUM function of a single range, because you need to add the values of three nonadjacent cells. If you were to construct the formula manually, you would make an addition formula that referred to three separate cells. For example, the grand total for 1975 would be calculated by the formula $=B15+B11+B7$. In the steps that follow, you will not build such an addition formula but will instead learn how AutoSum can automatically generate grand totals. If you select a range that contains subtotals and then select AutoSum, the AutoSum command will analyze the range and write grand total formulas in the first row of blank cells below the range.

To build the grand total formulas using AutoSum:

1 Select the range B5:E15, as shown in Figure 2.18.

	A	B	C	D	E	F	G	H
	B5	1485						
1	Shipments of Audio Recordings							
2	(in millions of dollars)							
3		1975	1980	1985	1990			
4	Phonograph Records							
5	LP Albums	1485	2290.3	1280.5	86.5			
6	Singles	211.5	269.3	281	94.4			
7	Total Records	1696.5	2559.6	1561.5	180.9			
8	Tapes							
9	8-tracks	583	526.4	25.3	0			
10	Cassettes	98.8	776.4	2411.5	3472.4			
11	Total Tapes	681.8	1302.8	2436.8	3472.4			
12	Compact Discs							
13	Regular CDs	0	0	389.5	3451.6			
14	CD Singles	0	0	0	6			
15	Total CDs	0	0	389.5	3457.6			
16	Grand Total							
17								

Figure 2.18

2 Select the AutoSum tool.
Grand total formulas appear in the grand total row, B16:E16.

3 Select cell B16.
The screen should now resemble Figure 2.19. The grand total formula for 1975, created by AutoSum, reads = SUM(B15,B11,B7).

	A	B	C	D	E	F	G	H
	B16	=SUM(B15,B11,B7)						
1	Shipments of Audio Recordings							
2	(in millions of dollars)							
3		1975	1980	1985	1990			
4	Phonograph Records							
5	LP Albums	1485	2290.3	1280.5	86.5			
6	Singles	211.5	269.3	281	94.4			
7	Total Records	1696.5	2559.6	1561.5	180.9			
8	Tapes							
9	8-tracks	583	526.4	25.3	0			
10	Cassettes	98.8	776.4	2411.5	3472.4			
11	Total Tapes	681.8	1302.8	2436.8	3472.4			
12	Compact Discs							
13	Regular CDs	0	0	389.5	3451.6			
14	CD Singles	0	0	0	6			
15	Total CDs	0	0	389.5	3457.6			
16	Grand Total	2378.3	3862.4	4387.8	7110.9			
17								

Figure 2.19

4 Double-click the **Sheet1** tab and rename the sheet **Audio Sales**
5 Save the file.

THE NEXT STEP

In this project, you built the functional parts of a worksheet. In the next project, your primary concern will be the appearance of the worksheet—its format. You will retrieve the worksheet, modify it, format it, print it, and learn more about several different formatting techniques.

This concludes Project 2. You can either exit Excel, or go on to work the Study Questions, Review Exercises, and Assignments.

SUMMARY AND EXERCISES

Summary

- The first step in building a large worksheet is to enter the row and column titles, followed by any other constant information. You can then construct formulas. You should complete the worksheet before doing detailed formatting.
- A cell's contents can be moved easily with the mouse.
- Excel can check the spelling of worksheet data.
- You can use preselection of a range to speed the entry of large amounts of data.
- You can copy a cell using the fill handle, the Copy tool, or the Copy command in the Edit menu. When a formula containing relative cell references is copied, those cell references will change relative to the new cell.
- A function is a built-in mathematical procedure that can be used in a formula. The SUM function, which totals a range of cells, can be typed in or entered using the AutoSum tool.

Key Terms and Operations

Key Terms
argument (to a function)
AutoSum
drag-and-drop
function
move
relative cell reference
result

Operations
Copy cell contents
Move cell contents
Paste cell contents
Spell check
Undo a command

Study Questions

Multiple Choice

1. What should usually be done first when building a large worksheet?
   a. formatting
   b. entry of text and number constants
   c. entry of formulas
   d. saving
   e. column-width adjustment

2. Which of the following best describes what happens when a cell is moved?
   a. The cell's contents are duplicated in another location and you have to erase the contents from the original.
   b. The cell's contents are removed from their original location and placed in a new location.
   c. The Move command is used to reposition the active cell in a new location.
   d. The Move command extends the current selection so it is larger than a single cell.
   e. none of the above

3. What key can be used to move within a preselected data-entry range?
   a. ↓   d. →
   b. ENTER   e. all of the above
   c. F1

4. What kinds of cell entries can be copied?
   a. formulas   d. all of the above
   b. text constants   e. none of the above
   c. number constants

5. Items of information provided to a function are called:
   a. values.   d. parameters.
   b. formulas.   e. arguments.
   c. variables.

6. What is a shorter way of computing
   $= C1 + C2 + C3 + C4 + C5 + C6 + C7 + C8$?
   a. $= ADD(C1..C8)$ d. $= SUMMATION(C1:C8)$
   b. $= TOTAL(C1:C8)$ e. $= C1:C8$
   c. $= SUM(C1:C8)$

7. What tool can be used to quickly create SUM formulas?
   a. Summation
   b. $= SUM$
   c. AutoSum
   d. Sum-O-Matic
   e. Sum command from the Formula menu

8. To have Excel skip all occurrences of a word that it doesn't have in its dictionary, what should you select in the Spelling dialog box?
   a. Ignore   d. Change All
   b. Ignore All   e. Cancel
   c. Change

9. When you use the mouse to copy a cell, the pointer will change to an:
   a. fill handle.   d. insertion symbol.
   b. double arrow.   e. hollow arrow.
   c. hollow plus sign.

10. Suppose the formula $= SUM(A1:A5)$ was entered in cell A6. What best describes the meaning of the formula?
    a. Total the cells A1 and A5.
    b. Total the five-cell range immediately above.
    c. Count the number of entries in the range A1 through A5.
    d. Total the cells A1, A2, A3, and A4.
    e. none of the above

Short Answer

1. What is a more efficient way to compute
   $= E7 + E8 + E9 + E10 + E11 + E12 + E13$ and what are the reasons to
   use it?

2. What effect does the Undo command have on a worksheet?

3. If the spelling checker pauses on a word in the worksheet, does this
   mean the word is misspelled? If so, what can be done?

4. What technique can be used to speed the entry of a block of data in a
   worksheet?

5. When a formula is copied to another cell, is it the value (result) of the
   formula that appears in the new cell?

6. What does the AutoSum tool do?

7. Approximately how many built-in functions does Excel have?

8. If the formula $= SUM(B2:B5)$ were entered into cell B6, how would
   the formula change if copied to cell C6?

9. What is a simple way to indent text entries?

10. What menu commands can be used to copy a cell?

For Discussion

1. Describe the general steps you should follow when building a worksheet.

2. Describe how to move a cell.

3. Describe how to copy a cell.

4. Describe relative cell referencing and how this affects the way formulas
   are copied.

5. Describe functions and their components. Use the example of the
   SUM function.

Review Exercises

Municipal Waste Trends

The Environmental Protection Agency (EPA) reports the information
shown in Figure 2.20 about the composition of municipal waste and how it
has changed over time (the figures reflect pounds per day per person).
Build a worksheet to present this data and calculate the various totals. Use
the SUM function to compute the required totals. Save an unformatted
version of the workbook to disk, under the name EPA1, for use in a Review
Exercise at the end of Project 3. After you save the workbook, experiment
with AutoFormat options but do not save the formatted version.

	A	B	C	D	E	F	G	H	I
1	Municipal Waste								
2		1960	1970	1980	1990				
3	Nonfood Wastes								
4	Paper	0.91	1.19	1.32	1.6				
5	Glass	0.2	0.34	0.36	0.28				
6	Plastics	0.01	0.08	0.19	0.32				
7	Total Nonfood	?	?	?	?				
8	Other								
9	Food	0.37	0.34	0.32	0.29				
10	Yard	0.61	0.62	0.66	0.7				
11	Total Other	?	?	?	?				
12	Grand Total	?	?	?	?				
13									

Figure 2.20

Winter Olympic Medals

Figure 2.21 shows the number of medals won by selected countries during the 1992 Winter Olympic Games. Create a worksheet that presents this information and calculates the required totals. Note that both row and column totals are computed. Save an unformatted version of the workbook to disk; use the name OLYMPIC1. Experiment with AutoFormat if you wish.

	A	B	C	D	E	F	G	H	I
1	1992 Winter Olympiad								
2									
3	Country	Gold	Silver	Bronze	Total				
4	Germany	10	10	6	?				
5	Unified Team	9	6	8	?				
6	Austria	6	7	8	?				
7	Norway	9	6	5	?				
8	Total	?	?	?	?				
9									

Figure 2.21

Assignments

Coffee House Income

Open the file COFFEE1 that you created in an assignment at the end of Project 1. Modify the worksheet, as shown in Figure 2.22, to show sales figures for other kinds of coffee. Note that the original formula for income uses relative addresses and can be copied down to compute income for the other coffee flavors. Create SUM formulas that compute totals for the number sold and income. Do not format the worksheet. Use the Save As command from the File menu to save the updated workbook under a new name, COFFEE2.

	A	B	C	D	E	F	G	H	I
1	Coffee	Cost	Selling Price	No. Sold	Income				
2	House Blend	0.39	0.95	60	?				
3	Espresso	0.61	1.25	12	?				
4	Cappuccino	0.74	1.5	22	?				
5	Cafe Mocha	0.55	1.45	35	?				
6	Total			?	?				
7									
8									

Figure 2.22

Personal Budget

Build a personal budget that describes your income and expenses for a typical month. Begin with income items such as salary, tips, and interest earned, grouped and indented under the heading *Income*. Build a formula that calculates a total of the income items. Similarly, group expense items such as food, rent, electricity, and insurance, and calculate their total. Finally, build a formula to calculate the difference between total income and total expenses. Do not format the worksheet, but save it to disk under the name BUDGET1 for use in another project.

Space Payloads

Figure 2.23 documents the number of payloads (objects carried into space) launched by various countries for the years 1988 through 1991. Construct a worksheet to present this data and compute the totals. You can use the SUM function to calculate column totals; you can calculate the average payloads per year for each country by dividing its row total by 4 or by using the AVERAGE function. Do not format the worksheet; save it to disk under the name SPACE1. You will use it in an assignment in Project 3.

	A	B	C	D	E	F	G	H	I
1	Space Payloads								
2									
3		1988	1989	1990	1991	Average			
4	USSR	107	95	96	101	?			
5	United States	15	22	31	30	?			
6	Japan	2	4	7	2	?			
7	Total	?	?	?	?	?			
8									

Figure 2.23

Objectives

After completing this project, you should be able to:

▶ Identify and analyze formulas in a worksheet

▶ Insert blank cells into a worksheet

▶ Recognize and correct circular references

▶ Clear cells

▶ Center titles across columns

▶ Change row height

▶ Print the worksheet

▶ Change the standard format

▶ Understand and modify styles

▶ Use information windows

CASE STUDY: SALES OF AUDIO RECORDINGS

In this project you will continue to work with the audio recordings worksheet from Project 2. Sales of cassette singles, shown below, will need to be included in the worksheet. The new data will appear in between the rows labeled *Cassettes* and *Compact Discs*.

	1975	1980	1985	1990
Cassette Singles	0	0	0	87.4

Once this information is added, some formulas in the worksheet will need to be adjusted to reflect the new information. In the final phase of the project, you will format the worksheet and learn about cell styles.

Designing the Solution

First you will need to make room for the new information on sales of cassette singles. You could move the lower half of the worksheet (A11:E16) down one row to create the needed space, but for this exercise you will use the Insert command. Using the Insert command is easier because it does not require that you select as large an area.

MODIFYING A WORKSHEET

When you modify a worksheet, you must consider how the change will affect other parts of the worksheet. You need to analyze carefully the way formulas depend on other cells. Usually formulas adjust automatically as you'd like them to, but in some cases they do not. Consider the consequences of inserting a new row: the area where you want to place extra cells might be quite small, but if you choose to insert an entire row, a new blank row will extend across the entire worksheet, perhaps inserting blank space through the middle of some other portion of the worksheet that you do not want to affect. Deleting an entire row or column is even more sensitive, because information is removed all the way across or down the worksheet.

Reminder You should save a workbook before performing a command that might significantly affect it. You should also consider the possible side effects of using a command. Save before you perform a command, then if the workbook is adversely affected by the command, you can close the damaged workbook without saving, return to your previously saved copy, and try again.

Tracing Precedents and Dependents

The Excel Auditing toolbar (and the Auditing option in the Tools menu) has several features that make it easier for you to understand the formulas in a worksheet. If you select a cell containing a formula and then select the Trace Precedents tool, Excel will draw *tracer arrows* on the screen from all the cells upon which that formula directly depends. These cells are called *direct precedents.* Selecting the Trace Precedents tool again will draw tracer arrows from *indirect precedents*—cells upon which the direct precedent cells depend. The Trace Precedents tool can be used repeatedly to trace back to the original precedents. If the precedent cells comprise a range, a box is drawn around the range.

You can also use the Trace Dependents tool to draw tracer arrows to direct and indirect *dependents*—cells that contain formulas that refer to (depend on) a particular cell. Whether you are tracing dependents or precedents, the tracer arrows have large dots on one end to show precedent cells and arrowheads on the other end to show dependent cells. The arrowheads indicate the direction of information flow.

In the following steps, you will use these tools to review how the formulas work in the audio sales worksheet.

 To open and prepare the AUDIO1 workbook:

1 Choose **File** and then **Open,** and open the AUDIO1.XLS workbook file you saved in Project 2.

2 Click the **Audio Sales** sheet tab, if necessary.

To display the Auditing toolbar:

1 Choose **View** and then **Toolbars,** and display the Auditing toolbar.

2 Dock the Auditing toolbar on the right side of the vertical scroll bar. The screen should resemble Figure 3.1.

	A	B	C	D	E	F	G	H
1	Shipments of Audio Recordings							
2	(in millions of dollars)							
3		1975	1980	1985	1990			
4	Phonograph Records							
5	LP Albums	1485	2290.3	1280.5	86.5			
6	Singles	211.5	269.3	281	94.4			
7	Total Records	1696.5	2559.6	1561.5	180.9			
8	Tapes							
9	8-tracks	583	526.4	25.3	0			
10	Cassettes	98.8	776.4	2411.5	3472.4			
11	Total Tapes	681.8	1302.8	2436.8	3472.4			

Figure 3.1

To trace direct precedents:

1 Select cell B16, which contains the formula for the grand total for 1975.

2 Click the **Trace Precedents** tool.

The screen should resemble Figure 3.2. Large dots appear in cells B7, B11, and B15; these dots mark precedent cells. The arrowhead points to cell B16, indicating that the information from the marked precedent cells feeds into the formula in cell B16.

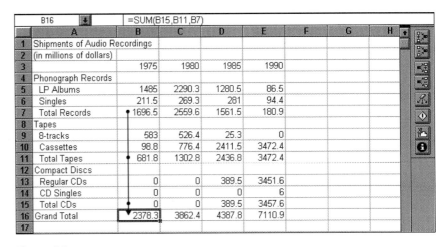

Figure 3.2

The formula in cell B16 depends *directly* on the three cells marked with dots. Remember that the three cells are themselves totals; in the next steps, you will select the indirect precedents of the grand total formula.

To trace indirect precedents:

1 Click the **Trace Precedents** tool again.
The screen should now resemble Figure 3.3, which shows indirect precedents along with direct precedents. For example, cell B11 depends on the range B9:B10, so this range is outlined, a dot appears in the first cell of the range, and the connected arrow points into cell B11.

B16	=SUM(B15,B11,B7)						
	A	**B**	**C**	**D**	**E**	**F**	**G**	**H**
1	Shipments of Audio Recordings							
2	(in millions of dollars)							
3		1975	1980	1985	1990			
4	Phonograph Records							
5	LP Albums	1485	2290.3	1280.5	86.5			
6	Singles	211.5	269.3	281	94.4			
7	Total Records	1696.5	2559.6	1561.5	180.9			
8	Tapes							
9	8-tracks	583	526.4	25.3	0			
10	Cassettes	98.8	776.4	2411.5	3472.4			
11	Total Tapes	681.8	1302.8	2436.8	3472.4			
12	Compact Discs							
13	Regular CDs	0	0	389.5	3451.6			
14	CD Singles	0	0	0	6			
15	Total CDs	0	0	389.5	3457.6			
16	Grand Total	2378.3	3862.4	4387.8	7110.9			
17								

Figure 3.3

2 Click the **Trace Precedents** tool again.
Excel beeps, signaling that there are no further precedents to be traced.

 3 Click the **Remove Precedent Arrows** tool.
The last traced precedence arrows are cleared; the screen should once again resemble Figure 3.2.

It is sometimes useful, when analyzing a worksheet with multiple levels of precedent cells, to be able to jump quickly from a cell to its precedent. The following steps demonstrate this feature.

 To use tracer arrows to activate dependent and precedent cells:

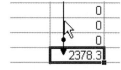

1 Position the pointer so it forms an arrow shape, just touching anywhere along the tracer arrow.

2 Double-click.
The active cell switches to cell B7, at the opposite end of the tracer arrow.

3 Make sure the pointer arrow just touches the tracer arrow and double-click.
The active cell switches back to cell B16.

 4 Click the **Remove All Arrows** tool.
No precedence arrows are visible now. The Remove Precedent Arrows tool could also have been used.

To trace dependents:

1 Select cell B5, LP album sales for 1975.

2 Click the **Trace Dependents** tool.
A tracer arrow appears, showing that cell B7, which computes total record sales for 1975, depends on the selected cell. The screen should resemble Figure 3.4.

B5	⏷	1485						
	A	B	C	D	E	F	G	H
1	Shipments of Audio Recordings							
2	(in millions of dollars)							
3		1975	1980	1985	1990			
4	Phonograph Records							
5	LP Albums	1485	2290.3	1280.5	86.5			
6	Singles	211.5	269.3	281	94.4			
7	Total Records	1696.5	2559.6	1561.5	180.9			
8	Tapes							

Figure 3.4

3 Click the **Trace Dependents** tool again.
Another tracer arrow appears, showing that cell B16, which computes the grand total for 1975, depends indirectly on the selected cell. The screen should resemble Figure 3.5.

B5	⏷	1485						
	A	B	C	D	E	F	G	H
1	Shipments of Audio Recordings							
2	(in millions of dollars)							
3		1975	1980	1985	1990			
4	Phonograph Records							
5	LP Albums	1485	2290.3	1280.5	86.5			
6	Singles	211.5	269.3	281	94.4			
7	Total Records	1696.5	2559.6	1561.5	180.9			
8	Tapes							
9	8-tracks	583	526.4	25.3	0			
10	Cassettes	98.8	776.4	2411.5	3472.4			
11	Total Tapes	681.8	1302.8	2436.8	3472.4			
12	Compact Discs							
13	Regular CDs	0	0	389.5	3451.6			
14	CD Singles	0	0	0	6			
15	Total CDs	0	0	389.5	3457.6			
16	Grand Total	2378.3	3862.4	4387.8	7110.9			
17								

Figure 3.5

4 Click the **Trace Dependents** tool again.
There are no further dependent cells.

5 Click the **Remove All Arrows** tool.
No tracer arrows should be visible.

Bearing in mind the modification planned for this worksheet, you will want to make sure that the data for sales of cassette singles, once entered into the worksheet, is also included in the total tape sales formula. You shouldn't have to worry about the grand total formula in this case, because it depends on the total tape sales formula.

Inserting Cells in a Worksheet

A range of blank cells needs to be inserted directly above the total tapes row. Excel lets you insert either a range of cells or an entire column or row. It is often safest to insert a range, because the effect doesn't stretch as far across the worksheet as it does when an entire column or row is inserted.

To insert blank cells:

1 Select cell A11, the cell containing the text *Total Tapes*, and then select the range A11:E11.

2 Choose **Insert** and then **Cells.**

The Insert dialog box appears, as shown in Figure 3.6. Because the selected range is wider than it is deep, Excel presumes that you want to shift the selected range (and everything underneath it) down, which is correct.

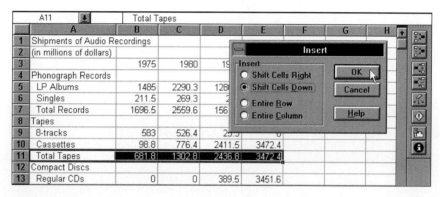

Figure 3.6

3 Select **OK.**

A new range of blank cells is now available.

To enter the new information:

1 Select cell A11.

2 Press (SPACE) twice and enter `Cassette Singles`

3 Enter `0` in cells B11, C11, and D11.

4 Enter `87.4` in cell E11.

Your worksheet should now resemble Figure 3.7.

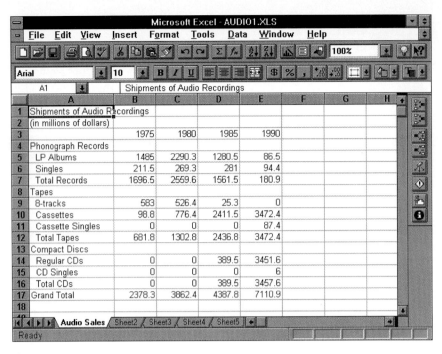

Figure 3.7

Assessing the Effects of a Command

Now that the data for sales of cassette singles is entered, you can determine whether adjustments are required to accommodate the new information. The sales of cassette singles should be included in the computation of total tapes, so you should examine the formulas in the total tapes row.

To examine the total tapes formulas:

1 Select cell E12.

The formula reads =SUM(E9:E10), so the range being summed does *not* include the new information in cell E11.

2 Trace the direct precedents of cell E12.

As shown in Figure 3.8, this confirms visually that the range being totaled, B9:B10, is not correct. For the total tape sales formula to be correct, it should depend not only on the sales of 8-tracks and cassettes, but on cassette singles as well.

8	Tapes				
9	8-tracks	583	526.4	25.3	0
10	Cassettes	98.8	776.4	2411.5	3472.4
11	Cassette Singles	0	0	0	87.4
12	Total Tapes	681.8	1302.8	2436.8	3472.4
13	Compact Discs				

Figure 3.8

3 Remove all tracer arrows.

Because cassette singles had no sales for 1975 through 1985, you might conclude that the only formula that needs to be fixed is the one for 1990. But leaving the other total tape sales formulas unchanged would be a serious design mistake; it would create an inconsistency in the worksheet that could later prove troublesome. What if the worksheet were reused and different years' data (all with sales of cassette singles) was entered over the older data? If the incorrect tape sales formulas were still present, their results would not include the new amounts.

You may have wondered why the range referred to in the SUM function did not automatically adjust. Excel will automatically adjust a range reference within a formula if the newly inserted row is *within* the existing top and bottom rows of the range, but not if the inserted row lies outside the existing range. Had the row for cassette singles been inserted between the 8-track and cassette rows, Excel would have adjusted the range reference in the formula.

In the steps that follow, you will build a new SUM formula for total tape sales for 1975 and copy the formula to the other total tape cells. Please follow the steps carefully, because the steps will purposefully instruct you to make a common mistake that you will then learn how to correct. *Do not use AutoSum for these steps.*

To build a self-referential SUM formula:

1 Select cell B12, where the formula for total tape sales for 1975 resides.

2 Type =sum(

3 Select cell B9, 8-track tape sales for 1975.

4 Drag the selection down through cell B12 to highlight the range B9:B12.

5 Type) and press (ENTER)
A dialog box appears with the message "Cannot resolve circular references."

6 Select **OK** to bypass the dialog box.

7 Select cell B12.

8 Trace the direct precedents of cell B12.

9 Select another cell away from the tracer area to see the tracer arrow more clearly.
As shown in Figure 3.9, cell B12 is dependent upon itself. Note that the Status bar shows "Circular: B17."

	A	B	C	D	E	F	G	H
1	Shipments of Audio Recordings							
2	(in millions of dollars)							
3		1975	1980	1985	1990			
4	Phonograph Records							
5	LP Albums	1485	2290.3	1280.5	86.5			
6	Singles	211.5	269.3	281	94.4			
7	Total Records	1696.5	2559.6	1561.5	180.9			
8	Tapes							
9	8-tracks	583	526.4	25.3	0			
10	Cassettes	98.8	776.4	2411.5	3472.4			
11	Cassette Singles	0	0	0	87.4			
12	Total Tapes	0	1302.8	2436.8	3472.4			
13	Compact Discs							
14	Regular CDs	0	0	389.5	3451.6			
15	CD Singles	0	0	0	6			
16	Total CDs	0	0	389.5	3457.6			
17	Grand Total	2378.3	3862.4	4387.8	7110.9			
18								

Audio Sales / Sheet2 / Sheet3 / Sheet4 / Sheet5

Ready   Circular: B17

Figure 3.9

10 Remove all tracer arrows.

Understanding Circular References

A *circular reference* occurs when a formula refers, either directly or indirectly, to itself. This kind of formula usually doesn't make any sense, so it is considered an error. The erroneous formula you just entered is an example of one of the more common places where circular references can occur. When using the mouse or arrow keys to select a range within a formula, you should drag or select away from the formula: this will reduce the chance of inadvertently including the formula's own cell within the selected range.

In the following steps, you will rebuild the formula. Although it is not necessary to clear the old formulas first, you will do so to learn about the Clear command.

To clear a range of cells:

1 Select the range B12:E12, which contains the total tape formulas.

2 Choose **Edit** and then **Clear.**
The Clear submenu appears.

3 Select **All.**
The formulas in the range B12:E12 should now be erased.

> **Tip** Another way to clear the contents of a selection is click the right mouse button to access the shortcut menu, and then choose Clear Contents. An even quicker way is to press ⌐DEL⌐ after making the selection.

Clearing cells is not the same as deleting them. When cells are cleared, their contents are erased but the cells themselves remain. Deleting cells, which you haven't done yet, removes the cells from the worksheet and shifts neighboring cells into take up the space.

You will now create the correct formula, copy it to the total tapes cells, and save the workbook.

To build the correct total tapes formula:

1 Select the range B12:E12, the cells that will contain total tape sales for each year.

2 Click the **AutoSum** tool.
SUM formulas appear in each of the selected cells.

3 Select cell B12.
The correct formula, =SUM(B9:B11), is visible in the formula bar.

4 Click the **Trace Precedents** tool, and then select another cell away from the trace area.
A tracer arrow and range outline appear, confirming that the range being totaled is correct, as shown in Figure 3.10.

8	Tapes				
9	8-tracks	583	526.4	25.3	0
10	Cassettes	98.8	776.4	2411.5	3472.4
11	Cassette Singles	0	0	0	07.4
12	Total Tapes	681.8	1302.8	2436.8	3559.8
13	Compact Discs				

Figure 3.10

5 Click the **Remove All Arrows** tool.

6 Undock and close the Auditing toolbar.
The screen should look like Figure 3.11.

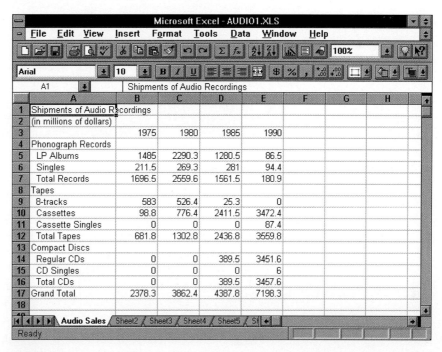

Figure 3.11

7 Save the workbook using the Save command from the File menu
or the Save button.
It is very important to save at this point, because in later steps you will
need to use this version of the workbook.

ENHANCING THE WORKSHEET

As in Project 1, you will use AutoFormat to format a worksheet. The
AutoFormat command works best on worksheets that have a relatively
simple and consistent structure. This worksheet will require several manual
adjustments after you use AutoFormat.

To use AutoFormat with the worksheet:

1 Select the range A1:E17.
A quick way to do this, provided you did not type any extraneous information
after the grand total for 1990, is to select cell A1 by pressing (CTRL) + (HOME)
and then press (CTRL) + (SHFT) + (END) (use (END) on the numeric keyboard
with (NUM LOCK) off).

2 Choose **Format** and then **AutoFormat.**
The AutoFormat dialog box appears.

3 Select the **Accounting 1** table format and select **OK,** as shown in
Figure 3.12.

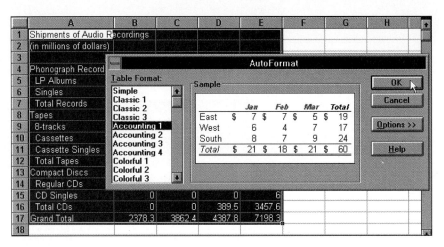

Figure 3.12

The worksheet is automatically formatted. Notice that in the Accounting 1 table format, values of zero are displayed as centered hyphens.

4 Select cell A1 to cancel the larger selected range.

You will notice that AutoFormat made column A too wide. It based its decision on the length of the worksheet's main title, *Shipments of Audio Recordings*. You will center this title across all the columns of the worksheet in the next series of steps, so column A does not need to be this wide.

5 Adjust the width of column A to about 22, so it is slightly wider than Phonograph Records, as shown in Figure 3.13.

Width: 22.00	Shipments of Audio Recordings					
	A	B	C	D	E	F	G
1	**Shipments of Audio Recordings**					
2	**(in millions of dollars)**					
3		*1975*	*1980*	*1985*	*1990*	
4	***Phonograph Records***					
5	LP Albums	$1,485.00	$2,290.30	$1,280.50	$ 86.50	
6	Singles	211.50	269.30	281.00	94.40	
7	*Total Records*	$1,696.50	$2,559.60	$1,561.50	$ 180.90	
8	***Tapes***					
9	8-tracks	$ 583.00	$ 526.40	$ 25.30	$ -	
10	Cassettes	98.80	776.40	2,411.50	3,472.40	
11	Cassette Singles	-	-	-	87.40	
12	*Total Tapes*	$ 681.80	$1,302.80	$2,436.80	$3,559.80	
13	***Compact Discs***					
14	Regular CDs	$ -	$ -	$ 389.50	$3,451.60	
15	CD Singles	-	-	-	6.00	
16	*Total CDs*	$ -	$ -	$ 389.50	$3,457.60	

Figure 3.13

Centering Text across Columns

The main title, *Shipments of Audio Recordings*, and the subtitle, *(in millions of dollars)*, would look better centered over the worksheet. You can use the Center Across Columns tool in the Formatting toolbar to center the contents of one cell over a selected group of columns. This tool requires that you select a range whose leftmost cells contain the text you want to center; the selected range should extend across the columns that you want the text centered within.

To center text across columns:

1 Select cell A1, which contains the text *Shipments of Audio Recordings*.

2 As shown in Figure 3.14, extend the selection to include A1:E2, which includes the subtitle row (row 2) and the column for 1990 (column E).

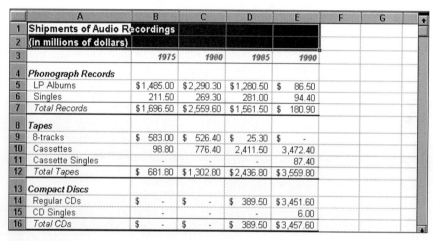

	A	B	C	D	E	F	G
1	Shipments of Audio Recordings						
2	(in millions of dollars)						
3		1975	1980	1985	1990		
4	Phonograph Records						
5	LP Albums	$1,485.00	$2,290.30	$1,280.50	$ 86.50		
6	Singles	211.50	269.30	281.00	94.40		
7	Total Records	$1,696.50	$2,559.60	$1,561.50	$ 180.90		
8	Tapes						
9	8-tracks	$ 583.00	$ 526.40	$ 25.30	$ -		
10	Cassettes	98.80	776.40	2,411.50	3,472.40		
11	Cassette Singles	-	-	-	87.40		
12	Total Tapes	$ 681.80	$1,302.80	$2,436.80	$3,559.80		
13	Compact Discs						
14	Regular CDs	$ -	$ -	$ 389.50	$3,451.60		
15	CD Singles	-	-	-	6.00		
16	Total CDs	$ -	$ -	$ 389.50	$3,457.60		

Figure 3.14

3 Release the mouse button and click the **Center Across Columns** tool on the Formatting toolbar.

4 Click any cell to cancel the selection.

The title and subtitle should now be centered above the worksheet, as shown in Figure 3.15. *Note that the text for these titles is still stored in cells A1 and A2.*

	A	B	C	D	E	F	G
1	Shipments of Audio Recordings						
2	(in millions of dollars)						
3		1975	1980	1985	1990		
4	Phonograph Records						
5	LP Albums	$1,485.00	$2,290.30	$1,280.50	$ 86.50		
6	Singles	211.50	269.30	281.00	94.40		
7	Total Records	$1,696.50	$2,559.60	$1,561.50	$ 180.90		
8	Tapes						
9	8-tracks	$ 583.00	$ 526.40	$ 25.30	$ -		
10	Cassettes	98.80	776.40	2,411.50	3,472.40		
11	Cassette Singles	-	-	-	87.40		
12	Total Tapes	$ 681.80	$1,302.80	$2,436.80	$3,559.80		
13	Compact Discs						
14	Regular CDs	$ -	$ -	$ 389.50	$3,451.60		
15	CD Singles	-	-	-	6.00		
16	Total CDs	$ -	$ -	$ 389.50	$3,457.60		

Figure 3.15

Changing Row Height

The worksheet might look better if there were more vertical space between the titles and the years. To create this extra space, you could insert a new row. However, you will have more precise control over the spacing if instead you change the height of the years' row. This process is very similar to that of changing the width of a column.

Whereas the width of a column is measured in characters, the height of a row is measured in **points,** a traditional type-measurement unit employed by printers and typographers. A point, abbreviated as *pt.,* is equal to one-72nd of an inch.

To change row height:

1 Position the pointer so it is over the *lower* edge of the heading for row 3 (on the line separating rows 3 and 4). The pointer should change to a vertical double arrow.

2 Hold down the mouse button and drag downward slightly to extend the lower edge of row 3. The reference area in the formula bar shows the height. Drag the mouse to set the height anywhere between 23 and 28 points, and then release the mouse button, as shown in Figure 3.16.

Height: 25.50							
	A	B	C	D	E	F	G
1	Shipments of Audio Recordings						
2	(in millions of dollars)						
3		1975	1980	1985	1990		
4	Phonograph Records						
5	LP Albums	$1,485.00	$2,290.30	$1,280.50	$ 86.50		
6	Singles	211.50	269.30	281.00	94.40		
7	Total Records	$1,696.50	$2,559.60	$1,561.50	$ 180.90		

Figure 3.16

Saving the Workbook under a Different Name

The worksheet has once again changed significantly. In the steps that follow, you will save the workbook before you print it. Because you will need to work with the earlier, unformatted version of the audio worksheet in later steps, you will save this formatted workbook with a different name.

To save the workbook with a different name:

1 Choose **File** and then **Save As.**
The Save As dialog box appears.

2 Type `audio2` for the file name and select **OK.**

EXIT If necessary, you can quit Excel now, and continue this project later.

PRINTING THE WORKSHEET

Before you print a worksheet, you should check your printer to make sure it is turned on, has paper, and is online (communicating with the computer). If it is a dot-matrix printer, you should ensure that the paper is properly lined up.

 To print the worksheet:

1 Make sure your printer is ready.

2 Choose **File** and then **Print.**
The Print dialog box appears.

3 Select **OK.**
You may notice dotted lines on the screen—these indicate page breaks in the worksheet.

Removing Cell Gridlines

Your printout should look something like Figure 3.17. Worksheets that have been formatted with border lines usually look better (and are less confusing to use) if the cell gridlines are turned off.

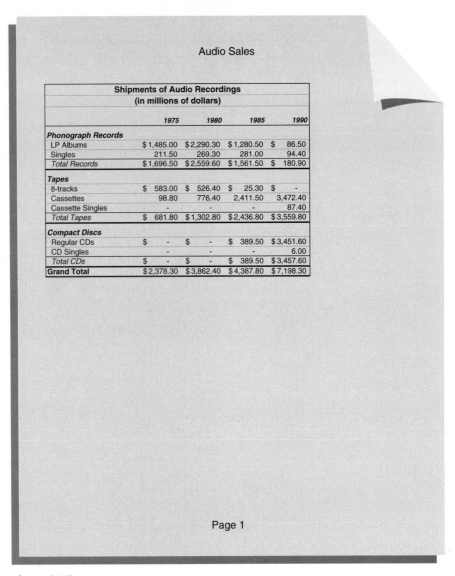

Shipments of Audio Recordings (in millions of dollars)			
1975	1980	1985	1990
Phonograph Records			
LP Albums	$1,485.00	$2,290.30	$1,280.50	$ 86.50
Singles	211.50	269.30	281.00	94.40
Total Records	$1,696.50	$2,559.60	$1,561.50	$ 180.90
Tapes			
8-tracks	$ 583.00	$ 526.40	$ 25.30	$ -
Cassettes	98.80	776.40	2,411.50	3,472.40
Cassette Singles	-	-	-	87.40
Total Tapes	$ 681.80	$1,302.80	$2,436.80	$3,559.80
Compact Discs			
Regular CDs	$ -	$ -	$ 389.50	$3,451.60
CD Singles	-	-	-	6.00
Total CDs	$ -	$ -	$ 389.50	$3,457.60
Grand Total	$2,378.30	$3,862.40	$4,387.80	$7,198.30

Audio Sales

Page 1

Figure 3.17

To remove cell gridlines:

1 Choose **Tools** and then **Options.**
The Options dialog box appears.

2 Click the **View** tab.

3 Clear the **Gridlines** check box and select **OK,** as shown in Figure 3.18.

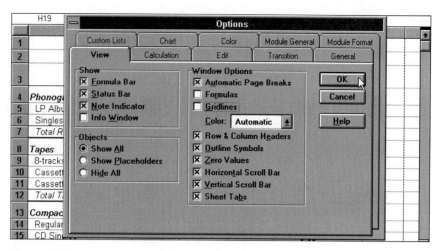

Figure 3.18

The worksheet now appears without gridlines. It will also print without gridlines.

4 Click the **Print** tool as a shortcut to print the file again. Your printout should look similar to Figure 3.19.

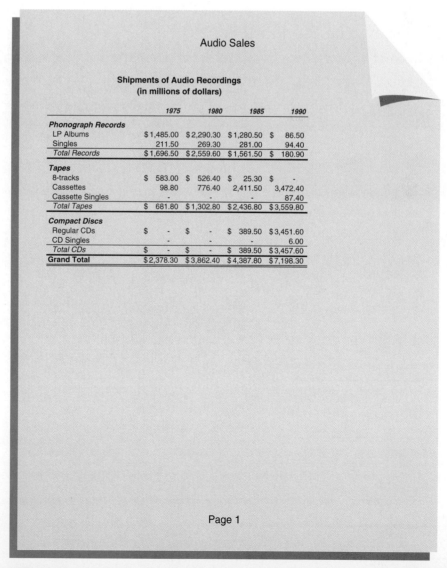

Figure 3.19

5 Close (and save) the AUDIO2 workbook. You will use the original AUDIO1 workbook for the remainder of this project.

Tip If you want to preserve cell gridlines on-screen but do not want to have them appear on printouts, first choose Options from the Tools menu, select the View tab, and select the Gridlines check box so it is checked. Then choose Page Setup from the File menu, select the Sheet tab, and clear the Gridlines check box.

WORKING WITH STYLES

In Excel, a *style* is a group of format settings that are collected and referred to by a name. The Normal style is what is used by default for all cell entries, unless you specify a different style.

In the steps that follow, you will work with the original, unformatted AUDIO1 workbook. You will be changing some of the characteristics of the Normal style, but you will not be switching any cells from one style (Normal) to another (such as Comma style). Normal style is the only style used in this project.

Changing the Standard Font

With most printers, you will achieve the best printouts with the smoothest lines and clearest type if you use TrueType fonts. A *font* in Excel is a typeface—the form or design of letters and characters. The TrueType font technology is built directly into Windows. Several basic TrueType fonts are also provided with Windows. TrueType has the additional advantage of making the screen appear very similar to the printout. Excel's default font, called Arial, is a TrueType font.

The Style dialog box includes a brief description of the style. Six check boxes correspond to the formatting attributes that a style can include: Number, Alignment, Font, Border, Patterns, and Protection. The Normal style specifies all of these. In this section, you will learn how to change the Normal style setting for a worksheet so Courier New, another TrueType font, is used.

 To change the standard font:

1 Open the AUDIO1 workbook.

2 Choose **Format** and then **Style.**
The Style dialog box appears.
The name Normal should appear in the Style Name list box. The font currently being used for the Normal style is Arial 10 (Arial, size of 10 points). You will change this to Courier New.

3 Select **Modify.**
A Format Cells dialog box appears, with tabs for each formatting attribute, as shown in Figure 3.20. You will now change the font.

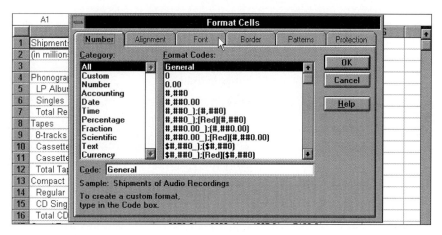

Figure 3.20

4 Click the **Font** tab.
The Font tab appears. Names of TrueType fonts are preceded by a "TT" logo.

5 Select the TrueType **Courier New** font in the list box (you may need to scroll through the alphabetical list) as shown in Figure 3.21, and then select **OK**.

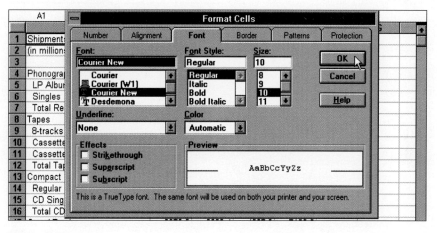

Figure 3.21

6 Select **OK** in the Style dialog box to complete the new definition of the Normal style.
All existing cell entries in this worksheet are in the Normal style and now appear in the TrueType Courier New font. The Normal style will also be in effect if you type new cell entries, so future entries will also appear in the Courier New font.

Formatting the Worksheet

In the steps that follow, you will format and adjust the worksheet, just as you did at the beginning of this project. These steps are condensed; refer back to the beginning of the project if necessary.

To format the worksheet:

1 Perform an AutoFormat on the range A1:E17, using the Accounting 1 table format.

2 Narrow column A to a width of about 20.

3 Center the main title and subtitle across columns A through E.

4 Turn off cell gridlines.

5 Increase the height of row 3 to about 25 points.

Your worksheet should look similar to Figure 3.22.

	A	B	C	D	E	F
1		Shipments of Audio Recordings				
2		(in millions of dollars)				
3		1975	1980	1985	1990	
4	Phonograph Records					
5	LP Albums	$1,485.00	$2,290.30	$1,280.50	$ 86.50	
6	Singles	211.50	269.30	281.00	94.40	
7	Total Records	$1,696.50	$2,559.60	$1,561.50	$ 180.90	
8	Tapes					
9	8-tracks	$ 583.00	$ 526.40	$ 25.30	$ –	
10	Cassettes	98.80	776.40	2,411.50	3,472.40	
11	Cassette Singles	–	–	–	87.40	
12	Total Tapes	$ 681.80	$1,302.80	$2,436.80	$3,559.80	
13	Compact Discs					
14	Regular CDs	$ –	$ –	$ 389.50	$3,451.60	

Figure 3.22

6 Save the workbook under the name AUDIO3.

7 Print the worksheet.

Compare your new printout with the earlier ones you made. Notice that the Courier New font resembles typewriter-style characters. You may wish to experiment with the other TrueType fonts on the system you are using.

USING INFORMATION WINDOWS

You have seen that several kinds of data can be stored in a cell and that a wide variety of formatting attributes can be applied to a cell. An *information window* lets you examine a cell's contents more closely. In the steps that follow, you will open an information window and then use it to find out more about the cells in your worksheet. Remember that some of these cells were extensively changed by the AutoFormat command. By studying these changes, you will better understand how to control worksheet formatting without using AutoFormat.

To activate an information window:

1 Select cell A1.

2 Choose **Tools** and then **Options.**
The Options dialog box appears.

3 Click the **View** tab.

4 Make sure the Info Window option is checked, and then select **OK.**

A new window will appear. If the AUDIO3 workbook was maximized prior to this, the new information window will completely cover the worksheet window, as shown in Figure 3.23; otherwise, a small information window will appear on top of the worksheet window. Notice that a different menu appears on the menu bar: this is because an information window is not a worksheet, and a different set of commands applies.

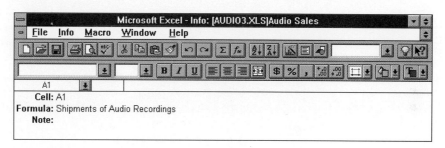

Figure 3.23

Switching between Windows

If several windows are visible on the screen at once, you can make a particular window active by clicking anywhere in that window. The active window will appear with a darker title bar. You can also use the list in the Window menu to choose a window by name; the names of currently open windows are included in the Window menu.

To switch between windows using the Window menu:

1 Activate the AUDIO3.XLS workbook window by opening the **Window** menu and choosing **AUDIO3.XLS.**
The information window seems to disappear, but it is just underneath the AUDIO3 worksheet window.

2 To reactivate the information window, open the **Window** menu and choose **Info: [AUDIO3.XLS]Audio Sales.**

Arranging Multiple Windows

For you to use the information window effectively, both it and the worksheet window must be visible at the same time. One way to achieve this is to *tile* the windows; doing so places them side by side, rather than one on top of the other. In the following steps, you will tile the two windows and then decrease the width of the information window to make more room for the worksheet window. Figure 3.24 shows the two windows tiled with their sizes being adjusted.

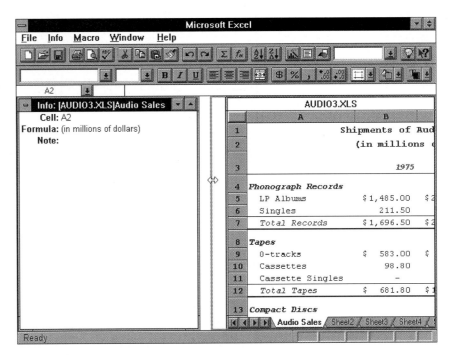

Figure 3.24

To arrange windows:

1 Choose **Window** and then **Arrange.**
The Arrange Windows dialog box appears.

2 Select **Tiled,** and then select **OK.**
The two windows are now tiled.

3 Select the information window by clicking it.

4 Decrease the width of the information window slightly by dragging its sizing border.

5 Select the worksheet window and increase its width, as shown in Figure 3.24.

Setting Up an Information Window

The standard display of an information window is not very informative. You can control what information about a cell is shown. In the following steps, you will instruct the information window to provide more details about a cell.

To set up an information window:

1 Activate the information window.

2 Choose **Info** and then **Value.**
Notice that Cell, Formula, and Note are already checked in the menu.

3 Choose **Info** and then **Format.**
Cell, Formula, Value, Format, and Note should all be checked.

4 Select the worksheet window.

5 Select cell G1.
Observe the information window. It should appear similar to Figure 3.25.

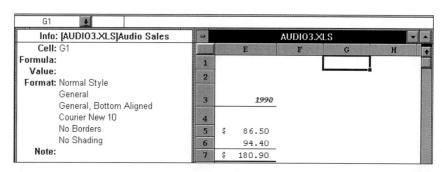

Figure 3.25

Using Information Windows to Examine Styles and Formats

The information window indicates that the active cell is G1; nothing appears next to Formula and Value because cell G1 is blank. The first line of the Format section reads *Normal Style.* This tells you that the Normal style applies to this cell. The subsequent lines provide details on what specifications of the Normal style apply. Because this cell was not included in the AutoFormat range, it has only the basic formatting attributes of the Normal style (without any additions or modifications).

General means the General Number format applies; this format does not include any special punctuation for numerical values.

General, Bottom Aligned describes the horizontal and vertical ***alignment*** of information in a cell. The horizontal alignment is *General;* this will cause numbers (and the results of formulas) to appear aligned right in their cells, and text to appear aligned left. The vertical alignment is *Bottom Aligned,* meaning that a cell's contents will appear to "sit" on the bottom edge of the cell.

Courier New 10 refers to the font—10-point Courier New. You will recall that earlier in this project you changed the font for Normal style to Courier New.

No Borders means no border lines will appear for this cell.

No Shading means no shading will be used in the cell.

To see information on cell A1:

1 Select cell A1.

2 Observe the information window; it will be similar to Figure 3.26.

A1	⬇	Shipments of Audio Recordings		

Info: [AUDIO3.XLS]Audio Sales		AUDIO3.XLS		▾ ▲
Cell: A1		A	B	C ▲
Formula: Shipments of Audio Recordings	1	Shipments of Audio I		
Value: "Shipments of Audio Recordings"	2	(in millions of d		
Format: Normal Style	3		1975	
General	4	*Phonograph Records*		
+ Center Across, Bottom Aligned	5	LP Albums	$ 1,485.00	$ 2,290
+ Courier New 11, Bold	6	Singles	211.50	269
+ No Borders	7	Total Records	$ 1,696.50	$ 2,559
+ No Shading	8	*Tapes*		
Note:	9	8-tracks	$ 583.00	$ 526

Figure 3.26

The Formula line shows what was literally typed into the cell (similar to what you would see in the formula bar); the Value line indicates, in the case of formulas, what the result of the formula is. The quotation marks around *Shipments of Audio Recordings* serve to remind you that this is a *text* entry.

The Format section indicates that the Normal style applies to this cell; certain aspects of this style still apply, but others have been overridden. The Format section of an information window will first name the style that applies to the cell, list the aspects of the style that have *not* changed (if any), and then list the formats that preempt those originally specified in the style. These overriding formats are preceded by a plus sign.

You may have noticed that some of the overriding formats (such as *No Shading*) do not differ from those in the original Normal style. These are still considered to be overriding because they were set specifically by the AutoFormat command.

The definition of the Normal style has not changed; rather, some cells in the worksheet have been given customized formats that take precedence over the formats indicated in the Normal style. If you were to change the definition of the Normal style—for example, if you changed the font specified in the style—the change would affect any cell to which the Normal style had been applied, provided that an overriding format had not been applied to the cell.

In this worksheet, if you redefined the Normal style to use the font Times New Roman 12, cell A5 would reflect the change, but not cell A4. Examine both of these cells (A4 and A5) in the information window to make sure you understand why a redefinition of the Normal style would affect cell A5 but not cell A4.

To see information on cell B7:

1 Select the cell that contains total records for 1975 (B7). Note that the cell's literal contents are =B5+B6, as indicated on the Formula line of the information window. The *value* of the cell is the result of this formula, 1696.5. Do not be alarmed by the strange-looking number format. Examine other cells with the information window.

2 Close the information window by selecting it and then double-clicking in its Control menu box.

3 Maximize the workbook window.

CUSTOMIZING TOOLBARS

Suppose that you frequently made use of information windows and wanted to avoid having to repeatedly use the Options dialog box. You could keep the Auditing toolbar open most of the time—it contains a button, called the Show Info Window tool, that creates information windows. But if you didn't want the extra screen space used up by the entire Auditing toolbar, you could add just the Show Info Window tool to one of the toolbars already on-screen.

Excel allows you to customize toolbars—to decide which tools you want to display on any toolbar. You do this graphically by dragging the desired tool from the Customize dialog box to the toolbar you want to contain the tool. You can remove a tool from a toolbar by dragging it from the toolbar to the Customize dialog box.

The Customize dialog box groups the dozens of available tools by category. For example, the show Info Window tool is in the Auditing category. You may need to examine several different categories before you find the particular tool you want to add to a toolbar.

In the steps that follow, you will customize the Standard toolbar by removing the Drawing button and adding a Show Info Window tool.

To customize a toolbar:

1 Choose **View** and then **Toolbars.**
The Toolbars dialog box appears.

2 Select **Customize.**
The Customize dialog box appears.

3 Click the **Drawing** tool on the Standard toolbar, drag its outline into the Customize dialog box (as shown in Figure 3.27), and release the mouse button.
The Drawing tool is removed from the Standard toolbar.

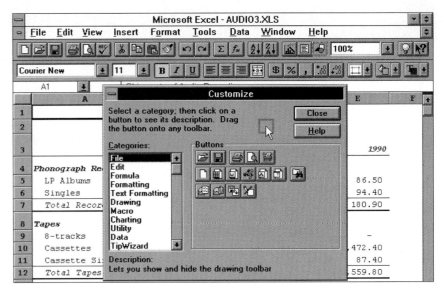

Figure 3.27

4 Scroll down the list of tool categories and click the **Auditing** category. This category contains the same set of buttons and tools that are on the Auditing toolbar.

5 Click the **Show Info Window** tool, as shown in Figure 3.28. A description of the tool appears in the Customize dialog box.

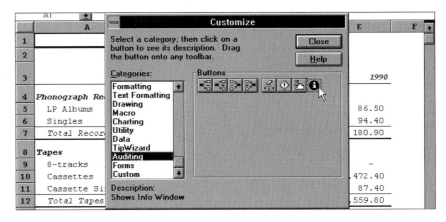

Figure 3.28

6 Drag the tool to the Standard toolbar, so it is placed where the Drawing tool used to be.

7 Select **Close.**
The Standard toolbar is now customized, as shown in Figure 3.29.

Figure 3.29

In the steps that follow, you will return the Standard toolbar to its default set of tools. You can reset a toolbar by opening the Toolbars dialog box, making sure the toolbar name is selected and checked in the list, and then selecting the Reset button.

To reset a toolbar to its default tools:

1 Choose **View** and then **Toolbar.**

2 Make sure the Standard toolbar is selected (highlighted) *and* checked.

3 Select the **Reset** button, and then select **OK.**
Notice that the Standard toolbar reverts to its default collection of tools.

4 Exit Excel, saving the workbook if necessary.
For many Excel operations, the most convenient access method is through a toolbar tool. You should feel free to customize toolbars to suit your particular needs as you work with Excel.

Tips You can create a fully customized toolbar with a name of your choice by choosing Toolbars from the View menu, double-clicking in the Toolbar Name box, typing a name, and then selecting OK. A floating toolbar will appear along with the Customize dialog box. You can then drag whatever tools you want to the new toolbar.

The file EXCEL5.XLB, normally stored in the Windows subdirectory, contains the most recently saved toolbar settings, including any customized toolbars you may have created. If you want to guarantee that Excel reverts to all of its original toolbar settings, you can delete this file before starting Excel. You can also rename the file (preserving the .XLB extension) and open it later, using the Open command from the File menu in Excel, to activate .XLB file's particular toolbar settings. Placing the file in the XLSTART subdirectory will cause the file to automatically open whenever Excel is started.

THE NEXT STEP

You are now ready to build a larger and more powerful worksheet. With the insight you have gained about formatting, you will be able to begin taking direct control over the formatting of your worksheets, because, as you have seen, AutoFormat won't always do what you want it to.

In the next project, you will build and format a worksheet on energy conservation that estimates the electricity used by a household and allows you to identify high-energy-cost appliances.

This concludes Project 3. You can either exit Excel, or go on to work the Study Questions, Review Exercises, and Assignments.

SUMMARY AND EXERCISES

Summary

- When you make major additions or changes to a worksheet, you must consider the effect those changes might have on existing parts of the worksheet—especially formulas.
- A formula's precedents are those cells on which the formula depends; a cell's dependents are other cells containing formulas that refer to that cell.
- You can insert blank cells into a worksheet, shifting existing cells to make room. However, if you do this, formulas do not always automatically adjust the way you might want them to.
- A circular-reference error occurs when a cell either directly or indirectly refers to itself.
- Clearing a range of cells erases the contents of the cells but does not remove the cells from the worksheet. Deleting removes both the contents and the cells.
- You can center cell entries across multiple columns; this is especially useful for worksheet titles.
- Row height can be changed in a manner similar to that for changing column width.
- You can remove the cell gridlines from a worksheet if you do not want them to appear on the screen or on printouts.
- A style is a named set of format attributes that can be applied to a cell to affect the cell's appearance. The default style is called *Normal.*
- TrueType fonts are preferable in most cases, because their appearance on-screen and on printouts is nearly identical, and because they produce sharper type on printouts.
- Information windows are used to find out detailed information about a cell, including its contents, value, and format.
- Customized formats applied to a cell override corresponding formats specified in the cell's style.

Key Terms and Operations

Key Terms
alignment
circular reference
dependent
direct precedent
font
indirect precedent
information window
points
style
tile
tracer arrow

Operations
Arrange
Clear a cell or range
Insert a cell or range
Print a worksheet
Trace Dependents
Trace Precedents

Study Questions

Multiple Choice

1. The cells that a formula either directly or indirectly refers to are called its:
   - a. descendants.
   - b. ancestors.
   - c. lineage.
   - d. dependents.
   - e. precedents.

2. Cells (containing formulas) that refer either directly or indirectly to a particular cell are called that cell's:
   - a. referents.
   - b. dependents.
   - c. terminal nodes.
   - d. signs.
   - e. descendants.

3. Which statement about the Edit Insert command is correct?
   - a. Any information present in the insert area is automatically cleared before the inserted text is added.
   - b. The command will prompt you to type the text or numeric constants to be inserted.
   - c. The command works on cells containing formulas.
   - d. Existing cells in the insertion range will be shifted to accommodate the inserted, blank cells.
   - e. None of the above.

4. The formula =SUM(B3:E3) is stored in cell E3. What (if anything) is the problem with the formula?
   - a. It contains a circular reference, and should probably be =SUM(B3:D3).
   - b. It should be =SUM(B3+C3+D3+E3).
   - c. It contains a circular reference, and should probably be =SUM(E3:B3).
   - d. It should be =B3+C3+D3+E3.
   - e. Nothing is wrong with the formula.

5. What font technology, built into Windows, can usually improve the printed quality of worksheets?
   - a. TrueType
   - b. PostScript
   - c. TypeTrue
   - d. Linotype
   - e. monotype

6. What menu command is used to arrange multiple windows?
   - a. Window Sort
   - b. Sort Window
   - c. Edit Arrange
   - d. Window Arrange
   - e. Format Windows

7. What menu command can be used to change from one window to another?
   - a. Options Goto
   - b. Edit Window
   - c. Window
   - d. File Window
   - e. Only mouse and keyboard shortcuts are available for this action.

8. What feature can be used to get detailed information on a particular cell?
   a. an information window
   b. the reference area
   c. the formula bar
   d. the Edit menu
   e. the Format menu

9. What term is used to describe a particular typeface design in Excel?
   a. style
   b. face
   c. font
   d. format
   e. regular

10. What command should be used to save a file under a new name?
    a. New in the File menu
    b. Save in the File menu
    c. Rename in the File menu
    d. Save As in the File menu
    e. Save As in the Edit menu

Short Answer

1. The formula $=A1-A2+A3$ is stored in cell A2. What (if anything) is wrong with the formula?

2. What mouse action or command is used to find the direct precedents of the currently selected cell?

3. Will centering text across columns change the cells where the text is stored? Will it break up the text and distribute the pieces to be stored in various cells?

4. List the formatting settings that can be included within a style.

5. Is inserting a blank row the best way to increase the space between rows of information in a worksheet? If not, what is a better way?

6. Are cell gridlines and border lines the same thing?

7. What font technology is usually the best choice for clear printouts?

8. What menu command is used to switch among multiple windows?

9. What kinds of information can be displayed in an information window?

10. What command is used to arrange multiple windows?

For Discussion

1. Why should you be careful when making major changes to a worksheet? What things should you do before you make a change? What should you check after the change?

2. What is a circular reference? Give an example.

3. Describe what happens when a customized format is applied to a cell. How does this affect the corresponding formats specified in the cell's style?

Review Exercises

Municipal Waste Trends

In the first review exercise in Project 2, you built a workbook about municipal waste and saved it under the name EPA1. If you haven't already created that worksheet, refer to Project 2 to build it. Then proceed to add the new information shown in Figure 3.30 for metals in the nonfood category.

	A	B	C	D	E	F	G	H	
2		1960	1970	1980	1990				
3	Nonfood Wastes								
4	Paper	0.91	1.19	1.32	1.6				
5	Glass	0.2	0.34	0.36	0.28				
6	Plastics	0.01	0.08	0.19	0.32				
7	Metals	0.32	0.38	0.35	0.34				
8	Total Nonfood	1.44	1.99	2.22	2.54				
9	Other								
10	Food	0.37	0.34	0.32	0.29				
11	Yard	0.61	0.62	0.66	0.7				
12	Total Other	0.98	0.96	0.98	0.99				
13	Grand Total	2.42	2.95	3.2	3.53				
14									

Figure 3.30

Use the Insert command to create a blank row for this new information; the information should be between the rows for plastics and total nonfood. Check, adjust, and copy formulas as necessary. Format the worksheet using AutoFormat with a nonaccounting table format. Additional opportunity for numeric formatting will be possible after you complete the next project. Save the workbook under the name EPA2.

Winter Olympic Games Medals

In the second review exercise of Project 2, you built and saved OLYMPIC1, a workbook that tabulates medals won by selected countries during the 1992 Winter Olympic Games. If you haven't already created that workbook, refer to Project 2 to build it.

Use the information shown in Figure 3.31 to add Italy to the worksheet. Use the Insert command to create a blank row for this new information; Italy should be the last country in the list. Check, adjust, and copy formulas as necessary. Format the worksheet using AutoFormat with a nonfinancial table format. Additional opportunities for numeric formatting will be possible after you complete the next project. Save the workbook under the name OLYMPIC2.

	A	B	C	D	E	F	G	H	I	
1	1992 Winter Olympiad									
2										
3	Country	Gold	Silver	Bronze	Total					
4	Germany	10	10	6	26					
5	Unified Team	9	6	8	23					
6	Austria	6	7	8	21					
7	Norway	9	6	5	20					
8	Italy	4	6	4	?					
9	Total	34	29	27	90					
10										

Figure 3.31

Assignments

Space Payloads

In the third assignment in Project 2, you built and saved SPACE1, a workbook that tabulates rocket payloads put into space by selected countries. If you haven't already created that workbook, refer to Project 2 to build it.

Add the information for the European Space Agency (ESA) as shown in Figure 3.32. Try using Move rather than Insert to make space for the new information. Adjust and copy formulas as necessary, change the standard font to a TrueType font of your choice, format the worksheet using AutoFormat and a nonaccounting table format, and save the workbook under the name SPACE2.

	A	B	C	D	E	F	G	H	I
1	Space Payloads								
2									
3		1988	1988	1988	1988	Average			
4	USSR	107	95	96	101	99.75			
5	United States	15	22	31	30	24.5			
6	ESA	2	2	1	4	?			
7	Japan	2	4	7	2	3.75			
8	Total	126	123	135	137	130.25			
9									

Figure 3.32

Coffee House Income

Starting with the third assignment in Project 1 and continuing in the first assignment in Project 2, you built and saved COFFEE2, a spreadsheet that calculates the income derived from sales of various coffees at Clem's Coffee Clutch. If you haven't already created that workbook, refer to Projects 1 and 2 to build it.

Add information for Cafe Royale, as shown in Figure 3.33. Adjust and copy formulas as necessary, change the standard font to a TrueType font of your choice, format the worksheet using AutoFormat, and save the workbook under the name COFFEE3.

	A	B	C	D	E	F	G	H
1	Coffee	Cost	Selling Price	No. Sold	Income			
2	House Blend	0.39	0.95	60	33.6			
3	Espresso	0.61	1.25	12	7.68			
4	Cappuccino	0.74	1.5	22	16.72			
5	Cafe Mocha	0.55	1.45	35	31.5			
6	Cafe Royale	0.68	1.85	55	?			
7	Total			184	89.5			
8								

Figure 3.33

Open an information window, set it to display values and formats, adjust the COFFEE3 and information windows in a tiled arrangement, and examine the format and style settings in the worksheet.

Additions to AUDIO3

Modify the AUDIO3 worksheet to include data for 1991, as well as figures for shipments of music videos, as shown in Figure 3.34. After inserting the new information, adjust and copy formulas as necessary, reformat the worksheet, and save the workbook under the name AUDIO4.

	A	B	C	D	E	F	G
1	Shipments of Audio Recordings						
2	(in millions of dollars)						
3		1975	1980	1985	1990	1991	
4	Phonograph Records						
5	LP Albums	$1,485.00	$2,290.30	$1,280.50	$86.50	$4.80	
6	Singles	211.50	269.30	281.00	94.40	22.00	
7	Total Records	$1,696.50	$2,559.60	$1,561.50	$180.90	$26.80	
8	Tapes						
9	8-track	$583.00	$526.40	$25.30	$0.00	$0.00	
10	Cassette	98.80	776.40	2,411.50	3,472.40	360.10	
11	Cassette Singles	0.00	0.00	0.00	87.40	69.00	
12	Total Tapes	$681.80	$1,302.80	$2,436.80	$3,559.80	$429.10	
13	Compact Discs						
14	Regular CDs	$0.00	$0.00	$389.50	$3,451.60	$333.30	
15	CD Singles	0.00	0.00	0.00	6.00	5.70	
16	Total CDs	$0.00	$0.00	$389.50	$3,457.60	$339.00	
17	Music Videos	$0.00	$0.00	$0.00	$9.20	$6.10	
18	Grand Total	$2,378.30	$3,862.40	$4,387.80	$7,207.50	$801.00	

Figure 3.34

PROJECT 4: USING FORMULAS IN A WORKSHEET

Objectives

After completing this project, you should be able to:

▶ Create customized numeric formats

▶ Magnify or reduce your view of a worksheet

▶ Change the alignment of cell entries

▶ Define and use names for constants and ranges

▶ Copy to nonadjacent selections

▶ Recognize and use absolute cell references

▶ Change the font style and size of a cell entry

▶ Apply borders to the worksheet

▶ Produce landscape printouts

CASE STUDY: ANALYZING HOME ENERGY USAGE

One way to decide how to save on home-electric bills—and reduce electricity consumption and related power-plant pollution—is to determine how each electrical appliance in your home or apartment contributes to your total monthly bill. Along with your personal electricity-usage patterns, many other factors, such as season, climate, and the availability of alternative energy sources, will influence the total bill. Excel is the ideal tool for making sense of these variables and simplifying the task of estimating electricity consumption.

Designing the Solution

In this project, you will build a worksheet that lists various electrical appliances and estimates their monthly consumption of electricity. The worksheet will describe a basic, all-electric home during a mild winter month in a moderate climate. Constructing this worksheet will involve calculating the monthly energy used by each appliance, a calculation based on each appliance's energy-consumption rate and the amount of time the appliance is used during a month.

There are several ways you could design a worksheet to implement the calculation described above. You could construct one giant formula to perform all calculations on all variables, but the worksheet will be easier to understand and modify if you break the process into smaller steps comprising a series of simpler formulas. This is the approach you will take in this project.

Figure 4.1 shows the completed worksheet. Separate columns designate each of the major variables involved in the calculation. The flexibility of this electronic worksheet will make easy experimentation and adaptation possible with variables such as different appliances, different electricity-usage habits, and so on.

Residential Electricity Usage
Based on a cost of
$0.08 per kilowatt-hour

Appliance	Wattage	Hours Cycled-On							Operating Hours per Month	Kilowatt-hours per month	Estimated Cost per Month
		Mon	Tue	Wed	Thu	Fri	Sat	Sun			
Heating/Cooling											
Heat pump (3 ton)	4,800	4.00	4.00	4.00	4.00	4.00	6.00	6.00	128	614	$49.15
Portable heater	1,500	1.00	1.00	1.00	1.00	1.00	2.00	2.00	36	54	4.32
Water heater	4,100	2.00	2.00	2.00	2.00	2.00	4.00	4.00	72	295	23.62
Kitchen											
Frost-free refrigerator	460	15.00	15.00	15.00	15.00	15.00	15.00	15.00	420	193	15.46
Convection oven	3,000	0.00	0.00	0.00	0.00	0.00	3.00	3.00	24	72	5.76
Microwave oven	1,500	0.25	0.25	0.25	0.25	0.25	0.50	1.00	11	17	1.32
Dishwasher	1,200	1.00	0.00	1.00	0.00	1.00	1.00	1.00	20	24	1.92
Laundry											
Washing machine	510	0.00	0.00	0.00	0.00	0.00	3.00	3.00	24	12	0.98
Clothes dryer	4,850	0.00	0.00	0.00	0.00	0.00	3.00	3.00	24	116	9.31
Lighting											
Incandescent	150	5.00	5.00	5.00	5.00	5.00	5.00	5.00	140	21	1.68
Fluorescent (twin)	96	5.00	5.00	5.00	5.00	5.00	5.00	5.00	140	13	1.08
Fluorescent (compact)	18	5.00	5.00	5.00	5.00	5.00	5.00	5.00	140	3	0.20
Electronics											
Color television	145	2.00	2.00	2.00	2.00	4.00	6.00	7.00	100	15	1.16
Personal computer	160	1.00	1.00	1.00	1.00	1.00	2.00	3.00	40	6	0.51
Total											$116.46

(Page 1)

Figure 4.1

ENTERING THE WORKSHEET CONSTANTS

You will first enter some of the worksheet titles and number constants. You will do some formatting early, to make subsequent data entry and formula construction easier to follow. You can refer to Figure 4.2 to see a partial, unformatted version of the worksheet. As in the previous project, the more intricate formatting steps will be completed in the final phase of worksheet construction.

	A	B	C	D	E	F	G	H	I	J	K	L	M
1	Residential Electricity Usage												
2	Based on a cost of												
3		0.08											
4				Hours Cycled-On									
5	Appliance	Wattage	Mon	Tue	Wed	Thu	Fri	Sat	Sun	Operating F	Kilowatt-hc	Estimated	Cost per Month
6	Heating/Cooling												
7	Heat pump (3 ton)												
8	Portable heater												
9	Water heater												
10	Kitchen												
11	Frost-free refrigerator												
12	Conventional oven												
13	Microwave oven												
14	Dishwasher												
15	Laundry												
16	Washing machine												
17	Clothes dryer												
18	Lighting												
19	Incandescent												
20	Fluorescent (twin)												
21	Fluorescent (compact)												
22	Electronics												
23	Color television												
24	Personal computer												
25	Total												
26													

Figure 4.2

To enter the main title and first subtitle:

1 Open a new workbook, select the **Sheet1** tab, and ensure that the font of the Normal style is Arial 10.

2 Enter **Residential Electricity Usage** in cell A1.

3 Enter **Based on a cost of** in cell A2.

Creating Customized Formats

In Figure 4.1, the second subtitle, *$0.08 per kilowatt-hour*, might appear to be a text entry. If it *were* a text entry, formulas in the worksheet could not meaningfully refer to it when calculating. In fact, it is a numeric entry, 0.08, assigned a *customized format.* Any time you want to have a value appear in some form other than the standard formats available, you can create your own format. For example, you might want a special date format, a format designed to represent amounts in a foreign currency, or a format that includes an abbreviation for a special unit of measurement. For this worksheet, you will create a format that will display whatever number is typed in the cell, preceded by a dollar sign and followed by the phrase *per kilowatt-hour*.

To enter and custom-format the second subtitle:

1 Enter **0.08** in cell A3.

2 Make sure cell A3 is still selected; choose **Format** and then **Cells.** The Format Cells dialog box appears.

3 Select the **Number** tab, if necessary. The Number format tab is displayed.

4 Double-click in the **Code** edit box. The Code edit box is where you can enter formatting codes to specify how you want numbers to appear.

5 Type the formatting code **$0.00 "per kilowatt-hour"** in the **Code** box.

Note the use of quotation marks. The screen should resemble Figure 4.3. The format code instructs Excel to display a value in cell A3 with a leading dollar sign, show a leading zero before the decimal point for numbers less than one, always show two digits to the right of the decimal, and follow the number with the phrase *per kilowatt-hour*.

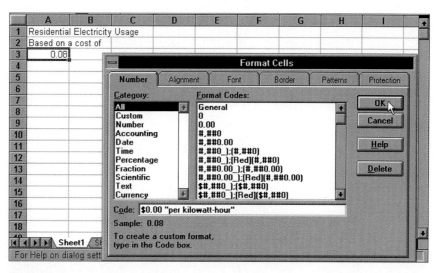

Figure 4.3

6 Select **OK** to complete the format specification.
Now you have assigned a customized format to cell A3. Number signs (#) appear in the cell, indicating that the column is too narrow to display the number 0.08 in the new format.

7 Widen column A to about 25 characters, so that all three cell entries (A1, A2, and A3) are accommodated.

It is very important to recognize that for calculation purposes, cell A3 contains the *number* 0.08. Formatting affects the way a cell entry *appears* but does not change the value of the entry or its data type (text constant, number constant, or formula).

Tip If you want to force every entry in a range to be converted to text, you can choose the Text format from the Number tab of the Format Cells dialog box. The Text format is the only format that actually changes the underlying data type of a cell entry.

Changing the View of a Worksheet Window

At normal magnification, a worksheet is rarely visible in its entirety; the screen and the worksheet window restrict your view. Excel is capable of *zooming out* (reducing) or *zooming in* (magnifying) to let you see more or less of the worksheet.

Occasionally, you will zoom in for a closer look, but more often you will zoom out to see more of the worksheet at once. A disadvantage of zooming out is that because you see more of the worksheet in a reduced size, it is more difficult to position correctly on specific cells.

You can also change to *full-screen view,* which temporarily removes the toolbars and status bar to allow more room for the worksheet itself. Switching to full-screen view does not in itself change the magnification of the worksheet, though full-screen view can be used in conjunction with the zoom command.

In the steps that follow, you will experiment with the Zoom and Full Screen commands.

To magnify a worksheet:

1 Open the **Zoom Control** list box on the Standard toolbar. A list box opens, showing various magnifications.

2 Select **200%** in the **Zoom Control** list box. Each worksheet cell appears much larger, but you can't see as many cells.

To reduce a worksheet:

1 Open the **Zoom Control** list box on the Standard toolbar.

2 Select **50%** in the **Zoom Control** list box. You can see many more cells in the worksheet, but individual cells become more difficult to read. This is especially true when Windows is running with standard VGA video (rather than with SuperVGA).

To set a custom magnification:

1 Click on the **50%,** which is currently displayed in the **Zoom Control** box.

2 Type **85** for the magnification and press (ENTER)

To return to 100% magnification:

1 Click the **Zoom Control.**

2 Select **100%** in the **Zoom Control** list box.

Tip If you want to magnify or reduce the worksheet so it accommodates a particular range of cells, select the range first and then choose Selection from the Zoom Control list box.

The Zoom commands are also available by selecting Zoom from the View menu.

From now on, you should change your view of the worksheet whenever you want.

To change to full-screen view:

1 Choose **View** and then **Full Screen.**
The toolbars and status bar disappear, and more rows of the worksheet are visible. A single-tool floating toolbar also appears, called the Full Screen toolbar; if you select this tool, you can switch back to normal view. You will now close the toolbar so it does not clutter the screen.

2 Click the Control menu box of the floating toolbar to close the toolbar. The toolbar disappears. You can always return to normal view by using the View menu. Excel will now remember your preference of not having the Full Screen toolbar appear in full-screen view.

3 Choose **View** and then **Full Screen.**

This "unchecks" the Full Screen option, returning the screen to normal view.

Using Series Fill

In the sections that follow, you will enter and partially format the column titles. To make it easier to see what you're typing, you will first zoom to a 75% magnification of the worksheet. As you work, you can refer to Figure 4.4.

You could manually enter the days of the week as the column headings in C5:I5, but Excel provides a shortcut called *AutoFill* that you can use when entering the days of the week or names of months. When you use the fill handle to copy information that represents part of a standard sequence or series, Excel automatically fills in the other members of the series. For example, if you use the fill handle to copy a cell that contains the text *Feb* and select a range three cells to the right, Excel will enter *Mar*, *Apr*, and *May*. If you don't want the series-fill effect to take place, hold down (CTRL) while dragging the fill handle.

A1		Residential Electricity Usage									
	A	B	C	D	E	F	G	H	I	J	K
1	Residential Electricity Usage										
2	Based on a cost of										
3	$0.08 per kilowatt-hour										
4			Hours Cycled-On								
5	Appliance	Wattage	Mon	Tue	Wed	Thu	Fri	Sat	Sun	Operating F	Kilowat
6											
7											

Figure 4.4

To enter the column titles:

1 Use the **Zoom Control** list box to reduce magnification of the worksheet to 75 percent.

2 Enter `Appliance` in cell A5.

3 Enter `Wattage` in cell B5.

4 Enter `Mon` in cell C5.

5 With cell C5 selected, position the pointer at the lower-right corner of the cell so the pointer forms the fill handle; drag the fill handle to cell I5 and release the mouse button.
The range now contains abbreviations for the days of the week, as shown in Figure 4.4.

6 In cell C4, *above* the column title *Mon*, enter `Hours Cycled-On`

7 In cell J5, enter `Operating Hours per Month`
This column is used to estimate how many hours per month an appliance is used. Do not be concerned if a column title or other cell entry appears either to spill over into a neighboring cell or to be cut off by a neighboring cell.

8 In cell K5, enter `Kilowatt-hours per Month`
Later you will construct a formula to calculate the number of kilowatt-hours used each month.

9 In cell L5, enter `Estimated Cost per Month`

This column will contain a formula that computes the electricity cost.

10 Press (CTRL) + (HOME)

The worksheet should resemble Figure 4.4.

Adjusting the Width of Multiple Columns

The columns for weekdays should be narrowed. Instead of setting each column width separately, you can adjust the width of a group of columns by selecting the group and then adjusting the width of any column in the group.

To adjust the width of a group of columns:

1 Select columns C through I by dragging across column headings C through I, and then release the mouse button.

2 Position the pointer on the *right* edge of any selected column heading. Using the width information provided in the reference area, drag the mouse to select a new width of about 5 characters, as shown in Figure 4.5.

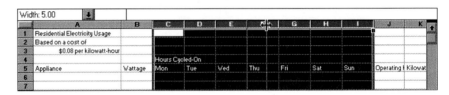

Figure 4.5

3 Release the mouse button.

Changing the Alignment of Cell Entries

A text entry is automatically aligned against the left edge of its cell, and a number entry against the right edge, but you can change this alignment. Text titles appearing above numeric entries will look better if they are aligned at the center or to the right.

Notice that Figure 4.1 shows the long column titles, such as *Operating Hours per Month*, wrapping in their cells. **Wrapping** means to break a long entry into separate lines.

In the steps that follow, you will align to the right the column titles *Wattage* through *Estimated Cost per Month* and specify that long entries be wrapped.

To align to the right and wrap selected column titles:

1 Select cell B5.

2 Select B5:L5, the range of text entries to be aligned.

3 Choose **Format** and then **Cells.**

The Format Cells dialog box appears.

4 Select the **Alignment** tab.

The Alignment tab appears.

5 Select the **Right** option button in the **Horizontal** group.

6 Select the **Wrap Text** check box if it is not already checked. The screen should resemble Figure 4.6.

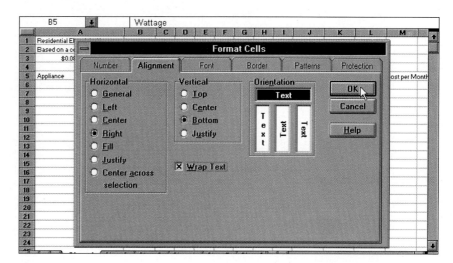

Figure 4.6

7 Select **OK** to complete the alignment.

The column headings should now be aligned to the right and, where necessary, wrap within their cells. Notice that wrapping automatically adjusted the height of row 5.

8 To make the worksheet look less cramped, increase the width of columns J, K, and L to about 10 characters.

Entering the Remaining Text Constants

In the following steps, you will enter the text constants for the row titles. Note that two levels of indentation are used for the row titles to visually outline the list of appliances. Section titles such as *Heating/Cooling* are indented two spaces, and individual appliance names, such as *Water heater*, are indented four spaces. You can use Figure 4.7 as a reference.

	A	B	C	D	E	F	G	H	I	J	K	L
1	Residential Electricity Usage											
2	Based on a cost of											
3	$0.08 per kilowatt-hour											
4					Hours Cycled-On							
5	Appliance	Wattage	Mon	Tue	Wed	Thu	Fri	Sat	Sun	Operating Hours per Month	Kilowatt-hours per Month	Estimated Cost per Month
6	Heating/Cooling											
7	Heat pump (3 ton)											
8	Portable heater											
9	Water heater											
10	Kitchen											
11	Frost-free refrigerator											
12	Conventional oven											
13	Microwave oven											
14	Dishwasher											
15	Laundry											
16	Washing machine											
17	Clothes dryer											
18	Lighting											
19	Incandescent											
20	Fluorescent (twin)											
21	Fluorescent (compact)											
22	Electronics											
23	Color television											
24	Personal computer											
25	Total											
26												

Figure 4.7

To enter the row titles:

1 Select A1:L5, the entire functional area of the worksheet.

2 Click the **Zoom Control** list box and choose **Selection** to fit the magnification to the selected range.

3 Select cell A6.

4 In cell A6, press (SPACE) twice, type **Heating/Cooling** and press (ENTER)

5 In cell A7, press (SPACE) four times, type **Heat pump (3 ton)** and press (ENTER)

6 Refer to Figure 4.7 to enter the remaining row titles.
Note that *Total* is not indented; *Kitchen*, *Laundry*, *Lighting*, and *Electronics* are indented by preceding the text with two spaces, and the remaining titles are indented four spaces.

7 Press (CTRL) + (HOME) and then choose **Tools** and then **Spelling** to check the spelling of the worksheet.

8 Save the worksheet under the name ENERGY1. The worksheet should resemble Figure 4.7.

Tip If you are building a worksheet that requires several levels of indentation, you can use separate columns for each indentation level, rather than using spaces. Although this approach slightly increases the complexity of the worksheet, adjustment (via column-width changes) of the amount of indentation for each level is much easier.

Entering the Number Constants

You will now enter the constants for wattage and hours cycled-on. Note that the numbers in the hours cycled-on section are ordinary decimal numbers: an hour-and-a-half is written as 1.50, not 1:30. In the following steps, you will also learn a data-entry shortcut that allows you to fill a large selection easily with a single entry.

The first step in calculating the energy used by an appliance over the course of a month is to determine the appliance's power consumption, or the rate at which it uses up energy. The amount of electrical power an appliance consumes is measured in *watts*. A typical light bulb uses 100 watts; a typical microwave oven uses 1500 watts.

If you need to know how many watts an appliance uses, check the appliance's operating manual or look on the appliance itself. If watts are not listed on the appliance, then volts (V) and amps (A) will likely be listed. You can multiply volts by amps to calculate watts. Note that sometimes the appliance's power supply will list the maximum rated power consumption, not what the appliance actually uses under normal operating conditions.

To enter the appliance-wattage constants:

1 Enter **4800** in cell B7.
This is the wattage of the 3-ton heat pump.

2 Referring to Figure 4.1 or 4.8, carefully enter the remaining number constants for the wattage column *only*.

> **Reminder** Because all punctuation is added through formatting, do not type commas in any of the numbers.

	A	B	C	D	E	F	G	H	I	J	K	L
					Hours Cycled-On					Operating Hours per Month	Kilowatt-hours per Month	Estimated Cost per Month
1	Residential Electricity Usage											
2	Based on a cost of											
3	$0.08 per kilowatt-hour											
4					Hours Cycled-On							
5	Appliance	Wattage	Mon	Tue	Wed	Thu	Fri	Sat	Sun	Operating Hours per Month	Kilowatt-hours per Month	Estimated Cost per Month
6	Heating/Cooling											
7	Heat pump (3 ton)	4800	4	4	4	4	4	6	6			
8	Portable heater	1500	1	1	1	1	1	2	2			
9	Water heater	4100	2	2	2	2	2	4	4			
10	Kitchen											
11	Frost-free refrigerator	460	15	15	15	15	15	15	15			
12	Conventional oven	3000	0	0	0	0	0	3	3			
13	Microwave oven	1500	0.25	0.25	0.25	0.25	0.25	0.5	1			
14	Dishwasher	1200	1	0	1	0	1	1	1			
15	Laundry											
16	Washing machine	510	0	0	0	0	0	3	3			
17	Clothes dryer	4850	0	0	0	0	0	3	3			
18	Lighting											
19	Incandescent	150	5	5	5	5	5	5	5			
20	Fluorescent (twin)	96	5	5	5	5	5	5	5			
21	Fluorescent (compact)	18	5	5	5	5	5	5	5			
22	Electronics											
23	Color television	145	2	2	2	2	4	6	7			
24	Personal computer	160	1	1	1	1	1	2	3			
25	Total											
26												

Figure 4.8

Your next step is to estimate how many hours per month the appliance is used. With many appliances you can estimate how many hours the appliance runs each day of the week, total these times, and then approximate a month's worth of use by multiplying the total by four (since there are about four weeks in a month).

Notice in Figure 4.8 that all three types of lighting are estimated to run at five hours per day, every day of the week. Rather than using the Copy command or typing 5 in each of the 21 cells, you will use an alternative method for this type of repetitive entry.

To quickly enter the usage times for lighting:

1 Select C19:I21, the range encompassing hours cycled-on for each of the lighting types for all of the days.

2 Type **5** and press (CTRL) + (ENTER)
The number 5 should be entered in all the cells of the selected range.

Other appliances vary in their consumption of electricity. For example, an air conditioner or oven consumes significant amounts of electricity, but only when actually in use. When calculating the hours cycled-on in your own home, you may need to refer to published approximations of typical running times for certain appliances.

To enter the remaining usage times:

1 Enter the remaining numbers for hours cycled-on. Use the various shortcut methods you've learned so far to do this quickly and easily.

2 Save the worksheet.
Your worksheet should now resemble Figure 4.8.

Electric bills are based on the number of hours each appliance runs, and the billing units are *kilowatt-hours*. A kilowatt is 1000 watts, and one kilowatt-hour is the energy consumed by running a 1000-watt appliance for one hour. If you run a 1000-watt hair dryer for three hours a month, you have consumed 3000 watt-hours or 3 kilowatt-hours of energy. The formula for energy consumption is generally written as (watts/1000) * hours. Remember to divide watts by 1000 when converting to kilowatts.

To estimate the monthly energy cost of an appliance, multiply the kilowatt-hours the appliance consumes by the cost per kilowatt-hour. With typical residential electric rates, electricity costs between $0.03 and $0.15 per kilowatt-hour. Check an electric bill or call your utility company to find out the rate for your area. The worksheet you build in this project will presume that electricity is billed at a flat rate.

You have already entered an electric rate of 8 cents ($0.08) per kilowatt-hour in cell A3. The monthly cost of the hair dryer mentioned above is 24 cents. As you can see in Figure 4.1, large appliances used for heating or cooling are the major consumers of electricity in the home.

Documenting Formulas

The total time an appliance is operated in a month is calculated by multiplying a week's operating time by four, because there are about four weeks in a month. For example, to compute the total monthly operating hours for the heat pump, the formula =SUM(C7:I7)*4 could be entered in cell J7. The SUM function computes a week's operating hours, and the result is then multiplied by 4.

It may seem that anyone examining the formula would understand that the 4 represents the four weeks in a month, but the 4 is a rather benign example of a *magic number*. Magic numbers are undocumented constants that show up in formulas. The problem with magic numbers is twofold. First, magic numbers carry little intrinsic meaning, so when people (even the worksheet's author) examine the worksheet long after it was first created, they may not understand the purpose of the number. Second, magic numbers buried within formulas make it harder to change the worksheet. For example, suppose you created and copied the formula just described and later wanted to use a more precise definition of a typical month as 4.345 weeks. You would have to first edit or rebuild the formula and then recopy it to replace the old formula.

Defining Names

One alternative to using magic numbers is to present such constants explicitly in the worksheet, in their own easily changed cells. This is an approach that you have already taken when you entered the information about the electric rate of $0.08 per kilowatt-hour. Excel offers another approach: defined names.

A *defined name* is a name you create that refers to other cells or to constants, such as the number of weeks per month. Each workbook has its own dictionary of defined names to which you can add or delete definitions.

In the following steps, you will define the name *WeeksPerMonth* to stand for 4. You will then use this name in the formulas for operating hours per month.

To define names for constants:

1 Choose **Insert** and then **Name.**

2 Choose **Define.**
The Define Name dialog box appears.

3 Type WeeksPerMonth in the **Names in Workbook** box, replacing any text that might have initially appeared in the box.
Remember to type the name with no spaces, and with mixed upper- and lowercase letters.

4 Type 4 in the box labeled **Refers to,** replacing any text that might have initially appeared in the box.

5 Select the **Add** button.
The dialog box should now resemble Figure 4.9. The newly defined name is added to the dictionary, which is listed under Names in Workbook. An equal sign is also automatically inserted.

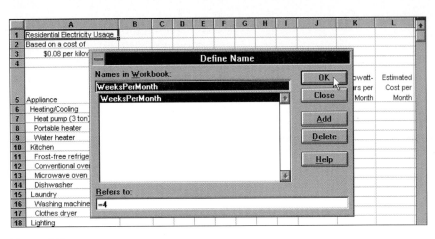

Figure 4.9

6 Select **OK** to close the dialog box.

Instead of typing the constant *4*, you can now use the name *WeeksPerMonth* in formulas within this worksheet.

> **Tip** When you define a name, follow these guidelines:
>
> ■ Make the name meaningful. Don't use names such as *X* or *N*. If a name refers to the marginal tax rate then make the name *MarginalTaxRate*, not *X*.
> ■ Make the name readable by mixing uppercase and lowercase letters; *MarginalTaxRate*, not *MARGINALTAXRATE*. You can also use underscores: *Marginal_Tax_Rate*.
> ■ Use only letters, underscores, and numbers in a name; never use spaces; and don't make a name look like a cell address or formula. Excel will prevent you from creating invalid names, such as *F16*, *B1*, and *Quarter-1*, which are all ambiguous.

Using Names in Formulas

To use a defined name within a formula, you type the name as part of the formula. When computing the formula's result, Excel automatically refers to the dictionary and substitutes the name with its definition. In the following steps, you will build and copy a formula to compute the operating hours per month for each appliance.

To build the formula for operating hours per month:

1 Select cell J7, which will contain the operating hours per month for the heat pump.

2 Type **=sum(**

3 Using point mode, select the range to be summed, C7:I7, by selecting away from the formula (Sunday's through Monday's operating hours).

4 Type **)*WeeksPerMonth** and then press (ENTER)

The formula reads =SUM(C7:I7)*WeeksPerMonth, and it means "total the seven cells to the left and multiply the total by WeeksPerMonth."

The formula's relative addressing will work when you copy the formula to the other cells in the column.

The result of this formula is 128. If you want to change the value of WeeksPerMonth, you can do so in the Define Name dialog box. The change would then be reflected in every formula that uses the name *WeeksPerMonth*.

Copying to Nonadjacent Selections

The formula you just completed needs to be copied to calculate operating hours per month for the other appliances. The fill handle could be used in a single step to copy the formula; however, this would leave copies in certain cells that should be blank (J10, for example). In the following steps, you will copy the formula to a nonadjacent selection—only those cells that should receive the copy.

To copy to a nonadjacent selection:

1 Select cell J7, which contains the formula to be copied.

2 Click the **Copy** tool from the Standard toolbar.

3 Hold down (CTRL) while dragging to select the ranges of cells that should receive the copy: J8:J9, J11:J14, J16:J17, J19:J21, and J23:J24, as shown in Figure 4.10.

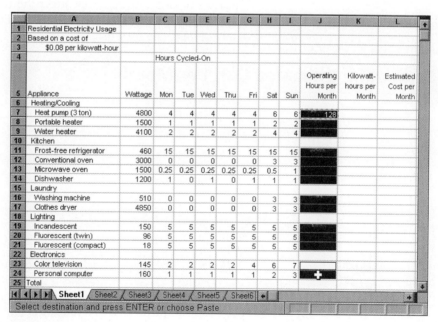

Figure 4.10

4 Press (ENTER) to paste the formula into the selected cells.

Calculating Kilowatt-hours per Month

The kilowatt-hours of energy used by an appliance in a month are the number of kilowatts it consumes multiplied by the number of hours it is cycled-on.

To build the formula for kilowatt-hours per month:

1 Select cell K7, which will contain kilowatt-hours per month for the heat pump.

2 Type **=(**

3 Select the wattage for this appliance, in cell B7.

4 Type **/1000)***

5 Select the operating hours per month for this appliance, in cell J7.

6 Press **(ENTER)** to complete the formula.
The result of the formula is 614.4. This formula's relative addressing will work when the formula is copied to other cells. The completed formula, =(B7/1000)*J7, can be interpreted as "Take what is nine cells to the left, divide it by 1000, and multiply that result by what is one cell to the left."

7 Copy the completed formula to the cells in column K that should contain the formula.

The parentheses inserted in this formula are not required by the rules of operator priority, nor do they affect the result of the formula. They are used to help convey the logic of the computation to people who might later examine the formula.

Computing Estimated Cost per Month

The final column will compute the monthly cost of operating each appliance. This value is calculated by multiplying the cost per kilowatt-hour (currently 0.08, in cell A3) by the kilowatt-hours calculated for each appliance in column K.

Follow the next steps carefully. You will first change the view of the worksheet and then, to illustrate a common error, you will build a formula that is mathematically correct but does not work when copied to other cells. Later, you will correct the formula and copy it again.

To change the view of the worksheet:

1 Press **(CTRL)** + **(HOME)**, then choose **View** and then **Full Screen.** Close the floating Full Screen toolbar if it appears.
The toolbars and status bar disappear. You will need the Standard toolbar for quick adjustment of magnification and access to the Copy tool, and you will need the Auditing toolbar to analyze formulas.

2 Choose **View** and then **Toolbars,** select the Standard and Auditing toolbars, and then select **OK.**

3 Drag the Auditing toolbar toward the upper-right corner of the worksheet window so the toolbar is positioned above blank cells but does not cover the column headings, as shown in Figure 4.11.

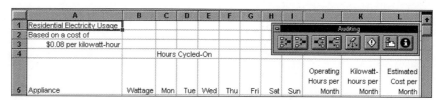

Figure 4.11

4 Choose **View** and then **Formula bar.**
The Formula bar appears.

5 Select the range A1:L25, the entire area of the worksheet that is needed. *Make sure column L is included in the selection.*

6 Click the **Zoom Control** list box and choose **Selection** to fit the magnification to the selected range.
The screen should resemble Figure 4.12.

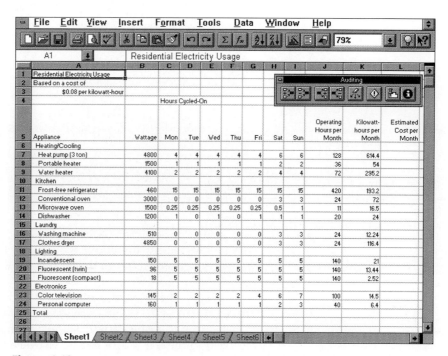

Figure 4.12

Reminder The cost per month is the cost per kilowatt-hour multiplied by the number of kilowatt-hours used in a month.

To build the formula for estimated cost per month (first attempt):

1 Select cell L7, which will contain the cost per month of the heat pump.

2 Type **=**

3 Select the cost per kilowatt-hour, in cell A3.

4 Type *

5 Select the number of kilowatt-hours used, in cell K7.

6 Press (ENTER)

The completed formula reads =A3*K7.

7 Using the skills you learned earlier for copying to nonadjacent selections, copy this formula to the other cells that require it in column L. The worksheet should now resemble Figure 4.13.

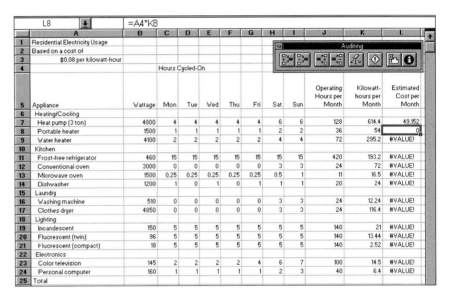

Figure 4.13

Analyzing Problem Formulas

There is obviously something wrong with the copied formulas. The formula in cell L8 gives a result of 0, and the other cells display the error message *#VALUE!*.

Consider the original formula in cell L7. As do the other formulas you have created, =A3*K7 uses relative cell references. The formula means "Take what is 4 cells up and 11 cells to the left, and multiply that by what is 1 cell to the left." This can be visualized by tracing the precedents of the formula.

To trace the precedents of the original formula:

1 Select cell L7, the estimated cost per month for the heat pump.

2 Click the **Trace Precedents** tool.

The direct precedents are cell A3, the cost per kilowatt-hour, and cell K7, the kilowatt hours used per month for this appliance.

To trace the precedents of a copy of the formula:

1 Select cell L8, the estimated cost per month for the portable heater.

2 Click the **Trace Precedents** tool.

The screen should resemble Figure 4.14. The direct precedents are cell A4, which is blank, and cell K8, the kilowatt hours used per month for this appliance.

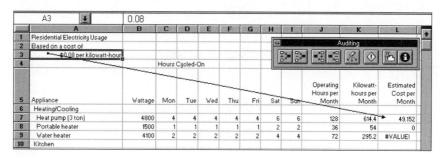

Figure 4.14

The formula in cell L8 attempts to take the contents of cell A4, which is 4 cells up and 11 cells to the left, and multiply those contents by cell K8, which is 1 cell to the left.

The K8 part is correct; the A4 reference is wrong. Cell A4 is blank, and because blank cells have a value of zero, the result of the formula is 0. The results of the other formulas give the error message *#VALUE!* because the other formulas attempt to multiply by cells that contain text, which is considered an error.

Another way of analyzing these formulas is to consider cell A3, which contains the cost per kilowatt-hour. This cell should be a direct precedent of all the formulas that compute estimated cost per month.

To trace the dependents of cell A3:

1 Click the **Remove All Arrows** tool.
All tracer arrows disappear.

2 Select cell A3, the cost per kilowatt-hour.

3 Click the **Trace Dependents** tool.
Your screen should resemble Figure 4.15. Only one cell, L7, depends on cell A3.

Figure 4.15

4 Click the **Remove All Arrows** tool.

Using Absolute Cell References

The formula in cell L7 (and in all the other cells in the estimated cost per month column) should instead mean "Take what is in cell A3, and multiply it by what is one cell to the left (of the cell in which this formula is located)." Using Excel terminology, the reference to cell A3 should not be a relative reference, but an ***absolute reference.***

An absolute cell reference in a formula is frozen so the reference will not change even if the formula that contains the reference is copied. A fully absolute reference is indicated with dollar signs preceding both the column letter and the row number. For example, in $A$3, the dollar sign in front of the *A* means "Don't change the *A*," and the dollar sign in front of the *3* means "Don't change the *3*."

The most convenient way to make a reference absolute is with the Absolute function key, (F4), which will work either while you are building a formula in point mode or when you are editing a formula. You can also type the dollar signs directly into a formula. In the steps that follow you will rebuild the formula, this time making the reference to cell A3 absolute.

Tip Any time you are pointing to a cell while building a formula, and that cell alone provides the required information for the formula and for future copies of the formula, the reference to the cell should be absolute. In short: if you're building a formula to be copied, any references to specific cells should be made absolute.

To build the formula for estimated cost per month (second attempt):

1 Select cell L7, which will contain the cost per month of the heat pump.

2 Type =

3 Select the cost per kilowatt-hour, in cell A3, and press (F4)
Notice that the dollar signs for absolute addressing appear in the formula bar. Don't hold down (F4), because it will cycle through absolute, mixed, and relative address forms. If this cycling happens, tap (F4) several times to cycle back to where both the row and the column part of the address are frozen.

4 Type *

5 Point to the number of kilowatt-hours used, in cell K7.

6 Press (ENTER)
The completed formula reads =$A$3*K7.

7 Copy this formula to the other cells that require it in column L.
The worksheet should now resemble Figure 4.16.

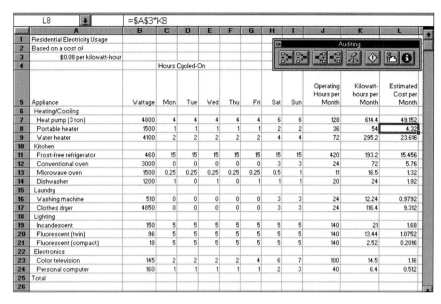

Figure 4.16

Once again, the formula you just created and copied means "Take what is in cell A3 and multiply it by what is one cell to the left (of the cell containing this formula)." You can use tracer arrows to confirm that all the estimated cost per month formulas now depend on cell A3.

 To trace the dependents of cell A3:

1 If necessary, select the **Remove All Arrows** tool.
All tracer arrows disappear.

2 Select cell A3, the cost per kilowatt-hour.

3 Click the **Trace Dependents** tool.
The screen should resemble Figure 4.17. All the cells that calculate estimated cost per month now depend on cell A3.

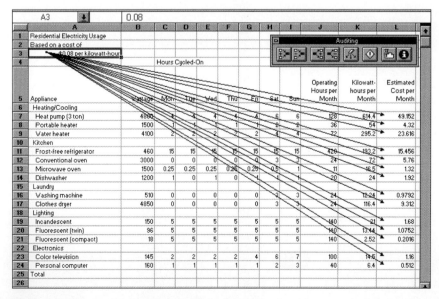

Figure 4.17

4 Click the **Remove All Arrows** tool.

Tip Printouts will include tracer arrows unless you clear the arrows before printing.

Building the Grand Total Formula

The only remaining formula to enter on the spreadsheet is the grand total of estimated monthly electricity costs.

To build the total formula:

1 Select cell L25, which will contain the total monthly cost of all appliances.

2 Type =sum(

3 Select the range encompassing all the cost formulas, L7:L24.
You can select the range by moving backward, if you wish. It's okay for the range to include blank cells—they won't affect the total.

4 Type) and press (ENTER)
The completed formula reads = SUM(L7:L24). The worksheet should now resemble Figure 4.18.

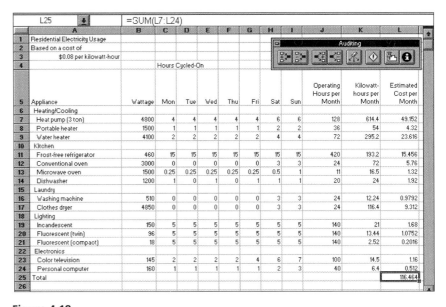

Figure 4.18

5 Rename the Sheet1 tab `Electricity`

6 Close the Auditing toolbar.

7 Save the workbook.

EXIT If necessary, you can quit Excel now and continue this project later.

FORMATTING THE WORKSHEET

As you can see from Figure 4.1, the finished worksheet has several formatting features. In the remainder of this project, you will assign formats to the worksheet and arrive at a completed document very similar to Figure 4.1.

Changing Numeric Formats

Apart from the custom-formatted 0.08 in the subtitle, three kinds of numeric formats are appropriate for this worksheet:

■ A comma-punctuated format with zero decimal places, used for wattage, operating hours per month, and kilowatt-hours per month.
■ A format showing values two digits to the right of the decimal, used for the hours cycled-on and for most of the values in the estimated cost per month columns. Although the values in these areas are currently small numbers, in later use of the worksheet they could become larger, so a comma-punctuated format wouldn't hurt.
■ A currency or accounting format, showing two decimal places, for the first entry and grand total in the estimated cost per month column.

You can change numeric formats in a worksheet in two ways: you can apply a style that contains the desired format or you can apply the numeric format directly. The main advantage to using styles is that you can later change the style definition and have the change take effect on all cells that have that style. There are six standard styles that will work for most situations; however, if no existing style includes the format you want, you can create your own style or modify an existing one.

In the following steps, you will use both approaches—styles and direct formatting—to change numeric formats. You will start by applying the Comma style to a nonadjacent selection composed of the columns for wattage, operating hours per month, and kilowatt-hours per month.

To apply the Comma style to a selection:

1 Staying in full-screen view, display the Formatting toolbar.

2 Zoom the worksheet to 73 percent magnification.

3 Make a nonadjacent selection that includes the values in the wattage, operating hours per month, and kilowatt-hours per month columns.

4 Click the **Comma Style** tool.
The screen should resemble Figure 4.19.

	A	B	C	D	E	F	G	H	I	J	K	L	M
1	Residential Electricity Usage												
2	Based on a cost of												
3	$0.08 per kilowatt-hour												
4				Hours Cycled-On									
5	Appliance	Wattage	Mon	Tue	Wed	Thu	Fri	Sat	Sun	Operating Hours per Month	Kilowatt-hours per Month	Estimated Cost per Month	
6	Heating/Cooling												
7	Heat pump (3 ton)	4,800.00	4	4	4	4	4	6	6	128.00	614.40	49.152	
8	Portable heater	1,500.00	1	1	1	1	1	2	2	36.00	54.00	4.32	
9	Water heater	4,100.00	2	2	2	2	2	4	4	72.00	295.20	23.616	
10	Kitchen												
11	Frost-free refrigerator	460.00	15	15	15	15	15	15	15	420.00	193.20	15.456	
12	Conventional oven	3,000.00	0	0	0	0	0	3	3	24.00	72.00	5.76	
13	Microwave oven	1,500.00	0.25	0.25	0.25	0.25	0.25	0.5	1	11.00	16.50	1.32	
14	Dishwasher	1,200.00	1	0	1	0	1	1	1	20.00	24.00	1.92	
15	Laundry												
16	Washing machine	510.00	0	0	0	0	0	3	3	24.00	12.24	0.9792	
17	Clothes dryer	4,850.00	0	0	0	0	0	3	3	24.00	116.40	9.312	
18	Lighting												
19	Incandescent	150.00	5	5	5	5	5	5	5	140.00	21.00	1.68	
20	Fluorescent (twin)	96.00	5	5	5	5	5	5	5	140.00	13.44	1.0752	
21	Fluorescent (compact)	18.00	5	5	5	5	5	5	5	140.00	2.52	0.2016	
22	Electronics												
23	Color television	145.00	2	2	2	2	4	6	7	100.00	14.50	1.16	
24	Personal computer	160.00	1	1	1	1	1	2	3	40.00	6.40	0.512	
25	Total											116.464	

Figure 4.19

5 Click the **Decrease Decimal** tool twice.
The affected values will now always appear with no digits to the right of the decimal and with commas in values of 1000 and higher.

To apply a number format directly from the Format menu:

1 Select C7:I24, the range for hours cycled-on for Monday through Sunday.

2 Choose **Format** and then **Cells.**

3 Click the **Number** tab.

4 Select **0.00** from the **Format Codes** list box.
The screen should resemble Figure 4.20.

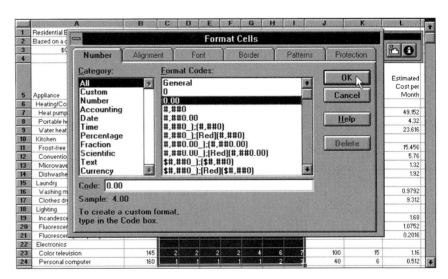

Figure 4.20

5 Select **OK** to apply the format.

The numbers for hours cycled-on now appear with two digits to the right of the decimal point.

The final numeric formatting involves the column for estimated cost per month. Because the numbers in this column are dollar amounts, they should appear with two digits to the right of the decimal. Even though all the figures in the column represent dollar amounts, preceding each by a dollar sign would make the column more difficult to read. In traditional financial-spreadsheet style, a dollar sign is used only in the first entry and the total of such a column.

The regular Comma style displays two digits to the right of the decimal; the regular Currency style is similar to Comma, except that a dollar sign precedes the displayed value.

To apply the Comma style to a selection:

1 Make a nonadjacent selection of L8:L24, the values for estimated cost per month, *excluding* the first and last figures.

2 Click the **Comma Style** tool to apply the style.

To apply the Currency style to a selection:

1 Select the estimated cost per month for the heat pump and the total estimated cost in L7 and L25, respectively.

2 Click the **Currency Style** tool.

The worksheet should resemble Figure 4.21.

	A	B	C	D	E	F	G	H	I	J	K	L	M
1	Residential Electricity Usage												
2	Based on a cost of												
3	$0.08 per kilowatt-hour												
4					Hours Cycled-On								
5	Appliance	Wattage	Mon	Tue	Wed	Thu	Fri	Sat	Sun	Operating Hours per Month	Kilowatt-hours per Month	Estimated Cost per Month	
6	Heating/Cooling												
7	Heat pump (3 ton)	4,800	4.00	4.00	4.00	4.00	4.00	6.00	6.00	128	614	$ 49.15	
8	Portable heater	1,500	1.00	1.00	1.00	1.00	1.00	2.00	2.00	36	54	4.32	
9	Water heater	4,100	2.00	2.00	2.00	2.00	2.00	4.00	4.00	72	295	23.62	
10	Kitchen												
11	Frost-free refrigerator	460	15.00	15.00	15.00	15.00	15.00	15.00	15.00	420	193	15.46	
12	Conventional oven	3,000	0.00	0.00	0.00	0.00	0.00	3.00	3.00	24	72	5.76	
13	Microwave oven	1,500	0.25	0.25	0.25	0.25	0.25	0.50	1.00	11	17	1.32	
14	Dishwasher	1,200	1.00	0.00	1.00	0.00	1.00	1.00	1.00	20	24	1.92	
15	Laundry												
16	Washing machine	510	0.00	0.00	0.00	0.00	0.00	3.00	3.00	24	12	0.98	
17	Clothes dryer	4,850	0.00	0.00	0.00	0.00	0.00	3.00	3.00	24	116	9.31	
18	Lighting												
19	Incandescent	150	5.00	5.00	5.00	5.00	5.00	5.00	5.00	140	21	1.68	
20	Fluorescent (twin)	96	5.00	5.00	5.00	5.00	5.00	5.00	5.00	140	13	1.08	
21	Fluorescent (compact)	18	5.00	5.00	5.00	5.00	5.00	5.00	5.00	140	3	0.20	
22	Electronics												
23	Color television	145	2.00	2.00	2.00	2.00	4.00	6.00	7.00	100	15	1.16	
24	Personal computer	160	1.00	1.00	1.00	1.00	1.00	2.00	3.00	40	6	0.51	
25	Total											$ 116.45	

Figure 4.21

3 Save the worksheet.

Tip The Currency Style tool uses an Accounting number format. If you would prefer having a format that places dollar signs immediately in front of numbers, you should use one of the Currency number formats available on the Number tab of the Format Cells dialog box. You can also redefine the Currency style to use a different number format.

If you use the Increase Decimal or Decrease Decimal tool on a cell, the tool overrides the number format specified in the cell's style. Unfortunately, this means subsequent changes to the style definition will not affect the cell (unless you reapply the style).

Changing the Font Style and Size

As you learned in a previous project, a *font* is a typeface design. Arial, New Courier, and Times New Roman are names of different fonts.

Along with choosing a font, you can decide whether the font should appear in a particular *font style.* The basic font styles, which should not be confused with worksheet-cell formatting styles, are Regular, **Bold**, *Italic*, and <u>Underline</u>. You can also combine font styles, as in ***Bold Italic.*** The size of a font is measured in units called *points.* One point is 1/72 of an inch; the default font size in Excel is 10 points.

Figure 4.22

As shown in Figure 4.22, the Formatting toolbar contains a group of convenient controls that can be used for the following functions: changing the font; changing the point size; turning bold formatting on or off; turning italic formatting on or off; and turning underline formatting on or off. More extensive control over fonts is available in the Font tab, accessed from the Format Cells menu command.

The only font used in the completed version of this worksheet is Arial, although a variety of point sizes and font styles are employed. In the next series of steps, you will change the main title to appear in 18-point bold italic.

To change the font style and size for the main title:

1 Select cell A1, which contains the title *Residential Electricity Usage.*

2 Select **18** points from the **Font Size** list box.

3 Click the **Bold** tool.

4 Click the **Italic** tool.

The screen should resemble Figure 4.23.

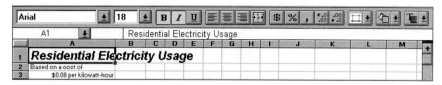

Figure 4.23

The title text should now appear in bold and italic and in a larger point size. Notice that the Bold and Italic buttons on the toolbar are highlighted; this indicates that the current selection has both the bold and the italic font styles.

The two subtitle lines each use a font size of 11 points. You can change this with the Font Size tool on the Formatting toolbar or in the Font tab of the Format Cells dialog box.

To increase the font size of the two subtitles:

1 Select A2:A3, the range containing the two subtitles.

2 Click inside the **Font Size** list box and change the size to 11 points.

Changing Font Style and Size for Other Cell Entries

Here's a list of the remaining cell entries whose font styles and sizes need to be changed:

- The title *Hours Cycled-On* should be 10-point bold.
- All of the column titles in B5:L5 should be 10-point italic.
- The titles *Appliance* and *Total* should be 16-point bold.
- The titles *Heating/Cooling, Kitchen, Laundry, Lighting,* and *Electronics* should be 11-point bold.
- The formula result for total estimated cost per month in cell L25 should be 11-point bold.

To change other font attributes in the worksheet:

1 Select cell C4, which contains the text *Hours Cycled-On.*

2 Click the **Bold** tool.

3 Select the range B5:L5, which contains the column titles.

4 Click the **Italic** tool.

This changes the font style to italic. On some systems, it may be necessary to slightly adjust the width of the columns after changing the column titles to italic.

5 Select cell A5, which contains the text *Appliance.*

6 Change the font size and style to 16-point bold.

Copying Only the Format of a Cell

The title *Total* in cell A25 is supposed to have the same font style and size as *Appliance* in cell A5. Excel has the ability to copy just the format (and not the contents) of one cell to another cell.

To copy the format of cell A5 to cell A25:

1 Select cell A5, which contains *Appliance*.

2 Select the **Format Painter** tool on the Standard toolbar. The pointer changes to a paintbrush.

3 Scroll down if necessary, and then select cell A25, which contains *Total*.

Tip The Paste Special command from the Edit menu can also be used to copy selected attributes of a cell and to change these copies in various ways.

To complete the font settings for the worksheet:

1 Press (CTRL) + (HOME)

2 Make a nonadjacent selection to include *Heating/Cooling* (cell A6), *Kitchen* (cell A10), *Laundry* (cell A15), *Lighting* (cell A18), *Electronics* (cell A22), and the grand total formula in cell L25.

3 Set these cells to 11-point bold.

Centering Selected Titles

The titles in A1:A3 should be centered across the whole worksheet; the title *Hours Cycled-On* should be centered across the weekday columns.

To center titles across selected columns:

1 Select the range A1:L3, as shown in Figure 4.24.

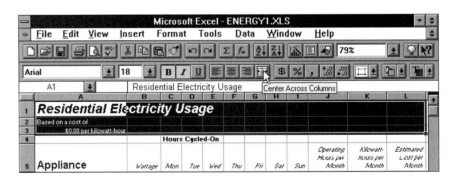

Figure 4.24

2 Click the **Center Across Columns** tool, as shown in Figure 4.24.

3 Change the height of row 4 to about 30 points.

4 Select the range C4:I4. This is the selection in which *Hours Cycled-On* should be centered.

5 Center *Hours Cycled-On* across the selection.

6 Save the workbook.

Adding Borders to a Worksheet

A *border* is a line that lends visual organization to the information in a worksheet. The completed worksheet will have several kinds of borders. You may want to turn cell gridlines off after performing a Border command, because the gridlines make it harder to see the borders.

> **Tip** When you are applying borders, it is usually a good idea to work from within the worksheet toward the outside perimeter: that is, you should create the innermost borders first, and then proceed to the next layer, and so forth.

The innermost borders in this worksheet are those for the hours cycled-on values. Next you will add the horizontal section borders, separating appliance categories. Finally, you will set the thick outer border.

To add borders to the hours cycled-on cells:

1 Remove the Formatting toolbar from the screen.

2 Select the range C5:I24, the hours cycled-on column headings and values.

3 Choose **Format** and then **Cells.**

4 Click the **Border** tab.

The Border dialog box appears. Notice that in the Style section, a rectangle surrounds the currently selected line style. Figure 4.25 shows the names of the various line styles.

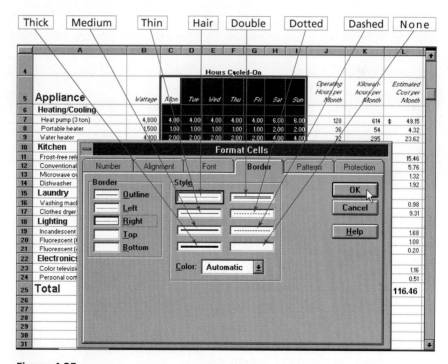

Figure 4.25

5 Select **Outline** in the **Border** group.

A thin line appears next to Outline indicating that this line style will be used to form an outline around the entire selected area.

6 Select **Left** in the **Border** group.
The left edge of each cell in the selected range will have a thin border.

7 Select the Hair line in the upper left of the **Style** group.
This selects a different line style—one that will be used for the left and right borders for each cell in the selected range.

8 Select **Right** in the **Border** group.
The Hair line style should appear for both the Left and Right borders, and the Thin line for the Outline, as shown in Figure 4.25.

9 Select **OK** to apply the chosen borders.

10 Choose **Tools** and then **Options,** click the **View** tab, and turn off cell gridlines, and then select OK.
The effect of the Border command is now more apparent, as shown in Figure 4.26. Notice that outline borders override individual cell borders.

	A		B	C	D	E	F	G	H	I	J	K	L	M
1			**Residential Electricity Usage**											
2						Based on a cost of							
3						$0.08 per kilowatt-hour							
4							**Hours Cycled-On**							
5	**Appliance**		*Wattage*	*Mon*	*Tue*	*Wed*	*Thu*	*Fri*	*Sat*	*Sun*	*Operating Hours per Month*	*Kilowatt-hours per Month*	*Estimated Cost per Month*	
6	**Heating/Cooling**													
7	Heat pump (3 ton)		4,800	4.00	4.00	4.00	4.00	4.00	6.00	6.00	128	614	$ 49.15	
8	Portable heater		1,500	1.00	1.00	1.00	1.00	1.00	2.00	2.00	36	54	4.32	
9	Water heater		4,100	2.00	2.00	2.00	2.00	2.00	4.00	4.00	72	295	23.62	
10	**Kitchen**													
11	Frost-free refrigerator		460	15.00	15.00	15.00	15.00	15.00	15.00	15.00	420	193	15.46	
12	Conventional oven		3,000	0.00	0.00	0.00	0.00	0.00	3.00	3.00	24	72	5.76	
13	Microwave oven		1,500	0.25	0.25	0.25	0.25	0.25	0.50	1.00	11	17	1.32	
14	Dishwasher		1,200	1.00	0.00	1.00	0.00	1.00	1.00	1.00	20	24	1.92	
15	**Laundry**													
16	Washing machine		510	0.00	0.00	0.00	0.00	0.00	3.00	3.00	24	12	0.98	
17	Clothes dryer		4,850	0.00	0.00	0.00	0.00	0.00	3.00	3.00	24	116	9.31	
18	**Lighting**													
19	Incandescent		150	5.00	5.00	5.00	5.00	5.00	5.00	5.00	140	21	1.68	
20	Fluorescent (twin)		96	5.00	5.00	5.00	5.00	5.00	5.00	5.00	140	13	1.08	
21	Fluorescent (compact)		18	5.00	5.00	5.00	5.00	5.00	5.00	5.00	140	3	0.20	
22	**Electronics**													
23	Color television		145	2.00	2.00	2.00	2.00	4.00	6.00	7.00	100	15	1.16	
24	Personal computer		160	1.00	1.00	1.00	1.00	1.00	2.00	3.00	40	6	0.51	
25	**Total**												$ 116.46	

Figure 4.26

11 Turn gridlines back on to make it easier to position the active cell.

To set the horizontal section borders:

1 Make a nonadjacent selection to include the rows for the appliance categories and the total. The selected ranges are A6:L6, A10:L10, A15:L15, A18:L18, A22:L22, and A25:L25.

2 Choose **Format** and then **Cells,** select the **Border** tab, and specify a Thin top border, as shown in Figure 4.27.
In the dialog box, the Left and Right boxes are shaded because not all cells within the selection currently have the same setting for left and right borders.

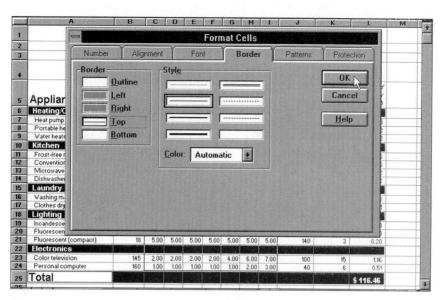

Figure 4.27

3 Select **OK** to apply the border.

To set an outline around the entire worksheet:

1 Select the entire functional area of the worksheet, A1:L25.

2 Choose **Cells** from the **Format** menu, select the **Border** tab, and set a Medium outline border for the worksheet. Medium is just under the Thin line style.

3 Turn cell gridlines off after completing the Border command. The worksheet should resemble Figure 4.28.

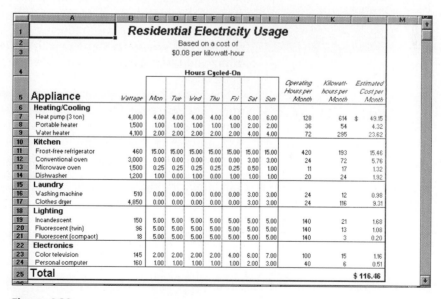

Figure 4.28

4 Turn cell gridlines back on.

5 Switch out of full-screen view and display the Formatting toolbar.

6 Save the workbook.

PRINTING AND MAKING FINAL MODIFICATIONS

In the steps that follow, you will learn how to suppress cell gridlines on the printout only (and keep gridlines on the screen). After printing the worksheet and examining the printout, you will notice areas that require adjustments. You will then print the worksheet again.

To suppress cell gridlines on a printout:

1 Make sure the printer is powered on and is online.

2 Choose **File** and then **Print.**

3 Select **Page Setup** in the Print dialog box.

4 Click the **Sheet** tab, clear the **Gridlines** checkbox, and then select **OK.**

5 Select **OK** in the Print dialog box.
The worksheet prints on two pages on most printers.

6 Zoom to 25 percent magnification.
If you examine the worksheet on-screen, you will see horizontal and vertical dashed lines placed by Excel at page breaks for your reference.

7 Zoom to 75 percent magnification.

Changing the Orientation of a Printout

Because the worksheet is printed on two pages, you would need to trim one of the sheets and tape the two pages together to have a single printed image of the worksheet. If you want this worksheet to fit on a single page, you can change the *scaling* (reducing it to fit) and you can flip the printout from *portrait orientation* (the default) to *landscape orientation.* Both the scaling and the orientation controls are in the Page tab of the Page Setup dialog box.

The text of a landscape printout reads along the long dimension of the paper. The terms *portrait* and *landscape* derive from the world of art, where portrait paintings are usually oriented with the long side on the vertical and landscape paintings with the long side on the horizontal.

You will also notice that the days of the week might look better if they were aligned in the centers of their cells, rather than aligned to the right. In the following steps, you will modify the alignment of the weekday names, and instruct Excel to produce a landscape printout centered on the page.

To adjust and reprint the worksheet:

1 Select the weekday names, *Mon* through *Sun*, and select the **Center** tool on the Formatting toolbar.

Reminder The Center tool has the same effect as choosing Center in the Alignment dialog box. It means to center each entry within its cell, and is not the same as centering an entry across columns.

2 Save the worksheet.

3 Choose **File, Print,** and then select **Page Setup.**

4 Click the **Page** tab.
The Page tab appears.

5 Select the **Landscape** option under **Orientation.**

6 Click the **Margins** tab.
The Margins tab appears.

7 Click the check boxes to center the printout horizontally and vertically, and then select **OK.**

8 Select **OK** in the Print dialog box to print the worksheet.
The completed landscape printout should resemble Figure 4.1.

Defining Named Ranges

Earlier in this project, you saw how to define names for constants. You can also define names for cells or larger ranges on the worksheet. You can then use the name as you enter new formulas. If formulas that refer to the named range already exist in the worksheet, you must *apply* the name to those formulas before the name will show up within the formulas.

Consider the formula for estimated cost per month in cell L7. It currently reads = $A$3∗K7. The same reference, $A$3, is used in every one of the estimated cost formulas. The formula would be a little more understandable if it looked like this: = CostPerKilowattHour∗K7. In the following steps, you will define the name *CostPerKilowattHour* to refer to cell $A$3. You will then apply the name to the cells containing the estimated cost formulas.

A quick way to define names that refer to ranges on the worksheet is to use the Name box in the formula bar.

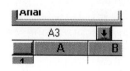

To define and apply a named range:

1 Select cell A3, which contains *0.08*, the cost per kilowatt-hour.

2 Click in the Name box in the formula bar.

3 Type **CostPerKilowattHour** in the Name box and press (ENTER)
Remember to type the name as a single word with mixed upper- and lowercase letters.

4 Select cell L7, the estimated cost per month for the heat pump.
Notice that the formula still reads = $A$3∗K7.

5 Select L7:L24, the range containing the formulas for estimated cost per month.

6 Choose **Insert, Name,** and then select **Apply.**
The Apply Names dialog box appears.

7 Select **OK** to apply the name *CostPerKilowattHour*, as shown in Figure 4.29.

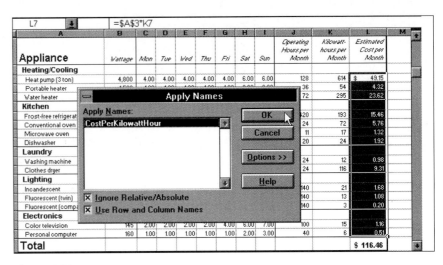

Figure 4.29

If you examine any of the formulas for estimated cost, you will discover that the name *CostPerKilowattHour* is now used instead of *$A$3*.

8 Save the workbook.

The dictionary of defined names is part of the workbook. Because the dictionary has changed, you should save the workbook.

THE NEXT STEP

Many of the commands you used in this project will help in constructing and managing larger worksheets. When the functional part of a worksheet grows to encompass thousands of cells, the increased complexity can be tamed somewhat by spending time initially on design, using named ranges, and using the Zoom Control command to view the worksheet from afar.

You have also worked with several sophisticated formatting features. Remember that the important thing about any worksheet is its results—usually numerical values resulting from formulas. Fonts, font styles, borders, and so on enhance the legibility of the worksheet and should not in themselves become a distraction to the person who reads the worksheet.

Perhaps one of the best ways to make the results of worksheets more legible is to present the information in pictures using Excel's superb charting capability. That is the subject of the next project.

This concludes Project 4. You can either exit Excel, or go on to work the Study Questions, Review Exercises, and Assignments.

SUMMARY AND EXERCISES

Summary

- Customized number formats allow you to attach special abbreviations and other text to a numeric entry.
- You can use the Zoom Control to magnify or reduce the view of the worksheet. Smaller magnifications are especially helpful for comprehending the arrangement of a large worksheet. Selecting full-screen view temporarily removes the toolbars and status bar to allow more room for the worksheet on-screen.
- You can use series fill to automatically fill a range that begins with a standard sequence or series.
- You can change the horizontal and vertical alignment of cell entries; titles above columns of numbers are usually easiest to read if they are aligned at the right or center. You can also make the text in cells wrap onto several lines.
- You can assign names to constants and to cells and ranges. Defined names make formulas more intelligible by eliminating constant numbers typed into formulas.
- You can copy to nonadjacent selections; this often saves you from using the Copy command repeatedly.
- Absolute cell references are usually necessary when you are copying a formula that contains a reference to a single cell in the worksheet.
- The font size (measured in points) and style (regular, italic, bold, underline, or bold italic) can be changed in selected cells or in a named cell style.
- Borders in a variety of thicknesses can be applied to cells and to larger selections.

Key Terms and Operations

Key Terms
absolute reference
AutoFill
border
customized format
defined name
fonts
font style
full-screen view
landscape orientation
points

portrait orientation
scaling
wrapping

Operations
Apply a style
Boldface text
Center across columns
Define a name
Format a cell
Italicize text
Zoom out or in

Study Questions

Multiple Choice

1. Excel displays number signs (#) in a cell when:
   a. A formatted number is too long to fit in the column.
   b. There is an error in a formula.
   c. A text entry is too long to fit in the column.
   d. An absolute cell address is required in a formula.
   e. The cell has an invalid customized format.

2. To conveniently enter a single value into a selected range, type the value in a cell within the selected range and then press:
   a. (ENTER)   d. (CTRL) + (ENTER)
   b. (SHIFT) + (ENTER)   e. (SHIFT) + (TAB)
   c. (TAB)

3. In the formula =SUM(G3:G12)*0.12115, *0.12115* is called a(n):
   a. defined name.   d. formula modifier.
   b. number constant.   e. relative address.
   c. absolute address.

4. In the formula =SUM(G3:G12)*ExpenseFactor, *ExpenseFactor* is a(n):
   a. text constant.   d. absolute address.
   b. manifest constant.   e. defined name.
   c. hidden number.

5. In the formula =$A$3*K7, *$A$3* is called a(n):
   a. defined constant.   d. relative cell address.
   b. defined name.   e. manifest constant.
   c. absolute cell address.

6. If the formula =A1+$A$2 were entered in cell A3 and then copied to cell B3, the copy in cell B3 would read:
   a. =B1+$A$2   d. =B1+b2
   b. =A1+$A$2   e. =B1+B2
   c. =A1+$B$2

7. Bold and Italic are examples of:
   a. font styles.   d. font names.
   b. patterns.   e. cell styles.
   c. alignments.

8. When adding several levels of borders to a worksheet, it is best to:
   a. Start from the innermost level and work outward.
   b. Start with the overall outline and work in.
   c. Proceed column by column.
   d. Zoom to a high magnification.
   e. Print with cell grid lines on.

9. Printing that is oriented along the long dimension of the paper is referred to as:

   a. portrait orientation.   d. anisotopic mapping.

   b. panoramic orientation.   e. landscape orientation.

   c. wide-angle printing.

10. Writing an incorrect formula that attempts to perform math by referring to a text entry causes Excel to display what in the formula's cell?

   a. ERROR   d. #VALUE!

   b. 0   e. !!!!!

   c. #####

Short Answer

1. How can you adjust the magnification of the worksheet so the selected range occupies the entire worksheet area?

2. What term is used to describe breaking a long text entry into several lines within its cell?

3. What type of format should be used when a numeric entry, such as 45, needs to appear in a single cell with text (for example, 45 degrees)?

4. What is the easiest way to enter the month names *Jan*, *Feb*, *Mar*, and so on in a range of cells?

5. Arial and Times New Roman are examples of what?

6. What unit of measurement is used when referring to the size of characters in a font?

7. If a formula refers to a specific, single cell, and the formula will be copied to other cells, how should the reference to the single cell appear in the formula?

8. If you want a border line to appear around all four sides of a selection, what command should you use?

9. How is a text entry normally aligned when it is entered into a cell?

10. How will numbers appear if they are formatted using the Comma Style tool?

For Discussion

1. What is the difference between using a style and applying a numeric format directly? What are the advantages of using styles?

2. What is the difference between relative and absolute cell addressing? Under what circumstances should a formula contain an absolute cell reference?

3. Explain the difference between portrait and landscape orientation. When is landscape printing appropriate?

4. In general, what steps are required to suppress gridlines on a printout, yet maintain them on the screen?

Review Exercises

Projecting Coffee House Income

Follow the steps below to construct a worksheet similar to Figure 4.30. The question marks in the figure indicate cells that will contain formulas.

Begin by entering all of the text constants (use AutoFill to enter the month names), and then enter the numbers for cost and price, and all the values for number sold. Enter the formula for income per cup as selling price per cup minus our cost per cup. Calculate the income for January by multiplying the number sold by the income per cup. Remember, the reference to income per cup should be absolute. Copy the formula to the other months.

	A	B	C	D	E	F	G	H	I
1			Clem's Coffee Clutch						
2			Projected Income from Cappuccino Sales						
3	Coffee	Our Cost per Cup	Selling Price per Cup	Income per Cup					
4	Cappuccino	$ 0.74	$ 1.50	?					
5									
6		Jan	Feb	Mar	Apr	May	Jun	Total	
7	Number Sold	440	350	370	340	290	220	?	
8	Income	?	?	?	?	?	?	?	
9									

Figure 4.30

Create formulas (using the SUM function) for total number sold and total income. Style in bold and center across columns the title and subtitle. Make the title a slightly larger size than the subtitle and make the subtitle italic. Format the column headings for our cost, selling price, and income per cup as bold, aligned to the right, and set to wrap. Format the month names and *Total* as bold, italic, and aligned to the right.

Apply the Currency style to the cost, price, and income per cup cells. Apply Currency style with no decimal places to the monthly income formulas and Comma style with no decimal places to the values for number sold each month. Adjust column widths and row heights as necessary, turn off cell gridlines, and apply borders so the worksheet resembles Figure 4.30. Save the workbook as COFFEE41, and then print the worksheet.

Computing Coffee Brand Income as Percent of Total Income

Figure 4.31 shows an enhanced version of the COFFEE3 worksheet from Assignment 2 in Project 3. A column has been added to show the income from each flavor of coffee expressed as a percent of the total income. For a particular flavor of coffee, this value is calculated by dividing its income amount by the total income. If such a formula is to be successfully copied to all the cells in the Percent of Total Income column, the reference to the total income must be absolute. The worksheet is also formatted with various alignments, borders, cell styles, and font styles.

	A	B	C	D	E	F	G	H
1	Coffee	Cost	Selling Price	No. Sold	Income	Percent of Total Income		
2	House Blend	$ 0.39	$ 0.95	60	$ 33.60	?		
3	Espresso	0.61	1.25	12	7.68	?		
4	Cappuccino	0.74	1.50	22	16.72	?		
5	Cafe Mocha	0.55	1.45	35	31.50	?		
6	Cafe Royale	0.68	1.85	55	64.35	?		
7	Total			184	$ 153.85	?		
8								

Figure 4.31

Refer to Figure 4.31 and build a similar worksheet. Add the new column first, and then proceed with formatting and borders. Apply the Currency and Comma cell styles as indicated in the figure. Use the Percent style for the new column of formulas.

Define the name *TotalIncome* to refer to the cell containing the total income, and then apply the name to the new formulas. Save the workbook under the name COFFEE42.

Assignments

Developing Your Own Electricity Worksheet

Construct a worksheet to calculate your monthly consumption of electricity. If necessary, look up energy consumption figures for the appliances in your home, apartment, or dorm room. Is there any appliance whose usage you can affect to such an extent that substantial amounts of electricity are saved? Save the workbook under the name MYENERGY.

Enhancing the Municipal Waste Worksheet

Figure 4.32 shows an enhanced version of the EPA2 workbook from the first Review Exercise in Project 3. The formula that computes the percent of the total for a particular category takes the 1990 value and divides it by the 1990 grand total (this is similar to the second review exercise in this project). Note that the borders have been customized, titles have been added, and numeric formatting has been adjusted.

	A	B	C	D	E	F	G	H
1	**Municipal Waste Trends**							
2	*in pounds per day per person*							
3	Category	1960	1970	1980	1990	Percent of Grand Total (for 1990)		
4	**Nonfood Wastes**							
5	Paper	0.91	1.19	1.32	1.60	?		
6	Glass	0.20	0.34	0.36	0.28	?		
7	Plastics	0.01	0.08	0.19	0.32	?		
8	Metals	0.32	0.38	0.35	0.34	?		
9	**Total Nonfood**	1.44	1.99	2.22	2.54	?		
10	**Other**							
11	Food	0.37	0.34	0.32	0.29	?		
12	Yard	0.61	0.62	0.66	0.70	?		
13	**Total Other**	0.98	0.96	0.98	0.99	?		
14	*Grand Total*	2.42	2.95	3.20	3.53	?		
15								

Figure 4.32

Build the new formulas and adjust the formatting as necessary to create a completed worksheet similar to Figure 4.32. Use Percent cell style for the new formulas. Save the modified workbook under the name EPA3.

Adapting to Off-Hours Discounts

Some electric utilities offer energy-savings time, a two-tier residential-electricity rate system, where customers who use electricity during off-peak hours receive a special reduced rate (for example, $0.05 per kilowatt-hour) and have to pay a premium rate (for example, $0.15 per kilowatt-hour) for electricity used during peak-demand hours. In the summer and fall, off-peak hours are usually from 9:00 p.m. to noon on weekdays and all day on weekends; in the winter and spring, off-peak hours are usually from 9:00 a.m. to 5:00 p.m. on weekdays and all day on weekends.

Adapt the ENERGY1 worksheet to accommodate a two-tier electricity price schedule. Save the workbook under the name ENERGYDL.

Objectives

After completing this project, you should be able to:

▶ Translate a verbal description and a sketch of a chart into a completed Excel chart

▶ Identify the major components of a chart

▶ Create column charts, pie charts, and 3-D perspective column charts

▶ Create both embedded charts and chart sheets

▶ Resize, position, and customize charts

▶ Link chart text to the worksheet

▶ Print charts

CASE STUDY: COMPARING PRIME-TIME TV SHOWS

Television has reigned as the predominant communications medium in the United States since shortly after the end of the Second World War. Figure 5.1 is a worksheet that shows the popularity of various kinds of prime-time TV shows in the United States from 1950 through 1990. This information is a snapshot of mid- to late twentieth-century U.S. popular culture.

The Most Popular Prime Time TV Shows
Genre by Decade (1950–1990)

Genre	1950s	1960s	1970s	1980s
Crime	8	4	13	16
Drama	10	7	8	14
Variety	20	14	2	0
Western	21	16	2	0
SitCom	23	48	61	54
Other	18	11	14	16
Total	100	100	100	100

Figure 5.1

For purposes of the worksheet, a television program is considered popular if it was among the ten most-watched *prime-time* (evening) programs each year. For each decade, there were 100 top programs. The worksheet condenses the data by considering whole decades and by classifying television shows by genre—or category—of show.

It's possible to see patterns in this table of numbers, but for most people, the best way to identify trends and interrelationships in data is to present the data visually as a ***chart,*** using lines, bars, geometric symbols, and colors.

In this project, you will construct several types of charts to display the information shown in Figure 5.1. Each type of chart emphasizes a certain aspect of the data or lends itself to a certain way of viewing or interpreting the information. Excel offers many more chart types than are needed for this project. Table 5.1 lists a few of the chart types you are likely to use for most of your charting needs.

Table 5.1

Chart Type	Description	Application
Bar	Compares individual values at a specific time. Emphasizes comparison rather than time flow.	Product launch, budget
Column	Similar to bar, but emphasizes variation over a period of time.	Quarterly sales forecast
Pie	Shows relationship between portions of a whole.	Sales levels in various cities
Line	Shows trends or changes over time. Emphasizes time flow and the rate of change rather than the amount of change.	Price index

Designing the Solution

If you want to build a chart, first decide what it is that you want to display in the chart and the type of chart that is most appropriate for the data you will plot. You can then figure out how the various aspects of the planned chart translate into Excel commands and charting options.

Suppose you want to show how the popularity of crime and drama shows changed between 1950 and 1990, and you want your chart to resemble Figure 5.2. Crime show popularity and drama show popularity are the variables that make up the *data series* that you wish to plot as a chart. A **data series** is a set of related values appearing in either a column or a row. A column chart like the one in Figure 5.2 is one way to view this kind of information.

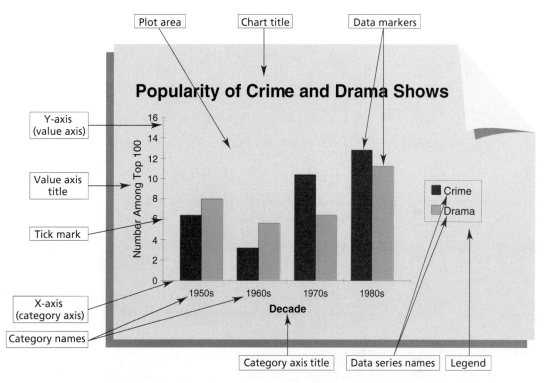

Figure 5.2

The labels along the bottom edge of the chart often correspond to worksheet column headings to tell you what the ***chart categories*** are. For example, the Drama data series has the value 7 in the 1960s category.

The graphic elements of the plot area include axes and the ***data markers*** that represent data points. Depending on the chart type, data markers can take the form of bars, lines, pictures, pie wedges, or other symbols. Each data series is graphically distinguished by the same pattern, color, or symbol. Each category, scale, or data series is marked off on the axis with a tick mark. There are generally two axes that act as the major frame for plotting. The horizontal or category axis—also referred to as the ***X-axis***—plots categories of the data series. The vertical or value axis—also called the ***Y-axis***—is the ruler for plotting data values. In addition to the graphical elements of the chart, text such as titles, a legend, and labels help to convey the interpretation of the data you are plotting.

In the worksheet, categories correspond to rows or columns, usually with titles that become the chart ***category names,*** used as labels along the axes. As shown in Figure 5.3, the categories for the example chart are 1950s, 1960s, 1970s, and 1980s.

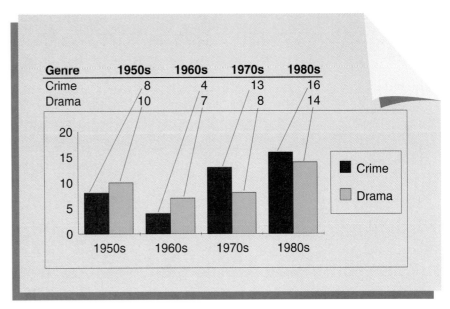

Figure 5.3

Figure 5.3 shows the relationship between a worksheet and a chart created from the worksheet. Each bar in the chart is a data marker. There are two data series: one for crime shows (represented by the red bars on the chart and the numbers 8, 4, 13, and 16 in the worksheet) and the other for drama shows (the green bars on the chart, and the numbers 10, 7, 8, and 14 in the worksheet). In a worksheet, you can often identify the data series as a group of values, in a column or a row, that *change over time*.

If a data series is a row, as is the number of shows each decade, then the chart categories of that data series—the decades—are represented in columns. Alternatively, if a data series is presented in a column, its chart categories are shown in rows. Figure 5.4 shows what the graph would look like if you switched the chart categories used in Figure 5.2 to data series, and the data series to chart categories. Whether you make the chart categories rows or columns depends entirely on the focus of the chart.

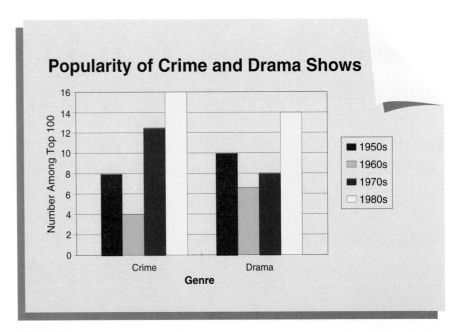

Figure 5.4

CREATING THE UNDERLYING WORKSHEET

In this section, you will make a worksheet similar to the one shown in Figure 5.1 and use that worksheet to create charts in the remainder of this project. You can refer to Figure 5.5 (which has been zoomed to 150 percent magnification) while typing the worksheet. The worksheet contains only four formulas, which compute totals for each column; their primary purpose is to help you check that you correctly typed the number constants.

	A	B	C	D	E	F
1	*The Most Popular Prime Time TV Shows*					
2	**Genre by Decade (1950-1990)**					
3	**Genre**	**1950s**	**1960s**	**1970s**	**1980s**	
4	Crime	8	4	13	16	
5	Drama	10	7	8	14	
6	Variety	20	14	2	0	
7	Western	21	16	2	0	
8	SitCom	23	48	61	54	
9	Other	18	11	14	16	
10	**Total**	100	100	100	100	

Figure 5.5

To build the basic worksheet:

1 Enter the title **The Most Popular Prime Time TV Shows** in cell A1.

2 Make the title in cell A1 11-point bold italic.

3 Enter the subtitle **Genre by Decade (1950-1990)** in cell A2, and make the subtitle bold.

4 Change the height of row 3 to about 28 points.

5 Referring to Figure 5.5, enter the column titles (*Genre* in A3 through *1980s* in E3), and make the titles bold.

6 Use the **Align Right** tool to adjust the column headings from *1950s* to *1980s*.

7 Refer to Figure 5.5 and enter the row titles (*Crime* in A4 through *Other* in A9) and the number constants (in the range B4:E9).

8 Enter **Total** in cell A10, and make the word bold.

9 Use the **AutoSum** tool to create total formulas where they are required in row 10.

10 Select A1:E2, and click the **Center Across Columns** tool.

Using a Tear-Off Palette

The Borders tool on the Formatting toolbar contains a group or *palette* of buttons that represent various commonly used border styles. If you want to keep the palette visible for repeated uses, you can "tear off" the palette and use it like a small floating toolbar. In the steps below, you will tear off the Borders palette and then apply a thin bottom border to the column headings, as well as a thin top and double bottom border to the totals row.

To tear off the Borders palette:

1 Click the arrow part of the **Borders** tool.
The Borders palette opens.

2 Click inside the **Borders** palette, drag its outline to the center right of the window, and then release the mouse button.

To apply borders using the Borders palette:

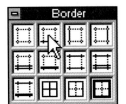

1 Select the column headings in the range A3:E3.

2 Click on the button for a thin bottom border in the **Borders** palette.

3 Select the range A10:E10, the totals row.

4 Click on the button for a thin top border and double-line bottom border.

5 Close the **Borders** palette.

6 Rename the Sheet1 tab to **TV Data**

7 Save the workbook as TV1.

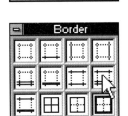

BUILDING A COLUMN CHART WITH CHARTWIZARD

The easiest way to build basic charts is to use *ChartWizard,* a special command accessible only as a toolbar tool. In this section, you will build a column chart based on the plan in Figure 5.2. This first chart will be an *embedded chart;* that is, it will exist as an object embedded within the TV Data worksheet. Later you will create charts as separate *chart sheets.*

When working with embedded charts, you will usually need to see a large area of the worksheet. In the steps that follow, you will change the view of the worksheet by reducing magnification to 75 percent and temporarily removing the status bar from the window.

To change the view of the worksheet:

1 Zoom the window to 75 percent magnification.

2 Remove the status bar, if it is visible, by choosing **View** and then **Status Bar.**
The status bar disappears from the window.

To specify the range to be charted:

1 Select the range A3:E5, as shown in Figure 5.6, which encompasses the data to be charted and the associated category and data series names. Excel will ignore the corner cell containing *Genre,* because it is neither a data series nor a chart category.

	The Most Popular Prime Time TV Shows											
	Genre by Decade (1950-1990)											
Genre	1950s	1960s	1970s	1980s								
Crime	8	4	13	18								
Drama	10	7	8	14								
Variety	20	14	2	0								
Western	21	16	2	0								
SitCom	23	48	61	54								
Other	18	11	14	16								
Total	100	100	100	100								

Figure 5.6

2 Click the **ChartWizard** tool.
The pointer changes to crosshairs. You can drag the mouse to select a location and size for the chart.

3 Position the crosshairs in the middle of cell G3, then hold down the mouse button and drag to the middle of cell K12, as shown in Figure 5.7, and then release the mouse button.

	The Most Popular Prime Time TV Shows											
	Genre by Decade (1950-1990)											
Genre	1950s	1960s	1970s	1980s								
Crime	8	4	13	16								
Drama	10	7	8	14								
Variety	20	14	2	0								
Western	21	16	2	0								
SitCom	23	48	61	54								
Other	18	11	14	16								
Total	100	100	100	100								

Figure 5.7

The ChartWizard Step 1 dialog box appears. Because you have already specified the range to be charted, you do not need to change anything in this dialog box.

4 Select **Next** in the ChartWizard Step 1 dialog box.
The Step 2 dialog box appears to let you pick one of the 15 major chart types.

To set the chart type and format:

1 Select the **Column** chart type if necessary, and then select **Next,** as shown in Figure 5.8.

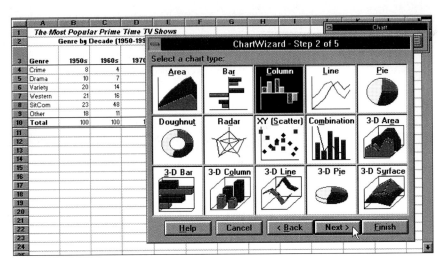

Figure 5.8

The Step 3 dialog box appears to let you pick the specific format for the chart type selected in the previous step.

2 Select chart format **1,** and then select **Next,** as shown in Figure 5.9.

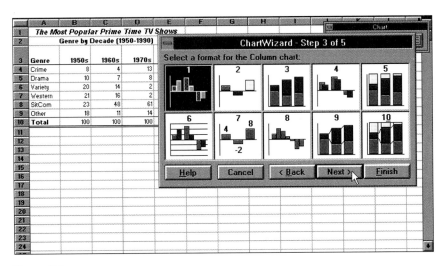

Figure 5.9

The Step 4 dialog box appears, as shown in Figure 5.10. You can use this dialog box to determine whether the data series will be in rows or columns and whether cells in the initially selected range should be used for data series and chart category names. Excel works on the assumption that you want fewer data series than chart categories, which means that for this worksheet, the data series are initially presented in rows.

6 Select **Finish** to complete the chart.
The screen should resemble Figure 5.14. The completed chart appears, embedded in the worksheet, and a floating Chart toolbar also appears. If necessary, you can drag the Chart toolbar so that it does not obscure the worksheet or chart.

	A	B	C	D	E	F	G	H	I
1	*The Most Popular Prime Time TV Shows*								
2	Genre by Decade (1950-1990)								
3	**Genre**	**1950s**	**1960s**	**1970s**	**1980s**				
4	Crime	8	4	13	16				
5	Drama	10	7	8	14				
6	Variety	20	14	2	0				
7	Western	21	16	2	0				
8	SitCom	23	48	61	54				
9	Other	18	11	14	16				
10	Total	100	100	100	100				
11									
12									
13									
14									

Figure 5.14

Working with Embedded Charts

The embedded chart is part of the worksheet, but it does not fill any cells and it doesn't have a cell address. Instead, think of an embedded chart as existing in its own layer that floats on top of the worksheet cells. This means the chart can easily be moved and resized. Small black boxes, called *handles,* appear on the chart's corners and sides when the chart is selected. The Chart toolbar also may appear when a chart is selected. You can select a chart by clicking anywhere inside its rectangle. If you click in the chart and then drag the mouse, you can reposition the chart in the worksheet. If you click and drag one of the chart's handles, you can resize the chart window.

To reposition the embedded chart:

1 Select cell A1.
Notice that the Chart toolbar and the handles on the chart rectangle disappear—the chart is no longer selected.

2 Click once anywhere inside the chart rectangle.
The Chart toolbar and handles reappear, signaling that the chart is selected.

3 With the pointer positioned inside the chart rectangle, hold down the mouse button.

4 Drag the chart's outline so it is below the worksheet data (in rows 12 to 22), similar to Figure 5.15.

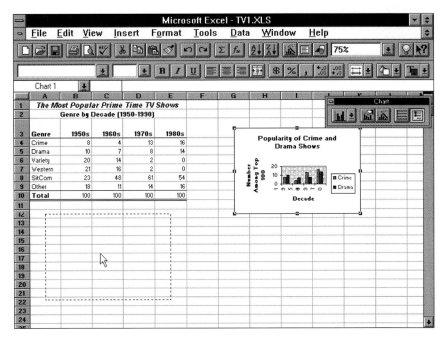

Figure 5.15

5 Release the mouse button.
The chart should now appear below the worksheet data.

The chart will be easier to read if you make it larger. You can change the width of the chart by dragging the middle handle of the left or right edge of the rectangle; change the height of the chart by dragging the middle handle at the top or bottom edge; and change both the width and the height of the chart simultaneously by dragging one of the corner handles.

It is often convenient to use the Print Preview command to see how the chart will appear on the printed page. After you use Print Preview, dotted lines will appear on the worksheet, showing you the boundaries of each printed page. You can then zoom out to 50 or even 25 percent and make adjustments to the chart location and size.

To preview the chart and worksheet printout:

1 Click the **Print Preview** tool on the Standard toolbar.
The Print Preview window appears, showing a simulated printout of the worksheet and chart. If you close the Print Preview window, you will still be able to see dotted reference lines showing page breaks.

2 Select **Close.**
The worksheet again appears, but with dotted reference lines.

3 Zoom to 25 percent magnification.
The placement of individual printout pages is more obvious if you zoom out.

To resize the embedded chart:

1 Zoom to 65 percent magnification.

2 Select the chart by clicking once in it.

3 Hold down the mouse button on the lower-right handle of the chart rectangle.

4 Drag the corner handle to the middle of cell G28, so the chart is wider and taller, similar to Figure 5.16.

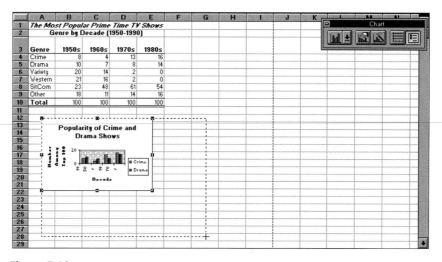

Figure 5.16

5 Release the mouse button.
The screen should now appear similar to Figure 5.17.

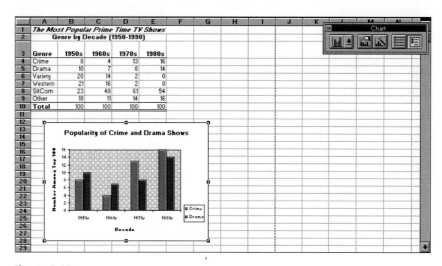

Figure 5.17

The chart you just created is ***linked*** to the worksheet: if the data upon which the chart depends changes, the chart will automatically update to reflect the change. In the following steps, you will change the value for crime shows in the 1960s to see the effect of this linkage. You will then use the Undo command to undo the entry and revert back to the original value.

To observe the effect of linkage:

1 Select cell C4, which contains *4*, the number of crime shows popular during the 1960s.
Note the bar on the chart that corresponds to this value.

2 Type **20** and press (ENTER)
The chart changes immediately to show the change in the worksheet.

 3 Click the **Undo** tool on the Standard toolbar.

4 Save the workbook.

Reminder Undo, also available from the Edit menu, reverses the effect of the most recently issued command.

EXIT If necessary, you can quit Excel now and continue this project later.

Printing Embedded Charts

An embedded chart is part of the worksheet document and it will print with the surrounding worksheet data looking much as it does on-screen. The printing commands you have already learned will work with charts as well. In the following steps, you will use the Print Preview command to see a simulated printout on-screen; then you will print the worksheet. Print Preview is useful, because it allows you to detect problems with the printout without wasting paper, ink, or time.

 To print the embedded chart with its worksheet:

1 Choose **File** and then **Print**.

2 Select **Print Preview**.
A simulated printout page appears. When the pointer is positioned over this page, the pointer shape changes to a magnifying glass; if you click the page, Excel will zoom in on the printout at the point you selected. Clicking again will zoom back out. You can also access other printing commands from the Print Preview window.

3 Position the pointer over the chart and click.
Excel zooms in at the point you clicked.

4 Click again to zoom out.
Notice that cell gridlines will appear on the printout, though it might look better without them.

5 Select **Setup**.
The Page Setup dialog box appears.

6 Select the **Sheet** tab.

7 Clear the **Gridlines** check box and then select **OK**.

8 Make sure the printer is ready, and then click the **Print** button.

Deleting Embedded Charts

You can have many different embedded charts in a worksheet. You can delete an embedded chart by selecting the chart and pressing (DEL) or choosing Clear from the Edit menu.

To delete the embedded chart:

1 Click within the chart to select it.

2 Press (DEL)

Plotting Nonadjacent Data

Suppose you wanted to make another column chart that showed the popularity of dramas and westerns for the 1950s and the 1970s only. This is *nonadjacent* information in the worksheet; that is, the ranges that contain the names and values are separated by cells that contain information that is not required for the chart.

Excel can easily make a chart from a nonadjacent selection, *provided that the pieces of the nonadjacent selection can be assembled into a rectangular range.* When you select the various ranges that comprise the nonadjacent selection, make sure the selections are each the same size and, if put together, that they form a rectangle. Any multicell ranges in the nonadjacent selection should be selected by dragging through the necessary cells, *not* by clicking each of the individual cells comprising the range. In the steps that follow, you will make a nonadjacent selection identical to Figure 5.18 (which is magnified for your reference), and then you will build a column chart based on that selection.

To make the nonadjacent selection:

1 Zoom to 75 percent magnification.

2 Select cell A3, which contains *Genre*, by clicking it. Keep the pointer in the middle of cell A3.

3 Hold down the mouse button and drag to the right to extend the selection to include cell B3, which contains *1950s*, and then release the mouse button.

4 Hold down (CTRL) and then click cell D3, which contains *1970s*.

5 Hold down (CTRL) and then click and drag to select A5:B5, which contains *Drama* and *10*.

6 Hold down (CTRL) and then click cell D5, which contains *8*.

7 Hold down (CTRL) and then click and drag to select A7:B7, which contains *Western* and *21*.

8 Hold down (CTRL) and then click cell D7, which contains *2*.

The completed nonadjacent selection should be identical to Figure 5.18.

Notice that the selection includes the names that should be used on the chart and that, if assembled, the nonadjacent parts would form a rectangle. As before, the upper-left cell (containing *Genre*) will not be used in the actual chart, but it is required if the combined selection is to be rectangular.

	A	B	C	D	E	F
1	*The Most Popular Prime Time TV Shows*					
2	**Genre by Decade (1950-1990)**					
3	**Genre**	**1950s**	**1960s**	**1970s**	**1980s**	
4	Crime	8	4	13	16	
5	Drama	10	7	8	14	
6	Variety	20	14	2	0	
7	Western	21	16	2	0	
8	SitCom	23	48	61	54	
9	Other	18	11	14	16	
10	**Total**	100	100	100	100	
11						

Figure 5.18

To build a column chart using the nonadjacent selection:

1 Select the **ChartWizard** button on the Standard toolbar.

2 Drag to select a chart area from about cell B12 to cell H23.

3 Select **Next** from the Step 1 dialog box.

4 Select the **Column** chart type and **Next** from the Step 2 dialog box.

5 Select chart format **1** and **Next** from the Step 3 dialog box.
The Step 4 dialog box appears.

6 Select **Next.**
The Step 5 dialog box appears.

7 Select **Finish** to create the chart.
You will not bother to add titles to this chart. The completed chart should resemble Figure 5.19.

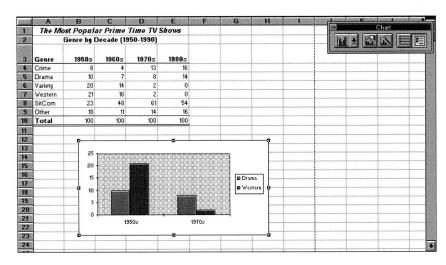

Figure 5.19

8 Delete the chart, and click on any single cell to cancel the selection.

BUILDING PIE CHARTS

A pie chart is different from most of the other chart types, because it shows just one data series. Pie charts are ideal for showing the relationship between a part and the whole—the relative share that each of the various categories represents.

In the following steps, you will create a pie chart showing the breakdown of different kinds of TV shows for the 1960s. This time, the data series will be in a column—the column for the 1960s—and the chart categories will be the different kinds of shows.

To build a pie chart:

1 Make a nonadjacent selection of the ranges A3:A9 and C3:C9, as shown in Figure 5.20. *Remember to drag to select multicell ranges.*

	A	B	C	D	E	F
1	The Most Popular Prime Time TV Shows					
2	Genre by Decade (1950-1990)					
3	Genre	1950s	1960s	1970s	1980s	
4	Crime	8	4	13	16	
5	Drama	10	7	8	14	
6	Variety	20	14	2	0	
7	Western	21	16	2	0	
8	SitCom	23	48	61	54	
9	Other	18	11	14	16	
10	Total	100	100	100	100	
11						

Figure 5.20

2 Click the ChartWizard button on the Standard toolbar.

3 Drag to select a chart area from about cell F2 to cell L23.

4 Select **Next** in the Step 1 dialog box.

5 Select the **Pie chart** type and then **Next** from the Step 2 dialog box.

6 Select chart format **5** and then **Next** from the Step 3 dialog box, as shown in Figure 5.21.

This pie chart format shows labels next to each slice of the pie.

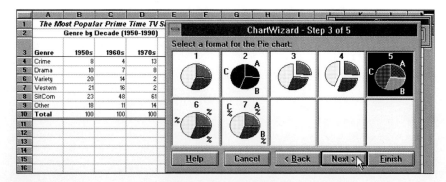

Figure 5.21

Note that the first column should be used for pie slice labels, and the first row for the chart title.

7 Select **Next** in the Step 4 dialog box, as shown in Figure 5.22. The Step 5 dialog box appears. A legend is not really necessary for this chart, because each slice is labeled.

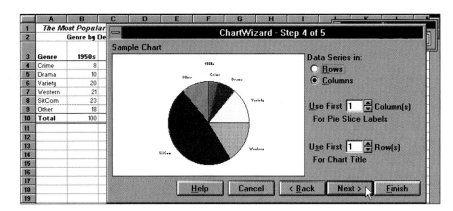

Figure 5.22

8 Select **Finish** in the Step 5 dialog box to create the chart.

9 Drag the Chart toolbar to the unused, lower-left part of the worksheet. The screen should resemble Figure 5.23.

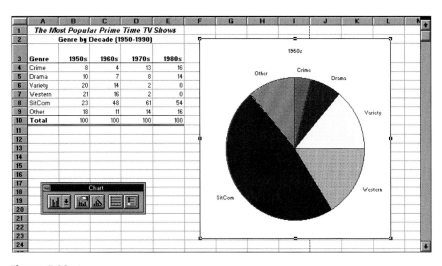

Figure 5.23

Editing an Embedded Chart

If you want to make extensive modifications to the text and graphic objects on a chart, you must first *activate* the chart for editing by *double-clicking* within the chart rectangle. In the following steps, you will activate and modify the pie chart.

Once a chart is activated, you can select an object within the chart by clicking that object. If several objects are in close proximity, you must pay close attention to which object is actually selected. Selected objects appear with handles that can be used to position or resize the object.

To modify an embedded chart:

1 Double-click in the pie chart.
The pie chart should now have a thick striped border, indicating that the chart is activated. Notice that the menu bar is different from the normal worksheet menu bar—it contains commands appropriate to working with charts.

2 Click once directly on the title *1960s.*
A box with handles appears around the text, indicating that the text is selected.

3 Type `Popular TV Shows in the 1960s` and press (ENTER)
The text you typed is used for the chart title.

4 Use the **Font Size** and **Bold** tools to make the title text 14-point bold.

5 Click once directly on the word *Variety.*
Notice that handles appear on all of the pie slice labels—the entire group of labels is selected.

6 Use the **Font Size** tool to change the size to 10 points.
All the pie slice labels are affected.

Suppose you wanted to emphasize or draw attention to the slice for the Western category. One way to do this is to *explode*—or pull out—that slice from the pie.

To explode a pie slice:

1 Position the pointer in the middle of the slice for Western and click.
Notice that all slices are selected.

2 Click again in the middle of the slice for Western.
Now the handles appear just on that slice.

3 Hold down the mouse button on the slice for Western and drag slightly to the right, as shown in Figure 5.24.

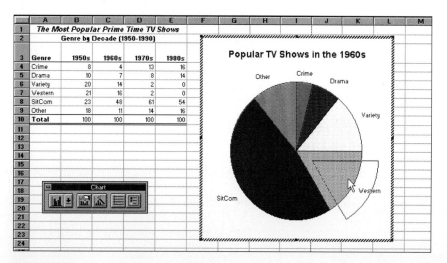

Figure 5.24

The slice for Western should now be pulled out from the pie. Once the mouse button is released, handles once again appear on the slice, which means the slice is still selected within the chart. Do not be concerned if the slice label *Western* is partly cut off.

4 Clear the slice handles by pressing (ESC) once.

Changing the Chart Type

Perhaps a fancier pie chart—such as a 3-D pie chart—would look better. You can change the chart type by using the Chart toolbar or by choosing Chart Type from the Format menu.

To change the type of a chart:

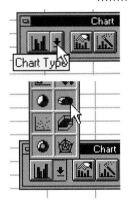

1 Click the list-box arrow on the **Chart Type** tool in the Chart toolbar.

2 Click the 3-D pie chart type.
The chart now appears as a 3-D pie chart. The slice for Western would appear more prominent if the chart were rotated clockwise.

3 Choose **Format** and then **3-D View.**

4 Click the clockwise rotation button three times so the chart is rotated 30 degrees clockwise, and then select **OK,** as shown in Figure 5.25.

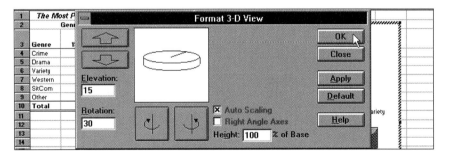

Figure 5.25

5 Click outside of the chart to deactivate it.

6 Close the Chart toolbar.

BUILDING A 3-D COLUMN CHART ON A SEPARATE CHART SHEET

What type of chart would help you to visualize the changing popularity of all the genres for the entire time span of the worksheet? A regular column chart would be cramped, as shown in Figure 5.26. A three-dimensional (3-D) column chart, which you can think of as a group of column charts seen in perspective, might be better.

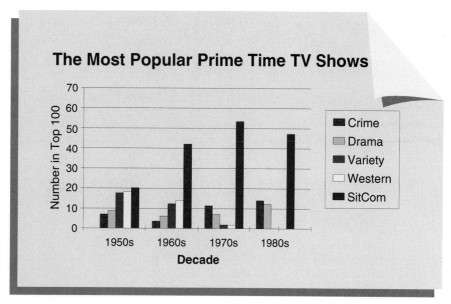

Figure 5.26

In this section, you will create a 3-D perspective column chart on a separate *chart sheet* within the workbook. Like embedded charts, charts in separate chart sheets are still linked to worksheet data. The primary advantage of having separate sheets for various charts is to organize your work and prevent having a single sheet cluttered with a variety of different charts.

To create a chart in a separate chart sheet:

1 Select A3:E8, as shown in Figure 5.27. *Do not include the Other category.*

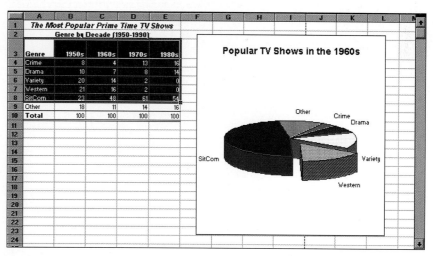

Figure 5.27

2 Choose **Insert, Chart,** and then **As New Sheet.**
The ChartWizard Step 1 dialog box appears.

3 Select **Next** in the Step 1 dialog box.

4 Select the **3-D Column** chart type and then **Next** from the Step 2 dialog box.

5 Select chart format **6** and then **Next** from the Step 3 dialog box. The Step 4 dialog box appears. It will be easier to see the various columns of the chart if the data series is in rows, rather than in columns.

6 Select **Rows** from the Step 4 dialog box, and then **Next**, as shown in Figure 5.28.

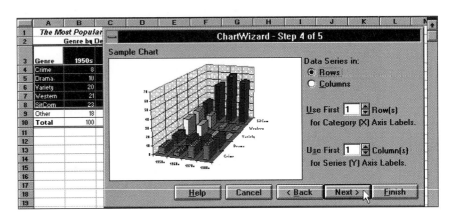

Figure 5.28

The Step 5 dialog box appears.

7 Select **Finish** to create the chart.
The chart appears in its own sheet, whose tab is named Chart1.

8 Double-click the **Chart1** sheet tab and rename it **3-D Column**

9 Drag the 3-D Column sheet tab so the chart sheet is layered after the TV Data worksheet.
The screen should resemble Figure 5.29.

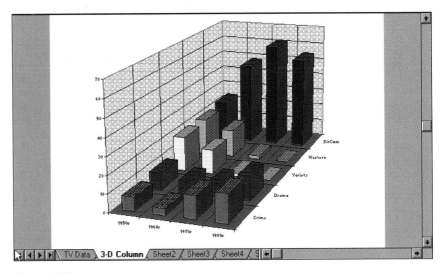

Figure 5.29

Changing the View of a 3-D Chart

The columns of the chart would be a little easier to see if the chart were viewed from a "higher" vantage point and if it were rotated clockwise slightly. It might also look better if the perspective—the three-dimensional effect—were exaggerated. The 3-D View command from the chart sheet's Format menu allows you to experiment with and set different viewing angles and perspectives.

To change the view of the 3-D chart:

1 Choose **Format** and then **3-D View.**

2 Move the pointer to the title bar of the 3-D View dialog box, and drag the dialog box to the upper-left area of the screen so most of the chart is visible, as shown in Figure 5.30.

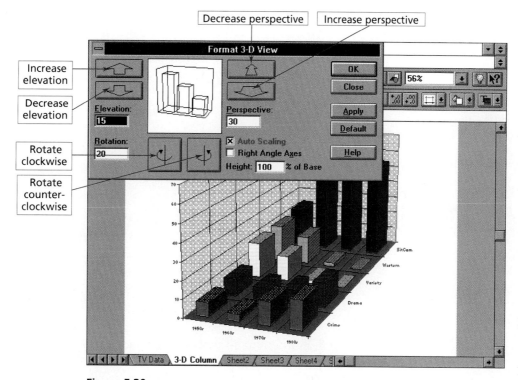

Figure 5.30

3 Use the **Increase Elevation** button to increase the degrees of elevation to 25.

Notice that the small wire-frame example chart in the dialog box changes slightly.

4 Select **Apply** to see the 3-D view settings applied to the actual chart.

5 Click the **Rotate Clockwise** button twice, until the chart is rotated to 40 degrees, and then select **Apply.**

6 Change the perspective to 40 degrees, and then select **OK,** as shown in Figure 5.31.

Selecting OK automatically applies the new 3-D view settings.

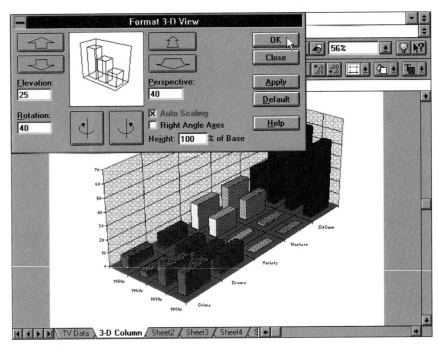

Figure 5.31

Attaching Titles to a Chart

In the following steps, you will add a main chart title that is linked to the worksheet. You will also enter titles for each of the axes.

To attach text to a chart:

1 Make sure the 3-D Column chart sheet is selected (click its tab, if necessary).

2 Zoom to 50 percent magnification; if the chart is not centered on-screen, use the scroll bars to center the chart.

3 Choose **Insert** and then **Titles.**
The Titles dialog box appears.

4 Click all of the check boxes: **Chart Title, Value (Z) Axis, Category (X) Axis,** and **Series (Y) Axis.**

5 Select **OK.**
The word *Title* appears above the chart; the letters *X, Y,* and *Z* label their respective axes.

6 Click on the word *Title* at the top of the chart.

7 Type =

8 Click on the **TV Data** sheet tab, and then select cell A1 (which contains the title text), as shown in Figure 5.32.

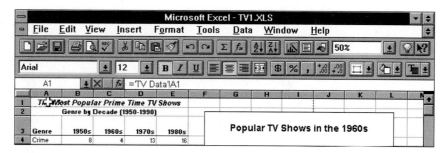

Figure 5.32

9 Press (ENTER) or click the **Enter** box on the formula bar.
The formula ='TV Data'!$A$1 means "get the contents of cell A1 from the sheet named TV Data."

10 Use the Formatting toolbar to change the main title font to Times New Roman 24-point bold italic.

To enter the other chart titles:

1 Click the label *Z*.
The Z-axis in a 3-D chart is marked with the measurement units of the data.

2 Type **Number in Top 100** and press (ENTER)

3 Change the font to Times New Roman 14-point bold italic.

4 Click the label *Y*.
The Y-axis is composed of the data series.

5 Type **Genre** and press (ENTER)

6 Change the font to Times New Roman 14-point bold italic.

7 Click the label *X*.
The X-axis is composed of the chart categories.

8 Type **Decade** and press (ENTER)

9 Change the font to Times New Roman 14-point bold italic.

To print the chart:

1 Choose **File** and then **Print Preview.**
A simulated printout appears. Notice that it includes a header and a footer—information at the top and bottom of the page. (In the next project, you will learn how to specify your own header and footer.) In this case, the header and footer are not necessary and reduce the space available for the chart itself, so they should be removed.

2 Select **Setup.**
The Page Setup dialog box appears.

3 Click the **Header/Footer** tab.

4 Scroll to the top of the **Header** list box and select **(none).**

5 Scroll to the top of the **Footer** list box and select **(none).**

6 Select **OK** in the Page Setup dialog box.

7 Select **Print** in the Print Preview window.
The Print dialog box appears.

8 Click **OK** to print the chart.
The printout should resemble Figure 5.33.

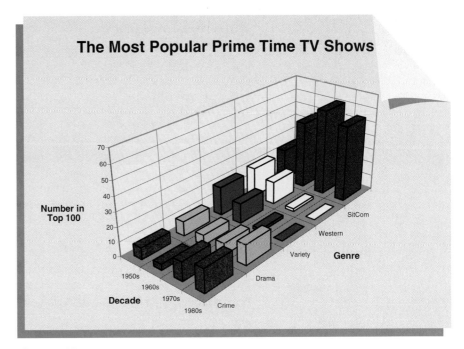

Figure 5.33

9 Save the workbook.

10 Exit Excel.

> **Tip** If a color or shade that Excel uses in a pie slice or bar on the printout is unacceptable (for example, too dark to show detail), double-click the specific object whose color you want to change, and select a different color and pattern from the Patterns tab of the Format Data Series dialog box.

The 3-D column chart conveys information more effectively than does the original table of numbers. If you follow a group of bars of a single color, you are tracing through time, following the changing popularity of a particular genre of TV show. If you read from lower left to upper right across the chart, you can examine the relative popularity of different kinds of shows for a particular decade.

THE NEXT STEP

Charts can help you analyze information, and they can also help you convey worksheet information more effectively to other people. If you are building a worksheet to make a point—to convince or educate other people about some conclusion or decision— charting can be a powerful tool.

However, you will encounter some worksheets, such as the one in the next project, for which a chart would not be of primary value. Use charting as you would use fonts and formatting: to support the understanding of information in worksheets, and not to distract or confuse.

This concludes Project 5. You can either exit Excel, or go on to work the Study Questions, Review Exercises, and Assignments.

SUMMARY AND EXERCISES

Summary

- Charting makes it easier to visualize and identify patterns in a table of numbers.
- Excel has 14 major types of charts, and many variations can be made of each type.
- The data you want to plot (display) in a chart is called a data series; each member of the data series corresponds to a chart category.
- If data series are in columns on the worksheet, their chart categories are in rows, and vice versa.
- Chart-category names appear along the horizontal (X) axis of a chart. The vertical axis is called the Y-axis.
- The symbols used to plot a value—such as the columns of a column chart—are called data markers.
- Using the ChartWizard tool is the quickest way to build a basic chart. You begin by selecting the range you want to chart, including any names that you want to appear on the chart.
- An embedded chart is a chart within a worksheet; a chart sheet exists in a workbook and is accessed using a worksheet tab.
- Charts are linked to the worksheets upon which they are based; if the worksheet data changes, the chart changes.
- Nonadjacent worksheet selections can be charted, provided the selections can be assembled into a rectangle.
- Embedded charts can be repositioned and resized in the worksheet and will print along with surrounding worksheet data.

Key Terms and Operations

Key Terms
category name
chart
chart category
chart sheet
ChartWizard
data marker
data series
embedded chart
explode

handle
legend
linked (chart)
palette
X-axis
Y-axis

Operations
Format a chart
Insert a chart
Insert titles

Study Questions

Multiple Choice

1. The labels that appear along the bottom edge of a chart are known as the chart:
   a. series.
   b. variables.
   c. categories
   d. data markers.
   e. data points.

2. A chart that appears within a worksheet is referred to as a(n):
   a. bar chart.
   b. column chart.
   c. category chart.
   d. worksheet chart.
   e. embedded chart.

3. How many major chart types are there in Excel?
   a. 1
   b. 2
   c. 3
   d. 4
   e. 14

4. On a chart, what is used to indicate what each color or symbol stands for?
   a. the X-axis
   b. a legend
   c. a data series
   d. a category
   e. a title

5. Line charts are most appropriate for:
   a. showing trends or changes over time.
   b. comparing individual values at specific times.
   c. showing relationships among portions of a whole.
   d. All of the above.
   e. None of the above.

6. Column charts are most appropriate for:
   a. showing trends or changes over time.
   b. comparing individual values at specific times.
   c. showing relationships among portions of a whole.
   d. All of the above.
   e. None of the above.

7. Pie charts are most appropriate for:
   a. showing trends or changes over time.
   b. comparing individual values at specific times.
   c. showing relationships among portions of a whole.
   d. All of the above.
   e. None of the above.

8. A nonadjacent range to be charted should:
   a. assemble into a rectangle.
   b. contain only text.
   c. contain only values.
   d. contain more chart categories than data series.
   e. contain more data series than chart categories.

9. If you want to modify an embedded chart, you must:
   a. Double-click it.
   b. Choose Edit from the Chart menu.
   c. Choose Chart from the Edit menu.
   d. Insert the chart into a chart sheet.
   e. Link the chart to an empty cell.

10. Embedded charts are especially useful when:
    a. The chart is to be displayed or printed along with the worksheet itself.
    b. Several charts are needed, all based on the same worksheet.
    c. A chart should exist in a separate chart sheet.
    d. The worksheet contains a large number of formulas (rather than number constants).
    e. The worksheet contains a large number of number constants (rather than formulas).

Short Answer

1. What is often the best way to identify trends and interrelationships in data?

2. If the data series is horizontal (in rows) in a worksheet, how are the chart categories arranged?

3. Which axis is the X-axis? Which is the Y-axis?

4. What are chart handles used for?

5. How is a pie chart different from most of the other chart types?

6. What term is used to describe a pie slice that has been pulled out of the pie for emphasis?

7. What type of chart would be most appropriate for showing month-by-month profits for a 48-month series?

8. What type of chart would be most appropriate for showing the relative market share of various brands of automobiles?

9. How do you modify an embedded chart? How do you delete an embedded chart?

10. Can chart sheets change if the worksheets upon which they were originally built change?

For Discussion

1. In what ways might a column chart provide a deceptive view of data? What about a 3-D perspective column chart? What do certain charts imply that may not really be present in the data?

2. When is a pie chart an appropriate chart type? When is a column chart appropriate?

3. What is a chart legend, and why is it usually important?

Review Exercises

Creating a Column Chart of Audio Sales for 1975–1990

Open the AUDIO2 workbook that you completed in Project 3. Using the ChartWizard tool and making nonadjacent selections, construct an embedded column chart that shows how sales of total records and total tapes changed over the time period of 1975 through 1990. The data series for this chart are in rows. The chart should resemble Figure 5.34. Print the embedded chart along with the worksheet. Save the workbook.

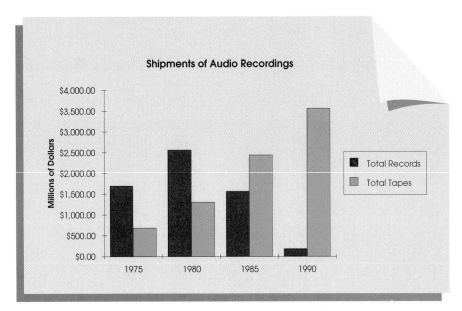

Figure 5.34

Creating a 3-D Pie Chart of Audio Sales for 1985

Open the AUDIO2 workbook that you completed in Project 3. Using the ChartWizard tool and making nonadjacent selections, construct a chart sheet that contains a 3-D pie chart that shows sales of total tapes, total records, and total CDs for 1985. Rotate the chart so the Total CD slice is in front. Explode the Total CD slice. Name the sheet AUDIOPIE. Print the chart. Save the workbook.

Assignments

Creating a 3-D Column Chart of Audio Sales for 1975–1990

Open the AUDIO2 workbook from Project 3. In a separate chart sheet, construct a 3-D column chart showing sales of LP albums, singles, 8-tracks, cassettes, and regular CDs over the 1975 to 1990 time period. Rotate the chart as needed to provide a good view of the columns. Print the chart and save the workbook.

Creating a Pie Chart of Energy Usage of Home Appliances

Open the ENERGY1 workbook from Project 4. Construct a pie chart in a separate chart sheet, with a legend but without labels for each slice, showing the share of the total monthly energy bill for each appliance in the worksheet. Add appropriate titles to the chart. Make another pie chart that graphs only the major users of electricity. Print the charts and save the workbook.

Creating a 3-D Column Chart of Daily Appliance Usage

Using the ENERGY1 worksheet from Project 4, construct a chart sheet containing a 3-D perspective column chart that shows, for each day of the week, the number of hours the following appliances are used: conventional oven, microwave oven, dishwasher, and clothes dryer. Rotate and format the chart as needed. Print the chart and save the workbook.

PART IV

Integrated Project 1

INTEGRATED PROJECT 1: EMBEDDING AN EXCEL WORKSHEET IN A WORD DOCUMENT

Objectives:

After completing this project, you should be able to:

▶ Create an object

▶ Embed an object in a Word document

▶ Update the embedded object

▶ Crop the embedded object

▶ Move the embedded object

▶ Size the embedded object

▶ Format the embedded object

Now that you have worked with the Microsoft Office products Word and Excel separately, you will learn how to integrate these two software packages. This means creating different document files in Word and Excel and putting them together into one file. This first project is the beginning of a large presentation project that you will create for the president of an expanding company. You will first create the body, or shell, of a report in Word and then include a worksheet as part of the document. This project will introduce you to object linking and embedding, which you will explore in greater detail as you complete your presentation throughout the other projects.

CASE STUDY: CREATING A REPORT

The company you work for wants to expand its business with a new product. They have hired various marketing firms to do national taste-test surveys to discover the potential sales market for fat-free potato chips. Taste-test surveys are being done on college campuses to determine whether collegians prefer the taste of greasy, regular potato chips or the taste of the new, light, fat-free chips your company has created. As the survey results come in, you will record them in an Excel worksheet.

Designing the Solution

The company president, Dr. Gardent, called you this morning and asked you to keep him updated on the progress of the national taste-test surveys. He wants you to prepare a simple report that shows the survey results, which states have been reported, which have not, and so on. This report will be given to his staff every morning so they can monitor the survey's progress.

You have two options: create and print separate worksheet report files, or create separate files and then incorporate the worksheet into the Word document. Because you have done work for Dr. Gardent in the past, you know that his simple projects usually take on a life of their own! So, to make updating and adding to the report easy, you decide to create the report in Word and include the worksheet in the Word document.

CREATING THE WORKSHEET AND DOCUMENT

Your first step is to enter the survey result into an Excel worksheet.

Tip When you see a button or icon next to a numbered step, you can select that button or icon in place of the menu command in the numbered step, as in step 4 in the following numbered steps.

To create an Excel worksheet:

1 Select the Excel button in the upper-right corner of the screen or, if the Microsoft Office suite does not start automatically when Windows starts, select the Office icon from the Program Manager window and then select Excel.

2 Select the Font button from the toolbar, and then select a 10-point sans serif font, such as Arial or Helvetica.

3 Create the spreadsheet as shown in Figure 1.1. Enter the State column heading in cell A4. Enter a formula in each cell that has the word *Total* in it to calculate the total sums of the row or column.

Fat Free Potato Chip Survey

State	Total	Fat Free		Regular	
		Salted	BBQ	Salted	BBQ
CA	Total	15000	9500	925	450
WY	Total				
AZ	Total				
VT	Total				
VA	Total				
WA	Total				
OR	Total				
TN	Total				
Total	Total	Total	Total	Total	Total

Figure 1.1

4 Choose Save from the File menu, or select the Save button.

5 Type **SURVEY.XLS** as the file name, select the A: drive, and then select OK to accept the file name and save the document.

Caution The drive called A: refers to the 3-½ inch floppy drive on your computer. On your system, it might be called B: or by another letter, depending on your system's configuration.

6 Exit Excel.

Now that you have created the worksheet, you can write the body of the report in Word.

Reminder All Word documents for this and the remaining integrated projects should be created in Page Layout view. To activate this view mode, start Word and select Page Layout from the View menu.

To create the Word document:

1 Select the Word button in the upper-right corner of the screen.

2 Choose Font from the Format menu.

3 Select a 14-point serif font, such as Times New Roman, and then select OK to accept the font settings.

4 Type **NEW PRODUCT DAILY REPORT**

5 Center and boldface the title.

6 Press (ENTER) eight times.

7 Type the following two paragraphs:

  This report is a daily update of the national research project. The listing below shows the results from the taste-test surveys as they are reported by the market researchers.
  It is our hope that this new product will be successful in the fat-free marketplace.

8 Press (ENTER) three times.

Your Word document should look like the document in Figure 1.2.

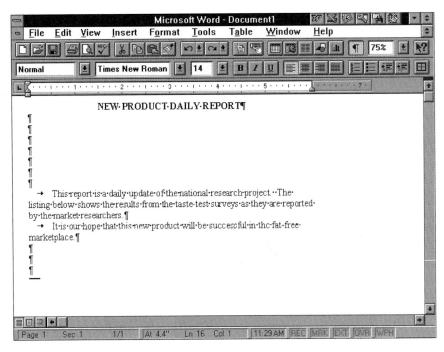

Figure 1.2

9 Choose Save from the File menu.

10 Type **REPORT.DOC** as the file name, select the A: drive, and then select OK to accept the file name and save the document.

EMBEDDING THE EXCEL WORKSHEET IN THE WORD DOCUMENT

You have created separate Word and Excel documents, so now it's time to put them together into one updatable document. There are three ways to include the worksheet in the Word document:

1. Copy the object to the clipboard and paste it into the document.

2. Embed the worksheet in the Word document.

3. Link the worksheet to the Word document.

These three methods are summarized in Table 1.1. The first method, copying and pasting, is very limiting. This method simply pastes an image of the object, like a camera snapshot, into the document. The image cannot be updated or edited. The other two methods, embedding and linking, are part of the *OLE* process. OLE (pronounced "oh-lay"), which stands for object linking and embedding, is the powerful process of connecting or combining objects created in different software packages into one updatable file. Each object's image has a ***source file*** associated with it. An object's source file, as you learned earlier in the Word 6 projects, can be a graphic image file, a clip art file, an equation constructed through the equation editor, or other types of files.

When an object is ***embedded,*** the source file is inserted into an existing file called the ***target file.*** Because the source file is included as part of the target file, the object can be updated directly from the target file if its application is loaded on the computer you are using.

Linking is very similar to embedding. When an object is linked to the target file, the target file stores the location of the object but not the object's source file; it displays only an image of the object. In this project you will learn how to use the embedding method of inserting objects. You will work with linking in the next project.

Table 1.1

Method	What Is Stored in the Target File?	Can the Object in the Target File be Updated?	If the Object Is Updated While in the Target File, Will Those Changes Be Saved in the Source File?
Copy/Paste method	Object's image	No	Not applicable
Embed method	Object's image and source file	Yes (if the source file's application is loaded)	No, the source file is not updated
Link method	Object's image and location of the source file	Yes (if the source file's application is loaded)	Yes, since the source file is actually updated

When you embed an object, you begin by opening the target file. Next you insert the object through the Insert menu. The computer automatically opens the object's source file application on top of the target file. Either you will see a separate window that shows only the source file's application (the title bar changes to display the source file's application title) or, as shown in Figure 1.3, you will see a secondary small window that displays the target application's toolbars and some menus changing to the source file's application toolbars and menus (the title bar does not change but shows the target application's title).

Word title bar
(target file)

Excel buttons
(source application)

Secondary
window
(source file)

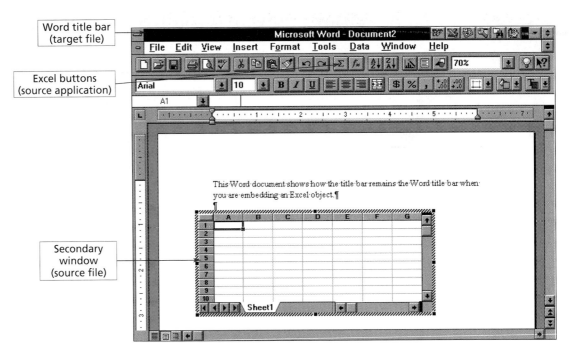

Figure 1.3

You can create an object in the source application before you embed it, or you can create an object directly from within the target application. You do not have to exit Word to create an embedded Excel worksheet if both the target and the source applications are loaded on the computer you are using.

Think about how you study at your desk. When you study for an exam, you probably have your textbook and class notes on your desk. You might pick up the class notes and put them on top of the textbook you were reading. It would be ridiculous to put your textbook away in a drawer every time you wanted to refer to your class notes. This concept relates to layering objects in a document. Instead of putting the word processing document away to work with the worksheet, you can open the worksheet on top of your word processing document. You can move the embedded worksheet around in the document to a different page, center the worksheet on the page, and so on, just as if you were physically moving a printed worksheet around on top of a printed word processing document. You just don't need a glue stick to connect the two documents together!

To embed the Excel worksheet in the Word document:

1 Position the insertion point at the end of REPORT.DOC, before the last (ENTER) symbol.

2 Choose Object from the Insert menu.
A dialog box appears, offering two options for inserting an object: Create New and Create from File.

3 Select Create from File.
This option enables you to select an object file that has already been created. The screen now looks like Figure 1.4.

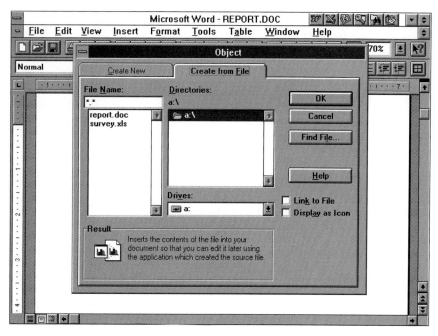

Figure 1.4

4 Select the SURVEY.XLS file from the A: drive.

5 Select OK to embed this worksheet.
The screen now looks like Figure 1.5.

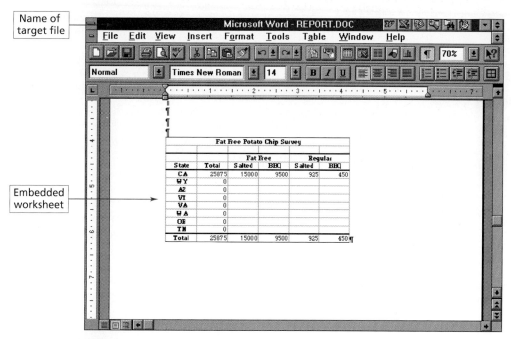

Figure 1.5

Wait until the hourglass icon disappears and you hear the drive activity noises stop before you try to continue.

Quick Fix If the embedded worksheet displays the actual row numbers and column labels (A, B, C...) and the toolbar looks like the Excel toolbar, move your mouse pointer to the top of the Word document and click once so that the insertion point is moved from the worksheet back into the Word document.

6 When the computer is finished embedding the worksheet, save your Word document.

When you saved your Word file, you saved the embedded worksheet as part of the Word document. The original source worksheet (SURVEY.XLS) was not saved. When you edit the embedded object from the Word document, the changes will not be written to the Excel source file. Be careful, because the target file size will grow as you edit the embedded worksheet. Files with embedded objects can become very large and difficult to maintain on floppy disks.

Tip Embedding is a good tool when you are using a small (in bytes) object. Because the entire object file resides in the target file (in this case, the Word document), the target file size can grow dramatically. You'll want to keep an eye on the target file size as you work with embedded objects.

EXIT If necessary, you can exit Word now and continue this project later.

UPDATING EMBEDDED OBJECTS

The survey results have started to come in, and your first report is due in Dr. Gardent's office. Instead of updating the spreadsheet in Excel and then re-embedding the worksheet in Word, you will edit the worksheet while working in the open Word document. You will also *crop* and *size* the worksheet window in the Word document. Currently, the worksheet window reveals only a portion of the entire Excel worksheet. When you *crop* the window, you move its edges so the window reveals more or less of the object. *Sizing,* on the other hand, retains the boundaries of the work-sheet but stretches the entire window so that the displayed worksheet is made larger or smaller.

Some source applications open a full window on top of the target document or file when the source file is edited. However, when you edit this worksheet, the computer will temporarily replace *some* of the Word menus and toolbars with some Excel menus and toolbars, and it will keep the Word window open.

Tip Check the title bar to confirm which type of window is being used. To exit from applications that change the title bar to the source application, choose Exit or Quit from the source application's File menu. When the title bar remains the target application's title bar, return to the target document by clicking outside of the embedded object.

To update the worksheet:

1 Start Word if necessary.

2 Open the Word document, REPORT.DOC, if necessary.

3 Double-click in the worksheet window.

The screen now looks like Figure 1.6. Notice that the Excel toolbar is displayed, although the title bar remains the Word title bar. The worksheet window also changes so that now you can see the row-and-column labels of the worksheet.

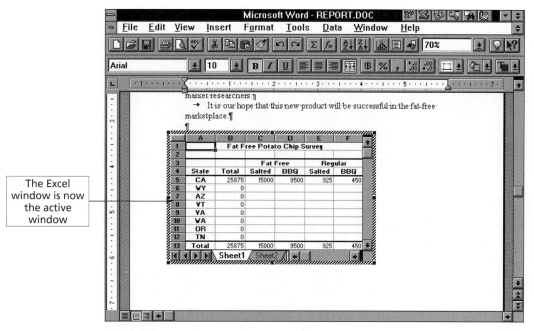

The Excel window is now the active window

Figure 1.6

4 Enter the new survey figures for the other states, as shown in Figure 1.7.

Fat Free Potato Chip Survey					
		Fat Free		Regular	
State	Total	Salted	BBQ	Salted	BBQ
CA	25875	15000	9500	925	450
WY	8100	400	500	4200	3000
AZ	14700	8000	5000	1200	500
VT	0				
VA	0				
WA	0				
OR	0				
TN	0				

Figure 1.7

5 Use the handles of the window to crop the worksheet object so that the last row in the window is row 15 and the right column is column G. The worksheet window now looks like Figure 1.8.

	A	B	C	D	E	F	G
1		Fat Free Potato Chip Survey					
2							
3			Fat Free		Regular		
4	State	Total	Salted	BBQ	Salted	BBQ	
5	CA	25875	15000	9500	925	450	
6	WY	8100	400	500	4200	3000	
7	AZ	14700	8000	5000	1200	500	
8	VT	0					
9	VA	0					
10	WA	0					
11	OR	0					
12	TN	0					
13	Total	48875	23400	15000	6325	3950	
14							
15							

Sheet1 / Sheet2 / Sheet3 /

Figure 1.8

6 Click outside of the embedded object, anywhere in the Word document.

7 Save the Word document.
The system saves the Word document, not the Excel worksheet.

MOVING UNFRAMED EMBEDDED OBJECTS

Objects can be moved once they are embedded in the document. Currently, the object is at the bottom of the document. In the following numbered steps, you will move the worksheet so that it is located before the first paragraph.

To move an embedded object:

1 Select the object by clicking once inside the object.

2 Drag the object so that the placement icon is before the first paragraph, as shown in Figure 1.9, and then release the mouse button.

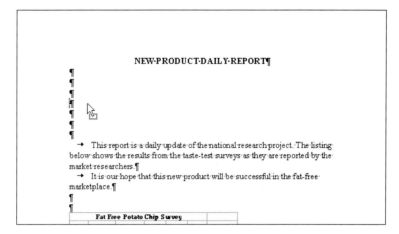

Figure 1.9

3 Click outside the embedded object.
The document now looks like Figure 1.10.

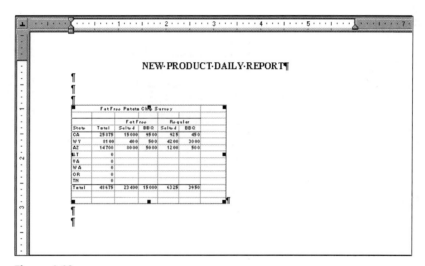

Figure 1.10

Your object can also be made larger or smaller. In the steps that follow, you will make the worksheet window larger.

 To size an embedded object:

1 Select the worksheet window.

2 Use the lower-right handle to increase the size of the window and release the handle when the window meets the right margin.
The new worksheet window looks like Figure 1.11.

Fat Free Potato Chip Survey

| State | Total | Fat Free | | Regular | |
		Salted	BBQ	Salted	BBQ
CA	25875	15000	9500	925	450
WY	8100	400	500	4200	3000
AZ	14700	8000	5000	1200	500
VT	0				
VA	0				
WA	0				
OR	0				
TN	0				
Total	48675	23400	15000	6325	3950

Figure 1.11

3 Decrease the window's size so that it fills approximately one half of the document width.
The worksheet window looks like Figure 1.12.

Figure 1.12 (shown above as part of the reduced worksheet illustration)

Figure 1.12

4 While your worksheet window is selected, click on the Center button. Notice that your worksheet is now centered between the left and right margins on the page.

5 Save your document.

FORMATTING AN EMBEDDED OBJECT

In the Word 6 projects you learned that frames give objects greater mobility. You can place a framed object anywhere on the page (except in a footnote, endnote, or annotation) by dragging the frame into position or by typing coordinates to place it in a precise location. You can make text flow around the framed object or bypass the object entirely. Frames and objects can be formatted by adding borders and shadows, and if you have a color printer, borders can be colorized to produce a sharp and professional presentation.

To add a border to an embedded object:

1 Select the object.

2 Choose Borders and Shading from the Format menu.

The Picture Borders dialog box appears.

3 Select the Borders tab.

4 Select the Shadow option in the Presets box.

5 Select the 1 ½-point double line from the Style column.

6 Select a color in the color menu (blue is chosen below, but you can select the color of your choice).
The screen now looks like Figure 1.13.

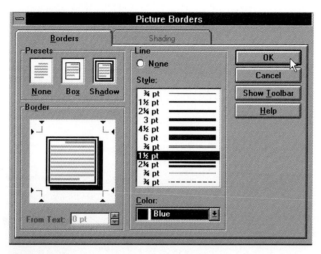

Figure 1.13

7 Select OK to accept the border options.
You are returned to the document.

8 Select the Print Preview button from the toolbar to see what your finished document would look like if you printed it on a color printer.
The document now resembles Figure 1.14.

NEW PRODUCT DAILY REPORT

Fat Free Potato Chip Survey					
		Fat Free		Regular	
State	Total	Salted	BBQ	Salted	BBQ
CA	25875	15000	9500	925	450
WY	8100	400	500	4200	3000
AZ	14700	8000	5000	1200	500
VT	0				
VA	0				
WA	0				
OR	0				
TN	0				
Total	48675	23400	15000	6325	3950

This report is a daily update of the national research project. The listing below shows the results from the taste-test surveys as they are reported by the market researchers.

It is our hope that this new product will be a successful product in the fat-free marketplace.

Figure 1.14

9 Save your document.

THE NEXT STEP

This project introduced you to a new concept, embedding. You embedded a worksheet in a word processing document. There are many other types of files that you can embed, for example, database data and graphic files such as clip art and photographs. And, provided that the computer you use has both the target and source applications installed, you can easily edit and update your objects as necessary.

Spreadsheets are great for compiling rows and columns of data, but they are not the best for displaying the data to the reader in a meaningful way. Charts and graphs are much better vehicles for communicating a message. Take another look at your spreadsheet. What information is meaningful for the president's staff? What states have the greatest sales potential for these chips? What states have the least potential? Where should the company begin to sell its product? Should the company market those states where the response was low? These are the types of questions managers and executives ask when they are facing business decisions. These questions are more easily answered when the data is displayed in a meaningful form, such as a chart or graph. The reader can see relationships between the data quickly and easily, without having to concentrate on the rows and columns of numbers. Seeing the data displayed graphically helps the reader assimilate the data and make logical conclusions based on the data.

Remember that when you combine applications to form documents, you usually are trying to communicate some sort of message to someone. Whether it is a newsletter, a brochure, a thesis paper, or a resume, you are communicating a message. Objects can be used to enhance the written word so that your message is reinforced and quickly assimilated by the reader.

This concludes Project 1 of the integrated projects. You can exit Word now or go on to work the Study Questions, Review Exercises, and Assignments.

SUMMARY AND EXERCISES

Summary

- Objects can be pasted, embedded, or linked to a target document.
- Copied objects cannot be updated.
- Object linking and embedding (OLE) is the process of combining objects from different source applications.
- An embedded object's entire source file is inserted into the target document and becomes part of the target document.
- Embedded objects can be updated.
- Only the location of the object is stored in the target file when the object is linked.
- A linked file's image is displayed in the target file.
- Objects can be created before or during the OLE process.
- An embedded object's source file is not saved after the object is embedded.
- Some applications temporarily replace the target application's toolbars and menus.
- Some applications open a separate window on top of the target window.
- Objects can be moved and sized after they are embedded.
- A framed object can be positioned anywhere on the page.
- Objects can be enhanced with colorful borders.

Key Terms and Operations

Key Terms	Operations
crop	Create an object from a file
embed	Crop an embedded object
link	Embed an object
OLE	Format an embedded object
size	Position an embedded object
source file	Size an embedded object
target file	Update an embedded object

Study Questions

Multiple Choice

1. An embedded object is a
   a. separate file attached to the end of a document.
   b. file inserted in a document, and the source file is no longer needed.
   c. file which is inserted in a document and the source file is needed.
   d. graphic file which cannot be changed once it is embedded.

2. Cropping is a process whereby
   a. the edges of a window are manipulated to display all or part of the object.
   b. the frame is formatted to match the size of the object.
   c. you define the size of the object file.
   d. the object file size is made smaller to fit onto the disk.

3. An embedded object
   a. is always created before the target document.
   b. can never be updated without the source file.
   c. is made a part of the target document file.
   d. must always remain in the original insertion place in the document.

4. The target document
   a. size will grow as the embedded document is edited and grows.
   b. must always be a word processing document.
   c. is always the first document created.
   d. must be stored on the computer's hard drive.

5. An object must always have
   a. a frame inserted around it.
   b. its application loaded on the computer in order to update the object.
   c. its application loaded on the computer in order to see the object in the target document.
   d. the source file available to update the object.

6. The target application is
   a. always a word processor.
   b. where the object is embedded.
   c. never opened.
   d. where the object is created.

7. Once an object is embedded
   a. it can never be edited.
   b. it should be edited straight from the source application.
   c. it must be saved separately from the target application.
   d. it is saved as a part of the target document.

8. Including an object when a document is saved means
   a. that you must save both the target document and the object separately.
   b. you save the document and the object into the target document file.
   c. you must save the object first and then include it when you save the target document.
   d. the object cannot be saved unless it was first created outside of the target document.

9. Using a frame to format an object means that
   a. you can add borders and color the borders of the frame.
   b. the object cannot be sized without the frame.
   c. you can edit the object within the frame only if the frame was inserted before the object was embedded.
   d. the object can be placed anywhere on the page.

10. Never use an object
    a. to display a graph.
    b. if you embed a scanned photograph.
    c. to include one word processing document within another.
    d. when you want to update the graphic file.

Short Answer

1. What does OLE stand for and what does it do?

2. What is the name of the file where the original object is created?

3. Which file stores the embedded object?

4. Which OLE method option puts a snapshot of the object into the file.

5. What helps make the object more mobile?

6. How do you size an object?

7. Which menu option lets you put a frame around an object?

8. What verifies which toolbars and menu items are active when you are editing an object?

9. What is the term that means to shrink and enlarge the window over the object?

10. When you save a file that contains an embedded object, where is the embedded object saved?

For Discussion

1. Explain the difference between embedding, linking, and copying and pasting.

2. When would you use the copy and paste method instead of the embedding method of inserting a graph or worksheet into the document?

3. What are some important things to remember when you are saving documents with embedded objects?

4. Besides a report, what are some other practical scenarios for using embedding?

Review Exercises

Updating the Worksheet's Format

Update the president's report to include new data. The additional data includes new columns, rows, and formulas that were not part of the original worksheet.

1. Open REPORT.DOC.

2. Save this document as UPDATE.DOC.

3. Edit the worksheet to include new columns, as shown in Figure 1.15.

	A	B	C	D	E	F	G	H
1			Fat Free Potato Chip Survey					
2								
3				Fat Free		Regular		
4	State	Total	Salted	BBQ	No Salt	Salted	BBQ	No Salt
5	CA	30875	15000	9500	5000	925	450	350
6	WY	8200	400	500	100	4200	3000	2000
7	AZ	17700	8000	5000	3000	1200	500	600
8	VT	3900	250	100	50	2000	1500	800
9	VA	8735	100	85	50	3500	5000	4500
10	WA	15300	7500	6200	500	500	600	100
11	OR	11850	5300	5500	600	300	150	75
12	TN	4700	650	500	50	2000	1500	500
13	Total	101260	37200	27385	9350	14625	12700	8925
14								
15								

Sheet1 / Sheet2 /

Figure 1.15

4. Save the document.

Moving and Formatting the Embedded Object

When you insert an object into a document you may find that you need to move the object to another page or to another section of the document. You may also decide to change the object's border style, color, or shading. Sometimes you need to modify the way the object looks to conform to a company standard or please a client. This exercise gives you some additional experience moving and formatting the embedded object.

1. Move the object so that your document looks like Figure 1.16.

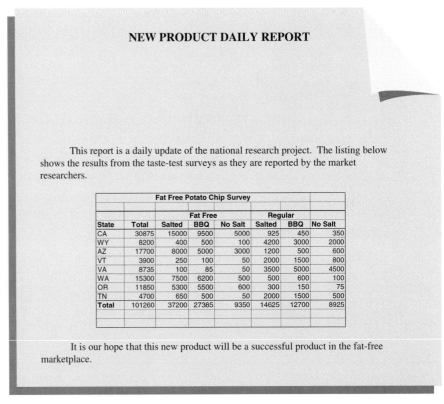

NEW PRODUCT DAILY REPORT

This report is a daily update of the national research project. The listing below shows the results from the taste-test surveys as they are reported by the market researchers.

Fat Free Potato Chip Survey							
			Fat Free		Regular		
State	Total	Salted	BBQ	No Salt	Salted	BBQ	No Salt
CA	30875	15000	9500	5000	925	450	350
WY	8200	400	500	100	4200	3000	2000
AZ	17700	8000	5000	3000	1200	500	600
VT	3900	250	100	50	2000	1500	800
VA	8735	100	85	50	3500	5000	4500
WA	15300	7500	6200	500	500	600	100
OR	11850	5300	5500	600	300	150	75
TN	4700	650	500	50	2000	1500	500
Total	101260	37200	27385	9350	14625	12700	8925

It is our hope that this new product will be a successful product in the fat-free marketplace.

Figure 1.16

2. Modify the borders so that there is no shadow behind the object. Select a different border line and color.

3. Save the document.

Assignments

Creating a Word Document with Embedded Objects

Write a letter to your family about the classes you are taking this semester. In the letter embed an Excel worksheet that lists your classes. Rate each class on an enjoyment scale from 1 to 50, following the example in Figure 1.17. Format the object so that the box has a shadow, and experiment with colored borders. Practice putting the worksheet in the middle, beginning, and end of your letter. Save this document as CLASSES.DOC on drive A:.

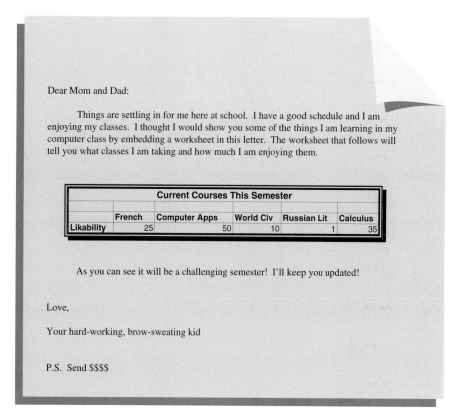

Dear Mom and Dad:

Things are settling in for me here at school. I have a good schedule and I am enjoying my classes. I thought I would show you some of the things I am learning in my computer class by embedding a worksheet in this letter. The worksheet that follows will tell you what classes I am taking and how much I am enjoying them.

Current Courses This Semester					
	French	Computer Apps	World Civ	Russian Lit	Calculus
Likability	25	50	10	1	35

As you can see it will be a challenging semester! I'll keep you updated!

Love,

Your hard-working, brow-sweating kid

P.S. Send $$$$

Figure 1.17

Embedding a Chart

Write a second letter home and call it FAVES. DOC. Use the worksheet data from CLASSES.DOC to embed a pie chart into this document. This will help those reading your letter to see at a quick glance which courses are your favorites, and which courses you'd rather not be taking. Your finished document should resemble the example in Figure 1.18.

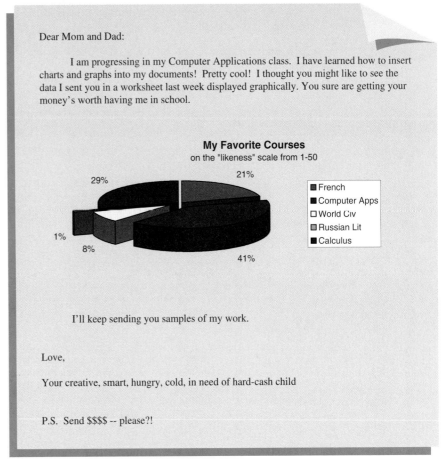

Dear Mom and Dad:

I am progressing in my Computer Applications class. I have learned how to insert charts and graphs into my documents! Pretty cool! I thought you might like to see the data I sent you in a worksheet last week displayed graphically. You sure are getting your money's worth having me in school.

I'll keep sending you samples of my work.

Love,

Your creative, smart, hungry, cold, in need of hard-cash child

P.S. Send $$$$ -- please?!

Figure 1.18

Turn the Tide: Embedding a WordArt Document in an Excel Worksheet

Objects can be embedded in word processing documents, but they can also be embedded in other applications. From Excel, select Object from the Insert menu. Choose Microsoft WordArt 2.0 from the Create New option, and then select OK. Type your full name into the text box. Use the WordArt features to shadow and shape your name, something like Figure 1.19. Save the Excel file as NAME.XLS on drive A:.

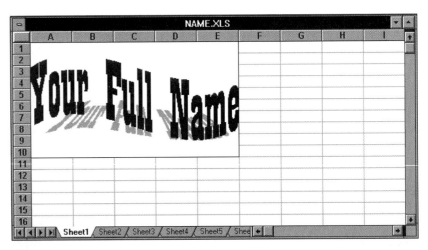

Figure 1.19

PART V

Microsoft Access 2

Overview

Objectives

After completing this overview, you should be able to:

► Start Access

► Describe the components of the Access main window

► Work with menus and the Tool bar using a mouse or the keyboard

► Display online Help for a variety of topics

► Exit Access

Every application manages data. However, word processing and spreadsheet applications can only use the data for which they were designed. Imagine trying to load and edit a spreadsheet with a word processing program. The word processor will refuse to load the spreadsheet file. ***Database management software,*** by contrast, is designed to handle generic data. In recent years, in fact, some database programs have become so powerful that there are spreadsheet and word processing interfaces to them. Microsoft Access 2 for Windows isn't quite that powerful. However, it is a straightforward program that simplifies the process of setting up and using a database.

USING DATABASE MANAGEMENT SOFTWARE

You have had experience with a database, although you might not have called it that. Your address book is a database of people with whom you have regular contact. The information it stores includes names, addresses, cities, states, zip codes, and (most important of all) telephone numbers. Let's use this example when defining a few terms common to database operations.

Since database software is more generic than other application packages, you must supply more information when you set up the database. However, once you have set up the database and entered the data, a database program simplifies some of your tasks a great deal. Among those tasks are *sorting*, *searching*, and *retrieving* data.

Sorting data means presenting it in a different sequence from the way it's stored in the database. Your address book is probably sorted by last name or, perhaps, by first name. However, if you do a mailing to all your friends, the post office will appreciate it if you sort the letters by zip code. Access will let you do this in an instant.

Searching data means looking for an entry that meets certain criteria. For example, suppose you wanted to find the name Chris Smith in your address book. You'd search the book for the last name Smith. If there was more than one Smith, you'd continue the search by looking for someone in the Smiths with the first name Chris. If there was more than one Chris Smith, you'd have to add more criteria to narrow the scope of the search. For example, you might search middle names or cities of residence to select the correct Chris Smith.

Retrieving data means finding groups of entries that meet certain criteria and copying them to another location. For example, suppose you were planning a trip to San Francisco and wanted a list of the names of everyone you know there. Database management software makes it simple to pull out all the entries, selecting them using the criterion that the city name is San Francisco.

Sometimes retrieving data takes some clever thinking. Suppose you wanted to retrieve the names of everyone you know in the San Francisco Bay Area. Using the city name as a criterion would not work; there are too many cities in the Bay Area. However, if you knew that all Bay Area zip codes begin with 94 or 95, you could use that as the search criterion instead.

All this may seem like a waste of time if your address book contains only a few hundred entries. After all, you can search that many without a computer. But imagine if there were thousands (or millions) of entries. That's the scale of the problems Access and other database managers are designed to handle.

USING MICROSOFT ACCESS

Microsoft Access 2 is a full-featured database management software package that takes advantage of the Windows graphical user interface (GUI). This interface lets you easily use database management features using a mouse, menus, dialog boxes, and the buttons displayed on the screen.

You can enter or change data, pointing to the specific location with the pointer. You can scroll through your data using scroll bars. You can delete one or more entries by selecting them and deleting them as a block. Searching, sorting, and retrieving are simple operations. You can also create good-looking data screens that take full advantage of Windows features such as list boxes and option buttons. You can create (and print) reports that mix various printer fonts.

The Help feature provides information about all the features of Access. The Help feature is discussed later in this overview.

A NOTE TO THE STUDENT

Access uses standard Windows operations. The only major exception is that you cannot use the keyboard for certain operations; some operations require a mouse. The first example of this you'll encounter is setting up a relationship, which is covered in Project 2.

STARTING ACCESS

You can start Access the same way you start any other Windows program. First you must locate the Access program icon in the Access program group (Figure 0.1). The screen may look somewhat different depending on how Access was installed.

Figure 0.1

> **Tip** When you see a button or icon next to a numbered step, you can select that button or icon on the screen in place of the menu command in the numbered step.

To start Access:

Microsoft Access

Microsoft Access

1 Start Windows if it isn't already running.

2 Double-click the Access group icon if it's shown on the screen. (If the Access group window is already open, skip to the next step.)

3 Double-click the Access program icon.
A copyright screen will be shown for a few seconds, followed by the Access main window, as shown in Figure 0.2. Access is a large program, so it will probably take a few seconds to load; be patient.

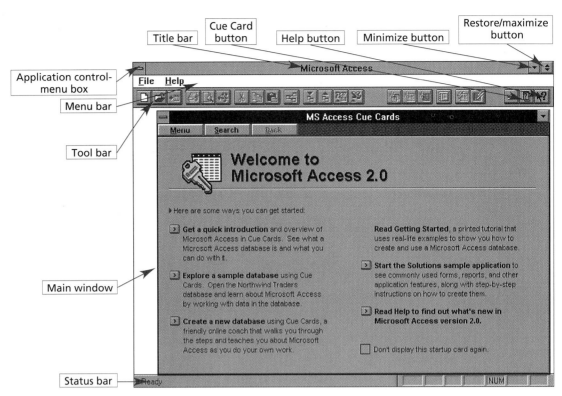

Figure 0.2

EXAMINING THE ACCESS MAIN SCREEN

Unlike many other application programs, when Access is started you can't do anything useful immediately. Before you can do anything, you must either create a new database or open an existing database. In Project 1, you'll learn how to create and open (and close) a database. For now, let's explore the Access main screen. Figure 0.2 shows where the various items are placed on the screen.

The bar across the top of the screen is the ***application title bar.*** It shows the name of the application running in that window. In this case, of course, it's Microsoft Access. The button at the left end of the application title bar is the ***Application Control-menu box.*** Clicking it once brings up the standard Windows application Control menu. Double-clicking closes the application. The two buttons at the right end of the application title bar are the standard ***Minimize*** and ***Restore/Maximize buttons,*** which you can use to change the size of the Access main screen.

The menu bar lies immediately below the application title bar. Below that is the ***Tool bar,*** which consists of buttons that let you quickly accomplish tasks instead of working through a sequence of menu selections. For example, the button at the right end of the Tool bar is the Help button, which you can use to get help on various topics.

Finally, the ***status bar*** at the bottom of the screen gives you information about the current status of the computer as well as feedback from the last operation you asked Access to perform.

Most of the screen, however, is occupied by the blank ***main window,*** which is the area in which you do most of your work. We'll begin filling this window shortly.

CHOOSING MENU OPTIONS

Most Access tasks are accomplished by selecting one or more menu items in sequence. Sometimes one menu selection opens a new menu, called a ***cascade menu.*** Figure 0.3 shows the File pull-down menu from the Access main screen. The Add-Ins item has an arrow next to it. This tells you there's a cascade menu attached to that item. Menu items with three dots next to them open dialog boxes.

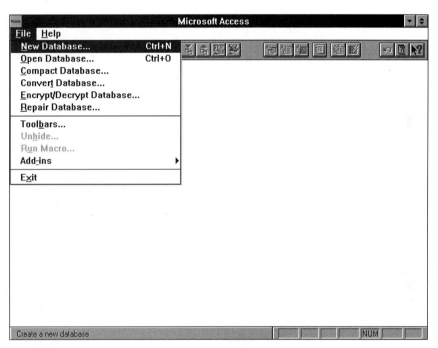

Figure 0.3

You can choose items from menus using the mouse or the keyboard. Clicking a menu item will select it. You can also press (ALT) and then type the first letter of the menu item. For example, pressing (ALT) + **F** will open the File menu. You must then press the arrow keys ((↓), (↑)) and press (ENTER) to select the item you want.

Some menu items have keyboard shortcuts as well. For example, pressing (CTRL) + **O** will select the Open Database menu item.

However, it's often possible to perform the same task by selecting a button on the Tool bar. This is both faster and easier than making selections from cascading menus. For example, suppose you want to open a database. You can either choose Open Database from the File menu or just click the Open Database button on the Tool bar.

GETTING ONLINE HELP

Access has an elaborate online *context-sensitive Help* system. ***Context-sensitive Help*** gives you information about the operation you're currently working on. The easiest way to get help is to click the ***Help button*** on the Tool bar. You can also select Help from the menu bar or press the ⒻⒷ function key. When you select the question mark at the far right edge of the Tool bar, you'll see the standard Windows Help system.

Access also includes a set of ***Cue Cards,*** which lead you through specific processes such as creating a table or report. Cue Card Help is similar to the numbered steps used in these projects. The Cue Card button is immediately to the left of the Help button.

To display online Help:

1 Click the Help button on the Tool bar.
A large question mark will appear next to the pointer.
When the pointer has the question mark attached, Help will be displayed for your next selection, whether it's from the menu, Tool bar, or a dialog box.

2 Choose New Database from the File menu.
The screen will look like Figure 0.4.

3 Double-click the window Control-menu box in the upper-left corner of the Help window to close it.

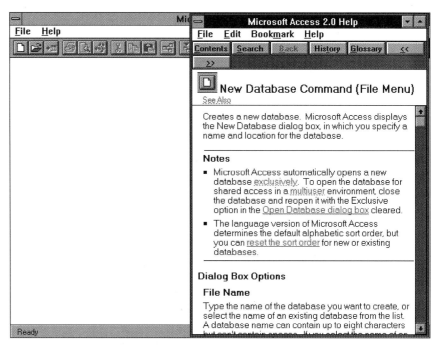

Figure 0.4

Tip When you select an item from a Help screen, the Back button becomes active. The Back button is very handy. It lets you back up to the previous Help screen.

EXITING ACCESS

It's important to exit Access when you're finished working with it. There are three ways to exit Access and return to the Windows Program Manager window. You can choose Exit from the File menu, you can press (ALT) + **FX** to make the same menu selections, or you can double-click the application Control-menu box.

File

This concludes the Overview. You can either exit Access or go on to work the Study Questions.

SUMMARY AND EXERCISES

Summary

- Database management software handles more generic data than other applications such as spreadsheet and word processing programs.
- Access is a complete database management system.
- You can start Access by double-clicking its program icon.
- You can get help by clicking either the Help button or the Cue Card button. You can also get help by pressing (F1).
- You can exit Access by choosing Exit from the File menu or double-clicking the Control-menu box.

Key Terms and Operations

Key Terms
application Control-menu box
application title bar
cascade menu
context-sensitive Help
Cue Card
database management software
Help button
main window
Minimize button
Restore/Maximize button
retrieve

search
sort
status bar
Toolbar

Operations
Exit
File
Help
New Database

Study Questions

Multiple Choice

1. Database software can be used to
   a. sort information.
   b. search for a specific piece of information.
   c. retrieve several pieces of related information.
   d. All of the above.

2. Context-sensitive Help means
   a. the Help screen will be related to the current operation you're attempting.
   b. help is provided in the context of database management software.
   c. help is related to Microsoft Access.
   d. the Help screen will walk you through certain operations.

3. Cue Card Help means
   a. the Help screen will be related to the current operation you're attempting.
   b. help is provided in the context of database management software.
   c. help is related to Microsoft Access.
   d. the Help screen will walk you through certain operations.

4. The difference between searching for data and retrieving data is
   a. searching implies locating a single entry in the database.
   b. retrieving implies selection of a group of entries in the database.
   c. retrieving usually means copying the group of entries to another location.
   d. All of the above.

5. To make a selection from a menu, which key should you should press in combination with the underlined letter of the menu?
   a. (ALT)   c. (ENTER)
   b. (ESC)   d. (↓)

Short Answer

1. Explain the differences between searching and retrieving data.

2. Explain how to start Access and two ways to get help.

3. What does "sorting data" mean?

4. You must perform one of two operations from the Access main screen before you can do useful work. What are they?

5. List three ways to exit Access and return to the Windows Program Manager.

For Discussion

1. List three things for which database software can be used. Explain each briefly.

2. Explain the differences between context-sensitive Help and Cue Card Help.

PROJECT 1: DESIGNING, CREATING, AND CHANGING A DATABASE

Objectives

After completing this project, you should be able to:

▶ Design a database

▶ Identify the different field types available in Access

▶ Create an Access database and its tables

▶ Change the structure of an Access table

▶ Format fields

▶ Use simple validation rules

CASE STUDY: SIMIAN SOFTWARE HAS A PROBLEM

Simian Software publishes two word processing packages that run under Microsoft Windows. ApeWord is a full-featured desktop publishing program that sells for $199.95. MonkeyWrite is a lower-level word processor designed to allow users to write memos and other short documents quickly and easily. Its price is $49.95. Both products are sold only in mail-order catalogs; the company does not sell through retail outlets or distributors.

The president of Simian Software, Jennifer Hudson, has asked you to help automate their operations. She is especially concerned with record keeping. She would like to keep track of customers, what products they have bought, and when. She wants to be able to call up any combination of information at any time.

Your job is to design the database and create it using Microsoft Access. In subsequent projects, you will enter the company's current data, design and set up several screen forms for data entry; produce a few reports; and set up queries to allow Ms. Hudson to select the data she wants to examine.

Designing the Solution

You should always design the database using paper and pencil before you even start Access. Once you have designed the database, you should divide it into several different tables to avoid entering data more than once. When you have completed both these steps, you're ready to start creating the database using Access. This project will lead you through the Access database design and creation process.

USING A RELATIONAL DATABASE MANAGEMENT SYSTEM

Access is a ***relational database management system***—a system that uses related data stored in different *tables*. A ***table*** is a collection of closely related information. The address book you use every day is a table. You use it to keep track of information about your friends. The information includes names, addresses, and telephone numbers. It may also include information on the city, state, and zip code for each of your friends, and perhaps other pertinent information such as the names of others in their families, birthdays, and so on.

In your address book, you most likely keep track of the names in alphabetical order. However, there are times when a different sequence could be more useful. Suppose you are going on a vacation to San Francisco, and you want a list of people you know in the Bay Area. If you could somehow get your address book's entries in zip code order, you'd be able to find those people with no problem. It would be even more useful if you could just find the zip codes that begin with 94 or 95, the first two digits of Bay Area zip codes. If your address book was set up as an Access table, you could get the answers to either of those questions in a matter of minutes and have enough time left to produce a nice-looking printed report, too.

Searching Your Database

"Wait a minute," you're saying. "I only have 73 names in my address book. And I know I don't know anyone in San Francisco. Even if I did, it would be faster for me just to read the darn thing from cover to cover instead of setting up an entire database."

And you're right. Searching a data table by reading each consecutive entry is called a ***sequential search***. You've been doing sequential searches all your life and probably didn't even know it. This technique may work fine for your address book. But imagine trying to use a sequential search on a table with 73,000 names. Once you learn to use Access, problems like this will become trivial.

Since an Access database is a collection of related data tables the process of searching 73,000 names is not impossible. Suppose you want to keep track of the class schedules of each person in your address book. You could write in the schedule at the beginning of each academic year. However, your address book would soon fall apart from all the erasing and corrections. It makes more sense to create a different data table for the class-schedule information, probably in the form of a separate class-schedule book. The data that connects the two tables is each person's name. Because it is a relational database system, Access can relate different tables, thus making your searching tasks much easier.

Fields, Records, and Keys

A table is made up of ***fields*** (columns) and ***records*** (rows). The fields describe characteristics of the data. For example, fields in your address book include last name, first name, address, city, state, zip code, and telephone number. These items describe characteristics of the people listed in your address book. The list of fields is called the ***table structure***. Each record contains information about one person. The ***primary key*** is the record used to link one table with another in the database.

If the process of linking tables seems a little abstract, that's because it is. This concept will be easier to understand after you have worked with tables and data. So be patient. Learn the terms used in this module and you will see how they apply to real-world situations very shortly.

DESIGNING THE DATABASE

Most problems people run into using database software are caused by poor database design. It may seem easier just to sit down at the computer, set up a database structure, and start entering data. If you do this, however, inevitably you will find you need something different after you have already entered several thousand records. Then you'll be forced to call in an expensive consultant to straighten out the database structure. Designing the database saves time and money in the long run. So get out some paper and a couple of pencils. You're going to design a database for Simian Software using the following five steps:

- Write down your objectives for the database.
- List the output you'll need from the database.
- List the different sequences in which you'll want to display the data. For example, you may want to list customer information in zip code order for mailings.
- Decide what *data type*, *field width*, and name to assign each field.
- Divide the fields into separate tables to avoid entering the same data more than once.

The first step in database design is to write down the main objective of the database. One possible statement of the objective of the Simian Software database is as follows: *The objective of Simian Software's database is to give the company quick, up-to-date information about customers and the orders Simian receives from them. We want to be able to summarize quickly the state of a customer's relationship with Simian Software.*

Once you know what you want to accomplish, you're ready to think about the structure of the database.

The second step in the database design process is to list the output— printed and on-screen—that Simian Software will want from this database. They'll surely want basic customer information: the name of the company, its address, city, state, country, zip code (or postal code); the company telephone number; and the name of your primary contact person. They'll also want the last contact date, the credit limit, the sales region, and a field for comments. It's always a good idea to include a separate field that contains an identification (ID) number. After all, several companies could have the same name; you'll need some easy way to keep track of which is which. (There are other good reasons for including an ID number, which will be discussed shortly.) For simplicity, several of the fields in this list will be omitted from the actual database, including country, postal code, and a second address field.

The next part of the database is order information. Simian Software will certainly want to know the name of the product that was ordered; the date and time the order was placed; the price the customer paid, sales tax, and shipping charges; how the order was to be shipped (U.P.S., Federal Express, or some other carrier); and the date the order was shipped. A field to describe any problems that may have occurred with the order will also be helpful.

The third step is to think about different ways you might want to search and/or sequence the data in your database. For example, you will undoubtedly need to produce reports in zip code order, if only to print mailing labels. You will probably want to sort the database in order of the last name of the contact person at the customer company. That implies the contact name field should be split into last name and first name fields. Addresses can be quite long; you'll want two fields for the address to make it simple to include an office number, suite number, or division name within a company. A good rule to follow is "When in doubt, divide the field." It's always easier to combine two fields into a single string than it is to split a single field into two different strings.

The fourth step is to decide the *data type* and *field width* for each field. The **data type** restricts the kind of data you can enter. For example, Number type fields allow you to enter only numbers. The **field width** is the maximum length entry that can be made in a field. For example, you'll want to restrict the State field to two characters maximum.

The eight data types available in Access with their maximum field widths are shown in Table 1.1.

Table 1.1

Data Type	Maximum Field Width	Description
Counter		Number type data that is automatically incremented
Currency		Number type data formatted for currency
Date/Time		Dates and/or times
Memo	32,000	Long text data not searched often
Number		Data on which you will perform numeric operations
OLE Object		Linked to an object external to Access via Object Linking and Embedding (OLE)
Text	255	Any characters available on the keyboard
Yes/No	1	Can contain only Y or N

Most of your fields will be Text type because most data is text data. The only fields you should make Number type are those you intend to use in numeric operations such as addition, subtraction, multiplication, and/or division. Date/time type fields contain dates and/or times. Counter type fields are similar to number type fields. However, counter fields automatically create a unique sequential value for each record. Currency type field data is similar to number data. The difference is that commas, a decimal point, and the currency symbol ($ in the U.S.) are automatically added on-screen and to printed output. Yes/no type fields can contain either yes or no.

Yes/no fields are called *logical* type in many other database products. They can be used to flag particular groups of records. For example, you may want to know whether each customer is allowed to make purchases on credit. A yes/no field can help you track that.

Memo type fields can contain large amounts of text type data. They're often used for notes, comments, and other lengthy entries. However, searching and retrieving records based on memo field data can be quite slow because they usually contain large amounts of data. It's usually better to use several text type fields if their contents must be searched frequently.

OLE object fields are used to link Access fields with data created by other programs via Micosoft's Object Linking and Embedding (OLE) standard. That's a little beyond anything we want to take on right now.

Counter type fields are automatically incremented each time a new record is added to the table, which is helpful for assigning identification numbers. Unfortunately, counter fields are numeric type; they are really nothing more than long integer number fields. Therefore you immediately face a choice. You can make the ID number field text type and write a program to update the ID numbers and to eliminate duplicates. The alternative is to make the ID number field numeric type and let Access do the work for you. The main advantage to making ID numbers text type is that text type data is easier to handle in screen forms and reports. However, you will take advantage of the counter data type and use it for the ID number field in the Customer table. When you actually set up the Orders table later in this project, you'll see another disadvantage to this decision.

> **Tip** Always make the Field width longer than the longest entry you can think of for that field. If you think you'll never run into a company name longer than 30 characters, make the field 35 characters wide. It's dangerous and time-consuming to make a field larger once the database is actually in use. Longer fields consume more disk space. However, disk space is usually cheaper than the cost of losing data because the database fields are too narrow.

Field names that are easy to comprehend will make your database most useful. Access field names can be up to 64 characters long. You can use any combination of letters, numbers, and blank spaces to make up a field name. Since you have so much flexibility, you should make the field name as descriptive as possible. For example, rather than calling the field that will contain customer identification numbers something obscure like CUSTID, call it Customer ID Number and everyone will immediately recognize what kind of data it contains. Here's one possible list of field types and widths for the Simian Software database.

Name	Type	Width
Customer ID Number	Counter	5
Name	Text	35
Address	Text	25
City	Text	25
State	Text	2
Zip Code	Text	10
Phone	Text	12
Contact Last Name	Text	16
Contact First Name	Text	16
Last Contact	Date/Time	
Credit Limit	Currency	
Sales Region	Text	5
Comments	Memo	
Product Ordered	Text	11
Order Date	Date/Time	
Order Time	Date/Time	
Order Sequence	Counter	
Price Paid	Currency	
Sales Tax	Currency	
Shipping Charge	Currency	
Order Total	Currency	
Shipped Via	Text	10
Order Problems	Memo	

Once you've created the list of fields, you can move on to the fifth step: dividing the fields into separate tables to avoid entering data more than once. Let's see how to accomplish that with the Simian Software database.

AVOIDING REDUNDANT DATA

There are quite a few fields in this list. In order not to waste disk space, it's important to avoid entering data more than once whenever possible. You should split the database into several tables so you don't enter the same data more than once. Technically, this procedure is called *normalizing* the database.

For example, suppose a customer, Windy City Writers, has purchased one copy each of ApeWord and MonkeyWrite. If you kept all the Simian Software data in a single table, you would have to type in the customer ID number, name, address, and all the other customer information twice—once for each order. That would waste disk space.

You can avoid repeating this information by keeping customer information in one table and order information in a second table. You can then connect these tables using the customer ID number—the field that both tables have. This connection is called *linking* the tables. You will call the two tables Customer and Orders. (Like field names, table names can be up to 64 characters long and can include letters, numbers, and blank spaces.) There will be one record in the Customer table for each customer. If a customer places more than one order, only information about each order will be entered in the Orders table. The sole field that will be included in both tables is the Customer ID Number field. We will use that field to link the tables. This ability to set up a relationship between tables is why Access and other similar database products are called relational database management systems.

Access will process data much faster if you define a *primary key* for each table. The **primary key** is a field (or combination of fields) used for searching and linking tables. The primary key must be unique; that is, no duplicate values will be allowed.

The primary key for the Customer table is clearly the Customer ID Number field. Each customer will have a unique identification number, so that's not an issue. The primary key for the Orders table is less clear. It seems as if the primary key for this table should also be the Customer ID Number field. However, Simian Software may receive several orders from each customer. Therefore, the customer identification number will appear more than once in each table and it will no longer be unique. Primary keys must be unique.

The way to handle this problem is to make more than one field the primary key. You will tack one or two other fields onto the Customer ID Number to make the key unique. For the Orders table, the primary key will be Customer ID Number, Order Date, Order Time, and Order Sequence. That means Order Date will be the second field in the Orders table, Order Time third, and Order Sequence fourth.

> **Tip**   You may have been tempted to use Customer ID Number, Order Date, and Product Ordered as the primary key for the Orders table. However, what if the same customer ordered more than one copy of a product on the same date but in separate orders? That would cause a duplicate primary key value.

Many books and articles have been written on the subject of normalization. You've barely scratched the surface of this interesting topic. However, if you heed the following simple rule, you'll avoid 90 percent of the pitfalls of database design: *Avoid entering and storing redundant data whenever possible.*

Table 1.2 Customer Table

Name	Type	Width
Customer ID Number	Counter	5
Name	Text	35
Address	Text	25
City	Text	25
State	Text	2
Zip Code	Text	10
Phone	Text	12
Contact Last Name	Text	16
Contact First Name	Text	16
Last Contact	Date/Time	
Credit Limit	Currency	
Sales Region	Text	5
Comments	Memo	

Table 1.3 Orders Table

Name	Type	Width
Customer ID Number	Number (Long Integer)	5
Order Date	Date/Time	
Order Time	Date/Time	
Order Sequence	Counter	
Product Ordered	Text	11
Price Paid	Currency	
Sales Tax	Currency	
Shipping Charge	Currency	
Order Total	Currency	
Shipped Via	Text	10
Order Problems	Memo	

Tables 1.2 and 1.3 show one way to divide the Simian Software database into two tables. Notice that in the Customer table, the Customer ID Number field is a counter type field, but in the Orders table, it is a number (long integer) type field. Remember, counter type fields are basically number type fields that automatically create a unique value for each record. Since we want to allow more than one entry for each customer identification number, the field must be a number type. Number fields that are designated as long integers can be used to match values stored in counter type fields.

CREATING THE DATABASE

When creating a new database, you'll work with the New Database dialog box shown in Figure 1.1. Take a minute to familiarize yourself with the elements of this dialog box. The File Name text box displays the default file name DB1.MDB. You will change this to a more appropriate name for your database. The Directories and Drives text boxes display the available directories and disk drives, respectively. Your instructor will assign a directory and disk drive where you will store your data.

To create the database:

1 Select the New Database button on the Tool bar, or choose New Database from the File menu.
The New Database dialog box is displayed, as shown in Figure 1.1.

2 In the Drives text box, select the letter designating the drive where you are to store your data.

3 In the Directories text box, select the directory where you are to store your data.

4 Select the File Name text box.

5 Change the default database file name to SIMIAN.MDB.
Figure 1.2 shows the New Database dialog box with SIMIAN.MDB being created in the \ACCESS\DATA directory on the D: drive. Your entries may be different.

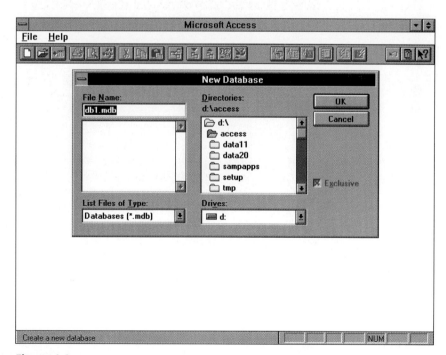

Figure 1.1

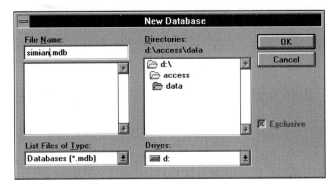

Figure 1.2

6 Look over the screen to be sure you have typed the name of the database correctly and are using the correct drive and directory.

7 When you are sure everything is correct, select the OK button to inform Access that you're ready to move on.
You will see the Database window shown in Figure 1.3.

Creating the database itself is just the beginning. Before you can do anything useful with the database, you will need to create tables and enter data. You will use the Database dialog box to create, open, or change the structure of tables, queries, forms, reports, macros, and modules.

Figure 1.3

CREATING THE CUSTOMER TABLE

In the following numbered steps you will create the Customer table in the Simian Software database. You've already defined the table structure earlier in this project, so you'll need to get out your database design notes. You'll be working in the Table dialog box, which is divided into two sections. The top portion is called the *field definition area.* It's where you enter the field names, and their data types, widths, and descriptions. The *field properties area* makes up the lower half of this dialog box. In it, you place restrictions on the data that can be entered in each field. For example, you will want to make sure that state names are always entered in uppercase: MA instead of ma. A field property can ensure this.

You'll make notes in a *data dictionary* as you work through the rest of this project. A **data dictionary** is a list of all fields in the database. Each field includes its data type and width if necessary; the table(s) in which it appears; screen(s) and reports in which it is used; and any *validation rules* to be applied to the field. (Validation rules will be defined later in this project.)

A data dictionary can take many forms. It can be a paper notebook in which you keep a record of work you've done with a database. It can be a computer file. It can even be another Access database. For our purposes, it's easiest to keep your data dictionary on paper. Make it part of your course notebook so you'll be able to update it quickly whenever you make any addition, deletion, or change in your database.

To create the table:

1 Be sure the Table button in the Database window is depressed.

2 Select the New button to open the New Table dialog box, or choose New Table from the File menu.

3 Select the New Table button instead of using the TableWizard. This will open the Table dialog box.

4 Select the first row of the Field Name column. The screen should look like Figure 1.4.

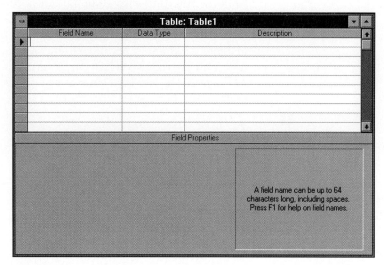

Figure 1.4

5 Type **Customer ID Number** and press (TAB)

6 Press (ALT)+⊕ to open the list box in the Data Type column.

7 Press ⊕ four times and then press (ENTER) to select the Counter data type.
The text cursor should move to the Description column.

8 Type **Customer identification number** but don't press (ENTER) or any other key. The screen should look like Figure 1.5.

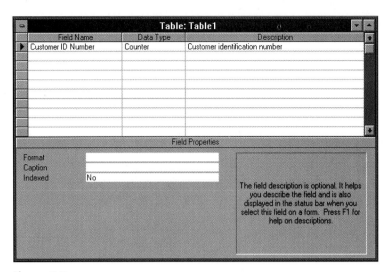

Figure 1.5

Next, you must *initialize* the Customer ID Number field. ***Initializing*** a field means assigning the first value that will be used in the field. Since Customer ID Number is a counter type field, the default initial value (where counting begins) is the number 1. ID numbers, however, are easier to work with if they all have the same number of digits. It's usually safe to begin counting with 10,000 because that leaves 9999 numbers available before the leading digit will change. (Naturally, you could use 100,000 or even 1,000,000 as an initial value. The appropriate number you choose depends on the number of customers you expect to have. Optimists will undoubtedly want to select larger initial values.)

Fortunately, there's a simple way to initialize counter type fields. You will use the Format text box in the Field Properties box.

To initialize a field:

1 Make sure the cursor is still in the Customer ID Number field definition row.

2 Click the Format text box in the Field Properties box or press (F6) to move to the Field Properties box.

3 Type **\10000**
The \ character tells Access to treat the number 1 as a number instead of as an instruction. Note this in your data dictionary.

4 Move the cursor back to the Customer ID Number field definition row in the top half of the dialog box.

Caution You've successfully initialized the Customer ID Number field. However, you have not actually added 10,000 to each ID number Access assigns. You've just changed the way the data is displayed by preceding each value with a 1 and the appropriate number of zeros. If the counter field reaches 19,999, the next number displayed will also be 19,999; the 1 displayed by the formatting will be replaced with the 1 generated by the counter field. Therefore, if you really need 99,999 ID numbers, make the format \100000.

Finally, you want the Customer ID Number field to be the primary key for this table. You will use the Tool bar.

To designate a field as the primary key:

1 Be sure the cursor is in the Customer ID Number field definition row.

2 Select the Key button on the Tool bar, or choose Set Primary Key from the Edit menu.
The screen should look like Figure 1.6. Notice the Key icon displayed to the left of the Customer ID Number field name. Remember to record the name of the field that makes up the primary key in your data dictionary.

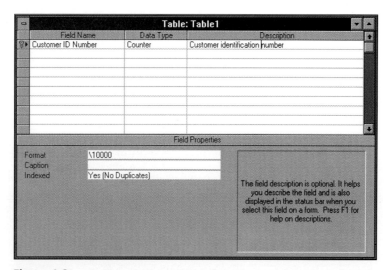

Figure 1.6

Recall that the primary key must contain unique values. It's used as the basis for sequencing records in the table. The primary key also can be used to join different tables, allowing you to use fields from different tables at the same time.

Now you're ready to set up the rest of the fields in the Customer table.

To add the remaining fields to the table:

1 Select the Field Name column in the blank row below Customer ID Number.

2 Type **Name** and press ⌈TAB⌉ to go to the Description column. Type **Customer company name**

3 Move to the Field Size property text box in the Field Properties box. Change the field size from 50 to 35.

4 Select the next blank row in the Field Name column.

5 Type **Address** and then press ⌈TAB⌉ to go to the Description column. Type **Address**

6 Move to the Field Size property text box. Change the field size from 50 to 25.

7 Move to the next blank row in the Field Name column.

8 Type `City` and press (TAB) to go to the Description column. Type `City`

9 Move to the Field Size property text box. Change the field size from 50 to 25.

10 Repeat steps 7 through 9 for the following text type fields:

Field Name	Description	Field Width
State	State	2
Zip Code	Zip Code (U.S. addresses only)	10
Phone	Voice Telephone	12
Contact Last Name	Contact last name	16
Contact First Name	Contact first name	16

11 Choose Save As from the File menu and type `Customer` as the table name.

12 Double-click the Control-menu box in the upper-left corner of the Table window to close the table or select Close from the File menu.

13 Note in your data dictionary that you've created the Customer table. Include the date and time it was first created.

Access makes creating a table fairly simple. However, you've only worked with two field types: counter and text. You still have date/time, currency, and memo type fields to work with. Let's see what happens when we add the rest of the fields to the table.

CHANGING THE STRUCTURE OF A TABLE

Changing the structure of a table means adding, modifying, or deleting fields. This is a simple process when you're using Access since you can use normal Windows procedures. For example, to delete a field, you can mark the field and press (DEL). Two buttons on the Tool bar are useful when modifying a table's structure. The Insert Row button inserts a blank row above the currently selected one. The Delete Row button deletes the current row.

If you want to add only a few fields to the end of the table structure, all you have to do is move the pointer to the blank row at the bottom of the table structure. In the following numbered steps, you will add some new fields to the Customer table.

Caution Never change the data type of a field. Also, avoid shortening a field width. If you shorten a width and there's some data too long for the new width, any data longer than the new width will be chopped off. You can also lose data changing field types.

To change the structure of a table:

1 Select the Customer table, then select the Design button in the Database window.

This opens the Customer table in Design view, which allows you to change the table structure.

2 Select the first available line to add a new field.

3 Type **Last Contact** and press ⟨TAB⟩

4 Open the Data Type list box, select the Date/Time data type, and then press ⟨TAB⟩

5 Type **Last contact date** and press ⟨ENTER⟩ to move to the next blank line.

6 Type **Credit Limit** and press ⟨TAB⟩

7 Open the Data Type list box, select Currency, and then press ⟨TAB⟩

8 Type **Credit limit (dollars)** and press ⟨ENTER⟩

9 Type **Sales Region** and press ⟨TAB⟩ twice to move to the Description column. (Since text is the default type, you don't need to choose it.)

10 Type **Sales region** but don't press ⟨ENTER⟩ yet.

11 Move to the Field Size property. Change the field size to 7.

12 Move to the next blank row in the Field Name column of the Table dialog box.

13 Type **Comments** and press ⟨TAB⟩ to move to the Data Type column.

14 Open the Data Type list box, select Memo type, and then press ⟨TAB⟩

15 Type **Comments**

16 Click the Save Object button on the Tool bar to save the table structure, or choose Save from the File menu.
At this point, the screen should look like Figure 1.7.

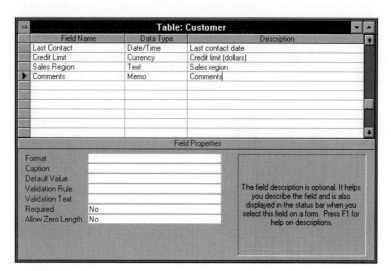

Figure 1.7

17 Close the Table window.

18 Note the changes to the Customer table in your data dictionary.

Step 15 is extremely important. Up to that point, all the changes you had made had not been saved to disk. Your modified Customer table existed only in the computer's internal memory (RAM). If the power had gone off, you would have lost all your work. It's important to save your work to disk frequently, using either the Save menu or the Save Object button.

EXIT   If necessary, you can exit Access now and continue this project later.

CREATING THE ORDERS TABLE

Using the database design you developed earlier, you can create the Orders table. Remember to make the Customer ID Number field the first in the table so it will become the first part of the primary key. The second, third, and fourth fields must be Order Date, Order Time, and Order Sequence, respectively.

To create the table:

1 Be sure the Table button is depressed.

2 Select the New button.

3 Select the New Table button (not the TableWizard button).

The Orders table differs from the Customer table in a number of ways. First, you must allow duplicate values for the Customer ID Number field in the Orders table. That means it can't be a counter type field. Instead, make it a number type with the Field Size property set to Long Integer.

To add fields to the table:

1 Select the first row of the Field Name column.

2 Type **Customer ID Number** and press TAB

3 Select Number as the Data Type and then press TAB

4 Type **Customer identification number** but don't press ENTER or any other key.

5 Move to the Field Size text box in the bottom half of the Table dialog box.

6 Select Long Integer for the Field Size.

Now, you must initialize the Customer ID Number field. If you don't, ID numbers entered in the Orders table won't match those in the Customer table.

To initialize a field:

1 Move to the Format text box.

2 Type **\10000**

Next, you will specify the Format property for the Order Date and Order Time fields, choosing from Access' selection of date and time formats.

To format a Date/time field:

1 Move to the Field Name column in the blank row below Customer ID Number.

2 Type **Order Date** and press (TAB)

3 Select Date/Time type.

4 Move to the Field Size text box in the lower half of the Table dialog box.

5 Select Short Date.

6 Move to the Description column in the upper half of the Table dialog box.

7 Type **Order date** and press (ENTER)

8 Type **Order Time** and press (TAB)

9 Select Date/Time type.

10 Move to the Field Size text box in the lower half of the Table dialog box.

11 Select Medium Time.
The screen should look like Figure 1.8.

12 Move to the Description column in the upper half of the Table dialog box.

13 Type **Order time** and press (ENTER)

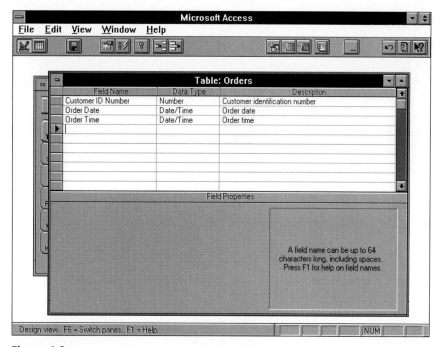

Figure 1.8

Now you are ready to set up the rest of the fields.

To add the remaining fields to the table:

1 Type **Order Sequence** and press (TAB)

2 Select Counter type.

3 Move to the Description column.

4 Type **Order sequence number** and press (ENTER)

5 Type **Product Ordered** and press (TAB)

6 Select Text type.

7 Move to the Field Size property in the lower half of the Table dialog box.

8 Type **11**

9 Move to the Description column in the upper half of the Table dialog box.

10 Type **Product ordered** and press (ENTER)

11 Type **Price Paid** and press (TAB)

12 Select Currency type.

13 Move to the Description column in the upper half of the Table dialog box.

14 Type **Price paid (dollars)** and press (ENTER)

15 Repeat steps 11 through 14 for the following Currency type fields:

Field Name	Description
Sales Tax	Sales tax charged (dollars)
Shipping Charge	Shipping and handling charge (dollars)
Order Total	Order total amount (dollars)

16 Move to the blank text box below Order Total in the Field Name column.

17 Type **Shipped Via** and press (TAB)

18 Select Text type.

19 Move to the Field Size property in the lower half of the Table dialog box.

20 Type **10**

21 Move to the Description column in the upper half of the Table dialog box.

22 Type **Shipping carrier** and press (ENTER)

23 Type **Order Problems** and press (TAB)

24 Select Memo type.

25 Type **Problems with order**

26 Select Save As from the File menu.

27 Type **Orders** and press (ENTER)

28 Select No when Access asks if you want to create a primary key.

Finally, remember that you'll need to use more than one field for the primary key to make the key unique for each record.

To use more than one field in the primary key:

1 Be sure the Orders table is open in Design view.

2 Select the Customer ID Number field in the field definition area.

3 Move to the Order Sequence line. Hold down (SHIFT) while you select it to mark a block made up of the first four fields in the table structure.

4 Select the Key button on the Tool bar or choose Set Primary Key from the Edit menu to create the primary key.

5 Note the addition of the Orders table and its primary key in your data dictionary.

The screen should look like Figure 1.9, which also shows the structure of the completed Orders table. (The window in Figure 1.9 has been maximized to display all fields; the screen you're looking at probably won't look exactly like this.) When you're done, select Save As from the File menu to save your table as ORDERS. After closing the window, the two tables should appear in the database window, as shown in Figure 1.10.

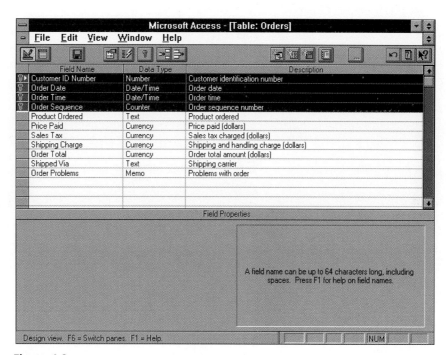

Figure 1.9

Figure 1.10

FORMATTING A FIELD

One of the biggest problems facing anyone who works with data is incorrect data entry. Spelling errors are far and away the most common source of this difficulty. Unfortunately, it's difficult to check for correct spelling all the time, especially when it comes to names. However, you can make sure that a few *validation rules* are included in your table. A **validation rule** is a restriction on the data that can be entered in a field. Formatting a field is one type of validation. One of the easiest formatting tools to implement guarantees that everything typed into a text type field is uppercase. The obvious field this applies to is State, in which every entry should be all uppercase.

To add a format to the State field:

1 Open the Customer table in Design view.

2 Select the State field.

3 Move to the Format text box in the field properties area.

4 Type >

5 Move back to the field definition area.
The screen should look like Figure 1.11.

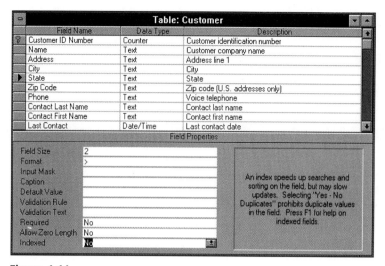

Figure 1.11

6 Close the Customer table, making sure you save the change you've just made.

7 Note this change in your data dictionary.

The > character tells Access to convert anything typed in the State field to all uppercase. If you type **ny**, it will be automatically converted to NY when you move the cursor out of the State field.

PRINTING THE TABLE STRUCTURE

You can print the table structure along with all table and field properties using the Print Definitions option from the File menu. You can print reports about your table structures, validations, formatting, and so on. However, analyzing the table and producing the report takes some time. Don't start the following procedure unless you're sure you have ten minutes to devote to getting the output.

To print a table definition:

1 Be sure the SIMIAN database is open and the Customer table is selected.

2 Choose Print Definition from the File menu.

You'll see the Print Table Definition dialog box shown in Figure 1.12.

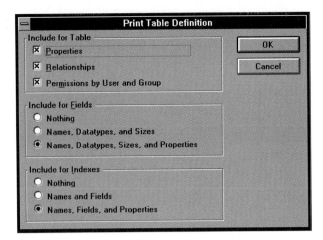

Figure 1.12

3 Select the OK button to accept all default values for the report. After a few minutes, you'll see the Object Definition window, as shown in Figure 1.13.

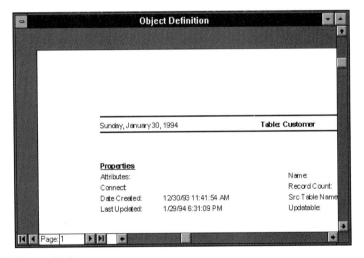

Figure 1.13

 4 Click the Print button on the Tool bar, or choose Print from the File menu.
You'll see the Print dialog box, as shown in Figure 1.14.

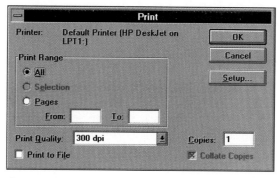

Figure 1.14

5 Select the OK button to print the report. It should look like Figure 1.15.

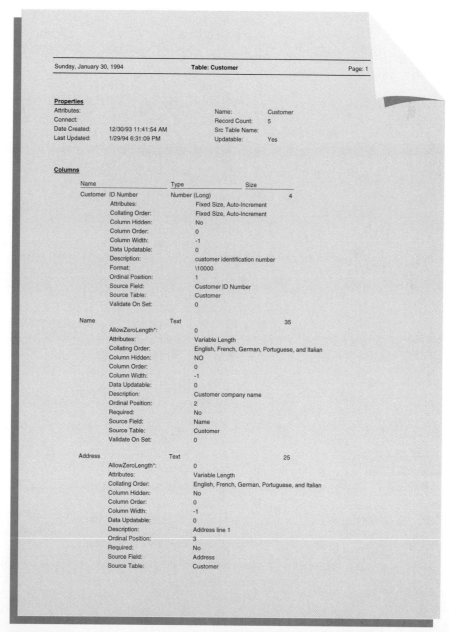

Figure 1.15

6 Close the Object Definition window.

7 Double-click the control button in the database window to close the Simian database.

8 Add a description of the report to your data dictionary.

THE NEXT STEP

You can add many validation rules and formatting options to tables. A complete list would be impossible, because every database has its own set of validations that depend on the requirements of the users. Additional discussion is well beyond the scope of this module.

One common validation is ensuring that zip codes contain either five digits or nine digits and a hyphen (in the form *nnnnn-nnnn*). A similar validation can be applied to Social Security numbers (*nnn-nn-nnnn*). Others include making sure the first letters of names are capitalized and restricting dates to be no earlier than the current date. The Access manuals show many examples. Interested students should read Chapter 3 of the *Access User's Guide*.

This concludes Project 1. You can either exit Access or go on to work the Study Questions, Review Exercises, and Assignments.

SUMMARY AND EXERCISES

Summary

- A database is a collection of related information.
- A database is made up of tables.
- A table is made up of fields (columns) and records (rows).
- When you need information from two or more tables, you must link them via a linking field, usually the primary key field.
- Access is a popular relational database management program. A relational database management program allows you to link multiple tables based on matching values from given fields.
- You should always design the database before starting Access.
- The first step in database design is to clearly state the objective.
- The second step in database design is to list all the outputs you want from the database.
- Next, list all the fields you might want to use to sort or search the data.
- The last step in database design is normalizing the database to eliminate redundant data.
- You should give a new database a name when you set it up for the first time.
- To create tables, use the Table icon and the New button.
- The Tool bar changes when you start a new activity.
- Each field has a set of properties that are useful for validating the data.
- You can use the Format property to initialize a counter type field.
- The Key icon on the Tool bar lets you set a primary key for each table.

- A long integer type field can be used with counter type fields to allow multiple entries with the same value.
- You should never change the data type of a field or make a field's width shorter.
- Placing a > character in the Format field property for a text type field converts the data entered in that field to all uppercase characters.

Key Terms and Operations

Key Terms
data dictionary
data type
field
field definition area
field properties area
field width
format
initialize
link
normalization
primary key
record
relational database management
    system

secondary key
sequential search
table
table structure
validation rule

Operations
New Database
New Table
Print
Print Definition
Save
Save As
Set Primary Key

Study Questions

Multiple Choice

1. A table is made up of related
   a. records.
   b. fields.
   c. linkages.
   d. relations.

2. A database is a collection of related
   a. kcy ficlds.
   b. tables.
   c. fields.
   d. records.

3. When setting up a new database, the first step is to
   a. clearly state your objectives.
   b. select New Database from the File menu.
   c. decide what fields it should contain.
   d. normalize it.

4. Memo fields are where you store
   a. long text strings.
   b. a memorandum from your boss.
   c. pictures.
   d. numbers.

5. The key field used to connect two tables in your database is called
   a. the linking field.
   b. the primary key.
   c. the main field.
   d. the secondary field.

6. It's dangerous to make a field
   a. too wide.
   b. a memo type.
   c. too narrow.
   d. part of a table.

7. Normalizing the database will
   a. save disk space.
   b. make searching more efficient.
   c. make your data relate logically.
   d. All of the above.

8. When you want to link a counter type field with a field in a second table that contains duplicate entries, you should make the field in the second table
   a. counter type.
   b. number type, short integer.
   c. number type, long integer.
   d. It is not possible to link two fields of those types.

9. Number type data should be used for
   a. fields that will only contain numbers.
   b. fields that will be used only for numeric operations.
   c. most fields in the table.
   d. Number data should never be used.

10. Text type data should be used for
    a. fields that will only contain numbers.
    b. fields that will be used only for numeric operations.
    c. most fields in the table.
    d. Text data should never be used.

Short Answer

1. What are the rows in a table called? What are the columns called?

2. Explain the meaning of the term *relational database management system*.

3. How can you change the structure of a table?

4. Explain the difference between fields and records in a table.

5. It's important to place restrictions on what can be entered in a field. What are these restrictions called?

6. What process is used to eliminate redundant data from a database?

7. List the data types available in Access and discuss briefly the uses for each type.

8. Explain how you start a counter type field at a number other than 1.

9. When a text type field has a > Format property, what happens to data entered in that field?

10. What are the pros and cons of using a text type field for an identification number?

For Discussion

1. Why didn't we normalize the Customer table even further by putting sales region information in a separate table? List other information that you might want to store in other tables. Under what circumstances would you want to make each change?

2. Why did we decide to use a counter type field to hold customer ID numbers in the Customer table? Why didn't we make the Customer ID Number field in the Orders table a counter type field?

3. We made the Order Date and Order Time separate fields in the Orders table. Discuss the pros and cons of making these a single field called Order Date and Time.

4. Why is sequencing an important part of the database design process? In other words, how does the fact that you'll want to list your data in a variety of arrangements influence the design of a database?

Review Exercise

Suppose Simian Software wants to keep track of the number of calls to their technical support department by each customer.

1. Design a field to hold this data, including its data type, width and format.

2. Add it to the appropriate table.

3. Add the appropriate field properties.

4. Save the result in a table called Customer Technical Support. You'll use this table in future exercises.

Assignments

Printing the Orders Table Structure

Print the definitions for the Orders table. Add this report to your data dictionary.

Adding Technical Support Calls to the Simian Software Database

Ms. Hudson is so pleased with your work that she has asked you to set up another table to keep track of customer telephone calls to Simian Software's technical support department. Calls come in from customers requesting a variety of information about using ApeWord and MonkeyWrite. Your new table must keep track of when each call was received, what technicians handled it (initials will be sufficient identification), and a summary of the question and the solution provided. Design the necessary table using the database design process described in this project. Then create the new table using Access. Print the resulting table, and turn in a listing of the table structure along with your database design notes.

Adding Inventory Control to the Simian Software Database

You've been asked to add inventory control to Simian Software's database. What fields and/or tables will you need to add? How will they be related to the existing fields and tables? Design the new tables and create them using Access. Turn in a listing of the table structure and your database design notes.

Adding Billing to the Simian Software Database

You've been asked to add billing to Simian Software's database. What fields and/or tables will you need to add? How will they be related to the existing fields and tables? Design the new tables and create them using Access. Turn in a listing of the table structure and your database design notes. (*Hint:* You'll have to normalize this part of the database.)

PROJECT 2: CREATING TABLE RELATIONSHIPS, ADDING DATA, AND CHANGING DATA

Objectives

After completing this project, you should be able to:

► Create relationships between tables

► Add data to tables

► Quickly print a report showing the data in a table

► Move the cursor to different locations in a table

► Change and delete data

CASE STUDY: WORKING WITH THE SIMIAN SOFTWARE DATABASE TABLES

"Naturally, we'll want some data in those tables," said Ms. Hudson. "Add about ten records to each so we can develop screens and reports."

"And it looks to me like there's a problem here. Suppose I want data that includes both customer and order information. For example, I might want the customer's name, telephone number, and the products they've ordered. How can I pull fields from two tables at the same time?"

Designing the Solution

So far you've set up the skeleton of your database consisting of the table structures. However, the tables themselves are empty. Think of an empty table as a house with no furniture or people in it. The house is an empty structure. It's not particularly interesting until some people and their belongings move in. Empty tables are no more interesting than empty houses. It's time to get some data into these empty table structures to make them interesting.

You need to establish a permanent link between the Customer and Orders tables. Since a customer may have placed more than one order, we'll have to be sure that all orders for each customer can be accessed. Once that's done, we'll move on to adding, changing, and deleting records from the tables. Fortunately, that's a fairly simple process; Access uses standard Windows procedures to change and erase data.

SETTING UP RELATIONSHIPS

Before we start entering data, you must tell Access what sort of *relationship* exists between the Customer and Orders tables; that is, you need to tell Access which order(s) go with each customer. While you could probably see this relationship intuitively, you'll have to teach the Simian Software database to accomplish the same task using Access.

The technique is straightforward. You will link the Customer table with the Orders table using the Customer ID Number field. Before moving on to the mechanics of getting this done in Access, there's some more terminology you must learn.

Relating Parent and Child Tables

In the Simian Software database, the Customer table is the parent table and the Orders table is the child table. The *parent table* (also called the *primary table*) is the one that is used as the main table in the relation. The *child table* is also called the *related table.* To fully understand the idea of parent and child tables, you should know something about the *record pointer,* the device that keeps track of which record is currently available for editing, copying, and other activities. The parent table controls the movement of the record pointer through the child table. (When more than one person is using the same table, each user is assigned a separate record pointer.)

A little more explanation will clarify this relationship. Each table has its own record pointer. Movement of the record pointer in the child table is controlled by the value of the linking field in the parent table. If Customer is the parent table, Orders is the child, and the Customer ID Number field in the parent table has a value of 10002, then the record pointer in the child table will point to the first record with a customer ID number of 10002. (Another way of defining the parent table is that it's the currently *active table,* the one in which the record pointer moves down one record when you press ⊕ and up one record when you press ⊛.)

Before you try to link the Customer and Orders tables, you need to establish what type of relationship will exist between them. A *one-to-one relationship* will have exactly one child record for each parent record. If there is more than one child for each parent, it's called a *one-to-many relationship.* If there are several parent records with matching keys in the child and several child records with matching keys in the parent, you have a *many-to-many relationship.*

The most common type of relationship is one-to-many. One-to-one relationships are rare. After all, if two tables are in a one-to-one relation, you have to ask yourself why all the records weren't just placed in the first table to begin with. While there may be a good reason for this (for example, there may be several child tables associated with a single parent table), the question should at least be raised.

Many-to-many relations sometimes mean the database has been badly designed. They are difficult to work with. One way of handling many-to-many relations is to use a third table set up solely to relate the other two. Each record in this *cross-reference table* contains a key value from the original parent and a key from the child. Any time the two original tables are used together, the cross-reference table is used to link them, effectively making the link a one-to-one relation.

The Simian Software database has a single one-to-many relationship because each customer has potentially several orders.

LINKING THE CUSTOMER AND ORDERS TABLES

There are two techniques available to link Access tables. The first uses relationships, which are *permanent* links between tables. The second uses **transient links,** which are temporary links often used to produce a report. In this project, you'll focus on relationships. Project 3 will show you how to use query-by-example to set up transient links.

You have determined that a one-to-many relationship should be established between the Customer and Orders tables. In the following numbered steps, you will use the Relationships dialog box to set up this relationship.

To establish a link between two tables:

1 Be sure all tables are closed and the Simian database is open with the Database window active. Also make sure the Customer table is selected.

2 Choose Relationships from the Edit menu.
The Add Table dialog box shown in Figure 2.1 will open automatically.

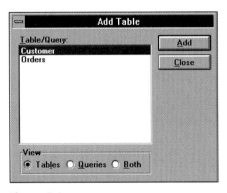

Figure 2.1

3 Select the Customer table, and then select the Add button. Repeat this process with the Orders table.

4 Close the Add Table dialog box.

5 Drag the Customer ID Number field from the Customer table structure onto the same field in the Orders table structure. Release the button to establish the relationship.
The screen should briefly look like Figure 2.2.

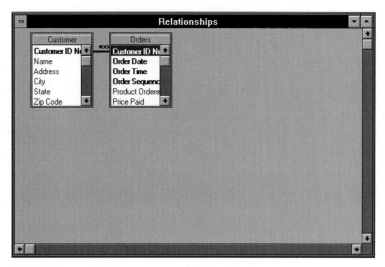

Figure 2.2

6 The Relationships dialog box should open automatically, as shown in Figure 2.3. If it doesn't, repeat the drag process (step 6) on the fields. This will open a Help window. Select the Cancel button in the Help window to open the Relationships dialog box.

You will continue to use the Relationships dialog box to establish certain characteristics of the relationship, which will be discussed in the following section.

Setting Up Referential Integrity

Just as some children have no parents, a child record may have no matching record in the parent table. Continuing the analogy, such records are called *orphan records*. The decision you must make is whether to allow orphan records in this relationship. In other words, are you going to allow orders that have no record in the Customer table?

Allowing orphan records is not a very good idea because you would have no way of knowing which customer placed those orders. Disallowing orphan records tells Access to enforce referential integrity in the relationship between the Customer and Orders tables. *Referential integrity* means there are no orphan records in any child table in the database.

Once you have established referential integrity, what happens when you delete a record from the Customer table? Should all the child records in the Orders table be deleted, too? You probably want that to happen to guarantee there will be no orphan records. Having made these two decisions, you can go ahead and set up the referential integrity between Customer and Orders. You will continue using the Relationships dialog box.

To establish referential integrity:

1 Select the Enforce Referential Integrity check box.

2 Select the Cascade Delete Related Records check box.

3 Make sure the Many button is checked in the One To box.
The screen should look like Figure 2.3.

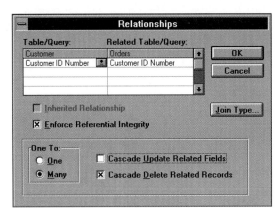

Figure 2.3

4 When referential integrity has been established, select the OK button.

5 Close the Relationships window. Select the Yes button when Access asks if you want to save the relationships.

> **Tip** Suppose you change a customer ID number. You'd like that change to be reflected in all orders from that customer. Access will do this for you if you check the Cascade Update Related Fields check box in the Relationships dialog box. However, since we've set up Customer ID Number as a counter type field, you aren't allowed to change the ID number. Therefore, you need not check that box for this relationship.

ENTERING DATA

Now you're ready to enter some customer records. In the steps that follow, you'll enter two customer records. Your instructor may ask you to enter the remaining records, or you may be given the finished database. When entering data in the Customer table, remember you won't be allowed to type anything into the Customer ID Number field because it's a counter type field; values will be entered automatically as you add records to the table. Here's how to add customer records.

> **Tip** There's a straightforward way to copy data from the same field in the previous record. While in the record you want to copy the data to, press CTRL+".

 To add customer records:

1 Be sure the Customer table is selected in the Simian database window.

2 Select the Open button. The screen should look like Figure 2.4.

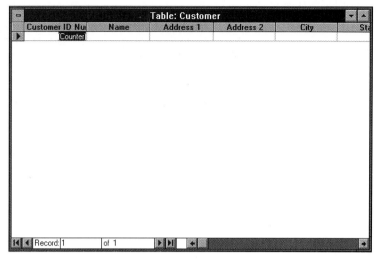

Figure 2.4

3 Press (TAB) to bypass the Customer ID Number field.

4 Type **Andy Jackson Associates** and press (TAB)

5 Type **123456 Some St.** and press (TAB)

6 Type **San Carlos** and press (TAB)

7 Type **ca** and press (TAB)

8 Type **94070-2316** and press (TAB)

9 Type **415-555-1234** and press (TAB)

10 Type **Jackson** and press (TAB)

11 Type **Andy** and press (TAB)

12 Type **1/2/94** and press (TAB)

13 Type **10000** and press (TAB)

14 Type **West** and press (TAB)

15 Type **A new customer with a lot of growth potential** and press
(ENTER)

16 Press (TAB) to bypass the Customer ID Number field.

17 Type **AllWays Desktop Publishing, Inc.** and press (TAB)

18 Type **9876 All Ways** and press (TAB)

19 Type **Wilkes-Barre** and press (TAB)

20 Type **pa** and press (TAB)

21 Type **17777** and press (TAB)

22 Type **717-555-5555** and press (TAB)

23 Type **Jones** and press (TAB)

24 Type **June** and press (TAB)

25 Type **11/7/93** and press (TAB)

26 Type **50000** and press (TAB)

27 Type **East** and press (TAB)

28 Type **This customer uses technical support a lot. We may have to start charging them for calls.** and press (ENTER)

At this point, the screen should look like Figure 2.5.

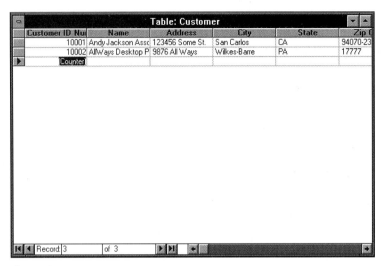

Customer ID Nu	Name	Address	City	State	Zip C
10001	Andy Jackson Assc	123456 Some St.	San Carlos	CA	94070-23
10002	AllWays Desktop P	9876 All Ways	Wilkes-Barre	PA	17777
Counter					

Record: 3 of 3

Figure 2.5

29 Choose Close from the File menu to close the Customer table and save your work.

30 Note in your data dictionary that you've added these two records to the Customer table.

> **Tip** When entering a large amount of data, you can save your work frequently by selecting Save Record from the File menu. That way, when a power failure occurs, the only work you'll lose is what you've done since you last saved to disk. (Data is automatically saved when you close a table or file.)

If necessary, enter the remaining data as shown in the following tables. Be sure to enter both the remaining customer records and all the orders records. (Don't try to enter data that's already been added.) When entering orders, you need only type the last digit of the Customer ID Number. The field format (\10000) will automatically add 10,000 to each number you enter.

Regardless of whether or not you enter the data, note the changes to the database in your data dictionary.

Table 2.1 Customers Table

	Customer 1	Customer 2	Customer 3	Customer 4
Date	28-Feb-94	28-Feb-94	28-Feb-94	28-Feb-94
Customer ID	10001	10002	10003	10004
Name	Andy Jackson Associates	AllWays Desktop Publishing	Gulfport Documentation	Windy City Writers
Address	123456 Some St.	9876 All Ways	4567 Gulf Ave.	111 Michigan Ave.
City	San Carlos	Wilkes-Barre	Gulfport	Chicago
State	CA	PA	MS	IL
Zip Code	94070-2316	17777	39505	60614
Phone	415-555-1234	717-555-5555	601-555-7777	312-555-6789
Contact Last Name	Jackson	Jones	Shettlemore	DePue
First Name	Andy	June	Walt	David
Last Contact	1/2/94	11/7/93	12/14/92	5/28/90
Credit Limit	$10,000.00	$50,000.00	$100,000.00	$1,000,000.00
Sales Region	West	East	South	Midwest
Comments	A new customer with a lot of growth potential.	This customer uses technical support a lot. We may have to start charging them for calls.	An exceptionally good customer.	Long-term customer who's fairly good.

Table 2.2 Customers Table

	Customer 5	Customer 6	Customer 7	Customer 8
Date	28-Feb-94	28-Feb-94	28-Feb-94	28-Feb-94
Customer ID	10005	10006	10007	10008
Name	Northern Publishing	Bay Area Writers	Tinsel Town Screenplays, I	The Writing Factory
Address	789 A St.	38791 Dan St.	47932 Sunny St.	17632-A 110 St.
City	Toronto	Concord	Los Angeles	Mexico City
State	ON	CA	CA	MX
Zip Code		94518	90024	
Phone	416-555-3456	510-555-7654	310-555-2938	525-555-5555
Contact Last Name	LeBlanc	Hillman	Brown	Lopez
First Name	Chris	Debra	Bruce	Trini
Last Contact	7/16/91	9/13/92	4/15/91	11/7/93
Credit Limit	$500,000.00	$1,000,000.00	$500.00	$100,000.00
Sales Region	North	West	West	South
Comments	Our first customer from Canada.	A small shop that does a lot of business.	Very slow to pay their bills. We may want to ship COD only.	A new customer that should benefit from passage of NAFTA.

Table 2.3 Orders Table

	Order 1	Order 2	Order 3	Order 4
Date	31-Jan-94	31-Jan-94	31-Jan-94	31-Jan-94
Customer ID	10001	10002	10002	10003
Order Date	1/2/94	11/7/93	12/14/93	12/14/92
Order Time	11:45 AM	01:23 PM	06:19 PM	07:45 AM
Order Sequence	1	2	3	4
Product Ordered	ApeWord	MonkeyWr	ApeWord	MonkeyWr
Price Paid	$199.95	$44.95	$179.95	$49.95
Sales Tax	$16.50	$0.00	$0.00	$0.00
Shipping Charge	$10.00	$10.00	$15.00	$15.00
Order Total	$226.45	$54.95	$194.95	$64.95
Shipped Via	UPS	UPS	FedEx	FedEx
Order Problems				Need rapid delivery

Table 2.4 Orders Table

	Order 5	Order 6	Order 7	Order 8
Date	31-Jan-94	31-Jan-94	31-Jan-94	31-Jan-94
Customer ID	10003	10004	10005	10005
Order Date	7/30/93	4/7/88	7/17/91	11/7/92
Order Time	09:36 AM	10:21 AM	12:58 PM	09:34 AM
Order Sequence	5	6	7	8
Product Ordered	ApeWord	ApeWord	MonkeyWr	ApeWord
Price Paid	$179.95	$199.95	$49.95	$179.95
Sales Tax	$0.00	$0.00	$0.00	$0.00
Shipping Charge	$10.00	$15.00	$10.00	$15.00
Order Total	$189.95	$214.95	$59.95	$194.95
Shipped Via	UPS	FedEx	UPS	UPS
Order Problems				Referral from technical support

Did you notice that as soon as the cursor left the State field, characters were automatically converted to uppercase? The > format you entered in Project 1 caused that to occur automatically. You may also have noticed that each figure you entered for the credit limit was converted to currency format with commas, a decimal point, and a dollar sign. That's because you made Credit Limit a currency type field.

 EXIT If necessary, you can exit Access now and continue this project later.

Tip Fields containing dates are date/time type. To enter a time after the date, just leave a blank space and type the time as HH:MM [AM|PM]. For example, you could type 7/16/91 11:34 am.

PRINTING THE DATA

The easiest way to print your data is to open the table and then select the Auto Report button on the Tool bar. Once Access creates the report, you can print it by selecting the Print button.

 ### *To print the Customer table:*

 1 Open the Customer table.

2 Select the Auto Report button on the Tool bar.

 3 Select the Print Report button on the Tool bar.

The report produced is pretty fancy. In Project 5, you'll learn how to modify reports like this. If you want to see just the data, without fancy fonts and other special features, you can open the table and choose Print from the File menu.

CHANGING DATA

Access makes it easy to *edit*, or change, data. You will move the cursor to the field you want and type the new data. You can move the cursor using the cursor control (arrow) keys or just click in the field and record area you want to edit. You can press (DEL), (BKSP), and other standard editing keys to make changes. If you press (INS) once, Access will toggle between insert and overwrite mode. In insert mode, characters are inserted starting at the text cursor. In overwrite mode, characters are overwritten one at a time as you type their replacements.

Memo fields require a different approach to editing data. Use the ⊝ and ⊜ keys to move the cursor to the part of the data you want to change.

THE NEXT STEP

Access has a number of built-in validations. Open either the Customer or Orders table and try to enter an illegal date, such as 2/29/93, in a date type field. You'll see the error box shown in Figure 2.6. Data entered in Access fields must conform to the data type of that field. That's the most fundamental type of data validation; it's handled automatically in Access.

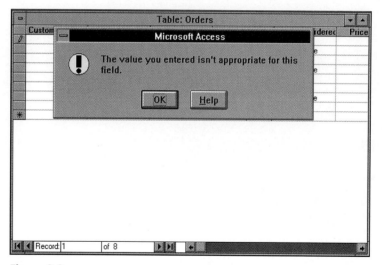

Figure 2.6

A more subtle form of illegal data involves referential integrity. If you try to enter a customer ID number in the Orders table that has no matching record in the Customer table, you'll be told you're trying to violate referential integrity. Remember we set up the relationship between the two tables, disallowing orphan records in the Orders table.

This concludes Project 2. You can either exit Access or go on to work the Study Questions, Review Exercises, and Assignments.

SUMMARY AND EXERCISES

Summary

- Setting up relationships is an essential part of establishing a database.
- Understanding the concepts of parent and child tables and referential integrity is necessary before creating relationships.
- You press (TAB) to move between fields within a single record.
- A table must be opened before data can be entered.
- You should save work frequently with the Save option from the File menu.
- You can change data quickly using standard editing keys.

Key Terms and Operations

Key Terms
active table
child table
cross-reference table
edit
many-to-many relationship
one-to-many relationship
one-to-one relationship
orphan record
parent table

primary table
record pointer
referential integrity
related table
relationship
transient link

Operations
Add Table
Edit
Relationships

Study Questions

Multiple Choice

1. When you enter data into a table, it is saved
   a. in memory.
   b. on the disk.
   c. on the monitor.
   d. It's not saved at all.

2. How often should you save data when you're entering or editing?
   a. once a day
   b. once a week
   c. as often as possible
   d. never, since Access saves the data automatically

3. When you need to match a field that contains several identical entries with a counter type field, you should make it
   a. a long integer number.
   b. a short integer number.
   c. a fixed decimal number.
   d. text.

4. When finished entering data in a field, what key should you press to move to the next field?
   a. (TAB)
   b. (ENTER)
   c. click in the new field
   d. All of the above.

5. The record pointer keeps track of the current
   a. field.
   b. table.
   c. record.
   d. database.

6. When you're done entering data, you should
   a. turn the computer's power off.
   b. choose Save from the File menu.
   c. choose Save As from the File menu.
   d. press (CTRL)+(ALT)+(DEL).

7. You should set up a relationship between two tables
   a. when you need a temporary link to print a report.
   b. when the link is a permanent part of the database.
   c. when you don't want to normalize the database.
   d. None of the above.

8. To open a table,
   a. double-click on the table name.
   b. click once on the table name, and then click the Open button.
   c. select the table name and press (ENTER).
   d. All of the above.

9. If you type 2/29/93 in a date/time type field, Access will
   a. do nothing.
   b. tell you 1993 was not a leap year.
   c. tell you February 29, 1993, is an illegal date.
   d. tell you that you've tried to enter an illegal value.

10. If you try to enter 98765 in a text type field, Access will
    a. do nothing.
    b. tell you 1993 was not a leap year.
    c. tell you February 29, 1993 is an illegal date.
    d. tell you that you've tried to enter an illegal value.

Short Answer

1. How can you use data from different tables at the same time?

2. Before you can enter data in a table, what steps should you take?

3. How often should you save your work when entering or editing data?

4. When you enter a new record in a table, where does Access store it?

5. List all the ways in which the cursor can be moved in a table.

6. Why did we make the Customer ID Number field in the Orders table long integer type instead of counter type?

7. List all the ways in which the record pointer can be moved to the next field in an open table.

8. What function does the record pointer serve?

9. What keys should you press to copy data from the previous record into the current record?

10. Explain the difference between one-to-one and one-to-many relationships.

For Discussion

1. What other fields might you want to include in the Orders table?

2. The only field used to relate the Orders table to the Customer table is Customer ID Number. Explain why Order Date, Order Time, and Order Sequence are included in the primary key for the Orders table.

3. This project introduced the idea of parent and child tables in relationships. What should you take into account when deciding which table is to be the parent and which the child? More specifically, why did we make the Customer table the parent and the Orders table the child? Can you think of any circumstances under which you'd reverse their roles, making Orders the parent and Customer the child?

Review Exercises

Test your knowledge of referential integrity by following these steps:

1. Open the Orders table.

2. Add a new record with the customer ID number 10050.

3. Explain why Access will not allow you to enter this number.

Test your knowledge of the meaning of cascading deleted records by following these steps:

1. Open the Customer table.

2. Delete the last record.

3. Write down the results of this action and explain why they occurred.

4. Add the record back to the Customer table.

Assignments

Adding Data to the Technical Support Table

If you set up a Technical Support table in Project 1, continue working with it by first establishing relationships between it and the other two tables and then adding some sample data. Print the table structure using the Print Definitions option from the File menu, and then print your data using the Auto Report button.

Adding Data to the Inventory Table

In Project 1, you may have designed and set up an inventory table for Simian Software. Review that design and make changes based on what you learned in this project. Be sure to relate the inventory table to one or more other tables in the Simian database. Then add some sample data to the table to see how well your design works. Print the table structure using the Print Definitions option from the File menu, and then print your data using the Auto Report button.

Adding Data to the Billing Database

If you set up a billing system in Project 1, review that design and make changes based on what you learned in this project. Be sure to relate the tables to one or more other tables in the Simian database (as well as relating the billing tables to each other). Then add some sample data to the table to see how well your design works. Print the table structure using the Print Definitions option from the File menu, and then print your data using the Auto Report button.

Objectives

After completing this project, you should be able to:

▶ Sort data to present the records in different sequences

▶ Search a table for a given value

▶ Use the relational operations select, project, and join

▶ Set up queries to search and sort data

▶ Use the permanent relationships between tables to create queries

CASE STUDY: GETTING MORE INFORMATION FROM A DATABASE

You've finished presenting the Simian Software database to Ms. Jennifer Hudson, the company president. "The database looks like it's in pretty good shape," said Ms. Hudson. "Now we need to learn how to put the data in order by the last date each customer contacted us. We also need to be able to search for specific pieces of information and retrieve groups of information. For example, we need to be able to find all customers who have had any activity on a particular date. Finally we want to look at information about customers from a particular state. We want this information for later use with screen forms and reports."

That sounds like a lot of work. Fortunately Access simplifies these tasks considerably.

Designing the Solution

Access tools will help you sort and search for data. Sorting is done using Tool bar buttons. Searching requires that you tell Access what you want to search for, which means you must understand how Access handles different data types.

Searching for a specific record is simply a matter of selecting a button from the Tool bar. However, you need to know how the various buttons can help you search data, ranging from exactly matching the value with the field contents to searching for the first (or next) occurrence of a text string anywhere in any field.

Access has *query by example (QBE)* capabilities that allow you to search and/or sort data by setting up examples of the data you want. It is used for complex searching and sorting tasks. You will see how to use QBE after learning about simple sorting and searching operations.

SORTING A TABLE

As you learned earlier, sorting a table means presenting the records in a different sequence from the one specified by the primary key. For example, suppose you want to see a list of customers in alphabetical order by state. Access gives you two options: You can sort the data in *ascending order* or *descending order*. **Ascending order** is A to Z for text fields, lowest to highest value for number and currency fields, and oldest to newest for date/time fields. You will use the A-Z button on the Tool bar (or choose Quick Sort/Ascending from the Records menu) to effect an ascending sort. **Descending order** is Z to A for text fields, highest to lowest value for number and currency fields, and newest to oldest for date/time fields. You will select the Z-A button on the Tool bar (or choose Quick Sort/Descending from the Records menu) to effect a descending sort. In the following numbered steps, you will sort the Customer table in order by state.

To sort the Customer table in order by state:

1 Open the Customer table in Datasheet view.

2 Move to the first record of the State field.

3 Select the A-Z button on the Tool bar.
The data will be sorted from CA to PA, as shown in Figure 3.1.

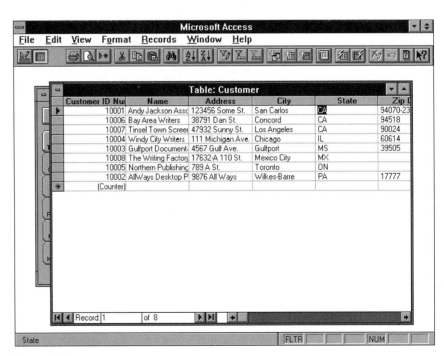

Figure 3.1

4 Select the Z-A button. The data will be sorted from PA to CA, as shown in Figure 3.2. Records from the same state may appear in a different sequence from that shown.

Figure 3.2

When you sort a table, the records are merely displayed in a different sequence. Closing the table and reopening it causes the record order to revert to the order specified by the primary key (which is the Customer ID Number field for the Customer table).

To print mailing labels, for example, you will need to sort data in zip code order. You may also want to see which customers have high (and low) credit limits and which haven't contacted you recently. In the following numbered steps, you will accomplish these tasks.

To sort the Customer table in other sequences:

1 Move to the first record in the Zip Code field.

2 Select the A-Z button from the Tool bar.
Your table will look like Figure 3.3, sorted from blank values to 94518. The two records with no zip code may appear in a different sequence.

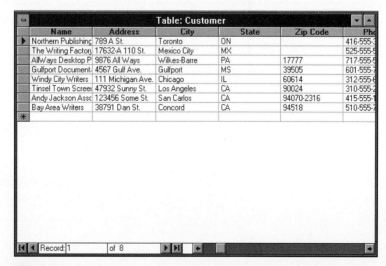

Figure 3.3

3 Move to the first record in the Last Contact field.

4 Select the A-Z button from the Tool bar.

Your table will look like Figure 3.4, sorted from oldest (5/28/90) to newest (1/2/94).

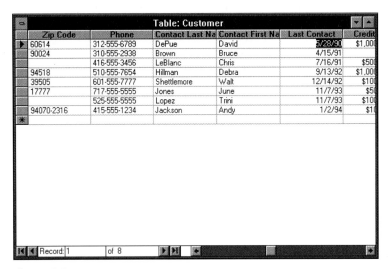

Figure 3.4

5 Move to the first record in the Credit Limit field.

6 Select the A-Z button from the Tool bar.

Your table will look like Figure 3.5, sorted from smallest value ($500) to largest value ($1,000,000).

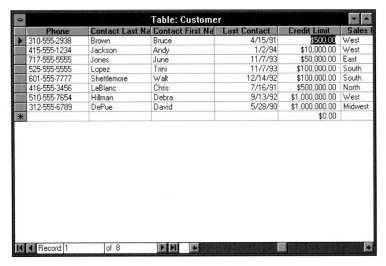

Figure 3.5

You should have noted several things while sorting the Customer table. Records with blank zip codes appear first when the table is sorted in ascending order. *Null fields*—those containing no data—will usually be sorted first when you specify ascending order. When you specify descending order, null fields will be sorted to the end of the table. At the end of this project, you'll learn how to eliminate null fields by using query by example to sort the table.

Take another look at Figure 3.3. The zip code 94070-2316 was the seventh record in the sorted table, despite the fact that its numeric value is far larger than any other. The Zip Code field is text type, which means records are sorted from left to right. Any record that has a lower leading digit will sort before one with a higher leading digit, regardless of the value of the digits that follow it. The zip code 94070-2316 sorts before 94518 because 940 is a lower value than 945. Numeric data types, on the other hand, sort in the order you'd expect for numbers, taking into consideration all digits in the number. Figure 3.5 shows that clearly. Be sure you understand why the Zip Code and Credit Limit fields were sorted in these sequences.

SEARCHING A TABLE

 To search a table for the first occurrence of a value in a field, you will use the Find button on the Tool bar.

Before you begin a search, you need to look at the options available in Access. When you select the Find button, you'll see the Find in Field dialog box, as shown in Figure 3.6. Table 3.1 summarizes the various Find in Field options.

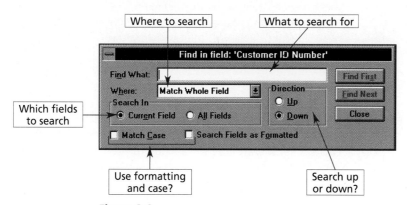

Figure 3.6

Table 3.1

Box or Button Name	Option	Description
Find What		Data to be found
Where	Any Part of Field	Search data can be anywhere in the field
	Match Whole Field	Search data must match entire field contents
	Start of Field	Search data must match first part of field contents
Search In	Current Field	Confine search to current field
	All Fields	Search all fields for the search string
Direction	Up	Search from current record to top of table
	Down	Search from current record to bottom of table
Match Case (checked)		Upper- and lowercase characters not treated the same
Match Case (not checked)		Upper- and lowercase characters treated the same
Search Fields as Formatted (checked)		Include field formatting for match with search string
Search Fields as Formatted (not checked)		Ignore field formatting

Before using Access to find a record, you should think about exactly what you're searching for and consider the options available in Access. For example, you can search for the first occurrence of a value or the next occurrence, starting from the current record. If you search for the next occurrence, you can tell Access to search either up or down in the table—toward the first record or toward the last record. You can specify whether you want Access to match the *case* of the value you give with the value in the field. The ***case*** of a text string can be either ***uppercase*** (as in CA) or ***lowercase*** (as in pa). If you elect to match the case, the letters *pa* won't be treated as a match for *PA*.

You can also tell Access to match the values in the entire field, match the value anywhere in the field, or match the value at the beginning of the field. When searching for a value in the State field, you'll usually want to match the whole value. However, when searching for a zip code, you may want to match only the first few characters. For example, if you're looking for a record in San Francisco, you may want to search for zip codes that begin with 94. In that case, you would select the option to match the value at the beginning of the field. Matching the value anywhere in the field means Access will stop at the first record in which the characters *pa* appear anywhere. If a record contains the word *apparent*, Access will stop there because the string *pa* is in the middle of the word. This feature can be useful, but a search for a value that occurs anywhere in a field can be slow.

If you click the Search Fields as Formatted check box, Access searches data that you have formatted in a particular way. For example, you can search dates using the date format specified for a date/time field. You may have set up a worksheet so that dates are displayed in the form d mmm yy, as in 5 Jan 92. If you select the Search Fields as Formatted box, you can search only for dates that you entered in that format. For the Customer table you will want to check this box when searching for a particular customer ID number, since the field is formatted with a leading value of 10000.

You will want to avoid searching all the fields of a large table for a single value. Searches that search anywhere in any field will be even slower than searching anywhere in a single field because there is more data to be examined. Before you start a search that will encompass an entire table, try to find some way of narrowing the search specification. (Of course, if your table has only a dozen records, Access will search it in a matter of seconds no matter what specifications you set. This advice only applies to large tables.)

In the steps that follow, you will set up the search for the first record in the table that contains information about a company located in Pennsylvania. That means we want to tell Access to search for the first record in which the State field contains a value of PA.

To search for the first Pennsylvania record:

1 Make sure Access is loaded and the Customer table is open in Datasheet view.

2 Move to the first record of the State field.

3 Select the Find button.
You should see the Find in Field dialog box displayed in the lower portion of the screen.

4 Move to the Find What text box.

5 Type **pa** but don't press (ENTER) yet.

6 Move to the Where box and select Match Whole Field from the list box.

7 Select the Find First button.
Look at the lower-left corner of the screen to see the message "Search succeeded."

8 Drag the Find in Field dialog box down if necessary.
The screen should look like Figure 3.7. Note that the record pointer is in the second record, and *PA* is selected.

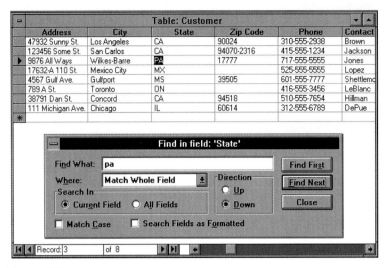

Figure 3.7

9 Select the Find Next button.

You'll see an information box, shown in Figure 3.8, telling you that Access has reached the end of the table and asking if you want the search to start again at the beginning of the table.

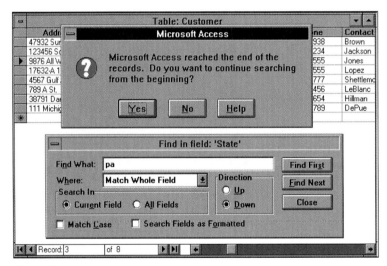

Figure 3.8

10 Select the No button.

Another information box will open.

11 Select the OK button.

12 Select the Close button to close the Find in Field dialog box.

Tip You could search every field in the table for the character string *pa* by selecting All Fields in the Search In box. Since you've already selected "Match Whole Field," the only likely matches are in the State field. However, suppose you also selected Any Part of Field in the Where list box. The entire table—every part of every field—would be searched for the character string *pa*. If the word *part* appeared in a record somewhere, that record would be selected. Similarly, if the word *apart* appeared, that record also would be selected. A search like that could take a very long time in a large database. Be careful how you set up a search!

USING SPECIAL SEARCH TECHNIQUES

There are some common techniques that have been developed for searching tables. While it would be impossible to present a complete list of search techniques, you may be able to adapt one of the following ideas to your particular needs:

- If you want to find all the records in a particular region, use the first few characters of the Zip Code field. For example, to find all records in California, Oregon, and Washington, search for zip codes that start with 9. (You can't do this if you make Zip Code a number type field.)
- Another way of searching for a specific area is to search for a specific telephone area code. In the Customer table, the first three characters in the Phone field entries are the area codes, so you can use the Start of Field option in the Where list box. For example, 415 is the area code for San Francisco and the area immediately south, so to search for records in that area you would type **415** in the Find What text box and select Start of Field. If you're having trouble narrowing a search, you can check the area code map found in your telephone book.
- You can use wildcard characters in your search. Use * to represent a string of any length. Use ? to hold the place for a single character. That means, of course, that searching for *pa** is the same as searching for the letters *pa* and specifying that they are to appear at the beginning of the field.

In the steps that follow, you will use wildcard characters in a search to find the first record with a last contact date in 1992. In other words, you want to search for any day and any month, as long as the year is 1992. You will search for */*/92. The result of this search will be the third record, which has a last contact date of 12/14/92. Note that if you were to search for ?/?/92, you would get no match because the question mark restricts the search to single-digit month and day numbers.

To find the first record with a last contact date in 1992:

1 Be sure Access is running and the Customer table is open in Datasheet view.

2 Move to the first record of the Last Contact field.

3 Select the Find button to open the Find in Field dialog box.

4 Be sure the text cursor is in the Find What text box, then type ***/*/92** and press (ENTER)

You'll see 12/14/92 selected, as shown in Figure 3.9.

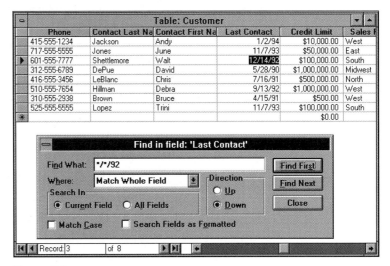

Figure 3.9

5 Select the Close button to close the Find In Field dialog box.

As you saw earlier, you can find the first zip code that starts with a given character. For example, in the steps that follow you will find the first zip code that starts with 6 (Illinois).

To find a regional zip code:

1 Move the cursor to the first record of the Zip Code field in the Customer table.

2 Select the Find button to open the Find in Field dialog box.

3 Move to the Find What text box and type **6**

4 Move to the Where list box and select Start of Field.

5 Select the Find First button.
The screen should look like Figure 3.10. Notice that the record for Windy City Writers in Chicago is selected.

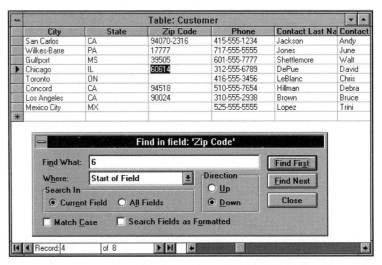

Figure 3.10

6 Close the Find in Field dialog box.

7 Close the Customer table.

EXIT   If necessary, you can exit Access now and continue this project later.

MOVING THE RECORD POINTER

The most straightforward way to move the record pointer is to use the scroll bars, located at the bottom of the table window, until the field-record combination you want is visible. Then you can select that cell. However, sometimes you want to move to the first or last record in the table. You can use the Top Record and Bottom Record buttons to make such moves quickly. These buttons appear in the lower-left corner of the table window, as shown in Figure 3.11. Clicking the Top Record button moves the pointer to the first record in the table, and clicking the Bottom Record button moves it to the last record. The button immediately to the right of the Top Record button moves the pointer up one record. The button to the left of the Bottom Record button moves the pointer down one record. However, you will usually find it easier to use the scroll bar or click in the record you want. (You will use these buttons in Project 6 when you work with screen forms).

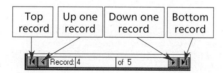

Figure 3.11

PERFORMING A QUERY USING QUERY BY EXAMPLE

For many purposes, simply being able to search for a specific record using one field is all you need. Sometimes, however, you'll want to be able to treat a record, or group of records, as if it were a separate table. Or you may want to search the table based on criteria in more than one field. For example, you might want to search for a record using both the Contact Last Name and Contact First Name fields. Query by example (QBE) is the tool you need. First developed by IBM in the late 1960s, QBE wasn't available in personal computer DBMS programs until the mid-1980s. The debut of Paradox in 1986 brought this powerful tool to personal computer software.

A *query* lets you ask the database simple or complex questions. You can use queries to

- Choose some of a table's fields
- Choose some of a table's records
- Sort a table
- Perform arithmetic calculations, such as totals
- Create reports, forms, and graphs
- Link several tables and then do any query operation

When you run a query, the results look like another table. However, it is not an actual table but rather a *view*—a set of data selected from the underlying tables and quickly updated. A view exists only in the computer's memory as long as Access maintains it. Unless you save the view on disk as a table, it will vanish when you leave QBE, close the database, or exit Access.

Setting Up a Simple Query

Access uses ***graphical query by example,*** which allows you to drag fields into the view and use standard Windows techniques to set up your view. When a query is executed, the result is a *view* based on the underlying records. This view is different from the underlying data. If you're running on a network and someone else changes data in the Customer table, it may take some time for those changes to appear in the query view. (On the other hand, if you're looking at the Customer table, changes made by other users will appear almost immediately in your copy of the table.)

Suppose you want to perform the same search you did at the beginning of this project: You want to find all customers in Pennsylvania. Here's how you do this with a query.

To find all the Pennsylvania customers:

1 Select the Customer table in the Database window.

2 Select the New Query button on the Tool bar.

You'll see the New Query dialog box, as shown in Figure 3.12.

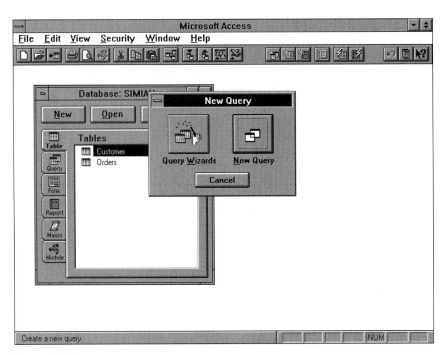

Figure 3.12

3 Select the New Query button from the dialog box.

You'll see the Select Query dialog box as shown in Figure 3.13. Notice that the first character in the fields list is an asterisk (*). That means to include all fields from the table in the query.

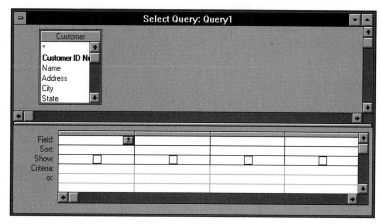

Figure 3.13

4 Drag the asterisk down to the first column of the Field row on the bottom part of the screen.

The screen should look like Figure 3.14.

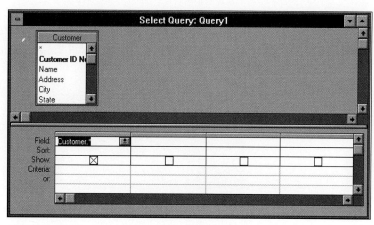

Figure 3.14

5 Select the Run button on the Tool bar.

The view should look like Figure 3.15. Even though this view looks identical to the Customer table, it's not the same because it's a view produced by the query.

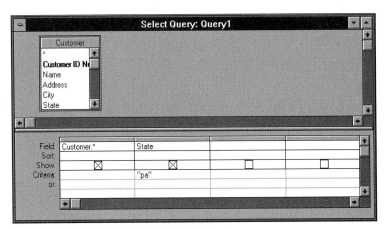

Figure 3.15

6 Select the Design button on the Tool bar to switch to Design view.

7 Scroll down the field list in the top half of the Query dialog box until the State field appears.

8 Drag the State field onto the second column of the Field row.

9 Select the Criteria box in the same column.

10 Type **pa** and press (ENTER)
The screen should look like Figure 3.16. Access recognizes that State is a text type field and automatically encloses *pa* in quotation marks to make this clear.

Figure 3.16

11 Select the Run button on the Tool bar.
The screen should look like Figure 3.17. Only one record is shown in this view. Unlike searching, which showed the original table, a view includes only the records selected by the query. Fortunately, Access makes it simple to experiment with query design until you get what you're after.

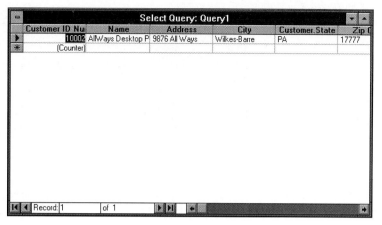

Figure 3.17

12 Choose Save As from the File menu.

13 Type **States** to name the query.

14 Close the Select Query window.

EXIT   If necessary, you can exit Access now and continue this project later.

SELECTING RECORDS FOR TWO STATES

Now suppose you want to see records for customers located in either Pennsylvania or California, or perhaps you want to see records for customers who are in California and have credit limits over $500,000. To accomplish these tasks, you will need to set up Or queries or And queries.

- Criteria that appear in the Select Query dialog box on different lines or are connected by the word *Or* are Or queries. Records that meet any of the selection criteria will be included in the view. Selecting the records of customers who have addresses in Pennsylvania or California is an example of an Or query.
- Criteria that appear in the Select Query dialog box on the same line or are connected by the word *And* are And queries. Records must meet all criteria to be included in the view. Selecting customers from California who also have credit limits over $500,000 is an example of an And query.

To select records from two different states:

1 Open the States query in Design view.

2 Move the cursor to the box under "*pa*".

3 Type **ca** and press (ENTER)
The screen should look like Figure 3.18.

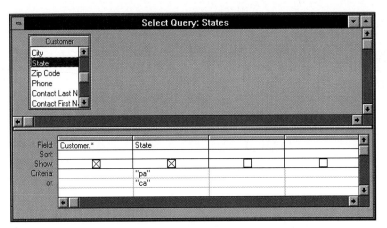

Figure 3.18

4 Select the Run button to see the records of the four customers from Pennsylvania and California, as shown in Figure 3.19.

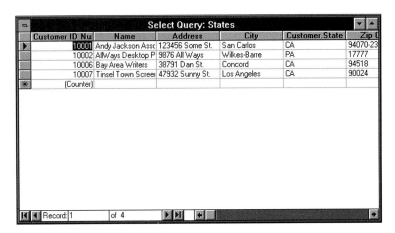

Figure 3.19

5 Select the Design button to return to the Select Query dialog box.

6 Choose Save As from the File menu.

7 Type **PA & CA Customers** and press (ENTER)
The title bar on the Select Query dialog box will change to show the new name.

8 Close the query window.

To see a list of all the queries in a database, select the Query icon in the database window. Anytime you want to see a list of the customers in a particular state, you can now use the States query, entering the appropriate state abbreviation for the selection criterion. Or if you want to see a list of customers in California and Pennsylvania, you can run the PA & CA Customers query.

USING RELATIONAL OPERATORS

In standard relational database terminology, the query by example procedures you've just performed are *select operations*. **Select** means to pick *records* from one or more tables based on specified criteria. If you had selected several *fields* from the table, you would have performed a **project** operation. In other words, a select operation picks records, and a project operation picks fields. The third major relational operator is **join,** which means to link two tables to form a view.

The main problem you'll encounter when setting up queries is working with different data types. In the following numbered steps, you will use number and date/time data types to select records. You will also pick a limited number of fields, building a combined select and project operation.

When working with numbers, you will use standard comparison operators, which are summarized in Table 3.2. In the following numbered steps, you will use these operators to select customers with a certain credit limit.

Table 3.2

Comparison Operator	Meaning with Number Data	Meaning with Date/Time Data
>	Greater than	Later than
>=	Greater than or equal to	Later than or on this date
<	Less than	Earlier than
<=	Less than or equal to	Earlier than or on this date
<>	Not equal to	Not on this date
=	Exactly equal to	On this date

Let's see how to select records based on Credit Limit ranges. Since Credit Limit is a Number type field, we'll use several of the operators listed in Table 3.1.

To select records using comparison operators:

1 Make sure the Customer table is selected in the Database window.

2 Select the New Query button on the Tool bar to open the New Query dialog box.

3 Select the New Query button to open the Select Query dialog box.

4 From the field list choose the Name, Phone, and Credit Limit fields, and drag them in that order to the Field row in the bottom part of the screen.

5 Move to the Criteria box in the Credit Limit column.

6 Type `>=100000 and <=1000000` and press (ENTER)

7 Drag the right edge of this column to the right until you can see all of the material you just typed.

The screen should look like Figure 3.20.

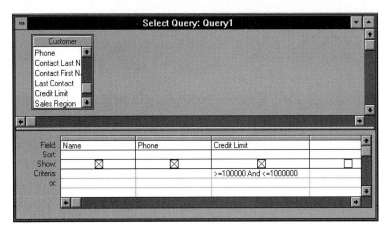

Figure 3.20

8 Select the Run button on the Tool bar.
The screen should look like Figure 3.21.

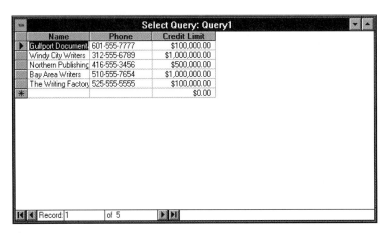

Figure 3.21

In the steps that follow, you will add one more criterion to this query. You want to select customers in Mississippi with credit limits between $100,000 and $1,000,000. However, you will not include the State field in the view.

To select records using both state and credit limit criteria:

1 Select the Design button on the Tool bar to switch back to Design view.

2 Drag the State field to column 4 of the dialog box.

3 Move to the Criteria box in the State column.

4 Type **ms** and press (ENTER)

5 Click the check box in the Show row in this column to clear the box to remove the checkmark.
The screen should look like Figure 3.22.

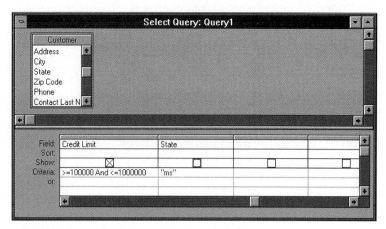

Figure 3.22

6 Select the Run button on the Tool bar.
The screen should look like Figure 3.23, which shows that only one customer meets all the criteria.

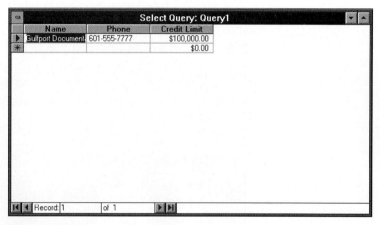

Figure 3.23

7 Close the Query dialog box.

8 When Access asks if you want to save the changes to Query1, select No.

Tip If you want to use the data produced by a previously defined query in another query, select the Query icon in the Database window and choose the query you want from the displayed list of queries. A view created with a query can be used just as a table can be used in another query.

LINKING TWO TABLES WITH A QUERY

In Project 2, you learned how to set up permanent links, called relationships, between tables as part of the structure of your database. Sometimes you will want to establish temporary links among several tables. These links are only needed for as long as it takes to produce a report, after which the query can be discarded.

Suppose you want to see all the activity that occurred on November 7, 1993, in both the Customer and Orders tables. In the following numbered steps, you will solve this problem using QBE.

To select records for all activity on a given date:

1 Select the Query icon in the Database window.

2 Select the New button in the Database window to open the New Query dialog box.

3 Select the New Query button.
The Add Table dialog box is displayed.

4 Add the Customer and Orders tables to the query.

5 Close the Add Table dialog box.

6 Choose Save As from the File menu.

7 Type **Activity by Date** and then select OK.
The screen should look like Figure 3.24. Note that the permanent relationship between the two tables is automatically shown as a connecting line in the query.

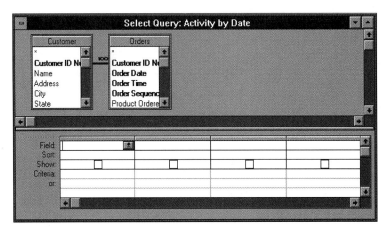

Figure 3.24

8 Drag the Name and Last Contact fields from the Customer table to the first two columns in the view.

9 Drag the Order Date field from the Orders table to the third column.

10 Drag the Last Contact field in the Customer table in the top half of the Select Query dialog box onto the Order Date field in the Orders table. You'll see a jagged line connecting the two fields, as shown in Figure 3.25.

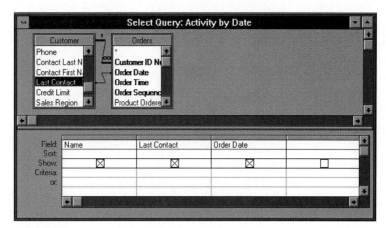

Figure 3.25

11 Move to the Criteria box in the Order Date column of the view.

12 Type **11/7/93** and press (ENTER)

13 Select the Run button from the Tool bar.
The screen should look like Figure 3.26.

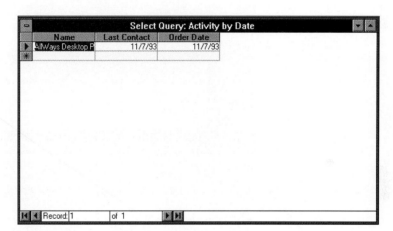

Figure 3.26

14 Switch back to Design view.

15 Close the Select Query dialog box.

16 Select Yes when Access asks if you want to save the changes to this query.

Did you notice that Access replaced 11/7/93 with #11/7/93#. The **#** *delimiters* tell Access to expect date/time type data between them. A ***delimiter*** is a character used in pairs to surround some data, often indicating the data type as well. The " delimiter indicates text type data, for example.

USING PERMANENT RELATIONSHIPS IN QUERIES

If you use a permanent relationship to link two tables, Access will make the process of building the query even easier. Access will recognize the permanent relationship and automatically add it when you add the tables involved in the relationship to a query. In the following numbered steps, you will take advantage of a permanent relationship to look at customer and order information in a single view.

To create a view with both Customer and Orders records:

1 Be sure you're looking at the Tables list in the Database window.

2 Open a new query that includes both the Customer and Orders tables.

3 Close the Add Table dialog box.
The screen should look like Figure 3.27.

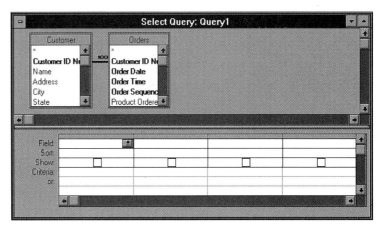

Figure 3.27

4 Add the following fields from the Customer table to the query view: Customer ID Number, Name, Phone. Then add these fields from Orders: Order Date, Product Ordered and Price Paid.

5 Select the Run button on the Tool bar to run the query.
The query view should look like Figure 3.28.

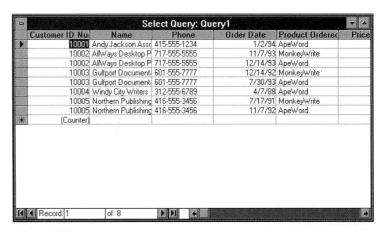

Figure 3.28

6 Close the Select Query window.

7 Select No when Access asks if you want to save this query.

Look closely at the query design as shown in Figure 3.27. The thick line connecting the two tables via the Customer ID Number field indicates the presence of a permanent relationship. The number *100* next to the Orders table indicates that this is the "many" end of the one-to-many relationship that exists between the two tables.

Now inspect the data as shown in in Figure 3.28. While records from both tables are included, the customer information is sometimes appears in more than one record in the view. There will be one copy of the customer data included for each order the customer has placed.

Finally, because you used the permanent relationship, you didn't have to set up a temporary link in QBE.

This isn't a particularly appealing way of displaying the data because the customer information is repeated for each order. In Project 4, you will learn how to create a screen form that displays the customer information once while showing all the orders for that customer.

SORTING WITH QBE

As you learned earlier in this module, sorting a table or view means rearranging the records in an order based on the values in one or more fields. Access gives you two ways to sort data. In this section, you'll learn how to use QBE to sort data. This procedure is useful when you want to sort the view that's created by select, project, and/or join operations. Project 5 will show you how to sort data using the report generator.

In the following steps, you will use QBE to sort the Customer table in order by the contacts' last names.

To sort the Customer table by contacts' last names:

1 Open a new query with the fields from the Customer table.

2 Drag the Contact Last Name field into the Field row in the first column of the query view.

3 Drag the * to the next column to add all the fields in the Customer table to the view.

4 Open the Sort list box in the Contact Last Name column.

5 Select Ascending from the list box.
The screen should look like Figure 3.29.

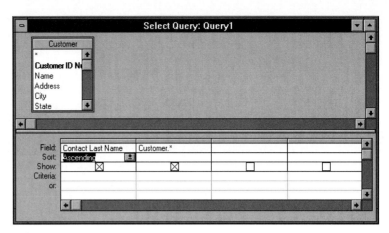

Figure 3.29

6 Select the Run button from the Tool bar to run the query.
The screen should look like Figure 3.30 with the view sorted by Contact
Last Name.

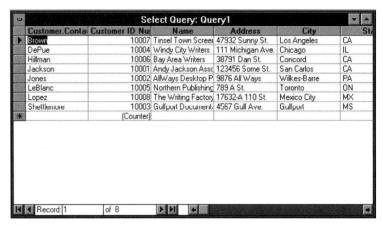

Figure 3.30

Now suppose you want to sort on more than one field. For example,
you want Contact Last Name to be the first field sorted. However, you
want people with the same last name to appear in order by first names.
That means you want to use Contact First Name as the second sort field.
You can't do this with the Sort button on the Tool bar; you must use QBE
instead.

To sort on more than one field:

1 Select the Design button on the Tool bar to switch to Design view.

2 Move the pointer over the second column of the view until you see a
solid downward-pointing arrow.

3 Click once to select the entire column.
The screen should look like Figure 3.31.

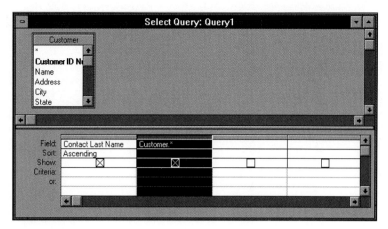

Figure 3.31

4 Press (DEL) once to delete the column's contents.

5 Drag Contact First Name from the list of fields in the Customer table to the second column of the query view.

6 Select an Ascending sort for the Contact First Name column. The screen should look like Figure 3.32.

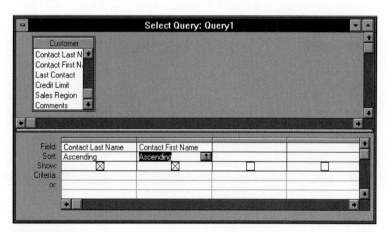

Figure 3.32

7 Select the Run button on the Tool bar to run the query. The screen should look like Figure 3.33.

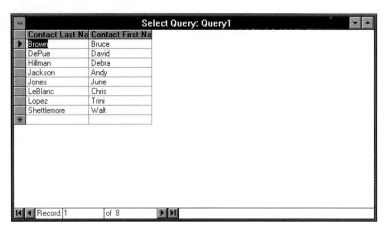

Figure 3.33

8 Close the Query design window without saving the query.

THE NEXT STEP

When working with tables that contain thousands of records, searching, retrieving, and sorting data can become very slow. One way to speed up each of those activities is by creating an appropriate *index*. (Unlike some other database products, indexing is not required for most Access operations.) Indexing is covered in Project 6.

Searching, retrieving, and sorting are complex topics. When working with large tables, it's usually a good idea to test complex query conditions on a sample of the data (50 to 100 records) to make sure your query is actually asking the question you intended. People often confuse *and* with *or* in their initial query design.

Sorting date type data in combination with other data types can present special problems. Access handles most of these difficulties for you. However, if you're interested in learning more about date type data, it's discussed at the end of Project 6.

SUMMARY AND EXERCISES

Summary

- The best way to search for a field value is to use the Find button on the Tool bar.
- Access allows searches on all or any part of a field's values.
- Access allows searches that are either case-sensitive or case-insensitive.
- Access allows searches up or down in the database.
- You can use the record pointer buttons to move quickly to the top or bottom of a table.
- Query by example (QBE) allows you to create a subset of records called a view.

- You can use QBE to pick several fields from a table. This is called a project operation.
- You can use QBE to pick several records from a table based on any criteria you specify. This is called a select operation.
- You can use QBE to link two or more tables and select values based on the fields in those tables.
- QBE recognizes permanent relationships built into the database structure and uses them automatically when you select the tables they link.
- Sorting data can be simplified using the Sort list box in the query view.

Key Terms and Operations

Key Terms
ascending order
case
delimiter
descending order
graphical query by example
join
lowercase
null fields
project
query

query by example
select
uppercase
view

Operations
add fields
query by example
search for a record
select records
sort a table

Study Questions

Multiple Choice

1. What is the main difference between searching a single table with the Find button and searching with query by example?
    a. QBE produces a new table, and the Find button shows you data in the original table.
    b. QBE allows multiple search criteria, and the Find button doesn't.
    c. The Find button can search parts of fields, which is more difficult in QBE.
    d. All of the above.

2. Which relational operation picks a group of records from a table?
    a. select
    b. project
    c. join
    d. No operation can pick records.

3. Which relational operation picks a group of fields from a table?
    a. select
    b. project
    c. join
    d. No operation can pick fields.

4. Which relational operation links two tables?
   a. select
   b. project
   c. join
   d. No operation can link tables.

5. When you select records and/or fields from query by example, the view you create is
   a. always saved as a new table.
   b. only saved as a new table if you tell Access to do this.
   c. cannot be saved as a new table.
   d. will be automatically saved as a new table after a predetermined time has passed.

6. To create a query with two And criteria, you put the two conditions in
   a. different Criteria rows.
   b. the same Criteria row connected with the word *Or*.
   c. different queries.
   d. the same Criteria row connected with the word *And*.

7. Which of the following will select records based on a field's value but not include the field in the query view?
   a. move the field to a column in the query
   b. move the field to a column in the query and check the Show box
   c. move the field to a column in the query and uncheck the Show box
   d. All fields in the query must be shown in the view.

8. When sorting a table based on a text type field, an ascending sort means the table will be sorted from
   a. A to Z.
   b. Z to A.
   c. differently depending on the exact values in the field.
   d. oldest to newest.

9. When sorting a table based on a Date/Time type field, an ascending sort means the table will be sorted from
   a. A to Z.
   b. Z to A.
   c. newest to oldest.
   d. oldest to newest.

10. Which type of search will cause a match between ACME and Acme?
    a. do not match case
    b. match case
    c. special case
    d. Access will always match ACME and Acme.

Short Answer

1. What is the name given to the result of a relational select, project, or join operation?

2. What is the difference between And and Or operations?

3. The default sort order is ascending, regardless of the data type of the field. What data type(s) would you rather see sorted in Descending order? Why?

4. What aspect of a database is picked by each of the relational operators select, project, and join?

5. What delimiters are used for text, number, and date type data?

6. Would you ever want to sort a table based on the fields in its primary key? Why?

7. What difficulties can you foresee sorting a table based on a memo type field?

8. Under what circumstances might you want to use a field in a query but not include that field in the resulting view?

9. What differences can you see between using number type fields and using currency type fields in queries?

10. Suppose you wanted a view that included records for all Customers whose zip codes begin with 9. How would you do this in QBE?

For Discussion

1. How should you decide whether to make a relationship a permanent part of the database structure?

2. Explain the difference between the results of the following two selection criteria: *>= 10 and <= 20* versus *>= 10 or <= 20.*

3. One problem with sorting a table is that the sorted table will have the same number of records and fields as the original. That means it will take up just as much disk space. What could you do to reduce the size of the sorted table? (Hint: think about what data you need from the sorted table.)

Review Exercises

Think about the problem of locating information on companies located outside the U.S. One way of finding those records is to search for a blank zip code field. Follow these steps to obtain non-U.S. records.

1. Open a new query with the Customer table.

2. Add the Zip Code field to the first column.

3. Add all fields to the second column.

4. Type **Null** and press (ENTER)

Access will replace the word *Null* with *Is Null.* (Null means the Zip Code records must be blank.)

5. Switch to Datasheet view to see the two non-U.S. records.

Assignments

Sorting the Orders Table

Set up a query to sort the Orders table in descending sequence of Order Date. For orders on the same date, sort in ascending sequence of Order Total.

Searching the Technical Support Table

If you have been working with the Technical Support table in Projects 1 and 2, search for the first technical support call: (a) from a specific customer; (b) to a specified technician; and (c) on a particular date. Then use QBE to link it with the Orders table without using the Customer table.

Searching the Billing Tables

If you have been working with the billing tables in Projects 1 and 2, search for invoices: (a) from a specific customer; (b) to a specified technician; and (c) on a particular date. Then link it with the Orders and Technical Support tables without using the Customer table.

Searching the Inventory Table

If you have been working with an Inventory table in Projects 1 and 2, search for inventory items: (a) ordered on a specific date; (b) with a specific dollar value of inventory on hand; and (c) with a specific number of units on hand.

After completing this project, you should be able to:

► Develop attractive data entry screen forms using the Access FormWizards

► Add combo boxes to a form

► Add totals to a form

► Create a screen form that uses data from two related tables

CASE STUDY: MAKING THE DATABASE MORE READABLE

"The database is very nice," Ms. Hudson tells you, "but it's very difficult to read. The data entry people can see only a few fields at a time. Can you set up some sort of screen form for us?"

Designing the Solution

Usually, to build a screen form, you start with one of the standard layouts provided by the Access FormWizards. Once you have built the form, you can easily modify the standard layout to suit your particular needs.

In this project, you will first build a simple single-column screen, with the field names in the left column and their values in the right. You will add a combo box to the screen to handle the Sales Region field. After that, you will move to a tabular form in which the field names are at the top of the screen and the values appear under the name. Although this layout is similar to the Datasheet view used by Access, the screen form version is much more attractive. Finally, you will create a screen form that draws data from both the Customer and Orders tables.

EXPLORING THE FORM BUILDER

A *screen form* is used to display, enter, and edit data on the screen. You can use the Access Form tool to create screen forms and graphs. However, screen forms are not the same as reports. Reports (which will be covered in Project 5) are designed to be printed or displayed on the screen. They do not allow data entry or editing. (You will want to keep this distinction in mind when you work through this project as well as Projects 5 and 6.)

Access forms are designed in *bands*. Each form has a **Form Header band** displayed at the top of the form. The **Form Footer band** is at the bottom of the form. Most of the data is in the **Detail band** located between the header and footer bands.

Tip The distinction between forms and reports isn't nearly as clean as it may sound. Many Access "screen" forms include an option that allows you to print them like reports.

USING FORMWIZARDS

Access lets you use *FormWizards* for forms and reports. A **FormWizard** is a sequence of windows and dialog boxes that leads you through the process of building a screen form or report. When you start a FormWizard, you are first given a choice of the style of form you want, as shown in Figure 4.1.

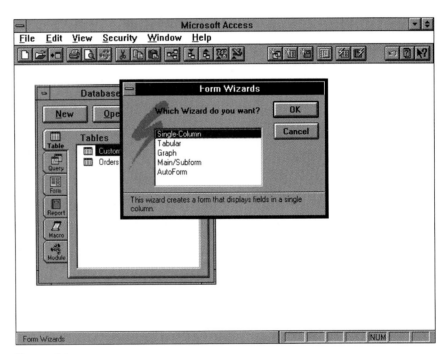

Figure 4.1

Forms are made up of *controls* and, in most cases, an attached *label*. A **control** contains a piece of information. For example, when a field is placed on a form, it's called a control. A **label** is usually text that describes something about the form itself or one of the controls the form contains. The screen form shown in Figure 4.2 contains a number of labels and controls.

Each label and control has an associated set of **properties** which can include the position on the screen; whether a control originates in a field or elsewhere; the name of the field that acts as the source for a control; and many other facts. Properties can be displayed and changed by selecting the screen object then selecting the properties button on the Tool bar. That will open the Properties window for the selected object.

A *single-column* FormWizard displays controls in a column, with labels in another column to the left, as shown in Figure 4.2.

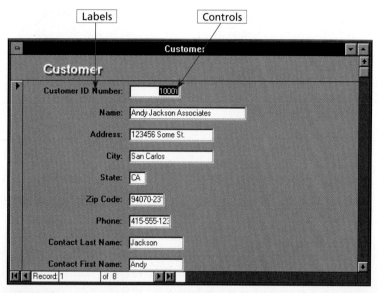

Figure 4.2

The *Tabular* Wizard displays labels at the top of columns with controls immediately below them, as shown in Figure 4.3.

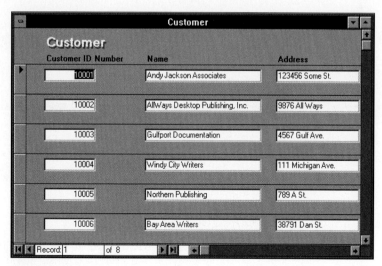

Figure 4.3

The *Graph* Wizard is used to display data as a graph. Figure 4.4 shows the Credit Limit field displayed as a pie graph. The Graph Wizard can easily build six different two-dimensional graphs as well as five three-dimensional graph forms. Graph forms are discussed in Project 6.

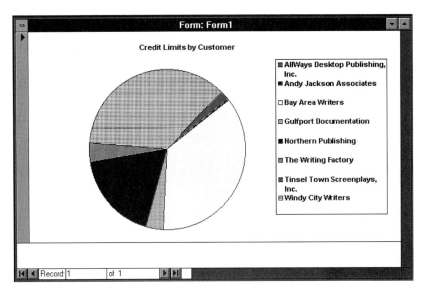

Figure 4.4

The *Main/Subform* Wizard is used to embed one form in another. Figure 4.5 shows two orders from a single customer on one screen. The orders are the subform and the customer information is the main form.

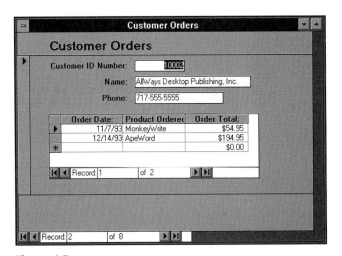

Figure 4.5

Finally, the *Auto-Form* Wizard is set up as a single-column form and automatically displays the data as shown in Figure 4.2.

When you start the screen form builder, you're given a choice between using the FormWizards or starting with a blank form. While a blank form gives you maximum flexibility, it's usually a good strategy to use the FormWizards for the initial layout. You will find it easier to customize a form after you've built a rough draft with the FormWizards.

In the following steps, you will use the FormWizards to build a simple screen form.

To build a single-column form:

1 Select the Customer table.

2 Select the New Form button on the Tool bar.

3 Select the FormWizards button.
You'll see the Form Style Selection dialog box shown in Figure 4.6.

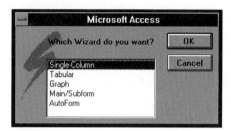

Figure 4.6

4 Select Single-Column style.
A dialog box will open that asks you to pick the fields you want, as shown in Figure 4.7.

Figure 4.7

5 Select the >> button to select all the fields for the form.

6 Select the Next> button to move to the next dialog box, which is shown in Figure 4.8.

Figure 4.8

7 Select the Embossed style.

8 Select the Next> button.
The screen should look like Figure 4.9.

Figure 4.9

9 Select the Finish button to accept the default title (Customer).
The screen should look like Figure 4.10.

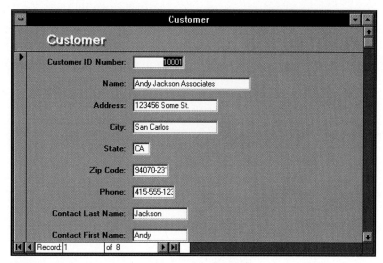

Figure 4.10

10 Choose Close from the File menu.

11 Select the Yes button when Access asks if you want to save the form.

12 Type **Customer** and press (ENTER)

EXIT If necessary, you can exit Access now. When you continue this project later, be sure to reopen the Customer form.

Now that you have a simple form set up, you can begin changing it. You'll want to move some controls to different screen locations. For example, rather than placing the City, State, and Zip Code fields on separate lines, you'll probably want them displayed on the same line. Here's how to modify the form you just created.

Tip Access places the fields on the screen in the order in which you add them. Add fields to your form in the order in which you want them to appear, and you'll find developing your forms will be much easier.

When you open a form in Design view, the Tool bar changes substantially, reflecting the numerous options available for screen design. Figure 4.11 shows the Tool bar for forms and gives a brief explanation of what each means.

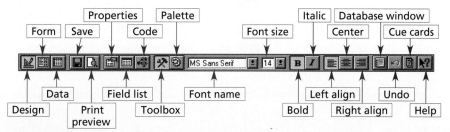

Figure 4.11

Tip When you open a form in Design view, the Toolbox window will open automatically. If you don't like having the Toolbox window open, just click the Toolbox button on the Tool bar to close it. Clicking the button again will reopen the window.

To modify the Customer form:

1 Open the Customer form in Design view.

2 Select the word *Customer* in the Form Header band.
You'll see a box around the word Customer with the usual Windows box handles.

3 Grab the left handle and stretch the box to the left margin.

4 Grab the right handle and stretch the box to the right margin.

5 Select the center text alignment button to center the Customer title. (The drop shadow may not have moved with the title. If not, stretch its box and select Center. You may have to choose Snap To Grid from the Format menu to turn off the grid and allow the fine alignment you need.) When you're done, the screen should look like Figure 4.12.

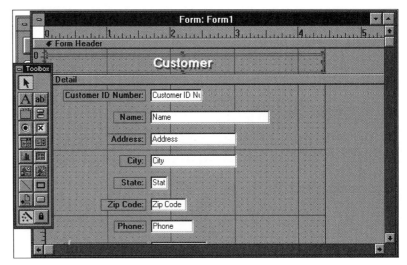

Figure 4.12

6 Choose the Format menu, and make sure Snap To Grid is marked with a checkmark. If it's not, choose Snap To Grid to turn the grid on.

7 Close the Format menu.

8 Drag the State label and control to the right of the City control.

9 Drag the Zip Code label and control to the right of the State control. The screen should look like Figure 4.13.

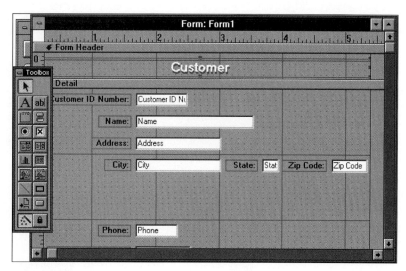

Figure 4.13

10 Move the remaining fields to create a screen that takes somewhat less space, roughly like Figure 4.14.
Your screen may not look exactly like Figure 4.14 because the window has been maximized so all the labels and controls are visible.

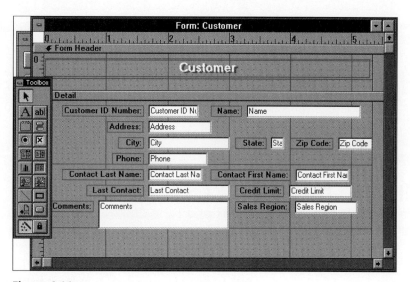

Figure 4.14

 11 Select the Form button on the Tool bar.
The data is displayed in the form you've just created, roughly like Figure 4.15.

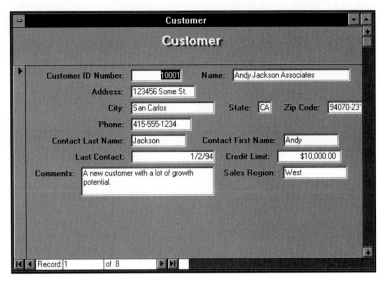

Figure 4.15

12 Before you do anything else, choose Save from the File menu to save the changes you've made.

13 Close the form.

EXIT If necessary, you can exit Access now and continue this project later.

···

Tip You can move a group of objects by drawing a rectangle around them and then dragging the entire rectangle. Be sure the Pointer icon on the Toolbox window at the left of the screen is selected before you try to drag an entire area.

USING COMBO BOXES

Most major problems you'll run into when working with a database involve working with bad data, such as misspelled names, unorthodox abbreviations, and incorrect identification numbers. The most common source of bad data is data entry errors—simple typing mistakes. The best way to avoid this problem is to let people make a selection from a list and use the selection to automatically fill in one or more fields. That way, there's no typing involved at all—and no possibility of typographical errors.

Access allows you to select data by using *list boxes* and *combo boxes.* Both of these screen tools let you make choices from lists, and the value you choose is automatically entered in the database. A combo box also allows you to type in data, but a list box restricts you exclusively to values on the list. A combo box is used most often. In the following steps, you will add a combo box for the Sales Region field to the Customer form. You'll then set up the combo box to restrict data entry to the entries on the list.

To add a combo box to a form:

1 Open the Customer form in Design mode. Be sure the Toolbox window is switched on and that the FormWizard button at the lower-left corner of the Toolbox window is depressed.

2 Select the Sales Region control and label.

3 Press (DEL) once to delete both the control and the label.

4 Select the Combo Box icon in the Toolbox window.

5 Move the crosshairs to the place where you want the upper-left corner of the Sales Region control to appear.

6 Click once to open the Combo Box Wizard, as shown in Figure 4.16.

7 Select the box in front of *I will type in the values that I want.*
The screen should look like Figure 4.16.

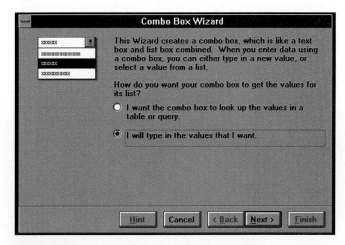

Figure 4.16

8 Select the Next> button.

9 Type **1** for the number of columns, and then press (ENTER)

10 Select the first row in the column of blank cells.

11 Type **East** and press (ENTER)

12 Type **Central** and press (ENTER)

13 Type **South** and press (ENTER)

14 Type **Midwest** and press (ENTER)

15 Type **West** and press (ENTER)

16 Type **North** and press (ENTER)
The screen should look like Figure 4.17.

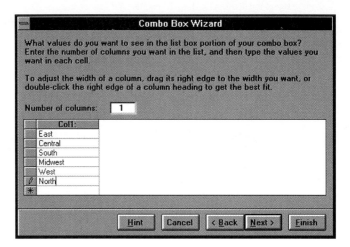

Figure 4.17

17 Select the <Finish> button.

18 Select the *Store that value in this field* button.

19 Select the Sales Region field from the list box.
The screen should look like Figure 4.18.

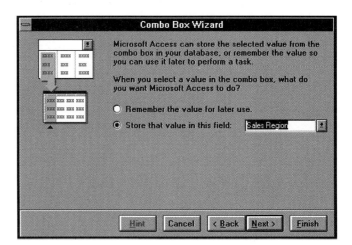

Figure 4.18

20 Select the Next> button.

21 Type **Sales Region:**
The screen should look like Figure 4.19.

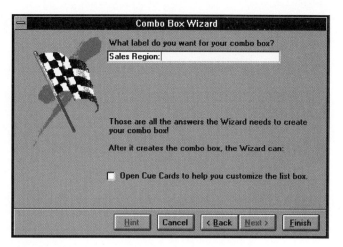

Figure 4.19

22 Select the Next> button.

23 Drag the bottom of the Sales Region label down one line. The screen should look like Figure 4.20.

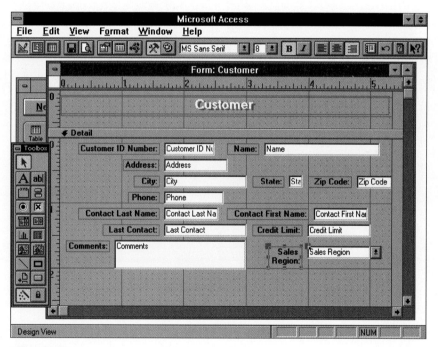

Figure 4.20

24 Select the Form button on the Tool bar to show the form with data. The screen should look like Figure 4.21.

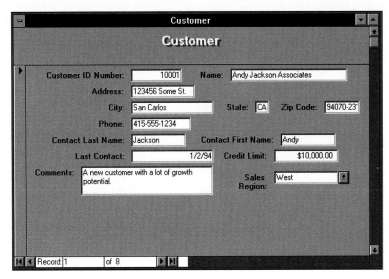

Figure 4.21

 25 Select the Design button on the Tool bar to switch back to Design view.

26 Select the Sales Region control.

27 Select the Properties button on the Tool bar.

28 Move to the Limit To list box.

29 Select Yes from the list.
The window should look like Figure 4.22.

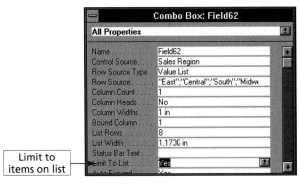

Figure 4.22

30 Close the Combo Box Properties dialog box.

31 Save the Customer form.

32 Close the form window.

EXIT   If necessary, you can exit Access now and continue this project later.

> **Tip** Combo and list boxes are useful, but one way to make them even more useful is to get the values from a table instead of typing them. You can easily do this using the FormWizards by selecting that option button. For example, you might want to use an inventory table to fill the Product Ordered field in the Orders table, as shown in Figure 4.16.

BUILDING A TABULAR FORM

As noted earlier in this project, a tabular form displays the fields in columns, with the field label above the contents. Each screen contains as many records as can fit. Tabular forms are more useful for tables, like the Orders table, that have a limited number of narrow fields that can be displayed in a single row on the screen. Tabular forms are also useful as a subform in a main/subform form (you will develop such a form at the end of this project). In the following steps, you will build a simple tabular form for the Orders table.

To build a tabular form:

1 Make sure the Orders table is selected, and then select the New Form button on the Tool bar.

2 Select the FormWizards button.

3 Select Tabular style.

4 Add the following fields to the form: Customer ID Number, Order Date, Product Ordered, Price Paid and Order Total.
The FormWizard dialog box should look like Figure 4.23.

Figure 4.23

5 Select the Next> button.

6 Select the Next> button on the Form Style Selection screen to leave the style as Embossed.

7 Select the Finish button to leave the Form Title as Orders.
The screen should look like Figure 4.24.

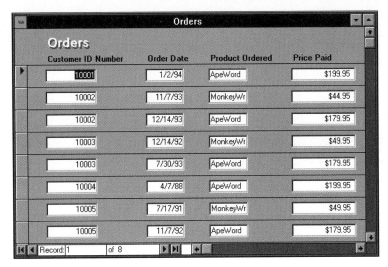

Figure 4.24

8 Select the Design button on the Tool Bar.

9 Select the Customer ID Number label.

10 Change the caption in the text box to read Customer ID.

11 Drag the rest of the fields and labels to the left until they all fit comfortably on one screen width.

12 Center the title (Orders) in the Form Header band.
The screen should look roughly like Figure 4.25.

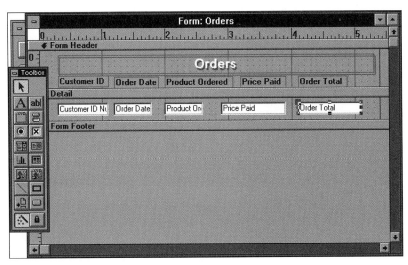

Figure 4.25

13 Select the Form Data button on the Tool bar to see what your form looks like with data.
The screen should look like Figure 4.26.

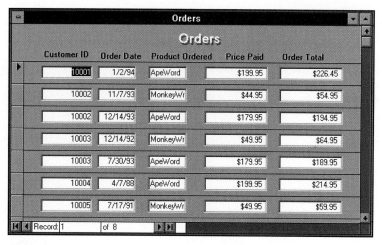

Figure 4.26

14 Choose Save from the File menu.

15 Type **Orders** for the name of the form.

  If necessary, you can exit Access now and continue this project later.

ADDING TOTALS TO A FORM

It's often useful to see totals for some fields. Specifically, you would like to know the total revenue from orders. This task is straightforward with Access. You will create a *summary field* in the *Form Footer band*. A ***summary field*** summarizes some aspect of another field in the table. The Form Footer band is the part of the form created after a screenful of records have been displayed. One common summary is adding up all the values in a field. For example, you may want to see the total amount spent on Simian Software products. You can get that total by telling Access to sum the Order Total field.

The three most common summary controls for numeric type data are sum, average, and count. Sum summaries simply add the values in the control. Count is the number of records in the control. Average divides the sum by the count.

In the steps that follow, you will summarize the Order Total field (control) and put the resulting sum on the form.

To place a summary control in the Form Footer band:

1 Open the Orders form in Design mode.

2 Drag the bottom of the Form Footer band down to create four or five blank lines.

3 Select the Text Box control button.

4 Place the crosshairs under the right edge of the Order Total field in the Form Footer band.

5 Click once to place the control.

The screen should look like Figure 4.27.

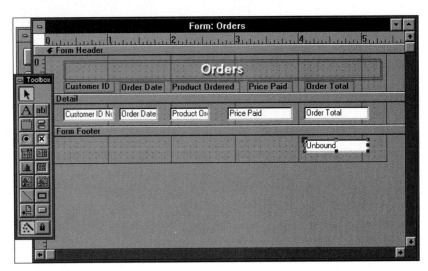

Figure 4.27

 6 Select the Properties button on the Tool bar to open the Text Box Properties dialog box.

7 Move to the Name text box and type **Total:**

8 Move to the Control Source text box and type **=Sum([Order Total])** This expression tells Access to use its built-in Sum( ) function to add the values in the Order Total field. (The name of the field must be enclosed in square brackets to let Access know that it's a field and not a control or label.)

9 Move to the Format text box.

10 Select Currency format.

The screen should look like Figure 4.28.

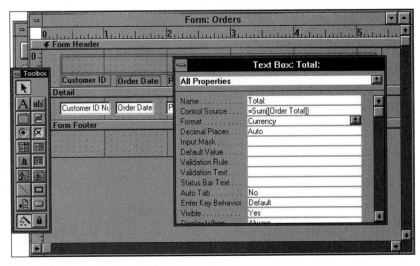

Figure 4.28

11 Close the Text Box Properties dialog box.

12 Select the Label button from the Toolbox window.

13 Place the crosshairs somewhere in the left part of the Form Footer band and click once.

14 Type **Total:** in the text box.

15 Drag the new text box to position it to the left of the Total Order Total control.

16 Resize the text box and move it until the screen looks like Figure 4.29.

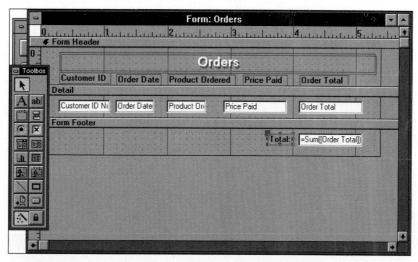

Figure 4.29

17 Select the Form Data button on the Tool bar. The screen should look like Figure 4.30.

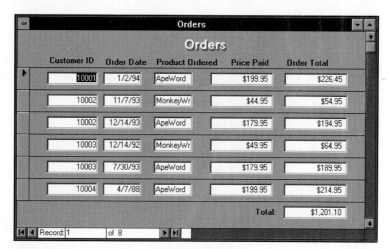

Figure 4.30

18 Select the Design button on the Tool bar.

19 Close the form, saving the changes you've made.

EXIT If necessary, you can exit Access now and continue this project later.

 Tip Access will help you if you need a function but don't know the name. When you move the cursor into the Control Source text box in any Properties window, a button labeled . . . opens next to the button that opens the list box. This button opens the Expression Builder, which will walk you through the process of assembling an expression for a particular control.

BUILDING A MAIN/SUBFORM FORM

When you're working with two tables that have a one-to-many relationship, it's often useful to see the parent record along with all its child records. Access includes the Main/Subform FormWizard to simplify this process. Let's see how to build a simple two-table form.

 ### To build a Main/Subform form:

1 Be sure the Customer table is selected.

2 Select the New Form button on the Tool bar.

3 Select the FormWizards button.

4 Select Main/Subform from the list of form types.

5 Select the Orders table when Access asks for the name of the child table or query.

6 Select the Next> button.

7 Add the Customer ID Number, Name, and Phone fields from the Customer table.

8 Select the Next> button.

9 Select Order Date, Product Ordered, and Order Total fields from the Orders table.

10 Select the Next> button.

11 Select Standard style for the form.

12 Select the Next> button.

13 Type `Customer Orders` for the name of the form.

14 Select the Finish button.

15 Select the OK button when Access tells you that you haven't saved the subform.

16 Type `Orders Subform` in the Save As dialog box.

17 Select the OK button, and you should see the form.

18 Move the record pointer to the next record to see the first customer with more than one order.
The screen should look like Figure 4.31.

19 Choose Save Form As from the File menu.

20 Type `Customer Orders`

21 Close the form.

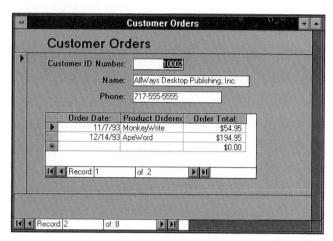

Figure 4.31

Tip Access makes it simple to turn your form into a printed report. With the form in Form data mode, choose Print from the File menu. Selecting the OK button will print the file using the form as a model.

THE NEXT STEP

Access lets you use all the standard Windows controls in screen forms, including option buttons, check boxes, buttons, and graphical images. What fields in the Customer and Orders tables do you think might be able to use one of these controls? Experiment with adding them to the appropriate screen form.

Graphs are a special type of form. The basics of creating a graph form are covered in Project 6.

SUMMARY AND EXERCISES

Summary

- A screen form should be used for data entry and editing.
- Access lets you design a form from scratch or use FormWizards.
- A form is made up of controls and labels.
- Controls are fields and calculated values.
- Labels are text that describe one or more controls.
- FormWizards uses four standard graph types: single-column, tabular, graph, and main/subform.
- A single-column form displays labels in the left column and controls in the right, one record per window.

- A tabular form displays labels in the Form Header band and controls in the Detail band, with multiple records per window.
- A graph form displays a graphical representation of your data using the Windows graph tool.
- A main/subform form embeds a multirecord child form in a single record parent form.
- A combo box or list box is a good way to control the contents of a field and prevent inaccurate data entry.

Key Terms and Operations

Key Terms
auto-form form
combo box
control
Detail band
Form Footer band
Form Header band
FormWizard
graph form
label

list box
main/subform form
properties
screen form
single-column form
summary field
tabular form

Operations
Create Form
Create Subform

Study Questions

Multiple Choice

1. You should use a screen form instead of entering data directly into a table because
   a. screen forms are easier to read than the table layout.
   b. screen forms allow longer, more descriptive labels than the table layout.
   c. screen forms allow additional validations.
   d. All of the above.

2. A label is usually
   a. text attached to a control.
   b. a field attached to text.
   c. a control attached to text.
   d. None of the above.

3. A control is usually
   a. text attached to a control.
   b. a field attached to text.
   c. a control attached to text.
   d. None of the above.

4. The difference between a list box and a combo box is
   a. a combo box lets you make selections from several fields, whereas a list box restricts selections to a single field.
   b. a combo box lets you type in data as well as making selections from a list, whereas a list box restricts selections to the list.
   c. a combo box will automatically fill in a field from selections made in a list, whereas a list box will only store the selection to a temporary storage area.
   d. a combo box will only store selections to a temporary storage area, whereas a list box will automatically fill in a field.

5. In a single column screen form, the labels and controls are displayed
   a. in columns with the controls beneath the labels.
   b. in columns with the controls to the right of the labels.
   c. in columns with the labels to the right of the controls.
   d. according to the layout you select when you set up the screen.

6. In a tabular screen form, the labels and controls are displayed
   a. in columns with the controls beneath the labels.
   b. in columns with the controls to the right of the labels.
   c. in columns with the labels to the right of the controls.
   d. according to the layout you select when you set up the screen.

7. The Form Header and Form Footer bands can contain:
   a. labels
   b. controls
   c. values from fields
   d. All of the above.

8. Which of the following items cannot have associated properties?
   a. labels
   b. controls
   c. fonts
   d. values from fields

9. When using a list box, you are restricted to
   a. values you type in to the list.
   b. a single column of data.
   c. automatically storing values in a field in the table.
   d. None of the above.

10. The Form Footer band can
    a. display the "footprint" of the form.
    b. show totals for one or more fields.
    c. not display text labels.
    d. All of the above.

Short Answer

1. What is the major difference between a single-column form and a tabular form?

2. When you created the main/subform form, you didn't have to tell Access how to select records from the Orders table. Why is this instruction unnecessary?

3. The Form Footer band can be used to display summaries of controls in the form. List two other items you might want to place in the Form Footer band? (*Hint:* Think of the ways you might query the database.)

4. What are the differences between a combo box and a list box?

5. When centering an item in a form, why must you first stretch the box that contains it?

6. How can you display data in a form in a sequence different from what is specified by the primary key?

7. What three operations can you perform on number type data in the Form Footer band?

8. If you try to summarize a text type field, Access will not allow you to sum or average. Why not?

9. You can use either tables or query views to create a form. Under what circumstances might you want to use a view?

10. Suppose you wanted a form that included the records of all customers whose zip codes begin with 9. Describe briefly how you would do this.

For Discussion

1. Since validations can be included in the table structure, why go to all the trouble of creating screen forms?

2. When might you want to print a screen form like a report? (*Hint:* Think about some of the forms you built in this project. Would you want to print any of them? Which ones? Why?)

3. What summary operators would you expect to be available for date type data? Use the Access manual and/or online Help to see the operators that are included.

Review Exercises

Adding a Combo Box for Product Ordered

Add a combo box to the Orders subform for the Product Ordered field by following these steps:

1. Open the Orders subform form in Design view.

2. Erase the Product Ordered label and control.

3. Add a combo box for the Product Ordered control.

4. Add a text box for the Product Ordered label.

5. Save the resulting form, print it with data, and turn in the results.

Adding a Lookup Table for the State Field

Add a combo box to the Customer form for the State field by following these steps:

1. Create a table called States.

2. Add the two-letter state abbreviations used in the Customer table to the States table.

3. Open the Customer form in Design view.

4. Erase the State label and control.

5. Add a combo box for the States control.

6. Be sure to select the option button *I want the combo box to look up the values in a table or query* in the first Combo Box Wizard screen.

7. Specify States as the table that will be the source for the field values.

8. Add a text box for the States label.

9. Save the resulting form, print it with data, and turn in the results.

Assignments

Designing an Orders Screen with Different Sequencing

Set up a screen form that displays orders in descending sequence of order dates. Print the result and turn it in.

Creating a Screen Form for the Technical Support Table

If you created a Technical Support table in the previous projects, set up a screen form that displays its data. Then modify this form to show calls handled by each support technician. (*Hint:* You will need to use a Form Header band for this.) Print the result and turn it in.

Creating Screen Forms for the Billing Tables

If you created Billing tables in the previous projects, create several screen forms that display invoicing information in ways you might want to see it. Print the results and turn them in.

Objectives

After completing this project, you should be able to:

▶ Create a single-column report

▶ Print different date formats

▶ Create a report using data from two tables

▶ Divide the report into groups

▶ Create subtotals for groups as well as a grand total for the report

▶ Add page numbers and other properties to the report

▶ Set up a report to print mailing labels

CASE STUDY: CREATING REPORTS FOR SIMIAN SOFTWARE

"We'd like to see some output," Ms. Hudson tells you. "My people are frustrated having to look at the data on the screen. Can't you give us some printed reports we can distribute for discussion in meetings? We need a customer list and a summary of recent orders that includes basic customer information. We'd also like you to design a few other reports that you think will be useful to management."

Designing the Solution

In some ways designing and printing reports completes a circle begun in Project 1. There you learned that the database design process begins by examining the output you want to get from your data. If your design was 100 percent accurate, you could just go back to those reports and create them using your original specification. For better or worse, that rarely happens. It's far more common to be asked for an ad hoc report that is needed in a matter of minutes, not days. Fortunately, the Access report writer can help you get the job done quickly and easily.

This project will show you how to use the Access Report Wizards to create attractive reports. You will work exclusively with the Report Wizards because they usually provide a faster way for you to create a report and then modify its structure to suit your particular needs.

You will start by creating a simple single-column report containing basic customer data—ID number, name, state, and telephone number.

Then you will create another report using data from the Customer and Orders tables. This report will include the ID number, name, order date, product ordered, and order amount. You will add groupings to this report, creating subtotals and a grand total of the order amount. Then you will add formatting touches that make the report easier to read, including dates, page numbers, and other formatting devices (including fonts). You will also create a report that you will use to print mailing labels.

REDESIGNING YOUR DATABASE

Database design is rarely as straightforward as it may have seemed to you after reading Project 1. You will discover that the database will change as you work with it. When you create a new query, screen, or report, there's a chance you will discover a way to make operations more efficient. Programmers are fond of pointing out that a good program is never finished, because people will always find new uses for it; every new use, however, requires changes to the program. A database is very much the same: people will always find new questions to ask of the data. Sometimes these questions will suggest different ways of organizing the data.

One change that might be made to the Simian Software database is eliminating the Order Total fields in the Orders table. In most reports this field can be calculated on the fly as the sum of the Price Paid, Sales Tax, and Shipping Charge fields. However, it's convenient to use the Order Total field for screen forms. The possibility of redesigning the database is something that should always be kept in mind. However, changes should only be made when you're sure they will make your job easier.

USING THE REPORT GENERATOR

Access uses a *band-oriented report generator,* which divides the report into bands:

- The contents of the *Report Header band* will be printed at the top of the first page of the report.
- The contents of the *Page Header band* will be printed at the top of each page of the report.
- The contents of the *Detail band* will be printed between the Page Header and Page Footer bands (unless the report includes groups, which will be explained later in this project).
- The contents of the *Page Footer band* will be printed at the bottom of each page of the report.
- The contents of the *Report Footer band* will be printed at the bottom of the last page of the report.

Reports can also include *groups,* which cluster records that are similar in some respect. Grouping will be explained later in this project.

Figure 5.1 shows where each of these bands lies in a standard report design, and Figure 5.2 shows part of the report created by this layout. However, the best way to learn about report bands is by using them.

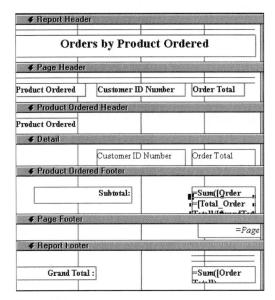

Figure 5.1

Figure 5.2

CREATING A SINGLE-COLUMN REPORT

Just as you used FormWizards extensively in Project 4, you will use ReportWizards in this project. It's faster to let the ReportWizards do most of the work setting up a report; then you can modify it to suit your particular needs. In this section you will create a simple single-column report. Reports are similar to screen forms: They are made up of bands, labels, and controls.

There are six ReportWizards: Single-Column, Groups/Totals, Summary, Tabular, AutoReport, and Microsoft Word Mailmerge. In this project you will use the Single-Column, Groups/Totals, and Mailing Labels ReportWizards.

The ReportWizards also let you choose one of three looks for your report: Executive, Presentation, or Ledger. In the following numbered steps, you will create the first report Ms. Hudson wants—a simple report showing each customer's ID number, name, state, and telephone number. When you reach the style selection screen (in step 8), you can select each of these buttons in turn and watch the sample part of the window to see how it looks.

To design and print a single-column report:

1 Be sure Access is started and the Simian database is open.

2 Select the Customer table.

3 Select the New Report button on the Tool bar.

4 Select the ReportWizards button.

5 Select the Single-Column style.
The Single-Column ReportWizard dialog box should appear on the screen.

6 Select the Customer ID Number, Name, State, and Phone fields.
The screen should look like Figure 5.3.

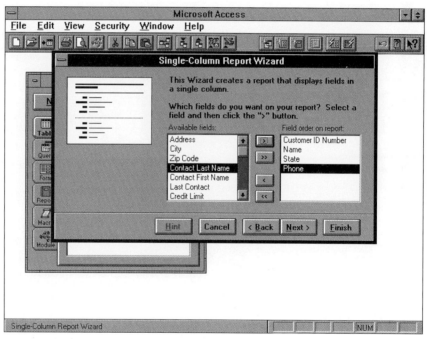

Figure 5.3

7 Select the Next> button.

8 Select the Next> button again to leave the report in primary key sequence and access the style selection dialog box.

9 Select Presentation style from the style selection dialog box.

10 Select the Next> button.

11 Type `Customer Table Report`

12 Select the Finish button.
The screen should look like Figure 5.4.

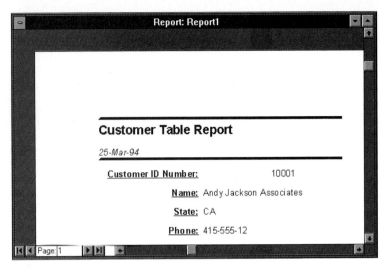

Figure 5.4

13 Move the pointer onto the report, and then click once to switch to Page Preview view. The screen should look like Figure 5.5.

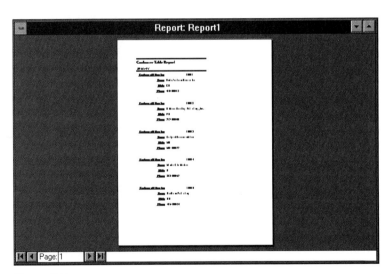

Figure 5.5

14 Move the pointer onto the report, and click once to return to the normal view of the report.

15 Choose Save As from the File menu.

16 Type **Customer Table Report**

17 Close the report.

This report doesn't quite have the professional look you want. The first problem is the date. The default date format is Medium Date, in which dates are written as DD-Mon-YY. That means September 6, 1993, will be written as 06-Sep-93, which is not very attractive.

The second problem is that the values in the Customer ID Number field are aligned to the right, making them distant from the label. We want them aligned to the left, next to the label. Finally, the telephone numbers are being truncated without printing the entire field. We want to print the entire number.

Like screen forms, report controls and labels have properties. When working with properties you will use the Access built-in functions. In the following numbered steps, you will fix this report, using the built-in function *Now( )*. Access uses its **Now( )** function to read the computer's clock and give you the current date (and time, if you want).

To change some properties of the Customer Table Report:

1 Select the Report icon in the database window.

2 Select the Customer Table Report.

3 Select the Design button.
The screen should look like Figure 5.6.

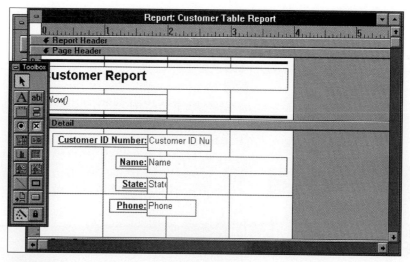

Figure 5.6

4 Select the *Customer Report* title text box in the Page Header band.

5 Select the Center button on the Tool bar.

6 Select the text box below the *Customer Report* title box that contains =Now( ).

7 Select the Properties button on the Tool bar to open the Properties dialog box.

8 Open the Format list box on the line immediately below the Control Source text box.

9 Select Long Date format.

10 Select the Customer ID Number control (not the label).

11 Scroll down the Text Box window until you reach the next to last item, Text Align.

12 Open the Text Align list box and select Left alignment.
The screen should look like Figure 5.7.

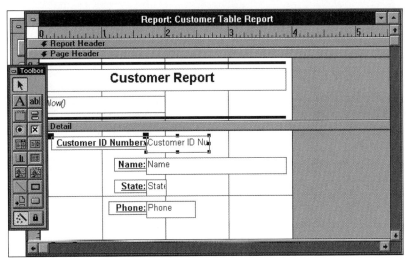

Figure 5.7

13 Close the Properties dialog box.

14 Select the phone control.

15 Drag the right edge of the control box to the right to make it large enough to display the entire telephone number.

16 Move to the Page Footer band.
The expression *=Page* in this band shows where the page number will be printed, as well as its font and style.

17 Select the Print Preview button on the Tool bar.
The screen should look like Figure 5.8.

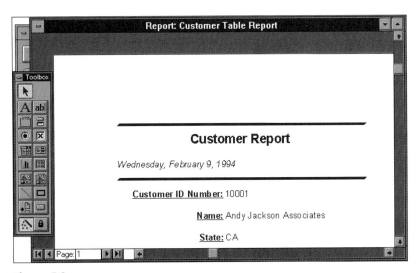

Figure 5.8

18 Select the Print button on the Tool bar to print the report.
Your report will print on two pages as shown in Figure 5.9.

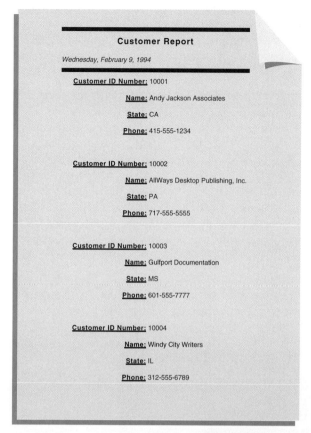

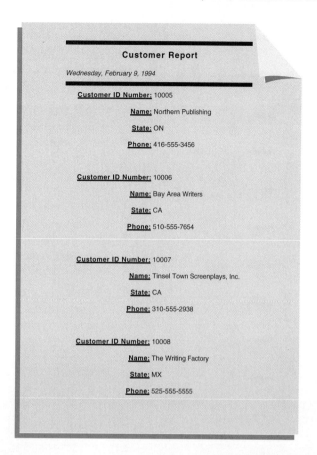

Figure 5.9

19 Close the Print Preview window.

20 Close the Report window, saving the changes you've made to the report design.

21 Write the name of this report, the table it relies on, and the fields it contains in your data dictionary.

CREATING A MULTITABLE REPORT

You also want to create a report showing customer and order activity broken down by date. The report should show all activity, whether it involves contact with the customer or is simply an order, on each date. Think back to Project 3 where you learned to use query by example. You've already built a query that supplies this data. The only problem is that the query currently selects activity only on November 7, 1992. You want to select all activity.

If the tables are linked with a permanent relationship, creating a report based on data from two linked tables is straightforward. Access keeps track of the relationship for you; all you must do is design the report. However, you can also use data from a view created by a query in a report. That's convenient because you will occasionally need reports based on links between tables.

Once the query is prepared, you'll be given a choice of how you want to handle the activity grouping. Remember a group is a collection of records that are related to each other according to some specified criteria. You can choose from

- normal grouping, in which records with the same value for the date (given the current date format) are kept together
- year grouping, in which records with the same year are kept together
- quarter grouping, in which records within the same calendar quarter (January–March, April–June, July–September, October–December) are kept together
- month grouping, in which records with the same month are kept together
- week grouping, in which records with the same week are kept together
- day grouping, in which records with the same day are kept together
- hour grouping, in which records with the same hour are kept together
- minute grouping, in which records with the same minute are kept together.

The grouping options are shown in the Grouping dialog box. You also can open the Group list box to see the options, as shown in Figure 5.10.

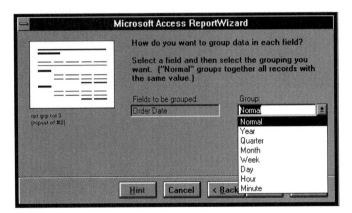

Figure 5.10

Other data types have different grouping options. These options are listed at the end of this project.

The report you will create in the following numbered steps will show each customer's name, the date of last contact with this customer, and the date of each order from each customer. To create the report, you will use the Activity by Date Query you created in Project 3. The report will be grouped by order date. All orders on a single date will be sorted in alphabetical sequence by name.

To create a report that groups activity by date:

1 Open the Activity by Date query in Design view.

2 Move to the Criteria line that contains the date 11/7/92.

3 Erase the date so the screen looks like Figure 5.11.

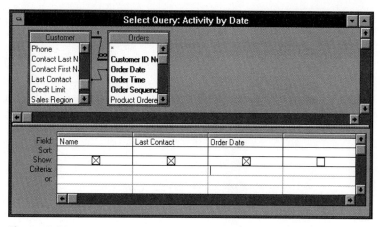

Figure 5.11

4 Save the query, but don't close the Query window.

5 Select the New Report button on the Tool bar.

6 Select the ReportWizards button.

7 Select Groups/Totals from the report type list.

8 Select the >> button to include all fields from the Query view in the report.

9 Select the Next> button.

10 Select the Order Date field as the basis for grouping.

11 Select the Next> button.

12 Select Normal grouping.

13 Select the Next> button.

14 Select the Name field as the basis for sorting within a group.

15 Select the Next> button twice.

16 Select the Presentation option button.

17 Select the Next> button.

18 Select the Finish button to leave the report title as it is.

19 Select Save As from the File menu, and type `Order & Technical Support Activity by Date` as the name of the report.

You will see the Print Preview view shown in Figure 5.12.

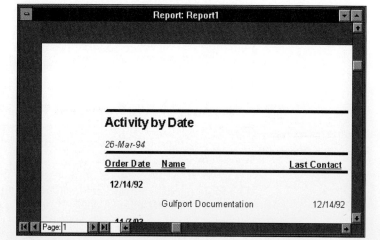

Figure 5.12

20 Scroll down the Report window until it looks like Figure 5.13.

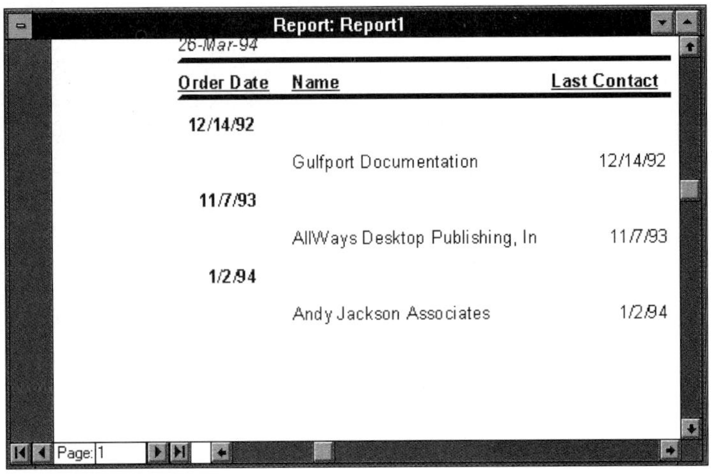

Figure 5.13

EXIT If necessary, you can exit Access now and continue this project later.

CREATING JOINS

There's a problem with the report: It includes only three records even though the Customer table has eight records. Before you pick up the telephone to call Microsoft and report a bug, think about that query. You told Access to match the Order Date field in the Orders table with the Last Contact field in the Customer table. What should Access do if there are records in one table for which there are no matching values in the other table?

The default Access uses is to select only records that have matching values in both tables. This is called an *inner join.* However, for your report you want an *outer join,* which displays all records from each table whether or not there's a matching record in the other table. (Naturally, if there are records with matching key values, they will be grouped together in the view.)

The link you've established between the Customer and Orders tables is a many-to-many relation, with several possible records in each table matching several other possible records in the other. Many-to-many relations are difficult to work with because there's no direct, easy way to link them. One of two techniques is usually used to handle many-to-many relations.

The Access manual recommends creating another table that contains one record for each record pair in the two tables you want to join. This has the disadvantage of cluttering your database with temporary tables. It also consumes disk space.

However, adding such a table is one solution to the current problem. The table needs only one field called Activity Date. It should contain the date that either an order was received, a technical call was received, or both. (An assignment at the end of this project lets you complete this exercise.)

The second method is to take advantage of the fact that you already have the table you need. Why not simply use the Customer table as the basis for the link? Take advantage of the inherent relationship between the Customer and Orders tables and use it to implement the many-to-many relation. The problem with this solution is that there's usually one field in the two tables you want to merge into a single field. In this example you want the Order Date and Tech Call Date fields to appear in a single column, which you will call Activity Date. That's difficult to do if you use the Customer table as the basis for the many-to-many relation. In the following numbered steps, you will create the outer join.

To create an outer join:

1 Close the Print Preview window.

2 Select the Activity by Date Query window.

3 Be sure the query is in Design view.

4 Select the line connecting the Last Contact and Order Date fields in the two field lists in the upper half of the window.

5 Choose Join Properties from the View menu to open the Join Properties dialog box.

6 Select option button 2 (*Include ALL records from 'Customer'* ...) The screen should look like Figure 5.14.

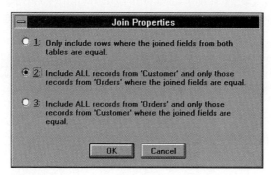

Figure 5.14

7 Select OK to add the link.
Note that the line linking the two tables has turned into a small arrow pointing away from the table whose records are all to be included.

8 Select the Relationship line connecting the Customer ID Number fields.

9 Press (DEL) to delete the permanent relationship.
The screen should look like Figure 5.15.

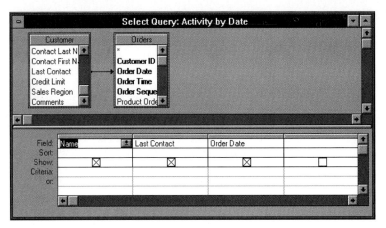

Figure 5.15

 10 Select the Save button on the Tool bar to save the changes to this query.

 11 Select the Run Query button on the Tool bar to see the results of the query.

The Query window should contain eight records. In the following numbered steps, you will turn this data into a report.

 ### To use the outer join in a report:

1 Select the Order & Technical Support Activity by Date report window.

2 Select the Print Preview button from the Tool bar.
You'll see all the records from the Customer table, as shown in Figure 5.16.

Figure 5.16

3 Select the Close button on the Tool bar to close the Print Preview window.

4 Close the Report and Query windows.

5 Write the following in your data dictionary: the name of this report, the query it relies on, the fields it contains, and the tables where each originate.

CREATING REPORT GROUPINGS

In this section you will create a grouped report. You want the report to show sales subtotals for each of our two products, with the sales of each product grouped together.

You've already worked with several groupings in the Simian Software database. For example, whenever you look at orders broken down by customer ID number, you're looking at a grouping based on ID. In the previous section, when you looked at customers and orders by date, you were grouping the data by date.

When you add a group to a report, you automatically add two bands: the *Group Header band* and the *Group Footer band*. The **Group Header band** contains labels and controls that will be printed before each group of data. It usually contains the values from the field(s) that serve as the basis for the grouping. The **Group Footer band** contains labels and controls that will be printed after each group of data. It is often used to hold summary data for the group such as a subtotal. Either or both can be removed from the report if you wish.

 ### To create a report grouped by product ordered:

1 Select the Orders table in the Database window.

2 Select the New Report button on the Tool bar.

3 Select the ReportWizards button.

4 Select Groups/Totals.

5 Add the Customer ID Number, Product Ordered, and Order Total fields to the report.

6 Select the Next> button.

7 Select Product Ordered as the field you want to group by.

8 Select the Next> button.

9 Select Normal grouping.

10 Select the Next> button.

11 Select the Next> button two more times to bypass sorting options and leave the report with an Executive style.

12 Type **Orders by Product Ordered** for the report name.

13 Select the Modify the Report's Design button.

14 Select the Finish button.
The screen should look like Figure 5.17.

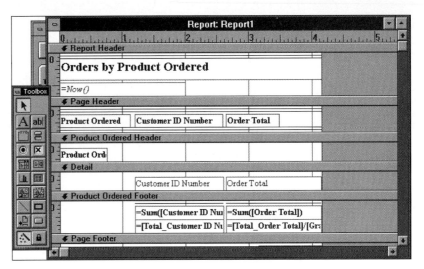

Figure 5.17

To print and save the report:

1 Choose Print Setup from the File menu.

2 Select the Portrait button for the print orientation.

3 Select OK.

4 Choose Print from the File menu to open the Print dialog box.

5 Select OK.

Your report should look like Figure 5.18.

Orders by Product Ordered

26-Mar-94

Product Ordered	Customer ID Number	Order Total
ApeWord		
	10005	$194.95
	10004	$214.95
	10003	$189.95
	10002	$194.95
	10001	$226.45
	10015	**$1,021.25**
	60.00%	**85.03%**
MonkeyWr		
	10005	$59.95
	10003	$64.95
	10002	$54.95
	10010	**$179.85**
	40.00%	**14.97%**
	10025	**$1,201.10**

Figure 5.18

6 Choose Save As from the File menu.

7 Type **Orders by Product Ordered** for the report name.

8 Select OK to save the report.

9 Close the Report window.

10 Write the following in your data dictionary: the name of this report, the table it relies on, and the fields it contains.

Take a good look at the report you've just printed. It has several problems. The most obvious is that the name of the second product is printed as *MonkeyWri*. You'll want to lengthen the box for that control so the entire name fits. Another problem is that subtotals and totals are being produced for the Customer ID Number field. The Access ReportWizards automatically produce subtotals, totals, and percentages for each Number type field (including Currency and Counter types). However, since adding up customer numbers doesn't make sense, you'll want to delete those subtotals and totals from the report design.

Finally, you want to make the usual cosmetic changes: centering the title, changing the date format to Long Date, and adding the label Grand Total in the appropriate places.

To change the report header design:

1 Open the Orders by Product Ordered report in Design view.

2 Select the Toolbox button on the Tool bar to close the Toolbox.

3 Select the report title box in the Report Header band.

4 Select the Center button on the Tool bar.

5 Select the box containing the expression =*Now( )* immediately below the title box.

6 Open the Properties window.

7 Change the format to Long Date.

8 Close the Properties window.

9 Select the Save button from the Tool bar.

To change the design of the Group Header and Group Footer bands:

1 Scroll the report design window until you see the report band labeled Product Ordered Header.

2 Select the text box containing the Product Ordered control.

3 Stretch the box to the right until it's a few characters wider.

4 Scroll further down the report design window until you see the Product Ordered Footer band.

5 Select the controls that sum and total the Customer ID Number field.

6 Delete the two selected controls by pressing (DEL)

7 Select the horizontal line above the controls you just deleted.

8 Delete the line by pressing (DEL)

9 Select the Toolbox button on the Tool bar to open the Toolbox.

10 Select the Text button.

11 Position the crosshairs in the Product Ordered Footer band to the left of the Sum control and stretch a box there.

12 Type **Subtotal:** in your new label box.

13 Select the new label box.

14 Drag the box until it's immediately to the left of the Sum control.

15 Select the Right Alignment button on the Tool bar.
The screen should look like Figure 5.19.

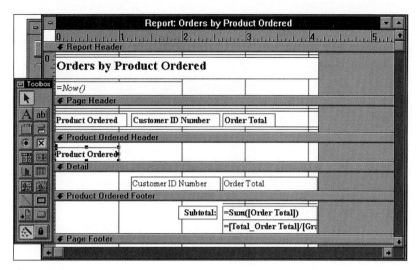

Figure 5.19

16 Select the Save button from the Tool bar.

Next, you will remove the page number as well as the report total for the Customer ID Number field. You will use the Sample Preview button, which shows the report using only a few of the records in the table. This can be much faster than Page Preview, which uses all the records.

To change the Page Footer and Report Footer bands:

1 Scroll down the report until you see the Page Footer and Report Footer bands.

2 Select the control and the two horizontal lines under Customer ID Number in the Report Footer band.

3 Delete the selected control and lines.

4 Select the =Page control in the Page Footer band.

5 Delete the selected control.

6 Drag the top of the Report Footer band up until the Page Footer band is entirely closed.
The screen should look like Figure 5.20.

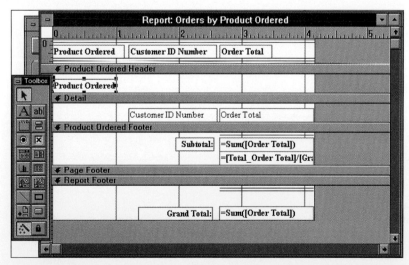

Figure 5.20

7 Select the Sample Preview button on the Tool bar. The screen should look like Figure 5.21.

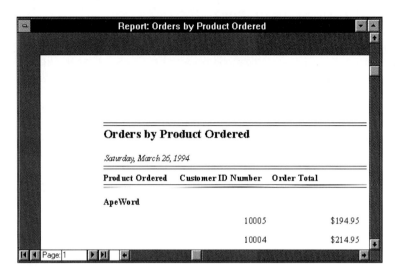

Figure 5.21

8 Scroll around the Sample Preview screen.

 9 If you don't like some aspect of the report, select the Close button on the Tool bar to return to Design view. Make changes as required until you're happy with the report. Be sure the report is in Design view before continuing.

10 Select the Save button from the Tool bar to save the report design.

11 Select the Print Preview button on the Tool bar.

 12 Select the Printer button on the Tool bar to open the Print dialog box.

13 Select OK to print the report.
Your report should look like Figure 5.22.

Orders by Product Ordered

Saturday, March 26, 1994

Product Ordered	Customer ID Number	Order Total
ApeWord		
	10005	$194.95
	10004	$214.95
	10003	$189.95
	10002	$194.95
	10001	$226.45
Subtotal:		**$1,021.25**
		85.03%
MonkeyWr		
	10005	$59.95
	10003	$64.95
	10002	$54.95
Subtotal:		**$179.85**
		14.97%
Grand Total:		**$1,201.10**

Figure 5.22

14 Close the report, saving the changes.

15 Note the changes to this report in your data dictionary.

Reminder As you were working with this report, you probably noticed that you saved the report design several times. Develop the habit of saving your work every ten minutes. That way you won't lose very much when the inevitable system crash or power failure occurs.

EXIT If necessary, you can exit Access now and continue this project later.

CREATING MAILING LABELS

Mailing labels simplify the task of sending letters to all (or some of) your customers, vendors, clients, or any other group. Sometimes you'll use them to send invoices. Other times you may want to send a notice that your hours of operation or prices have changed. The ability to quickly generate and print stick-on mailing labels can save hours of time.

There are a seemingly infinite number and variety of labels available. There are labels for dot-matrix, laser, daisy wheel, and line printers. There are labels for disks and magnetic tapes of all sizes. The most common labels are those produced by Avery Products for laser printers. Access includes a ReportWizard to handle Avery labels, so this section will focus on those products. Specifically, in the following numbered steps, you will use Avery 5260 labels, which are 3 across, 1 inch high and 2⅝ inches wide. With 10 rows per sheet, there are 30 labels per sheet.

You will set up an Access report to print labels for mailings to Simian Software customers. The Access Mailing Label Wizard will do most of the work for you. In fact, you don't even have to type. Figure 5.23 shows the Mailing Label Wizard dialog box. Before starting the Wizard, take a minute to examine this dialog box.

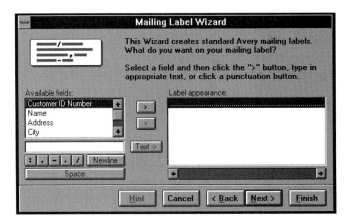

Figure 5.23

To add fields and punctuation marks, you must use the buttons below the Available Fields list box. If you want to place the next field on a new line, you must click the Newline button. If you don't select Newline at the end of a line, the next field or punctuation mark you select will be placed on the current line. When you select the Text-> button, you can type text on the label.

To set up mailing labels for Simian Software customers:

1 Select the Customer table in the Database window.

2 Select the New Report button on the Tool bar.

3 Select the ReportWizards button.

4 Select the Mailing Label Wizard.
The screen should look like Figure 5.23.

5 Select the Name field.

6 Select the Newline button.

7 Select the Address field.

8 Select the Newline button.

9 Select the City field.

10 Select the comma button and then the Space button.

11 Select the State field.

12 Select the Space button twice.

13 Select the Zip Code field.

The screen should look like Figure 5.24.

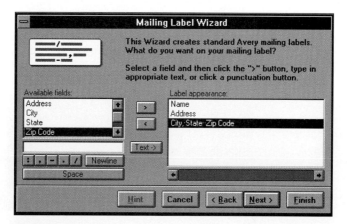

Figure 5.24

14 Select the Next> button to open the Print Order dialog box.

15 Select the Zip Code field to print the labels in Zip Code order.

16 Select the Next> button to display a pick list of standard Avery labels.

17 Scroll down the label list until you see 5260, and then select this label.

18 Select the Next> button to display a Text Appearance dialog box.

19 Select Arial 12-point bold for the font and style. Be sure italics and underlining are not selected.

The screen should look like Figure 5.25.

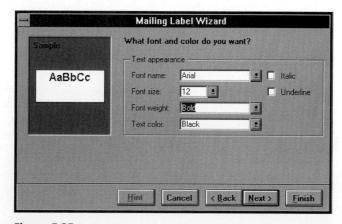

Figure 5.25

20 Be sure the screen looks like Figure 5.25, then select the Next> button.

21 Select the Modify the Mailing Label Design button.

22 Select the Finish button.

23 Choose Save As from the File menu.

24 Type **Customer Mailing Labels**

25 Select OK.

The screen should look like Figure 5.26.

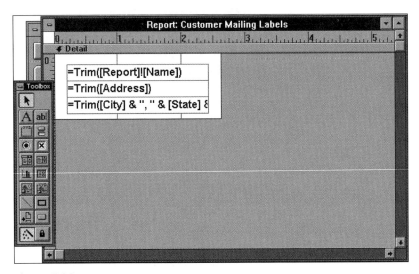

Figure 5.26

Look carefully at the labels in Figure 5.26. You will notice two unusual features of Access illustrated there. First is the appearance of the Trim( ) function, which is used to remove trailing blanks from a field. Trim( ) is particularly needed for the third line of the labels, which reads

```
Trim([City]&", "&[State]&" "&[Zip Code])
```

Without the Trim( ) function, the third line of the addresses would be printed like this:

```
Chicago , IL 60614
```

The second feature you will notice illustrated is the expression [*Report*]!/[*Name*]. The word *Name* is used internally by Access to refer to labels and controls. Preceding it by the word *Report* and connecting the two with a *!* tells Access to use the Name field instead of the name of the control or label when printing the labels.

You are now ready to print your labels. Before you can do this, however, you must fix one minor problem. As the labels are currently set up, the state names will be printed lowercase. In the steps that follow, you will see this using the Print Preview button on the Tool bar. You will then use the **Ucase( )** function to cause lowercase text to be printed as uppercase and print the labels.

To change lowercase state names to uppercase and print the labels:

1 Select the Print Preview button on the Tool bar. Notice that the state names are printed in lowercase.

2 Select the Close button on the Tool bar to return to Design view.

3 Place the text cursor immediately in front of [*State*].

4 Type **Ucase(**

5 Place the text cursor immediately after [*State*].

6 Type **)**

The expression should look like Figure 5.27.

& UCase([State]) &

Figure 5.27

7 Select the Print Preview button on the Tool bar.

8 Select the Print button on the Tool bar to print the labels. They should look like Figure 5.28.

The Writing Factory
17632-A 110 St.
Mexico City, MX

Northern Publishing
789 A St.
Toronto, ON

AllWays Desktop
Publishing, Inc.
9876 All Ways
Wilkes-Barre. PA 17777

Gulfport Documentation
4567 Gulf Ave.
Gulfport, MS 39505

Windy City Writers
111 Michigan Ave.
Chicago, IL 60614

Tinsel Town Screenplays,
Inc.
47932 Sunny St.
Los Angeles, CA 90024

Andy Jackson Associates
123456 Some St.
San Carlos, CA 94070-2316

Bay Area Writers
38791 Dan St.
Concord, CA 94518

Figure 5.28

REPORT GROUPING OPTIONS

Available grouping options will vary depending on the data type of the field being used to set up the group. Here's a summary of the available options.

Text Type Data

Table 5.1

Normal grouping	Set up the new group when field value changes.
1st character	Set up the new group based on first character of field value.
1st 2 characters	Set up the new group based on first two characters of field value.
1st 3 characters	Set up the new group based on first three characters of field value.
1st 4 characters	Set up the new group based on first four characters of field value.
1st 5 characters	Set up the new group based on first five characters of field value.

Number Type Data (including Currency and Counter)

Table 5.2

(Grouping options will be scaled to range of values in field.)

Normal grouping	Set up the new group when field value changes.
10s	Set up the new group when value changes by 10.
50s	Set up the new group when value changes by 50.
100s	Set up the new group when value changes by 100.
500s	Set up the new group when value changes by 500.
1000s	Set up the new group when value changes by 1,000.
5000s	Set up the new group when value changes by 5,000.
10000s	Set up the new group when value changes by 10,000.
50000s	Set up the new group when value changes by 50,000.
100000s	Set up the new group when value changes by 100,000.
500000s	Set up the new group when value changes by 500,000.

Date/Time Type Data

Table 5.3

Normal grouping	Keep records with the same value for the date (given the current date format) together.
Year	Keep records with the same year together.
Quarter	Keep records within the same calendar quarter (January–March, April–June, July–September, October–December) together.
Month	Keep records with the same month together.
Week	Keep records with the same week together.
Day	Keep records with the same day together.
Hour	Keep records with the same hour together.
Minute	Keep records with the same minute together.

THE NEXT STEP

Access has many functions that are part of the Access Basic language. You've already seen the Now( ) function in several reports in this project. If you're interested in extending your knowledge of this aspect of Access, a good place to start is the manual.

There are several other ReportWizards we didn't explore at all. Summary reports have no Detail band. Tabular reports look very much like tabular forms. The AutoReport Wizard will attempt to show your data in the way that makes the most sense, at least to the Wizard. The final Wizard, MS Word Mailmerge, exports data in a format that Microsoft Word's Mailmerge feature can read. This is handy for producing customized form letters.

Experiment with fonts and print styles, areas in which Access excels.

SUMMARY AND EXERCISES

Summary

- Access includes ReportWizards for single-column, grouped, and tabular formats, as well as mailing labels. Wizards are also included that will generate automatic reports and export data to Microsoft Word's Mailmerge format.
- To build a report with fields from two or more tables, you can use query by example to create a view first and then create the report based on that view.
- Grouping lets you create reports with records collated according to the values in one or more fields.
- Grouping also lets you create subtotals for groups as well as a grand total for the report.
- You can display today's date with the Now( ) function.
- You can change the format in which the date is printed.
- The mailing label ReportWizard handles standard Avery label layouts.
- To insert text characters in a mailing label, you must use the Text –>button provided by the Mailing Label ReportWizard.
- The UCase( ) function is helpful when you want to make sure report output is entirely uppercase.

Key Terms and Operations

Key Terms
band-oriented report generator
Detail band
group
Group Footer band
Group Header band
inner join
Now( )
outer join
Page Footer band

Page Header band
Report Footer band
Report Header band
UCase( )

Operations
Create New Report
Preview Page
Design Report
Preview Sample

Study Questions

Multiple Choice

1. The band that is printed only at the top of the first page of a report is called the
   a. Page Header   c. Report Header
   b. Page Footer   d. Report Footer

2. The band that is printed at the bottom of each page of a report is called the
   a. Page Header   c. Report Header
   b. Page Footer   d. Report Footer

3. When creating a group within a report, subtotals are usually placed in which band?
   a. Page Header   c. Group Header
   b. Page Footer   d. Group Footer

4. When creating a group within a report, the grand total of a numeric field is usually placed in which band?
   a. Report Header   c. Group Header
   b. Report Footer   d. Group Footer

5. The fastest way to create a new report based on data in a table is to select
   a. the Report button in the Database window and then the Design button in the Database window.
   b. the table name or Query view in the Database window and then the New Report button on the Tool bar.
   c. View/Reports from the menu and then the Design button in the Database window.
   d. the table name or Query view in the Database window and then the AutoReport button on the Tool bar.

6. Creating a report that uses data from more than one table can be accomplished by
   a. using any permanent relationship between the tables.
   b. using a query that links the two tables.
   c. joining the two tables to create a third table and then using the new table to create the report.
   d. All of the above.

7. A single-column report places
   a. labels in the leftmost column and controls immediately to their right.
   b. labels above each column and controls below them.
   c. field names above each column and record values below them.
   d. None of the above.

8. A tabular report places
   a. labels in the leftmost column and controls immediately to their right.
   b. labels above each column and controls below them.
   c. field names above each column and record values below them.
   d. None of the above.

9. The Now( ) function tells you
   a. the current date and time, according to the computer's built-in clock.
   b. the current time, according to the computer's built-in clock.
   c. the current date, according to the computer's built-in clock.
   d. any of the above, depending on the format setting selected.

10. The UCase( ) function
    a. converts the first letter of each word in the text to uppercase.
    b. converts all letters in the text to uppercase.
    c. converts the first letter of each word in the text to lowercase.
    d. converts all letters in the text to lowercase.

Short Answer

1. What is the difference between a single-column report and a tabular report?

2. Why do we need to create groupings in a report? Give two examples of useful ways the Customer table might be grouped.

3. When you created the report for the Orders table grouped on Product Ordered, subtotals and a grand total were automatically added for the Customer ID Number field. Why did this happen?

4. Describe where each of the following report bands are placed: Report Header, Report Footer, Page Header, Page Footer, Detail.

5. Describe how you could prevent a band from printing on the report.

6. What options are available for grouping a Date type field? Briefly describe how each behaves.

7. What is the difference between an inner join and an outer join?

8. Why did we need to use the UCase( ) function to convert state names to uppercase for mailing labels. (*Hint:* You may want to review the database design specifications for the State field in your data dictionary.)

9. What does the Now( ) function do?

10. What does the expression =*Page* do?

For Discussion

1. When you created the report for the Orders table grouped on Product Ordered, subtotals and a grand total were automatically added for the Customer ID Number field. Explain why this happened. Then discuss how you could change the structure of the Orders table to eliminate this problem.

2. Using the Customer and Orders tables as examples, make up three reports for which you would use an inner join rather than an outer join. (Don't actually create the reports in Access, just design them.) Explain why an inner join is appropriate for each report.

Review Exercises

Creating a Cross-reference Table

When working with two tables that have a many-to-many relationship, the Access manual recommends creating a table that contains one record for each record pair in the two tables you want to join. Follow these directions to create such a cross-reference table.

1. Open a new table structure in Design view.

2. Add one field called Activity Date.

3. Add data to this table consisting of the date that either an order was received or a customer contact was made, or both.

4. Use your new table to duplicate the multitable report created in this project.

Using Reports to Sort Data

When working with the report for the Orders table grouped on Product Ordered, you may have noticed that records for ApeWord were in the first group and MonkeyWrite records were in the second group. In the following steps you will see how report groups can be used to sort data without a query.

1. Open a new grouped report for the Customer table.

2. Add some fields. Be sure Contact Last Name is the first field.

3. Group the report based on Contact Last Name.

4. Look at the finished report in Design view.

5. Delete all labels and controls from the Group Header and Group Footer bands.

6. Add the Contact Last Name field to the Detail band.

7. Look at the report in Print Preview view. The data should be shown in alphabetical order by the Contact Last Name field.

Assignments

Grouping a Numeric Field by Range

Suppose you wanted a report that showed your credit exposure to customers. You want the report grouped in $100,000 increments. Work with the Groups/Totals ReportWizard to accomplish this. When you're satisfied with your results, print the report.

Reports for the Technical Support Table

If you've been working with a Technical Support table, create three reports. The first should simply list the data. The second should group the data by product name. The third should include customer information as well as the technical support data.

Reports for the Billing Tables

If you've been working with billing tables, create three reports. The first should be a summary of invoices. The second should be an invoice form. (You'll have to include the Customer table as well as both billing tables.) The third should group invoices by the month in which they were issued. (This report can serve as the basis for an aged accounts receivable report.)

Reports for the Inventory Table

If you've set up an Inventory table, create three reports. The first should list the inventory file. The second should list only inventory items that have quantities on hand below their reorder points. The third should show inventory item information along with data about orders for each item.

PART VI

Integrated Project 2

Objectives

After completing this project, you should be able to:

▶ Link a Word document to an Access database object

▶ Display the linked object as a data field in the Word document

▶ Display the linked object as a table in the Word document

▶ Update the linked object in the Word document

▶ Link a query to the Word document

▶ Format the linked object

The first integrated project introduced you to OLE, object linking and embedding. In that project you embedded an Excel worksheet by inserting the source file into a Word document. You then updated the object by updating the Word document. In this project you will also insert an object, an Access database. Instead of embedding the source file, however, you will create a link between the Word document and the source file. A linked object is treated differently than an embedded object.

When you link an object you do not actually insert the object into the target file. The target file stores only the location of the source file. This means that each time an object is updated, the source file must be available. The source file must have the same name and location as it did when it was first linked; otherwise, Word won't be able to find the source file.

Linking displays an image of the source file in the target file. When the object is an Access database, the image displayed is a Word table. You can also display the link itself, which is displayed as a *field code.* The field code contains only the location of the source file and not the contents of the source file. Because the source file is not included in the target file, you do not have the same file size concerns you have when you embed a file. The contents of the source file remain separate from the target file, so the size of the target file doesn't grow as large as it can when you embed an object.

CASE STUDY: CREATING A LINK

The report you created in the first integrated project collected survey results from a national taste-test. Respondents tasted a variety of fat-free and regular potato chips. The results were tallied by state and entered into an Excel worksheet. You created a Word document to present the data and embedded the Excel worksheet into the report. Dr. Gardent and his staff are so excited about tracking the survey on a daily basis that they have asked you to expand the contents of the report. They want to see the results from another survey the marketing department is taking. This survey queries food stores to see if they will sell the new fat-free potato chips. The presidential staff wants to know which stores have been contacted and which stores have agreed to carry the new chips.

Designing the Solution

You could create another worksheet and embed it in your Word document, just like you did in the first integrated project. The challenge, however, is that this data will be collected by the marketing department. They have their own computers, which are connected to the network, and they have control over the database in their department. This data will constantly change, as the marketing department collects new data and modifies the database to meet the needs of the presidential staff. It is impractical to reproduce the data from the marketing database every day for the daily report. The best option is to create a link to the marketing database. Then each morning you can update the Word document with the new data from the database and print the report.

CREATING THE ACCESS DATABASE

Even though this database will be maintained by the marketing department, your boss asked you to create it for them.

To create an Access database:

1 Select the Access button in the upper-right corner of the screen or, if the Microsoft Office suite does not start automatically when Windows starts, select the Office icon from the Program Manager window and then select Access.

2 Choose New Database from the File menu, or click on the New Database button.
The New Database dialog box appears.

3 Select the A: drive from the Drives list box.

4 Type **STORES.MDB** in the File Name text box.
The screen now looks like Figure 2.1.

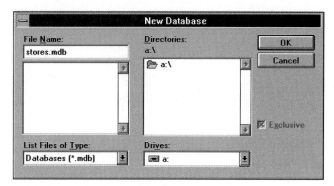

Figure 2.1

5 Select OK to close the dialog box.

6 Create a small database, using the skills and steps you learned in the Microsoft Access projects.
Table 2.1 shows the database structure.

Table 2.1

Field Name	Data Type	Width
ID	Counter (primary key)	n/a
Store Name	Text	35
Answer	Text	10

7 Save the table as SURVEY.

8 Open the database table and enter the data as shown in Figure 2.2

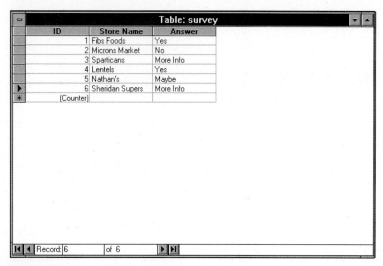

Figure 2.2

9 Save the table and exit Access.

UPDATING THE WORD DOCUMENT

Now it's time to get your report ready to receive the new database data. In the steps that follow, you will open the Word document you created in the first integrated project and revise it slightly.

To update the Word document:

1 Open Word and UPDATE.DOC file.

If you did not complete the review exercises at the end of Integrated Project 1, please ask your instructor for the file: UP__1.DOC. Save this as UPDATE.DOC and use this file to continue on in Integrated Project 2.

2 Modify the font setting so that all of the text of your Word document is now a 12 point font.

3 Position the insertion point at the end of the document, and type the following paragraph:

   As a result of the positive feedback from the taste-test surveys, we are petitioning grocery stores to see if they will carry our new product. The database below shows the stores which have been contacted, and their response to carrying the fat-free chips.

4 Press (ENTER) three times.

5 Save UPDATE.DOC.

The document now looks like Figure 2.3.

NEW PRODUCT DAILY REPORT

This report is a daily update of the national research project. The listing below shows the results from the taste-test surveys as they are reported by the market researchers.

Fat Free Potato Chip Survey							
		Fat Free			Regular		
State	Total	Salted	BBQ	No Salt	Salted	BBQ	No Salt
CA	30875	15000	9500	5000	925	450	350
WY	8200	400	500	100	4200	3000	2000
AZ	17700	8000	5000	3000	1200	500	600
VT	3900	250	100	50	2000	1500	800
VA	8735	100	85	50	3500	5000	4500
WA	15300	7500	6200	500	500	600	100
OR	11850	5300	5500	600	300	150	75
TN	4700	650	500	50	2000	1500	500
Total	101260	37200	27385	9350	14625	12700	8925

It is our hope that this new product will be a successful product in the fat-free marketplace.

As a result of the positive feedback from the taste-test survyes, we are petitioning grocery stores to see if they will carry our new product. The database below shows the stores which have been contacted, and their response to carrying the fat-free chips.

Figure 2.3

LINKING THE DATABASE

With your descriptive paragraph in place, you can now link to the STORES database. Your first step will be to activate the field code box so the linked data will be displayed as a code.

To activate field codes:

1 Choose Options from the Tools menu.

2 Select the View tab, and then select the Field Codes option so it is checked.
If a checkmark already appears next to the Field Codes option, do not select the option.

3 Select OK to close the dialog box.

Now you can create the link between the two documents.

To link the Access database:

1 Choose Database from the Insert menu.
The Database dialog box appears as shown in Figure 2.4.

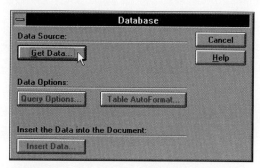

Figure 2.4

2 Select Get Data.
The Open Data Source dialog box appears.

3 Select MS Access Databases (*.mdb) from the List Files of Type box as shown in Figure 2.5. Notice that Confirm Conversions is not selected. If it is selected on your screen, turn this option off before you continue.

4 Select the A: drive, select STORES.MDB, and then select OK.

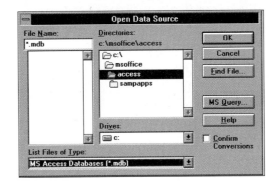

Figure 2.5

The Microsoft Access dialog box appears as shown in Figure 2.6.

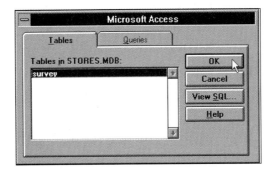

Figure 2.6

5 Select the Tables tab and the SURVEY table, and then select OK. The Database dialog box appears as shown in Figure 2.7.

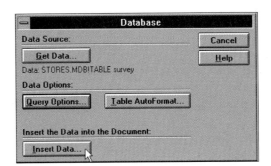

Figure 2.7

6 Select Insert Data.
The Insert Data dialog box appears as shown in Figure 2.8.

This option
creates the link.

Figure 2.8

7 Select Insert Data as Field.
Selecting this option ensures that the database will be a linked object and cannot be updated in Access. If this option is not selected, the data will be inserted into a Word table.

8 Select OK.
The screen now looks like Figure 2.9.

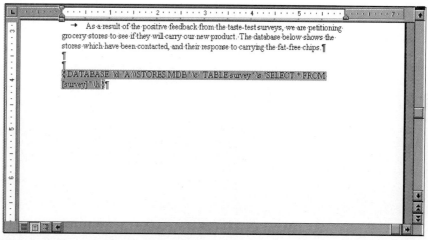

Figure 2.9

Quick Fix If your data looks like a Word table and not the database field shown in Figure 2.9, you probably did not select the View options properly. Choose Options from the Tools menu. Select the View tab, and then select the Field Codes option. If this option is already selected, select the table in your document and press (DELETE). Go back to step 1 and insert the database again. This time, don't forget to check the Insert Data as Field option from the Insert Data dialog box.

To save and view the linked document:

1 Select the Save button from the toolbar to save UPDATE.DOC.

2 Select the Print Preview button to view the document.
Notice that even though the database field code was displayed in the document, the actual data is displayed just as it will print.

3 Close the Print Preview window.

VIEWING THE LINKED OBJECT IN THE WORD DOCUMENT

When you created the linked object, you selected the Insert Data as Field option. This is the option that actually established the link by inserting a field code in the document that stores the location of the database. You then used Print Preview to see the image of the data. It is possible, however, to display the object's image in the Word document without having to activate Print Preview. This is done through the Options choice on the Tools menu. As you turn the Field Code option on and off, the linked database is displayed as either a field code, as shown in Figure 2.10, or as a Word table, as shown in Figure 2.11.

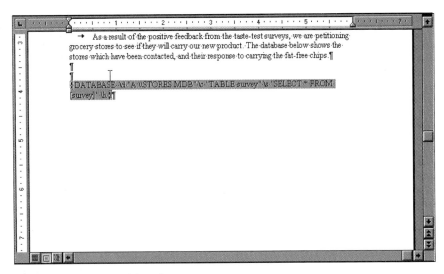

Figure 2.10   With Field Codes On

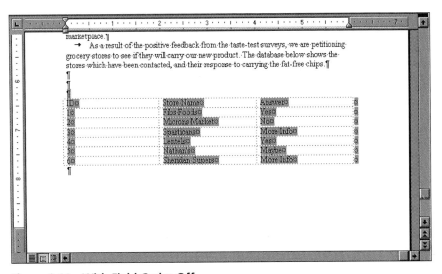

Figure 2.11   With Field Codes Off

Notice that the object is displayed as a table, and the table is shaded to help you see that it is not an ordinary Word table.

To view the linked data image:

1 Choose Options from the Tools menu.

2 In the View tab select the Field Codes option so that it is not checked and click OK.

3 Scroll through UPDATE.DOC and see the object's image. It should look like Figure 2.11.

EXIT If necessary, you can exit Word now and continue this project later.

UPDATING THE LINKED DATA

As the marketing department updates this database, you will be able to update the data in your document with only two keystrokes. This is because what you see in your document is actually an image of the real data located in another file. Since the Word document stores only the location of the database and displays only an image of the data, the image must be updated to reflect any changes that have been made to the database.

To update the linked data in the Word document:

1 Start Word and open UPDATE.DOC, if necessary.

2 Start Access, and open the STORES.MDB database.

3 Add records 7–10 to the SURVEY table, as shown in Figure 2.12.

ID	Store Name	Answer
1	Fibs Foods	Yes
2	Microns Market	No
3	Sparticans	More Info
4	Lentels	Yes
5	Nathan's	Maybe
6	Sheridan Supers	More Info
7	Parker Town	Maybe
8	Breaker's Barn	No
9	Ventura Market	Yes
10	People's Plaza	Yes
(Counter)		

New records ⎨ 7–10

Figure 2.12

4 Save the table, and exit Access.

5 Make sure the object is displayed in the Word document as a table. If the object is displayed as a field code, select Options and then change the Field Code so you can see the object in a Word table format.

6 Position the insertion point anywhere in the displayed table, and click once.

7 Press (F9) to complete the updating process.

The newly added records are displayed in the object's updated image, as shown in Figure 2.13.

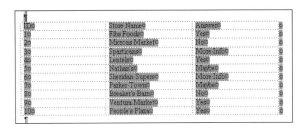

Figure 2.13

QUERYING THE LINKED DATABASE

The report you have created displays all of the data in the database. But what if you wanted only the stores answering yes to the survey question? You can do this by inserting a database *query* into the report. A query, as you learned in the Access 2 projects, lets you ask the database simple or complex questions. When you insert a query object, you can insert either a query made from within Access or a new query created through the Query Options dialog box. You can also sort the data into a meaningful order through a query. When you link to a query, Word remembers the query questions you answered in the Query Options dialog box. Each time you press (F9) to update the object, Word repeats the query instructions behind the scenes and inserts the updated data from the source file.

You will use the Query Options dialog box to establish **selection rules** for the query. Selection rules allow you to extract or display certain records from the database. To set up a selection rule, you will follow three basic steps:

- Identify field names in the database
- Select a comparison phrase, such as *Greater Than* or *Equal To*
- Enter numbers or characters (text) that will be compared to the data in the database field

You can create up to six selection rules in a query and connect them by using AND or OR. For example, if you wanted to select all store names that begin with *A* through *F*, you would enter the selection rules shown in Figure 2.14.

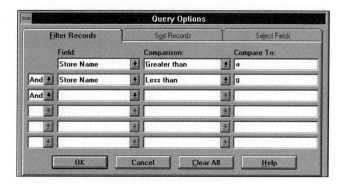

Figure 2.14

Tip Fields containing text and numbers are sorted and compared differently. Word uses the ANSI (American National Standards Institute) sorting order, which means that *corn* is "less than" *potatoes* because *corn* comes before *potatoes* alphabetically.

To begin the query process, you will enter text into the Word document and prepare a place to insert the new table that will result from the query.

To prepare the Word document for the query:

1 Insert a page break at the end of the document, after the linked object.

2 Type the following paragraph:
The following stores have agreed to carry our product without reservation. The marketing team will contact production and arrange for the first shipment of fat-free potato chips to arrive next month.

3 Press (ENTER) three times.

4 Save UPDATE.DOC.

Now you are ready to designate the database that will be the source of the data.

To establish a data source for the query:

1 Choose Database from the Insert menu.

2 Select Get Data from the Database dialog box.

3 Select MS Access Databases (*.mdb) from the List Files of Type box.

4 Select the A: drive from the Drives list box.

5 Select STORES.MDB in the File Name box.

6 Select OK to accept the data source. Make sure that Confirm Conversions is not selected on your screen.

Caution Do not select MS Query from the Open Data Source dialog box. This is not the query option you will use in this project.

7 Select the Tables tab from the Microsoft Access dialog box.

8 Select SURVEY as the table, and then select OK.

You can now set up the selection rules for the query.

To establish selection rules:

1 Select Query Options from the Database dialog box.
The screen now looks like Figure 2.15.

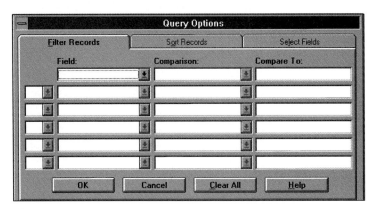

Figure 2.15

2 Select the Filter Records tab.

3 Select the field Answer from the Field List box.
The comparison list box displays Equal to.

4 Type **yes** in the first row of the column labeled Compare To.
The screen now looks like Figure 2.16. Notice that the query is not case sensitive; you can enter upper- or lowercase letters.

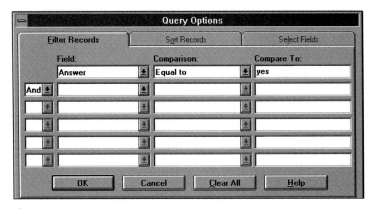

Figure 2.16

In the steps that follow you will complete the query by designating how you want the object displayed. You will then insert the object in the report.

To sort and delete records from the database:

1 Select the Sort Records tab.

2 Select Store Name from the Sort By list box.
The screen now looks like Figure 2.17.

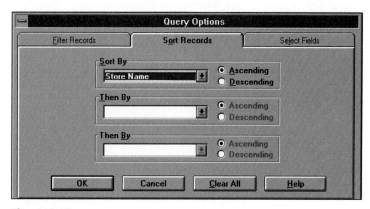

Figure 2.17

3 Select the Select Fields tab.

4 Select the ID field and then select Remove to delete the ID field from the object's displayed image.
The screen now looks like Figure 2.18.

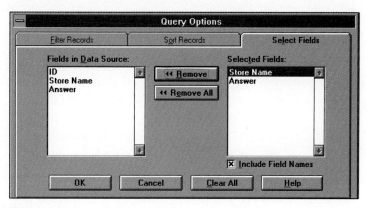

Figure 2.18

5 Select OK to accept the query.

To insert the query object:

1 Select Insert Data from the Database dialog box.

2 Select Insert Data as Field from the Insert Data dialog box, and then select OK.

3 Save UPDATE.DOC.

Word displays only the data that matches the query you created: the four stores with Yes in the Answer field, as shown in Figure 2.19.

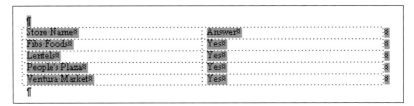

Figure 2.19

FORMATTING THE LINKED OBJECT

The linked object looks like a Word table, and you can format it as you would a Word table. You can add grid lines, create a border, and add shading to the object's image. However, any formatting, such as sizing the table columns, modifying or adding borders, and adding colors or shading, is lost each time you use (F9) to update the data. To help you maintain the formatting when you update your linked object, you will format the data with one of the Access *templates*, or patterns, provided in the Table AutoFormat feature.

To format a linked object:

1 Click once anywhere in the first complete database object on page 1, not the query object.

2 Choose Database from the Insert menu.

3 Select Get Data from the Database dialog box.

4 Select MS Access Databases (*.mdb) from the List Files of Type list box in the Open Data Source dialog box.

5 Select the A: drive and STORES.MDB, and then select OK.
Make sure that Confirm Conversions is not selected on your screen.

6 Select the Tables tab from the Microsoft Access dialog box.

7 Select SURVEY as the table, and then select OK.

8 From the Database dialog box select Table AutoFormat, as shown in Figure 2.20.

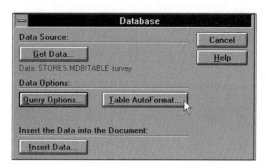

Figure 2.20

The Table AutoFormat dialog box appears.

9 Select Grid 8 from the Formats list box to designate the template.

10 Make sure the other dialog box settings are the same as those shown in Figure 2.21, and then select OK.

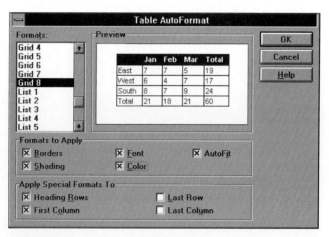

Figure 2.21

Now you can replace the unformatted object currently in the document with the newly formatted object.

To insert the formatted object:

1 Select Insert Data from the Database dialog box.

2 Select Insert Data as Field from the Insert Data dialog box, and then select OK.

The message box shown in Figure 2.22 appears, warning you that if you continue you will replace the existing linked object with a new linked object.

Figure 2.22

3 Select Yes to continue the link process.

4 Save UPDATE.DOC.

The database object now looks like Figure 2.23.

ID	Store Name	Answer
1	Fibs Foods	Yes
2	Microns Market	No
3	Sparticans	More Info
4	Lentels	Yes
5	Nathan's	Maybe
6	Sheridan Supers	More Info
7	Parker Town	Maybe
8	Breaker's Barn	No
9	Ventura Market	Yes
10	People's Plaza	Yes

Figure 2.23

5 Use Print Preview to see what the formatted object will look like when it is printed on paper.

THE NEXT STEP

What if the president's staff wants the contents of the marketing database to change? Marketing may expand the contents of the database to include the suggested retail price of the fat-free chips, the date the store wants delivery of the chips, and the number of bags sold during the first month. As the requirements for the report grow and change, you can use linking and querying to change the type of data reported and to modify how the data looks. You can sort it in a different order, include other fields, and keep it up to date.

If the database you are querying has hundreds or thousands of records, you should query only a small portion of the data. A sample of 50 to 100 records is a good test to verify that your query will really produce the data you want to see. Always test the query before you put it in your final report. Another important point to remember when you are creating an advanced query is AND and OR are not necessarily interpreted by the computer the same way you interpret the words when speaking. Suppose the president said, "Give me a report of all the stores answering yes and all the stores in Ohio." Should the report show all stores in Ohio, regardless of their answer and all stores answering yes regardless of their state or should the report contain all Ohio stores answering yes? You must clarify exactly what has been requested, because what the requester says is not necessarily what he or she really wants!

This concludes Project 2 of the integrated projects. You can exit Word now or go on to work the Study Questions, Review Exercises, and Assignments.

SUMMARY AND EXERCISES

Summary

- The target file stores the location of the linked source file, not the contents.
- The source file must be available every time the linked object is updated.
- Linking displays an image of the source file in the target file.
- When the target file contains a linked object, it does not grow as large as it does when it contains an embedded object.
- A linked database's image is displayed as a Word table.
- A linked object can be displayed as a field code, which contains the link—the location of the object.
- The Insert Data as a Field option in the Insert Data dialog box is the option that establishes the link.
- Field codes can be turned on and off by choosing Options from the Tools menu. Turning on Field Codes displays the database as a field code. Turning off Field Codes displays the database as a Word table.
- To update the linked database, you click anywhere in the displayed table and press (F9).
- You can link to a database query.
- A query can have up to six selection rules and can be sorted.
- A linked database object can be formatted using Table AutoFormat.
- Always test a query on a sample of records to verify the accuracy of the query instructions.

Key Terms and Operations

Key Terms
field code
query
selection rule
template

Operations
Create a query
Format a linked object

Get a data source
Insert data as a field
Link a database
Sort records in a query
Turn on field code display
Update a linked object's data

Study Questions

Multiple Choice

1. The main difference between a linked object and an embedded object is
   a. a linked object can never be updated in the target file.
   b. embedded objects must always have the source file available.
   c. the linked object's source file's location is stored in the target file.
   d. All of the above.

2. The linked object is displayed in the target file as
   a. an image of the source file.
   b. an icon representing the source file.
   c. a framed empty box.
   d. an image of the target file.

3. The field code contains
   a. the list of fields in the database object.
   b. the database data in encrypted form.
   c. a password needed to access the linked object.
   d. the location of the database source file.

4. You should link an object when
   a. you don't need the source file to update the object.
   b. you want the target file's byte size to remain as small as possible.
   c. the source file is not on a network.
   d. the target file is on a network.

5. To insert an Access database as a linked object you
   a. use the copy and paste method to create the link.
   b. choose Object from the Insert menu.
   c. choose Database from the Insert menu.
   d. always use the embed method.

6. If you want to insert an Access database as a linked object you must
   a. select Insert Data as Field from the Insert Data dialog box.
   b. never select Insert Data as Field from the Insert Data dialog box.
   c. always choose Options from the Tools menu to turn field codes on.
   d. first create a Word table to hold the database data.

7. To view the linked object's data you must
   a. use Print Preview to see how the data will look when it prints.
   b. insert the database as a Picture from the Insert menu.
   c. use the Zoom feature of Word to magnify the field code.
   d. turn the field code display off by choosing Options from the Tools menu.

8. To update a linked database object you will
   a. re-establish the link by deleting the old object and inserting the database again.
   b. select AutoUpdate from the Database dialog box.
   c. double-click the insertion point in the linked database object to make the changes.
   d. position the insertion point in the database object and press (F9)

9. A query
   a. must be made in Access before the linked object is created.
   b. must be repeated manually every time you update the database object.
   c. can be created through the Query Options dialog box.
   d. can be created through MS Query if Access is not available.

10. To sort a query, Word uses
    a. the ASCII standard rules of sorting.
    b. the ANSI standard rules of sorting.
    c. the Excel sort feature.
    d. the ACQV standard rules of alphabetizing.

Short Answer

1. When a database is linked to a target file, what does the target file actually store?

2. What is the field code?

3. When should you use link to create an object instead of embed?

4. How does linking affect the size of the target file?

5. What Word option changes the way the image of the database is displayed in the document?

6. How do you update the database object after it has been linked to the document?

7. What option do you use to format the database object with colors and borders?

8. What is the purpose of a query?

9. What are the three steps involved in creating a selection rule?

10. How many selection rules can you use when you create a query?

For Discussion

1. Explain what happens when an object is linked to a target file.

2. What is a field code? Why is it important?

3. Explain which Word option actually creates the link. How does this relate to turning field codes on and off?

4. Explain what a query is. Why is it important to test your queries with sample data? What would happen in this integrated project if the president's staff saw incorrect data in the report? How would that affect their business decisions?

5. What do you need to remember when someone asks you to build an advanced query?

Review Exercises

Linking a Query

Save UPDATE.DOC as QUERY.DOC and create another linked database at the end of QUERY.DOC. This time, insert a query to display all stores that answered no to the survey question. Display the image as a table, not a field code. Add an opening paragraph to identify this new table in the report. Your new query object and text should resemble Figure 2.24.

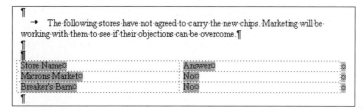

Figure 2.24

Formatting a Linked Database Object

Create another linked database and format it using the AutoFormat feature. The query should display all stores that answered maybe to the survey. Do not display the store's ID in the object. Choose one of the format templates available, and display the table in color. Save your updated document as LINKED.DOC. Use Print Preview to see what the object will look like when it prints.

Assignments

Creating an Advanced Query

In Access, add new fields to the SURVEY table in the STORES database, as shown in Table 2.2.

Table 2.2

Field Name	Data Type	Description	Field Size
Region	Text	Region of US	10
Years	Number	Length of time in business	Double
Zip Code	Number	Postal Code	Double

Update the data in the SURVEY table as shown in Figure 2.25. Use the AutoFormat feature to create a pleasing color effect.

ID	Store Name	Answer	Region	Years	Zip Code
1	Fibs Foods	Yes	Western	10	94632
2	Microns Market	Yes	Western	3	87555
3	Sparticans	Yes	South	15	76111
4	Lentels	Yes	North	4	14088
5	Nathan's	Yes	Western	20	92662
6	Sheridan Supers	Yes	Western	2	94773
7	Parker Town	Yes	South	13	74223
8	Breaker's Barn	Yes	North	25	15445
9	Ventura Market	Yes	Eastern	16	22998
10	People's Plaza	Yes	Eastern	20	22075
(Counter)				0	0

Figure 2.25

Suppose the president called you and said, "Create a report showing all stores that said yes they would carry the new product, but only display them if they are in states in the western region of the country. And, if a store has been in business less than 5 years, I don't want it on the report." This requires an advanced query. Create a new Word document named ADVANCE.DOC and link to the president's new query. Sort the records by store name in descending order. Do not display the store ID. Your report should resemble Figure 2.26.

FAT-FREE POTATO CHIP SURVEY REPORT

At the request of the president, this report queried the STORES database kept by Marketing. This report is based upon the following:

- All stores agreeing to carry the new product
- In the Western region
- No store which has been in business less than 5 years

Store Name	Answer	Region	Years	Zip Code
Nathan's	Yes	Western	20	92662
Fibs Foods	Yes	Western	10	94632

Figure 2.26

Querying a Range of Values

The president wants one last query. Save ADVANCE.DOC as ZIPCODE.DOC. Modify the report, and create a query that will eliminate all stores with a zip code of 50000 through 80000. Your report should resemble Figure 2.27.

FAT-FREE POTATO CHIP SURVEY REPORT

At the request of the president, this report queried the STORES database kept by Marketing. This report is based upon the following:

Σ All stores with a zip code between 50000 and 80000.

Store Name	Answer	Region	Years	Zip Code
Sheridan Supers	Yes	Western	2	94773
Fibs Foods	Yes	Western	10	94632
Nathan's	Yes	Western	20	92662
Microns Market	Yes	Western	3	87555
Ventura Market	Yes	Eastern	16	22998
People's Plaza	Yes	Eastern	20	22075
Breaker's Barn	Yes	North	25	15445
Lentels	Yes	North	4	14088

Figure 2.27

PART VII

PowerPoint 4

Overview

Objectives

After completing this overview, you should be able to:

▶ Start PowerPoint

▶ Describe the components of the PowerPoint screen

▶ Execute commands using menus and toolbars

▶ Navigate dialog boxes

▶ Access on-screen Help

▶ Exit PowerPoint

In the past an articulate and substantive presentation, delivered from a podium with the help of notes, was sufficient to capture and hold the attention of your audience. Today's listeners, however, have grown accustomed to speakers conveying their key points by highly visual means, such as presentations supported by professional graphics, animated slide shows, and coordinated handouts.

The technology is now in place to develop computer-generated and computer-controlled presentations. A powerful microcomputer, color monitor, and projection device comprise the necessary equipment for on-screen presentations. Letter-quality printers allow you to produce overheads when a projection system is unavailable. Add an easy-to-use presentation graphics program and you can quickly develop professional, eye-catching presentations.

USING A PRESENTATION GRAPHICS PROGRAM

A *presentation graphics program* is a software tool you use to develop professional-looking presentations in the form of paper copies, overhead transparencies, 35mm slides, and automated slide shows. This type of program offers many features to help you develop the content of your presentation, such as outlining, word processing, drawing, charting, and spell-checking. You can polish your final product by adding background designs and color. Within seconds you can also generate an outline of your presentation and audience handouts that duplicate several slides on each page.

USING POWERPOINT 4.0

Microsoft PowerPoint is among the best-selling presentation graphics programs in the world. Using this program you can quickly and easily display text in bulleted lists as well as add art, tables, or business graphs to the slides. PowerPoint includes *AutoContent Wizard,* which helps you set up a basic theme for the presentation and guides you through the steps to create all the slides. This wizard provides suggested outlines for common types of presentations, such as sales reports, training programs, and news bulletins, that you can adapt to reflect your ideas. Figure 0.1 illustrates several slides created using AutoContent Wizard.

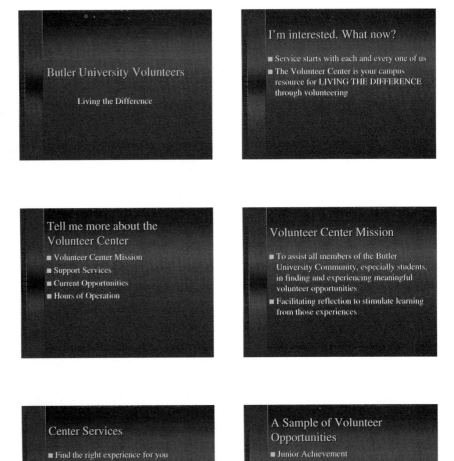

Figure 0.1

You can also use *Pick a Look Wizard* to choose among 57 predefined background settings; determine the type of output, such as 35mm slides or an on-screen presentation; and specify types of printouts, including speaker's notes and audience handout pages. Figure 0.2 illustrates several slides created using Pick a Look Wizard.

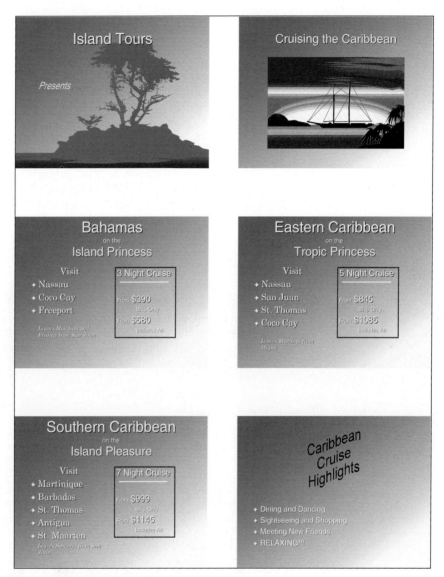

Figure 0.2

If a suggested outline or predefined setting does not meet your needs, you can also build a professional-looking presentation from scratch.

A Note to the Student

The projects in this module assume that your system is equipped with a mouse and that you are comfortable working in a Windows environment. For a quick refresher of Windows terms and techniques, you might want to review the *Introduction to Windows* segment provided at the beginning of this module.

Because PowerPoint allows you to customize the work area, the screen displays on your system may vary slightly from the figures in this module. For example, PowerPoint allows you to display one or more toolbars on your screen. A **toolbar** contains buttons representing commands that can be executed by positioning the mouse pointer and clicking the button. Figures in the module usually show only the Standard, Formatting, and Drawing toolbars provided by PowerPoint, but you may have set a different combination to display.

The projects in this module present several popular applications for presentation graphics. We suggest that you first read this overview to learn about basic PowerPoint screens and PowerPoint's powerful Help feature. Then, as you work through Projects 1 and 2 in sequence, you will use AutoContent Wizard to create a presentation on volunteerism. In the process you will learn to enter and edit text as well as save and print your slides. You can then turn your attention to creating a presentation promoting Caribbean cruises: In Project 3 you will learn to use Pick a Look Wizard and position text, and in Project 4 you will add shapes, draw lines, and insert clip art. You might then proceed to Project 5 so that you know how to present an on-screen slide show. Projects 6–8, which discuss graphs, tables, and charts, may be worked through in any order. Let's begin!

Starting PowerPoint

You can start PowerPoint from the Microsoft PowerPoint group window, Microsoft Office group window, or the Microsoft Office toolbar. Your PowerPoint software may also be installed in a different window, such as one named Applications or PowerPoint. Figure 0.3 shows the PowerPoint icon within the Microsoft Office group window.

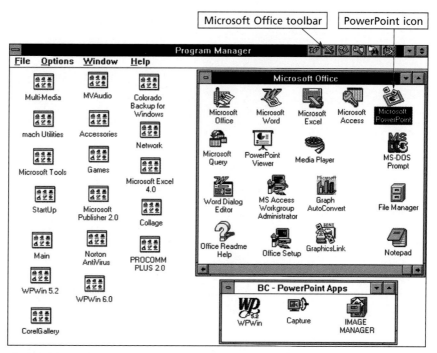

Figure 0.3

An *icon* is an on-screen symbol that represents a program file, data file, or some other function. You can select an icon by positioning the mouse pointer on the symbol and clicking the left mouse button.

Reminder The icons on your screen will likely vary from those shown in Figure 0.3.

If Microsoft Office software is installed on your system, you will see the Microsoft Office toolbar in the upper-right corner of the screen. By clicking the appropriate icon in this toolbar, you can start other Microsoft applications such as Word (word processing), Excel (spreadsheet), and Access (database).

After selecting the PowerPoint icon you will see a Tip of the Day dialog box, unless this feature has been turned off. You can read the information and view additional tips if you choose, and then you can select OK to see the initial Microsoft PowerPoint screen shown in Figure 0.4.

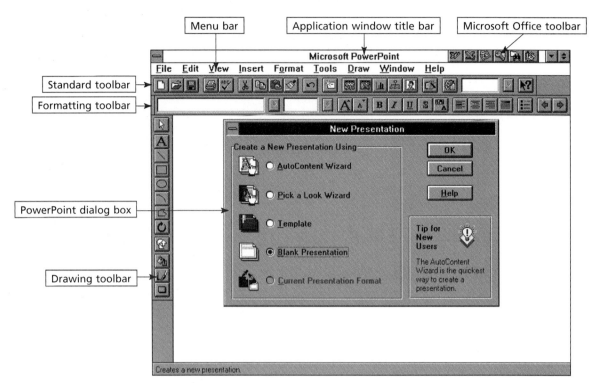

Figure 0.4

The application window title bar indicates you are using Microsoft PowerPoint. As soon as you save a presentation to disk or open an existing presentation, the name of the presentation file also appears in the title bar.

The *menu bar*, located just below the title bar, is a horizontal listing of PowerPoint commands. Selecting an option on the menu bar causes related commands to appear in a *pull-down menu,* in which each new option is listed below the previous one.

When you start PowerPoint for the first time, several toolbars appear on the screen, as shown in Figure 0.4. You decide which of the toolbars you want to display and where they will appear on-screen, as described later in the Overview. Clicking an icon on a toolbar executes the associated PowerPoint command.

The PowerPoint dialog box occupies most of the remainder of the screen. A *dialog box* appears whenever additional information is needed to complete a task. Why don't you take a look at this screen for yourself? In the steps that follow, you will start the PowerPoint program.

To start PowerPoint:

1 Open the window containing the PowerPoint icon.
The PowerPoint icon shown in Figure 0.3 appears.

2 Double-click the PowerPoint icon.
After a brief display showing copyright information, the Microsoft PowerPoint screen shown in Figure 0.4 appears. If a Tip of the Day dialog box appears instead, select OK to remove it.

USING MENUS AND DIALOG BOXES

Tip If you are already familiar with using menus and dialog boxes in another Windows product, you might want to skip this section and continue with the section called "Using Toolbars."

PowerPoint includes a powerful set of commands grouped within the nine options in the menu bar shown in Figure 0.5. Choosing an option on a menu bar displays a pull-down menu in which options are arranged vertically—each additional option appears beneath the previous one.

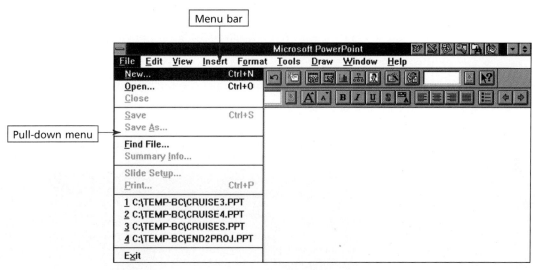

Figure 0.5

Options that appear dimmed, such as Close and Save in Figure 0.5, are not currently available. Choosing an option followed by three dots (...) opens a dialog box. One letter of every menu, called a mnemonic letter, is underlined. You can choose a menu bar option by using a mouse to click the option name, by pressing ⒜ᴸᵀ in combination with the mnemonic letter, or by pressing ⒡¹⁰ and then pointing to the selection from the keyboard (pressing arrow keys to select the desired option and then pressing ⒠ⁿᵗᵉʳ). You can choose a pull-down menu option by using the mouse to click the option name, by typing the mnemonic letter, or by pointing to the selection from the keyboard.

For some common command sequences, PowerPoint has assigned a key or key combination. Using these *shortcut keys* (sometimes called accelerator keys), you can bypass several menu selections. For example, four shortcut keys are available for file-management tasks, such as ⒞ᵀᴿᴸ+O to open a file and ⒞ᵀᴿᴸ+P to print. If a shortcut key is available, it appears to the right of its associated command in a pull-down menu (see Figure 0.5).

Tip If you start to choose from menus and do not wish to continue, you can click the left mouse button after positioning the mouse pointer anywhere outside the menu, or you can press (ESC) one or more times.

Choosing a command generally opens a dialog box, which gives you the opportunity to provide additional information for completing a task. You can select a dialog box option by positioning the mouse pointer and clicking the left mouse button or by pressing (TAB) until the desired option is highlighted and then pressing (ENTER).

Some options within a dialog box appear in sets called *radio buttons.* These options are so named because, as on a radio, you can specify only one choice from a set of items. For example, look again at the Power-Point dialog box shown in Figure 0.4, and note the five options preceded by circles. You may select only one of the options at a time, such as using AutoContent Wizard or opening an existing presentation. In Figure 0.4, Blank Presentation is selected.

Some dialog boxes, like the one shown in Figure 0.6, display more information and require additional interaction.

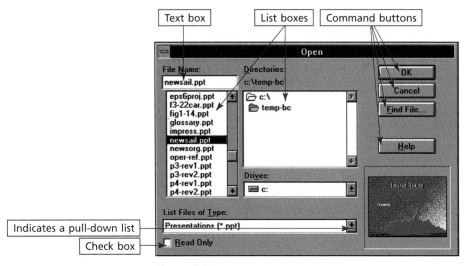

Figure 0.6

The upper-right corner of a dialog box, like the one shown in Figure 0.6, usually contains one or more ***command buttons,*** which you can select to execute the named operation. If an ellipsis (...) appears after the name in a command button, selecting that button opens another dialog box. OK, Cancel, Find File, and Help are the command buttons shown in Figure 0.6.

You will use a ***text box*** to type information such as the name of a file. ***List boxes*** display alphabetized lists of choices. In Figure 0.6 the list box in the middle of the screen shows the directories that exist on the current disk drive. The list box below the File Name text box displays the names of files stored in the current directory.

You can use a **check box** to turn an option on or off. An X within the box indicates an option is on. The absence of an X in a check box indicates an option is off. In Figure 0.6, for example, the Read Only feature is not selected, which means that you can edit an existing presentation and store it under its current name. If Read Only were selected, you would not be able to save changes using the same file name.

An underscored down arrow in a dialog box indicates the existence of a **pull-down list,** which shows related options. If you were to select the arrow in the Drives box shown in Figure 0.6, you would see a list of the disk drives available on your computer.

The PowerPoint dialog box should still be displayed on your screen from the previous steps. Let's take a look at another dialog box. In the process you will make several selections from menus.

To view another dialog box:

1 Select Cancel (a command button) to close the PowerPoint dialog box and display a blank screen.

2 Choose File from the menu bar.
The File pull-down menu shown in Figure 0.5 appears.

3 Choose Open from the File pull-down menu.
The Open dialog box shown in Figure 0.6 appears.

To view the contents of a pull-down list:

1 Click the underscored arrow in the Drives box.
A list of the drives available on your computer system appears.

2 Click anywhere on the dialog box surface to close the pull-down list.

3 Select Cancel.

> **Tip** If necessary, you can use a keyboard instead of a mouse for most PowerPoint activities. For example, after pressing (TAB) to move to the Drives section of the dialog box, you would press (↓) to view the list of drives.

USING TOOLBARS

The six toolbars shown in Figure 0.7 provide quick access to PowerPoint commands. Each toolbar contains buttons representing commands, each of which can be executed by clicking the appropriate button.

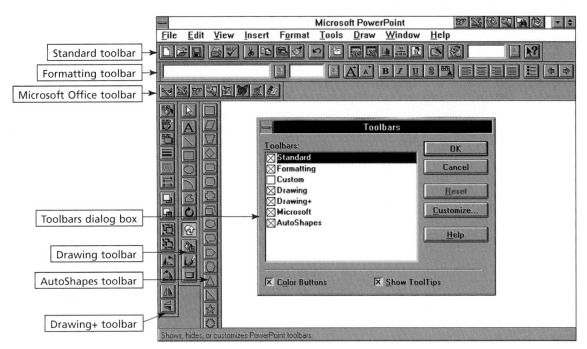

Standard toolbar →

Formatting toolbar →

Microsoft Office toolbar →

Toolbars dialog box

Drawing toolbar

AutoShapes toolbar

Drawing+ toolbar

Figure 0.7

Some buttons replace two or more menu selections. For example, clicking the open file folder button (the second button on the standard toolbar) can substitute for choosing Open from the File menu. When you have such a choice in this module, you will see a picture of the button in the left margin next to the associated step describing the menu sequence. The button will only be shown the first time you can use it in a project.

Other commands, like the ones on the AutoShapes toolbar, can be applied only by using the toolbar. When you first start PowerPoint and open a presentation, the Standard and Formatting toolbars are displayed just below the menu bar, and the Drawing toolbar is displayed vertically on the left side of the window, as shown in Figure 0.4. You can, however, display any or all toolbars on your screen, as well as drag them to different locations. When you exit the program, PowerPoint remembers which toolbars were active and displays the same arrangement when you access PowerPoint again.

Tip If you do not know the purpose of each button, you can choose Toolbars from the View menu and select the Show ToolTips check box in the Toolbars dialog box. When this feature is active, the name of the button appears each time the mouse pointer rests on the button.

GETTING ON-SCREEN HELP

PowerPoint provides information about the program on the screen. This information can either be ***context-sensitive Help,*** which provides information about the operation in progress, or information of a more general nature. You can display context-sensitive Help about the current task by selecting the Help command button in a dialog box or by pressing (F1). For example, if you were to select Help or press (F1) after choosing Toolbars from the View menu, you would see information about the Toolbars dialog box. Other help is available through options on the Help menu and a Help button, as described in the following sections.

Using Contents to Get Help

From the PowerPoint Help Contents screen, as shown in Figure 0.8, you can choose among four options on a menu bar, select among seven buttons to navigate the Help system, press (F1) to learn how to use Help, or select one of three icons to display the information described in the center of the screen.

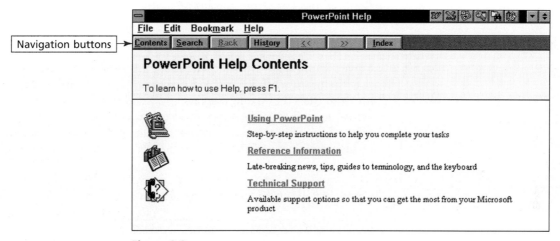

Figure 0.8

In the following steps, you will view several screens accessed through the PowerPoint Help Contents screen. By exploring other topics on your own, you will have a better idea of the help available on-screen.

To learn how to use Help:

1 Choose Contents from the Help menu (or press (F1)).
The PowerPoint Help Contents screen appears as shown in Figure 0.8.

2 Press (F1) to learn how to use Help.

3 Read the information on how to choose a help topic, and then select Help Basics.

4 View other Help topics of your choice.

5 Choose Exit from the PowerPoint Help File menu.

Tip Clicking the Back button moves you back through Help screens one at a time. Choosing Exit from the PowerPoint Help File menu terminates the Help session immediately.

To display information represented by an icon:

1 Choose Contents from the Help menu (or press (F1)).

2 Click the icon to the left of *Using PowerPoint*.
A window appears in which topics are arranged according to the chapters in the *PowerPoint User's Guide*.

3 Scroll through the list of topics under each of the seven chapters.

4 Select one or more topics within any chapter to view the associated information.

5 Choose Exit from the PowerPoint Help File menu.

Using Search to Get Help

When you don't know the exact name of the feature about which you need help, PowerPoint will help you search. Choosing Search for Help on from the Help menu displays the Search dialog box. If Help is already active, selecting the Search button below the menu bar produces the same effect. Instructions to use the box appear near the top and in the middle, as shown in Figure 0.9.

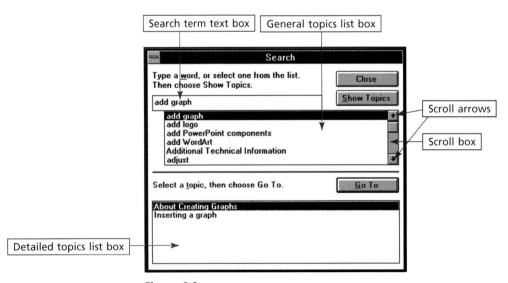

Figure 0.9

As you start to type your search word or phrase, PowerPoint displays an alphabetized list of topics that start with the same letters. If you see the general topic you have in mind, you can select Show Topics to view a more detailed list, if available. In the following steps you will use this feature to display information about adding a graph to a PowerPoint presentation.

To use the Search feature of on-screen Help:

1 Choose Search for Help on from the Help menu.
A blank Search dialog box appears.

2 Type **add graph** in the search term text box.
Notice that you only have to type *add g* to select the term.

3 Select Show Topics.
The related topics appear as shown in Figure 0.9. Shading indicates the current selection, which you can change by clicking another topic.

4 Select Go To to display information on the selected topic (*About Creating Graphs*).

5 Choose Exit from the PowerPoint Help File menu.

Using Index to Get Help

If you know the exact name of the feature about which you need help, you can look up information about the topic by choosing Index from the Help menu. Instructions to use the Index feature appear below a horizontal list of letter buttons, as shown in Figure 0.10.

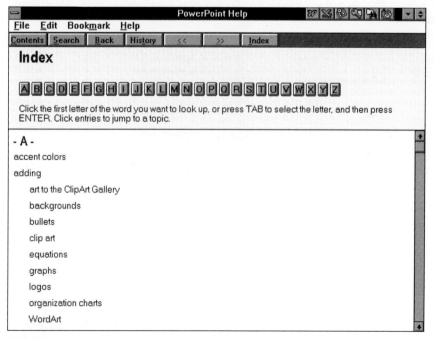

Figure 0.10

After you select the first letter of the word you want to look up, PowerPoint displays an alphabetized list of topics that start with the same letter. If the list is longer than the current screen display, you can use the scroll bar to view the complete list of topics. In the following steps you will use this feature to display information about ToolTips.

To use the Index feature of on-screen Help:

1 Choose Index from the Help menu.
The Index screen shown in Figure 0.10 appears.

2 Click the T button.

3 Use the scroll bar to bring the word *ToolTips* into view.

4 Click ToolTips.
Information about ToolTips appears.

5 Choose Exit from the PowerPoint Help File menu.

Using Cue Cards to Get Help

For a few common but somewhat intricate procedures, PowerPoint provides a *cue card,* which gives detailed instructions on how to accomplish the task. Cue cards stay on the screen until you close them. Figure 0.11 shows the cue card list that appears after you choose Cue Cards from the Help menu.

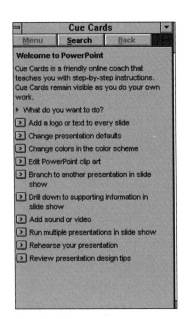

Figure 0.11

To tell PowerPoint what you want to do, click the button to the left of the desired procedure. One or more cue cards will lead you through the process step by step. You will not use cue cards in this module because detailed instructions are provided in the projects. On your own, however, you might find that cue cards make it easier to complete unfamiliar tasks.

Using the Help Button

If you are using a mouse, PowerPoint provides a Help button, which allows you to view information about a command or window item on the screen. To do this, you must first click Help at the right end of the Standard toolbar. The pointer changes to an arrow with a question mark. You then position the pointer on the item you would like to know more about, and click again. In the following steps you will use the Help button to view information about the Open button.

To use the Help button:

 1 Click the Help button at the right end of the Standard toolbar. The mouse pointer changes to an arrow with a question mark.

2 Move the pointer until it rests on the Open button (an open folder symbol near the left end of the Standard toolbar).

3 Click the left mouse button.
Information about opening a presentation appears on the Help screen.

4 Choose Exit from the PowerPoint Help File menu.

EXITING POWERPOINT

When you finish working on a presentation, you can save or discard your changes and then continue developing another presentation or exit Power-Point. You will start the process to leave the current presentation by choosing one of several options (or the corresponding shortcut keys) on the File menu shown in Figure 0.5.

You will choose Close if you want to close the current presentation but continue working in PowerPoint. You will choose Exit if you want to quit working in PowerPoint. Whichever option you select, you will be prompted to save a presentation if it contains any unsaved changes (saving a presentation is discussed in Project 1).

To exit PowerPoint:

1 Choose Exit from the File menu.

The Next Step

At this point you have a lot of information about the PowerPoint work environment. As you complete subsequent projects, you will have many opportunities to choose from menus, select buttons, and indicate your preferences in dialog boxes. However, these step-by-step instructions do not include using on-screen Help. Starting now, get in the habit of viewing on-screen Help about each new topic you encounter.

You might also take another look at PowerPoint features, some of which were described in the opening paragraphs of this overview. Rather than reread those sections, however, choose Quick Preview from the Help menu to view a short, animated, attention-grabbing presentation on-screen.

This concludes the Overview. You can either exit PowerPoint, go on to work the Study Questions, or proceed to Project 1.

SUMMARY AND EXERCISES

Summary

- PowerPoint is an outstanding presentation graphics program you can use to develop professional-looking presentations in the form of paper copies, overhead transparencies, 35mm slides, and automated slide shows.
- PowerPoint includes AutoContent Wizard that guides you through the steps to create multiple slides around a common theme, and Pick a Look Wizard to choose background settings and output forms.
- You can execute commands using menu bars, pull-down menus, and toolbar buttons. Quite often you must also specify settings in a dialog box to complete an operation.
- Whenever you want information about some feature of PowerPoint, you can use the extensive on-screen Help feature.

Key Terms and Operations

Key Terms
AutoContent Wizard
check box
command button
context-sensitive Help
cue card
dialog box
icon
list box
menu bar
Pick a Look Wizard
pull-down list

presentation graphics program
pull-down menu
radio button
shortcut keys
text box
toolbar

Operations
Start PowerPoint
Exit PowerPoint
Get on-screen Help

Study Questions

Multiple Choice

1. Which of the following is not a method to choose a menu bar option?
   a. Using a mouse to click the name of the option.
   b. Pressing (CTRL) in combination with the mnemonic letter.
   c. Pressing (F10) and then pointing to the selection from the keyboard.
   d. All of the above are methods to choose a menu bar option.

2. Which of the following is not a true statement about toolbars?
   a. A toolbar can be positioned vertically or horizontally on the screen.
   b. A toolbar can be moved and sized.
   c. You can select a button on a toolbar using a mouse or the keyboard.
   d. All of the above.

3. Which type of box will you use to turn an option on or off?
   a. text box
   b. check box
   c. list box
   d. pull-down box

4. Which of the following is not a PowerPoint toolbar?
   a. Standard
   b. Formatting
   c. Drawshapes
   d. All of the above are PowerPoint toolbars.

5. Which option on the Help menu should you select if you don't know the exact name of the feature about which you need help, but you want to type in a word or phrase?
   a. Index
   b. Quick Preview
   c. Cue Cards
   d. Search for Help on

Short Answer

1. On-screen Help can be general in nature or provide information about the operation in progress. What is the term used to describe help related to the operation in progress?

2. If an option on a pull-down menu is not currently available, how does that option appear relative to options that are available?

3. If you make a mistake while choosing from menus, what key can you press one or more times to restore the appropriate screen for restarting the sequence?

4. Which PowerPoint wizard would you use to choose among predefined background settings?

5. What do you call the on-screen Help feature that gives detailed instructions on how to accomplish a task and stays on the screen while you complete the task?

For Discussion

1. Describe features generally found in presentation graphics programs. In addition to those related to appearance, include a discussion of the types of output and features that help you develop the content of a presentation.

2. You frequently have to issue commands to perform various presentation graphics functions. Explain the various ways you can issue a command using PowerPoint. Include a description of the menu structure, toolbars, and shortcut keys in your discussion.

3. PowerPoint provides quite a few buttons on seven toolbars. If you do not know the purpose of one of the buttons, what action(s) might you take to find out?

PROJECT 1: CREATING A PRESENTATION

Objectives

After completing this project, you should be able to:

▶ Create a presentation using AutoContent Wizard

▶ Save a presentation

▶ Open an existing presentation

▶ Enter and edit text in Outline view

▶ Switch among alternative views of a presentation

CASE STUDY: PROMOTING VOLUNTEERISM

Assume that you are a student actively involved with the volunteer center on your campus. You are working with the staff to increase student awareness and participation in volunteer activities coordinated by the center. Just recently the center acquired PowerPoint 4.0 for Windows software, and you see an opportunity to develop a series of slides that you or other center representatives can present during classes and meetings of student organizations.

Designing the Solution

Before you begin to develop the content of your slides, you need to decide on the length of the presentation. For example, you might allocate 15 minutes or so to make your comments and provide additional time for questions. You must also know what equipment will be available, such as an overhead projector for black-and-white transparencies or a computer with color projection capabilities for an on-screen slide show.

Next you need to plan what you want to say, using slides for visual support during your presentation. For increased readability, the slides should generally show key points in short phrases preceded by bullets. A **bullet** is a symbol, such as a solid square block or open circle, that you use to set off an item in a list. You can add detail as you speak. PowerPoint includes AutoContent Wizard, which helps you set up a basic theme for the presentation and guides you through the steps to create all the slides.

USING AUTOCONTENT WIZARD

When you access PowerPoint or start a new presentation, the PowerPoint dialog box shown in Figure 1.1 appears automatically. The tip for new users in the lower-right corner suggests that AutoContent Wizard is the quickest way to create a presentation.

Figure 1.1

Selecting AutoContent Wizard starts a four-step process in which you create a title slide and choose one of six predefined presentation outlines with which to work: Recommending a Strategy; Selling a Product, Service or Idea; Training; Reporting Progress; Communicating Bad News; and General. PowerPoint then displays content suggestions for a series of slides in outline form. You will edit the outline, adding or deleting bulleted items and adding or deleting slides.

In this project you will use the General outline in AutoContent Wizard to create slides containing text shown in bulleted lists. In subsequent projects you will learn to present ideas in columns and tables as well as add artwork, graphs, and organizational charts.

To start AutoContent Wizard:

1 Open the group window containing the PowerPoint icon.

2 Double-click the PowerPoint icon.
After a brief display showing copyright information, the PowerPoint dialog box shown in Figure 1.1 appears. If a Tip of the Day dialog box appears instead, select OK to remove that box.

3 Click the radio button in front of AutoContent Wizard if a black circle does not already appear in front of that option.

4 Select OK.
The AutoContent Wizard - Step 1 of 4 screen shown in Figure 1.2 appears.

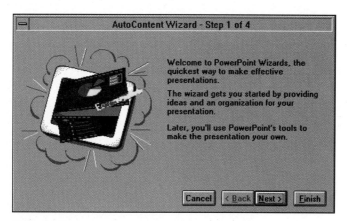

Figure 1.2

5 Select Next> or press (ENTER)
The AutoContent Wizard - Step 2 of 4 screen shown in Figure 1.3 appears. Two of the text boxes may already contain information provided by the registered owner of the program, as shown in Figure 1.3. You can change this text as described later.

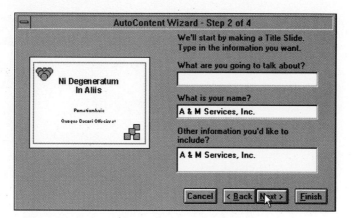

Figure 1.3

To create a title slide:

1 Select the What are you going to talk about? text box if the flashing cursor does not already appear there.

Tip You can select a box by clicking within the box or by pressing (TAB) until the box is highlighted.

2 Type **Butler University Volunteers** (do not press (ENTER)).

Quick Fix If you accidentally press (ENTER) and the AutoContent Wizard - Step 3 of 4 screen appears, click <Back to return to the preceding screen.

3 Select the What is your name? text box.

4 Press (DEL) or (BKSP) until existing characters in the text box disappear.

5 Type **Living the Difference**

Tip You do not need to show a name in this box, which appears as the second line in the slide. In this case, for example, the slides will be used by more than one presenter.

6 Select the Other information you'd like to include? text box.

7 Press (DEL) or (BKSP) until existing characters in the text box disappear.
The text for your title slide should appear as shown in Figure 1.4. If necessary, select a text box and make changes.

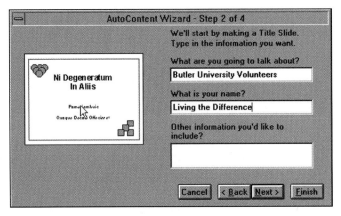

Figure 1.4

8 Select Next>
The AutoContent Wizard - Step 3 of 4 screen shown in Figure 1.5 appears.

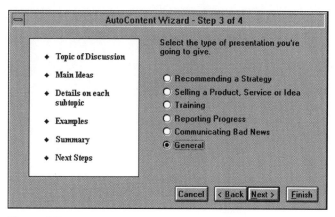

Figure 1.5

 ## To select a predefined presentation type:

1 Select General if that option is not already selected.
The bulleted list in the left side of the dialog box is a condensed version of the General outline.

2 Select each presentation radio button one at a time to view those outlines.

3 Select General.

4 Select Next> or press (ENTER)
The AutoContent Wizard - Step 4 of 4 screen appears as shown in Figure 1.6. At this point you can still change the type of presentation by selecting <Back.

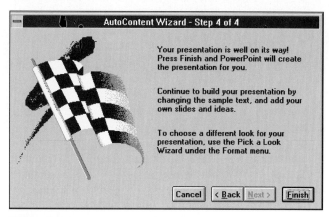

Figure 1.6

5 Select Finish or press (ENTER)
The General outline of your presentation appears on the screen as shown in Figure 1.7.

Tip If a cue card appears also, remove the information by clicking the minus sign in the upper-left corner of the cue card window and then choosing Close from the pull-down menu.

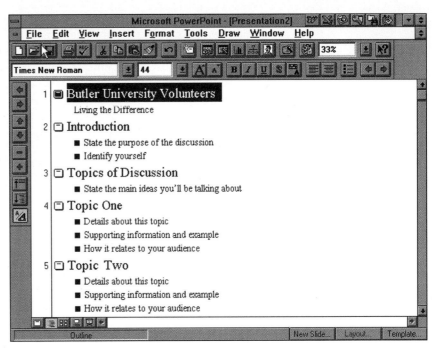

Figure 1.7

Caution Once you have finished using AutoContent Wizard, the outline that results can only be changed by editing. To select a different outline, you must start a new presentation using AutoContent Wizard.

SAVING A PRESENTATION

During an editing session, changes to the contents of a presentation are stored in the computer's internal memory (often called RAM, for random access memory). However, the ability to save a presentation on disk is the real power of a presentation graphics program or any computer program. Once saved on disk, the presentation may be called back on the screen, changed, and saved again. If you develop a habit of frequently saving on disk the presentation you are editing, you will save substantial retyping time should a power outage occur during a work session.

When you save a file, you must specify both its name and location on disk. The file name can contain one to eight characters without spaces. The program supplies the three-character extension .PPT, identifying a PowerPoint presentation.

A *path* describes the route PowerPoint must follow to locate a presentation on disk. This route includes a *disk drive* specification and may include one or more *directories* separated by backslashes. A *disk drive* writes data to and reads data from a disk. A letter designates a specific disk drive, such as disk drive A, which manages data on a removable 3½- or 5¼-inch disk, or disk drive C, which manages data on a hard disk sealed inside the computer. A *directory* provides a way to group related files.

Because most school computer labs do not allow you to save files on the hard disk or network, the illustrations in this module assume that you are saving your files on a disk in drive A. If you prefer to save a presentation in a different location, in the following numbered steps, replace any drive A designation with the drive you want.

If you want to save a presentation on disk and continue to work on the presentation, you can select the Save button, or you can choose the Save or Save As command on the File menu. You will choose Save to replace the copy of a presentation on disk with the version of the presentation on the screen. When you save a presentation for the first time, PowerPoint automatically displays the Save As dialog box shown in Figure 1.8, regardless of whether you chose Save or Save As from the File menu.

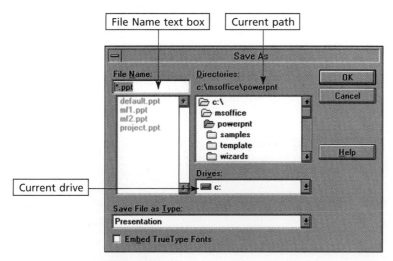

Figure 1.8

Tip You also can choose the Save As command if the current presentation has been saved previously, but you want to change its name or its storage location on disk.

Caution If you select the Save button or choose the Save command on the File menu, the presentation on the screen is automatically saved under its current name. You do not have an opportunity to verify the file name.

After you specify a file name and location, a Summary Info dialog box appears, giving you the opportunity to store additional information about the subject and author of the presentation. This information will not appear in the presentation. If you create a lot of presentations or have multiple users on the computer, it is a good practice to complete this dialog box.

Tip You can access this dialog box to modify the information by choosing Summary Info from the File menu.

A new presentation is labeled Presentation until you save it. Thereafter, the name of the presentation displays in uppercase letters within square brackets in the title bar at the top of the screen. In the following steps you will save the initial general outline for the presentation on promoting volunteerism.

Tip When you see a button or icon next to a numbered step, you can select that button or icon on your screen to execute the instructions in the step.

To save a presentation and close the file:

1 Choose Save from the File menu.
The Save As dialog box shown in Figure 1.8 appears.

2 Click the drive icon or the underscored down arrow in the Drives box.
A pull-down list of the drives attached to your computer appears, similar to the one shown in Figure 1.9.

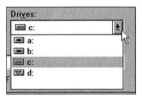

Figure 1.9

3 Select a:
The pull-down list disappears, and a: appears in the Drives box.

Reminder Substitute the appropriate drive and path if you are saving your presentation in another location.

4 Select the File Name text box in the upper-left corner of the Save As dialog box.

5 Delete the asterisk and type **service**
Check that the name SERVICE.PPT appears in the File Name text box.

6 Select OK or press (ENTER)
After a brief delay, the Summary Info dialog box appears.

7 Select Subject and type **Volunteerism**

8 Select Author and type your name.
Compare your title, subject, and author information to that shown in Figure 1.10. Make changes as necessary.

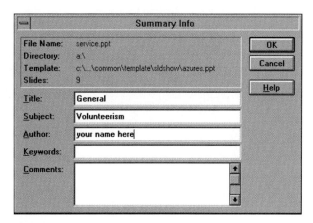

Figure 1.10

9 Select OK or press (ENTER) to complete saving the file and to restore the display of the presentation outline.

Your presentation should now be saved under the name SERVICE.PPT on the disk in drive A. [SERVICE.PPT] appears in the title bar at the top of the screen.

10 Choose Close from the File menu to close the presentation.

EXIT   If necessary, you can exit PowerPoint now and continue this project later.

OPENING A PRESENTATION

A major advantage of a presentation graphics program is the ability to store presentations on disk and access them again for editing and viewing. To open a previously stored presentation, you will select the Open button, choose the Open command on the File menu, or select Open an Existing Presentation from the PowerPoint dialog box. The Open dialog box appears, similar to the one shown in Figure 1.11.

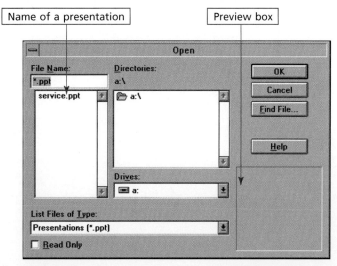

Figure 1.11

Recall that you must specify a drive, path, and file name in a dialog box in order to *save* a file. You will work with the same specifications to *open* a file. After you select a presentation in the File Name text box, the first slide appears in the preview box, allowing you to verify that this is the file you want. If you have many files stored on disk, you can use the Find File command to locate the one you want quickly.

Tip With PowerPoint you can use files you created in other programs. For example, if you typed an outline using Word (Microsoft's word processor), you can open the file in PowerPoint. Each heading becomes a slide, and subtopics under each heading appear in bulleted lists.

You can open several presentations at a time. The one you are currently working on, called the ***active presentation***, appears in the top window. To see a list of open presentations, you can choose Window from the menu bar.

In the following steps you will open the SERVICE.PPT presentation, which you set up using AutoContent Wizard earlier in the project. Remember to substitute the correct drive and directory if you did not store this file on a disk in drive A.

To open an existing presentation:

1 Click Open in the Standard toolbar.
The Open dialog box appears, similar to the one shown in Figure 1.11.

Tip If you previously exited PowerPoint, you can load the program and select Open an Existing Presentation from the PowerPoint dialog box to produce the same result.

2 Select the drive on which you are storing your PowerPoint files.

3 Select SERVICE.PPT in the list of file names at the left side of the dialog box.
After a brief delay, the title slide of the selected presentation appears in the preview window.

4 Select OK or press (ENTER)
The selected presentation appears in Outline view, as shown in Figure 1.12.

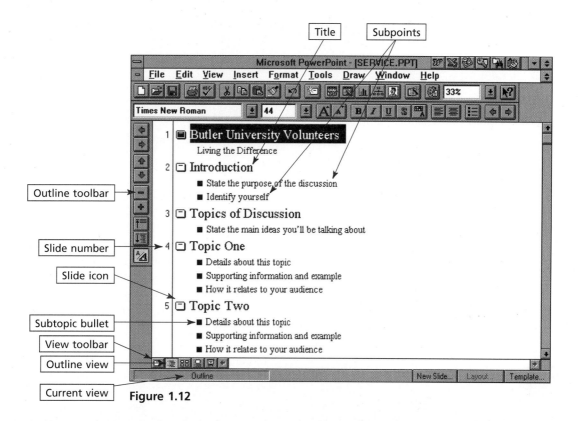

Figure 1.12

Tip If you are sure of the name of the presentation you want to open, you can double-click the desired file name in place of steps 3 and 4.

WORKING IN OUTLINE VIEW

A *view* is a way to look at the slides in a PowerPoint presentation. You can work with a presentation in any one of five views. The name of the current view appears in the lower-left corner of the screen. You can change views by clicking the appropriate icon in the View toolbar.

In **Outline view,** you work with slide titles and main text, with each additional slide appearing below the previous one, as shown in Figure 1.12. A slide icon indicates the title of the slide, and subtopic bullets precede key points. You select Outline view when you want to see the organization of your presentation, edit text, add and delete bulleted items, add and delete slides, and change the order of slides.

Using the Outline Toolbar

The Outline toolbar includes the nine buttons shown in Figure 1.13. The first four buttons help you change the arrangement of text, and the next four buttons control the level of detail shown. You can use the last button to switch between a display of *formatted text*, which shows variations in font and type size, and unformatted text.

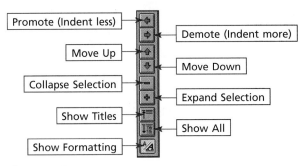

Figure 1.13

Before selecting one of the first four buttons, you must position the *insertion point* within the paragraph you want to move. The ***insertion point*** is the blinking vertical bar that marks the position where text will be inserted or deleted when you type on the keyboard. If you ***promote*** a topic, the selected text shifts left one level in the outline, and the bullet character changes to match other bullets at that level. If you ***demote*** a topic, the selected text shifts right one level in the outline, and the bullet character changes to match other bullets at that level, as you will see in Project 2. The Move Up and Move Down buttons move the paragraph containing the insertion point above the preceding item and below the next item, respectively.

You can use the Collapse Selection button to display only the title of the slide containing the insertion point. A line appears below the title, indicating the text is collapsed. The Expand Selection button expands text that has been collapsed in one slide. The next two buttons collapse all levels of text for all slides (Show Titles) and expand the outline so all levels of text for all slides appear (Show All).

In the following steps you will change the view from formatted text to unformatted text, switch to a collapsed view of the outline, and then restore the expanded display.

 ### *To display unformatted text in Outline view:*

1 Check that the volunteerism presentation (SERVICE.PPT) appears on the screen in Outline view, as shown in Figure 1.12.

2 Press (CTRL)+(HOME) if the insertion point is not at the top of the outline.

 3 Select Show Formatting on the Outline toolbar so that formatting (boldface and larger type size) disappears from the outline.
The smaller type size in the unformatted display allows you to see more of the outline on-screen.

To collapse and expand the outline:

1 Select Show Titles.
Only slide titles appear in the outline. The line beneath a title indicates that slide is collapsed.

2 Select Show All to expand the outline.

Editing Text in Outline View

Whether you use one of the predefined presentation types available through AutoContent Wizard or develop a presentation from scratch, you will find that Outline view provides an easy-to-use work surface on which to make text changes. You will edit text in Outline view in much the same way as you edit text in your favorite word processor. For example, you can delete the character preceding the insertion point by pressing (BKSP) and remove the character at the insertion point by pressing (DEL). To add text, you will simply move the insertion point to the location where you want new characters to appear and start typing.

If you want to replace an entire phrase, however, you do not have to delete the unwanted text in a separate step. Instead, you will select the block of text to replace and then start typing. The highlighted text disappears automatically as the first new character appears. You can select text using a mouse by positioning the mouse pointer at the beginning of the phrase, pressing and holding down the left mouse button, dragging the mouse pointer until the rest of the phrase is highlighted, and releasing the mouse button. In PowerPoint's Outline view you can also select all text in a subpoint by clicking its bullet or select the contents of an entire slide by clicking the slide icon (see Figure 1.12).

In the following steps you will work in Outline view to edit the presentation on promoting volunteerism that you created using AutoContent Wizard. The title slide changes are done, but the remaining topics still show AutoContent Wizard's suggested organization and hints for developing the content. For example, the General presentation form shown in Figure 1.12 suggests that after you explain the purpose of the presentation and identify yourself (slide 2), you provide an overview of the key points you intend to address (slide 3). You will now replace this outline with your own speaking points, as shown in Figure 1.14. Remember to save your work frequently.

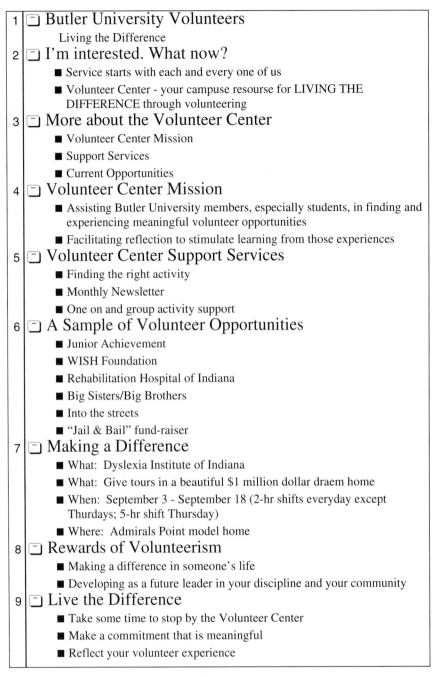

1 ▢ Butler University Volunteers
   Living the Difference

2 ▢ I'm interested. What now?
- Service starts with each and every one of us
- Volunteer Center - your campus resourse for LIVING THE DIFFERENCE through volunteering

3 ▢ More about the Volunteer Center
- Volunteer Center Mission
- Support Services
- Current Opportunities

4 ▢ Volunteer Center Mission
- Assisting Butler University members, especially students, in finding and experiencing meaningful volunteer opportunities
- Facilitating reflection to stimulate learning from those experiences

5 ▢ Volunteer Center Support Services
- Finding the right activity
- Monthly Newsletter
- One on and group activity support

6 ▢ A Sample of Volunteer Opportunities
- Junior Achievement
- WISH Foundation
- Rehabilitation Hospital of Indiana
- Big Sisters/Big Brothers
- Into the streets
- "Jail & Bail" fund-raiser

7 ▢ Making a Difference
- What: Dyslexia Institute of Indiana
- What: Give tours in a beautiful $1 million dollar draem home
- When: September 3 - September 18 (2-hr shifts everyday except Thurdays; 5-hr shift Thursday)
- Where: Admirals Point model home

8 ▢ Rewards of Volunteerism
- Making a difference in someone's life
- Developing as a future leader in your discipline and your community

9 ▢ Live the Difference
- Take some time to stop by the Volunteer Center
- Make a commitment that is meaningful
- Reflect your volunteer experience

Figure 1.14

Caution Pressing (ENTER) at the end of an outline item causes a blank new item to be inserted below. If this is not the effect you want, position the insertion point to the right of the new bullet and press (BKSP) to remove the bullet.

To edit the second slide:

1 Locate slide 2 and select the title.
The title of slide 2 appears highlighted, as shown in Figure 1.15.

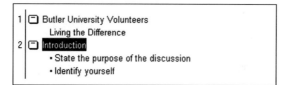

Figure 1.15

2 Type **I'm interested. What now?** (do not press (ENTER)).
The highlighted text disappears, replaced by the text you typed.

Quick Fix Pressing (ENTER) at the end of a slide's title will insert a new slide. If this happens, press (BKSP) to delete the slide and move the insertion point to the previous title.

3 Select the first bulleted subtopic in slide 2.
The subtopic *State the purpose of the discussion* appears highlighted on the screen.

Reminder Clicking the bullet preceding a subtopic automatically selects the associated text on that line. This technique cannot be used to highlight only a title line, because clicking the bullet preceding a slide's title selects all text on the slide.

4 Type **Service starts with each and every one of us** (do not press (ENTER)).

5 Select the second bulleted subtopic in slide 2.

The subtopic *Identify yourself* appears highlighted on the screen.

6 Type (including any spelling errors) **Volunteer Center - your campuse resurse for LIVING THE DIFFERENCE through volunteering** (do not press (ENTER)).
Check that slide 2 of your outline view matches the text shown in Figure 1.16. Make changes if necessary.

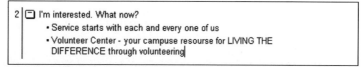

Figure 1.16

To edit the remaining slides:

1 Locate slide 3 and select the title.
The original slide title *Topics of Discussion* appears highlighted on the screen.

2 Type **More about the Volunteer Center** (do not press (ENTER)).
The new text replaces the original title.

3 Select the first bulleted subtopic.
The subtopic *State the main ideas you'll be talking about* appears highlighted on the screen.

4 Type **Volunteer Center Mission** and press (ENTER)
The new text replaces the original subtopic, and PowerPoint inserts a new blank line preceded by a bullet.

5 Type **Support Services** and press (ENTER)

6 Type **Current Opportunities** (do not press (ENTER)).
Check that the text on your slide 3 matches that shown for slide 3 in Figure 1.14. Make changes as necessary.

7 Edit the remaining slides 4 through 9 to match those shown in Figure 1.14 (be sure to delete the third bulleted item in slide 4 and include the spelling errors in slide 7).

Caution Be sure to save your work frequently during any long editing process.

8 Save the file.

EXIT If necessary, you can exit PowerPoint now and continue this project later.

SWITCHING VIEWS

In the previous section you edited a presentation in Outline view. PowerPoint provides four other views within which you can see the results of your work and make changes. You will switch views using the View toolbar shown in Figure 1.17.

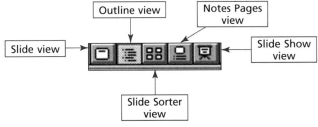

Figure 1.17

Recall that Outline view displays the entire presentation in outline form, the preferred work surface on which to make major text changes. You see one slide at a time in **Slide view**, and on this work surface you can add graphics, draw shapes, and change the slide layout in addition to editing text. In **Notes Pages view** you also see one slide at a time, but a slide occupies only the top half of the work surface. In the bottom half you can add speaker's notes.

Slide Sorter view displays reduced images (text and graphics) of all slides on a single screen. In this view you can change the order of slides as well as set timing between slides for an on-screen presentation. After making changes in this view, you can see the complete electronic presentation in **Slide Show view**, in which each slide fills the screen.

In the following steps you will view the volunteerism presentation in each view.

To look at a presentation in Slide view:

1 Load PowerPoint and open the SERVICE.PPT presentation if necessary.

2 Locate slide 1 in the Outline view.

3 Select Slide view from the View toolbar.
Slide 1 appears as shown in Figure 1.18.

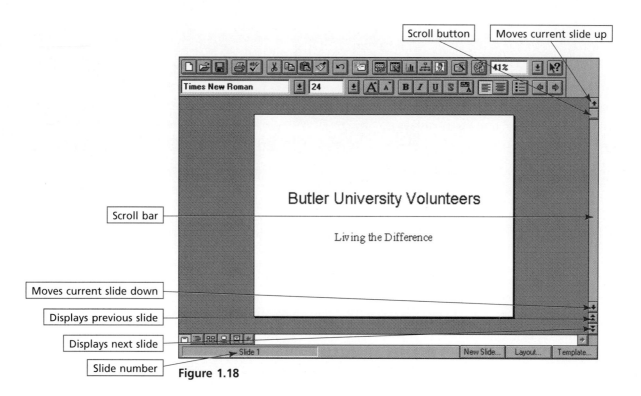

Figure 1.18

Tip You can move among the slides by clicking the double-arrow buttons at the bottom of the vertical scroll bar (up arrows to see the previous slide and down arrows to see the next slide). You can also drag the scroll button on the vertical scroll bar or press (PGUP) and (PGDN).

4 Display the next slide.
The slide number changes in the lower-left corner of the screen.

5 Continue to view the other slides.

 ### *To look at a presentation in Slide Sorter view:*

 1 Select Slide Sorter view from the View toolbar.
Slides appear three across as shown in Figure 1.19. A heavy black border indicates the current slide.

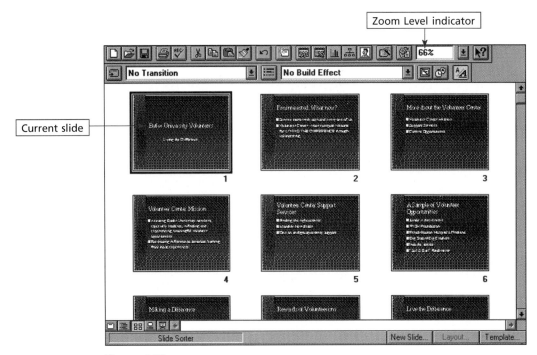

Figure 1.19

Tip Clicking the underscored down arrow to the right of the Zoom Level indicator produces a pull-down list of predefined percentages at which you can view the slides. You can select a smaller view such as 33% or a larger view such as 200%.

2 View the remaining slides using the vertical scroll bar.

3 Click slide 1 to make it the current slide.

 ### *To look at a presentation in Notes Pages view:*

 1 Select Notes Pages view from the View toolbar.

A box in which you can add speaker's notes appears below the current slide, as shown in Figure 1.20.

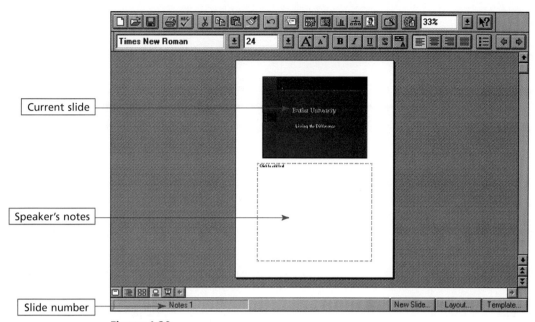

Current slide

Speaker's notes

Slide number

Figure 1.20

2 Use the vertical scroll bar to switch from slide to slide in Notes Pages view.

3 Click slide 1 to make it the current slide.

 ### *To look at a presentation in Slide Show view and then close the file:*

1 Choose Slide Show from the View menu.
The Slide Show dialog box appears as shown in Figure 1.21. Current settings indicate that you will see all slides by manually advancing to the next slide.

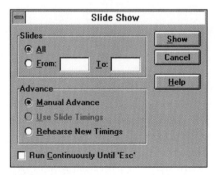

Figure 1.21

2 Select Show.
The Windows operating environment disappears, and the first slide fills the entire screen.

Tip Selecting Slide Show from the View toolbar allows you to bypass the Slide Show dialog box and immediately start a full-screen display of slides.

3 Click the left mouse button or press (SPACE) or (PGDN) to see the next slide.

Tip You can view a previous slide in a slide show by clicking the right mouse button or by pressing (PGUP).

4 Press (SPACE) or (PGDN) until you have viewed all the slides.
At the end of the slide show, the most recent view appears on the screen (in this case, Notes Pages).

5 Close the file.

THE NEXT STEP

In this project you modified a General type multislide presentation suggested by AutoContent Wizard and then looked at various ways to show the slides on the screen. You will work within the various views throughout subsequent projects, but you won't have a guided tour using another predefined presentation type. On your own you might select one of the other five types, such as Selling a Product, Service or Idea, and then modify the suggested organization and hints for content to suit your needs.

This concludes Project 1. You can either exit PowerPoint or go on to work the Study Questions, Review Exercises, and Assignments.

SUMMARY AND EXERCISES

Summary

- Before you begin using PowerPoint to develop a graphics presentation, you should decide on the length of the presentation, find out what type of equipment will be available, and plan what you want to say.
- PowerPoint includes AutoContent Wizard, which helps you set up one of six basic themes for a presentation and guides you through the steps to create all the slides.
- When you save a presentation, you must specify both its name and location on disk. The file name may contain one to eight characters. PowerPoint supplies the .PPT extension.
- PowerPoint provides two options to save a presentation: Save and Save As. Choose Save to replace the copy of a presentation on disk with the version of the document on the screen. Choose Save As to save a presentation for the first time or to change the name or location of a previously saved document.
- To open a presentation, you must specify both its name and location on disk. You can open several presentations at a time.

- Outline view provides an easy-to-use work surface on which to make text changes. You will edit text in Outline view in much the same way you edit text in your favorite word processor.
- A view is a way to look at the slides in a PowerPoint presentation. You can work with a presentation in any one of five views: Slide, Outline, Slide Sorter, Notes Pages, and Slide Show.

Key Terms and Operations

Key Terms

active presentation
bullet
demote
directory
disk drive
formatted text
insertion point
Notes Pages view
Outline view
path
promote

Slide view
Slide Show view
Slide Sorter view
view

Operations

Create a presentation using Auto-Content Wizard
Edit text in Outline view
Open a presentation
Save a presentation
Switch from one view to another

Study Questions

Multiple Choice

1. Which of the following PowerPoint views shows more than one slide per screen?
   a. Slide
   b. Slide Sorter
   c. Slide Show
   d. Notes Pages

2. Which of the following is a false statement about PowerPoint?
   a. Files created in other programs cannot be used in PowerPoint.
   b. You can open several presentations at a time.
   c. When you save a presentation for the first time, PowerPoint automatically displays the Save As dialog box.
   d. When you access PowerPoint or start a new presentation, the PowerPoint dialog box appears automatically.

3. To save an existing presentation under a different name, use the PowerPoint command
   a. Save
   b. Save As
   c. Rename
   d. Replace

4. Which of the following buttons on the Outline toolbar would you select to show only the title of the slide containing the insertion point?
   a. Collapse Selection
   b. Show Titles
   c. Demote
   d. None of the above.

5. While working in Outline view, which key could you press at the end of a slide's title to insert a new slide?
   a. ⊘
   b. PGDN
   c. ENTER
   d. None of the above.

6. Which of the following is a false statement about AutoContent Wizard?
   a. Once you have finished using AutoContent Wizard, the outline that results can only be changed by editing.
   b. To select a different outline, start a new presentation using AutoContent Wizard.
   c. You can choose among eight predefined basic presentation types.
   d. AutoContent Wizard is one of the options in the PowerPoint dialog box that you can use to create a new presentation.

7. To view the previous slide during a slide show,
   a. press PGUP.
   b. click the right mouse button.
   c. Both a and b.
   d. None of the above.

8. In which of the following PowerPoint views does a slide occupy the entire screen?
   a. Slide
   b. Slide Sorter
   c. Slide Show
   d. Notes Pages

9. Which of the following terms describes the route PowerPoint must follow to locate a file on disk?
   a. disk drive
   b. path
   c. RAM
   d. directory

10. Which of the following is not one of the basic presentation types you can select using AutoContent Wizard?
    a. Recommending a Strategy
    b. Communicating Good News
    c. Training
    d. Selling a Product, Service or Idea

Short Answer

1. What is the term describing the flashing vertical bar that marks the position where text will be inserted or deleted when you type on the keyboard?

2. Which dialog box would you use to document the title, subject, and author of a presentation? (This information would not appear on any slide in the presentation.)

3. What is the term for a symbol such as a solid square block or open circle used to set off an item in a list?

4. In some software a three-character extension identifies the type of file. What is the extension that identifies a PowerPoint presentation?

5. Which button on the Outline toolbar would you select to expand a collapsed outline so that all levels of text for all slides appear?

6. What key can you press to delete a character to the left of the insertion point?

7. What term describes shifting selected text left one level in an outline?

8. Which button on the Outline toolbar would you select to switch between showing plain text and showing text with changes in print style and size?

9. In which PowerPoint view can you set up speaker's notes?

10. What key can you press at the end of an outline item to insert a blank new item below?

For Discussion

1. Before you start creating a presentation using the PowerPoint software, describe some of the actions you should take to plan the presentation.

2. Selecting AutoContent Wizard starts a four-step process. Describe the actions you must take during the process and the results you achieve.

3. You can work with a PowerPoint presentation in any one of five views. Briefly describe the primary reason(s) to use each view.

4. Describe how you would insert, delete, and replace text while working in Outline view.

5. When you are working in Outline view, you can hide some of the text. Explain what text can be hidden and how you know from looking at an outline that some text is not in view.

Review Exercises

Promoting a Service

1. Load PowerPoint and select AutoContent Wizard.

2. On the AutoContent Wizard - Step 2 of 4 screen, type **First Impressions** in the What are you going to talk about? box.

3. Type **For students, by students** in the What is your name? box. Also delete text, if any, in the Other information you'd like to include? box.

4. On the AutoContent Wizard - Step 3 of 4 screen, select Selling a Product, Service or Idea, and then select Finish to see PowerPoint's suggested organization and content in Outline view.

5. Edit the suggested outline to match the text shown in Figure 1.22. Include the spelling errors in slides 6 and 7.

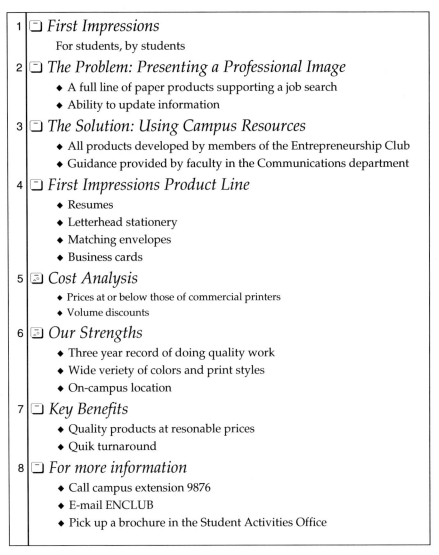

Figure 1.22

6. Save your work using the name IMPRESS.PPT (you will use this file in the Project 2 review exercises). During the save process, enter appropriate subject and author information in the Summary Info dialog box.

Buying a Computer

1. Load PowerPoint and select AutoContent Wizard.

2. On the AutoContent Wizard - Step 2 of 4 screen, type **BUYING A COMPUTER** in the What are you going to talk about? box.

3. Type your name in the What is your name? box. Also delete any text that appears in the Other information you'd like to include? box.

4. On the AutoContent Wizard - Step 3 of 4 screen, select General and then select Finish to see PowerPoint's suggested organization and content in Outline view.

5. Edit the suggested outline to match the text shown in Figure 1.23.

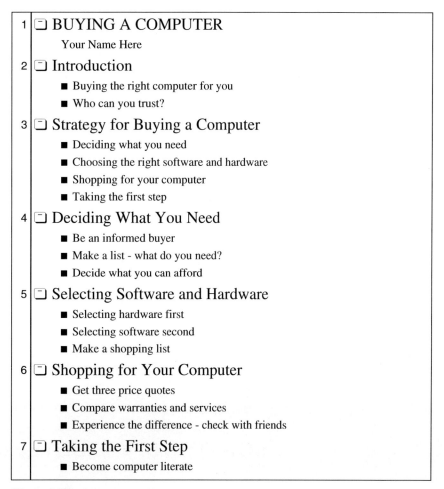

1 ❏ BUYING A COMPUTER
   Your Name Here

2 ❏ Introduction
   ■ Buying the right computer for you
   ■ Who can you trust?

3 ❏ Strategy for Buying a Computer
   ■ Deciding what you need
   ■ Choosing the right software and hardware
   ■ Shopping for your computer
   ■ Taking the first step

4 ❏ Deciding What You Need
   ■ Be an informed buyer
   ■ Make a list - what do you need?
   ■ Decide what you can afford

5 ❏ Selecting Software and Hardware
   ■ Selecting hardware first
   ■ Selecting software second
   ■ Make a shopping list

6 ❏ Shopping for Your Computer
   ■ Get three price quotes
   ■ Compare warranties and services
   ■ Experience the difference - check with friends

7 ❏ Taking the First Step
   ■ Become computer literate

Figure 1.23

6. Save your work using the name COMPUTER.PPT (you will use this file in the Project 2 review exercises). During the save process, enter appropriate subject and author information in the Summary Info dialog box.

Assignments

Using Help's Index Feature

Use Index in on-screen Help to look up information about finding a file. Write a brief summary of what you learned about the Find File button.

Using Help's Search Feature

Use Search in on-screen Help to learn more about selecting text in an outline. Summarize how to select the entire outline, one slide, a paragraph and all its sublevels, and one word.

Reporting on Progress

Create a new presentation using the AutoContent Wizard. Select Communicating Bad News as the presentation type. Modify the suggested organization and content to reflect the assumption that goals have not been met for participation in a school, sport, or charity event. Save the file using the name UPDATE.PPT.

PROJECT 2: POLISHING A PRESENTATION

Objectives

After completing this project, you should be able to:

▶ Proofread a presentation

▶ Move and copy text

▶ Promote and demote topics

▶ Add, delete, and duplicate slides

▶ Create speaker's notes

▶ Spell-check a presentation

▶ Print a presentation

CASE STUDY: PROMOTING VOLUNTEERISM II

Very few individuals can produce a perfectly worded, well-organized, and complete presentation on the first attempt. For example, in Project 1 you edited an outline suggested by PowerPoint's AutoContent Wizard. In this project you will examine this first draft with a critical eye toward improving organization, completeness, and grammar. After you are satisfied that the slides convey your message and have no misspelled words, you can concentrate on techniques to improve delivery.

Designing the Solution

You must check every presentation you create for accuracy, completeness, organization, proper grammar, and correct spelling. The wrong date for a volunteer activity would indicate a problem with accuracy. If you suggested that viewers contact the Volunteer Center and failed to include a phone number, the presentation would not be complete. When you check organization, you might ask yourself if the words flow easily and if there are logical transitions between slides. Perhaps you'll notice that an apostrophe is missing or several words run together. Using PowerPoint, you can easily retrieve the initial draft of a presentation and make revisions. It is up to you, however, to review your work carefully and decide what revisions you need to make.

In the following sections you will continue editing the SERVICE.PPT presentation you created in Project 1. The changes include correcting grammar, inserting a new slide, duplicating a slide, adding and demoting bulleted subtopics, and moving text to another location. After adding the finishing touches—speaker's notes and correction of spelling errors—you will print the slides.

PROOFREADING A PRESENTATION

When you ***proofread*** a presentation, you read the text on each slide, noting omissions as well as corrections to be made in content and organization. After making the desired changes, you should always proofread the revised presentation. Several editing sessions may be required before you are satisfied with the quality of the slides.

If you are comfortable proofreading text on the screen, you can display the presentation in Outline view, which shows the title and bulleted subtopics from all slides. You can also print an Outline view of the presentation and mark your revisions on paper. The handwritten annotations in Figure 2.1 describe changes to make after proofreading the initial draft of the volunteerism presentation.

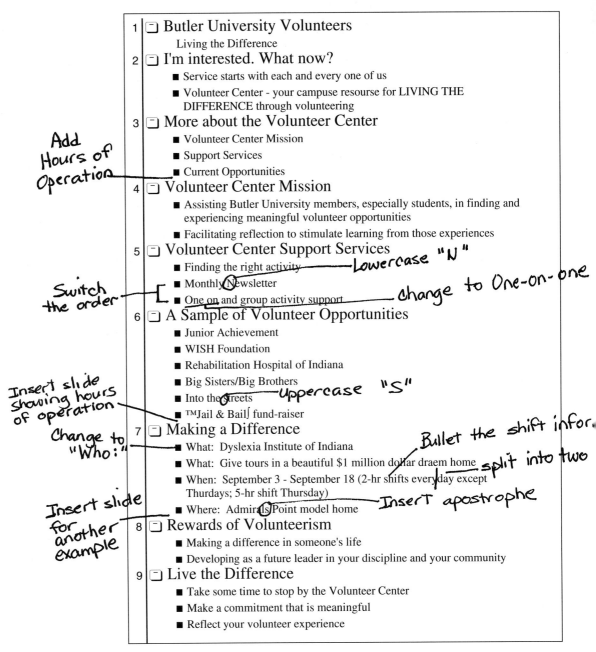

Figure 2.1

In the following sets of numbered steps, you will make the changes shown in Figure 2.1. You will begin by inserting and deleting text in existing slides.

Reminder It may be necessary to correct spacing around newly edited text.

To open an existing presentation:

1 Load PowerPoint 4.0 for Windows.

2 Open the SERVICE.PPT presentation.
The initial nine-slide volunteerism presentation you created in Project 1 appears in Outline view. The printed text should match that shown in Figure 2.1.

Tip If the presentation is not in Outline view, switch now. Check the formatting mode to make sure the presentation looks like Figure 2.1.

To insert a new bulleted topic:

1 Position the insertion point at the end of the last bulleted topic in slide 3.

2 Press (ENTER) to insert a new line preceded by a bullet.

3 Type **Hours of Operation**
The text in your slide 3 should match that shown in Figure 2.2.

> 3 ☐ More about the Volunteer Center
> • Volunteer Center Mission
> • Support Services
> • Current Opportunities
> • Hours of Operation

Figure 2.2

To edit existing text and save the revisions:

1 Locate the second and third bulleted topics in slide 5.

2 Lowercase the *N* in *Newsletter*, and type **One-on-one** in place of *One on.*
Your revisions to slide 5 should match those shown in Figure 2.3.

> 5 ☐ Volunteer Center Support Services
> • Finding the right activity
> • Monthly newsletter
> • One-on-one| and group activity support

Figure 2.3

3 Locate the fifth bulleted topic in slide 6, and capitalize the *s* in *streets.*

4 Locate slide 7.

5 Revise the first bulleted topic by typing **Who** in place of *What.*

6 Revise the third bulleted topic by inserting a space to separate *everyday* into the words *every* and *day.*

7 Revise the fourth bulleted topic by inserting an apostrophe before the *s* in *Admirals*.

Your revisions to slide 7 should match those shown in Figure 2.4.

7 ▭ **Making a Difference**
- Who: Dyslexia Institute of Indiana
- What: Give tours in a beautiful $1 million dollar draem home
- When: September 3 - September 18 (2-hr shifts every day except Thurdays; 5-hr shift Thursday)
- Where: Admiral's Point model home

Figure 2.4

8 Locate the third bulleted topic in slide 9, and type **on** between *Reflect* and *your*.

Your revision to slide 9 should match that shown in Figure 2.5.

9 ▭ **Live the Difference**
- Take some time to stop by the Volunteer Center
- Make a commitment that is meaningful
- Reflect on your volunteer experience

Figure 2.5

9 Save the file.

EXIT   If necessary, you can exit PowerPoint now and continue this project later.

MOVING AND COPYING TEXT

As you make changes to the initial draft of a presentation, you may want to move text from one position to another. To move selected text, you can choose the Cut command to cut (remove) the block from its current position, and then choose the Paste command to paste (insert) the block in a new location. You can also click the block and drag the selected text to a new location.

 Tip In Outline view you can use the Move Up or Move Down button on the Outline toolbar to switch the selected topic with one that precedes or follows.

Using PowerPoint, you can avoid typing the same text twice. To copy a block of text, you can choose the Copy command to duplicate the selected text, and then choose the Paste command to insert the block. Although the new location can be in the current set of slides, you are more likely to copy selected text to another presentation or a blank presentation window.

Tip If you press and hold down (CTRL) after you click a selected block, you can drag the highlighted text to a second location.

When you first cut or copy a block of text, the text is stored on the **clipboard,** a temporary storage area located in the computer's memory. Each time you cut or copy a new block, the previous contents of the clipboard are erased.

Quick Fix Using PowerPoint's Undo feature, you can reverse the most recent editing action. For example, if you cut or copy the wrong block of text, you can reverse the action if you immediately choose Undo from the Edit menu.

In the following steps you will use the Cut and Paste buttons in the Standard toolbar to switch the second and third bulleted topics in slide 5, restore the moved text to its original position using the Move Up button on the Outline toolbar, and then repeat the move process using the mouse to drag selected text.

To move text using Cut and Paste:

1 If necessary, load PowerPoint and open the SERVICE.PPT presentation in Outline view.

2 Locate slide 5 and click the bullet next to *Monthly newsletter*. PowerPoint automatically selects (highlights) all text in the bulleted topic, as shown in Figure 2.6.

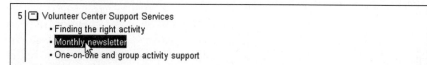

Figure 2.6

3 Click Cut in the Standard toolbar.
The selected text disappears, and two bulleted topics remain in slide 5.

4 Position the insertion point at the end of the second bulleted topic.

5 Click Paste in the Standard toolbar.
Monthly newsletter becomes the third bulleted topic and the highlighting disappears, as shown in Figure 2.7.

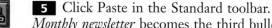

Figure 2.7

To move text using the Outline toolbar:

1 Click the bullet next to *Monthly newsletter* in slide 5.

2 Click Move Up on the Outline toolbar.
The selected text moves up one bulleted topic to its original position. The text remains selected (highlighted).

To move text using the mouse and then save your change:

1 Position the mouse pointer on the selected text as shown in Figure 2.6.

2 Press and hold down the left mouse button.

3 Drag the pointer to the end of the third bulleted topic.
The hollow square at the bottom of the mouse pointer indicates that you are dragging text.

4 Release the mouse button.
Monthly newsletter becomes the third bulleted topic, as shown in Figure 2.7. The highlighting remains.

5 Click text or white space to unselect the highlighted block of text.

6 Save the file.
The change in topic order on slide 5 is saved to disk. The outline of the presentation remains on the screen.

PROMOTING AND DEMOTING TOPICS

In Outline view an item's position indicates its importance in relation to other items, as shown by the levels in Figure 2.8. If you have set the display to show formatting, a different bullet character precedes each level, such as a square for level 2 and a diamond for level 3.

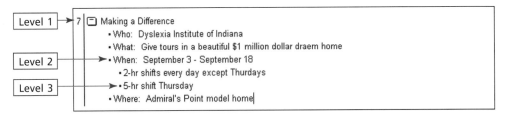

Figure 2.8

The title of a slide displays at level 1. Each major point within a slide appears at level 2. Each subpoint supporting a major point occupies a level-3 position.

If you demote a topic, the selected text shifts to the right, forming a subtopic at the next level in the outline. The bullet character changes to match other bullets at that level. You will use the Demote (right-arrow) button on the Outline toolbar for this change. If you promote a topic, the selected text shifts to the left, forming a topic at the previous level in the outline. The bullet character changes to match other bullets at that level.

The Promote button (the left arrow) on the Outline toolbar executes this action.

In the following steps you will edit slide 7 to show shift information in level-3 subpoints, as shown in Figure 2.8. You will start by placing shift-related text on two separate level-2 lines. To complete the process, you will demote the two phrases to level 3.

To demote topics and save the changes:

1 Locate slide 7 in Outline view, and position the insertion point immediately after *September 18* in the third bulleted topic.

2 Press (ENTER) to shift the remaining text to a new bulleted topic.

3 Position the insertion point before the semicolon at the end of the text describing 2-hour shifts.
The insertion point should be just after the *s* in *Thurdays*.

4 Press (ENTER) to create another bulleted topic.

5 Delete the semicolon, the parentheses, and the extra spaces preceding the text.
The shift information appears as shown in Figure 2.9.

7 | Making a Difference
- Who: Dyslexia Institute of Indiana
- What: Give tours in a beautiful $1 million dollar draem home
- When: September 3 - September 18
- 2-hr shifts every day except Thurdays
- 5-hr shift Thursday
- Where: Admiral's Point model home

Figure 2.9

6 Select only the text describing 2-hour shifts.

Reminder You can select a level-2 or lower bulleted subtopic by clicking the associated bullet.

7 Click Demote (the right arrow) on the Outline toolbar.
The selected text shifts to the right to form a subtopic under the range of dates.

8 Select only the text describing a 5-hour shift.

9 Click Demote.
The selected text shifts to the right to form a subtopic under the range of dates.

10 Click text or white space to unselect the highlighted block of text.
Your changes to slide 7 should match those shown in Figure 2.8.

11 Save the file.

If necessary, you can exit PowerPoint now and continue this project later.

ADDING AND DELETING SLIDES

As you revise a presentation, you may need to add or delete a slide. Adding a slide involves a two-step process: positioning the insertion point within the slide you want to precede the new slide and then choosing New Slide from the Insert menu or clicking the New Slide button near the lower-right corner of the screen.

Deleting a slide requires a similar two-step process: selecting the slide to remove and then executing the delete operation. In Outline view you can select the slide by clicking the symbol to the left of the slide's title. You can then press (DEL) or choose Delete Slide from the Edit menu.

You can add or delete slides while you work in any view mode. In the following steps you will insert a new slide in Outline view after the current slide 6. The new slide will show the hours of operation for the Volunteer Center.

To add a slide:

1 If necessary, load PowerPoint and open the SERVICE.PPT presentation in Outline view.

2 Position the insertion point on any text within slide 6.

3 Click New Slide at the lower-right corner of the screen.
A new slide appears as shown in Figure 2.10. Subsequent slides are renumbered automatically.

Figure 2.10

To add text to the new slide and save your changes:

1 Check that the insertion point appears to the right of the slide 7 symbol.

2 Type **Hours of Operation** and press (ENTER)

Reminder Pressing (ENTER) in Outline view inserts a line at the same level. In this case pressing (ENTER) has created an unwanted new slide.

3 Click Demote on the Outline toolbar.
The slide 8 symbol changes to a level-2 bullet under slide 7.

4 Type **Monday 8:00 a.m. - 8:00 p.m.** and press (ENTER)

5 Type **Tuesday 9:00 a.m. - 5:00 p.m.** and press (ENTER)

6 Type **Wednesday 8:00 a.m. - 5:00 p.m.** and press ⏎ENTER

7 Type **Thursday 10:00 a.m. - 8:00 p.m.** and press ⏎ENTER

8 Type **Friday 8:00 a.m. - 3:00 p.m.**
The text on your new slide 7 should match that shown in Figure 2.11.

---

7 ☐ Hours of Operation
- Monday 8:00 a.m. - 8:00 p.m.
- Tuesday 9:00 a.m. - 5:00 p.m.
- Wednesday 8:00 a.m. - 5:00 p.m.
- Thursday 10:00 a.m. - 8:00 p.m.
- Friday 8:00 a.m. - 3:00 p.m.

Figure 2.11

9 Save the file.

DUPLICATING A SLIDE

In the previous section you typed all of the text on a new slide. If the content you have in mind for a new slide corresponds closely to the layout on an existing slide, you might save keystrokes by duplicating and then editing the similar slide. Duplicating a slide involves a two-step process: selecting the slide to copy and then choosing Duplicate from the Edit menu.

Tip Duplicating a slide automatically inserts the copy immediately after the current slide. If you want to make a copy of a slide at another location, you must use a Copy and Paste command sequence.

In the following steps you will duplicate slide 8, which shows an example of a volunteer activity. You will then edit the new slide 9 to illustrate a second volunteer opportunity, as shown in Figure 2.12.

---

9 ☐ Making a Difference
- Who: Parkside Community Center
- What: Working with Children
  - Tutoring school age children
  - Working with crafts
  - Helping with preschool
- When: 2-4 hours per week
- Where: Downtown Indianapolis

Figure 2.12

To duplicate a slide:

1 Select slide 8 titled *Making a Difference*.

2 Choose Duplicate from the Edit menu.
The new slide 9 contains the same text as slide 8.

Quick Fix If you were not able to complete step 2 because the Duplicate option appeared dim, you may not have selected slide 8 properly. Check that you clicked the slide icon next to the slide title, and then repeat step 2.

 ### *To modify the duplicate slide:*

1 Select *Dyslexia Institute of Indiana* in the duplicate slide 9 (do not include *Who:*).

2 Type **Parkside Community Center**
The text you just typed replaces the original who information.

3 Select *Give tours in a beautiful $1 million dollar draem home*, type **Working with Children** and press (ENTER)
The text you just typed replaces the original what information, and PowerPoint inserts a blank bulleted topic.

4 Click Demote on the Outline toolbar to insert the first of three subtopics.

5 Type **Tutoring school age children** and press (ENTER)

6 Type **Working with crafts** and press (ENTER)

7 Type **Helping with preschool**

Quick Fix If a new subtopic bullet appears, you accidentally pressed (ENTER) again. Delete the unwanted blank subtopic by clicking its bullet and pressing (DEL) or by pressing (BKSP)

8 Select *September 3 - September 18*, and type **2-4 hours per week**
The text you just typed replaces the original when information.

9 Click the bullet in front of *2-hr shifts*, and press (DEL)

10 Click the remaining bullet in front of *5-hr shift*, and press (DEL)

11 Select *Admiral's Point model home*, and type **Downtown Indianapolis**
The text you just typed replaces the original where information.

12 Compare your edited slide 9 to Figure 2.12 and make changes as necessary.
Do not, however, change spelling errors. You will use a feature to check all spelling after you create speaker's notes in the next section.

13 Save the file.

EXIT If necessary, you can exit PowerPoint now and continue this project later.

ADDING SPEAKER'S NOTES

Slides generally show only key points in short phrases. Many speakers use printed notes, in addition to their presentation slides, to help them deliver a talk. Using PowerPoint, you can easily develop speaker's notes in Notes Pages view. As shown in Figure 2.13, Notes Pages view displays an image of the current slide at the top of the page and a box for your notes at the bottom of the page.

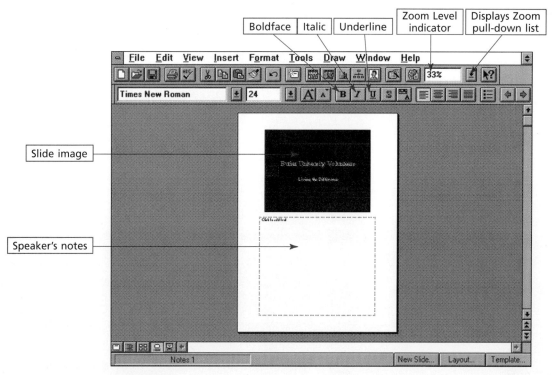

Figure 2.13

Many word processing features are available as you type your notes. For example, you can move and copy text as well as boldface, italicize, and underline selected text using the associated buttons on the Standard toolbar.

Zoom allows you to increase and decrease the size of the image on your screen in relation to its printed size (100%). The current zoom level appears in the Standard toolbar, such as 33% in Figure 2.13. You can easily change this setting by clicking the underscored down arrow to the right of the Zoom Level indicator and selecting one of the predetermined settings from a pull-down list.

Tip You can add and edit speaker's notes at any time during the process of developing a presentation. Rather than waiting until you have created all your slides, however, you might add notes while your thoughts about a specific slide are fresh in your mind.

In the following steps you will add speaker's notes to the first slide in the SERVICE.PPT presentation on volunteerism. You will also boldface key words and phrases in your notes so that you can tell at a glance what point you should be making next.

To change the view to Notes Pages:

1 If necessary, load PowerPoint and open the SERVICE.PPT presentation in Outline view.

2 Position the insertion point anywhere in slide 1.

3 Click Notes Pages in the View toolbar.
Your screen displays an image of slide 1 above an empty speaker's notes box with a narrow dotted border, as shown in Figure 2.13. The relative size of the display will vary if 33% is not the current zoom setting.

To change the zoom setting:

1 Click the underscored down arrow to the right of the Zoom Level indicator.

2 Select 50% in the pull-down list.

3 Click the underscored down arrow to the right of the Zoom Level indicator.

4 Select 100% in the pull-down list.

5 View the slide at other zoom settings, and then restore a 100% view.

To enter speaker's notes:

1 Click within the notes box where you see the phrase "Click to add text."
The border of the box changes to a wider pattern formed by a series of forward slashes.

2 Type `Welcome participants to the presentation` and press `ENTER` twice.

3 Type `Tell listeners who I am` and press `ENTER` twice.

4 Type `Get show of hands from audience - # students, faculty, staff` and press `ENTER` twice.

5 Type `Explain format and timing (a few slides, question/answer period)`

6 Check that your notes for slide 1 match the text shown in Figure 2.14, and make changes as necessary. You will add the boldface in the next set of numbered steps.

Welcome participants to the presentation

Tell listeners **who I am**

Get **show of hands** from audience - # students, faculty, staff

Explain **format and timing** (a few slides, question/answer period)

Figure 2.14

To boldface selected text and save the changes to your presentation:

1 Select *Welcome* in the first note, and then click Boldface in the Standard toolbar.

2 Select *who I am* in the second note, and then click Boldface.

3 Select *show of hands* in the third note, and then click Boldface.

4 Select *format and timing* in the fourth note, and then click Boldface. The notes display selected words and phrases boldface, as shown in Figure 2.14.

5 Save the file.

SPELL-CHECKING A PRESENTATION

Nothing ruins your credibility as a presenter faster than displaying a spelling error on a slide. PowerPoint uses the same powerful spell-checking feature used in other Microsoft programs to find and correct spelling errors in all slides, notes pages, and handout pages.

Spell-checking begins at the location of the insertion point. PowerPoint "looks up" each word in its dictionary. If a word is either misspelled or not found in the dictionary, the Spelling dialog box shown in Figure 2.15 appears, with the problem word displayed in the Not in Dictionary box. A suggested spelling appears in the Change To box. There may be other suggested spellings as well.

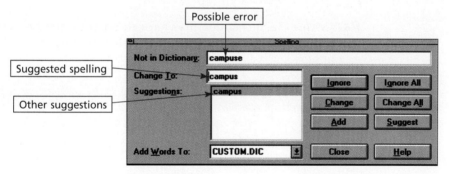

Figure 2.15

You may recognize one of the suggestions as the correct spelling. Clicking that word places it in the Change To box. If you know the correct spelling, you can also edit the word in the Change To box. You can then replace that particular instance of the misspelled word with the correct one by selecting Change, or for the rest of the presentation by selecting Change All.

Some suggested misspellings are not errors. For example, many proper names (such as Parkside), acronyms, abbreviations, slang words, and specialized terms are not in the dictionary. You can choose to ignore the suggested error one time only by selecting Ignore, or for the rest of the presentation by selecting Ignore All.

Tip If a word you will be using frequently shows as misspelled, you can add the word to the dictionary. Exercise caution, however, because you cannot remove a word from the dictionary once you have added it.

In the following steps you will check the spelling in the volunteerism presentation. The steps assume that you have typed the document exactly as directed, including spelling errors. If you already corrected one or more given misspelled words as you typed, you will need to skip one or more steps below. If you misspelled other words, you should correct those errors on your own.

To begin a spelling check, replacing misspelled words:

1 Choose Outline from the View menu.

Tip Spell-checking can be done from any view mode. However, it is easier to start with the most familiar view, which is the one that displays the most text on one screen.

2 Press (CTRL)+(HOME) to position the cursor at the beginning of slide 1.

3 Choose Spelling from the Tools menu.
The first possible error, *campuse*, appears at the top of the Spelling dialog box, followed by the most likely correction, *campus*, as shown in Figure 2.15.

Reminder Spell-checking may have stopped on another word if you made an unintentional spelling error earlier or you corrected *campuse* as you typed.

4 Select Change to replace the spelling error *campuse* with the suggested correction, *campus*.
The next possible error appears in the Not in Dictionary box.

5 Select Change to replace the spelling error *resourse* with the suggested correction, *resource*.

To complete spell-checking, ignoring some suggested changes:

1 Select Ignore All to bypass making changes to *a.m.* and again to bypass making changes to *p.m.*

2 Select Change to replace *draem* with *dream* and *Thurdays* with *Thursdays*.

3 Select Ignore to bypass the suggested spelling *Paradise* for *Parkside*.

4 Select OK to end the spelling check.

5 Click text or white space to remove the highlighting on the last word found in the spelling check.

6 Save the file.

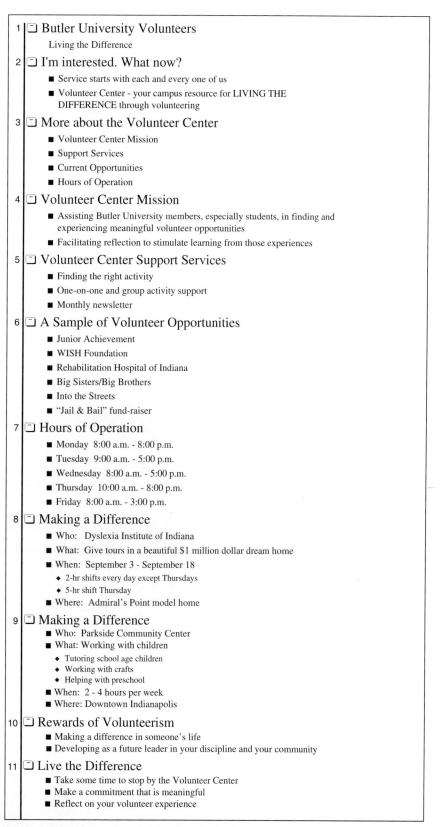

1. Butler University Volunteers
   Living the Difference

2. I'm interested. What now?
   - Service starts with each and every one of us
   - Volunteer Center - your campus resource for LIVING THE DIFFERENCE through volunteering

3. More about the Volunteer Center
   - Volunteer Center Mission
   - Support Services
   - Current Opportunities
   - Hours of Operation

4. Volunteer Center Mission
   - Assisting Butler University members, especially students, in finding and experiencing meaningful volunteer opportunities
   - Facilitating reflection to stimulate learning from those experiences

5. Volunteer Center Support Services
   - Finding the right activity
   - One-on-one and group activity support
   - Monthly newsletter

6. A Sample of Volunteer Opportunities
   - Junior Achievement
   - WISH Foundation
   - Rehabilitation Hospital of Indiana
   - Big Sisters/Big Brothers
   - Into the Streets
   - "Jail & Bail" fund-raiser

7. Hours of Operation
   - Monday 8:00 a.m. - 8:00 p.m.
   - Tuesday 9:00 a.m. - 5:00 p.m.
   - Wednesday 8:00 a.m. - 5:00 p.m.
   - Thursday 10:00 a.m. - 8:00 p.m.
   - Friday 8:00 a.m. - 3:00 p.m.

8. Making a Difference
   - Who: Dyslexia Institute of Indiana
   - What: Give tours in a beautiful $1 million dollar dream home
   - When: September 3 - September 18
     - 2-hr shifts every day except Thursdays
     - 5-hr shift Thursday
   - Where: Admiral's Point model home

9. Making a Difference
   - Who: Parkside Community Center
   - What: Working with children
     - Tutoring school age children
     - Working with crafts
     - Helping with preschool
   - When: 2 - 4 hours per week
   - Where: Downtown Indianapolis

10. Rewards of Volunteerism
    - Making a difference in someone's life
    - Developing as a future leader in your discipline and your community

11. Live the Difference
    - Take some time to stop by the Volunteer Center
    - Make a commitment that is meaningful
    - Reflect on your volunteer experience

Figure 2.17

5 Choose Close from the File menu.

THE NEXT STEP

In this project you added the finishing touches to your first PowerPoint presentation. After proofreading your work, you moved text, corrected grammar, added two slides, added speaker's notes, and checked spelling. Actions such as these allow you to turn an initial draft into a polished presentation.

To go beyond the material in this project, look for opportunities to experiment with activities that were described but not worked through. For example, you experienced moving text within a slide. Now try copying selected text in another presentation of your own. Add another slide to a presentation and then see if you can delete it. You added boldface. Use on-screen Help to find out how to remove that enhancement. Exploring can be fun!

This concludes Project 2. You can either exit PowerPoint or go on to work the Study Questions, Review Exercises, and Assignments.

SUMMARY AND EXERCISES

Summary

- As you proofread a presentation, you should check the set of slides for accuracy, completeness, organization, proper grammar, and correct spelling.
- Editing activities include moving and copying text, demoting and promoting topics, adding and deleting a slide, and duplicating a slide.
- Many speakers use printed notes, in addition to slides, to help them deliver a presentation. Using PowerPoint, you can develop speaker's notes in Notes Pages view.
- PowerPoint includes a powerful spell-checking feature to find and correct spelling errors in all slides, notes pages, and handout pages.
- You can print a presentation in several forms: slides, notes pages, handouts, and an outline.

Key Terms and Operations

Key Terms
clipboard
proofread

Operations
Add a slide
Add speaker's notes
Boldface text

Demote a topic
Duplicate a slide
Move text
Print the outline of a presentation
Proofread a presentation
Spell-check a presentation

Study Questions

Multiple Choice

1. Which of the following is not an option for printing handout pages?
   a. two slides per page
   b. three slides per page

c. four slides per page

d. six slides per page

2. As you drag selected text to a new location, which key do you press and hold down to copy instead of move?
   a. (ALT)
   b. (CTRL)
   c. (SHFT)
   d. None of the above.

3. Which of the following is not a true statement about developing speaker's notes?
   a. In Notes Pages view you see a box for your notes at the top of the page and an image of the current slide at the bottom of the page.
   b. You can boldface, italicize, and underline text in notes pages.
   c. You can add and edit speaker's notes at any time during the process of developing a presentation.
   d. All of the above are true.

4. If you do not have a color printer, you should always specify Black & White or Pure Black & White as a print setting unless the selected output form is
   a. Slides.
   b. Notes Pages.
   c. Handouts.
   d. Outline View.

5. To delete a selected slide, choose
   a. Remove from the Edit menu.
   b. Delete from the Layout menu.
   c. Delete from the Tools menu.
   d. None of the above.

Short Answer

1. What is the temporary storage area located in the computer's memory that holds text cut from a presentation?

2. If you demote a topic in an outline, in which direction does the selected text shift?

3. Explain the menu sequence you can choose to reverse the most recent editing action.

4. What command button do you select in the Spelling dialog box to replace the word in error with the suggested word throughout the remainder of the presentation?

5. What single action begins printing immediately, so that you do not have an opportunity to change default print settings?

For Discussion

1. What tasks are involved in proofreading a presentation?

2. Describe the process of spell-checking a presentation.

3. You can add a slide to a presentation by inserting a new blank slide or by duplicating an existing slide and editing the copy. Briefly explain why you might choose one method over the other and then describe the steps to take for each process.

Review Exercises

Promoting a Service (Part 2)

1. Open the IMPRESS.PPT presentation you created in the Project 1 review exercises (see Figure 1.22).

2. Locate slide 3 (The Solution) and uppercase the *d* in *department*.

3. Locate slide 4 (Product Line) and insert another bulleted item, *Cover letters*, after *Resumes*.

4. Locate slide 5 (Cost Analysis) and move the two bulleted topics to subtopics under *Quality products at resonable prices* in slide 7.

5. Delete slide 5.

6. Create a notes page for slide 4. Include two notes: one to tell the audience about a free sample available after the presentation, and the other to direct attendees to an exhibit of products in the hall outside the meeting room.

7. Spell-check the presentation.

8. Save your changes, print the revised presentation in outline form, and then close the file.

Buying a Computer (Part 2)

1. Open the COMPUTER.PPT presentation you created in the Project 1 review exercises (see Figure 1.23).

2. Make the handwritten changes for slides 5 and 7 as shown in Figure 2.18.

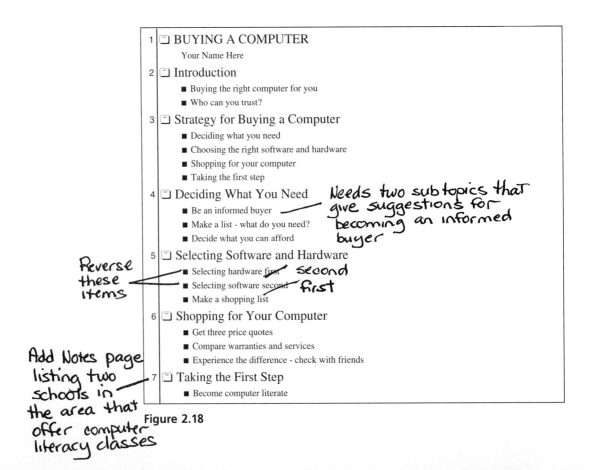

Figure 2.18

3. In slide 4 add two subtopics under *Be an informed buyer* that suggest ways to become an informed buyer (read computer magazines, talk to other users, and so on).

4. Add speaker's notes to slide 7 about two schools offering computer classes.

5. Spell-check your presentation.

6. Save your changes, print the revised presentation in outline form, and then close the file.

Assignments

Getting Help on Undo

Using Index in on-screen Help, look up additional information about undoing PowerPoint operations (select U as the first letter of the word you want to look up). Write a brief summary of what you learned, and include a sketch of the Undo button.

Getting Help on Boldface and Italics

Using Index in on-screen Help, find out if you can apply both boldface and italics to text. Also determine how to restore plain text. Write a brief summary of what you learned. (Hint: Explore various topics under formatting text.)

Getting Help on Hidden Slides

One of the options in the Print dialog box is Print Hidden Slides. Using Search in on-screen Help, find out what hidden slides are. Write a brief summary of what you learned. Include Help's example for using hidden slides and a sketch of the Hide Slide button.

Duplicating a Slide

Open the SERVICE.PPT presentation. Insert a duplicate of slide 9 (Making a Difference - Parkside Community Center) immediately after slide 9. Revise text on the new slide 10 to give one more example of a volunteer activity of your choice. Save your changes, print the new slide (optional), and then close the file.

PROJECT 3: WORKING WITH TEXT OBJECTS

Objectives

After completing this project, you should be able to:

▶ Use the Pick a Look Wizard

▶ Use AutoLayout to design a slide

▶ Create, edit, move, and size a text box

▶ Change text font and size

▶ Enhance text with special effects and color

▶ Set up two-column text and a bulleted list

▶ Center text

CASE STUDY: CRUISING THE CARIBBEAN

Assume that you are a summer intern at the Island Tours travel agency. Recently the agency acquired PowerPoint 4.0 for Windows software, and your supervisor has asked you to create a slide presentation explaining some of the firm's cruise packages.

Designing the Solution

You are well on your way to developing a well-received presentation because you have an interesting subject. Your objective now should be to develop slides that will grab and hold the attention of an audience.

Some presentations do not lend themselves to the text-only suggested outlines provided by AutoContent Wizard. You have an opportunity to include pictures as well as words on your cruise-related slides, and to arrange those items in creative ways. Figure 3.1 illustrates ideas for an eight-slide presentation combining text and pictures: a lead-in slide showing the firm's name; a title slide for the cruise-related presentation; three slides describing specific cruises (Bahamas, Eastern Caribbean, and Southern Caribbean); a sixth slide showing cruise highlights; a slide explaining how to plan the vacation through your agency; and a final slide repeating the firm's name.

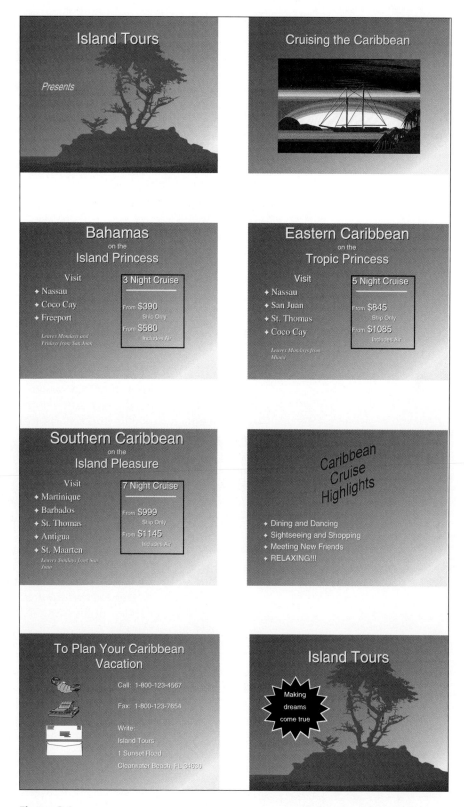

Figure 3.1

The suggested slides shown in Figure 3.1 contain text, clip art, lines, and other special effects. *Clip art* refers to a graphics image stored on disk, such as the image of a sail boat in slide 2. In slides 3, 4, and 5, a solid line forms a box. Within each box a horizontal line separates information about the length of the cruise from the associated prices. Changing the print style for selected text, such as italicizing departure information (slides 3, 4, and 5) and adding shapes containing text (slide 8), can also help to focus a viewer's attention.

Although you can create each complete slide before turning your attention to the next one, you might find it easier to build a text and graphics presentation in two phases. In the first phase you determine the general look of the slides, select a layout for each slide, add text to the slides, and format the text; these are the tasks you will accomplish in this project. Once you have the content established, you can add art work, lines, and other features that will transform the presentation to an effective, professional-looking product; you will do this phase of creating the presentation in Project 4.

USING PICK A LOOK WIZARD

Pick a Look Wizard provides a nine-step process for choosing a *template,* which tells PowerPoint how the various parts of your presentation should appear. For example, the template controls the background pattern and colors assigned to a slide and repeats text such as a company name, the date, or a slide number. This feature also allows you to select the type of slide and one or more supporting documents including outlines, audience handouts, and speaker's notes.

If an overhead projector is the only equipment you will be able to use during a presentation, you should select *Color Overheads* (color printer only) or *Black and White Overheads* as the type of slide. Some printers, such as laser printers, allow you to print directly on plastic transparencies. Otherwise, you can print paper copies of your slides and have transparencies made at a copy center. If you have computer projection equipment, which allows you to display the current monitor image on a screen, you should select *On-Screen Presentation* as the type of slide. PowerPoint provides one other slide output form, *35mm Slides,* which you can select if you have a desktop film recorder or you plan to send the file to a service bureau that will make the slides for you.

Tip Generally you will print overheads, outlines, audience handouts, and speaker's notes using **portrait orientation,** in which the image is longer than it is wide. Presentations projected from a computer monitor or 35mm slides should be set up with **landscape orientation,** in which the image is wider than it is long.

Figure 3.2 shows the first of the nine Pick a Look Wizard screens. Four buttons in the lower-right corner of the screen control movement through the screens. You will select Next to continue the process or Back to return to the previous screen. The other two command buttons allow you to quit using Pick a Look Wizard: You choose Finish to save your selections or Cancel to abort your settings.

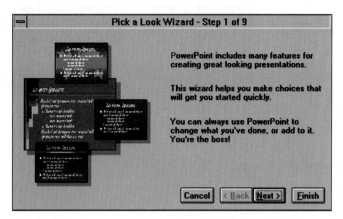

Figure 3.2

You can access this wizard at any time during the creation of a presentation by choosing Pick a Look Wizard from the Format menu. In the following steps you will establish the look of your presentation; later you will add slide content. This is an effective approach when putting together a presentation on a tight schedule, because you can select among dozens of professionally designed templates.

Tip After you complete an on-screen presentation of your own, you can also output the slides as overhead transparencies. By doing so you have an alternative means of presentation available in case your computer projection device does not work.

To start Pick a Look Wizard and select the type of output:

1 Open PowerPoint.
The PowerPoint dialog box appears. If a Tip of the Day dialog box appears instead, select OK to remove it.

2 Select Pick a Look Wizard if a black circle does not already appear in front of that option.

3 Select OK.
The Pick a Look Wizard - Step 1 of 9 screen shown in Figure 3.2 appears.

4 Select Next.
The Pick a Look Wizard - Step 2 of 9 screen shown in Figure 3.3 appears.

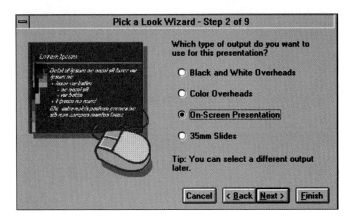

Figure 3.3

5 Select On-Screen Presentation as shown in Figure 3.3.

6 Select Next.

The Pick a Look Wizard - Step 3 of 9 screen shown in Figure 3.4 appears.

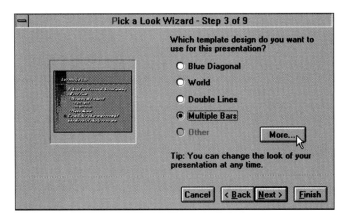

Figure 3.4

 To select a slide design:

1 Select More (see the mouse pointer in Figure 3.4).

The Presentation Template dialog box shown in Figure 3.5 appears.

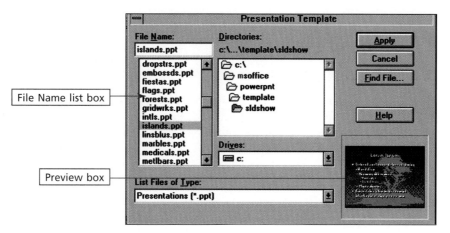

File Name list box

Preview box

Figure 3.5

2 Scroll through the display of names in the File Name list box until ISLANDS.PPT appears.

3 Select ISLANDS.PPT.
An image of the selected template appears in the preview box in the lower-right corner of the dialog box.

> **Tip** If minimum installation procedures were followed to set up PowerPoint on your system, ISLANDS.PPT may not be available. You can substitute another template, such as WORLDS.PPT.

4 Select Apply.
Pick a Look Wizard restores the display of the Step 3 of 9 screen. The ISLANDS.PPT template appears in the preview box.

5 Select Next.
The Pick a Look Wizard - Step 4 of 9 screen shown in Figure 3.6 appears.

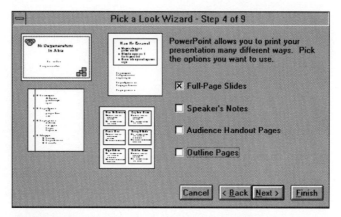

Figure 3.6

To select presentation and slide options:

1 Select the check box setting shown in Figure 3.6.

Reminder Recall that an X in a check box indicates the option is active, and the absence of an X indicates an option is off. Clicking the check box toggles (switches) between the two settings.

2 Select Next, and then select the setting shown on the Pick a Look Wizard - Slide Options screen in Figure 3.7.

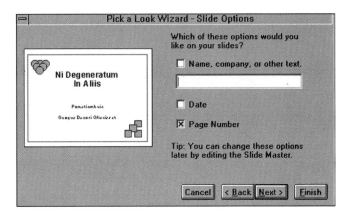

Figure 3.7

3 Select Next.
Pick a Look Wizard goes directly to step 9, skipping the other steps related to speaker's notes, audience handout pages, and outline pages (you eliminated these output forms on the Pick a Look Wizard - Step 4 of 9 screen).

4 Select Finish.
The first blank slide appears as shown in Figure 3.8. PowerPoint automatically inserts *placeholders* (boxes or other shapes that you can fill) for a title and subtitle.

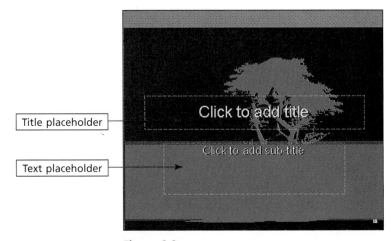

Figure 3.8

To save the new slide presentation:

1 Save the new presentation using the name CRUISES.PPT.

Tip If necessary, refer to the detailed instructions for saving a new PowerPoint presentation provided in Project 1.

2 Enter the title, subject, author, and comments information in the Summary Info dialog box as shown in Figure 3.9, and then select OK.

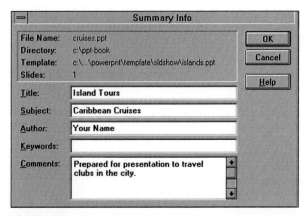

Figure 3.9

Reminder Save your presentation frequently to minimize the loss of your efforts should a power outage occur.

CREATING PLACEHOLDERS WITH AUTOLAYOUT

A slide may contain one or more *objects*. In PowerPoint an *object* can be text (such as a title or bulleted list), clip art, a table, a graph, or an organization chart.

The arrangement of objects on a slide is called the ***slide layout.*** PowerPoint provides an ***AutoLayout*** feature, through which you can select among 21 professionally designed layouts. You will select an AutoLayout using the New Slide or Slide Layout dialog box. Figure 3.10 shows the first nine designs. A heavy black surrounding border indicates the current selection.

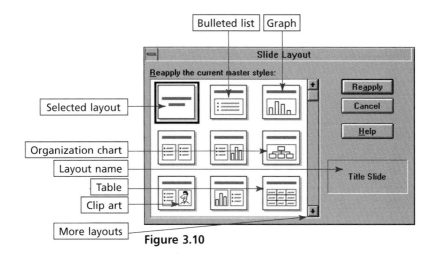

Figure 3.10

The first layout shown in the upper-left corner of Figure 3.10 is the design PowerPoint assigned to the initial slide in your cruises presentation. It sets placeholders for two objects, one a title text box and the other a subtitle text box. The other designs set up two or three objects. For example, the slide design in the lower-left corner of Figure 3.10 includes a title text box above a bulleted list on the left and a clip art image on the right.

In the following steps you will adjust the background shading and color intensity of all slides. You will then select a Title Only layout for the first slide in your cruises presentation.

To adjust background shading and color intensity:

1 Choose Slide Background from the Format menu.
The Slide Background dialog box shown in Figure 3.11 appears.

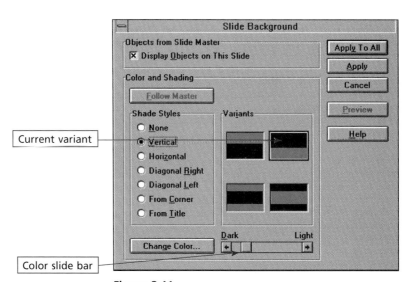

Figure 3.11

2 Select Diagonal Right from the Shade Styles list.

3 Select the upper-left of the four variants.

4 Slide the color slide bar to the lightest setting.

5 Select Apply To All.
The dialog box disappears. The screen displays the slide shown in Figure 3.8 with a lighter background and different shading pattern.

To select an AutoLayout and save your changes:

1 Select Slide Layout from the Format menu.
AutoLayouts appear as shown in Figure 3.10.

2 Scroll to the bottom of the layout designs.

3 Select the middle slide in the last row.
The words Title Only should appear in the layout name box.

4 Select Apply.
The revised layout displays a single text box, as shown in Figure 3.12.

Click to add title

Figure 3.12

5 Save the file.

EXIT   If necessary, you can exit PowerPoint now and continue this project later.

WORKING WITH TEXT BOXES

Think of a slide as a work surface on which you can set up placeholders for one or more objects. If a placeholder marks the position for text, you can click within the borders of the associated box and type the words you want to display. PowerPoint also supports a variety of features associated with word processing. For example, you can center text, alter line spacing, and change the style and size of characters.

Your ability to work with text boxes is not limited to content, however. Using a mouse, you can easily alter the dimensions of a box as well as move it to another position on the slide.

Creating and Editing a Text Box

PowerPoint's AutoLayout will create one or more predefined text boxes of your choice. You can also place a text box on the current slide by clicking the Text Tool button on the Drawing toolbar, positioning the mouse pointer where you want the upper-left corner of the box to appear, and then dragging the mouse down and to the right to form the boundaries of the box.

Tip Text that you type in title and main text placeholders will appear in Outline view. Text that you type with the Text Tool does not appear in Outline view.

To enter text in a blank box, click within the box borders and begin typing. To edit existing contents, click anywhere on the text. The object becomes a *selection box,* which you can recognize by the border of forward slashes shown in Figure 3.13. After you select a box, you can make corrections as you would on any word-processed document.

Selection box —

Figure 3.13

In the following steps you will turn on the Drawing toolbar. You will also add text in two places on slide 1: your firm's name in the title placeholder and additional text in a newly drawn box.

To turn on the Drawing toolbar:

1 If necessary, load PowerPoint and open the CRUISES.PPT presentation.

2 Choose Toolbars from the View menu.

3 Select the Drawing toolbar, if not already selected.
An X appears in the box to the left of the Drawing toolbar name. Standard and Formatting toolbars should already be selected.

4 Select OK.

Tip If necessary, review information about using toolbars provided in the Overview.

To enter text in an existing box:

1 Click within the borders of the title placeholder at the top of the slide.
The box border changes, and the message "Click to add title" disappears.

2 Type **Island Tours**

3 Click anywhere outside the box to cancel editing.
The new title appears centered near the top of the slide. PowerPoint automatically assigns a large print size.

To draw a box and enter text:

1 Select Text Tool on the Drawing toolbar.

2 Position the mouse pointer below the word *Island*, about midway between the top and bottom of the background tree.

3 Click and drag the mouse pointer down about 1 inch and to the right about 2 inches, forming a box on the screen.
While you are drawing the box, the mouse pointer changes from an arrow to a thin square cross at the lower-right corner of the box.

4 Release the mouse button.
A blank selection box appears near the middle of the slide.

5 Type **Presents . . .**
The newly created box resembles the one shown in Figure 3.13.

6 Click anywhere outside the box.
The slide resembles the first slide in Figure 3.1 except for the position of the most recent text entry. In the next section you will move that text away from the background tree.

Moving and Sizing a Text Box

Moving an object requires a two-step process: displaying the moving-and-sizing border shown in Figure 3.14 and then dragging the box to its new location.

Moving-and-sizing border

Resize handle

Figure 3.14

Clicking a border of the object's selection box will display the moving-and-sizing border. To *drag* the box, position the mouse pointer on a border (see Figure 3.14), click and hold down the left mouse button, move the box to its new position, and release the mouse button.

The square at each corner and midpoint of the moving-and-sizing border is a *resize handle*. With one exception, dragging a resize handle resizes the object. If you added text to an object you've drawn on the screen, the text won't resize. (You will learn to change the style and size of text later in this project.)

Tip To delete an object drawn with PowerPoint's drawing tools, display the moving-and-sizing border and then press `DEL`.

In the following steps you will improve the readability of text by moving it away from the background tree.

To move a text box and save your changes:

1 Position the mouse pointer on *Presents. . .* and click.
A selection box appears as shown in Figure 3.13.

2 Click anywhere on the selection box border.
The moving-and-sizing border displays as shown in Figure 3.14.

3 Click the moving-and-sizing border, and drag the box to the left side of the slide.
The text *Presents. . .* should appear in the clear area to the left of the background tree, as shown in Figure 3.1.

4 Click outside the box.

 5 Save the file.

 If necessary, you can exit PowerPoint now and continue this project later.

ENHANCING TEXT

Anytime you develop slides, you should think about how to focus a reader's attention on key points. For example, you might increase the size of selected text, **bold** a phrase, which displays it darker than the surrounding text, or use various colors. Effective use of such text enhancements is an art that you will develop as you examine techniques used by others and experiment on your own. Avoid using too many text enhancements, or the viewer may become distracted.

Changing Font Style and Size

Font refers to the shape (typeface) of characters. Size is expressed in terms of *points,* such as 12-point or 18-point. Each point equals 1/72 inch. You can change fonts and points using the Formatting toolbar or the Font dialog box, both of which are shown in Figure 3.15. Changes apply to selected text within a box.

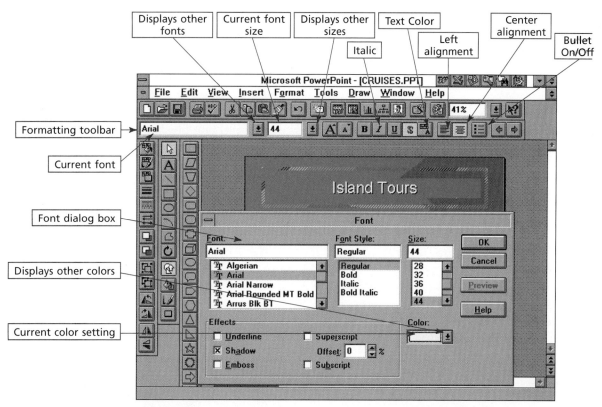

Figure 3.15

Tip Do not mix too many fonts in a presentation. You should also standardize fonts as much as possible, such as using the same font for all slide titles.

In the following steps you will alter the font and increase the text size on the current slide. First you will use the Formatting toolbar to make those changes to the slide title. You will then use the Font dialog box to make similar changes in remaining text.

To change font size using the Formatting toolbar:

1 If necessary, load PowerPoint and open the CRUISES.PPT presentation.

2 Click the slide title.
A selection box appears, surrounding the words *Island Tours*.

3 Select both words in the title.

Caution If you omit this step, PowerPoint will change only the word at the current insertion point position.

4 Click the underscored down arrow to the right of the current font size in the Formatting toolbar.

Caution Do not click the underscored down arrow to the left of the current font size, or you will view the font *style* options instead of the font *size* options.

5 Select 54 from the pull-down list of point sizes.
54 displays as the current font size in the Formatting toolbar.

6 Click outside the selection box.

To change font and font size using the Font dialog box:

1 Select the *Presents. . .* text box.

2 Choose Font from the Format menu.

3 Select Arial Narrow in the Font list box.
If Arial Narrow is not available on your system, substitute another font such as Times New Roman or Century Gothic.

4 Select 36 in the Size list box.

5 Turn off active features in the Effects section of the dialog box by clicking in the checked boxes (if any).

6 Select OK to apply the font changes.
Text within the selection box appears in a larger size.

7 Click outside the selection box.

Adding Special Effects

Several changes can be made to the appearance of characters. For example, you can bold, italicize, and underline text. When you ***shadow*** text you add a drop shadow behind the selected text. If you want text to take on the same color as the background and appear slightly raised, you can ***emboss*** it. Once in awhile you may want to change the position of a character, altering its location on a line in relation to other characters on the line. For example, you can position a ***superscript*** character slightly above characters on the same line or a ***subscript*** character slightly below characters on the same line.

In the following steps you will use the Italic tool on the Formatting toolbar to italicize a phrase.

To italicize selected text:

1 Select the *Presents. . .* text box.

2 Click Italic in the Formatting toolbar.
The selected text appears italicized.

Tip Choosing Font from the Format menu and selecting Italic in the Font dialog box produces the same result.

3 Click outside the selection box.

Applying Color

If you will be giving an on-screen presentation or using color slides, color can be a powerful tool for emphasizing text. Research has shown that "hot" colors such as red and yellow tend to excite or antagonize, while "cool" colors such as green and blue tend to relax or pacify.

Clicking the Text Color button in the Formatting toolbar, or selecting the color pull-down list in the Font dialog box, displays an initial 8-color palette. If the color you want does not appear in the initial color set, you can select Other Color to view the dialog box shown in Figure 3.16, which offers a color palette with 88 colors.

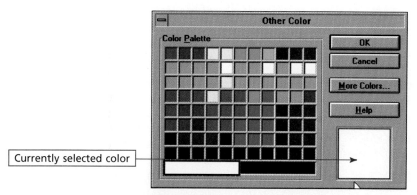

Currently selected color

Figure 3.16

Additional variations of shading and hues are available if you select the More Colors button. Exercise caution, however, in setting colors. Too many variations can be distracting to a viewer.

In the following steps you will change the color of selected text.

To apply color and save your changes:

1 Select the *Presents. . .* text box.

2 Click the Text Color button in the Formatting toolbar.

3 Select yellow from the color palette.

4 Click outside the selection box.

5 Save the file.

EXIT If necessary, you can exit PowerPoint now and continue this project later.

COMPLETING TEXT ENTRY

Throughout the remainder of this project, you will set up the *text* portions of slides 2 and 3 as shown in Figure 3.1 (you will add lines and clip art in Project 4). In the process you will work with variations of earlier activities, such as selecting a different AutoLayout design, and a few new features, such as centering text.

You will be instructed to save your changes at the end of each section. If necessary, you can exit PowerPoint after saving your work and complete the project later. To begin again, load PowerPoint, open the CRUISES.PPT presentation, and display the last slide you were editing.

Using Object AutoLayout

You want slide 2 to display a title over a picture of a sail boat (see Figure 3.1). To create this slide, you will select the AutoLayout named Object and add the title *Cruising the Caribbean*, as shown in Figure 3.17.

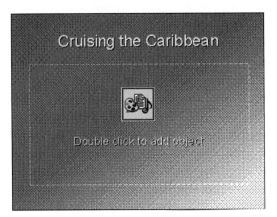

Figure 3.17

To create slide two:

1 If necessary, load PowerPoint and open the CRUISES.PPT presentation.

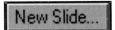

2 Click New Slide near the lower-right corner of the screen.
The New Slide dialog box appears.

3 Select the Object layout.

4 Select OK to create the slide.
Two placeholders appear, one for a title and the other for an object (in this case, clip art to be added in Project 4).

5 Choose Slide Background from the Format menu.

6 If an X appears in the Display Objects on This Slide check box, click the check box until it is blank.
The setting that controls display of background objects is turned off.

7 Select Apply.
The background tree disappears.

8 Click the title text box.

9 Type **Cruising the Caribbean** and then click outside either box. Check that your slide matches Figure 3.17.

10 Save the file.

Using 2 Column Text AutoLayout

Slides 3, 4, and 5 have a more complex layout than the first two slides (see Figure 3.1). Each title occupies three lines. Other text displays in two columns, one of which contains a bulleted list.

You could create each slide from scratch. However, once you set up the two-column text design on slide 3 using AutoLayout and then enter text, you can duplicate that slide twice to form slides 4 and 5 (which you will do in Project 4). It's a relatively simple task to then edit the two new slides to reflect different cruise packages.

In the following steps you will use AutoLayout to select a basic design for slide 3, remove the slide background, enter a three-line title, vary the font size in the title, and move the lower two boxes to add space below the title. Remember to save your work frequently during a long editing session.

To select the layout for slide 3 and remove the background:

1 Click New Slide.

2 Select 2 Column Text layout, and then select OK.
Three boxes appear: one for the title, and two other text boxes side by side. The bullet in the upper-left corner of each text box indicates the box is a placeholder for a bulleted list.

3 Remove the background tree from the slide.
If you do not remember how to complete this task, review steps 5 through 7 in the previous numbered steps.

Caution The Display Objects on This Slide check box must be blank. You may need to click the box twice, once to remove shading and again to remove the X.

To specify the title for slide 3 and vary font size:

1 Select the title box at the top of the slide.

2 Type **Bahamas** and press (ENTER)

3 Type **on the** and press (ENTER)

4 Type **Island Princess** (do not press (ENTER))

5 Select *Bahamas* and apply a 54-point Arial font.

Reminder If a font you are instructed to use does not appear on your font list, select another font.

6 Select *on the* and apply a 24-point Arial font.

7 Select *Island Princess* and apply a 44-point Arial font.

8 Click outside the slide to clear the text box outline.

To move the boxes and save your changes:

1 Select the left box below the title.

2 Drag the box downward by its border to add space below the title, as shown in Figure 3.18.

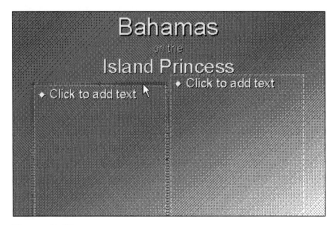

Figure 3.18

3 Select the right box below the title.

4 Drag the box downward the same distance as the left box.

5 Save the file.

Aligning Text

By default, text aligns at the left edge of a box. The Formatting toolbar contains Left Alignment and Center Alignment buttons. You can also choose Alignment from the Format menu to left-align, center, or right-align text. In the following steps you will finish entering the text for slide 3. You will also change fonts and alignment.

To apply a font to a blank text box:

1 Click within the left box below the title.

2 Apply a 32-point Century Schoolbook font to the box.
This font will apply to all text typed in the box unless you specify otherwise.

To center text:

1 Click Bullet On/Off in the Formatting toolbar.
The bullet in the text box disappears.

2 Type **Visit**

3 Click Center Alignment in the Formatting toolbar.
Text is now centered on the current line.

4 Press (ENTER) to position the insertion point on the next line.

 5 Click Left Alignment in the Formatting toolbar.

6 Click Bullet On/Off.
A bullet appears on the slide. The Bullet On/Off button appears slightly depressed and lighter in color compared to other buttons in the Formatting toolbar, which tells you that the feature is active.

 ### To complete the bulleted list:

1 Type **Nassau** and press (ENTER)

2 Type **Coco Cay** and press (ENTER)

3 Type **Freeport** and press (ENTER)

4 Click Bullet On/Off to turn bullets off.

5 Apply a 20-point Century Schoolbook font.

6 Press (ENTER) and then press (TAB)

7 Type **Leaves Mondays and Fridays from San Juan**
Text that won't fit on one line automatically wraps to the next line.

8 Select the text typed in the previous step, and then click Italic in the Formatting toolbar.

9 Click outside the box to deselect it.
The text on your slide should match that shown in Figure 3.19. Positioning may vary if you chose different font styles or sizes.

Figure 3.19

 10 Save the file.

To change fonts and enter text in the right text box:

1 Select the text box on the right side of the slide.

2 Apply a 32-point Century Schoolbook font to the box.

3 Click Bullet On/Off to remove the bullet.

4 Type **3 Night Cruise** and press (ENTER) twice.

5 Type **From $390** and press (ENTER)

6 Press (TAB) twice, type **Ship Only** and then press (ENTER)

7 Type **From $580** and then press (ENTER)

8 Press (TAB) twice, and then type **Includes Air**

9 Apply a 20-point Century Schoolbook font to four words and phrases: the word *From* preceding $390, the phrase *Ship Only*, the word *From* preceding $580, and the phrase *Includes Air*.

10 Click outside the box.

11 Check that the text on your slide matches that shown in Figure 3.20. Make changes as necessary.

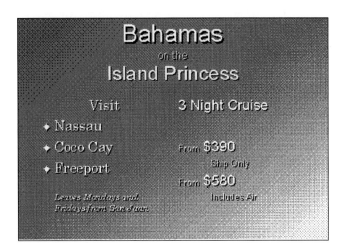

Figure 3.20

12 Save the file.

You have created the text portion of slide 3. After adding lines in the next project, you will use this slide to create two similar slides.

THE NEXT STEP

Think of all the PowerPoint features presented in this project! You used the Pick a Look Wizard to assign a template and specify the desired outputs. Several AutoLayout designs provided the starting points for new slides. You worked extensively with text boxes, entering and editing text as well as moving and sizing the boxes. Of course, you also enhanced text by varying font and size, changing color, and applying special effects.

To build on your skills, plan your own presentation combining text with other objects. Up to this point the decisions as to layout, font, text to type, and so forth were made for you. Now prepare to make your own decisions. Take a look at the available templates. View other AutoLayout slide designs, and imagine a slide in which you might use each layout. Try out options you read about but didn't work through, such as shadowing or embossing text. Type some words in a new presentation, and apply different fonts, font sizes, and special effects. By experimenting with the program on your own, you'll quickly gain confidence.

This concludes Project 3. You can either exit PowerPoint or go on to work the Study Questions, Review Exercises, and Assignments.

SUMMARY AND EXERCISES

Summary

- Pick a Look Wizard provides a nine-step process for choosing a template, picking the type of slide, and selecting support documents (outlines, audience handouts, and speaker's notes).
- A template controls how the various parts of your presentation should appear, including background patterns and colors.
- The options for type of slide include color overhead, black and white overhead, on-screen presentation, and 35mm slides.
- A slide may contain one or more objects. In PowerPoint an object can be text (such as a title or bulleted list), clip art, a table, a graph, or an organization chart.
- The arrangement of objects on a slide is called the slide layout. PowerPoint provides the AutoLayout feature, through which you can select among 21 professionally designed layouts.
- You work with objects in boxes on a slide. You can create, edit, move, and size a box.
- Font refers to the shape (typeface) of characters, and font size refers to height. You can make changes to font and font size as well as display text in color and with special effects.
- Text can appear left-aligned (the default), centered, and right-aligned.

Key Terms and Operations

Key Terms
35mm Slides
AutoLayout
Black and White Overheads
bold
clip art
Color Overheads
drag
emboss
font
landscape orientation
object
On-Screen Presentation
placeholder
point
portrait orientation
resize handle

selection box
shadow
slide layout
subscript
superscript
template

Operations
Use Pick a Look Wizard
Create placeholders with AutoLayout
Create and edit a text box
Move a text box
Change font and font size
Italicize text
Apply color to text
Center text

Study Questions

Multiple Choice

1. Which of the following is not a valid type of slide?
   a. Color Overheads
   b. On-Screen Presentation
   c. Landscape
   d. 35mm Slides

2. Which of the following refers to the arrangement of objects on a slide?
   a. slide layout
   b. resize handle
   c. AutoLayout
   d. AutoContent Wizard

3. Which of the following can be controlled by a template?
   a. background pattern
   b. colors
   c. repeating text such as a company name or the date
   d. All of the above.

4. What is the feature that provides 21 professionally designed arrangements of objects on a slide?
   a. Pick a Look
   b. AutoLayout
   c. object orientation
   d. None of the above.

5. What are the objects on a slide that reserve space and are filled in later?
   a. placeholders
   b. text boxes
   c. clip art boxes
   d. Both b and c are true.

6. The border of forward slashes that appears around the text box when you click the text indicates
   a. adjustment handles.
   b. sizing handles.
   c. a selection box.
   d. a border box.

7. What term refers to moving a box using a mouse?
   a. click
   b. move
   c. cut and paste
   d. drag

8. The term *points* refers to
   a. typeface.
   b. font size.
   c. italics.
   d. shadow effect.

9. Which is not a true statement about slide layouts?
   a. You can design your own layout.
   b. You can select a layout using AutoLayout.

    c. You can change the size of an object on the slide.
    d. You must delete a slide to select a new layout.

10. Which is not a true statement about aligning text?
    a. The default alignment is along the left edge of a box.
    b. You can center and right-align text by choosing Alignment from the Format menu.
    c. You can center and right-align text using the Formatting toolbar.
    d. All previous statements are true.

Short Answers

1. What is the term that refers to graphics images stored on disk?

2. If an overhead projector is all that you have to use during a presentation, what two types of slides should you create?

3. What wizard provides a nine-step process for choosing a template, which tells PowerPoint how the various parts of your presentation should appear?

4. What is the name of the AutoLayout displaying side-by-side text boxes below a title box?

5. When you click anywhere inside a text box, what kind of box does the object become?

6. When you click on a text box, what are the squares at each corner and the midpoints called?

7. What is the shape (typeface) of characters called?

8. Name three font styles or special effects.

9. What term refers to arranging text along the left edge of a text box?

10. What option, accessed from the Format menu, lets you adjust a slide's shading and color intensity?

For Discussion

1. Describe the process for dragging a text box to a different location.

2. Explain the options for aligning text in a box.

3. Why is it important to enhance the appearance of text? What are some of your options to make some characters look different than others?

4. Which of the 21 predefined layouts provide placeholders for text?

5. Discuss the purpose of Pick a Look Wizard.

Review Exercises

Buying a Car

Create a six-slide presentation showing the steps to buying a car. Figure 3.21 shows the plan for the completed presentation, which includes clip art, word art, lines, borders, and color fills.

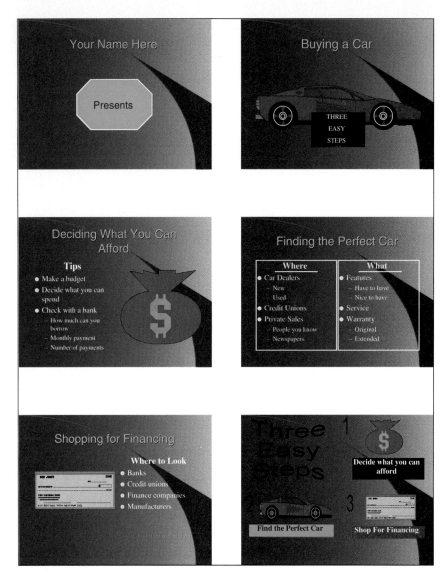

Figure 3.21

In this review exercise you will create each slide from AutoLayout and then add text (the other enhancements are part of the review exercises in Project 4). When you finish the following instructions, your presentation will include the layouts and text shown in Figure 3.22. Refer to this figure as you complete the following steps. Save your work after each new slide (use the name BUYCAR.PPT).

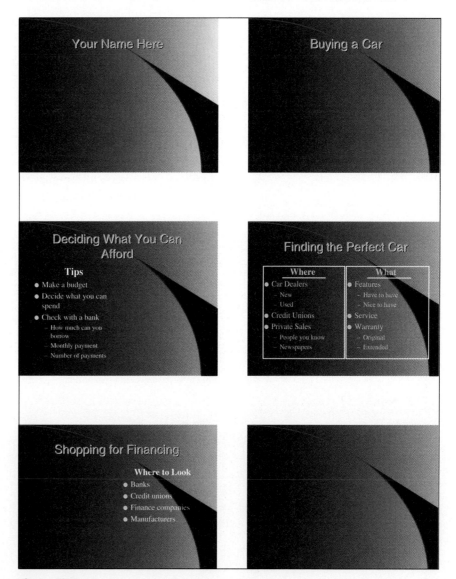

Figure 3.22

1. Load PowerPoint and select Blank Presentation. (If already in PowerPoint, choose New from the File menu.)

2. Create slide 1. Select a Title Only layout, and type your name in the Title text box.

3. Click Template near the bottom of the screen, and select SOARINGS.PPT from the list of file names in the Presentation Template dialog box (template files are stored in the TEMPLATE\SLDSHOW directory).

4. Create slide 2. Select a Title Only layout, and add the title shown in Figure 3.22.

5. Create slide 3. Select a Text & Clip Art layout, and enter the title and tips shown in Figure 3.22.

6. Create slide 4. Select a 2 Column Text layout, and enter the title as well as the *Where* and *What* information shown in Figure 3.22.

7. Create slide 5. Select a Clip Art & Text layout, and enter the title and *Where to Look* information.

8. Create slide 6. Select a Blank layout. (You will add the text summarizing the three steps after adding word art and clip art in the Project 4 review exercises.)

9. Review your BUYCAR presentation, and make changes as necessary.

Getting Involved in Campus Life

Create a six-slide presentation showing some of the ways that students can get involved in campus life. Figure 3.23 shows the plan for the completed presentation, which includes special text effects and clip art.

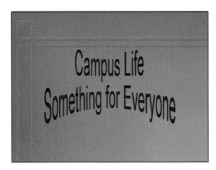
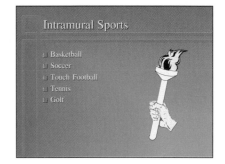

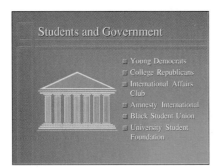

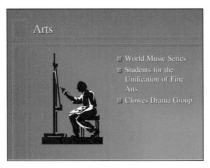
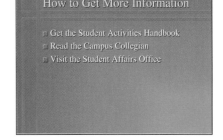

Figure 3.23

In this review exercise you will create each slide from AutoLayout and add text (the other enhancements are part of the review exercises after Project 4). When you finish the following instructions, your presentation will include the layouts and text shown in Figure 3.24. Refer to this figure as you complete the following steps. Save your work after each new slide (use the name GETALIFE.PPT).

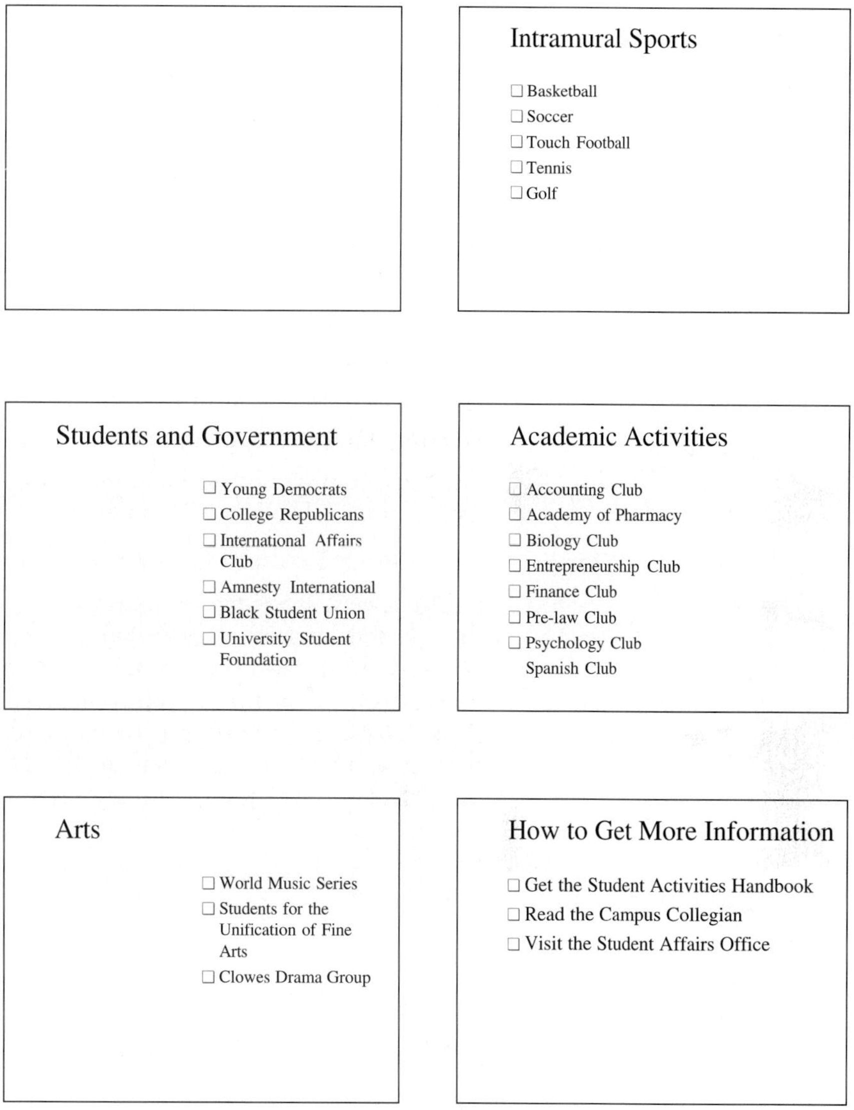

Intramural Sports

☐ Basketball
☐ Soccer
☐ Touch Football
☐ Tennis
☐ Golf

Students and Government

☐ Young Democrats
☐ College Republicans
☐ International Affairs Club
☐ Amnesty International
☐ Black Student Union
☐ University Student Foundation

Academic Activities

☐ Accounting Club
☐ Academy of Pharmacy
☐ Biology Club
☐ Entrepreneurship Club
☐ Finance Club
☐ Pre-law Club
☐ Psychology Club
   Spanish Club

Arts

☐ World Music Series
☐ Students for the Unification of Fine Arts
☐ Clowes Drama Group

How to Get More Information

☐ Get the Student Activities Handbook
☐ Read the Campus Collegian
☐ Visit the Student Affairs Office

Figure 3.24

1. Load PowerPoint and select Blank Presentation. (If already in PowerPoint choose New from the File menu.)

2. Create slide 1. Select a Blank layout. Leave the slide blank until Project 4.

3. Create slide 2. Select the Text & Clip Art layout, and then add the *Intramural Sports* title and text in a bulleted list, as shown in Figure 3.24.

4. Create slide 3. Select the Clip Art & Text layout, and then add the *Students and Government* title and text in a bulleted list, as shown in Figure 3.24.

5. Create slide 4. Select the Text & Clip Art layout, and then add the *Academic Activities* title and text in a bulleted list, as shown in Figure 3.24.

6. Create slide 5. Select the Clip Art & Text layout, and then add the *Arts* title and text in a bulleted list, as shown in Figure 3.24.

7. Create slide 6. Select the Bulleted List layout, and then add the *How to Get More Information* title and text in a bulleted list, as shown in Figure 3.24.

8. Review your GETALIFE presentation, and make changes as necessary.

Assignments

Getting Help on Typing Text

Use Search in on-screen Help to look up information about terms that apply to typing text. Write a brief summary of what you learned.

Getting Help on Moving Text

Use Search in on-screen Help to look up information about moving text with a mouse. Write a brief summary of what you learned.

Combining Text and Clip Art (Part One)

Create a new presentation. Select among the following topics (or substitute another of your choice): selling a product, organizing a social event, registering for classes, or repairing a broken item. The presentation should instruct viewers to follow at least a three-step process. First provide a sketch of the text and art you have in mind for each slide (try to include at least four variations in slide layout). Then look through the clip art gallery to find appropriate graphics. Create the slides, but enter only the text. Save your work using a name that helps you remember the presentation topic.

PROJECT 4: COMBINING TEXT AND ART

Objectives

After completing this project, you should be able to:

▶ Select and insert clip art

▶ Add lines and borders

▶ Duplicate slides in Slide Sorter view

▶ Use Word Art to enhance text

▶ Arrange multiple objects effectively

▶ Display AutoShapes containing text

CASE STUDY: CRUISING THE CARIBBEAN II

Think back to times you have walked down a hall past a bulletin board, thumbed through the telephone yellow pages, or watched billboards as you traveled on an interstate highway. What did you see that caused you to take a second look? In many cases you would say it was an image that first caught your attention. Viewing a combination of art and text on slide presentations can have a similar attention-grabbing effect.

In Project 3 you entered most of the text for an eight-slide presentation about Caribbean cruises. In this project you will add art, borders, lines, shapes, and color to emphasize your message.

Designing the Solution

Most of the design work is already done. Before you created the first cruise-related slide, you had an overall layout in mind (see Figure 3.1):

- An introductory slide showing your company's name, with a background of a tree on an island
- A second slide announcing the subject of the presentation (*Cruising the Caribbean*) with a picture of a sailing vessel occupying most of the slide
- Three slides promoting different cruise packages, with bulleted lists of destinations along with departure and rate information set apart from other text
- A slide summarizing cruise highlights

- A slide letting viewers know how to get more information (you'd like pictures of a phone, a fax machine, and an envelope placed next to associated numbers and address)
- A final slide showing your firm's name, along with a promotional message within an eye-catching shape

The remaining design work is very hands-on in nature. In this project you receive instructions on which clip art figures to select, the shape in which to type text, exactly where to draw a line, and so forth. For your own presentations, however, this phase will involve looking through a lot of clip art, moving and sizing selected objects, and experimenting with color and other visual effects until you are satisfied that the slides will capture the attention of an audience.

ADDING CLIP ART

Clip art pictures are created by computer drawing programs, digital cameras, and scanners that turn images into computer files stored on disk. Examples of this process can be found in retail outlets that place your image on t-shirts, calendars, and cakes. Some public and school libraries have scanners that you can use to digitize pictures as easily as duplicating pages on a copy machine.

Caution United States copyright laws apply to photographs and art as well as written material. They apply to images digitized from hard copy or downloaded from a network such as the Internet. Be aware that you may have to get permission to use an image, such as a Disney character.

PowerPoint provides an extensive gallery of more than 1000 clip art images organized into 40 categories such as Academic, Banners, Business and Finance, Cartoons, Energy, Technology, and Transportation. Choosing the Clip Art option from the Insert menu displays the initial Microsoft ClipArt Gallery dialog box shown in Figure 4.1.

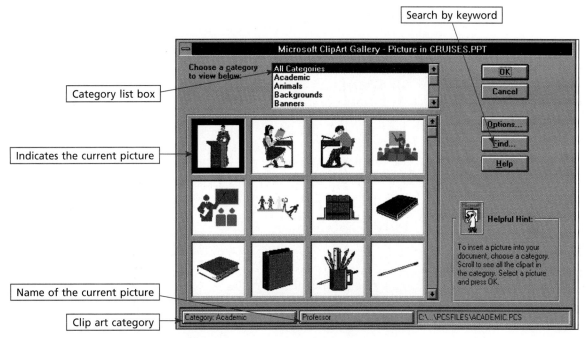

Figure 4.1

Directions to select a picture appear in a Helpful Hint box in the lower-right corner of the dialog box. A thick surrounding border indicates the current picture; its category and name are displayed at the bottom. You can select among other sets of pictures using the Category list box. The Find option helps you locate a specific picture or type of picture quickly. For example, you can display all clip art in a specified category or with names containing a certain word or phrase, such as sailing.

In the following steps you will add a sailing clip art figure to the object box in slide 2. (You will also add clip art to slide 7 near the end of the project.)

> **Tip** The full set of PowerPoint clip art may not be installed on your system. Therefore, one or more of the clip art pictures specified in this project may not be available. If you should encounter a message stating that a matching picture could not be found, select an appropriate substitute.

To add clip art to an existing object box:

1 Load PowerPoint and open the CRUISES.PPT presentation.
The opening slide appears, showing the title and background tree.

2 Display slide 2.

3 Double-click the icon within the object box.
The Insert Object dialog box appears on the screen.

4 Select Microsoft ClipArt Gallery in the Object Type list box.

5 Select OK.
The Microsoft ClipArt Gallery appears as shown in Figure 4.1.

6 Select Find.
The Find Picture dialog box appears.

7 Select With a Description Containing.

8 Type **sailing** and click OK.
Two pictures with a sailing theme appear, as shown in Figure 4.2. The selected figure (the first one) is the one you want.

Reminder If the specified clip art is not available, select an appropriate substitute. You might, for example, look in the Transportation or Travel categories.

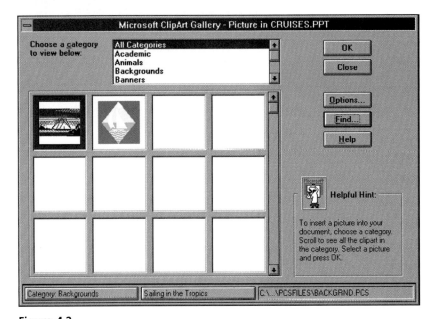

Figure 4.2

9 Click OK to select the current clip art.

10 Click outside the object box to deselect it.
The completed slide 2 is shown in Figure 4.3.

Figure 4.3

 11 Save the file.

ADDING LINES AND BORDERS

You can create interesting visual effects by using horizontal lines, vertical lines, and borders to separate sections of a slide, as shown in Figure 4.4. A *border* is a line drawn around the edge of an object.

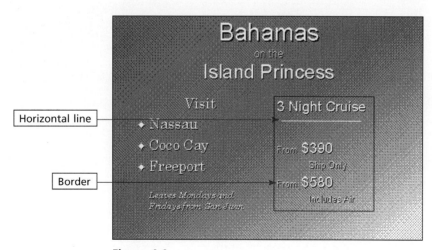

Figure 4.4

To draw a line, you will first select the Line Tool button on the Drawing toolbar. Next you will move the mouse pointer to the location where you want the line to start (the arrow pointer changes to a cross-hair pointer when you cross the boundary of the slide, as shown in Figure 4.5). You will then drag the pointer to the ending point.

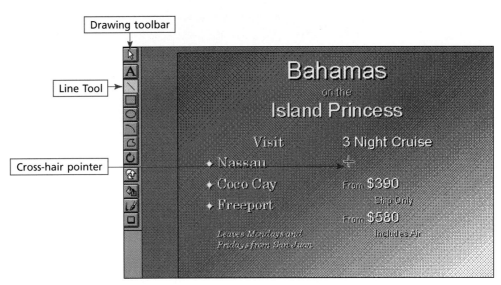

Figure 4.5

To create a border, you will select the object you want to surround with a line and then open the Colors and Lines dialog box shown in Figure 4.6. You can select among solid and dashed line styles, pick a color for the border from the Line pull-down list, and pick a color to fill the space within the border from the Fill pull-down list.

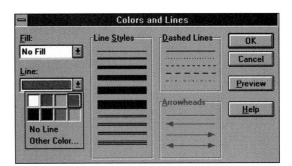

Figure 4.6

In the following steps you will enhance slide 3 by adding a horizontal line to separate the length of a cruise from the prices that follow. You will also add a colored border.

 To display the Drawing toolbar (skip these steps if the Drawing toolbar already displays):

1 Choose Toolbars from the View menu.

2 Click the box to the left of Drawing until an X appears in the box.

3 Select OK.

Tip Subsequent instructions will not contain the level of detail shown in steps 1 through 3. Instead, you will see a single instruction to turn on the Drawing (or some other) toolbar.

To add a horizontal line:

1 Display slide 3.

2 Select Line Tool from the Drawing toolbar, and position the cross-hair pointer as shown in Figure 4.5.

3 Hold down the left mouse button and move the cross-hair pointer to the right, as shown in Figure 4.7.

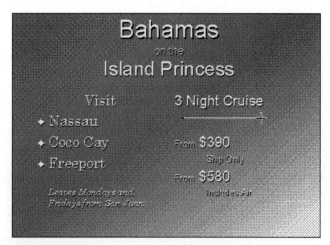

Figure 4.7

4 Release the left mouse button.

5 Click outside the line to deselect Line Tool.
A horizontal separator line appears as shown in Figure 4.4.

To add a border:

1 Select the text box on the right side of slide 3 that contains price information.

2 Choose Colors and Lines from the Format menu.
The Colors and Lines dialog box appears.

3 Click the first option in the Line Styles list (a thin solid line).

4 Click the underscored down arrow to the right of the Line box.
The pull-down list of eight colors appears.

5 Select Blue.

6 Select OK to close the dialog box.
A blue border appears around the text box.

7 Move and size the box until its location and size matches that shown in Figure 4.4.

8 Click outside the box to deselect it.

9 Save the file.

EXIT If necessary, you can exit PowerPoint now and continue this project later.

DUPLICATING SLIDES IN SLIDE SORTER VIEW

Look again at Figure 3.1. Slides 4 and 5 have the same text arrangements, fonts, font sizes, lines, and borders as slide 3. Duplicating slide 3 twice will save you time in developing the next two slides.

You can duplicate slides in Slide Sorter view or Outline view by choosing Duplicate from the Edit menu. PowerPoint automatically inserts the duplicate slide immediately after the original slide.

Tip To duplicate a slide in a nonadjacent position, use Copy and Paste commands on the Edit menu. For example, later in this project you will use copy and paste techniques to duplicate the contents of slide 1 on a new slide 8.

In the following steps you will duplicate a slide twice in Slide Sorter view. You will then edit the text in the new slides to display information about two other cruises.

To duplicate a slide in Slide Sorter view:

1 If necessary, load PowerPoint and open the CRUISES.PPT presentation.

2 Select Slide Sorter view.

3 Select slide 3.
A thick black border appears around slide 3.

4 Choose Duplicate from the Edit menu to create slide 4.

5 Choose Duplicate from the Edit menu to create slide 5.
Slides 3, 4, and 5 are identical for the moment. You will edit slides 4 and 5 in the following sets of numbered steps.

To change the title in slide 4:

1 Select slide 4.

2 Select Slide view.

Caution Slides 3, 4, and 5 are identical until you change them. Be sure you have accessed the correct slide by checking the slide number in the lower-left corner of the screen.

3 Click within the title text box.

4 Select *Bahamas* and type `Eastern Caribbean`
The new text replaces the selected text.

5 Select *Island* and type `Tropic`

To edit text in the left text box on slide 4:

1 Click within the left text box.

2 Select *Coco Cay* and type `San Juan`

3 Select *Freeport* and type `St. Thomas`

4 Press (ENTER) to insert a blank bulleted line.

5 Type `Coco Cay`

6 Edit the departure information by typing `Leaves Mondays from Miami` to replace *Leaves Mondays and Fridays from San Juan*.

7 Check that the text in your left text box matches that shown on slide 4 in Figure 3.1. Make changes as necessary.

To edit text in the right text box on slide 4:

1 Click within the right text box.

2 Select *3 Night Cruise* and type `5 Night Cruise`

3 Select *$390* and type `$845`

4 Select *$580* and type `$1085`

5 Click anywhere outside the box to clear the text box outline.

6 Check that your slide 4 matches Figure 4.8. Make changes as necessary.

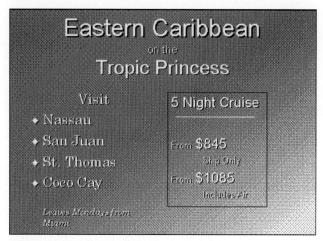

Figure 4.8

7 Save the file.

To change the title in slide 5:

1 Select slide 5.
Be sure that slide 5 is selected by checking the current slide number in the lower-left corner of the screen.

2 Click within the title text box.

3 Select *Bahamas* and type `Southern Caribbean`

4 Select *Princess* and type `Pleasure`

To edit text in the left text box on slide 5:

1 Click within the left text box.

2 Select *Nassau* and type `Martinique`

3 Select *Coco Cay* and type `Barbados`

4 Select *Freeport* and type `St. Thomas`

5 Press (ENTER) to insert a blank bulleted line.

6 Type `Antigua` and press (ENTER) to insert another blank bulleted line.

7 Type `St. Maarten`

8 Delete the blank line after St. Maarten.

9 Edit the departure information by typing `Leaves Sundays from San Juan` to replace *Leaves Mondays and Fridays from San Juan*.

10 Click anywhere outside the box.

11 Check that the text in your left text box matches that shown on slide 5 in Figure 3.1. Make changes as necessary.

12 Save the file.

To edit text in the right text box on slide 5:

1 Click within the right text box.

2 Select *3 Night Cruise* and type `7 Night Cruise`

3 Select *$390* and type `$999`

4 Select *$580* and type `$1145`

5 Click anywhere outside the box to clear the text box outline.

6 Check that your slide matches Figure 4.9. Make changes as necessary.

Figure 4.9

7 Save the file.

EXIT If necessary, you can exit PowerPoint now and continue this project later.

ADDING WORD ART

Word art refers to the special text effects created by slanting, curving, or otherwise manipulating text to form an eye-catching design. The phrase *Caribbean Cruise Highlights* above the bulleted list in Figure 4.10 is an example of word art.

Figure 4.10

PowerPoint includes the Microsoft WordArt application, which lets you select among 36 predefined special effects after typing your text. The choices are displayed in the special text effects gallery shown in Figure 4.11.

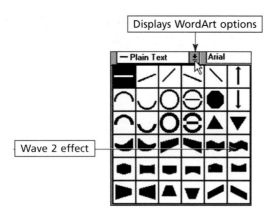

Figure 4.11

Tip For best results, use this feature on only one or two words or a short phrase.

In the sets of numbered steps that follow, you will add a blank slide 6 and create the word art and bulleted list shown in Figure 4.10.

To create a new slide without a background:

1 If necessary, load PowerPoint and open the CRUISES.PPT presentation.

2 Display slide 5, and then click New Slide.

3 Select the Object over Text layout, and then select OK.
A new slide 6 appears with placeholders for a title, an object, and a bulleted list. A tree on an island appears in the background automatically because you selected the ISLANDS.PPT template.

4 Choose Slide Background from the Format menu.

5 Click the Display Objects on This Slide check box until the box is blank.

6 Select Apply.
The setting that controls display of background objects is turned off.

To remove the unwanted title text box:

1 Click the border of the title text box at the top of the slide.
The resize handles appear.

2 Press ⌐DEL⌐ to remove the selected box.

To create curved text using Microsoft WordArt:

1 Double-click within the object box.
The Insert Object dialog box appears.

2 Select Microsoft WordArt 2.0, and then select OK.
The Enter Your Text Here dialog box appears.

3 Type the text as shown in Figure 4.12. Press (ENTER) after typing **Caribbean** and again after typing **Cruise**

Figure 4.12

4 Click the underscored down arrow to the right of the Plain Text box in the upper-left corner of the screen.
A gallery of 36 special effects appears as shown in Figure 4.11.

5 Select the last option in the fourth row of the special text effects gallery (Wave 2).
Check that your screen matches the one shown in Figure 4.13.

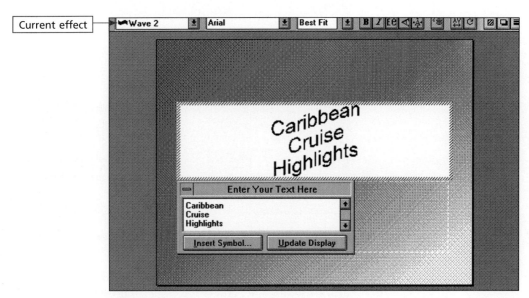

Current effect

Figure 4.13

6 Click outside the slide area to exit Microsoft WordArt.
The selected text effect with resize handles appears on the screen.

To move and size the word art and bulleted list:

1 Position the pointer within the word art object and drag it to the top of the slide.

2 Drag one or more resize handles until the word art occupies the space shown in Figure 4.10.

3 Click within the bulleted list box.

4 Enter the four lines of text shown in Figure 4.10.

5 Move and size the text box as necessary.

6 Save the file.

EXIT If necessary, you can exit PowerPoint now and continue this project later.

WORKING WITH MULTIPLE OBJECTS

You'll want viewers to pay attention to, rather than be distracted by, your slide layouts. Providing balance among objects can help to achieve the effect you want. In this section you will create slide 7 (see Figure 4.14), which combines text and pictures to let viewers know how to get more information.

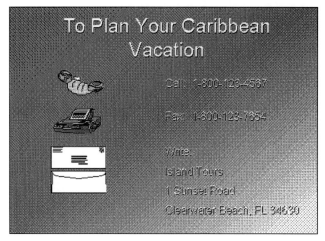

Figure 4.14

The design includes a title box across the top, three clip art boxes down the left side, and three associated text boxes down the right side.

Most of the tasks involved in creating slide 7—inserting clip art and creating text boxes—have already been described in detail in other sections of this project and Project 3. For those steps, only limited instructions will be provided. However, you will be adding clip art and text boxes without placeholders marking the locations (PowerPoint doesn't provide a predefined layout for three clip art boxes on the left and three text boxes on the right). Therefore it will be necessary to size and move each box.

Reminder Substitute similar clip art if a specified figure is not available on your system. If you can't find three suitable figures, limit the clip art to one or two.

To select a layout and turn off the background:

1 If necessary, load PowerPoint and open the CRUISES.PPT presentation.

2 Display slide 6 in Slide view, and then click New Slide.

3 Select Title Only as the layout, and then select OK.
A blank slide 7 with a palm tree background appears.

4 Choose Slide Background from the Format menu, and turn off the display of the tree in the background.

To add a slide title and three clip art figures (use Figure 4.14 as a guide, and save your work frequently):

1 Click the title box and enter the title To Plan Your Caribbean Vacation.

2 Click Insert Clip Art in the Standard toolbar.
The Microsoft ClipArt Gallery appears.

3 Select Find.
The Find Picture dialog box appears.

4 Select With a Description Containing.

5 Type hand and click OK.

6 Select the clip art of a hand holding a telephone receiver, and then click OK.
The selected clip art fills the center of the slide, as shown in Figure 4.15.

Figure 4.15

7 Move and size the clip art until its location and size resembles that shown in Figure 4.16.

Figure 4.16

Reminder Save your work frequently—in this case, after every step.

8 Repeat steps 2 through 7 and create the fax clip art object (use the word *fax* to find the desired clip art).

9 Repeat steps 2 through 7 and create the envelope clip art object (use the word *envelope* to find the desired clip art).

10 Save the file.
Now you will use Figure 4.14 as a guide to create the text boxes to the right of the clip art. Be sure to save your work frequently.

To create the three associated text boxes:

1 Click Text Tool on the Drawing toolbar, and create a text box to the right of the hand-holding-phone clip art.

2 Type **Call: 1-800-123-4567** in the text box.

3 Move and size the box until its location and size resemble that shown in Figure 4.14.

4 Click outside the slide to deselect the box.

5 Repeat steps 1 through 4 to create the fax information to the right of the fax clip art.

6 Repeat steps 1 through 4 to create the write information to the right of the envelope clip art (enter all four lines of text in one box).

7 Check that your final slide displays the content and layout shown in Figure 4.14. Make changes as necessary.

8 Save the file.

EXIT If necessary, you can exit PowerPoint now and continue this project later.

ADDING AUTOSHAPES WITH TEXT

An *AutoShape* is one of 24 complex predefined shapes, such as the seal shown in Figure 4.17. These shapes can be stretched over the top of a text box, or you can place one on the screen, fill it with color, and add text to it.

Figure 4.17

Drawing a predefined shape requires steps similar to those for drawing a text box or line. You begin by clicking the desired shape on the AutoShapes toolbar shown in Figure 4.18. Next you will move the mouse pointer to the location where you want the shape to start and then drag the pointer to the ending point. You can move an AutoShape by dragging on a border of its selection box, and you can change its size by dragging one of the eight resize handles.

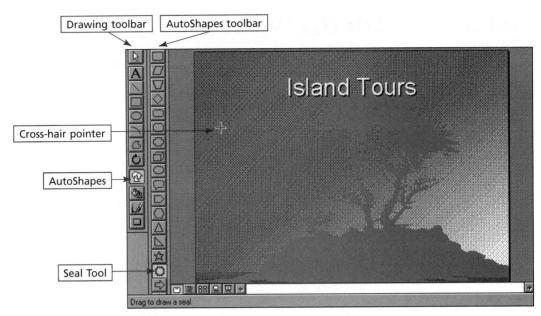

Figure 4.18

Tip If you intend to manipulate text inside a shape, add the shape to the screen first and then add text. Both objects can then be manipulated as one.

In the following steps you will use cut and paste commands to create the final slide 8 from slide 1. You will then modify slide 8 by deleting text below the title and substituting the seal and text shown in Figure 4.17.

To copy a slide:

1 If necessary, load PowerPoint and open the CRUISES.PPT presentation.

2 Select Slide Sorter view.

3 Click slide 1.

4 Click Copy in the Standard toolbar (or choose Copy from the Edit menu).

5 Click slide 7.

6 Click Paste in the Standard toolbar (or choose Paste from the Edit menu).
PowerPoint duplicates slide 1, automatically inserting it as a new slide 8 after slide 7.

7 Select Slide view.
The label Slide 8 appears in the lower-left corner of the screen.

To edit a slide and insert an AutoShape:

1 Click the selection box around *Presents* in slide 8, and then press DEL
The text box below the title disappears.

2 Select AutoShapes on the Drawing toolbar.
The AutoShapes toolbar appears as shown in Figure 4.18.

3 Select Seal Tool from the AutoShapes toolbar.

4 Position the cross-hair pointer where you want the upper-left corner of the shape to appear (use Figure 4.18 as a guide).

5 Click and drag the pointer down and to the right to create the seal.
The seal appears as shown in Figure 4.19.

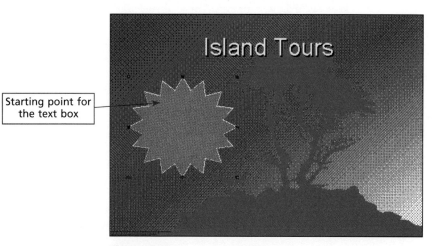

Starting point for the text box

Figure 4.19

> **Tip** If you are not satisfied with the selected shape, you can remove the shape by pressing (DEL) while the selection box is on. You can also move and size the shape until it is acceptable.

6 Choose Colors and Lines from the Format menu.

7 Select Blue from the Fill pull-down list, and then select OK.

8 Click outside the AutoShape to deselect it.

9 Save the file.

To add a text box to an AutoShape:

1 Select Text Tool from the Drawing toolbar.

2 Position the cross-hair pointer where you want the upper-left corner of the text box to appear (see the starting point marked on Figure 4.19).

3 Click and drag the pointer down and to the right to create the box within the seal.

4 Click Center Alignment on the Formatting toolbar.

5 Type the text shown in Figure 4.17.

6 Click outside the selection box, and then save the file.

To view the complete presentation in Slide Show view:

1 Display slide 1.

2 Click Slide Show.
The first slide appears, filling the screen.

3 Press (PGDN) or (SPACE) to view the next slide.

4 Repeat Step 3 until you have viewed all slides and exited Slide Show.

5 Choose Close from the File menu.

THE NEXT STEP

In this project you completed a second PowerPoint presentation. You used AutoLayout to select a predefined layout for each slide and then worked with many features designed to capture the attention of an audience—clip art, shapes, word art, colors, borders, and more. The next step involves putting those features to work in your own presentations, leaving behind the step-by-step guidance on choice of layout, content, special effects, and so forth. Combine imagination with experimentation!

This concludes Project 4. You can either exit PowerPoint or go on to work the Study Questions, Review Exercises, and Assignments.

SUMMARY AND EXERCISES

Summary

- Clip art pictures are images stored on disk. PowerPoint provides an extensive gallery of more than 1000 clip art images organized into 40 categories.
- You can create interesting visual effects by using borders, horizontal lines, and vertical lines to separate sections of a slide.
- PowerPoint includes the Microsoft WordArt application, which lets you choose among 36 predefined special effects including slanted and curved text.
- PowerPoint provides 24 complex predefined shapes, such as a star or seal, that you can create using the AutoShapes toolbar.

Key Terms and Operations

Key Terms
AutoShape
border
word art

Operations
Add AutoShapes
Add borders

Add clip art
Add lines
Add word art
Combine shapes and text

Study Questions

Multiple Choice

1. What is the term used to describe digitized pictures stored on disk?
   a. WordArt
   b. clip art
   c. borders
   d. AutoShapes

2. What command could you use to locate an image in PowerPoint's large clip art gallery?
   a. Locate
   b. Find
   c. Load
   d. Get

3. What is the term used to describe text displayed with special effects?
   a. WordArt
   b. clip art
   c. borders
   d. AutoShapes

4. Which key do you press to delete a selected object?
   a. ENTER
   b. CTRL
   c. SHFT
   d. DEL

5. What is the term used to describe lines placed around text boxes?
   a. WordArt
   b. clip art
   c. borders
   d. AutoShapes

Short Answer

1. Computer drawing programs, digital cameras, and scanners are used to produce what type of graphics?

2. What toolbar is used to access the predefined shapes PowerPoint offers?

3. What type of pointer appears on the screen when the Line tool is selected?

4. What do you call a line around the edge of an object?

5. Name the feature that allows you to slant or curve text.

For Discussion

1. What support does PowerPoint provide for adding images to slides? Also describe the process to insert an image.

2. What are AutoShapes? Explain the process to draw an AutoShape.

3. What is word art? When would it be appropriate to use word art?

Review Exercises

Buying a Car (Part 2)

The first review exercise at the end of Project 3 involved creating only the text objects in a six-slide presentation on buying a car. In this review exercise you will complete that presentation named BUYCAR.PPT by adding the clip art and other enhancements shown in Figure 4.20.

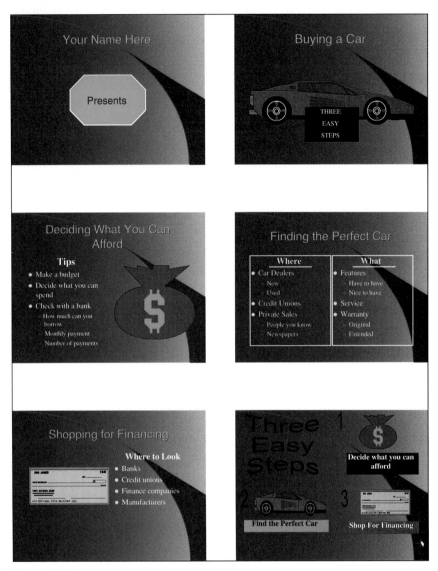

Figure 4.20

Refer to Figure 4.20 as you complete the following steps and move or size boxes as necessary. Save your work after revising each slide.

1. Open the BUYCAR.PPT presentation in Slide view.

2. Display slide 1. Add the octagon AutoShape with the text *PRESENTS*, and fill the AutoShape with a light blue color.

3. Display slide 2. Add the Red Sports Car clip art (Transportation category) file and the *THREE EASY STEPS* text box, and then fill the text box with black. Apply a 44 pt Braggadocio font to the slide title.

4. Display slide 3 and add the Bag of Money clip art (Currency category).

5. Display slide 4 and add the borders and lines.

6. Display slide 5 and add the Check clip art (Business category).

7. Display slide 6 and add the *Three Easy Steps* word art in the upper-left corner of the slide. Add also the money bag, car, and check clip art.

8. On slide 6, add the three text boxes *Decide what you can afford*, *Find the Perfect Car*, and *Shop For Financing*. Fill the text boxes with black, green, and red, respectively.

9. After saving your changes, run a slide show of the presentation.

Getting Involved in Campus Life (Part 2)

The second review exercise at the end of Project 3 involved creating only the text objects in a six-slide presentation on getting involved in campus life. In this review exercise you will complete that presentation named GETALIFE.PPT by adding the clip art and other enhancements shown in Figure 4.21.

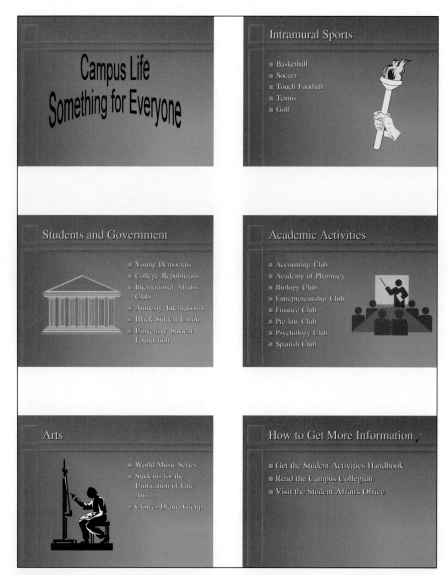

Figure 4.21

Refer to Figure 4.21 as you complete the following steps. Save your work after revising each slide.

1. Open the GETALIFE.PPT presentation in Slide view.

2. Display slide 1 and add the word art shown in Figure 4.21 (apply the Deflate (Bottom) effect).

3. Display slide 2 and add the Hand Holding Torch clip art (Sports & Leisure category).

4. Display slide 3 and add the Courthouse clip art (Buildings category).

5. Display slide 4 and add the Lecture clip art (Academic category).

6. Display slide 5 and add the Artist at easel clip art (People category).

7. Apply the EMBOSSDS.PPT template (you can use Pick a Look Wizard or select Template).

8. After saving your changes, run a slide show of the presentation.

Assignments

Getting Help on Clip Art and Word Art

Use Search in on-screen Help to look up information about inserting clip art, WordArt, and other pictures tips, which you will find under Clip Art.

Getting Help on AutoShapes

Use Search in on-screen Help to look up information about hints for working with shapes, which you will find under AutoShape. Also, review other topics about using AutoShapes.

Combining Text and Clip Art (Part Two)

Directions to begin your own presentation combining text and art were provided in the Assignments section at the end of Project 3. Open the presentation you started, and add clip art, word art, AutoShapes, borders, colors, and fills of your choice to complete the presentation.

PROJECT 5: PRESENTING A SLIDE SHOW

Objectives

After completing this project, you should be able to:

▶ Change the order of slides in Slide Sorter view

▶ Set transitions among slides

▶ Use builds to emphasize text in bulleted lists

▶ Rehearse a presentation

▶ Advance slides automatically

▶ Add freehand annotations to a slide

CASE STUDY: CRUISING THE CARIBBEAN III

In Project 4 you completed the eight-slide Caribbean cruise presentation you began developing in Project 3. If your presentation medium will be overhead transparencies or 35mm slides, you will print the results of your efforts and rehearse delivery on your own. Projecting slides from computer to screen, however, provides several opportunities for turning your slide show into a truly professional production.

Designing the Solution

Some PowerPoint features apply only to on-screen presentations. For example, you can select a *transition* between slides, which controls how each slide appears and disappears. You can also set up a *build*, which makes text in a bulleted list fly onto the screen from the left, right, top, or bottom—one line at a time. If you have a mouse, you can even draw attention to a specific area during a presentation by using the *Freehand Annotation* feature to point or draw on the slide. In addition to slide-specific content and display decisions, you can set a timer to switch slides automatically or advance to the next slide on your own.

> **Tip** Be sure to rehearse the delivery of your presentation. For a professional presentation, your accompanying remarks must be as polished as your slides.

In this project you will add the finishing touches to an on-screen presentation of the cruise slides. You will begin by using Slide Sorter view to make a final adjustment in the order of the slides. You'll have an opportunity to try out several transitions and builds before making your final selections. As you rehearse your presentation, you will set several slides to advance automatically and also experiment with using freehand annotation.

ORGANIZING SLIDES WITH SLIDE SORTER

The arrangement of slides should be well established by the time you finish developing a presentation. However, as you rehearse delivering your presentation, you may want to make a last-minute change to the order of your slides. In Project 4 you used Slide Sorter to duplicate slides. You can also use this view to change the arrangement of slides by dragging and dropping a slide into a new location.

When you begin to drag a slide, the pointer changes to a small arrow with a slide attached. A vertical dotted line shows where PowerPoint will place the slide.

In the following steps you will first save a slide show version of the presentation. Then you will reposition the information about the least costly Bahamas cruise (currently slide 3) after the more expensive Eastern Caribbean and Southern Caribbean cruises (slides 4 and 5).

To save a presentation under another name:

1 Load PowerPoint and open the CRUISES.PPT presentation.
The opening slide appears, showing a title and background tree.

2 Choose Save As from the File menu.

3 Type **SHOWSAIL.PPT** in the File Name text box, and then select OK.
The Summary Info dialog box appears.

4 Type **Version of presentation with transitions and builds** in the Comments box.

5 Select OK to close the dialog box and complete the save operation.

To change the order of slides:

1 Click Slide Sorter in the View toolbar.

2 Click slide 3 and hold down the mouse button.

3 Move the pointer between slides 5 and 6.
The pointer changes to a small arrow with a slide attached.
A dotted line appears between slides 5 and 6, showing where PowerPoint will place the slide.

4 Release the mouse button.
The slides appear in the revised order shown in Figure 5.1.

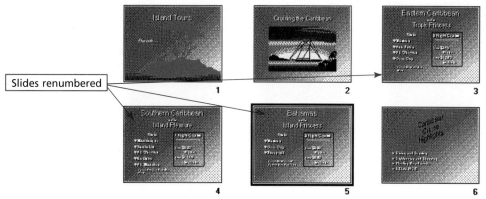

Slides renumbered

Figure 5.1

ADDING TRANSITIONS

Transitions are special effects controlling how slides appear and disappear. You can select among 45 transitions, including Blinds Horizontal or Vertical, Box In or Out, Checkerboard Across or Down, and Dissolve. You can also select Random Transition and let PowerPoint automatically select a variety of effects.

Although transitions can be applied in any view mode, you can see the results more easily in Slide Sorter view. A pull-down list of transition effects will appear when you click an underscored down arrow in one of two locations: at the right end of the Transition Effect box in the Slide Sorter toolbar, or at the right end of the Effect box in the Transition dialog box shown in Figure 5.2.

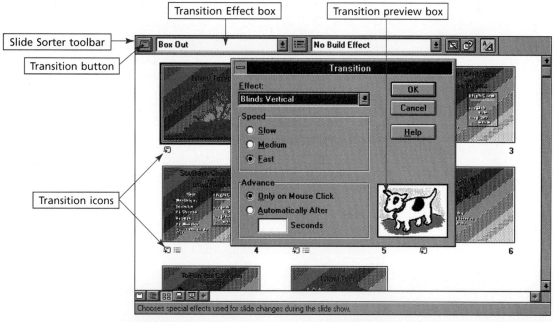

Transition Effect box

Transition preview box

Slide Sorter toolbar

Transition button

Transition icons

Figure 5.2

If you use the Transition dialog box to select an effect, you can also select two other settings: Speed and Advance. Speed controls the quickness of the transition (slow, medium, or fast). Advance lets you set an automatic or mouse-activated movement to the next slide. You can display the Transition dialog box by clicking the transition button at the left end of the Slide Sorter toolbar or by choosing Transition from the Tools menu.

Transitions can be applied to the current slide or to multiple slides. You can select multiple slides by holding down (SHFT) while you click the mouse on the desired slides. Choosing Select All from the Edit menu selects all slides.

Tip For consistency in a presentation, you will generally apply transitions to all slides.

When you select an effect or speed, the Transition preview box demonstrates that setting. In Slide Sorter view a Transition icon appears below the lower-left corner of a slide if a transition has been set. Clicking the icon lets you preview the effect.

In the following steps you will select all slides, view several transition effects, and save your final choice.

To select slides and display the Transition dialog box:

1 If necessary, display slides in Slide Sorter view.

2 Choose Select All from the Edit menu.
A thick black border appears around all slides.

3 Click the Transition button at the left end of the Slide Sorter toolbar.
The Transition dialog box appears. No Transition appears in the Transition Effect box. All slides remain selected.

Reminder If you want a transition style to apply to all slides, as you do in the next two sets of numbered steps, be sure to select all slides first.

To select a transition effect and speed using the Transition dialog box:

1 Click the underscored down arrow at the right end of the Effect box in the Transition dialog box.
A list of effects appears in alphabetical order except for No Transition and Random Transition, which appear first.

2 Select Blinds Vertical.
The pull-down list disappears, and Blinds Vertical appears in the Transition Effect box.

3 Select Fast in the Speed box if Slow or Medium is the current setting.

4 Select OK to close the dialog box.

5 Click the Transition icon under slide 1 to view the selected effect.

6 Click the Transition icon under several other slides in succession to continue viewing the selected effect.

To select other transition effects using the Slide Sorter toolbar and then save your final choice:

1 Click the underscored down arrow at the right end of the Transition Effect box in the Slide Sorter toolbar.

2 Select Box Out from the Transition pull-down list. Slide 1 displays the Box Out effect.

3 Click the Transition icon under several other slides in succession to continue viewing the selected effect.

4 Repeat steps 1 through 3, except select Checkerboard Across in step 2.

5 Repeat steps 1 through 3, except select Dissolve in step 2.

6 Repeat steps 1 through 3, except select Wipe Right in step 2.

7 Select other transition effects of your choice, and then specify Box Out as the transition setting for all slides.

8 Click anywhere between slides to deselect all slides.

 9 Save the file.

 If necessary, you can exit PowerPoint now and continue this project later.

ADDING BUILDS

You may have attended a presentation in which the speaker uncovered one line of text at a time on an overhead transparency. This technique focuses an audience's attention on the current point under discussion, rather than allowing the audience to read ahead.

You can produce this special effect during an on-screen PowerPoint presentation by specifying a build, sometimes called a ***progressive disclosure list***. When you first show a slide containing a build, bulleted items are hidden. Each time you press (ENTER) or click the left mouse button, the next line in the bulleted list appears.

You can select among 30 builds, including Fly from Left (also Fly from Bottom, Top, or Right), Blinds Horizontal or Vertical, Box In or Out, and Checkerboard Across or Down. You can also select Random Effects and let PowerPoint automatically select among a variety of effects.

> ***Tip*** If a slide contains one or more objects other than the bulleted list, select a build that displays text from the closest side. For example, if a bulleted list appears in the lower-left corner of the slide, select a build such as Fly from Left or Fly from Bottom. If you were to select Fly from Right or Top, the text would first have to cross other information, which could be distracting to viewers.

A pull-down list of build effects will appear when you click an underscored down arrow in one of two locations: at the right end of the Build Effect box in the Slide Sorter toolbar, or at the right end of the Effect box in the Build dialog box. Builds can be applied in any view mode. In Slide Sorter view a Build icon appears below each slide for which a build has been selected, as shown in Figure 5.3.

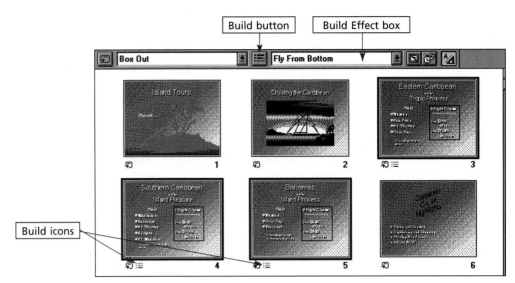

Figure 5.3

If you use the Build dialog box to select an effect, you can also dim previous points, as shown in Figure 5.4. The associated pull-down list provides color options for the dimmed items.

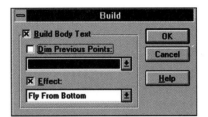

Figure 5.4

Builds can be applied to the current slide or to multiple slides. You can select multiple slides by holding down (SHFT) while you click the mouse on the desired slides.

In the following steps you will select the three slides in the cruise presentation that contain bulleted lists, view several build effects, select one build style for all three slides, and look at the results in Slide Show view.

To select a build using the Build dialog box:

1 If necessary, load PowerPoint and open the SHOWSAIL.PPT presentation and display slides in Slide Sorter view.

2 Select slides 3, 4, and 5.

Reminder You can select multiple slides by holding down (SHFT), clicking each desired slide in succession, and then releasing (SHFT). Thick black borders indicate the slides are selected.

3 Click the Build button in the Slide Sorter toolbar.
The Build dialog box appears.

4 Select Build Body Text.

5 Select Effect.

6 Select Fly from Bottom from the Effect pull-down list.
Your settings should match those shown in Figure 5.4.

7 Select OK to apply the selected build.

8 Click anywhere between slides.

To view a build:

1 Select slide 3.

 2 Select the Slide Show icon at the bottom of the screen.
The Eastern Caribbean cruise slide appears without the bulleted list
showing its ports of call, as shown in Figure 5.5.

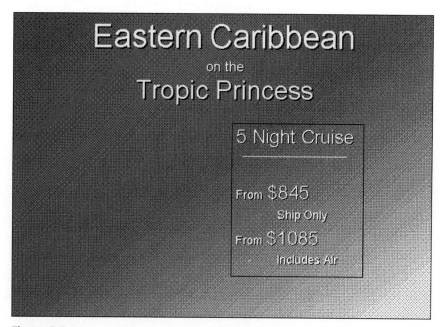

Figure 5.5

3 Press (ENTER) to see the first line in the hidden bulleted list.
The first line (the word *Visit*) moves into position from the bottom of the
slide.

4 Press (ENTER) to see the second line in the bulleted list, as shown in
Figure 5.6.

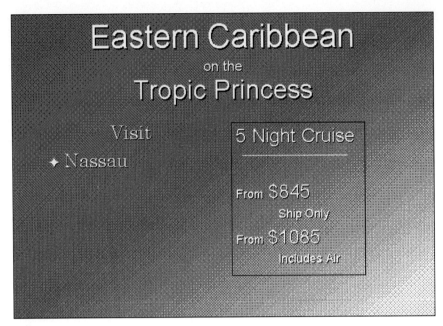

Figure 5.6

5 Press (ENTER) until the Southern Caribbean slide (slide 4) appears on your screen.

6 Press (ESC) to end the slide show and restore Slide Sorter view.

To select a build using the Slide Sorter toolbar, view the results, and save your settings:

1 Select slides 3, 4, and 5.

2 Click the underscored down arrow at the right end of the Build Effect box in the Slide Sorter toolbar.

3 Select Fly from Left from the Build pull-down list.

4 Click anywhere between slides, and then select slide 3.

5 Click Slide Show in the View toolbar.

6 Press (ENTER) to see the first line in the hidden bulleted list.
The first line (the word *Visit*) moves into position from the left edge of the slide.

7 Press (ENTER) until the Southern Caribbean slide (slide 4) appears on your screen.

8 Press (ESC) to end the slide show and restore Slide Sorter view.

9 Click anywhere between slides.

10 Save the file.

EXIT If necessary, you can exit PowerPoint now and continue this project later.

REHEARSING THE PRESENTATION

The amount of rehearsal needed for a slide show depends on the presentation environment. No practice is needed if your slides stand alone as part of an exhibit. You can set the show to play in a *continuous loop,* which means that PowerPoint automatically starts over with slide 1 after reaching the end of the set of slides. To set this display mode, choose Slide Show from the View menu and then select the Run Continuously Until 'Esc' check box.

It is more likely that you will be giving a live presentation, in which slides provide a framework for your personal comments. In this case it is essential that you practice your delivery. The content of your remarks is up to you. PowerPoint assists in the mechanics of delivery by providing manual or automatic shifts to the next slide and the tools to add freehand annotations as you speak.

Advancing Slides Automatically

During a slide show, you can manually advance to the next slide by pressing the left mouse button, (ENTER), or (SPACE). In other words, you manually set the *timing,* which determines the amount of time a slide stays on the screen. PowerPoint also allows you to advance slides automatically by setting slide timings.

> **Tip** You can use a combination of manual and automatic advances. For example, you can set the first few introductory slides to advance automatically after a few seconds and then use a manual advance after more complex slides.

You can set slide timings in the Transition dialog box by typing the desired number of seconds in the Seconds text box. You can also adjust the timing as you cycle through slides while you rehearse a presentation. To use the latter method, you will choose Slide Show from the View menu and then select Rehearse New Timings. PowerPoint notes the length of time each slide is displayed and sets the time intervals for you.

> **Tip** To remove one or more automatic advances, select the desired slides in Slide Sorter view, choose Transition from the Tools menu, and then select Only on Mouse Click.

In the following steps you will set timing for the first two slides in the cruise presentation.

To set an automatic advance using the Transition dialog box:

1. If necessary, load PowerPoint and open the SHOWSAIL.PPT presentation and display slides in Slide Sorter view.
2. Select slides 1 and 2.
3. Click the Transition button in the Slide Sorter toolbar.

4. Select Automatically After.

5 In the Seconds text box, delete the current number, and then type **5** as the number of seconds, as shown in Figure 5.7.

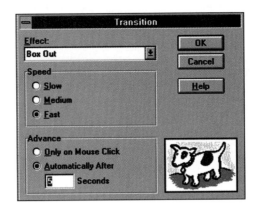

Figure 5.7

6 Select OK to apply the time intervals and close the dialog box. The notation :05 appears below slides 1 and 2, indicating the automatic slide timing.

7 Click anywhere between slides.

To view automatic advances:

1 Select slide 1.

2 Choose Slide Show from the View menu.
The Slide Show dialog box appears.

3 Select Use Slide Timings, and then select Show.
Slide 1 appears for five seconds, slide 2 appears for five seconds, and then slide 3 appears but does not advance.

Tip At this point you would begin rehearsing your presentation, manually advancing to the next slide after practicing the comments associated with the current slide.

4 Press (ESC) to end the slide show and restore Slide Sorter view.

Using Freehand Annotations

PowerPoint's Freehand Annotation feature is a line-drawing tool you can use during an on-screen presentation to draw attention to key points. For example, you might want to underline a phone number. Such annotations are temporary. They automatically disappear when you display the next slide, or you can type E to erase the lines from the current slide.

Moving the mouse slightly during a slide show causes the Freehand Annotation icon (a pencil tracing a wavy line) to display in the lower-right corner of the screen. When you click the icon, the arrow cursor changes to a pencil. You can then position the pointer, hold down the left mouse button, draw the desired line, and then release the mouse button. Clicking the icon again turns the Freehand Annotation feature off.

Tip Be sure to rehearse using the Freehand Annotation feature before incorporating it in a live presentation. Drawing a smooth line, such as one used to circle a key phrase, takes practice.

In the following steps you will underline one of the phone numbers on the last slide in the cruise presentation.

To add freehand annotations:

1 Select slide 7.

2 Click Slide Show in the View toolbar.

3 Shift the mouse until the Freehand Annotation icon appears in the lower-right corner of the screen.

4 Click the Freehand Annotation icon.
The mouse pointer changes from an arrow to a pencil, and the Freehand Annotation icon changes to an arrow.

5 Position the pencil pointer under *Call: 1-800-123-4567.*

6 Hold down the left mouse button and drag a line under *Call: 1-800-123-4567,* as shown in Figure 5.8.

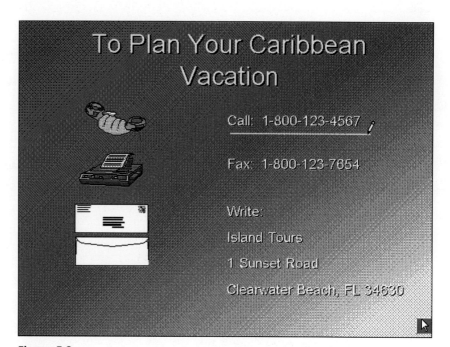

Figure 5.8

To erase the line without advancing a slide, turn off the Freehand Annotation feature, and save the timing changes:

1 Type **E** to erase the line.

2 Click the Arrow icon in the lower-right corner of the screen.
The icon changes back to a pencil, which indicates the annotation feature is turned off.

3 Press (ESC) to exit the slide show.

4 Save the file.

THE NEXT STEP

While Projects 3 and 4 focused on the creation of an eye-catching cruise presentation, this project focused on giving a well-rehearsed presentation. Prior to rehearsing, you added builds and transitions that produced special effects within and between slides during an on-screen slide show. You also learned a few techniques to polish the presentation, including advancing slides automatically and adding freehand annotations.

As a next step, you might learn how to use *PowerPoint Viewer,* a special application that allows you to run a PowerPoint presentation on a computer that does not have PowerPoint installed. This application is also useful if you want to send your presentation to someone who does not have PowerPoint. You cannot legally give someone a copy of PowerPoint, but it is legal to provide a copy of the PowerPoint Viewer. You will find information through on-screen Help if you use Search to look up PowerPoint Viewer.

This concludes Project 5. You can either exit PowerPoint or go on to work the Study Questions, Review Exercises, and Assignments.

SUMMARY AND EXERCISES

Summary

- In Slide Sorter view, you can change the order of slides by using a mouse to drag a slide to its new location.
- Some PowerPoint features, such as transitions, builds, slide timings, and freehand annotations, apply only to on-screen presentations.
- A transition controls how each slide appears and disappears. Using PowerPoint you can select among 45 transitions and set the speed of a transition at Slow, Medium, or Fast.
- A build—sometimes called a progressive disclosure list—causes text in a bulleted list to fly onto the screen one line at a time. Using PowerPoint, you can select among 30 builds.
- During a slide show, you can manually advance to the next slide by pressing the left mouse button, (ENTER), or (SPACE). You can also advance slides automatically by setting slide timings.
- During an on-screen presentation, you can draw lines to emphasize key points, such as underlining or circling a phone number. This freehand annotation disappears when you advance to the next slide.

Key Terms and Operations

Key Terms
build
continuous loop
Freehand Annotation
PowerPoint Viewer
progressive disclosure list
timing
transition

Operations
Advance slides automatically
Change the order of slides
Change the speed of transitions
Rehearse an on-screen presentation
Set builds
Set slide timings
Set transitions
Use Freehand Annotation

Study Questions

Multiple Choice

1. In Slide Sorter view, you can
   a. duplicate slides.
   b. rearrange the order of slides.
   c. Both a and b.
   d. None of the above.

2. During an on-screen presentation, what special effect relates to the appearance and disappearance of entire slides?
   a. build
   b. progressive disclosure
   c. transition
   d. 3-D advance

3. During an on-screen presentation, what special effect displays one line at a time from a bulleted list?
   a. 3-D advance
   b. freehand annotation
   c. transition
   d. build

4. Which of the following is not a true statement about transitions?
   a. Transitions can be applied in any view mode.
   b. Although PowerPoint provides 45 transition effects, only one transition style may be used in a presentation.
   c. Transition styles appear in a pull-down list in alphabetical order.
   d. If you prefer, you can select a transition for only one slide or a few slides—instead of all slides—in an on-screen presentation.

5. What is the name of the feature that you use to mark on slides during an on-screen presentation?
   a. On-screen Drawing
   b. Freehand Annotation
   c. Slide Rehearsal
   d. None of the above.

Short Answer

1. What is the phrase that describes automatically playing a slide show over and over?

2. What is an alternate term for the word *build?*

3. What settings are available for transition speed?

4. What actions advance a slide manually?

5. What key should you press and hold down prior to selecting multiple slides in Slide Sorter view?

For Discussion

1. What is a build? What purpose does it serve? Explain how you would establish builds in an on-screen presentation.

2. What is a transition? What purpose does it serve? Explain how you would establish transitions in an on-screen presentation.

3. Describe the process of reorganizing slides using the Slide Sorter view.

Review Exercises

Changing the SHOWSAIL Slide Show

1. Open SHOWSAIL.PPT and save it to disk as 5REVIEW.PPT.

2. Change the slide timings for slides 1 and 2 from 5 seconds to 10 seconds.

3. Change the builds for slides 3, 4, and 5 to Checkerboard Across, Strips Left-Up, and Wipe Up, respectively.

4. Select all slides and change the transition to Random Transition.

5. Rehearse the slide show. Try to draw a circle around a phone number on slide 7.

6. Save your changes and close the 5REVIEW.PPT file.

Presenting the GETALIFE Slide Show

1. Open GETALIFE.PPT and save it as SHOWLIFE.PPT (instructions to create this presentation were provided in Review Exercise 2 in Projects 3 and 4).

2. Access Slide Sorter view, and change the order of slides 2 through 5 to Academic Activities, Arts, Intramural Sports, and Students and Government.

3. Set the build effects for all slides to Random Effects.

4. Change the transition to each slide so that they alternate between Blinds Vertical and Blinds Horizontal.

5. Apply different effects of your choosing to slides 2 through 6.

6. Rehearse the slide show.

7. Save your changes and close the SHOWLIFE.PPT presentation.

Assignments

Getting Help on Slide Timings

Use on-screen Help to look up information about setting slide timings while rehearsing (see the Setting Slide Timings topic).

Getting Help on Slide Shows

Use Search in on-screen Help to review general information about slide shows (see the Terms That Apply to Slide Shows topic).

Adding Builds and Transitions to SERVICE.PPT

Open the SERVICE.PPT presentation you created by working Projects 1 and 2. Immediately save the file to disk as 5ASSIGN3.PPT. Add appropriate builds and transitions to all slides, and save your changes. Rehearse the presentation.

Adding Other Builds and Transitions

If you created another presentation as directed in end-of-project assignments for Projects 3 and 4, open that presentation. Immediately save the presentation as 5ASSIGN4.PPT. Add appropriate builds and transitions to all slides, and save your changes. Rehearse the presentation.

PART VIII

Integrated Project 3

Objectives

After completing this project, you should be able to:

▶ Work in multiple applications concurrently

▶ Embed into PowerPoint an object previously embedded into Word

▶ Embed into PowerPoint an object previously linked to Word

▶ Change the format of the embedded and linked objects in PowerPoint

▶ Update an Access database and display the changes in PowerPoint

Y ou have learned how to embed and link objects from Word, Excel, and Access into one updatable document. PowerPoint, a member of the Microsoft Office suite, can also be used to link and embed objects. In this project you will learn how to create a slide in PowerPoint and embed that slide into a Word document. You will also learn how to create a multiapplication presentation by embedding and linking Word documents, Excel worksheets, and Access databases in a PowerPoint slide.

CASE STUDY: CREATING A MULTIAPPLICATION PRESENTATION

The reports you have created and sent to the president's staff have caused quite a lot of excitement. Not only is the staff excited about the data in the reports, but also they are very impressed with the way you presented the reports. They are even more impressed that you were able to give them all of the data they wanted to see at a moment's notice. You have done such a great job that you have been promoted! You are now the new Director of Information Resources, and your first task is to produce a report for the stockholders' meeting at the end of the week. The president wants you to explain the progress of the fat-free potato chip versus regular potato chip taste-test surveys using a computer-generated slide presentation.

Designing the Solution

You know that you could display the Word reports you created for the daily staff meeting, but you really want to impress the stockholders with something exciting. So you decide to use PowerPoint to create the presentation. You know that PowerPoint has Wizards to help you create a snazzy background, and you won't need to retype all of the data from the Word reports. PowerPoint will let you create the presentation today and then update the statistics, if they change, right before the presentation.

CREATING THE PRESENTATION

Your first step in creating a four-slide PowerPoint presentation is to set up the type of presentation you want. You will then enter the text for the slides.

To set-up the PowerPoint presentation:

1 Select the PowerPoint button in the upper-right corner of your screen or, if the Microsoft Office suite does not start automatically when Windows starts, select the Office icon from the Program Manager window and then select PowerPoint.

The PowerPoint dialog box appears as shown in Figure 3.1.

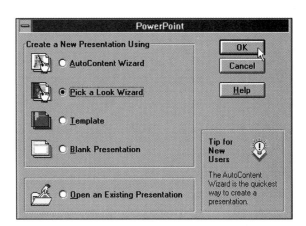

Figure 3.1

2 If your system displays the Tip of the Day, select OK to close the dialog box.

3 Select Pick a Look Wizard from the PowerPoint dialog box and then select OK.

The Pick a Look Wizard–Step 1 of 9 dialog box appears as shown in Figure 3.2.

Figure 3.2

4 Select Next to go to the Step 2 dialog box.

5 Select On-Screen Presentation, and then select Next.
The Step 3 dialog box appears as shown in Figure 3.3.

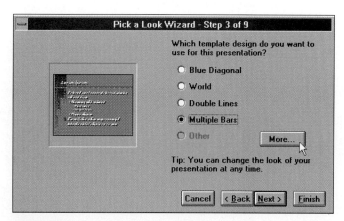

Figure 3.3

6 Select More.
The Presentation Template dialog box shown in Figure 3.4 displays the
default directory for the PowerPoint templates. If you have problems
locating the template files, check with your network administrator for help.

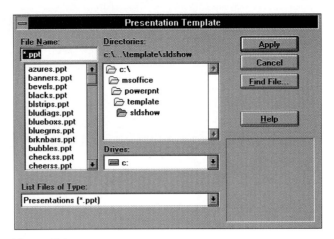

Figure 3.4

7 Select PATCHWKS.PPT, as shown in Figure 3.5.
If this template is not available, then select another template.

8 Select Apply.
You are returned to the Step 3 dialog box.

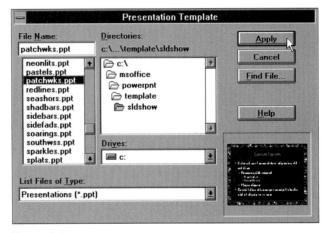

Figure 3.5

9 In Step 3, select Next.
The Step 4 dialog box appears as shown in Figure 3.6.

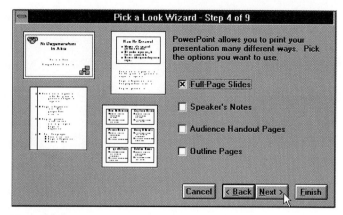

Figure 3.6

10 Select Full Page Slides by deselecting the other options and then select Next to go to the Slide Options dialog box.

11 Type **Fabulous Fat-Free Potato Chips**
The screen now looks like Figure 3.7.

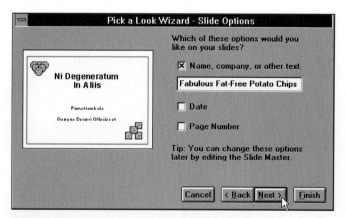

Figure 3.7

12 Select Next to go to the Step 9 dialog box shown in Figure 3.8, and then select Finish.
The first slide of your presentation is displayed.

Figure 3.8

13 Save your PowerPoint presentation on the A: drive under the name POTATO.PPT.

You can now enter the text you want to appear in your presentation slides.

Reminder Save your PowerPoint presentation often.

To enter text in the slides:

1 Click once in the top box of Slide 1 and type `Fabulous Fat-Free Potato Chips`

2 Click once in the bottom box and type `The Hot New Potato Product`

3 Click once outside of the subtitle box within the presentation window. The slide now looks like Figure 3.9.

Figure 3.9

4 In the lower-right corner of the screen, select New Slide. The New Slide dialog box appears as shown in Figure 3.10.

5 Select the Bulleted List AutoLayout, and then select OK.
The screen now displays a new slide with two text boxes.

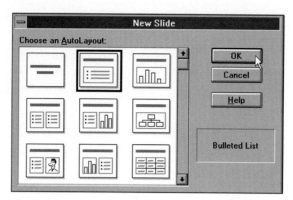

Figure 3.10

6 Enter the text into the two text boxes as shown in Figure 3.11.

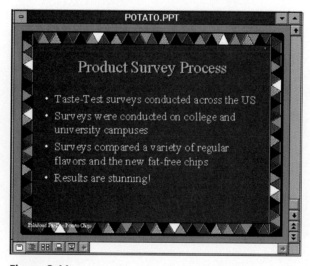

Figure 3.11

7 Select New Slide, select the Title Only AutoLayout, and select OK, as shown in Figure 3.12.

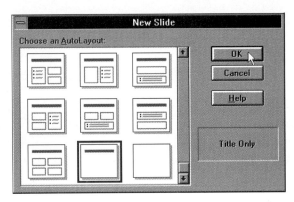

Figure 3.12

8 In the Title box type the text as shown in Figure 3.13 and deselect the text box.

Figure 3.13

9 Save your presentation.

EXIT   If necessary, you can exit PowerPoint now and continue this project later.

EMBEDDING THE EXCEL WORKSHEET INTO THE PRESENTATION

You have completed the basic skeleton of your presentation. The first section of data you will display is the Excel worksheet from UPDATE.DOC. You will embed this embedded object from Word into the PowerPoint slide by using the copy and paste method. Normally, this means that, once you copy the worksheet into the presentation you can not update it. The worksheet, however, is an embedded object in Word, which PowerPoint views as an embedded object, so you will be able to update it.

To embed Word's embedded worksheet in the PowerPoint presentation:

1 Start PowerPoint and open POTATO.PPT, if necessary.

2 Display the third slide, as shown in Figure 3.13.

3 Select the Word button from the upper-right corner of the screen.

4 Open UPDATE.DOC.

> **Note:** If you did not complete the review exercises at the end of Integrated Project 2, please ask your instructor for the file: UP__2.DOC. Save this as UPDATE.DOC and use this file to continue on in integrated Project 3.

5 Select the worksheet by anchoring the mouse in the paragraph symbol before the worksheet and dragging the mouse over the worksheet. The screen now looks like Figure 3.14.

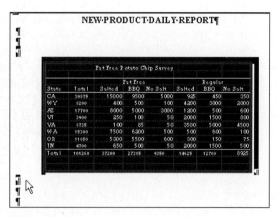

Figure 3.14

6 Select Copy.

7 Select the PowerPoint button in the upper-right corner of the screen.

8 Select Paste.
The slide now looks like Figure 3.15. You might have difficulty seeing the worksheet because of the colors. You will modify the colors later so that your presentation is easier to read.

9 Save your presentation.

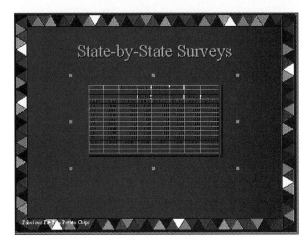

Figure 3.15

EMBEDDING THE ACCESS DATABASE INTO THE PRESENTATION

The fourth slide in your presentation will display the database data. You will move back into Word, select the linked database, and then copy and paste it onto the slide.

To embed the linked Access database to the presentation:

1 Select New Slide.

2 Select the Title Only AutoLayout.

3 Type **In the Marketplace** in the text box and then deselect the text box.

4 Select the Word button.

5 Using the same technique as you did when you copied the embedded worksheet, select the first database on page 1, as shown in Figure 3.16, and select copy.

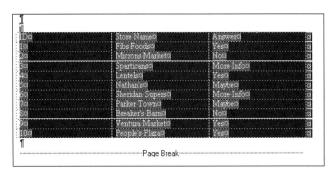

Figure 3.16

6 Select the PowerPoint button.

7 Display slide 4 if it is not already on the screen.

8 Select Paste.
The slide now looks like Figure 3.17.

Figure 3.17

The background of this figure is shown here as white to help you check your work. Your background should remain blue.

9 Save your presentation.

EXIT If necessary, you can exit PowerPoint now and continue this project later.

FORMATTING THE SLIDE PRESENTATION

Your data is now in the presentation, but the color scheme makes it difficult to read the black text from the worksheet and database. You will change the color of the object's fill, which is the background of the object.

> *Tip* You can experiment with colors other than those selected here. Keep in mind, however, that your screen may not look just like the examples in the text if you select different colors.

To format the presentation objects:

1 Open PowerPoint if it is not already open, and display POTATO.PPT on the screen, if it is not already displayed.

2 Display slide 3 on the screen. It is titled State-by-State Surveys.

3 Click once inside of the worksheet.

4 Select the Fill On/Off button.
The screen now looks like Figure 3.18.

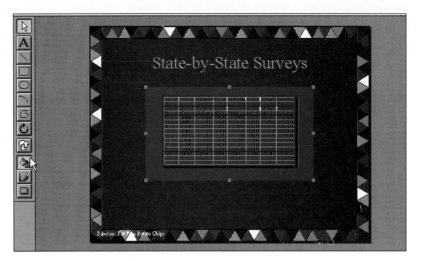

Figure 3.18

5 Choose Colors and Lines from the Format menu.

6 Select white as the fill color.

7 Select light green as the line color, with a triple border style, as shown in Figure 3.19 and select OK.

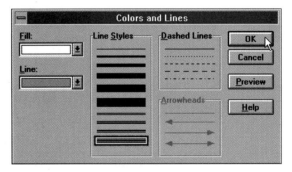

Figure 3.19

8 Save your presentation.

9 Display slide 4.

10 Repeat the formatting instructions for the database object.

11 Save your presentation.

UPDATING THE SLIDE PRESENTATION'S DATA

Today is the big day. The president has reviewed your slide show and is very pleased with the way it looks. The staff and stockholders are gathered in the lecture room, and the presentation will begin in about one hour.

Your phone just rang. The president called to tell you that the marketing department had convinced all of the stores to carry the new product. He wants to know if you can modify your presentation so that slide 4 shows all of the stores as answering yes to the survey. This is no problem, providing the database itself has been modified.

Since marketing has been so busy meeting with store managers, they haven't had time to update the database. You must update the database in Access before you update your presentation.

The objects you copied from Word into PowerPoint are now ***multiapplication objects*** in PowerPoint. This term describes an object that has been embedded or linked through a ***primary source application*** and through a ***secondary source application.*** In this project, Excel and Access are the primary source applications, because these are the applications where the objects were first created. Word takes on the role of the secondary application for the objects embedded in your presentation. What is actually embedded in PowerPoint is the secondary application's image of the data. If you double-click the worksheet or the database, the toolbars will change to reflect the secondary application's features. Any changes you make to the objects are restricted to the changes you would make if you were in Word when you selected the object. Once Word has been activated as the secondary source application and you double-click the Excel worksheet object, the primary source application opens so that you can change the worksheet data. Since the Access database is a linked object in the Word document, you cannot double-click the database to change the data. Instead, the data must be changed through Access. Then can you activate the secondary source application, Word, by double-clicking the object, locating the insertion point in the database, and pressing F9 to update the data.

To modify the embedded and linked data:

1 Open Access.

2 Open STORES.MDB.

3 Open the table SURVEY, and change all of the records' contents of the field Answer to Yes.

4 Save the table and exit Access.

5 Open PowerPoint if it is not already open.

6 Display slide 4 (In the Marketplace) if it is not already displayed.

7 Double-click the embedded database object.

The screen now looks like Figure 3.20. Notice that the database is being displayed as a Word object, with the Word ruler and toolbars.

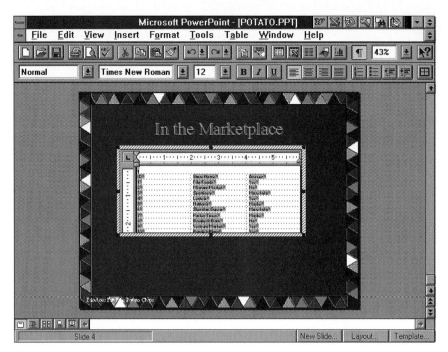

Figure 3.20

8 Click anywhere in the displayed database object in Word.

9 Press **F9** to update the data.

The screen now looks like Figure 3.21.

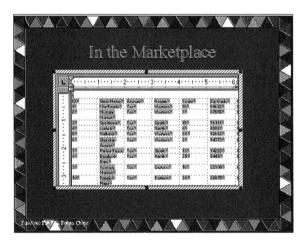

Figure 3.21

10 Crop, size, and move the Access database object so that only the first three columns are displayed and it is centered on the slide, and deselect the object.

The slide now looks like Figure 3.22.

Figure 3.22

THE NEXT STEP

As you can see, the power of OLE is very great. The problem of redundant construction of data has been solved. In the ever-increasing traffic on the information superhighway, data exchange needs to be fast, efficient, and accurate. Linking and embedding helps to ensure that sharing data *is* fast, efficient, and accurate.

Throughout the integrated projects you have seen several ways to connect objects from different applications. In PowerPoint you can insert an Excel worksheet or graph through the Insert menu, and you can follow the same steps to embed the worksheet into the presentation as you did with the Word document. You cannot, however, insert a database object into PowerPoint. There is no facility in PowerPoint to do this, except by passing the database through Word first.

You also saw that you can have as many applications open as your computer system can handle. Different systems have different amounts of RAM and hard disk space, so sometimes there are limitations. But the Microsoft Office product was designed so that you can move from one application to another with just the click of a button.

Think about ways you can use OLE to create the types of linked files you might use. What about creating a resume with your photograph embedded in it? If you apply to graduate school, you can include a summary sheet on the classes you are currently involved in, including your GPA. Keep your grade statistics in a worksheet or database, and then embed and link them into the graduate school application, the report home, or other documents you may create. You can even embed movies into your PowerPoint presentations. Wouldn't it be fun to send a friend a video of your class activity, embedded in a slide presentation?

This concludes Project 3 of the integrated projects. You can exit PowerPoint now or go on to work the Study Questions, Review Exercises, and Assignments.

SUMMARY AND EXERCISES

Summary

You can use OLE to create a multiapplication presentation.
You can copy and paste objects embedded in Word into PowerPoint.
The copied embedded-worksheet object can be updated from PowerPoint.
You can copy and paste objects linked in Word into PowerPoint.
The copied linked object can be updated from PowerPoint.
The color scheme of the objects can be changed in PowerPoint.
Objects can pass through multiple applications.

Key Terms and Operations

Key Terms
multiapplication object
primary source application
secondary source application

Operations
Create a presentation
in PowerPoint

Copy and paste objects into a
presentation
Format a presentation
Update embedded and linked data in
a presentation

Study Questions

Multiple Choice

1. A multiapplication presentation is
   a. a presentation made up of separate application files; that is, a Word file, a PowerPoint file, an Excel file, and an Access file, printed and bound into one document.
   b. a PowerPoint slide show.
   c. a presentation in one file with objects created in different applications.
   d. a Word document that is more than one page in length.

2. Once an object is embedded in Word and is then embedded in PowerPoint,
   a. it can no longer be updated.
   b. it can no longer be formatted.
   c. it can be updated from PowerPoint.
   d. it cannot be moved.

3. Objects in PowerPoint
   a. must be formatted and sized in Word first.
   b. cannot have primary source files.
   c. must have secondary source files.
   d. can be movies, Word documents, clip art, or other types of files.

4. The primary source application
   a. is always Word.
   b. is where the object is first created.
   c. is where the object will be placed.
   d. is never Word.

5. The secondary source application
   a. is where the object is first created.
   b. is where an embedded or linked object was first inserted.
   c. doesn't allow the object to be updated.
   d. None of the above.

6. An embedded object in PowerPoint
   a. cannot be edited if it was inserted through the copy and paste method.
   b. must always be edited in the primary application.
   c. can be edited if it was inserted through the copy and paste method.
   d. must never be edited in the primary application.

7. The difference between an embedded file and a linked file is that
   a. the embedded file's source file is a part of the target file, and the linked file's source file is not.
   b. the linked file can be updated, but the embedded file cannot.
   c. the linked file's source file is a part of the target file, and the embedded file's source file is not.
   d. an embedded file cannot be copied into another application like PowerPoint, but a linked file can be copied.

8. PowerPoint can
   a. only accept embedded objects from other applications.
   b. only accept Access databases as objects if a secondary source application exists.
   c. accept Access databases as objects without a secondary source application.
   d. only accept linked objects from other applications.

9. OLE is a tool that
   a. is very limiting in its capacity and scope.
   b. is very powerful if used well.
   c. cannot be used if you have more than one application open at a time.
   d. can only connect objects created in the Microsoft Office suite.

10. Copy and paste is a method that
   a. usually disallows updating of the copied object.
   b. lets you embed a linked Access database in Word to a PowerPoint slide.
   c. is a part of the OLE process.
   d. All of the above.

Short Answer

1. What is a primary source application file? When is it created?

2. What is a secondary source application file?

3. What is the difference between embed and link?

4. How do you embed an Access database file in PowerPoint?

5. What happens when you double-click on the Excel worksheet in PowerPoint?

6. What happens when you double-click on the Excel worksheet two times in a row in PowerPoint?

7. How do you update the Access database data in PowerPoint?

8. How many applications can you open at the same time?

9. What dictates how many applications can be open at the same time on a computer system?

10. What are some ways you can use OLE now? What about in the future?

For Discussion

1. What are the three OLE methods and how do they differ? How are they similar?

2. What are the advantages of using the embed method to create objects?

3. What are the advantages of using the link method?

4. Explain the concept of passing objects through multiple applications. Why is this a good tool?

Review Exercises

A Presentation to the Employees

1. Design a six-slide (or longer) PowerPoint presentation to include the worksheet showing the entire taste-test survey results, and include the database queries you created in Project 2.

2. Include some text to explain to the employees why the company has been so preoccupied lately.

3. Use a different Wizard, or come up with your own master slide background and color scheme.

4. Save this presentation as EMPLOYEE.PPT.

Update the Excel Data

1. Edit the Excel worksheet in the EMPLOYEE.PPT presentation. Add five rows of states and their responses to the taste-test survey. Make up the states you add and their responses.

2. Crop and size the edited worksheet so that it fits nicely on the PowerPoint slide.

Assignments

Presenting a Pie Chart

Create a PowerPoint presentation to present the pie chart you embedded in the first integrated project's assignment document, CLASSES.DOC. Use PowerPoint features to border the pie chart, and put some sharp colors in the slide. Save this presentation as HOME.PPT.

Creating a Hobby Poster

In Word write a two-paragraph description of your favorite hobby. Save the document as HOBBY.DOC. Then create a PowerPoint slide. Insert a clip art file that best represents your hobby. Choose Object from the Insert menu and select your HOBBY.DOC file. Size the two objects so that they create a poster of your favorite hobby.

PART IX

Additional Project

ADDITIONAL PROJECT: ELECTRONIC MAIL AND THE INTERNET

Objectives

After completing this project, you will be able to:

▶ Describe what e-mail is and how it is used

▶ Send e-mail to people around the world

▶ Describe the major tools of the Internet and how to use them

▶ Use the File Transfer Protocol

▶ Use the World Wide Web

▶ Access Benjamin/Cummings' FTP site on the Internet

▶ Access Benjamin/Cummings' WWW site on the Internet

DEFINING ELECTRONIC MAIL

Electronic mail, or *e-mail,* is both a product and a process. The product is a letter, memo, or message created on a computer. The process is transmitting this message to the recipient. Computer files, such as worksheets, clip art files, or graphic files, can be attached to the e-mail message and sent. It really is very similar to sending a letter through the postal service, only in this case it's all done electronically.

Electronic mail is used to communicate just about anything people usually communicate verbally or in written form. Businesses use e-mail when people are working together on a project to exchange information and to keep the momentum of the project from collapsing. It is a very helpful tool when people are working together closely on a daily basis but are geographically separated by tens or thousands of miles. Electronic mail also helps people communicate quickly and inexpensively, without relying on long distance phone calls or expensive overnight mail costs.

Another e-mail benefit is that it can help people become more productive. If you are working on a tight deadline for a project and you suddenly remember you need to tell someone something, you can quickly send an e-mail and return to your work. Sending an e-mail causes a minimum amount of interruption to your work because, for example, it can keep you from getting caught on the phone with someone who loves to talk yet lets you communicate an important concept or idea to the other person.

SENDING AND RECEIVING E-MAIL

If you want to send or receive mail electronically, you must have an *e-mail address.* This address uniquely identifies you, so that only you can receive the messages addressed to you. An e-mail address has two basic identifiers, separated by the @ sign. To the left of the @ sign is a name, which could be your name, a nickname, or set of numbers. To the right of the @ sign is a computer name. The computer name itself has several identifiers. Each identifier in the computer name is separated by periods, which in computer-speak are called *dots.*

The computer name identifies the computer's physical location on the Internet. Part of that location is called the *mail server.* The mail server is a computer that acts much like a local post office. It also has an address that identifies it on the Internet. E-mail sent to you is routed to the mail server, which holds the mail until you ask for it. This is much like going to your local post office and opening your own mailbox with a key. Likewise, when you send a letter to someone it goes to the local post office (mail server) and then on to the recipient's mailbox. Figure A.1 shows you an example of a fictional e-mail address.

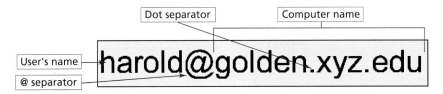

Figure A.1

Commercial companies often use e-mail to keep in touch with their clients or people who purchase their products. A television newsmagazine show, "Dateline NBC," uses e-mail to gather the opinions of the people who watch their program. Their e-mail address is dateline@nbc.com. They solicit e-mail from their viewers each week by presenting a question or a topic and then asking viewers to respond. While this is not a scientific survey, it does give them an idea of what a lot of their viewers think about the topics of their shows and helps them plan future presentations.

Many celebrities, sports figures, and politicians have e-mail addresses. If you know your favorite actress's e-mail address, you can send her a message. You can even e-mail the President of the United States at president@whitehouse.gov. Here are some others:

Table A.1

Name	Vocation	Address
Douglas Bell	Author of a series of science fiction books about a place called Infinity City.	dougbell@netcom.com
Al Gore	Vice President	vice.president@whitehouse.gov
Terry Pratchett	Humorous writer, author of *Discworld*	terryp@unseen.demon.co.uk

NETWORKING AND E-MAIL

Electronic mail can be sent within a *local area network*, or *LAN*, which is a group of computers that generally reside in the same building and are connected into one system. Some sort of e-mail software is used to send and receive e-mail messages on the LAN. Microsoft Office's Mail license can be used to send and receive e-mail on a network that uses Microsoft Mail as the mail carrier, or service. There are other commercial products that send and receive e-mail. Usually, everyone uses the same mail service within the same local area network. But what happens when you want to send an e-mail message to someone outside of your local area network? How do you send an e-mail message to someone who is in a different country? Computer networks' hardware and software vary throughout companies and organizations. This can make it difficult for computer systems to communicate. But there is a global network that can handle just about any type of computer and is used as a main artery for e-mail communications. It is called the *Internet*, also known as the *Net*.

DESCRIBING THE INTERNET

The Internet is a network of thousands of computers spanning the globe. It emerged out of ARPANET, which was started about 30 years ago by the United States military. ARPANET, the Department of Defense's Advanced Research Projects Agency network, was created to facilitate and protect military communications in the event of nuclear attack. This network was designed so that different computers using different hardware and software could communicate easily. In the 1970s and 1980s, as universities and researchers needed a way to communicate and share data, such as literature, photographs, research results, computer programs, and so on, computer systems began connecting to other computer systems, and through ARPANET the Internet network of computers was informally established.

ACCESSING THE INTERNET

You access the Internet by using a service that lets you in the Net gateway. Either your business or school provides access, or you can use the services of commercial providers of Internet access: Delphi, CompuServe, America Online, Netcom, or Prodigy, to name a few. There are also research networks, such as BITNET and Usenet, that offer gateways to the Net. There are also independent bulletin board services that offer e-mail services either for free or for a small fee, but you usually have to pay for the telephone call into the bulletin board service. If you access the Net through one provider, you can usually send mail to someone using a different provider as long as you have their Internet address.

Commercial providers of the Net usually charge a monthly fee and/or assess an hourly or minute-by-minute charge for their services. They provide you an Internet address and some sort of software program to help you move around, or *navigate*, the Net.

How the user will interact with the data on the screen is determined by a software program called the *interface.* When it was first established, the Internet's interface was solely a text-based system of government and educational computers connected through modems. It was crude compared to today's interface standard. When a person accesses the Net through a *text-based* or *character-based* interface, the computer presents a screen of words and numbers only. The user responds by typing a series of letters (words) and/or numbers.

GUI, or *graphical user interface,* is becoming a more common way to work on the Net and is emerging as the new interface standard. This means that you can use your mouse to point and click; you make selections from menus and icons and see graphic displays and photographs on your screens, rather than plain characters. While the movement today is toward GUI, text-based interfaces are still very accessible and widely used. In the next sections you'll see both text-based and GUI forms of access.

WORKING ON THE INTERNET

There are many different ways information is exchanged and used across the Net. The Net can be used to communicate messages from one person to another, to share ideas and exchange thoughts between groups of people, or to transfer files from one computer to another. Libraries can be accessed through the Net for research purposes, and many organizations and institutions offer information on the Net that can be used for commercial purposes or as informational resources.

One of the best ways to get information about the Internet is from the Internet itself through *Frequently Asked Questions,* or *FAQ,* documents. You can access FAQ documents through newsgroups, FTP sites, and Gopher sites, all of which are discussed in the following sections. These FAQ postings are very helpful because almost everyone has the same common questions when they begin to use the Internet. So the FAQ documents serve as a guide to help you get the most out of the Internet. FAQs have technical information, such as how to handle error messages on certain systems, how to download files, and how to use various Internet tools, like Telnet, Gopher, and the World Wide Web. They also help you understand the rules of social behavior on the Net. Even though the Internet is not a physical place, it is a kind of community. And, as such, there are community standards of social behavior and expectations. FAQs help Internet users to understand, make sense of, and exist in this virtual community.

NEWSGROUPS

Newsgroups provide a forum for the exchange of ideas and information. Newsgroups are formed around a specialized topic of interest: computer programming, bungee jumping, parenting, classical music, cycling, the theater—if there is a topic of interest, there is a group. If the group doesn't exist, you can create it. People write articles and post, or display, the articles to the members of the group. You can join any newsgroup, read any posted article, or post your own. You can also personally respond to writers of articles by e-mail.

Newsgroups are broken down into categories and have names that look much like e-mail addresses. The first level of the name identifies the type of group it is. There are specific first-level group types for Canada, Japan, and the United States. There are also first-level group types for regions of the United States, alternative newsgroups that have some strange and bizarre groups as well as semicommercial and education groups, and groups relating to recreation and sports, computer topics, science fields, social cultures, and a miscellaneous group for newsgroups that don't really fit anywhere else. After the first-level group type, the other parts of the name identify the group topic. As you read the name from left to right, the sections and subsections are separated by periods. Each name to the right of the period is a subset to the name to the left. It's much like the system of directories and subdirectories on a computer disk. For instance, the groups *alt.sports.basketball.nba.utah.jazz* and *alt.sports.basketball.nba.phx-suns* are subgroups that each focus on an individual basketball team. A group called *clari.sports.baseball* has a subset group called *clari.sports.baseball.games.* Figure A.2 shows a sample newsgroup article from the *rec.food.restaurants* group.

```
Subject: UK FOOD
Date: Tue, 2 May 1995 00:48:12 GMT

I am looking forward to our upcoming trip to London and the nearby
countryside;  I have heard a lot (negative mostly) about food and even one
recent post about fish and chips being not that great.  This can't be!  Help!
What are some good place to eat good british food...in London, around
Salisbury, Cornwall and Cotswolds?
```

Figure A.2

INTERNET RELAY CHAT

The ***Internet Relay Chat,*** or ***IRC,*** is an online communication tool. It is an interactive conversation between two or more users. The conversation takes place in a ***channel.*** You can think of the channel as a phone line or a room in a house where you sit and talk with someone. Channels are identified by names that describe the general theme of the conversations. IRC names begin with the pound sign. There is a channel for California (#california), Seattle (#seattle), and you can use the #chat and #friendly channels to become acquainted and familiar with the IRC. When you join a channel you can "listen" by reading the screen as others converse, or you can join in the conversation by typing your thoughts on your keyboard. You can join a channel using your own name or you can use a nickname or alias. You'll find many interesting nicknames and conversation topics on the IRC. And, just like at a party, if the conversation is dull or not interesting to you, you can leave and find another group of people to talk with. Figure A.3 shows a conversation taking place on the #california channel.

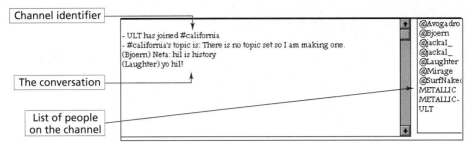

Channel identifier

The conversation

List of people
on the channel

Figure A.3

It is also possible to hold a private conversation with just one other user. You can do this by setting up a private channel and passwording the channel so that only those knowing the password can join it. But, since the IRC is a worldwide Internet feature, your conversation may travel through many systems. Computer systems administrators can look at and read these conversations because they pass through their systems. So, while you may feel like you are having a private conversation with another person, it is not a totally secure place to have a confidential conversation.

GOPHER

"The Internet Gopher is a distributed document search and retrieval system," according to a recent posting of the most frequently asked questions about *Gophers.* Gophers began at the University of Minnesota and have quickly spread throughout the Internet community. Gophers help you find information in files throughout the Internet. You can browse through document offerings and retrieve documents that reside on many different computers throughout the world. When you access a Gopher menu, you will generally see two types of data: another menu and a data file. The data file can be text, graphics, or sound. There is an icon next to each item on the Gopher menu to help you identify what you will receive if you select it. For instance, in Figure A.4 you will see several different types of icons on the Information About Gopher menu from the University of Minnesota.

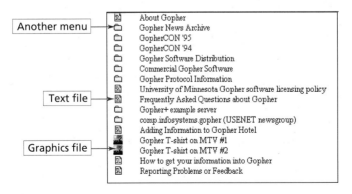

Another menu

Text file

Graphics file

Figure A.4

FILE TRANSFER PROTOCOL

One of the exciting uses of the Internet is the ability to share information. Files can be accessed on computers all over the world and **downloaded** to your computer system at home. Downloading is the process of copying files from one computer onto another through a modem. You can download antivirus software, gather data files to support a term paper, collect photos of interest—the possibilities are endless. **File Transfer Protocol,** or **FTP,** is the tool systems use across the Internet to send files. Many **sites,** which are computers you can access on the Internet, allow FTP access. When you access a site through FTP you need a username and password to connect to the site's **host** computer. It is called a host because the computer is letting you enter its system and use its resources, much like a host of a party grants you entrance to the party and provides you with food and drink. When you access a host computer, you need to identify yourself to the computer. Many sites accept the username "anonymous" if you enter your Internet address as the password. Once you are attached to the host computer, you can browse through its offerings and download any files that interest you.

FTP access is a special privilege, not a right. Most sites welcome anonymous access if you are courteous and conscientious about using their systems. Most FTP sites ask that you restrict your access to non-prime-time hours. Try not to connect to a site between 6:00 a.m. and 7:00 p.m., according to the time zone of the site. That's especially important when you are accessing a computer in a time zone different than yours. Also, don't spend too much time once you are connected. Look around, download interesting files, and then disconnect so that others can download.

An FTP site may display a welcome notice with information about that particular site. Often included in this notice is a request to read a file called README. Be sure to download and read that file before you access the site any further. Those files contain the rules for that site, when you are welcome, and anything you may need to know about using that system.

Tip If you get an error message when accessing a known FTP site, it may be that the site is not accessible because the host's computer is down for maintenance or software upgrades. Try again later.

The Benjamin/Cummings FTP site is available to you anytime you are able to gain access through your computer. If you have access to the Internet through your school or business, you can do the following numbered steps. Otherwise, follow the guiding text and look at the figures closely to get a feel for what it's like on the Net.

 ### To access Benjamin/Cummings FTP site:

1 Through your provider, school, or business, use your FTP command.

2 At the prompt type `ftp bc.aw.com`
The screen will resemble Figure A.5.

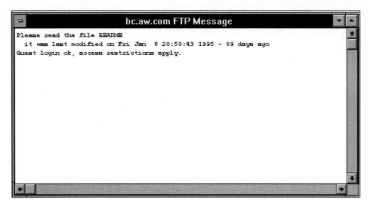

Figure A.5

3 If you are using GUI close the message box.

4 Use the c/d command to access the subdirectory bc/info. Or, if your provider's interface is GUI, access the subdirectory bc/info as shown in Figure A.6.

```
drwxrwxr-x  7 31      31         512 Jan 19 20:19 aw.innovations
drwxrwxr-x  3 32      33         512 Feb  7  1994 aw.mathematics
drwxrwxr-x  2 28      28        1024 Mar 30 09:37 aw.prof.comp.series
drwxrwxr-x  9 127     30         512 Jan  2 11:48 bc
drwxrwxr-x  2 0       1          512 Feb 14 15:26 bexpress
drwxrwxr-x  2 0       1          512 Jan  3  1994 bin
```

Figure A.6

5 Ask your computer lab staff or instructor to help you use your system to download the file: ftp-faq.asc

TELNET

Accessing and connecting to a computer, whether you are one block away or on the other side of the world, is the function of Telnet. To connect to another computer, you must have a user name and a password, which identifies you as a valid user. However, many computers will let you connect by using the word *anonymous*, or *guest*. Once connected via Telnet, you are an online user and can access anything the computer system will allow you to access. Usually the menus are lines of text, and you respond by moving the arrow key or typing a one-word response and pressing (ENTER).

Telnet lets you connect to libraries all over the world, where you can do research for term papers or special projects. Some computers provide programming helps, such as compilers, for Telnet users. Figure A.7 shows a Telnet connection to a job search service.

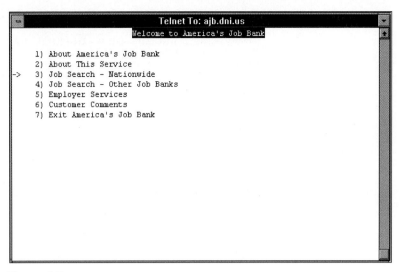

Figure A.7

WORLD WIDE WEB

One of the most interesting ways to move or navigate on the Net is through the *World Wide Web,* or *WWW.* The Web provides an easy way to move from one computer to another through a graphical user interface.

Web sites have what is called a *home page.* This home page usually displays the organization's name and logo, and maybe a photograph or two of the facility or important people. On this home page will be some textual information, and some of the words will appear in green or blue. If you point your mouse to a colored word or phrase, the pointer will change to an arrow. Click once and you will then see another screen.

The Benjamin/Cummings WWW site is available to you anytime you are able to gain access through your computer. If you have access to the Internet through your school or business, you can do the following numbered steps. Otherwise, follow the guiding text and look at the figures closely to get a feel for what it's like on the Web.

 To access the Benjamin/Cummings Home Page on the Web:

1 Use your computer's Web command to access http://bc.aw.com The screen will resemble Figure A.8.

Figure A.8

2 Use your scroll bar to move down the Addison-Wesley home page. You will see information on the home page similar to Figure A.9.

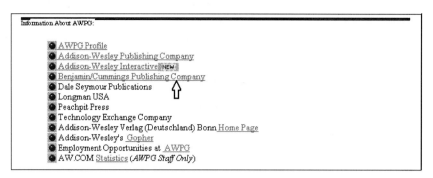

Figure A.9

3 Point to the colored words *Benjamin/Cummings* and click once. The screen will resemble Figure A.10.

Figure A.10

4 On the Benjamin/Cummings home page, scroll down to *Computer Information Systems* as shown in Figure A.11 and select it.

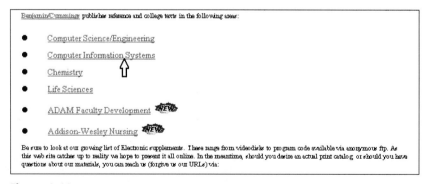

Figure A.11

The CIS titles page is displayed as shown in Figure A.12.
5 Click on *CIS Newsletter*.
The BC Link online newsletter appears.

*Computer Information Systems titles
at Benjamin/Cummings*

This page is under construction. Please bear with us. You are looking at preliminary links to remind us where we need to put up the joists and foundations!

Our CIS newsletter is online. More to come. You can contact the newsletter editor directly by sending e-mail to: bclink@bc.aw.com

Information about our books

Author Index

Title Index

For more information about our books, please send e-mail to: bookinfo@bc.aw.com

Figure A.12

6 Click *Student Access*, as shown in Figure A.13.

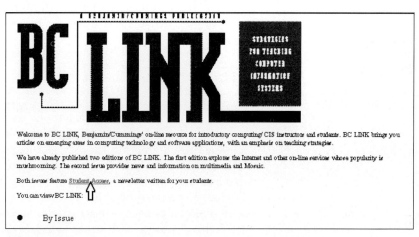

Figure A.13

The Student Access page appears as shown in Figure A.14.

BC LINK's

StudentAccess

Welcome to Student Access! This is your on-line resource for news and information on the latest computer technology and how it's being applied. This on-line newsletter was created by Benjamin/Cummings for Introductory Computing and Computer Information Systems students.

Please let us know what you think of our BC Link: Student Access site. You can e-mail us at

bclink@bc.aw.com

Figure A.14

7 Scroll down the page and select one of the topics, as shown in Figure A.15.

- **Computers in Action**

  - Earthquake BBS

  - CD-ROM Shopping

  - Haves and Have Nots

  - Wed in Cyberspace

  - Desktop Video

  - Pizza via the Internet

- **For Further Exploration**

  - Snow Crash

  - I Want My MTV...via E-mail

  - The 7th Guest

Figure A.15

Now that you have worked on the Internet, you may explore some more on your own, or you may exit your Internet service provider.

SURVIVING ON THE NET

Just as there are etiquette rules in our society, the phrase ***netiquette*** refers to rules of social behavior on the Net. While there are no Net police to enforce these standards, the Net is self-monitored by the user community. When you post articles in newsgroups, for example, don't ask questions that are found in the FAQ for that topic. If you do, you'll probably be ***flamed,*** or rebuked harshly by other members of the group. When you send e-mail messages or post articles to newsgroups, remember that you are communicating with other living, breathing, feeling human beings. And these other people cannot see your facial expressions or hear the intonations of your voice. They can only read your words. So, if you use all capital letters in a message or article, it is like SHOUTING VERY LOUDLY to someone. If you are making a wisecrack, the other people in the newsgroup might not understand that you are joking and take you seriously. There are some cute ***emoticons,*** or emotion icons, that have evolved to help communicate the feelings behind your words. These icons display certain feelings. Figure A.16 shows an example of some of the more common emoticons. You'll need to turn your text sideways to get the full impact of these little figures, as they represent faces.

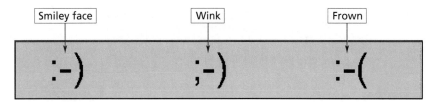

Figure A.16

Some other tips on behaving on the Net: Don't be easily offended by what you read in the newsgroups. The Net is an open forum for all ideas or thoughts. What some people think is hilarious, others may find distasteful. What some people call grotesque, others may view as simply bizarre and inoffensive. There are people who will post outrageous remarks to a newsgroup just to see how many people will vehemently respond. Be sensible, and if something offends you, ignore it or don't participate in that group. Try to keep articles short and to the point, and post articles to the appropriate newsgroup. An article about fly fishing should not be posted to a newsgroup that talks about poetry. All in all, a good dose of common sense and courtesy will take you a long way in your interactions with others on the Internet.

THE NEXT STEP

There are other tools you can use to find your way around the Internet. Spend some time researching the Archie (via FTP) and Veronica (via Gopher) tools. Go to your library and find some books on the Internet and read about European sites. Did you know that you can actually download pictures of paintings at the Louvre in Paris?

There are many interesting and fun FTP and Web sites available. The offerings are constantly changing, so don't be surprised if a site you accessed last month has changed dramatically or is no longer available. Here are a few Web sites you may want to experience at your leisure:

- webcrawler.cs.washington.edu/WebCrawler/WebQuery.html   Use this site to search the Net for other Web sites by entering a word or words. You can search on music, theater, sports, and so on, and get up to 500 Web sites to visit.
- http://www.nbctonightshow.com   Go visit Jay Leno and the "Tonight Show."
- http://www.cbs.com/alt-text.html   Check in with David Letterman and his show—a great place to go if you love his Top Ten List.
- http://white.nosc.mil/sandiego.html   The city of San Diego has a beautiful home page with lots of interesting photos.
- http://www.stones.com   Home page of the Rolling Stones.
- http://www.cba.uh.edu/ylowpges/yc.html   A listing of other Web sites, a "yellow pages" for the Web.

The electronic capabilities are mind boggling. Electronic mail, coupled with the power of the Internet, can actually make our planet smaller as we travel the globe and communicate with people all over the world—all without leaving the comfort of home.

SUMMARY AND EXERCISES

Summary

- Electronic mail is a product as well as the process of sending and receiving messages electronically.
- Electronic mail can be sent to anyone with an e-mail or an Internet address.
- An e-mail address is made up of two components: your name and a computer name.
- E-mail address components are separated by the @ sign, and the computer name identifiers are separated by dots.
- Microsoft Mail is a single workstation license that allows you to send and receive mail on a network using Microsoft Mail as its mail software.
- The Internet is a system of networked computers all over the world that began out of ARPANET about 30 years ago.
- The Internet can be accessed through a school or business if they have access, or through a commercial provider, bulletin board service, or an independent network offering the service.
- The Internet uses both text-based interfaces and graphical user interfaces.
- FAQs are answers to frequently asked questions about the Internet and should be read before using the Net.
- Newsgroups are forums for the exchange of ideas and information.
- IRC is an online communication tool and is not private.
- Gophers are computers that allow you to search and retrieve documents.
- Data can be downloaded from computers on the Internet onto your computer.
- File Transfer Protocol lets you download files from the Internet onto your home computer.
- Read the README file at each FTP site and observe access rules.
- Telnet allows you to connect to remote computers throughout the world, provided you have a valid user name and password.
- The World Wide Web is a graphical user interface to sites all over the world.
- Netiquette rules are important on the Net.
- Emoticons can help you express your true feelings when you communicate with others on the Net.

Key Terms and Operations

Key Terms

channel	home page
character-based	host
dot	interface
download	Internet (Net)
electronic mail (e-mail)	Internet Relay Chat (IRC)
e-mail address	local area network (LAN)
emoticons	mail server
File Transfer Protocol (FTP)	navigate
flamed	netiquette
Frequently Asked Questions (FAQs)	newsgroups
	site
Gopher	text-based
graphical user interface (GUI)	World Wide Web (WWW, or WEB)

Study Questions

Multiple Choice

1. The Internet is
   a. a network of thousands of computers spanning the globe.
   b. the term used to describe a network of computers residing in the same building.
   c. accessible only to government and education employees.
   d. a network of e-mail servers providing e-mail delivery to members of the Internet Association.

2. Microsoft Mail is
   a. a product providing Internet mail service.
   b. available to people using Microsoft Office products to send e-mail on the Internet.
   c. included in the Microsoft Office package, and is a workstation license only for use with the networked mail product.
   d. An interface for the World Wide Web.

3. A graphical user interface will
   a. always be needed to access the Internet.
   b. display data screens with icons and pictures that can be activated by clicking a mouse.
   c. never work on an IBM PC.
   d. display text and numbers so that the user doesn't need a mouse.

4. Electronic Mail is
   a. used extensively around the world as a means of communication.
   b. limited to communication between users on the same local area network.
   c. only used when people cannot send mail through the postal service.
   d. always confidential; only the recipient can read it.

5. File Transfer Protocol is
   a. a network of computers that can be accessed and looked at.
   b. a software tool that allows files to be downloaded from an FTP site to your computer.
   c. a way of sending attachments to your e-mail messages.
   d. another way of sending electronic mail.

6. If you have a computer, communications software, and a modem
   a. you can access the Internet directly.
   b. you can access the Internet only during the netiquette prime-time hours.
   c. you can access the Internet through your school, business, bulletin board, or a commercial provider.
   d. you can send e-mail to the Internet without a special e-mail address.

7. A mail server is
   a. an icon on the screen that looks like a waiter in a restaurant and is used to access the Internet.
   b. a computer that receives e-mail messages for users and holds them until the user picks up the e-mail.
   c. only found on local area networks.
   d. never used after midnight, according to netiquette rules.

8. The Internet is
   a. a complex network of computers run by the International Network Association.
   b. an informal organization designed to regulate standards of international networking hardware and software.
   c. a global network of computers that evolved from the United States Department of Defense Advanced Research Projects Agency network.
   d. an internal network organization in the United States for use by educational institutions only.

9. The difference between a graphical user interface and a character-based interface is that
   a. a graphical user interface requires use of a Macintosh computer to interpret the graphical images, and a character-based interface requires a DOS-based PC.
   b. the character-based interface was written in the BASIC programming language, and the graphical character interface was written in Visual BASIC.
   c. the graphical user interface relies on a complex, high-speed modem to process the images, and the character-based interface does not need a modem at all.
   d. a character-based interface presents a screen of words and numbers, and a graphical user interface uses the mouse to make selections from menus and icons, and displays graphic images and photographs on the screen.

Short Answer

1. How did the Internet come into existence?

2. What does Telnet do and how does it work?

3. What are newsgroups?

4. What is the IRC?

5. How are the newsgroups and the IRC used to communicate?

6. Explain netiquette and why it is important.

7. What are Gophers? What is their function?

8. What is a home page?

9. What are emoticons? Why are they important?

10. What are some of the uses of the Internet?

For Discussion

1. Why is the Internet a valuable tool?

2. Why is netiquette so important?

3. Would you or do you use the Internet? Explain why you use it or why you would not choose to use it.

EDIT

Button	Menu Option	Keys	Description	Word	Excel	Access	PowerPoint
↺	Undo	CTRL + Z	Undoes the last operation.	●	●	●	●
↻	Repeat	CTRL + Y	Repeats the last operation.	●	●		
✂	Cut	CTRL + X	Cuts selected text to clipboard.	●	●	●	●
📋	Copy	CTRL + C	Copies selected text to clipboard.	●	●	●	●
📋	Paste	CTRL + V	Pastes clipboard text segment into document.	●	●	●	●
	Paste Special		Pastes or embeds formats, values, or other attributes of information from the clipboard to a selection.	●	●		●
	Clear	DEL	Erases contents and/or formats from a selection.	●	●		●
	Delete	DEL (Access)	Deletes a marked block or object at the cursor.		●	●	
	Delete Sheet		Removes an entire sheet from the workbook.		●		
	Move or Copy Sheet		Changes order of sheets in workbook or duplicates sheets in workbook.		●		
🔗	Relationships		Sets up or modifies relationships between tables.			●	
	Select All	CTRL + A	Selects entire document.	●			●
	Duplicate	CTRL + D	Duplicates the selected slide or object.				●
	Delete Slide		Removes the selected slide from the presentation.				●
	Find	CTRL + F	Finds specified text.	●	●		●

Button	Menu Option	Keys	Description	Word	Excel	Access	PowerPoint
	Replace	CTRL + **H**	Replaces one text string with another.	●	●		●
	Go To	CTRL + **G**	Goes to certain page (or other marker).	●	●		
	Links		Connects an object in the active file with a file on disk.	●	●		●
	Object		Switches the selected object into the edit mode.	●	●		●
	Bookmark		Creates for selected text, graphics or other elements.	●			
	AutoText		Creates an AutoText entry from selected text or frequently used graphics. Inserts AutoText entry into a document.	●			

VIEW

Button	Menu Option	Keys	Description	Word	Excel	Access	PowerPoint
	Normal		Displays in normal editing view.	●			
	Slides		Selects the single Slide view mode.				●
	Outline		Displays in Outline view.	●			●
	Page Layout		Displays in Page Layout view.	●			
	Formula Bar		Displays/hides formula bar.		●		
	Status Bar		Displays/hides status bar.		●		
	Full screen		Displays file contents only (no menus, toolbars, etc.).	●	●		
	Slide Sorter		Selects the Slide Sorter view mode.				●
	Notes Pages		Selects the Notes Pages view mode.				●
	Slide Show		Selects the Slide Show view mode.				●
	Master		Accesses the Master slide menu.				●
	Toolbars		Displays or hides toolbars.	●	●	●	●
	Ruler		Displays or hides ruler(s).	●			●
	Guides		Turns on/off vertical and horizontal guides on the screen.				●
	Header and Footer		Shows headers and footers.	●			
	Footnotes		Opens Footnote window.	●			
33% ↧	Zoom		Increases/decreases document magnification.	●	●		●
Table	Tables		Displays a list of tables.			●	
Query	Queries		Displays a list of queries.			●	
Form	Forms		Displays a list of forms.			●	

Button	Menu Option	Keys	Description	Word	Excel	Access	PowerPoint
Report	Reports		Displays a list of reports.			●	
Macro	Macros		Displays a list of macros.			●	
Module	Modules		Displays a list of modules.			●	
	Code		Displays a list of code files.			●	
	Options		Sets screen options.			●	
	Master Document		Displays master document as an outline.	●			
	Annotations		Displays annotations from the document.	●			

SECURITY

Button	Menu Option	Keys	Description	Word	Excel	Access	PowerPoint
	Permissions		Sets table permission levels.			●	
	Users		Sets up user lists.			●	
	Groups		Sets up group lists.			●	
	Change Password		Changes the current password.			●	
	Change Owner		Changes the name of the owner of this database.			●	
	Print Security		Prints a report on the current security setup.			●	

INSERT

Button	Menu Option	Keys	Description	Word	Excel	Access	PowerPoint
	Break		Inserts page, column, or section break.	●			
	Symbol		Inserts special symbol.	●			
	Footnote		Inserts footnote reference.	●			
	File		Inserts another file into document.	●			
	Frame		Inserts selected text or object into frame.	●			
	Object		Inserts object, such as WordArt object, equation, graph, and so on.	●	●		●
	Database		Inserts a database into the document.	●			
	Cells		Inserts a range of cells, shifting worksheet contents to make room.		●		
	Rows		Inserts row(s) into worksheet, shifting other information down.		●		
	Columns		Inserts column(s) into worksheet, shifting other information right.		●		
	Worksheet		Inserts a new worksheet before current worksheet in workbook.		●		
	Chart		Creates a chart (as new sheet or as embedded chart).		●		
	Page Break		Forces a printout page break at the current cell location.		●		
	Function		Uses Function Wizard to step through building a function.		●		
	Name		Creates named range or names constant.		●		
	Note		Creates cell note.		●		

Button	Menu Option	Keys	Description	Word	Excel	Access	PowerPoint
New Slide...	New Slide	CTRL + M	Inserts a new slide following the current slide.				●
	Date		Inserts the current date on a master slide.				●
	Time		Inserts the current time on a master slide.				●
	Page Number		Inserts page numbering on a master slide.	●			●
	Slides from File		Inserts slides from a disk file in the active presentation.				●
	Slides from Outline		Creates slides from a text outline on disk.				●
(icon)	Clip Art		Adds an image from the clip art library to the current slide.	●	●		●
	Picture		Adds a graphic file to the current slide.	●	●		●
(icon)	Microsoft Word Table		Adds a Microsoft Word table to the current slide.				●
(icon)	Microsoft Graph		Adds a Microsoft graph to the current Slide.				●
	Annotation		Inserts an annotation mark.	●			
	Date and Time		Inserts the date or time.	●			
	Field		Inserts a field.	●			
	Form Field		Inserts a text check box or a drop-down form field.	●			
	Caption		Inserts captions to document items.	●			
	Cross-reference		Inserts a cross-reference to an item in a document.	●			
	Index and Tables		Creates indexes, Tables of Contents, figure tables and tables of authorities.	●			

FORMAT

Button	Menu Option	Keys	Description	Word	Excel	Access	PowerPoint
	Alignment		Controls the appearance, alignment, font characteristics, and so on, of cell contents.		•		
	Protection						
	Borders						
	Patterns						
Times New Roman	Font		Sets character formats.	•			•
	Paragraph		Sets paragraph formats.	•			
	Tabs		Sets, changes, and clears tabs.	•			
	Borders and Shading		Formats paragraphs and tables with borders and shading.	•			
	Row		Controls height of row and whether row is hidden.		•		
	Columns		Sets width and number of columns in Word, controls height and whether column is hidden in Excel.	•	•		
	Sheet		Sets name of sheet on tab, hides/displays sheet.		•		
	AutoFormat		Applies combinations of formats automatically.	•	•		
	Change Case	(SHFT) + (F3)	Switches from capital to lowercase letters or vice versa.	•			•
	Bullets and Numbering		Establishes bulleted or numbered lists. In PowerPoint, changes bullet character for selected text.	•			
	Style		Defines, edits, and applies styles.	•	•		

Button	Menu Option	Keys	Description	Word	Excel	Access	PowerPoint
	Frame		Adjusts size and position of frame.	●			
	Alignment		Aligns selected text left, right, or centered between margins.				●
	Line Spacing		Sets line spacing for selected text.				●
	Text Anchor		Adjusts the shape of a text object within a graphic object.				●
	Colors and Lines		Changes lines and fill colors.				●
	Shadow		Adjusts the shadow around an object.				●
	Pick Up Style		Copies the attributes of an object.				●
	Apply Style		Applies the previously picked up style to the selected object or default style.				●
Template...	Presentation Template		Applies the format of an existing presentation to the active presentation.				●
	Pick a Look Wizard		Designs a look for the active presentation.				●
Layout...	Slide Layout		Displays available AutoLayouts.				●
	Slide Background		Changes background color or shading.				●
	Slide Color Scheme		Changes color of one or more elements in a slide.				●
	Drop Cap		Formats paragraph with a drop cap.	●			
	Heading numbering		Creates a numbered list from a series of styled headings.	●			
	Style Gallery		Applies the style from a selected template to the active document.	●			
	Picture		Inserts a graphic from another application.	●			
	Drawing Object		Changes formatting elements of drawing objects.	●			

TOOLS

Button	Menu Option	Keys	Description	Word	Excel	Access	PowerPoint
	Spelling	F7	Checks spelling.	•	•		•
	Thesaurus	SHFT + F7	Suggests alternative word choices.	•			
	Word Count		Counts words, characters, paragraphs, lines, or pages.	•			
	AutoCorrect		Lists errors to be automatically corrected.	•			
	Auditing		Traces cell precedents, dependents, and errors; displays cell notes.		•		
	Protection		Activates/deactivates sheet and workbook protection.		•		
	Macro		Allows macros to be run or edited.	•	•		
	Record Macro		Records commands into a macro.		•		
	Replace Fonts		Replaces one typeface with another throughout the active presentation.				•
	Transition		Applies a special effect during a change from one slide to the next slide.				•
	Build		Causes items in a list to appear one at a time during a slide show.				•
	Hide Slide		Skips a slide during a slide show.				•
	Play Settings		Determines how and when embedded movies, sounds, and objects should be played during a slide show.				•

Button	Menu Option	Keys	Description	Word	Excel	Access	PowerPoint
	Recolor		Recolors the selected picture, graph, or slide.				●
	Crop Picture		Hides portions of the selected picture.				●
	Customize		Edits menus and toolbars.	●			●
	Options		Changes various options.	●	●		●
	Grammar		Checks document for grammar errors and displays suggested corrections.	●			
	Hyphenation		Inserts proper hyphens.	●			
	Language		Designates selected text's language.	●			
	Mail Merge		Merges main document with data source.	●			
	Envelopes and Labels		Prints envelopes and labels.	●			
	Protect Document		Protects documents from alterations.	●			
	Revisions		Traces revisions made to a document.	●			

TABLE

Button	Menu Option	Keys	Description	Word	Excel	Access	PowerPoint
	Insert		Inserts table, row, or column.	●		●	
	Delete		Deletes row or column.	●		●	
	Merge		Merges several cells into one.	●		●	
	Select Table	ALT + 5	Selects an entire table.	●		●	
	Table AutoFormat		Applies format options to a table.	●		●	
	Cell Height and Width		Changes height or width of rows or columns.	●		●	
	Convert Text to Table		Changes text into a table or a table into text.	●		●	
	Sort		Sorts text or rows in a table.	●		●	
	Gridlines		Turns table gridlines on or off.	●		●	
	Split Cells		Splits a cell horizontally.	●		●	
	Select Row		Selects row containing insertion point.	●		●	
	Select Table	ALT + 5	Selects table containing insertion point.	●		●	
	Select Column		Selects column containing insertion point.	●		●	
	Headings		Automatically repeats table headings for tables spanning more than one page.	●		●	
	Formula		Performs mathematical calculations.	●		●	
	Split Table		Divides a table.	●		●	

DATA

Button	Menu Option	Keys	Description	Word	Excel	Access	PowerPoint
	Sort		Sorts information in database or other selection.		●		
	Filter		Activates/deactivates database AutoFilter mode (to allow criteria to be used for controlling record display).		●		
	Form		Activates database data entry form.		●		

DRAW

Button	Menu Option	Keys	Description	Word	Excel	Access	PowerPoint
	Group		Combines selected objects into a group so they function as a single object.				●
	Ungroup		Breaks a group into its components.				●
	Regroup		Reapplies grouping to previously grouped items.				●
	Bring to Front		Moves an object in front of all other objects that may be covering it.				●
	Send to Back		Moves an object behind all other objects on the slide.				●
	Bring Forward		Moves a slide forward one layer at a time.				●
	Send Backward		Moves a slide backward one layer at a time.				●
	Align		Changes the alignment of selected objects in relation to each other.				●
	Snap to Grid		Attaches objects to an invisible grid.				●
	Rotate/Flip		Rotates an object to an exact position (Free Rotate) or 90 degrees to the left or right. Flips an object 180 degrees horizontally or vertically.				●
	Scale		Resizes selection by a precise percentage.				●
	Change AutoShape		Changes a selected Auto-Shape to another shape.				●

WINDOW

Button	Menu Option	Keys	Description	Word	Excel	Access	PowerPoint
	New Window		Opens new window into active document.	●	●		
	Tile		Tiles currently open windows.			●	
	Fit to Page		Fits active window to slide size.				●
	Cascade		Cascades currently open windows.			●	●
	Arrange Icons		Arranges current icons into neat rows.			●	●
	Hide		Hides current window.		●	●	
	Unhide		Unhides hidden window.		●	●	
	Arrange		Arranges open windows.		●		
	Freeze Panes		Freezes portion of worksheet so that portion is always visible.		●		

HELP

Button	Menu Option	Keys	Description	Word	Excel	Access	PowerPoint
	Contents	F1	Displays contents for Help.	●	●	●	●
	Search for Help On		Searches Help by keyword.	●	●	●	●
(Access)	Cue Cards		Opens cue card Help.			●	●
	Technical Support		Displays Microsoft technical support Help menus.	●	●	●	●
	About Microsoft		Displays information about the open software application and your computer system; can also be used to run another application.	●	●	●	●
	Index		Displays index for Help.	●	●		●
	Quick Preview		Provides a brief on-screen interactive introduction to the application.	●	●		●
	Tip of the Day		Displays a tip about a feature in the application.	●			●

Glossary

35mm Slides An output medium in which slides are displayed using a slide projector.

386 enhanced mode A Windows operating mode that provides access to the advanced memory management features of the Intel 80386 processor, including virtual memory capabilities and the ability to run non-Windows applications in sizable windows.

absolute cell reference A cell reference that does not change, even when the formula containing the reference is copied. Either the row, the column, or both the row and the column may be absolute. Examples: A$1, $A1, $A$1. Also called *absolute address*. Contrast with relative cell reference.

active cell The current, selected cell, as outlined by the thick border of the selection rectangle. The active cell is where the next action or command will take place. Its address is displayed in the reference area.

active presentation The presentation being viewed or edited when more than one presentation is open.

active table is the table in which the record pointer moves down one record when you press ⬇ and up one record when you press ⬆.

address A phrase which identifies an individual on the Internet network. Electronic mail is sent to a person's address. The computer user then accesses his or her mailbox and retrieves the mail. An address example: earthplanet@galaxy.com

aligned left Paragraph format in which lines are aligned along the left edge. Used for most text. Select the paragraph and then select the Align Left button on the Formatting toolbar, or press CTRL+**L**.

aligned right Paragraph format in which lines are aligned along the right edge. Difficult to read, but can be used for small amounts of text such as a figure caption or a short heading. To align text to the right, select the paragraph and then select the Align Right button on the Formatting toolbar, or press CTRL+**R**.

alignment How information (text or value) is oriented within a cell or range. Numerical values are usually right aligned, and text is either center or left aligned, though any choice of left, center, or right is possible. You can also wrap long text entries within a cell and center a title across a range of cells.

application A program designed to accomplish a particular task. Word processor programs and electronic spreadsheets are applications. Often used interchangeably with program.

application Control-menu boxes are the buttons at the left end of the application title bar.

application icon A Windows icon that represents a minimized program.

application title bars are the bars across the top of the main screen window.

application window A window that contains a running application in Windows.

argument A piece of information provided to a function. Some functions, such as =NOW(), require no arguments; others require one or several. Multiple arguments are separated by commas, as in =IF(A3>5,1,0).

ascending order is A-Z order for text type fields, oldest to newest for date fields, and smallest to largest for number fields.

AutoContent Wizard Provides suggested outlines for common types of presentations such as sales, training, and communicating news which you can adapt to reflect your ideas.

AutoLayout Provides twenty-one predefined slide layouts including placeholders for titles, text, clip art, tables, graphs, and organization charts.

AutoShape One of twenty-four complex predefined shapes that can be added to a slide.

band-oriented report generators allow you to design a report by dividing it into bands. (See also *report header, report footer, page header, page footer, groupings*.)

best fit A way to accommodate the longest entry in a column by double-clicking the mouse button. The width is adjusted automatically.

black and white overhead An output medium in which slides are printed on a black and white printer and displayed using an overhead projector.

body text The main text of a report, letter, or other document, as contrasted with headings or headlines.

bold Emphasizes text by making it appear darker than the surrounding text.

border A line drawn around the edge of an object.

border A decorative line attached to one or more sides of a cell. A variety of line styles is available. Borders are a kind of format.

build A special effect that displays items in a bulleted list, one at a time. The list is called a progressive disclosure list.

bullet A symbol, such as a solid square block or open circle, that precedes an item in a list. A small typographical device, usually a large dot, that indicates separate items in a list. Used to create bulleted lists.

Calculator A Windows utility program, or accessory, that operates as a typical calculator.

Calendar A Windows utility program, or accessory, that serves as an electronic appointment calendar.

Cardfile A Windows utility program, or accessory, that serves as an electronic set of index cards.

cascade menus are menu selections that open another menu.

cascading A method of arranging windows in which all windows are placed in an overlapping pattern with their title bars showing.

category In charting, a category describes a certain circumstance for a variable, which means that a variable has a particular value under a certain category. The categories appear along the bottom edge (X-axis) of a chart. Each category is labeled with a category name.

cell The basic building block of an electronic spreadsheet; the intersection of a column and a row. Cells are referred to by indicating their column and row. A cell is a holding place where you can store information.

cell reference A cell's address, usually expressed in terms of the cell's column and row on the worksheet. For example, the cell at the intersection of column C and row 15 has the reference C15.

center tab Centers text under a tab. You can choose from various tab options by selecting the Tab Alignment button at the left edge of the ruler.

centered alignment Paragraph format in which lines are centered between margins or column edges. Often used with headings or small amounts of text that require a formal presentation. To center text, select the paragraph and then select the Center button on the Formatting toolbar, or press CTRL+**E**.

channel A place on the Internet where two or more people hold an online conversation. Channels have names, like #chat or #friendly, and can be joined at any time. Channels are used by the Internet Relay Chat to provide a place for users to talk about the channel's current topic.

character-based See *text-based*.

chart A graph that displays quantitative information visually rather than using text and figures.

chart sheet A document or sheet type in Excel, designed to hold a chart; can be linked to worksheets.

chart type The kind of graph or chart. Excel has 14 major chart types, such as pie, line, and column charts.

check box Indicates an option in a dialog box that can be on or off. An "X" indicates the feature is active; the absence of an "X" indicates the feature is not active.

checkmark A mark next to a command name that indicates an active command.

child tables are those whose record pointers are controlled by parent tables. (See also *related tables*.)

circular reference A formula which directly or indirectly refers to itself. Circular references are almost always mistakes. Example: the formula =0.08*C15 if contained in cell C15 would be a circular reference.

click To press and quickly release the left mouse button after positioning the pointer on a character or object.

clip art Graphic images stored on disk.

clipboard A temporary storage location in the computer's memory used for transferring data from one document to another.

Clock A Windows utility program, or accessory, that displays the current time.

color overhead Output medium in which slides are printed on a color printer and displayed using an overhead projector.

column The vertical subdivision of a worksheet; columns are labeled with letters of the alphabet.

command buttons Buttons used to execute the named options in a dialog box. The two most common command buttons, OK and Cancel, are used to close dialog boxes.

constant A number or text entry which does not change; information typed in literally rather than a formula.

context-sensitive Help Takes you directly to Help information about a feature you have selected or are using without having to search through a list of Help topics.

continuous loop A function whereby PowerPoint automatically replays a presentation after reaching the end of the set of slides.

Control menu The pull-down menu from the Control menu box used to control a window.

Control menu box The box in the upper left corner of all windows from which the Control menu pulls down.

controls contain pieces of information in screen forms and reports. For example, when a field is placed on a form, it's called a control.

copy To duplicate some or all of the contents of a cell or range.

crop The process of shrinking or enlarging an object's window. The object's size under the window remains the same while the borders of the window are moved to reveal more or less of the underlying object.

cross reference tables contain a key value from the original parent and a key from the child.

cue card Provides detailed instructions to complete a task.

customized number format A user-defined cell format designed to display specialized number entries in a particular form. Common examples include formats for serial numbers, telephone numbers, Social Security numbers, zip codes, and part numbers.

data dictionary a list of all fields, queries, forms, reports, relationships, formatting instructions, and validations in the database.

data marker The graphic symbol used to plot information on a chart. Data markers include lines, bars, and other symbols.

data series Set of related data values or observations used in constructing charts. The gross national product for each year from 1970 to 1990 is an example of a data series.

data types are the kinds of data that can be stored in a table. Access data types include text, memo, number, date/time, currency, counter, yes/no, and OLE object.

databases are collections of related data tables.

decimal tab Aligns text—or, more commonly, numbers—on the decimal point under the tab. You can choose from various tab options by selecting the Tab Alignment button at the left edge of the ruler.

defined name A user-created name that refers to a constant, a cell, or a range of cells. Defined names can make formulas and macros easier to read and understand. Also called *range names*.

delimiters are characters used in pairs to surround some data.

demote Shifts selected text right one level in the outline and changes the bullet character to match other bullets at that level.

dependent cell Cell (containing a formula) that depends on a particular cell for information.

descending order is Z-A order for text type fields, newest to oldest for date fields and largest to smallest for number fields.

desktop The background screen of a graphical operating environment, which serves as a graphics-based work area.

Detail bands will be printed between the page header and page footer (unless the report includes groups).

dialog box A box that appears on the screen to prompt the user to enter more information; also displays information, warnings, and error messages.

dimmed commands Command names in menus appearing in a lighter shade to indicate that a command is not available at the current time.

directory Groups related files on a disk.

directory icon Icons that look like small folders and represent directories on the current disk.

directory path In the title bar of a directory window, a label that displays the current drive letter and directory.

directory window In the File Manager, a split window where the left half displays the directory structure of the current drive and the right half displays the contents of the current directory.

disk A floppy disk is a removable data storage medium either 3 1/2" or 5 1/4" in size. A hard disk is a rigid data storage medium, either inside or connected to a computer, usually rated in MB (millions of bytes) of storage.

disk drive Writes data to and reads data from a disk. A letter designates a specific disk drive, such as disk drive A:.

document A file created by an application program.

document window A window that contains a document.

dots The symbols used to separate the elements of an e-mail address. The period symbol is used to represent a dot.

double-click To press and quickly release the left mouse button twice in rapid succession.

download To copy or move a file electronically from one computer to another.

drag Moving an object using the mouse pointer.

drag and drop An operation that allows you to move selected text quickly by dragging it from one spot and dropping it in another using the mouse.

drive icon In a directory window, an icon that represents floppy and hard disk drives, optical drives, or other storage devices.

e-mail The abbreviated form of electronic mail.

Electronic mail Messages that are sent and received over a network through a software program designed to provide mail services. It functions much like the postal service with carriers that take the messages to and from post offices, or network servers.

ellipsis A series of three dots (...) following a command indicating that a dialog box with more information will appear before the command can be completed.

embed Part of the OLE process of inserting a source file created in one software program into a target file created in a different software program. The embedded file becomes part of the target file, and can be updated and edited. Once embedded and edited, the original source file will not change. Only the object in the target file is modified.

embedded chart A chart contained within a worksheet. Contrast with chart sheet.

emboss Emphasizes text by making letters appear slightly raised.

emoticons Little faces drawn in an e-mail message or newsgroup article using the colon, semicolon, hyphen and parentheses characters. They can be used to express the emotions of the writer.

endnote Like a footnote, a brief block of text used for citing authorities or making incidental comments. An endnote appears at the end of a section rather than at the bottom of a page.

end-of-document mark (end mark) A short horizontal line that marks the end of a document. You cannot insert characters after the end-of-document mark.

execute To run a program or macro; to cause the program or macro to perform the instructions that comprise it.

explode In pie charts, to emphasize a particular pie slice by pulling it out from the pie.

field code This code represents the location of a linked object. The code can be displayed in the target file, or an image of the object can be displayed in the target file by turning field codes on and off through the Options choice on the Tools menu.

field width is the maximum length entry that will be allowed in a field.

fields are characteristics of the data.

file A block of storage on disk that contains the text and formatting information for a document.

file icon In the directory window, the icon next to a file name. Different icons represent different types of documents and programs.

File Manager The Windows program that is used to manage files and directories.

file name The name assigned to a file stored on disk.

File Transfer Protocol A world-wide accepted standard of rules governing the transfer of files, used extensively across the Internet. With FTP files can be downloaded to your computer from another computer, or uploaded from your computer to another computer.

fixed-space font A type style, such as Courier New, in which all characters are allotted the same width regardless of the letterform.

flamed A strong rebuke on the Internet because of incorrect behavior on the Net. Harsh articles are posted to newsgroups, often containing foul language, when someone commits a major faux pas on the Net. Flames can be avoided if you read the FAQs carefully and follow their instructions.

font Refers to the shape (typeface) of characters; a kind of letterform. Each font has a name (such as Arial), a size (such as 12 point), and a style (such as italic).

footer A repeating block of text at the bottom of each page in a section. Might contain a chapter heading, page number, or similar information. Word allows different footers for even and odd pages.

footnote A brief block of text at the bottom of a page that is used for citing authorities or making incidental comments.

format The appearance of information within a cell. Font, alignment, and number format are among the more important aspects of a cell's format.

formatted text Shows variations in font and text size.

Formatting toolbar Contains information, menus, and buttons related to formatting a document.

Form Footers are the part of the form shown after a screenful of records have been displayed.

formula A kind of cell entry that performs a calculation. All formulas begin with an equal sign. Normally, the result of the formula (as opposed to the formula itself) appears within the worksheet. Formulas can automatically change their result if there are changes in the cells upon which they depend, and formulas are the main reason that electronic spreadsheets are so useful.

Freehand Annotation A PowerPoint feature that allows you to use a mouse to draw on a slide during a slide show.

Frequently Asked Questions (FAQs) Documents that contain the answers to the most frequently asked questions about using the Internet. These documents can be found by using the FTP tool, on the Web, and in newsgroups.

function A built-in mathematical operation in Excel. There are hundreds of functions with many uses. Perhaps the most common function is SUM, which totals the values in a range of cells. Example: =SUM(A3:A7) sums the range of cells from A3 to A7.

Gopher A system that helps you find information in files throughout the Internet. You can browse through document offerings and retrieve documents that reside on many different computers throughout the world.

graphical query by example allows you to drag fields into the view and use standard Windows techniques to set up your view.

graphical user interface (GUI) The interface in a graphical operating environment. Includes the use of icons, windows, and pull-down menus.

group icon In the Program Manager, an icon that represents a group of programs.

groupings cluster records that are similar in some respect.

group window A window that displays the items in a group within the Program Manager.

GUI Graphical user interface.

hanging indentation Paragraph format in which the first line is not indented but subsequent lines are indented. The fastest way to create a hanging indentation is to press `CTRL`+T.

header A repeating block of text at the top of each page in a section. Might contain a chapter heading, page number, or similar information. Word allows different headers for even and odd pages.

Help button the button at the right end of the toolbar used to obtain online help.

home page On the Internet's World Wide Web, the home page is a file which lets people visit the organization sponsoring the home page. When you access a home page, the Web is actually displaying a file on your computer. Home pages usually contain some type of graphics, a photograph, or logo, and some text to explain the organization's services or products.

host A computer recognized by the Internet. People can access a host computer by connecting as a registered user of that computer system, or sometimes the computer will let people connect anonymously.

icon A graphical representation of a Windows element, such as a program file, data file, or some other function.

indentation marker Triangular markers on the ruler. The marker at the top left controls the first-line indentation. The marker at the bottom left controls the left edge indentation. The marker at the right side of the ruler controls the right indentation.

information window A special window designed to provide additional information about the active cell in a worksheet. Information windows can be used to monitor such things as cell formats, protection, dependents, and precedents.

inner joins select only records that have matching values in both tables.

insert mode In insert mode, characters that you type on the keyboard are inserted into whatever text already exists in the document. Select the Overtype indicator (OVR) in the status bar to switch between insert mode and overtype mode.

insertion point A blinking vertical bar that marks the position where text will be inserted or deleted when you type on the keyboard.

integrates software An integrated software program is several programs in one product. The separate programs cannot be purchased alone. Most integrated packages have a word processor, a spreadsheet, a database and some type of communications software.

interface A software program which controls how information is displayed on the screen. The newest interface standard is the GUI.

Internet A system of computers informally connected together throughout the world.

Internet Relay Chat (IRC) A system of channels on which two or more people can hold online, live conversations. An IRC channel is not totally private; conversations can be heard by systems administrators as they pass through their computer systems.

join means to link two tables to form a view.

jump In a Help screen, a reference to related definitions or Help topics. A jump is displayed in a contrasting color. Select a jump to see that definition or related topic.

justified alignment Paragraph format in which lines are aligned along both left and right edges. Often used with text that appears in multiple columns on a page. To justify text, select the paragraph and then select the Justify button on the Formatting toolbar, or press CTRL+J.

labels are text in a screen form or report that describes something about the form itself or one of the controls the form contains.

landscape orientation A print option producing a slide that is wider than it is tall.

left tab Aligns text on the left side under the tab. You can choose from various tab options by selecting the Tab Alignment button at the left edge of the ruler.

legend On a chart, a legend shows how different colors and data markers correspond to the data series used to make the chart.

link To insert the location of an object file in another file. The object can be updated to reflect the changes in the linked object's source file.

linked text On a chart sheet, linked text is derived from a worksheet cell. If the original text changes in the worksheet, the linked text in the chart changes as well.

linking key fields are fields used to relate tables.

list box Displays an alphabetized list of choices in a dialog box.

local area network A system of computers connected together. Usually the computers all occupy the same building and are connected with cabling.

mail server A computer which receives incoming electronic mail and manages the outgoing electronic mail from the users.

many-to-many relationships have several parent records with matching keys in the child and several child records with matching keys in the parent.

maximize To fill the entire screen with one window.

maximize button The small box on the right corner of the title bar containing an up arrow. Used to enlarge a window to its maximum size.

menu A list of available commands in an application window.

menu bar A horizontal listing of commands located near the top of the screen. Selecting an option on a menu bar displays the associated pull-down menu.

minimize To shrink a window to an icon.

minimize button The small box on the right corner of the title bar containing a down arrow. Used to reduce a window to an icon.

mouse A palm-sized input device equipped with two or three control buttons. Movement causes movement of a mouse pointer in the same direction on the screen.

mouse pointer Indicates the area on the screen that the next action affects.

move To remove information from one location and place it in another. Unlike copying, moving "picks up" the contents of a cell or range and places them elsewhere.

multi-application object An object which has passed through more than one application before being linked or embedded in the final document file.

multitasking The capability of running multiple programs simultaneously.

navigating Moving from one electronic place to another on the Internet is called navigating.

netiquette A set of social and behavioral rules for the Internet.

newsgroups Forums on the Internet for the exchange of information, thoughts and ideas. Each newsgroup is dedicated to one topic or idea. People write and post articles in a newsgroup for others to read and respond to.

nonadjacent selection A compound selection of multiple ranges. A nonadjacent selection need not form a rectangle or be composed of a single selected area.

nonprinting characters Characters that can be displayed on the screen but will not be printed. Include spaces, paragraph marks, and tabs. You can toggle screen display of nonprinting characters on and off by selecting the Show/Hide ¶ button on the Standard toolbar.

non-Windows applications Programs not specifically designed to run under Windows and that cannot take advantage of many Windows' features, such as a consistent user interface.

normalizing The process of dividing the database into several tables so you don't enter the same data more than once.

Notepad A Windows utility program that serves as an electronic note pad.

Notes Pages view Displays a slide with speaker's notes, if any, below the slide.

number (number constant) Numbers are constant numeric values (such as 3 or -1.9) and are a basic kind of cell entry.

object Text, clip art, a table, a graph, or an organization chart attached to a slide.

OLE Object Linking and Embedding is the process of connecting or inserting files created in one software package into a file created in another software package so that the OLE files can be updated and modified.

on-screen presentation An output medium in which slides are viewed on a computer monitor or displayed on a screen using a computer projection device.

one-to-many relationships have more than one child for each parent.

one-to-one relationships have exactly one child record for each parent record.

operating environment A graphics-based work area allowing easy access to multiple programs.

operating system Software required for use on a computer to manage the computer's resources.

option button In a dialog box, round buttons that appear in small groups of related options from which you can select only one item.

orphan records are records in a child table that have no matching key in the parent table.

outer joins display all records from each table regardless of whether or not there is a matching record in the other table.

Outline view Displays slide titles and main text in outline format.

overtype mode In overtype mode, characters you type replace existing characters. Select the Overtype indicator (OVR) on the status bar to switch between overtype mode and insert mode.

Page Footer bands will be printed at the bottom of each page of the report.

Page Header bands will be printed at the top of each page of the report.

Paintbrush A Windows utility program used for creating drawings.

paragraph mark Marks the end of a paragraph in Word. Inserted with the (ENTER) key. Shows on-screen as a ¶ symbol.

parent tables are used as the main tables in a relationship. (See also *primary tables*.)

path Describes the route an application must follow to locate a document on disk.

Pick a Look Wizard Provides 57 pre-defined background settings and prompts the user to select one or more types of output.

placeholder An empty box or other shape that you can fill later.

point A measure of the type size of characters. A point equals 1/72 inch, thus 72-point type is 1 inch high. Text matter is usually from 8 to 12 points. Headings are usually 14 points or larger.

point (point mode) A method of building formulas that reduces the need to keep track of literal cell references and instead allows you to use the mouse or arrow keys to "point" to the cells or ranges that will be referred to in the formula.

pointer The arrow-shaped cursor that follows the movement of a pointing device to indicate which area will be affected when you press the mouse button. May change shape in different applications.

portrait orientation A print option producing a slide that is taller than it is wide.

PowerPoint Viewer A special application that allows you to run a PowerPoint presentation on a computer that does not have PowerPoint installed.

precedent cell Cell upon which formulas in other cells depend. A change in a precedent cell can cause the result of a dependent formula to change.

presentation graphics program A software tool for developing professional-looking presentations.

primary key fields are used to permanently link one table with another in the database. The records in a table will be in the order of its primary key. The primary key must be unique; that is, no duplicate values will be allowed unless it is sorted on another expression.

primary source application The application used to create an object's source file. An Access database object's primary source file is Access.

primary tables are used as the main tables in a relationship. (See also *parent table*.)

priority The relative "binding strength" of an Excel arithmetic operator. The priority of operators in a formula determines the order in which operations are performed. For example, because multiplication has higher priority than addition, the formula =2+2*10 has the result 22, not 40.

Program Manager An integral part of Windows that enables the user to easily start applications and logically organize programs.

program-item icon An icon chosen to start a program.

progressive disclosure list See *build*.

project means to pick fields from one or more tables.

promote Shifts selected text left one level in the outline and changes the bullet character to match other bullets at that level.

proofread Read the text on each slide, noting omissions and corrections to be made in content and organization.

proportionally spaced font A type style, such as Arial or Times New Roman, in which the width of a letter depends on the letterform. For example, the letter *i* is thinner than the letter *M*.

pull-down list A list of related items that appears after clicking an underscored down arrow in a dialog box or toolbar.

pull-down menu A menu that appears when a choice is made from the menu bar at the top of the screen.

query Lets you ask the database simple or complex questions.

radio buttons Used to specify only one choice from a set of items in a dialog box.

range A rectangular block of cells, identified by any two of its diagonal corner cells. A range can be as small as one cell or as large as the entire worksheet. Example: the rectangle of cells whose upper-left corner is A3 and whose lower-right corner is D5 is called A3:D5.

record pointer keeps track of which record is currently available for editing, copying, and other activities.

records are the information for each field.

Redo command Restores editing or typing that has been reversed with the Undo feature.

referential integrity means no orphan records are allowed in any child table. It can also mean that deleting a parent record will automatically delete all child records in all tables involved in a relationship.

related tables are those whose record pointers are controlled by parent tables. (See also *child tables*.)

relational database management systems can easily use related data that's stored in different tables.

relationships are permanent links between tables.

relative cell reference Within a formula, a cell reference that can change if the formula is copied. This is the default (standard) kind of cell reference in Excel formulas and is most often what will work best if a formula is copied. Contrast with absolute cell reference.

Report Footer bands will be printed at the bottom of the last page of the report.

Report Header bands will be printed at the top of the first page of the report.

resize handle A point on the border of a selected object. Dragging a resize handle changes the size of the object.

restore To return an icon or maximized window back to its former size.

restore button The small box on the right edge of the title bar containing up and down arrows. Used to restore a maximized window.

retrieving data means finding groups of entries that meet certain criteria and copying them to another location.

right tab Aligns text on the right side under the tab. You can choose from various tab options by selecting the Tab Alignment button at the left edge of the ruler.

row The horizontal subdivision of a worksheet. Rows are labeled with numbers.

ruler Displays and allows you to control margins, indentation, tab settings, and column widths. Page Layout view shows a vertical as well as a horizontal ruler.

sans serif font Typefaces that lack serifs, or small crosslines at the end of the main letter strokes. Arial is a sans serif font.

screen forms are used to display, enter, and edit data on the screen.

scroll arrow The arrow at either end of a scroll bar that enables the user to shift the screen display in the direction of the arrow.

scroll bar The bar at the right side and bottom edge of a window that enables the user to scroll through text and graphics that do not fit within a window's boundaries.

scroll box Within the scroll bar, the box that is dragged to scroll through a window.

searching data means looking for an entry that meet certain criteria.

secondary keys are index keys used to speed up searches.

secondary source application The application used to create the secondary source file in a multiapplication object. In the case of an Access database object linked to a Word document embedded in a third application, the secondary source application is Word.

section A portion of a document that can be formatted with specific margin settings, page orientation (portrait or landscape), page numbering sequence, multiple columns, or other features affecting page layout.

select means to pick records from one or more tables based on specified criteria.

selection A group of cells that have been marked to be affected by a command or other action. Selection is usually done by dragging with the mouse, though several other methods are available.

selection bar Allows you to select part of a document using a mouse.

selection box A box selected for editing. A selection box is surrounded by a border of forward slashes.

selection rule Selection rules are set up by identifying field names, selecting comparison phrases, and stating numbers or characters which are compared to the data in the database. You can extract or display certain records from the database based upon the selection rule.

sequentially searching a table means searching the data table by reading each consecutive entry.

serif font Typefaces that have small crosslines, called serifs, at the end of the main letter strokes. Times New Roman is a serif font.

shadow Emphasizes text by adding a drop shadow behind it.

shortcut keys Keystrokes used to bypass menu selections.

site A computer, accessible through the Internet, which lets you connect to it.

size Changing the size of an object's window. The object will grow or shrink proportionately as the window is sized. Use the mouse to grab one of the object's handles and drag the window edge to make the window larger or smaller.

sizing buttons The small boxes on the right edge of the title bar containing arrows. Used to quickly change the dimensions of the window.

slide layout The arrangement of objects on a slide.

Slide Show view Displays a presentation one slide at a time. Each slide fills the screen.

Slide Sorter view Displays reduced images (text and graphics) of all slides in order on the screen, three to a row.

Slide view Displays a presentation one slide at a time for edit. You can add graphics, draw shapes, and change the slide layout in addition to editing text.

software applications Software programs which perform specific functions like word processing, database, spreadsheet, drawing and painting, communications. Each individual program type is a software application.

software suite A set of programs which work together, especially in support of OLE. Microsoft Office is a software suite because the programs, while fully operational and available separately, work together as if they were one software program.

sorting data means presenting the data in a different sequence from the way it's stored in the database.

source application The software application or package being used to create an object file. This object file will be either linked or embedded into a target file.

source file The actual object which was created in the source application. This object will be linked or embedded into a target file.

spelling checker Word's spelling checker will compare every word in a document with an online dictionary. If a word is not in the dictionary, Word reports the word as a possible misspelling.

standard mode Windows' basic operating mode. A non-Windows application runs in a full-screen window that cannot be sized into a smaller window.

Standard toolbar Contains buttons that allow you to perform many word processing tasks with a click of a mouse.

status bar Gives basic information about a document or about word processing modes.

strikeover mode Characters are typed on the screen at the location of the cursor, and existing characters are replaced by the new characters.

style A collection of formatting characteristics that is given a name and is accessible from the Style box in the Formatting toolbar. In Excel, several predefined but modifiable cell styles are available; you can also create your own cell styles.

subscript A character slightly below characters on the same line.

summary fields summarize some aspect of another field in the table.

superscript A character slightly above characters on the same line.

table structures are lists of fields in tables.

tables are collections of closely related information.

target application The software application or package being used to create a file which will contain embedded or linked objects.

target file The actual file created to contain an embedded or a linked object. The source file will be inserted into the target file.

task A term that is sometimes used to refer to a program.

Task List A Windows utility program that enables the user to manage multiple running programs.

template A template is a formatting blueprint. Colors, lines, shadows, and other formatting settings are established in the template. This blueprint is used to format a new object or file when it is created.

text-based An interface made up of displaying numbers and characters only. This interface requires the computer user to respond to the screen by typing numbers and letters. A mouse is not used in a text-based interface.

text box Used to type information, such as a file name, in a dialog box.

text (text constant) Data, usually consisting of words, that serves to identify parts of the worksheet or to store non-numeric information.

thesaurus Word's built-in thesaurus can look up a word and provide a list of synonyms, or words with similar meanings.

tiling A method of arranging windows in which all windows are visible but are reduced in size so that they fit like tiles side-by-side on the screen.

timing The amount of time a slide stays on the screen.

title bar Bar at the top of all windows containing the title of the application and that of the current document file.

toggle To alternately turn commands or options on and off.

toolbar a series of buttons immediately below the menu bar that let you quickly accomplish tasks by clicking the button instead of working through a sequence of menu selections.

track ball A pointing device with a ball exposed on the top. Moving the ball with your fingers correspondingly moves a pointer on the screen.

transient links are temporary links between two tables.

transition A special effect that controls how each entire slide appears and disappears from the screen.

Undo Reverses a previous editing or typing step. You can usually undo several word processing steps in reverse order.

validations are restrictions on the data that can be entered in a field.

value A number constant or a formula that produces a numeric result. Values can participate in arithmetic calculations.

view A way to look at the slides in a PowerPoint presentation.

volume label A name for a disk. Usually assigned when a disk is formatted.

window A well-defined rectangular area on the desktop. Contains applications and documents.

window border Defines the outside edge of a window.

Windows application A program that is specially designed to take full advantage of all the powerful features of Windows.

Wizards are sequences of windows and dialog boxes that ask a series of questions about a document format and use your answers to lead you through the process of building a document, table, query, screen form, or report.

Word art A special text effect, such as slanting or curving.

word processing Using a computer to write, edit, format, store, and print documents.

word wrap A word processing feature that determines where line breaks need to fall and automatically begins a new line where necessary. You should press (ENTER) only to start a new paragraph.

workbook The basic file type in Excel. Workbooks can contain sheets of various kinds: worksheets, chart sheets, and modules (module sheets).

worksheet (spreadsheet) A table consisting of rows and columns of information, ideal for setting up calculations for a wide variety of applications. Originally implemented on green columnar paper, worksheets can now be manipulated with programs such as Excel.

workstation license Granted by Microsoft's Office product, one workstation license is granted to an Office purchaser. This license allows the holder to use the Microsoft Mail service on a PC network, provided the network has purchased and is using the Mail product.

World Wide Web A navigation system for the Internet. It is a GUI which allows people to move throughout the Internet to Web host sites by pointing to and clicking colored words or phrases on home pages. The user then moves directly to the site offering the service or information indicated by the colored words.

wrap To break a long line of text into two or more lines.

Write A Windows word processing program used for creating small documents.

WYSIWYG An acronym for "What You See Is What You Get," which refers to the fact that the screen shows the document formatted as it will be printed.

X-axis The horizontal axis (usually the bottom edge) of a chart. The X-axis is often broken into the various chart categories.

Y-axis The vertical axis (usually the left edge) of a chart. The Y-axis is often a numerical scale.

zoom To magnify or reduce the view of a worksheet or chart.

Windows 3.1

Microsoft Word 6

Microsoft Excel 5

Microsoft Access 2

Microsoft PowerPoint 4